THE LAW OF THE SEA CONVENTION

Center for Oceans Law and Policy

Series Editors

Myron H. Nordquist
John Norton Moore

VOLUME 15

For a full list of titles, see www.brill.nl/publications/center-oceans-law-and-policy

The Law of the Sea Convention

US Accession and Globalization

Edited by

Myron H. Nordquist,
John Norton Moore,
Alfred H. A. Soons,
Hak-So Kim

MARTINUS NIJHOFF PUBLISHERS

LEIDEN • BOSTON
2012

This book is printed on acid-free paper.

Library of Congress Cataloging-in-Publication Data

The Law of the Sea Convention : US accession and globalization / edited by Myron H. Nordquist...[et al.].
p. cm. – (Center for Oceans Law and Policy ; 15)
"Brought together on the occasion of the 34th Annual Conference of the Center for Oceans Law and Policy, University of Virginia School of Law (COLP)" – CIP galley.
ISBN 978-90-04-20136-1 (hardback : alk. paper) 1. United Nations Convention on the Law of the Sea (1982) – Congresses. 2. Law of the sea – Congresses. 3. Law of the sea – United States – Congresses. I. Nordquist, Myron H.

KZA1120.3.L395 2012
341.4'5 – dc23

2011053215

ISBN: 978 90 04 20136 1 (hardback)
ISBN: 978 90 04 20232 0 (e-book)

WASHINGTON PAPERS

The Law of the Sea Convention: US Accession and Globalization is part of a series of publications on oceans law and policy associated with the Center for Oceans Law and Policy, University of Virginia School of Law. Part I of this volume is based on presentations made May 20–21, 2010, at the Center's 34th Annual Conference, "United States Interests in Prompt Adherence to the Law of the Sea Convention" which was held in Washington, DC. Part II of this volume is based on presentations made at the conference "Globalization and the Law of the Sea" co-sponsored by the Korea Maritime Institute and the Netherlands Institute for the Law of the Sea in conjunction with the Center for Oceans Law and Policy which was held December 1–3, 2010, in Washington, DC.

TABLE OF CONTENTS

PART II

"Globalization and the Law of the Sea"

PREFACE

This volume, the *Law of the Sea Convention: US Accession and Globalization*, consists of two major sections. The first is based on the Center for Oceans Law and Policy, University of Virginia School of Law's (COLP's) 34th Annual Conference, "United States Interests in Prompt Adherence to the Law of the Sea Convention." This Conference, held in Washington, DC, May 20–21, 2010, featured many high-level dignitaries and experts who focused on the fact that the United States is not a Party to the United Nations Convention on the Law of the Sea, 1982 (UNCLOS). A unique contribution at this Conference was a spirited debate between a leading proponent and a leading opponent of US accession to UNCLOS.

The second part of this volume records the presentations given at a conference co-sponsored by the Korea Maritime Institute, the Netherlands Institute for the Law of the Sea and COLP, also held in Washington, DC, December 1–3, 2010. This meeting was concentrated on "Globalization and the Law of the Sea." Appropriate for both conferences was a Distinguished Lecture delivered by Dr. N. Hassan Wirajuda while he was Minister for Foreign Affairs, Republic of Indonesia. Minister Wirajuda completed his SJD at Virginia on a law of the sea subject under the supervision of Professor John Norton Moore, COLP's Director. For his lecture given in autumn 2009 at COLP, the Minister spoke on "The Law of the Sea and Ethical Maritime Order in Southeast Asia." His oral presentation was shaped into suitable written form by his daughter, Adhyanti S. Wirajuda Suryana, herself also a "lawyer by training and diplomat by choice." The central theme of the Distinguished Lecture was international peace and security in the ocean areas of Southeast Asia. Especially noteworthy was his discussion of Indonesia's leadership role in negotiating the ASEAN-China Declaration on the Conduct of Parties in the South China Sea.

Part I "United States Interests in Prompt Adherence to the Law of the Sea Convention"

Five keynote contributions were presented at the May 2010 conference on "US Interests in Prompt Adherence to the Law of the Sea Convention." The US Secretary of State, Hillary Rodham Clinton, wrote that accession to the Convention would restore US leadership in ocean affairs and fundamentally advance the rule of law in the world's oceans. US Senator Lisa Murkowski, representing the state of Alaska, stressed that her state made America an "Arctic Nation." Advances in technology were seen as opening opportunities to develop responsibly vast new oil and gas deposits as well as future shipping routes in the Arctic. She believes UNCLOS provides a necessary framework for the advancement of US interests in the Arctic.

Former Secretary of State Lawrence Eagleburger* deplored the fact that the United States was not a Party to UNCLOS and pointedly observed: "There is no reason not to join." Similar views were expressed by ADM Gary Roughead, Chief of US Naval Operations, who echoed the support for UNCLOS adherence by "all living former Chiefs of Naval Operations." He summarized "that it is in the best interests of this nation and the best interests of our Navy to finally join the Law of the Sea Convention." The fifth keynote speaker was Dr. Quenton Dokken, a widely recognized authority on the Deepwater Horizon blowout spill that was capped only approximately one month after his presentation. While he noted that the actual environmental impact may never be fully known, the "response to the blowout was fast, aggressive, comprehensive, extensive and effective."

The first panel on UNCLOS, "The Stakes for America," was chaired by Ambassador Mary Beth West. She cited a wide array of UNCLOS proponents from not only industry sectors but also ocean environmental and humanitarian organizations. The lead speaker on Panel I was Ambassador David A. Balton who is the Deputy Assistant Secretary for Oceans and Fisheries, US Department of State. True to his operatic background, he lists the eight greatest hits of the stakes for America in relation to UNCLOS which he drew from "countless" State Department statements before Congress. He added three points of his own for adherence to the treaty: to increase US clout to shape the future of the Arctic, to secure our legal rights to an extended continental shelf and to strengthen US multilateral engagements serving hard core US national interests. Thereafter, former Commandant of the US Coast Guard, Paul A. Yost, Jr., concluded that the "pundits and politicians who object to this treaty have very shallow grounds...." The next speaker was Margaret F. Spring, Chief of Staff, National Oceanic and Atmospheric Administration, who offered her agency's perspective on UNCLOS. She stated that "the Law of the Sea Convention provides a stable, predictable legal framework to strike the appropriate balance among often competing oceans interests."

Andrew Keller, Deputy Chief Counsel, Democratic Staff, Senate Foreign Relations Committee and Michael J. Mattler, Chief Counsel, Republican Staff, Senate Foreign Relations Committee, rounded out the presentations on Panel I. Mr. Keller reviewed the procedural processes in the Senate with respect to

* Editors' Note: Secretary Eagleburger passed away June 4, 2011.

UNCLOS, stressing the priorities on floor time. Mr. Mattler stated that the "core of the argument for the Convention is based upon national security considerations." He indicated that the key question with respect to granting floor time would be the extent of incremental benefits to the United States from joining the Convention.

Panel II, titled "Energy and Economic Development" was opened by Paul L. Kelly, a respected spokesman for the US offshore industry. At the end of the Panel, he explained that the United States had already given notice to operators bidding on leases close to the 200-mile EEZ limit in the Gulf of Mexico that leases may be subject to the payment of royalty fees to the ISA. He also commented on the large number of submissions to the Commission on the Limits of the Continental Shelf (CLCS). In introducing ADM James D. Watkins, Mr. Kelly noted that the former Chief of Naval Operations as well as former Secretary of Energy had recently chaired a presidential Commission on US Oceans Policy. ADM Watkins urgently called for the Senate to get its priorities straight and allocate floor time for UNCLOS commensurate with the national interests at stake. ADM Watkins stressed that the message supporters had to send to the US President was "to get oceans on a front burner" right now.

The next speaker, R. Bruce Josten, Executive Vice President, US Chamber of Commerce, stated that it was "imperative that the US accede to the treaty [UNCLOS] allowing our US economy, resource exploration, and commercial enterprises to sustain our economic position." The third oceans industry panelist was Randall Luthi, President of the National Ocean Industries Association. Mr. Luthi asserted that accession would increase, not decrease as opponents argue, US ocean jurisdiction through international shipping, commercial fishing, offshore oil/gas development as well as many newer technological advances. The last speaker on this representative industry panel was Brian T. Petty, Executive Vice President of the International Association of Drilling Contractors. Mr. Petty emphasized the Arctic's oil/gas potential, ice challenges in development and the key aspect of political will.

Panel III was devoted to the critical infrastructure component filled by submarine cables which carry 95% of US international Internet and data transfer traffic. Douglas R. Burnett, the moderator, spoke as the international law advisor to the International Cable Protection Committee, whose members include all the major companies from around the world involved in the submarine cable industry. He covered legal issues such as repair permits, taxes and fees and inadequate domestic law compliance with UNCLOS. As undersea telecommunications capability is indispensable for the global transmission of banking data, Stephen R. Malphrus of the Federal Reserve System gave an overview of the communication technology involved in financial transactions. Next, Robert Wargo, President of the North American Submarine Cable Association, described submarine cable organizations and outlined the international submarine cable network. He emphasized that UNCLOS is "cable friendly" and explained why cable companies urge accession to UNCLOS for increased protection for cables. The last speaker on the submarine cable panel was Dr. Ronald J. Rapp, Director, Tyco Electronics Subsea Communications, which is a full service provider of undersea telecommunication system construction and is a supplier of fiber-optic systems. He described the operation and repair of the global undersea fiber-optic network and its close relationship to compliance with coastal State maritime regulations.

Panel IV was moderated by Edwin D. Williamson, a former Legal Adviser, US Department of State. Directed to US national security, the panel was kicked off by VADM Bruce W. Clingan, Deputy Chief of Naval Operations for Plans and Strategy. He concisely, but comprehensively, reviewed the adverse impacts on Naval operations because the United States is not a Party to the Convention. RADM William L. Schachte, a retired head of Navy JAG and a combat-tested surface warfare officer, covered specific ways that UNCLOS protected US national security interests. He also highlighted inaccuracies relied upon by opponents of the Convention with respect to intelligence gathering, customary international law and loss of US sovereignty. RADM Nanette DeRenzi, speaking on behalf of the senior lawyer for the US Navy, stressed how important freedom of navigation is to counter-proliferation, counter-piracy, counter-terrorism and humanitarian relief operations.

The fifth Panel introduced a unique format, i.e., a lively debate on the proposition that the Senate should give prompt advice and consent to UNCLOS. Panel V was introduced and moderated by Thomas R. Pickering, a former US Under-Secretary of State for Political Affairs. The proponent for the proposition was John Norton Moore, Director of COLP and a former US Ambassador and negotiator for UNCLOS. He spoke on the background and importance of UNCLOS for the United States, misinformed arguments of opponents and the adverse impact for US non-adherence to UNCLOS. Steve Groves, a senior representative of the Heritage Foundation in Washington, DC, argued that "there is no guarantee that US interests will be advanced by acceding to the treaty." He pointed out abuses of the treaty by China and cited problematic benefits from its continental shelf text in Article 82, especially the revenue sharing provisions. Professor/Ambassador Moore responded that UNCLOS, unlike customary law, provided the certainty investors require and dramatically expanded US offshore resource jurisdiction, especially in the Arctic. As to revenue sharing, if the United States occupied its rightful place within the Convention, the tiny payments made could only go where the United States agreed. Steven Groves responded that the United States alone decided where its continental margin ended, not any international organization. He also rejected the notion of the common heritage of mankind as "silliness." Panel V concluded with a spirited audience question and answer session.

Part II "Globalization and the Law of the Sea"

The President of the Korea Maritime Institute (KMI) Hak-So KIM opened the Washington, DC, conference co-sponsored by KMI, the Netherlands Institute for the Law of the Sea at Utrecht University and the Center for Oceans Law and Policy at the University of Virginia School of Law (COLP). The title of this conference was "Globalization and the Law of the Sea". President KIM pointed out that there were many new issues to be resolved within the UNCLOS system, including piracy and terrorism at sea. The context for the Conference was then framed and illustrated by Dr. Barry Bosworth, a former presidential advisor now with the Brookings Institution located in Washington, DC. He noted the growing importance globally of Asian economics and addressed how the trans-Pacific relationship would evolve in future years.

The second keynote speaker at the Globalization and Law of the Sea conference was Sergey Tarasenko, Director, UN Division of Ocean Affairs and the Law of the Sea. He reviewed the UN's role in combatting piracy and terrorism at sea. He highlighted regional and international cooperation frameworks and identified key capacity building networks. He concluded by assessing current challenges. The third keynote speaker was José Luis Jesus, President of the International Tribunal for the Law of the Sea (ITLOS), who described the Tribunal's role in dispute settlement. President Jesus pointed out ITLOS's contentious as well as advisory jurisdiction and the fact that the Tribunal had entertained 18 cases since receiving its first case in 1998. He then described in detail the issues raised in several currently pending cases, including one on maritime delimitation and another, the first request for an advisory opinion. The final keynote speaker was Michael W. Lodge, Legal Counsel for the International Seabed Authority (ISA). He reflected on the precedent-setting submission in September 2010 for an advisory opinion from ITLOS's Seabed Disputes Chamber. The subject matter of the request concerned the responsibilities and liabilities of sponsoring States under UNCLOS relating to environmental protection in the seabed area beyond national jurisdiction.

Panel I of the Globalization Conference, moderated by Keun-Gwan LEE, took up the trends in commercial shipping with a review by Beom Shik PARK, a Korean expert on the impact of surging ship-owners' liability and compensation risks for the protection and indemnity marine insurance industry. Thereafter Professor Erik Franckx and Laura Boone from Brussels, Belgium, spoke on "New Developments in the Arctic: Protecting the Marine Environment from Increased Shipping." The IMO's work on the compatibility between climate change and shipping regimes was then addressed by Professor Nilufer Oral from Istanbul's Bilgi University. She critically assessed proposed market-based proposals considered by the IMO and their linkage with the 1992 UN Framework Convention on Climate Change.

Panel II was moderated by John Norton Moore and opened with a paper by Professor Robert Beckman and Tara Davenport prepared at the Centre for International Law, University of Singapore. Their overall content was captured in its title, "Maritime Terrorism and the Law of the Sea: Basic Principles and New Challenges." Commander James Kraska, JAGC, US Navy, from the US Naval War College faculty next detailed Group Two's work for the Contact Group on Piracy off the Coast of Somalia. The main purpose of its work has been to encourage the prosecution and imprisonment of piracy suspects within national legal systems. Professor Samuel Pyeatt Menefee followed with an examination of the possibility of predicting future piracies by looking at five major historical factors. The author suggested that these factors form a useful paradigm for assessing maritime risk.

Panel III, on the topic of "Islands and Rocks," was moderated by Alex Oude Elferink of the Netherlands Institute for the Law of the Sea (NILOS). Former ITLOS Judge David Anderson who was prevented by snow from attending the Conference, nevertheless provided a written text for Panel III on "Islands and Rocks in the Modern Law of the Sea." In his paper he reviews the legislative history of Article 121 in UNCLOS, discusses the roles of islands and rocks in delimitation between neighboring States and considers the issue of standing in disputes over maritime spaces around islands and rocks. Professor Clive Schofield from the University of Wollongong in New South Wales spoke on the importance of the regime of islands in the delimitation of maritime boundaries. He suggested that a clear means of distinguishing between types of islands did not exist but that a clear trend was emerging in terms of how small islands were dealt with in the delimitations of maritime boundaries. The next presenter on Panel III was Guifang (Julia) Xue, Director, Institute for the Law of the Sea, Oceans University of China. She focused on the Japanese claims to the "Okinotorishima Rocks" and their entitlement to extended jurisdictional zones. She concluded that these features are not legal islands as artificial construction by Japan had changed their natural status which was necessary for offshore resource entitlement.

Panel IV, moderated by ITLOS Judge Jin-Hyun PAIK, considered the subject of "Safety and Navigational Freedom." Kuen-chen FU, a Professor of Law at Shanghai Jiao Tong University spoke first. He emphasized the importance of the proportionality principles, i.e., relevance, necessity and balance of interests, for policing the sea with force. J. Ashley Roach, a retired US Navy lawyer and formerly the leading US State Department law of the sea attorney, then covered recent developments in enhancing safe navigation in the Arctic. His paper reviewed the steps underway to improve the safety of navigation in the Arctic Ocean, with particular emphasis on the 2009 *Arctic Marine Shipping Assessment* prepared under the auspices of the Arctic Council. Professor Ted L. McDorman, Faculty of Law, University of Victoria, Canada, next analyzed an August

2009 amendment to Canada's Arctic Exclusive Economic Zone statute that mandated that commercial vessels entering Canadian shipping control zones were to report to and receive clearance from national authorities. The United States believes that such mandatory reporting must be approved by the IMO while Canada's position is that its actions are consistent with relevant IMO instruments and Article 234 of UNCLOS.

Panel V, dealing with marine scientific research, was moderated by Alfred H.A. Soons, NILOS's Director. The first speaker was Captain Javier A. Valladares (Argentina, Ret.), Chairman of the Intergovernmental Oceanographic Commission (IOC). He was followed by a comprehensive description of the EU's Integrated Maritime Policy and its environmental pillar, the Marine Strategy Framework Directive aimed, *inter alia*, at new approaches to marine resource management, including the ecosystem approach. This extensive study was prepared by Professor Ronán Long, National University of Ireland, Galway. He noted that the EU itself and its Member States are Party to UNCLOS, including Part XIII dealing with the conduct of marine scientific research (MSR). Professor Long traced the progressive development of EU MSR policy and provided a relevant account of EU regulatory instruments. He concluded by suggesting steps to streamline EU's MSR consent regime to facilitate practical implementation of an ecosystem approach pertaining to collection of scientific data across the maritime boundaries of Member States. He predicted a gradual transition from the current fragmented authorization of ship-based MSR towards a fully integrated EU-wide governance system within the UNCLOS framework. He foresees that this would support the sustainable and integrated management of marine ecosystems. Ki-Jun YOU, a Korean diplomat, then presented in his academic capacity, consideration of the MSR issues in Northeast Asia which has many disputed maritime boundaries posing special complications. He commented that the text of UNCLOS was not clear on the definition of MSR and suggested several possible ways for improving the situation.

Panel VI, moderated by Myron H. Nordquist of COLP, dealt with "Emerging Global Ocean Policy Issues." The lead off speaker was VADM James W. Houck, Judge Advocate General, USN and DOD Representative for Ocean Policy Affairs. He stressed that the global security issues such as counter-proliferation, piracy and assertive coastal State controls threaten the traditional balance of high seas freedoms found in UNCLOS. In addition, the United States has national security interests in the Arctic and must be prepared to operate in this unique, harsh environment, either independently or with other nations. The next presentation was co-authored by Larry A. Mayer (a scientist at the University of New Hampshire), Capt. J. Ashley Roach (a retired sea lawyer), and Betsy Baker (Vermont Law School). They jointly addressed the question of whether there is a need for international regulation given the blowout of the Deepwater Horizon and the environmental challenges in opening the Arctic.

While Part XII of UNCLOS provides a start for international environmental and safety standards for offshore development, they conclude that neither the United States nor the global community currently have a satisfactory regulatory regime.

Panel VII, moderated by ITLOS Judge Jin-Hyun PAIK, wrapped up the program with a commentary and review of the Conference by four panelists selected because each was an outstanding graduate of the Rhodes Academy of Oceans Law and Policy, a summer program sponsored annually by several leading law of the sea academic centers including COLP, KMI and NILOS. Haryo Budi Nugroho (Indonesia) focused on PSSA's (Particularly Sensitive Sea Areas), Teoman Uykur (Turkey) on islands in delimitation and piracy off Somalia, Fernanda Millicay (Argentina) on globalization and UNCLOS norms pertaining to islands/rocks, piracy, and marine scientific research while Vita Onwuasoanya (UN Division for Oceans Affairs and the Law of the Sea) made general observations on UNCLOS within the context of the Conference's theme of globalization and the rule of law on the world's oceans.

ACKNOWLEDGEMENTS

The impetus for a conference in Washington, DC to be held in the early part of 2010 came from Professor John Norton Moore, Director, Center for Oceans Law and Policy, University of Virginia School of Law, who closely monitors the efforts to support or oppose US accession to the UN Convention on the Law of the Sea, 1982. He also suggested the unique debate format in this volume for a fair and highly effective way to demonstrate the arguments for and against US accession. Professor/Ambassador Moore also strongly advocated the successful airing of the Conference to a national television audience via CSPAN.

The idea for the Globalization and Law of the Sea Conference in December, 2010, grew out of an introduction of Dr. Hak-Bong Chang of the Korea Maritime Institute to Professor Myron H. Nordquist in Virginia by Alfred H.A. Soons, Director, Netherlands Institute for the Law of the Sea (Utrecht). The President of KMI, Hak-So Kim, and Dr. Chang were interested in co-sponsoring a significant conference on oceans policy and they, Professor Soons and Professor Nordquist were primarily responsible for organizing the program.

In Charlottesville Donna Ganoe and Kay Wood, from the Center for Oceans Law and Policy, provided invaluable administrative staff support for both conferences held in 2010. Judith A. Ellis contributed what can only be described as outstanding service as Technical Editor for both parts of this volume. Many others, of course, participated in a collegial spirit and since it would be impossible to name each, the Editors simply extend our heart-felt appreciation to all.

The University of Virginia Distinguished Lecture

THE LAW OF THE SEA AND ETHICAL MARITIME ORDER IN SOUTHEAST ASIA

Dr. N. Hassan Wirajuda[1] *and Adhyanti S. Wirajuda Suryana*

I am honoured and delighted to be here again at the Center for Oceans Law and Policy of the University of Virginia School of Law, mingling with eminent academicians and their bright-eyed students.

From where I stand I can see familiar faces among the members of the Center's Board of Directors. I do recognize Prof. John Norton Moore and Prof. Myron Nordquist who, through their writings, have contributed tremendously to the promotion of law and order at sea.

My being here today gives me a sense of *déjà vu*: the time I spent on this campus was filled with intellectual excitement and remains a very important part of my life. When I left after completing my studies in 1988, I brought with me not only pleasant memories of the University of Virginia and Charlottesville, but also a fine sense of anticipation that much can and should be done for the cause of law and order in a world that is mostly oceans, seas and waterways.

The world has radically changed since then – it has become so much more complex. New issues, new ideas and new realities are now prevailing in international affairs. A much welcome reality has been the coming into force of the United Nations Convention on the Law of the Sea of 1982.[2]

---

[1] Statement given by Dr. N. Hassan Wirajuda at the University of Virginia School of Law on September 30, 2009. Dr. N. Hassan Wirajuda was the Foreign Minister of Indonesia from 2001 to 2009. Currently he is a member of the Council of Presidential Advisors of the Republic of Indonesia and patron to the Institute of Peace and Democracy, Bali Democracy Forum. A lawyer by training and a diplomat by choice, Dr. Wirajuda has held several important posts including Director-General of Political Affairs of the Ministry of Foreign Affairs (2000–2001), Ambassador and Permanent Representative to the United Nations and other international organizations in Geneva (1998–2000), Ambassador Extraordinary and Plenipotentiary to Egypt (1997–1998), and Director of International Organizations of the Department of Foreign Affairs (1993–1997). Mrs. Suryana provided the footnotes for this paper.

In 2011, Dr. Wirajuda was awarded the Medal of Honor, the Bintang Mahaputera Adipradana, by the President of Indonesia.

[2] The United Nations Convention on the Law of the Sea entered into force on 23 November 1994.

This "Constitution of the Oceans" enjoys almost universal ratification, with 160 parties to it, making it the single legal framework for ocean governance.[3] Because of the Convention, all maritime spaces on the planet are now regulated.

The UNCLOS is a codification of longstanding customary laws as well as new legal principles in matters relating to oceans applicable to all states regardless of their geographical situation.

Thus, the Convention represents a breakthrough in transnational rule-making on the rights and responsibilities of states with regards to the world's oceans. Consequently, the Convention has brought about a great deal of legal certainty in interstate relations. Indonesia is proud of the fact that it was actively involved in the nine-year negotiations that led to the concluding of the Convention in 1982.

Of course, the tremendous advances in science and technology have also changed the world in the meantime: they have shrunk the world into a virtual village. But, they have not diminished the importance of the oceans and seas. They still have a vital role in food security, energy security, climate stability, human security and socioeconomic activities.

The oceans provide the only feasible means of transporting strategic materials – be they food or energy – in massive quantities in relatively short time. Without the oceans so much less commerce would be taking place. Sea-borne trade accounts for nearly 85 percent of world trade. And this is estimated to increase, albeit at a slower rate as compared to 2007.[4]

We in Indonesia are very much aware of this. As the largest archipelagic country in the world, we have a special regard for our maritime territory and resources: they are life-giving and they are a force for national unity and identity. That is why we refer to our country as *tanah-airku*, my land and waters.

We are aware of the strategic importance of our archipelago. Four of the ten straits vital to international navigation involve Indonesian waters: the Strait of Malacca, the Strait of Singapore, the Strait of Sunda and the Strait of Lombok.

One-third of all sea-borne trade and the energy supply from the Middle East to China, the Republic of Korea and Japan pass through the Straits of Malacca

[3] Update: as of March 2010, there are currently 160 State parties to the 1982 Convention as Chad acceded to the Convention on 14 August 2009.

[4] Following the global economic downturn and sharp decline in world merchandise trade in the last quarter of 2008, growth in international seaborne trade continued, albeit at a slower rate of 3.6 per cent in 2008 as compared with 4.5 percent in 2007. UNCTAD estimates the 2008 international seaborne trade at 8.17 billion tons of goods loaded, with dry cargo continuing to account for the largest share. It can also be noted that forecasts for seaborne trade have been marked downwards, with several shipbrokers (namely Fearnley's and Clarkson Shipping Services) that expect world seaborne trade to fall by 1.4 percent in 2009, before turning around and growing at a slower rate of 2.0 per cent in 2010. See pages 6–7 of the Review of Maritime Transport 2009, Report of the UNCTAD Secretariat, Chapter 1.

and Singapore.[5] Over 60,000 vessels pass through these straits every year, and the number is expected to increase by ten percent annually. Any disruption in this maritime traffic because of a collision of vessels would have an adverse impact on global trade and on the economies of the littoral states.

The other countries of Southeast Asia share Indonesia's marine and maritime concerns. The region as a whole boasts a mega-diversity of marine flora and fauna and other resources that can be exploited for economic purposes. Hence, all the countries of the region are seized with the task of integrated coastal management and environmental protection.

And because the seas of the region are semi-enclosed seas, the bordering states are mandated to cooperate closely with one another in the exercise of their rights and in the performance of their duties under the Convention. That is the idea behind the establishment of the Sulu-Sulawesi Seas Marine Eco-region in February 2004 and the Coral Triangle Initiative (CTI) in May this year.[6]

There is a great deal of cooperation on maritime matters among the countries of Southeast Asia today, not only because it is mandated by the Convention, but also because they learned several decades ago that cooperation was the only way to achieve prosperity and stability in a region that was once ravaged by proxy wars and civil wars. It was the best strategy for survival in an uncertain world.

That was why the Association of Southeast Asian Nations or ASEAN was established in 1967: to promote cooperation in political, economic and

[5] The Strait of Malacca links the Indian Ocean to the South China Sea and Pacific Ocean. Malacca is the shortest sea route between Persian Gulf suppliers and the Asian markets, notably China, Japan, South Korea and the Pacific Rim. Oil shipments through the Strait of Malacca supply China and Indonesia, two of the world's most populous nations, and it is the key chokepoint in Asia with an estimated 15 million bbl/d flow in 2006. *See* Country Analysis Briefs of the Energy Information Administration, <www.eia.doe.gov>.

[6] The Sulu-Sulawesi Marine Ecoregion (SSME) is an extraordinary ecoregion situated within the center of global marine biodiversity. Three countries – Indonesia, Malaysia and the Philippines – share, and directly benefit from, the rich resources of the SSME. The deterioration of environmental conditions in the ecoregion indicates that the resource extraction has exceeded the natural capacity of this marine ecosystem for recovery. Shared boundaries, ecosystem dynamics and resources, as well as transboundary environmental issues (including human migration) justify an ecoregion approach to conserve the SSME.

The Coral Triangle Initiative (CTI) in May 2009 was initially proposed by President Yudhoyono of Indonesia in August 2007. The CTI is a new multilateral partnership to safeguard the region's extraordinary marine and coastal biological resources. Twenty-one heads of states welcomed the Initiative at the APEC Summit in September 2007. The CTI was officially launched in December 2007 during the 13th Conference of the Parties to the UN Framework Convention on Climate Change in Bali.

socio-cultural fields so that there would be peace and progress in the region.[7] Today ASEAN is no longer just a loose association of nations in a given geographical area: it has a Charter that gives it a legal identity and imparts momentum to its efforts to become an ASEAN Community by 2015. As such, ASEAN will also be a Security Community, an Economic Community and a Sociocultural Community.[8]

When I speak of a Security Community, I do not refer to a military alliance. It means that we take responsibility for our own national and regional security so that we take every measure possible to ensure peace and stability. It also means that we attend to our political development through sharing and shaping of values – values that are conducive to peace and cooperation among ourselves, the regional nations and between us and external powers.

This shaping and sharing of values has been going on for some time. One significant process began in 1990 when Indonesia launched an annual informal workshop on Managing Potential Conflict in the South China Sea.[9]

The workshop was launched at a time when it was feared that the next flashpoints would be the South China Sea, as there are many unresolved maritime boundaries and sovereignty disputes in an area so important to international

[7] The Association of Southeast Asian Nations, or ASEAN, was established on 8 August 1967 in Bangkok, Thailand, with the signing of the ASEAN Declaration by the Founding Fathers of ASEAN, namely Indonesia, Malaysia, the Philippines, Singapore and Thailand. As set out in the ASEAN Declaration, the aims and purposes of ASEAN include promoting regional peace and stability through abiding respect for justice and the rule of law in the relationship among countries of the region and adherence to the principles of the United Nations Charter.

[8] The ASEAN Community is comprised of three pillars, namely the ASEAN Political-Security Community, ASEAN Economic Community and ASEAN Socio-Cultural Community. Each pillar has its own Blueprint, and, together with the Initiative for ASEAN Integration (IAI) Strategic Framework and IAI Work Plan Phase II (2009–2015), they form the Roadmap for an ASEAN Community 2009–2015. The blueprints can be accessed at the ASEAN website, <www.asean.org>.

[9] Despite many concerns and reservations at the time, ASEAN agreed to try to manage the potential conflicts in the South China Sea and to convert them as much as possible to cooperation. It was with this understanding in mind that a series of workshops were held in Indonesia, as Indonesia is not a claimant to any islands or rocks in the Spratly group. The first workshop was held in Bali in 1990, and was basically a meeting among ASEAN participants only. Topics identified at the first meeting include: (1) territorial and sovereignty issues; (2) political and security issues; (3) marine scientific research and environmental protection; (4) safety of navigation; (5) resources management; and (6) institutional mechanisms for cooperation. By the second workshop, several non-ASEAN countries also participated in the workshop process, namely China, Vietnam, Laos and Chinese Taipei. The workshops were held consecutively in: Bali (1990), Bandung (1991), Yogyakarta (1992), Surabaya (1993), Bukit Tinggi (1994), Balikpapan (1995), Batam (1996), Pacet (1997), Ancol (1998), Bogor (1999), Cengkareng (2001), Jakarta (Special Meeting – 2002), Medan (2003), Batam (2004), Anyer (2005) and Bali (2006).

navigation. China was locked with several ASEAN countries that were also engaged with one another in such disputes.

Not being one of the rival claimants to all or parts of the South China Sea, Indonesia was able to organize the workshop as a confidence building measure and as a venue for Track Two diplomacy. Experts and analysts from all over the region participated in this process – in their individual capacities and not as representatives of governments.

Over the years in the 1990s, a body of ideas and project plans grew out of the workshop, all of them aimed at promoting cooperation among the rival claimants. Several of these projects were carried out, benefiting those involved and enhancing mutual trust among the nations of the region.

The ideas developed in the workshop led to the adoption in 1992 of the ASEAN Declaration on the South China Sea, which not only committed the regional countries to peaceful resolution of their maritime boundary and sovereignty disputes but also to work together for the common good of all stakeholders.[10] This was followed by negotiations and the eventual conclusion, in 2002, of an ASEAN-China Declaration on the Conduct of Parties in the South China Sea.[11]

---

[10] The ASEAN Declaration on the South China Sea was concluded in Manila, Philippines, on 22 July 1992. The Declaration was mainly comprised of 5 paragraphs, as follows: (1) Emphasize the necessity to resolve all sovereignty and jurisdictional issues pertaining to the South China Sea by peaceful means, without resort to force; (2) Urge all parties concerned to exercise restraint with the view to creating a positive climate for the eventual resolution of all disputes; (3) Resolve, without prejudicing the sovereignty and jurisdiction of countries having direct interests in the area, to explore the possibility of cooperation in the South China Sea relating to the safety of maritime navigation and communication, protection against pollution of the marine environment, coordination of search and rescue operations, efforts towards combating piracy and armed robbery as well as collaboration in the campaign against illicit trafficking in drugs; (4) Commend all parties concerned to apply the principles contained in the Treaty of Amity and Cooperation in Southeast Asia as the basis for establishing a code of international conduct over the South China Sea; (5) Invite all parties concerned to subscribe to this Declaration of Principles.

[11] The ASEAN-China Declaration on the Conduct of Parties in the South China Sea was concluded on 4 November 2002 in Phnom Penh, Cambodia. The Declaration is comprised of 10 operative paragraphs, which, *inter alia,* emphasize that: (1) The Parties reaffirm their commitment to the purposes and principles of the Charter of the United Nations, the 1982 UN Convention on the Law of the Sea, the Treaty of Amity and Cooperation in Southeast Asia, the Five Principles of Peaceful Coexistence, and other universally recognized principles of international law which shall serve as the basic norms governing state-to-state relations; (2) The Parties are committed to exploring ways for building trust and confidence in accordance with the above-mentioned principles and on the basis of equality and mutual respect; (3) The Parties reaffirm their respect for and commitment to the freedom of navigation in and overflight above the South China Sea as provided for by the universally recognized principles of international law, including the 1982 UN Convention on the Law of the Sea; (4) The

By virtue of that Code, China and the ASEAN countries committed themselves to the peaceful resolution of their maritime territorial and sovereignty disputes.

Another process of shaping and sharing of norms was launched in Bangkok in 1994 – the ASEAN Regional Forum (ARF), a vehicle for political and security dialogue and cooperation on security matters that involves all countries that have significant influence and interest in the security of the larger Asia-Pacific region.[12] These include all the major powers.

Parties concerned undertake to resolve their territorial and jurisdictional disputes by peaceful means, without resorting to the threat or use of force, through friendly consultations and negotiations by sovereign states directly concerned, in accordance with universally recognized principles of international law, including the 1982 UN Convention on the Law of the Sea; (5) The Parties undertake to exercise self-restraint in the conduct of activities that would complicate or escalate disputes and affect peace and stability including, among others, refraining from action of inhabiting on the presently uninhabited islands, reefs, shoals, cays, and other features and to handle their differences in a constructive manner, and that pending the peaceful settlement of territorial and jurisdictional disputes, the Parties concerned undertake to intensify efforts to seek ways, in the spirit of cooperation and understanding, to build trust and confidence between and among them; (6) Pending a comprehensive and durable settlement of the disputes, the Parties concerned may explore or undertake cooperative activities; (7) The Parties concerned stand ready to continue their consultations and dialogues concerning relevant issues, through modalities to be agreed by them, including regular consultations on the observance of this Declaration, for the purpose of promoting good neighborliness and transparency, establishing harmony, mutual understanding and cooperation, and facilitating peaceful resolution of disputes among them; (8) The Parties undertake to respect the provisions of this Declaration and take actions consistent therewith; (9) The Parties encourage other countries to respect the principles contained in this Declaration; (10) The Parties concerned reaffirm that the adoption of a code of conduct in the South China Sea would further promote peace and stability in the region and agree to work, on the basis of consensus, towards the eventual attainment of this objective.

The ASEAN Political-Security Community Blueprint (APSC) further stipulates in section A.2.2 entitled "Ensuring Full Implementation of the Declaration on the Conduct of Parties for Peace and Stability in the South China Sea (DOC)" that there are three actions to be called for, namely: (1) to continue ASEAN's current practice of close consultation among member States to achieve full implementation of the DOC; (2) to explore and undertake cooperative activities identified in the DOC and eventually explore other cooperative measures on the basis of close consultations among the member countries, while respecting the sovereignty and integrity of each other; (3) to carry out on a regular basis the overview of the process of implementation of the DOC, thus ensuring timely and proper conduct of the parties in the South China Sea, in accordance with the DOC; and (4) work towards the adoption of a regional code of conduct in the South China Sea.

[12] The ASEAN Regional Forum (ARF) was established during the 26th ASEAN Ministerial Meeting and Post-Ministerial Conference which was held in Singapore on 23–25 July 1993. The inaugural meeting of the ARF was held in Bangkok on 25 July 1994. Objectives of the ASEAN Regional Forum as outlined in the First ARF Chairman's Statement (1994) include: (1) to foster constructive dialogue and consultation on political and security issues of common

The work of the Forum would cover progressively the fields of confidence building, preventive diplomacy and practical cooperation. Since then, the Forum has proven to be greatly effective in confidence building and has additionally begun to undertake preventive diplomacy activities. It has also opened up a Track Two process, involving non-governmental entities in the promotion of security in the Asia-Pacific region.

As a matter of course, since a large part of the Asia-Pacific is made up of an ocean and many seas, much of the work of the Forum has been directed at maritime safety and security. On 5–6 March 2009, the ARF met in Surabaya, Indonesia to consider exclusively maritime security matters.[13]

Taking a cue from the success of the ASEAN Regional Forum, we in the region are launching by the end of this year the ASEAN Maritime Forum (AMF) which will provide us a venue for developing common perceptions on threats to maritime security and enhance inter-governmental cooperation in fighting perpetrators of crimes at sea.[14]

---

interest and concern; and (2) to make significant contributions to efforts towards confidence-building and preventive diplomacy in the Asia-Pacific region. The 27th ASEAN Ministerial Meeting (1994) stated that "The ARF could become an effective consultative Asia-Pacific Forum for promoting open dialogue on political and security cooperation in the region. In this context, ASEAN should work with its ARF partners to bring about a more predictable and constructive pattern of relations in the Asia Pacific."

[13] Pursuant to the decision of the 15th Ministerial Meeting of the ASEAN Regional Forum (ARF) held in Singapore on 24 July 2008, the first meeting of the ARF Inter-Sessional Meeting on Maritime Security (ARF ISM MS) was held in Surabaya on 5–6 March 2009. The ARF ISM MS discussed several issues, namely: (1) A review of previous discussions on Maritime Security issues in the ARF, existing Bilateral and Plurilateral Cooperation to address these issues, and Major Related Events that have taken place in the Region; (2) Building Common Perceptions on Threats and Challenges in Maritime Security; and (3) Building Common Steps to Address Issues of Common Concern on Maritime Security.

[14] A workshop was held in Batam Island, Indonesia, on 7–8 September to specifically discuss the establishment of an ASEAN Maritime Forum. The workshop was of the view that the purposed ASEAN Maritime Forum would provide a forum to exchange ideas, not only on maritime security issues but also broad, cross-cutting issues such as the protection of the marine environment, illegal fishing, smuggling and maritime transportation. The workshop further recognized that the ASEAN Maritime Forum may also consider maritime issues involving enclosed and semi-enclosed seas and that it would also consider the particular concerns of the large archipelagic nations in ASEAN. Furthermore, section A.2.5 of the ASEAN Political-Security Community Blueprint (APSC) regarding Promotion of ASEAN Maritime Cooperation calls for four actions, namely: (1) the establishment of an ASEAN Maritime Forum; (2) to apply a comprehensive approach that focuses on safety of navigation and security concern in the regions that are of common concern to the ASEAN community; (3) to take stock of maritime issues and identify maritime cooperation among ASEAN member countries; and (4) to promote cooperation in maritime safety and search and rescue (SAS) through activities such as information sharing, technological cooperation and exchange of visits of authorities concerned.

These processes involving the sharing and shaping of norms were built on the solid foundation of the Treaty of Amity and Cooperation (TAC) in Southeast Asia, which was concluded in 1976.[15]

The TAC is essentially ASEAN's code of conduct committing its signatories to five principles of peaceful coexistence: mutual respect, non-interference, peaceful settlement of disputes, renunciation of the threat or use of force and cooperation for socioeconomic development. As of today 17 States have acceded to the Treaty, including major maritime powers like Russia, China, India, Japan, and recently the United States and the European Union.[16]

As a code of conduct, it has worked so well that for more than three decades, in spite of many maritime boundary disputes in the Asia-Pacific region, no armed conflict has broken out among the signatories and those who acceded to the Treaty.

And it is quite obvious to me that these processes of sharing and shaping of norms leading to good behavior between and among states have promoted faithful compliance to the mandates and stipulations of the UN Convention on the Law of the Sea. To my mind, this brings up an important point: the law is always vital because we must have an ordered society of individuals as well as of nations, but the law will never be strong enough until, and unless, it is supported by human values.

Ethics and a striving for virtue must complement the law: that is what we have been proving in the ASEAN region over the years that we have been growing and evolving to become a true community. On the other hand, the existence of law encourages and validates ethical behavior. I believe there is a synergy rather than conflict between law and ethics.

Knowing this, I do not think that we in ASEAN will ever become a litigious group of nations. A few years ago, a territorial dispute between Malaysia and Indonesia over the islands of Sipadan and Ligitan was decided by the

[15] In their relations with one another, the ASEAN Member States have adopted the Treaty of Amity and Cooperation (TAC) in Southeast Asia. TAC raised the provisions of the Kuala Lumpur Declaration to the level of a treaty to which other Southeast Asian countries could accede and with which the non-regional countries could associate themselves. The treaty enshrines the following principles: mutual respect for one another's sovereignty; noninterference in internal affairs; the peaceful settlement of intraregional disputes; and effective cooperation. The treaty also provides for a code of conduct for the peaceful settlement of disputes. And it mandates the establishment of a high council made up of ministerial representatives from the parties as a dispute-settlement mechanism. To this day, TAC remains the only indigenous regional diplomatic instrument providing a mechanism and processes for the peaceful settlement of disputes.

[16] Update: with the United States of America's accession on July 23, 2009, there are currently 27 countries that have acceded to the Treaty of Amity and Cooperation.

International Court of Justice in favour of Malaysia.[17] More recently a territorial dispute over the island of Pedra Branca between Malaysia and Singapore was decided in favor of Singapore.[18] I do not believe there will be many more adjudications like that in the future.

---

[17] Ligitan and Sipadan are two very small islands located in the Celebes Sea, off the north-east coast of the island of Borneo. Having found that neither of the Parties had a treaty-based title to Ligitan and Sipadan, the International Court of Justice (ICJ) next considered the question whether Indonesia or Malaysia could hold title to the disputed islands by virtue of the *effectivités* cited by them. In this regard, the Court determined whether the Parties' claims to sovereignty were based on activities evidencing an actual, continued exercise of authority over the islands, i.e., the intention and will to act as sovereign. Having rejected Indonesia's arguments based on its *effectivités*, the Court turned to consideration of the *effectivités* relied on by Malaysia. As evidence of its effective administration of the islands, Malaysia cited *inter alia* the measures taken by the North Borneo authorities to regulate and control the collecting of turtle eggs on Ligitan and Sipadan, an activity of some economic significance in the area at the time. It relied on the Turtle Preservation Ordinance of 1917 and maintained that the Ordinance "was applied until the 1950s at least" in the area of the two disputed islands. It further invoked the fact that the authorities of the colony of North Borneo constructed a lighthouse on Sipadan in 1962 and another on Ligitan in 1963, that those lighthouses exist to this day and that they have been maintained by Malaysian authorities since its independence. The Court notes that "the activities relied upon by Malaysia... are modest in number but... they are diverse in character and include legislative, administrative and quasi-judicial acts. They cover a considerable period of time and show a pattern revealing an intention to exercise State functions in respect of the two islands in the context of the administration of a wider range of islands". The Court further states that "at the time when these activities were carried out, neither Indonesia nor its predecessor, the Netherlands, ever expressed its disagreement or protest". As such, the International Court of Justice (ICJ) in its judgement of 17 December 2002, found, by sixteen votes to one, on the basis of the *effectivités*, that sovereignty over Pulau Ligitan and Pulau Sipadan belongs to Malaysia.

[18] The International Court of Justice (ICJ) rendered its Judgment in the case concerning Sovereignty over Pedra Branca/Pulau Batu Puteh, Middle Rocks and South Ledge (Malaysia/Singapore) on 23 May 2008. In its Judgment, which is final, binding and without appeal, the Court found: (a) by twelve votes to four that sovereignty over Pedra Branca/Pulau Batu Puteh belongs to the Republic of Singapore; (b) by fifteen votes to one that sovereignty over Middle Rocks belongs to Malaysia; (c) by fifteen votes to one that sovereignty over South Ledge belongs to the State in the territorial waters of which it is located. The Court concludes, especially by reference to the conduct of Singapore and its predecessors *à titre de souverain*, taken together with the conduct of Malaysia and its predecessors including their failure to respond to the conduct of Singapore and its predecessors, that by 1980 (when the dispute crystallized) sovereignty over Pedra Branca/Pulau Batu Puteh had passed to Singapore. The Court thus concluded that sovereignty over Pedra Branca/Pulau Batu Puteh belongs to Singapore. With respect to Middle Rocks, the Court observes that the particular circumstances which led it to find that sovereignty over Pedra Branca/Pulau Batu Puteh rests with Singapore clearly do not apply to Middle Rocks. It therefore finds that original title to Middle Rocks should remain with Malaysia as the successor to the Sultanate of Johor. As for South Ledge, the Court notes that this low-tide elevation falls within the apparently overlapping territorial waters generated by Pedra Branca/Pulau Batu Puteh and by Middle Rocks. Recalling that it has not been

That is because we have seen that adjudication, although it has the major virtue of being a peaceful process, almost inevitably leads to a winner-take-all situation. There is always something more to be desired from a situation where one party must accept the role of loser. The more prudent choice therefore is to sustain the various processes of norms setting and promoting ethical behavior while we settle our maritime and other disputes through consultation and negotiation.

Negotiations, of course, take a great deal of time and patience. But as long as the parties involved are committed to peace and cooperation, time is not of the essence. An accumulation of wisdom over the years, even decades, could eventually lead to a win-win solution to any dispute no matter how intractable it appears to be. Meanwhile, all parties benefit from the maintenance of peace and from the results of their cooperation.

We do have something right and good taking place in the ASEAN region: a process of sharing and shaping of norms that lead to nations becoming well-behaved and law abiding. It occurs to me that there is no similar process going on among the Indian Ocean rim nations – at a time when the Indian Ocean is becoming more than ever before an important strategic theatre. I think it would be worth the time of policy-makers, think tanks and thoughtful individuals to explore the potential of the ASEAN-led forums and processes as models for the promotion of peace and cooperation in other parts of the world that are not carrying out similar undertakings.

In sum, let me just say that one of the greatest achievements of the international community has been the virtually universal ratification of the UN Convention on the Law of the Sea. It has served humankind very well and imparted additional order to international relations.

It deserves our support and we need to support it. And the best way to support it is to develop the values, the sense of ethics that make human beings law-abiding. That is what we have been doing in the ASEAN region.

---

mandated by the Parties to draw the line of delimitation with respect to their territorial waters in the area, the Court concludes that sovereignty over South Ledge belongs to the State in the territorial waters of which it is located.

PART I

"United States Interests in Prompt Adherence to the Law of the Sea Convention"

Keynote Addresses

STATEMENT BY THE SECRETARY OF STATE HILLARY RODHAM CLINTON

May 20, 2010

I congratulate the Center for Oceans Law and Policy for convening this conference and for its continued support for US accession to the Law of the Sea Convention. Every administration – whether Democratic or Republican – since the treaty was first submitted to the Senate in 1994, has supported the United States' accession to the convention and ratification of the associated 1994 Agreement.

It is an important goal of this Administration to secure Senate approval of the Convention, which has the support of all living Chiefs of Naval Operations, four Commandants of the US Coast Guard, the endorsement of every Secretary of State since the Reagan Administration, various industry groups, environmental groups, and other affected associations, as well as security experts, practitioners, and scholars.

The United States' accession to the Convention would also help to restore US leadership in ocean affairs. By joining the Convention, the United States would be joining 159 other nations and the European Union as States Parties to a convention that fundamentally advances the rule of law in the world's oceans – one that also advances US national security interests, facilitates the exercise of US sovereign rights, benefits the US economy, and promotes the sustainable development of ocean resources.

US INTERESTS IN PROMPT ADHERENCE TO THE LAW OF THE SEA CONVENTION

Senator Lisa Murkowski[1]

It is my pleasure to address you today at the 34th annual Center for Oceans Law and Policy conference. I have to commend the Center for putting together a very impressive conference.

As all of us in this room are aware, the United States IS an Arctic nation because of Alaska. And I am very privileged to be the senior Senator for America's Arctic State. But, what does it mean to be an Arctic nation? I believe that the Federal Government is just waking up to this reality and we are trying to define exactly what that distinction means. In my view, being an Arctic nation means that the United States, by virtue of our land and waters, has a fundamental interest in the region and a responsibility and obligation to protect those interests.

I speak to you at a time of great change for the Arctic. That pace of change demands that greater attention be focused on the region. The implications of the dynamic changing Arctic for the residents and important international security, economic, environmental, and political interests, depend on it.

Interest in the Arctic, by both the general public, the media and Arctic and non-Arctic nations, continues to grow. The attention is primarily due to the impacts of climate change and subsequent loss of seasonal sea ice, and interest in shipping lanes, energy and natural resources.

Until recently, the resources of the Arctic were deemed to be too difficult and expensive to develop. But with increasing access and high energy and mineral prices, the Arctic's wealth is now being increasingly discovered, explored, and developed. This includes conventional oil and natural gas as well as methane hydrates and other less conventional forms. In offshore Alaska we are estimating fifteen billion barrels of oil in a concentrated area of the Chukchi Sea and eight

---

[1] US Senator Lisa Murkowski (R – Alaska). Senator Lisa Murkowski is the first Alaskan-born Senator and only the sixth United States Senator to serve the state. The state's senior senator, Lisa Murkowski is a third generation Alaskan, born in Ketchikan and raised in towns across the state: Wrangell, Juneau, Fairbanks and Anchorage. Since joining the Senate in 2002, Senator Murkowski has been a strong advocate for Alaska on the important issues facing the state, including energy, health care, education, military/veterans' affairs and infrastructure development.

billion barrels in the Beaufort Sea, and I am hopeful that exploratory wells will prove up this summer.

The United States Geological Survey tells us that the region has possibly up to 30 percent of the world's undiscovered gas and 13 percent of its oil. We also think it holds huge amounts of other minerals – like coal, nickel, copper, tungsten, lead, zinc, gold, silver, diamonds, manganese, chromium and titanium. But there's a natural, sometimes reflexive tendency to question how in the world it can ever be safe or even economical to drill and produce in such harsh, misunderstood, and distant environments. But it's happening, and the technology and engineering behind some of the existing and proposed activities are fascinating. We already know that the Russians are turning their eyes to the Arctic's vast energy reserves as they are building the first offshore oil rig that can withstand temperatures as low as minus 50 degrees Celsius and heavy pack ice. As their oil production is in decline, they are also reducing taxes and bureaucratic hurdles in order to encourage new oil development in the Arctic. They are also planning for a near wholesale replacement of their icebreaker fleet in order to better operate in the polar region. By the same token, an energy company from England is now seriously readying to explore for oil and natural gas for the first time off the coast of Greenland.

The spill in the Gulf of Mexico has shown that there will always be risks and impacts associated with producing energy. We must take every appropriate step to minimize the risks into the future. But we also need to be rational in our response to the Deepwater Horizon tragedy. We don't yet know exactly what failed. Until we do, we should be careful and not pass reactionary legislation that hasn't been fully thought through. We must learn the lessons from the Gulf accident, but we are still collecting information. Once we have a full understanding of the cause of the accident, it will guide us in our decision making on drafting new regulations and improving our safety procedures.

The Deepwater Horizon incident may have made us more reticent to drill in the deep offshore, but it did nothing to reduce our need for oil and gas and it did nothing to change the value of those resources in what is still a growing global economy. Even as we take steps to reduce our dependence on fossil fuels, we're going to continue to need oil and gas for decades to come.

I believe that we will rise from this tragedy not only as Americans, but also that the world will learn and grow stronger in terms of understanding the values and risks of energy production.

Alaska's offshore oil and natural gas resources are vital to the nation's strategic economic and energy security, and I remain committed to responsible exploration and production in the Beaufort and Chukchi seas. Since the Deepwater Horizon tragedy has been unfolding, we have demanded and achieved even greater protections surrounding those exploratory activities. There are differences between the deepwater Gulf activity and the Arctic – specifically, the relative shallow water depths and pressures in the Arctic. In addition, the Shell Oil Company permits have had more regulatory environment and judicial scrutiny than any other exploration permit in recent history. All eyes are on us in Alaska, and we need to be given the chance to prove we can explore safely.

The exploration activity in the Arctic, combined with declining summer sea ice, has positive implications for energy security across borders, because LNG and oil tankers will in some cases be able to have alternatives to their current, more dangerous and clogged routes through South-East Asian straits and the Gulf of Aden and of course the Suez Canal. So non-Arctic nations are going to benefit in this way, but importantly they can also benefit through the funding element of these huge projects. The exploration, the production, and certainly the construction necessary to develop Arctic resources is going to require all types of financing not just for the sheer scale and remoteness of the projects, but for the levels of technology needed to bring them online in a way that's safe for workers, safe for the environment, and as insulated from risk as possible.

Recently I had the experience of visiting a 4-D seismic room in New Orleans – where the images acquired through 3-D are basically animated to give a sense of shifting oil and gas reservoirs so that geologists can study trends and get a much more telling picture of the resource potential. It is almost surgical compared to the basic exploratory drilling which occurred in the last century – and it gives me confidence that a well can be targeted and explored with limited impacts to surrounding areas.

This is just one example of the ways in which technology is able to provide a reassuring answer to questions about whether the world is ready for increased energy development in the Arctic. Another great example – and specifically an Arctic example – is the Liberty project in Alaska. Some of you may already be familiar with this extended reach drill rig which Parker drilling helped develop for BP to access an oilfield directionally eight miles away. It's not quite there yet, but I'm hoping, and I'm betting, on good news from Alaska's North Slope on just how far we can continue to reach both literally and figuratively.

And this brings me to a point – technology is advancing because oil and natural gas are still the most economically valuable energy sources in the world. The term "easy oil" is being slowly redefined as these technologies develop, and I have to predict that we will see a measured but certain expansion into Arctic lands and waters. This is significant because the First Peoples of the Arctic have, I believe, a right to benefit by all of their resources, not just energy but the fisheries and marine mammals on which they depend for their nutrition and livelihoods. And I am encouraged by what I am seeing to be an increasing level of engagement, rather than opposition, from these constituencies. Thirty years ago in Alaska, we were able to establish production from America's largest single oilfield at Prudhoe Bay by involving our Native Peoples in almost every aspect of this new and substantial change to their land and lifestyle. There was engagement – sometimes contentious and sometimes very difficult – on the legislative level, on the administrative level, on the operational level, and on the personal level. The ultimate result has benefitted all Alaskans and our national energy security in ways beyond any of our predictions at the time.

It isn't just Arctic energy that is drawing increased activity into the region. The impacts of an ice-diminished Arctic are already affecting marine shipping. We recently saw two German vessels complete a commercial transit from Asia to Europe through the Arctic Ocean north of Russia. Two multipurpose heavy lift carriers transited through the North East-Passage or Northern Sea Route during August and September of last year [2009]. The route is now open for a short time in late summer that cuts about 4,000 nautical miles from the 11,000 miles long traditional journey through the Suez Canal and the Gulf of Aden.

We now have reports that a Russian shipping firm has announced that it will use one of its ice-strengthened Arctic tankers to carry oil from the Kara Sea across the Northern Sea Route to Japan this year. This would be a proof of concept that could also apply to LNG tankers based on the same dual-acting icebreaker-tanker design used for the oil tankers.

While the *Arctic Marine Shipping Assessment* predicts it will be decades before these routes are open for many months of the year, I think we must consider that this is only the beginning and if it proves to be economical, it will happen.

We know that there are national security and sovereign interests for all the Arctic coastal States in the region. The US Navy has a new roadmap for the Arctic and they are studying the feasibility of a deepwater port in the far north. In support of their efforts, I introduced legislation that directs the Department of Defense and the Department of Homeland Security to study the feasibility, location and resource needs for an Arctic deep water port. This study will determine whether it is in the strategic interest of the United States, as I believe it is, to build a port and where it might be located. A deep water port would not only serve our military and Coast Guard needs, but as we develop our offshore oil and gas reserves and see more shipping, tourism and vessel traffic in the Arctic, a deep water port could provide valuable support for these activities as well.

The Coast Guard has also embarked on a high latitude study to determine what assets and infrastructure for which it needs to be prepared for in an ice-diminished Arctic Ocean. With increased maritime activity in the Arctic and such a shortage of infrastructure, it is vital we determine what the needs are and actively work to provide resources to protect the Arctic residents and environment.

I believe we are at a very critical time in the Arctic right now. There seem to be two paths that we can go down in regards to international relations – one is a path of competition and conflict, and the other is one of cooperation and diplomacy. I believe the decision on which path we ultimately take will require dynamic leadership.

One of the first areas which we need leadership in the United States and in the Senate is for ratification of the Convention on the Law of the Sea. I believe it is crucial for the United States to be a party to this treaty and be a player in the process, rather than an outsider hoping our interests are not damaged. Accession to the Convention would give current and future administrations both enhanced credibility and leverage in calling upon other nations to meet Convention responsibilities. Given the support for the treaty by Arctic nations and the drive to develop natural resources, the treaty will also provide the environmental framework to develop these resources while minimizing environmental impacts.

The United States is the only Arctic State that is not a party to the Law of the Sea Convention, having first submitted the treaty to the US Senate for approval in 1994 but not yet having acceded to it. Canada and Denmark joined the treaty in 2003 and 2004 respectively.

There are some who do not see the point in joining the rest of the world in ratifying the treaty. They say that the United States already enjoys the benefits of the treaty even though we are not a member, and that by not becoming a party to the treaty, we can pick and choose which sections we abide by, while not subjecting our actions to international review. I respectfully disagree.

The United States MUST ratify the treaty but we remain at a stalemate: the White House looks to the Senate to lead and the Senate waits for stronger support from the Administration. In part, the Senate calendar is to blame. It is anticipated that should the majority leader move the treaty to the Senate floor, it would consume at least a week of floor time. And considering that there are less than 40 legislative days before the coming August recess, it is highly uncertain that such time will be carved out unless it becomes a priority for this Administration. Given the President's focus on advancing the START treaty, I see even less of an opportunity to schedule the Law of the Sea Convention this year. I wouldn't say it is impossible, but certainly would say it's unlikely. Unfortunately, failure to ratify continues to keep the United States at a disadvantage internationally and outside the process, without a seat at the table.

Until the United States accedes to the treaty it cannot submit its data regarding the extent of its extended continental shelf (ECS) to the Commission on the Limits of the Continental Shelf, established under the treaty. Without a Commission recommendation regarding such data, the legal foundation for ECS limits is much less certain than if the United States were a party to the treaty.

According to the US Arctic Research Commission, if the United States were to become a party to the treaty, we could lay claim to an area in the Arctic of about 450,000 square kilometers – or approximately the size of California.

While the United States has not ratified the treaty, we continue to map our extended continental shelf and have been working cooperatively with Canada the last two summers on extended continental shelf data collection in the Arctic and are scheduled to work again in the summer of 2010. The US icebreaker *Healy* completed the second summer of joint mapping with the Canadian icebreaker *Louis St. Laurent*. Though each ship has its own equipment in order to accomplish the mission, combining their efforts provides better data and they can cover more area together.

Canada is expected to make its submission to the Commission in December 2013, so as to meet its deadline under UNCLOS. The United States, as I have previously stated, will not be able to submit its claim until we ratify the Law of the Sea Convention.

I am pleased that ever so slowly, the United States seems to be waking up to the fact that we are, indeed, an Arctic nation. I am confident that with the leadership of members of Congress, of the Administration, and from the Arctic community at large, we can continue to highlight the strategic importance of the Arctic for the United States. Thank you.

REMARKS ON THE LAW OF THE SEA TREATY

Lawrence Eagleburger[1]

I noticed John Moore talked about encouraging the prompt adherence to the Law of the Sea treaty. That is a little bit of a misnomer. There hasn't been any prompt adherence to this treaty and that is disgusting when I think about it. I was reading about the history of this problem last night as I was trying to get ready for this morning and all I could see on pages and pages and pages was that the leadership in this country, both Republican and Democrat I am sorry to say, has not found it "necessary," I guess that is the right word, to push adherence to this treaty. I think that is a shame and it is a blot on the record of both Republican and Democratic Presidents and certain Secretaries of State who, if they had thought about it at the time, would have been able to push it themselves. I won't mention any names because mine is too long to pronounce.

It is disgusting when I think about it. There is no reason not to join. I have looked at this treaty again and again and again trying to figure out why anybody with a brain in his head and between his ears would want to do anything other than seek and get ratification of the treaty, and as fast as possible. John Bolton, for example, is a very good friend of mine and sometimes I hate to admit that, but nevertheless he is. Every time I have talked to John about why he doesn't want this treaty to proceed his only basic answer is that it is a blot on American sovereignty. I don't understand that.

I don't know if anybody can make a case that I can understand because the fact of the matter is that in reality this treaty *increases*, if possible, our sovereignty in the sense that it adds substantial "ground," if I may use the word ground, or territory above and below the sea, to US authority, if you will, and to its ability to make use of it with perfect adherence to the treaty. We could make use of "ground" that at this point is not possible for us to use. We are very nearly the only country that has failed to ratify this treaty, and that is a blot on the United States. If you can explain to me why we haven't done this,

---

[1] Lawrence Eagleburger was an American statesman and former career diplomat who served as the US Secretary of State (1992–1993) and US Deputy Secretary of State (1989–1992) under President George H.W. Bush. Previously, he served in other capacities under Presidents Richard Nixon, Jimmy Carter, Ronald Reagan, and George H.W. Bush. Sadly, this strong advocate of the Convention passed away June 4, 2011.

I would like to listen. I would like to hear it because I can't find any arguments that make any sense at all in terms of our failure to ratify this treaty, other than the failure of political leadership in this country from the time this treaty was first proposed until today.

I am asking the present President of the United States if he will change that record and provide the leadership necessary for this treaty to be ratified by the Senate during President Obama's time in office. I have not asked him for anything before this, and I am sure given what I have said in public too many times that he wouldn't give me anything anyway, but this is a little bit different. I think the President can demonstrate substantial leadership, unlike his predecessors, on this very important subject, if in fact he will tell the Senate that it is damn well time for them to grow up and ratify this treaty. I don't know if I have anything else to say to you. I know I am scheduled to speak for 30 minutes, but there is nothing I can say other than what I have already said about this treaty.

You all know the details and the only thing I can say is this is a failure of leadership of both parties and of the Presidents of the United States and of a lot of others, including Secretaries of States, although I should mention I have read through and very much admire what the present Secretary of State has said about the subject. Mrs. Clinton was very much in favor, obviously, when she was before the Senate Committee on Foreign Relations. She made it very clear that she believes this is a treaty that needs to be ratified soon. It is one thing to say that, and it is another thing to do something about it, and it is in fact that very issue. None of the leadership in this country that I can see at least in the past has been opposed to the treaty and they have all said it must pass. Then they have gone on to other things, and as I said, given no leadership.

This is an issue that is a loss to the United States for every day, every week, every month and every year we don't ratify it. We lose substantial benefits by not ratifying the treaty, and it makes no good sense. If I say that one more time you are going to say, "you don't understand much" I guess. The fact of the matter is, I *can't* understand why it is that these people say that we should not ratify the treaty, which does nothing but provide the United States authority it does not now have and is a benefit to the United States in ways that are not now pertinent to the abilities of the United States to proceed. Again President Obama, hear me please and ratify this treaty and propose a ratification of the treaty, push it, and I would have some nice things to say for a change. Thank you very much and I hope we will succeed this year in getting this damn thing done. We have deserved it for many years. Thank You!

REMARKS ON THE UN LAW OF THE SEA CONVENTION

Admiral Gary Roughead, USN[1]

Thank you very much John Norton Moore, it is great to be here and I appreciate the opportunity to come and speak. I'd also like to recognize one of my predecessors, Admiral Jim Watkins, for whom I have the greatest respect and who continues to give of himself to public service. Thank you so much for everything you continue to do.

There are a lot of lawyers here – which usually makes me quite nervous – so because of that, I'm not going to get into a lot of the exacting details of the Convention and finer legal points. What I would like to do is to come in here as a sailor, and operator and talk about the security implications of the Convention as I have seen them over 37 years of serving in our Navy, in both Fleets and around the world.

I have the great pleasure and privilege of being able to lead our fleets today with a Navy that is as busy as it has ever been; a Navy that remains global and a Navy that is always forward, representing and looking out for the interests of our country.

From a sailor's perspective, the basic concepts of freedom of navigation on, under and over the world's seas are well-established and, for the past 30 years, specifically embodied in the text of the Law of the Sea Convention. There are some who argue that becoming a party to the Convention would somehow constrain our Navy's ability to do its job. If I thought that was the case, I wouldn't be advocating it, advocating for it today, nor would I have been advocating for it in the years that I have been a voice for the Navy. It is a matter of public record that all living former Chiefs of Naval Operation support the Law of the Sea Convention because it is in our nation's best interest to ratify, to finally ratify and join the assembly of nations in supporting the maritime regime that we created and must continue to nurture.

[1] Admiral Roughead is a graduate of the United States Naval Academy. Among his six operational commands, Admiral Roughead was the first officer to command both classes of Aegis ships, having commanded USS *Barry* (DDG 52) and USS *Port Royal* (CG 73). As a flag officer, he commanded Cruiser Destroyer Group 2, the *George Washington* Battle Group; and US 2nd Fleet/NATO Striking Fleet Atlantic and Naval Forces North Fleet East. Ashore, he served as Commandant, United States Naval Academy, the Department of the Navy's Chief of Legislative Affairs, and as Deputy Commander, US Pacific Command.

The Convention provides the norms that I believe our sailors need to conduct the basic operations of our Navy. Right now, there are dozens of US Navy ships that are sailing the world's oceans. They are operating in the high seas, they are operating under the sea with our submarine force, they are transiting through Exclusive Economic Zones (EEZs), straits, and archipelagos all carrying out the needs of the nation. Clearly our Navy is as heavily involved as any of the armed services in the fight in the Middle East. In fact, I have 14,000 sailors on the ground and 10,000 at sea in the Central Command. But just for a ship to get into the fight in Iraq and Afghanistan, if you're in the Atlantic fleet, you have to pass through the Strait of Gibraltar, the Suez Canal, the Strait of Bab el Mendeb, the Gulf of Aden, and the Strait of Hormuz before you arrive on station in the Arabian Gulf. A Pacific Fleet ship must also transit some critical straits of the world and transit through archipelagic waters. Without the provisions contained in the Convention for freedom of navigation, and for the sovereign immunity of warships, passage through strategic waterways could be a lot more sporty for our sailors. Whether it is interdicting pirates off the coast of Somalia, go-fast boats smuggling narcotics in the western hemisphere, or disrupting terrorists who seek to come from the sea, the Law of the Sea Convention provides a stable and predictable framework for all our operations.

Also under the norms of the Convention, we as a nation, and operationally as a Navy, can challenge illegal maritime claims of other nations that threaten to affect and limit our navigational freedoms. For example, the right to conduct military activities in foreign EEZs without the need to obtain permission from, or provide advance notice to, a coastal State is extraordinarily important to us. And given the expanse of waters and the vital chokepoints that exist within foreign EEZs, and as I watch the continuous efforts of some coastal States to restrict military activities in EEZs, I deem this to be of particular importance. Clear examples of coastal nations seeking to establish new customs and new norms that threaten our traditional view of navigational freedoms are apparent from time to time. Most notably, not too long ago, one of our ships, the USNS *Impeccable* was challenged by China about the right to engage in legitimate military activities within an EEZ. We continue to conduct military operations in those EEZs, because those operations are legitimate and in this case, they prevent China's misinterpretations from solidifying into new customary law. We're going to continue to assert our navigational rights in this manner, but I would also like to have the ability to work within the framework of the Convention to ensure other nations remain committed to the norms the United States fought so hard to include in that agreement.

The Convention also has important implications for our Navy's operations and our nation's interests in the Arctic. There are some who believe we'll be seeing a lot of commerce in the Arctic in the very near term. I am not sure commercial traffic is that close because the Arctic is not yet ice-free. I prefer to refer to it as ice-diminished but not ice-free – and for a Navy person, any place where there is more water than there was before is always a good thing. But I do expect that in time there will be commercial traffic that will start to ply the waters of the Arctic.

Moreover, discoveries and claims to resources on the Arctic seabed are going to increase the competition that will soon take place there. The commerce and resource disputes that are likely to occur in the future will develop into legal questions that will take on significant importance. We're beginning to see this happen already with Russian assertions of sovereignty to the polar sea floor, Canadian claims that the Northwest Passage is internal waters and proposed regulations for mandatory position reporting in the Northern EEZ, and, recently, Chinese insistence on a role in Arctic matters.

Beyond specific operational freedoms that the Convention provides for in EEZs, straits, archipelagos and the Arctic, joining this treaty has strategic effects for global maritime partnerships and American maritime leadership and influence. While there may be times when the United States must act unilaterally, we must also acknowledge that leveraging the power of coalition efforts can bring much stronger presence to bear. As powerful as our Navy is, we cannot single handedly promote and achieve maritime safety and security across the globe – it's not always in our best interest to always be the sole actor. Our maritime strategy that we released in 2007, emphasized partnership and the latest Quadrennial Defense Review that was signed out by Secretary Gates, also reflected the importance of partnerships into the future. Creating partnerships that are in the strategic interests of our nation must be based on relationships of mutual respect, understanding, and trust – trust that can only be built over time. In fact, in our strategy we have a line and that has been often quoted, that trust cannot be surged, it has to be built over time. For the 159 nations who are parties to the Law of the Sea Convention, a basis for trust and mutual understanding is codified in black and white in that document.

The Convention is the obvious vehicle to further that trust and cooperation for our own interests, and it is the vehicle by which we can collectively provide continuing stability in the maritime domain. An example of how this can happen is found in the Proliferation Security Initiative, a framework through which like-minded states act in concert to prevent the proliferation of weapons of mass destruction. Some countries, and I speak from experience as a fleet commander in the Pacific, are reluctant to participate citing that the US failure to ratify the Law of the Sea Convention is evidence of a lack of support for accepted international law. If we are to succeed in the crucial task of guarding against the proliferation of weapons of mass destruction – and we must succeed in doing that – then we must close the seam that many countries see present.

The importance of the Convention for our partnerships has implications for our role as a global leader. There is no Navy more global or more powerful than ours and therefore our nation should be a leader in global maritime affairs. We played a leading role in the nine-year negotiation of the Law of the Sea Convention, as well as the subsequent negotiation of the 1994 Part XI Implementing Agreement. Yet, as the *only* permanent member of the UN Security Council outside the Convention, the only Arctic nation that is not a party, and one of the few nations still remaining outside one of the most widely subscribed international agreements in world history, we hinder our ability to lead. Our ability to positively influence and shape emerging trends is negatively influenced because we do not have a seat at the table. We cannot stand outside the Convention and watch as other nations inside the Convention accept the legal framework on issues of navigation, sovereignty, and resource rights that are critical to our nation. We don't have a voice at that table and I can't overstate the importance of this issue. Having a seat at the table is extraordinarily important and it will diminish our maritime interests in the future if we do not subscribe to this.

Let me circle back to where I began and reiterate the same thing that Admiral Watkins and all of my living predecessors have made particularly and extremely clear – that it is in the best interest of this nation and the best interests of our Navy to finally join the Law of the Sea Convention. We must demonstrate leadership and provide the men and women who serve in our Navy the most solid legal footing possible so they can carry out the daily tasks that our nation requires of them. It is an imperative and I appreciate all that you do to keep the discussion and the initiative and the debate going.

Thank you very much and I have some time for any questions that you may have.

THE SKY IS FALLING OR IS IT? DISSECTION OF THE GULF OF MEXICO "MACONDO" OIL SPILL

Dr. Quenton Dokken[1]

In an interview with Mr. Tom Zeller of the *New York Times* a few days after the blowout on the Deepwater Horizon drill rig, in response to headlines of unprecedented disaster and doom for the Gulf of Mexico I commented "...the sky is not falling..."; a statement that not everyone agreed with. Apparently some people believed the sky was/is falling, and at the time headlines certainly did not dissuade that impression. I believe that there is substantial ground on which to consider and measure spill impact and the future of the Gulf of Mexico and its coastal communities. The full impact of this blowout has not been measured, only speculated, and the history of spills suggests that the Gulf of Mexico will survive as a productive ecosystem and economic engine.

The blowout at the Deepwater Horizon drill rig in lease block *Mississippi Canyon 252* on April 20 was tragic – 11 men lost their lives leaving a hole in our hearts and history that can never be filled. Environmentally, it is still a disaster of undetermined magnitude. Certainly, the natural environment has been degraded and lives have been negatively impacted, but the full extent of this has not yet been measured. It is an ongoing disaster. Recovery within our coastal communities and impact assessment will not be complete until the well is plugged and the scientific and economic data is fully tabulated and analyzed.

Environmental Impact

Oil in the Gulf of Mexico is not new – it has been entering the Gulf of Mexico for as long as the Gulf has existed!

1) Natural seepage (1–2 supertankers/year or ~1,090,910 brls/yr);
2) Marine shipping disasters (just since 1990 145,234 brls and during WWII 56 ships were sunk in GoM);
3) Marine shipping operations (bilge cleaning);

[1] President/CEO Gulf of Mexico Foundation, Inc. <www.gulfmex.org>. This paper was presented on May 20, 2010, one month after the initial blowout. See also in this volume "Deepwater Horizon and the Arctic: Is There a Need for International Regulation?" by Mayer, Roach, and Baker.

4) Oil/gas production (IXTOC I in 1979 3,181,818 brls over a 10 month period);
5) Chronic spills in recreational and commercial marinas (significant);
6) Storm water runoff within the watershed of the Mississippi River and all other river systems feeding into the Gulf of Mexico and from coastal communities (perhaps the largest source of all);
7) Spills from hurricane impact (159,091 brls during Katrina); and
8) Other (refinery spill 71,000 brls).

Why is this important to know? Based on scientific measurement and history – hydrocarbons in the system have always been adequately dealt with by nature. It is not likely that the oil flowing into Gulf today will still be there a year from now. That being said, although oil and gas in the Gulf is not new, it is imperative that we reduce and eliminate human inputs where possible – anthropogenic inputs are not good!

Science does not have a clue as to the total capacity of the Gulf of Mexico to absorb pollutants that we dump into it. We do not know which straw "will break the camel's back." And, keep in mind; these human inputs are not just hydrocarbons but a diverse soup of contaminants coming from seemingly unlimited sources, both direct and non-point sources. Without question these human inputs can be stopped if we humans are willing to make the commitment to do so!

Economic Impact on the Communities of the Gulf of Mexico

The Gulf of Mexico is the most economically productive body of water within the United States and Mexico's nearby seas. The tourism and energy industries are the largest economic factors in the Gulf. Along with ports, shipping, and fisheries, these industries combined have an economic impact in excess of $280 billion/year! And the "oh wow!" message here is that all of these industries are interconnected and inseparable.

How robust do you think the tourist industry of Florida would be without hydrocarbon energy and chemistry? Tourists do not walk to Florida, they don't fish from row boats, and they don't stay in hotels made of mud. In Texas, Louisiana, Mississippi, and Alabama, since the first offshore production platform was installed a few hundred yards off the coast in 1947, citizens of these states have reaped countless billions of dollars in paychecks and business profits. The flow of taxes into the state coffers from this activity is significant.

The agriculture, tourism, forestry, chemical, and fishery industries of all Gulf States could not exist without the oil/gas industry! And conversely, if these non-oil/gas industries did not exist the demand for hydrocarbons would be vastly reduced, and consequently, our need for the oil and gas industry would concurrently be reduced.

Relative to the tourism and fisheries industries of the northern Gulf Coast, the Deepwater Horizon spill is having a serious immediate localized impact. As a precautionary move, areas are being closed to fishery harvest until this event is over and subsequent laboratory tests indicate that the seafood from those areas is safe. Seaside hotels are losing bookings as we speak. All in all, the normal flow of dollars through these industries and coastal communities is going to be distorted in the summer of 2010.

Note that I said "distorted" not stopped. I've never seen data and analysis of the ultimate financial impact on the people of Alaska caused by the *Exxon Valdez* spill. It would be interesting to see a scientific analysis of what the average and median incomes of the folks of Alaska were before the *Exxon Valdez* spill compared to data taken during the event and after the event.

After all the federal government dollars spent during and after the spill, the response jobs funded, vessels chartered, and all the personal injury lawsuits were settled to the advantage of the Alaskans, what was the true financial impact? It was Governor Sarah Palin of Alaska that championed the "Drill Baby Drill" slogan and this was after the *Exxon Valdez* spill. Is it possible that after the smoke cleared and the spill headlines were replaced by headlines of another catastrophe – the true financial impact was not the disaster predicted and portrayed? Alaska wants the oil and gas industry, and I bet the Gulf States do too.

Science and Technology Response

Catastrophic events are kind of "gotcha events." Our limits of knowledge and technology – the good – the bad – and the ugly – are thrust into the spotlight. The Deepwater Horizon spill has underscored our relative ignorance of deep water habitats and ecosystem. We know virtually nothing of the ecosystem dynamics 5,000 feet below the water's surface where light never shines, temperatures are always below freezing, and pressures are crushing! Why is this? Because these remote realms are expensive to study, out of sight and out of mind, and the powers that control funding for scientific research are more interested in funding research in those areas where people live and can see the results. And, other than hydrocarbons we have not developed any financial interests in these habitats. In the Gulf of Mexico all but one academic institution that I am aware of has sold or scrapped their deep water research vessels because there was not enough funding to support them!

This spill has also underscored the oil/gas industry's technological deficiencies in dealing with such un-intended events. The IXTOC I blowout in 1979 occurred at 200 feet below the sea's surface and flowed for nine months spilling nearly 3.2 million barrels of heavy oil into the southern Gulf of Mexico which eventually coated the barrier island beaches of Texas. At that time the IXTOC

I was considered a deep water well. And, although the technology to drill the well existed there was absolutely no technology developed, tested, and ready to employ should a blowout occur! Sound familiar? Before April 20th engineers in the oil and gas industry were convinced that such an event as the Deepwater Horizon blowout could not happen with a blowout preventer and other fail-safe mechanisms in place! They were confident that they had everything under control. Unfortunately, they were wrong and we must learn from this. Booms, dispersants, and skimmers are band aids, and as such, inadequate. The development of deepwater drilling technology must give equal attention to prevention and response technology as well as to the drilling and production technology. Wells are being drilled beyond depths of 10,000 feet! Response capabilities must match drilling and production capabilities – no exceptions!

Future of the Energy Industry in the Gulf of Mexico

Offshore oil and gas production will continue until we, nationally and globally, can wean ourselves from not only the energy of hydrocarbons, but just as importantly, the chemistry of hydrocarbons. With a push for alternative energy, we stand a much better chance on the energy front than we do on the chemistry front. Here is a challenge, where you are now sitting try to identify one man-made object that does not have hydrocarbon energy and/or chemistry involved in its manufacture. Now identify those man-made objects with hydrocarbon energy and chemistry that you are willing to give up!

The oil/gas industry is here for the foreseeable future; and that is not necessarily bad. For the most part those hydrocarbon based man-made elements in our lives have elevated and sustained our desired quality of life. I, for one, am not ready to move back into a cave, walk the raw ground barefoot, and beat my evening meal to death with a stick!

Absolutely we must use this invaluable resource wisely. As demonstrated by the Deepwater Horizon event, we've got serious work to do to ensure that we can extract this resource safely and sustainably. The same can be said for the consumption of hydrocarbons – technology must allow us to do so in a manner that does not destroy our home – Planet Earth.

Gulf of Mexico Foundation

The Gulf of Mexico Foundation was incorporated in May 1990 – this is our 20th anniversary. We are heavily involved in habitat restoration projects, more than 70, in all five US Gulf States and four Caribbean Territories. Our education programs stretch around the Gulf perimeter and into the watershed states. The Foundation is in the forefront of developing and implementing effective environmental collaborations with Mexico.

We have a program of retirees that migrate south across the Mississippi River watershed with the whooping cranes every winter; and we are now involved in an environmental/education project in Equatorial Guinea on the west coast of Africa! Why – this is where the hurricanes of the Gulf of Mexico originate as does the dust storms that affect the coral reefs of the Caribbean Sea – it is a small interconnected world. We sponsor teachers on underwater explorations to the Flower Garden Banks National Marine Sanctuary and along the Intracoastal Waterway between Louisiana and Texas. Our programs reach tens of thousands across the United States and beyond.

Private industry is a critical partner as we strive to fulfill the Foundation's mission. We have always felt that the Gulf of Mexico society is better served by the Gulf of Mexico Foundation working with industry to improve the environment and economy. The oil and gas industry has always been supportive with financial support, and human energy and intellect. They have always joined us asking, "What can we do to help?" We are grateful and proud of all of our partnerships, whether they come from retail, food service, agriculture, ports, fisheries, individuals, or energy!

Conclusion

In the title I posed a "this or that" riddle: The Sky is Falling! Or Is It? The answer; no the sky is not falling today, but if we do not take proactive steps to protect both the environment and economy, it may fall someday. The future is literally ours to paint.

POST-SCRIPT FEBRUARY 8, 2011

THE SKY HAS NOT FALLEN – YET

This presentation was an opinion based on the author's past experience with oil spills in the Gulf of Mexico, most notably, the 1979 IXTOC I blowout in the southern Gulf of Mexico, and on observations of the response to the Macondo blowout. During the period of the Macondo blowout/spill the author and his staff completed three tours along the coast from Galveston, TX to Dauphin Island, AL to observe the impacts and response. The author was interviewed numerous times by media interests from around the world.

The Mississippi Canyon 252 "Macondo" well was capped on June 15, 2010. From the blowout on April 20th to capping on June 15th, 4.9 million barrels of crude oil flowed into the northern Gulf of Mexico. It was recorded as the worst (i.e. largest volume) oil spill in US history.

The *DEEP WATER: The Gulf Oil Disaster and the Future of Offshore Drilling* Report to the President has been published and study of the long-term and regional impact has been initiated. It will be years, if not decades, before the dust settles and the Macondo blowout becomes known history. And, it is possible that the actual environmental impact will never be known because 1) pre-blowout baseline data was inadequate for rigorous comparisons, and in the case of deepwater habitats, non-existent and 2) future hurricanes through the area will dilute and confuse the spill impact making it extremely difficult to attribute negative impacts solely to the Macondo spill. What we do know is that the area impacted by the Macondo spill has been impacted by oil before and recovered each time.

The response to the blowout was fast, aggressive, comprehensive, extensive, and effective. All known response technologies were brought to bear including *in situ* burning, skimmers, tens of thousands of feet of oil booms, and significant quantities of dispersants applied at the well head. Ultimately, the majority of the released crude oil was collected, dispersed, diluted, and kept from the most vulnerable habitats, coastal marshes and estuaries. Granted, some oil did get into the marshes and estuaries, but not nearly the volumes that could have if the response had been less aggressive. The effectiveness of the response was enhanced by favorable weather and sea conditions during the initial weeks of the response.

The engineering feat of capping the Macondo well 5,000 feet below the sea surface was astounding, rivaling any other effort to respond to catastrophic events in other worldly conditions. Granted, industry did not heed the lessons of the 1979 IXTOC I blowout and plan for such an event in advance, but the response will no doubt be the basis of future text books.

Ecologically, the claims of "doom" have not come true. Scientific studies have described immediate and localized impact, but none have described scientifically "significant" impacts outside of the immediate time frame or the local area. In scientific environmental investigations a finding of "statistically significant" denotes a finding that is considered fact with a prescribed margin of error, typically five percent. A significant finding indicates that the researcher is 95% certain that the conclusions are correct. Hence, while an oiled pelican or turtle is emotionally devastating, it is not necessarily significant to the overall population of pelicans or turtles or the ecology of the area. No studies have yet proven scientifically significant impacts in a long-term or regional framework from Macondo. Long-term studies may do so, but those studies will require time to complete.

The media frenzy was astonishing and never has transparency been achieved to this extent during a catastrophic event! Twenty-four/seven the public had access to the well site and all events surrounding the response. Media representatives from around the world were combing the northern Gulf Coast for the next headline. Media pundits expected and demanded immediate answers to the most complex of questions. Industry representatives, government representatives, and many within the scientific community were caught in the harsh glare of a spotlight with a voracious appetite. The result, what the public often believed to be "facts" was no more than opinion uttered under pressure but presented with great drama and fanfare.

The scientific method requires that several steps be initiated and completed before facts can be stated: 1) a question is asked, 2) a hypothesis to state the question is formulated, 3) a research strategy to test the hypothesis is designed and testing of the hypothesis is undertaken, 4) data is collected and analyzed, and 5) truths are stated based on the facts uncovered. During Macondo, the "question" was often presented to the public as the truth determined by scientific fact.

The Macondo blowout/response quickly faded from the front pages of the national and international media once the well was capped. However, emotions remain high in the affected areas, mostly focused around the issue of compensation for those financially impacted. Billions of dollars were spent during the response event and hundreds of millions, if not billions more will be spent in the coming decades on studying the impacts, lawsuits, and fines levied against BP. People and businesses were negatively impacted but to what extent is still being assessed. In some areas of southern Louisiana state sales tax actually increased during the response. Hotels were sold out to response workers, restaurants were full, and thousands of marine vessels were contracted; all paid for by BP.

In the shadows the term "spillionaires" was coined to denote those who made significant money during the response; and as with any major catastrophe, fraud did ensue. Today, dozens of investigators are working to separate legitimate claims from fraudulent claims. BP, from the start, has committed to "making it right" with those affected. But, as with ExxonMobil following the *Valdez* spill, BP has been viewed as a "cash cow" ripe for the taking.

The event resulted in the reorganization of the Minerals Management Service into multiple oversight offices under the Bureau of Ocean Energy Management, Regulation, and Enforcement. Permitting and drilling activities in US Ocean territories was put on hold until safeguards are in place to minimize the chances of such an event occurring again. Much of the industry has been idled as new regulations and controls have been promulgated. In the interim, significant numbers of the offshore drilling rigs working in the Gulf of Mexico have left to drill in other areas of the world. The economic impact of this down time may eventually equal the impact during the spill event.

It is fact that we live in a world with an insatiable appetite for oil, and oil is the foundation of the global economy. And, the US consumer is the most voracious of all. The Gulf of Mexico oil and gas industry is here to stay for the foreseeable future. However, there are many issues that must be addressed.

The Macondo blowout was the result of bad decisions complicated by faulty technology; hence, technology development and human decision making strategies must improve significantly. And, regardless of the efforts of the federal government to provide oversight improvements to decision making strategies and technology, advance in these areas must primarily come from within the industry and those companies that comprise the industry. By and large, the knowledge, expertise, experience, and motivation to improve are encumbered within these companies.

Other priority concerns include:

1) Only the majors (i.e. largest of oil/gas companies) could have borne the cost of such a blowout/spill. The smaller companies working in the US continental shelf would be forced to declare bankruptcy and leave the burden to the US taxpayers;
2) The Gulf of Mexico is an international body of water and both Cuba and Mexico are pursuing deep water oil/gas production. It is questionable that either could respond to a blowout/spill in the Gulf of Mexico with the same level of resources as did the US government and BP. Due to current patterns a blowout/spill in Mexican or Cuban waters will affect the US mainland significantly; and
3) The US Gulf of Mexico oil/gas industry is the foundation of the economies of the Gulf States. And, all other Gulf industries, including tourism, fisheries, agriculture, forestry, shipbuilding, and ports are dependent upon the Gulf of Mexico oil/gas industry. The industry produces a product that our societies demand and money flowing through the Gulf of Mexico oil/gas industry flows throughout the Gulf States. The industry must remain active and productive.

In conclusion, the opinions of my presentation on May 20, 2010 have held true; not due to any clairvoyance on my part, but simply because my opinions were based on history. And, history has repeated itself. Although we need to incorporate renewable energy sources into our portfolio of energy sources, the oil/gas industry is here to stay and must remain strong. It must also operate in an environmentally benign manner. It is also imperative that as we develop strategies to sustain the oil/gas industry, we must also consider all other industries and their impacts upon the Gulf of Mexico. No one industry can exist without the others and all have impacts.

In discussing the oil/gas industry and all other industries that make up the economic structure of the Gulf of Mexico we are really discussing quality of life issues. The environment and economy are two cornerstones of the quality of life we desire and wish to pass on to future generations. As we consider how we are going to exploit these two cornerstones it is imperative that we get it right today. Our grandchildren's grandchildren are depending on us.

Panel I: UNCLOS – The Stakes for America

PANEL I: UNCLOS – THE STAKES FOR AMERICA: INTRODUCTION

*Ambassador Mary Beth West**

I want to thank you all for being here, and I thank the Center for Oceans Law and Policy for having this event at the Press Club and inviting us all to participate in it. As is clear from the statement that Secretary Clinton issued and from the film as well, the Law of the Sea Convention serves a wide number of important United States national interests. This can be seen, among other things, in the incredibly broad range of US industries and interest groups that have publically declared their support for US accession to the Convention. These include, as Secretary Clinton's statement noted, every US President and administration – Republican and Democratic – since the deep sea bed mining provisions of the Convention were modified to meet our needs and the Convention was signed and submitted to the Senate for advice and consent in 1994. Proponents also include an impressive list of current and former military service chiefs and combatant commanders, Secretaries of State, Cabinet and Sub-Cabinet officials, Senators, National Security Advisors, state and city officials and others. In addition, a broad list of industry CEOs from industry sectors such as energy, fisheries, shipping, marine manufacturing, bio-technology and telecommunications, to name a few, support the Convention. The list of supporters also includes a wide array of oceans environmental and humanitarian organizations, including the National Resources Defense Council, WWF, the Nature Conservatory, Defenders of Wildlife, the Center for International Environmental Law, the Monterey Bay Aquarium, the Pew Charitable Trusts, Humane Society International, the Ocean Conservancy, Oceana, and a number of others. John Norton Moore did not mention that I have recently assumed the position of Director of the Washington Office of IUCN, the International Union for the Conservation of Nature. The IUCN has also issued a statement

* Ms. West is the Director of the Washington, D.C. Office of the International Union for the Conservation of Nature (IUCN) and a consultant on international legal issues. From 1996 to 2003, she was Deputy Assistant Secretary for Oceans and Fisheries in the Bureau of Oceans and International Environmental and Scientific Affairs of the US Department of State, with the rank of Ambassador. Prior to 1996, Ms. West served in the Office of the Legal Adviser of the Department of State, and also in the Office of the General Counsel of the National Oceanic and Atmospheric Administration (NOAA).

supporting the Convention. In addition, the Joint Ocean Commission Initiative, research and scientific organizations, international affairs organizations, legal and professional societies, churches, and many others support the Convention. I don't know of any treaty before the US Senate that has such breadth and depth of support across such a wide variety of US industries, environmental, humanitarian groups and government officials.

In addition to the fact that joining the Convention is very much in the US national interest, there are particular reasons why joining now is important for the United States. We have a very distinguished panel here to talk further about the stakes for the United States.

First is Ambassador David A. Balton, the Deputy Assistant Secretary of State for Oceans and Fisheries with rank of Ambassador, who is responsible for coordinating the development of US foreign policy concerning oceans and fisheries. Prior to becoming the US Oceans Ambassador, Ambassador Balton served for six years as the Director of Office Marine Conservation at the Department of State and twelve years in the Department's Office of the Legal Adviser.

Admiral Paul Yost is a former Commandant of the US Coast Guard. He had a distinguished 39-year career in the US Coast Guard during which he served as a member of the US delegation to the Law of the Sea negotiations representing marine transportation. He also oversaw the 1989 *Exxon Valdez* oil spill clean-up. Admiral Yost has served as the President of the James Madison Memorial Fellowship Foundation for 20 years and is now the Church of Latter-Day Saints Representative to the United Nations.

Margaret Spring is Chief of Staff of the National Oceanic and Atmospheric Administration (NOAA) and in that capacity works directly with the Administrator of NOAA. Prior to her tenure at NOAA, she was the Director for Coastal and Marine Programs for the Nature Conservancy (California office), and, prior to that, the Senior Counsel to the Senate Committee on Commerce Science and Transportation. In the Senate, she worked on many seminal pieces of legislation, such as the Oceans Act of 2000 and the Magnuson-Stevens Fishery Act re-authorization and others under which we operate today. I know Margaret was on the phone on her way here this morning about the Deepwater Horizon oil spill in the Gulf; she is very, very involved in what is now going on.

Andrew Keller is the Deputy Chief Counsel for the Senate Foreign Relations Committee majority staff with responsibility for treaties, nominations, and other legal issues. Prior to that he was in the Office of Legal Adviser at the Department of State for seven years, during which he handled counter terrorism, law enforcement, and intelligence issues among others.

Mike Mattler is the Minority Chief Counsel for the US Senate Committee on Foreign Relations. He is the principal legal adviser to the committee's ranking minority member, Senator Lugar of Indiana. Prior to joining the Foreign Relations Committee, Mike also worked for twelve years in the Office of Legal Adviser at the US State Department.

You may be beginning to think something is in the water in the Office of the Legal Adviser, since four of us on this panel are alumni of that office!

PANEL I: UNCLOS – THE STAKES FOR AMERICA

*Ambassador David A. Balton**

Introduction

I would like to thank the Center for Ocean Law and Policy for inviting me to join this illustrious panel.

Given the time constraints, please allow me to come right to the point: The United States would advance many of its interests as a party to the UN Law of the Sea Convention. That was true in 1994, when President Clinton submitted the Convention and the Part XI Agreement to the Senate. It has remained true ever since. It remains true today. Indeed, I find it challenging to say anything truly new on this topic, or to say it better, than others have said countless times before – including many of the people in this room.

I recently re-read the statements of State Department witnesses who testified before Congress in favor of US accession since 1994, most of which I helped to draft.

What struck me – other than how well they were written – is the consistency of the main points in those statements. I have taken the liberty of distilling those main points into a sort of catechism – the eight "greatest hits" of the Stakes for America in relation to the UN Law of the Sea Convention:

The Stakes for America: "Greatest Hits"

1. The United States is the world's leading maritime power. Only as a party could we best invoke and ensure observance of the rules of the Convention protecting freedom of navigation to advance our commercial and national security interests.
2. The United States has the world's largest EEZ and a continental shelf that is likely to be the envy of most other States. Only as a party could we best ensure respect for our rights as a coastal State and best secure international recognition of and legal certainty with respect to, the outer limits of our continental shelf.

* Deputy Assistant Secretary for Oceans and Fisheries, US Department of State.

3. Only as a party could the United States make best use of the Convention's provisions on environmental protection to advance our agenda for protecting the marine environment and managing ocean fisheries.
4. Only as a party could the United States exert full influence over the development of rules for mining the seabed beyond national jurisdiction. Only as a party could the United States sponsor a US company seeking to engage in such mining.
5. Only as a party could the United States use the dispute settlement provisions of the Convention – which are at once comprehensive and flexible. Only as a party could we nominate a US national for a seat on the International Tribunal for the Law of the Sea and participate in elections for those seats.
6. Only as a party could the United States maximize our leadership and influence on international oceans issues under discussion within the Law of the Sea framework.
7. Only as a party could we best hope to maintain the careful balance of interests reflected in the Convention. We cannot rely solely on customary international law, or on operational and diplomatic challenges, to best protect our rights from erosion.
8. The only reason we did not become a party in the 1980s was due to our objections to Part XI of the Convention. The 1994 Implementing Agreement addressed those objections in a manner that is both satisfactory and legally effective.

So, is there anything really new or different to say? I would offer three ideas. You can be the judge of whether any of them are truly new.

Regional stake: The Arctic Ocean

The first idea I would submit for special consideration relates to a particular region of the world – the Arctic Ocean.

Last year [2009], the Center for Ocean Law and Policy devoted its annual conference to Arctic issues. The Arctic is hot – figuratively speaking – in large part because the region is warming, literally speaking.

The Convention provides the basic framework for managing the emerging issues in the Arctic Ocean, including increased shipping, hydrocarbon development, environmental protection, marine scientific research and, of course, determination of the outer limits of continental shelves. All other Arctic nations are parties. We are the odd ones out. At a minimum, this complicates our diplomacy and weakens our credibility and clout to shape the future of the Arctic Ocean to our liking.

Practical stake: ECS

A second idea relates to the benefits of adhering to the Convention in regard to the US extended continental shelf, or ECS.

As I mentioned, our status as a non-party puts us at a significant disadvantage in our endeavor to secure international recognition of and legal certainty about the outer limits of our continental shelf – in the Arctic and elsewhere. But this disadvantage has become much more apparent recently.

By last count, 43 other States have made partial or full submissions to the Continental Shelf Commission in support of their claims to continental shelf beyond 200 nautical miles. In addition, 34 States have submitted preliminary information. Thus, a total of 77 States are actively engaged with the Commission, with others soon to follow. But not the United States.

Initial estimates indicate the US ECS – just the portion beyond 200 nautical miles from shore – is at least one million square kilometers or about twice the size of California. The United States certainly has extended continental shelf off our Atlantic seaboard, in the Gulf of Mexico, in the Bering Sea, and in the Arctic Ocean. Recent analyses and data collection suggest an even larger ECS, in these and possibly other areas.

In our view, a State does not need to be a party to the Convention to be entitled to continental shelf beyond 200 nautical miles. But joining the Convention would provide at least three advantages:

- First, it would secure our sovereign rights with respect to our extended continental shelf as a matter of treaty law.
- Second, it would give us access to the Continental Shelf Commission, whose technical recommendations lend the necessary legal certainty and stability to exercise those rights – and without which US companies are unlikely to engage in exploration and exploitation of the resources of the ECS.
- Finally, it would allow us to nominate a US national to the Commission.

Some may say that the massive oil spill in the Gulf of Mexico will severely dampen enthusiasm for future exploitation of hydrocarbons in offshore areas, including areas of the US extended continental shelf. That may be true. But whether the United States chooses to exploit those resources or chooses not to, the point is that we are better off being the ones to make that choice over as large an area of seafloor as possible. Only as a party could we best secure our right to make that choice with respect to the full extent of our continental shelf.

Geopolitical Stake

As for my third idea: Perhaps the thing that is most new since a State Department witness last testified before Congress in support of accession is that a new President occupies the White House, one who is seeking to strengthen US multilateral engagement. No, the Obama Administration is not rushing to embrace each and every multilateral regime – or every proposal for a new multilateral regime.

But if we wish to demonstrate our commitment to hard-headed multilateral solutions, accession to the Law of the Sea Convention presents an excellent opportunity to do so. As many of you have argued, and as I have tried to summarize, the rules of this regime clearly benefit the United Sates. That's particularly true since 1994, when the seabed mining rules were changed to satisfy our earlier objections.

If we are serious about multilateral solutions, the time is ripe for US accession. Thank you.

PANEL I: UNCLOS – THE STAKES FOR AMERICA

*Admiral Paul A. Yost, Jr., USCG (Ret.)**

I have been asked to replace Admiral Thad Allen who is out in the Gulf of Mexico supervising the clean-up of the oil spill there. Ambassador Moore, I don't think anything ever changes. It seems like 20 some years ago, I worked for you as we started the Law of the Sea negotiations on your delegation and here we are again. I was responsible for cleaning up the *Exxon Valdez* oil spill and now I am replacing Admiral Thad Allen who is now out cleaning up the Gulf of Mexico spill. I don't think things ever change, they just repeat themselves. I don't know really why we are here because I felt this treaty would be acceded to long, long ago and here I am old and grey and we are still messing with this treaty. I don't represent the US Coast Guard and I am glad Captain Kenney is here for the Coast Guard's man involved at sea in case I make any mistakes or seem to represent the US Coast guard because I don't. I was a Commandant of the Coast Guard some 20 years ago and before becoming a Commandant of the Coast Guard, I had Captain Kenney's job with law of the sea, so there is hope, Captain, that you will still be doing this for a long time.

The delegation from the State Department, of course was represented by our ambassador, Ambassador John Norton Moore, and he did an excellent job and ran a very tight delegation and negotiated hard. Interestingly enough the 500-pound gorilla in the room for our delegation was the Department of Defense. I smile now, but I was very unhappy then. In Caracas [1974] the Department of Defense was represented by several members on the delegation. When I got to Caracas, I had to go back home for about three days because I had to move my family across the country since I had a transfer coming. So I ran back to the United States to move a whole family from Washington to Seattle. I went back to Caracas and my assistant was gone! The Coast Guard simply cannot afford two or three people on each delegation. I was the only one and I had three committees to cover. I found the Coast Guard officer who had been sent to the Naval War College for a course and he called me and said, "look Captain, I am teaching law of the sea here and is there any way I can come and help you on the delegation?" I said, "Praise the Lord. I can really use you here because I am all by myself and please come." So, he came while I left to move

* Former Commandant, United States Coast Guard and President, James Madison Memorial Fellowship Foundation.

my family for two or three days. I left him in charge, basically, and when I got back he was gone. I said, "What happened to him?" My newly-minted Navy admiral had found that I had an assistant and he felt my having an assistant might somehow harm the DOD and he called the president of the Naval War College and had my assistant recalled. I have never forgiven him for that, but this is the first time I have gone public on it. I can't believe it!

Well, at any rate I represented on that delegation the interests of the US Coast Guard, the Department of Transportation and the shipping interests and my concerns were largely identical to the Department of Defense's concerns. I think about that now and I can laugh about it, but I was not laughing then. I think we negotiated well and we struck hard bargains and we came out with a good treaty with a possible exception of the Seabed Authority. And as has been repeated here and described by others and will be again today I am sure, the Reagan Administration objected to some of the Seabed issues. But that was re-negotiated and worked out so everybody felt very good about it. So we met all of our requirements in Committee One, we met all of our requirements in Committee Two, and we met all of our requirements in Committee Three, which was the pollution committee on which I spent a lot of my time.

So now that we have met all of our objectives in all three committees and really we have met them in dispute resolution as well, why haven't we joined the treaty? Maybe that is the reason we are having this meeting Mr. Ambassador. We haven't joined the treaty. I will repeat, four of the last Presidents, four of the last Chiefs of Naval Operations, four of the last Secretaries of State, four of the last Commandants of the Coast Guard, maybe more, have strongly recommended it be ratified. So have countless scholars and industry groups. Others must have better answers than I do as to why we have not signed the treaty. The fear factor that we will be giving up sovereignty in some way is a red herring and most of the other arguments against the treaty are equally weak. Of the issues requiring our acceding to the treaty, the largest is the change in the Arctic, which has just been well covered by Ambassador Balton. I would say the Navy's statement on the issue reads something like this, "While the United States has stable relationships with other Arctic nations, the changing environment and competition for resources may contribute to increasing tension, or, conversely, provide opportunities for cooperative solutions. The importance of the Arctic region is identified in the strategic guidance of all Arctic nations, therefore this roadmap, the Navy's *Arctic Roadmap*, considers the requirement for the governments framework provided by the United Nations Convention on Law of the Sea and the 1994 Amendment." So the issues requiring us to accede to the treaty include: it provides a written treaty and countries are normally more comfortable with a treaty than they are with conventional international law or customary international law; agreed limits for the territorial sea; standards for drawing baselines; a legal framework for freedom of navigation;

transit through straits and archipelagoes; dispute resolution; protection of assets in the Exclusive Economic Zone and the continental shelf; US representation on the Seabed Authority; free market access to seabed mining; and port State ability to combat pollution and smuggling in their own ports.

So it is safe to say that all countries are much more comfortable with a treaty, including us, than they are with conventional or customary international law. As a military officer, delegation member, and former Commandant of the Coast Guard, I think that the pundits and politicians who object to this treaty have very shallow grounds in my view. They play a very dangerous game leading average Americans to believe that the Law of the Sea Convention can somehow rob the United States of its sovereignty. It is just not so! Thank you very much.

PANEL I: UNCLOS – THE STAKES FOR AMERICA

*Margaret F. Spring**

I see a lot of very familiar faces here today. This is a very important topic for us. I am Chief of Staff of NOAA and Dr. Lubchenco, our Administrator, really regrets not being able to be here today. She offers her best wishes for a productive conference on this very important topic to you and to NOAA (National Oceanic and Atmospheric Administration). I am going to be offering the NOAA perspective on the Law of the Sea Convention and I have been actively engaged while at NOAA and for most of my career from the NGO and Senate perspectives on the whole range of oceans' issues. In this case, I have been privileged to work with many of the visionaries here in this room today who are interested in elevating the national attention to oceans and I thank you. Much of this vision has been articulated of late to the US and Pew Oceans Commissions and their success in the Joint Oceans Commission. All of them identified the need to accede to the Law of the Sea treaty as a top priority. I recognize Admiral Watkins is here today. Thank you for your service.

NOAA is often referred to and refers to itself as the nation's oceans agency, but many agencies and entities play critical roles in this regard. It is clear that US oceans interests are broad and diverse as evidenced by the representation here at this meeting. NOAA's mission is one of stewardship, science and service: stewardship of marine and coastal resources of the United States, support for maritime commerce and industry, ocean science and research, and provision of services. That support includes weather forecast and warnings, oil spill response, support to coastal communities, planning and building resilience, and a new area of focus – climate services. As you might imagine we have been spending most of our attention for the past four weeks on the Deepwater Horizon oil spill in the Gulf of Mexico working closely with Ambassador Balton and the Department of State to ensure we are communicating with the governments in the region and responding to offers of assistance.

The Law of the Sea Convention provides a stable, predictable legal framework to strike the appropriate balance among often competing oceans interests. It is this balance that in many ways makes the Law of the Sea Convention unique and makes it able to withstand the test of time. The United States is both a

* Chief of Staff, National Oceanic and Atmospheric Administration.

coastal State and a maritime State and we value the range of rights and responsibilities accorded by the Convention. Of particular interest to NOAA are those provisions of the Convention that promote continuing improvement in the health of the world's oceans and their living resources as well as the scientific research that is essential to understanding, protecting, and sustainably managing the oceans. The United States leads the world in marine scientific research and in promoting the right to conduct scientific research in the marine environment. The Convention protects the right to conduct marine scientific research on the high seas, promotes access to coastal areas for scientists and importantly provides for the sharing of results. It provides important protection for scientists seeking access to coastal areas and promotes stability and predictability, which is essential to the planning and conduct of research projects. It also promotes international cooperation between states and through international organizations such as the Intergovernmental Oceanographic Commission.

NOAA's researchers and research vessels and those of our partners operate globally, taking advantage of these provisions of the Convention to work in other countries and to collaborate with international partners. The benefits to the United States from this research and from the partnerships established among researchers, institutions and countries are enormous. The science informs our management actions, commercial endeavors, and our understanding of the world around us, including our ability to cope with dangerous phenomena such as hurricanes. Let me provide a recent example. NOAA recently launched a new research vessel called the *Okeanos Explorer*, dedicated to exploration. Its first mission is scheduled to take it to Guam and then to Indonesia where it will participate in a joint exploration effort in a relatively unexplored part of Indonesia's waters in partnership with an Indonesian research vessel. The process to obtain the required research permits and associated visas to operate in Indonesian waters was very complex and difficult. Nevertheless, the process exists due to the Law of the Sea Convention and therefore this collaboration is possible.

The Convention is also a comprehensive environmental agreement addressing all sources of pollution to the marine and coastal environment, including from land-based, air and vessel sources. It has served as a launching point for a number of international agreements that give further definition to rights and obligations on specific topics. It recognizes that the coastal State has the authority to protect and manage coastal and ocean waters, including the environmental safeguards that are important for commercial, recreational and other societal benefits and services. It provides a mechanism to work internationally to achieve those goals.

We have learned through experience that managing competing ocean interests requires an integrated approach. Human uses of our oceans are increasing. Commercial fishing boats, cargo ships and pleasure crafts compete with offshore oil and gas exploration. New wind and wave energy sources are under development and underwater cables are being laid to connect the world. Of special concern in this regard is the Arctic, which Ambassador Balton has already noted. NOAA has a unique role to play in this effort through interagency collaboration and working with the States and stake holders. We are working to foster a comprehensive management approach that reduces human use and ecosystem conflicts, while still promoting economic activity and maintenance of critical ecosystem services. This reflects the balance and body of the Convention. Our ability as both a coastal and maritime nation to continue to explore and understand our oceans, to facilitate economic progress and to carry out our stewardship obligations, will be greatly strengthened by the United States joining the Law of the Sea Convention.

PANEL I: UNCLOS – THE STAKES FOR AMERICA

*Andrew Keller**

My name is Andrew Keller and I am the deputy counsel for the Majority Staff on the Senate Foreign Relations Committee. I would first like to thank Ambassador Moore for the invitation to speak here and to be part of the panel. It is humbling to be part of the panel with so many people who have such vast experience, from negotiation of the treaty to dealing with it for many years on a daily basis. I should let you know that I am a relative newcomer to the treaty; my experience has been in conjunction with my time in the Senate, which has been for the last year and half. So I don't bear all the joy and scars and other drama that is sometimes associated with the treaty. I should also let you know that I am here in my personal capacity and not on behalf of Senator Kerry or the other members of the Foreign Relations Committee.

I would like to speak to you about a few things today. One is the developments or perhaps the non-developments during the 111th Congress on the Law of the Sea treaty. The second is the procedural requirements for moving the treaty through the Senate and at this point what needs to be done both in Committee and on the floor. And then, lastly, some challenges that I see in getting the treaty to the Senate floor and beyond.

It is first important to know, as we are talking about the 111th Congress, that there was a transition in leadership on the Senate Foreign Relations Committee. It went from Senator Biden, who was a strong supporter of the treaty, to Senator Kerry. Senator Kerry has continued this tradition of support and has been a strong and public advocate of the treaty. He has made clear that bringing it to the floor and getting advice and consent is one of his top priorities. He and the other supporters of the treaty in the Senate really see this for what it is. It is one of the few issues that, as Ambassador West mentioned, the military, key industries, environmental groups and other stakeholders are on the same page and recognize that national security and environmental interests favor moving forward on the treaty.

As far as developments within the Senate go for this Congress, as many of you probably know, the Senate Foreign Relations Committee has not held hearings on the Law of the Sea during the 111th Congress. In fact, we have only

* Deputy Chief Counsel, Majority Staff, Senate Foreign Relations Committee.

moved a few noncontroversial tax treaties through the Senate. It is important to recognize that we have seven new members of the Committee that were not serving on the Foreign Relations Committee during the 110th Congress – the last time the Law of the Sea was taken up, so in a sense these members had not been really exposed to the Committee treaty process. The first big test of that is ongoing right now with the new START treaty, which is the bilateral arms control treaty with Russia that the administration recently submitted.

As far as committee action on Law of the Sea, it has been fairly sparse. We held a roundtable on Arctic issues, in which Senators Kerry and Murkowski raised the importance of the Law of the Sea and clearly noted how important it is that the United States join and participate in the treaty in relation to its framework for handling Arctic issues. One of the most notable moments came in February when Secretary Clinton was in front of the Committee testifying on the foreign affairs budget. She made some remarks that demonstrated the passion and support that she has for the treaty. She stated that, "Our country stands to gain immensely from this treaty. Everything we know from what we are picking up with respect to other countries' use of the tools under the Law of the Sea demonstrates that we will lose out, in economic and resource rights, in terms of environmental interests, and national security, if we do not accede to the treaty." She went on to say, "I believe with all my heart that we are going to be so sorry if we don't get this thing up and going. If there is more that we need to do from the administration side, Mr. Chairman, I will get it done. You give me the date and we will have people here to testify because I want everybody on the Committee and Congress to know what is at stake here." These remarks show, at least at the State Department and at the Secretary of State level, that there is incredible support for moving this forward. As many of you know, the White House has been less vocal in pushing the treaty during this Congress.

As far as other developments outside of Congress, the most important recently is what Ambassador Balton has mentioned, which is the Gulf of Mexico oil spill. As he said, the question is not necessarily substantively if the treaty will affect our decision whether we drill in the continental shelf. That is a decision that is left up to domestic processes, but it will be important to consider down the road how the oil spill affects the political landscape with regard to the treaty.

We end up getting a lot of questions on where the treaty is and why it is in front of the Committee even though it has been reported out previously, so I would like to take a few minutes to explain the basic process so folks can understand what is necessary to move forward. The Foreign Relations Committee has jurisdiction within the Senate on treaty issues and when a treaty is submitted by the President it is referred to the Foreign Relations Committee, which is what happened with Law of the Sea when President Clinton submitted it in 1994. The Committee has taken it up on two occasions – in 2004 and 2007. The treaty was not considered by the full Senate on either occasion.

Under the Senate rules, if a treaty is still pending on the Senate calendar at the end of Congress it gets referred back to Foreign Relations Committee. That is what happened to the Law of the Sea Convention because it was still pending at the end of last Congress. We have it in the committee again now. So to move it forward procedurally we would need to have new hearings, and then have a committee vote on a recommended resolution of advice and consent. Upon a successful vote, the treaty would be placed on the Senate calendar. If there were a decision to take it up on the floor, as you know, the Constitution requires that two-thirds of the Senators present concur, and, for Law of the Sea that would almost certainly take 67 votes.

With that in mind it is important and probably easy to identify the challenges going forward. The treaty, as I said, has been taken up twice by the Committee and reported out, but has never received Senate floor time and so the procedural challenge is really how do we get to that next step? It is not a small challenge. If there is one thing I have learned in my short time in the Senate it is that floor time is the equivalent of gold. Just think of all the competing priorities, including some at which the Senate and Congress have already taken a look and spent significant time and effort on like healthcare or the ongoing financial regulatory reform effort. There is also a Supreme Court nomination debate coming up, there is the new START treaty, potentially a climate bill, and other important legislative items. So I see the issue of floor time and the substantive challenges to Law of the Sea as linked. What is necessary is to find a way to hit the right policy and pressure points to convince the Administration to fully support taking up Law of the Sea at this time and to convince the Majority Leader that, among the many competing priorities, it makes sense to move forward on Law of the Sea and to give what would likely be several days of Senate floor time to do so. My colleague Mike Mattler is going to be speaking more about this so I will stop now. Thank you for your attention.

PANEL I: UNCLOS – THE STAKES FOR AMERICA

*Michael J. Mattler**

It is a pleasure to be here. This is my second opportunity to deliver a presentation at a COLP conference. The first opportunity was back in 2004 in St. Petersburg, Russia. That conference took place just after the Senate had reported the Convention for the first time out of Committee, and we thought we were on our way to the swift ratification. But the work continues. During that period of time, Senator Lugar, for whom I work, was the Chair of the Foreign Relations Committee and he is now the ranking Republican member. Throughout his tenure and leadership on the Committee he has been a strong supporter of the Convention, and, like Senator Kerry, and like the administration, very much would like to see the United States become party to the Convention.

When Andrew and I address groups like this, we play something like the role of anthropologists. This is not only for people from outside this country, but also for people inside this country. We play a role of trying to explain the peculiar habits of thought and behavior of the US Senate. So I think you can take Andrew's remarks and certainly my remarks in that spirit. Hopefully we can help to explain how it is the case that the Senate has not yet ratified a convention which is so clearly in our interests for all the reasons contained in Secretary Clinton's statement, the testimony Andrew quoted, and in Dave Balton's catechism, and on and on. We pushed the rock up the hill twice – in 2004 and 2007. But, as Andrew noted, on each occasion the Convention wasn't given floor time in the Senate by the Majority Leader, in the first instance by a Republican Majority Leader, Senator Frist, and in second instance by Democratic Senate Majority Leader Senator Reid.

This has led some to conclude – sort of a conventional wisdom that has developed – that we are just waiting for the right window or the right kind of leadership, and, if we can just get ourselves all organized and time things right, we will be off and running. Certainly, there are important organizational and political aspects to the job that will be required to obtain Senate advice and consent for the Convention. But these process issues aside, I would like to spend a moment thinking about some of the substance of the case for the Convention that will be important as we move forward. A framing device for

* Chief Counsel, Minority Staff, Senate Foreign Relations Committee.

this was Andrew's comment about the difficulty for any Senate and any Senate Majority Leader faced with a number of competing priorities to decide to which items to devote the Senate's time. This is a particularly important consideration in the case of the Convention, because there is enough opposition to the Convention in the Senate to require the Senate to take a substantial period of time – at least a week and possibly two weeks on the Senate floor to debate the Convention. As a result, the threshold for moving it forward is likely higher than it might be for other items, because if the Majority Leader decides to spend a week or two weeks on the Law of the Sea Convention he can't spend that time on other pressing matters.

Even among those who have concerns about the Convention there are few that would dispute that the vast bulk of the Convention, and certainly its provisions with respect to the traditional uses of the oceans, is enormously in the interests and to the benefit of the United States.

The core of the argument for the Convention is based upon national security considerations. Everyone agrees that it is critical to our national security that our military is able to exercise the freedom of navigation rights contained in the Convention. There are also very important economic arguments for the Convention such as the ability to develop the resources within our Exclusive Economic Zone and on the extended continental shelf.

But if you are a Senate Majority Leader, one question you might ask yourself is whether becoming party to the Convention is necessary to securing these benefits. In this regard, those who might try to sow doubt about moving forward with the Convention might argue that we enjoy many of these benefits now because much of the Convention is accepted as customary international law. On this basis, some might ask "why do we need to become party to the Convention, given that we already enjoy many of these benefits even as a non-party? Our Navy and Air Force move more or less freely. What is it that, in addition, is gained by actually becoming party to the Convention?"

I think this way of seeing things tends to distort the analysis of the Convention. It makes any perceived shortcomings of the Convention seem outsized, because it would appear that the United States would be assuming new burdens by joining the Convention, without getting substantial additional benefits beyond those we already enjoy. When presented with an argument in these terms, the Majority Leader of the Senate would have to make a decision about the value of the increment between enjoying the benefits in the way we do now and the extra sort of benefit we would get by actually being a party. He would then need to assess how those benefits compare with other benefits that might be attained by Senate action other matters that the Senate might otherwise take up.

Given the need for the Majority Leader to make decisions in these terms, answering this question will be important as supporters of the Convention seek ways of persuading members of the Senate and members of the administration to pursue approval of the Convention.

So why is it not sufficient for us simply to continue as we are now, claiming the things we like in the Convention as customary international law and standing apart from other aspects of the Convention that some might consider would have some impact on our sovereignty or restrain the United States in some way?

Most importantly, there is the importance of locking in and preserving in law rights contained in the Convention, particularly with respect to our navigation rights. Relying on customary international law alone for these purposes would risk erosion of these rights through state practice that would be harder to challenge. States might seek to deny passage through straits of transit. We would be on less solid ground as a non-party trying to invoke rights, whether diplomatically or through the Convention's procedures. If efforts were made formally through the Convention process to amend the Convention the United States would not have a seat at the table in the amendment process. Some might argue that we could become a party just on the eve of an effort to amend the Convention in ways that prejudice our interests – that we could have a deathbed conversion if there were to be some effort to upset the balance that we fought very hard to have in the Convention. I think that would be viewed skeptically and would not put us in a strong position to fight back to protect rights on which we rely.

Relying on the customary law status of the Convention would also not put us in a terribly good position with respect to securing our rights to the extended outer continental shelf. Others on the panel have discussed the continental shelf commission process, which is ongoing and which is moving. Other countries in that process will make claims which may overlap with ours. That process will likely be looked to by a number of countries as an important legitimate process in contrast to those claims that are made outside that process. It is very likely that claims that conflict with ours may come to gain acceptance elsewhere in the international community, so we would be in a much weaker position with respect to seeking recognition of our claims.

A third problem with relying on the customary international law status is something that goes beyond the Law of the Sea Convention itself and goes to our broader ability to engage successfully in multilateral negotiations. The Convention, and in particular the changes made to the Convention with respect to the Seabed Authority, were hard fought diplomatic victories for the United States. They involved many of our partners making concessions on matters they knew were important to the United States. If the United States asks our negotiating partners to make concessions on matters important to them, and then after securing those concessions decides that it will stand apart from the Convention, our credibility as negotiators not only on Law of the Sea issues, but also elsewhere, becomes compromised. And so when we engage in other multi-lateral negotiations we may have more difficulty in getting other countries to make concessions that may be difficult for them in order to address our concerns. They will conclude the United States won't become party to the convention being negotiated anyway, and will question why they should agree to make the concession being sought by the United States. One might consider in this regard the land mines convention, the Rome Statute of the International Criminal Court, or cluster munitions discussions. One narrative of the outcomes of each of these negotiations is that our partners concluded that it was just not worth it to address our concerns because the likelihood that the United States would join the Convention at the end of the day was remote enough. It is important to our multi-lateral diplomacy that when we get a deal we like, we get a deal we have fought for, we actually embrace that deal and become party to the convention and move forward.

These are some starting points toward an answer for why not only the content of the Convention is in our interests, but why it is important for us to be full-fledged members of the Convention and to accede to the Convention. Being able to make this case that not only are the rules important, but actual membership in the regime is also crucial, will be important to any effort to convince an administration to devote political capital and convince a Majority Leader of the Senate to devote floor time and finally get us over that hurdle and achieve accession to the Convention.

Panel II: Energy and Economic Development

PANEL II: ENERGY AND ECONOMIC DEVELOPMENT

*Paul L. Kelly**

It is a pleasure for me to be here with you this morning and moderate this panel on the topic of the relationship of the 1982 Convention to energy and economic development in the United States. I first became involved in treaty developments in the 1970s, when I was vice president and general counsel of Zapata Offshore Company, which was the offshore drilling company founded by George H.W. Bush. After President Bush left the company and dissolved his interests to go into public service the company got into fishing as a second business. Believe it or not, tuna fish and menhaden fishing is the same enterprise as offshore oil and gas drilling. I can tell you now, that as general counsel and manager of government affairs for the company, this is one area where we had no conflict. I went to Washington participating in activities with a lot of other lobbyists who were involved in the treaty and watching what John and his colleagues were doing, and, with respect to my company and its constituencies, there was never any conflict of interest. I mentioned this only because it is reflective of the variety of US business interests that have been supporting ratification of the treaty. This certainly continues today, as you will see with the presentations of our panel.

Our first speaker, as John said, is Admiral James D. Watkins, US Navy (Ret.) who recently served as chairman of the US Commission on Ocean Policy. The Commission's final report is entitled *An Ocean Blueprint for the 21st Century*. It was submitted to the President and Congress on September 20, 2004. The President responded positively to this ocean action plan on December 20, 2004. I could go on for the full length of this panel describing Admiral Watkins' activities over all these years. Many of you are aware of his involvement in ocean policy and ocean activities, all the way from his work with the Consortium for Oceanographic Research and Education and his outstanding work bringing various academic ocean interests together in that activity. Also, we are all very much aware that prior to all this good oceanographic work, Admiral Watkins served as the sixth Secretary of Energy under President George H.W. Bush. He served as the twenty-second Chief of Naval Operations 1982–1986, as well as

* Senior Vice President, Rowan Companies, Inc. (ret.) and Member, US Commission on Ocean Policy. The author's PowerPoint can be viewed at <http://www.virginia.edu/colp/pdf/Kelly-comments-presentation.pdf>.

chairman of the US Commission on the HIV epidemic 1987–1988. Again, this certainly explains so much of the diversity and capability that he has.

For his various work in these fields, Admiral Watkins has been awarded an honorary Doctor of Science degree from William and Mary and Oregon State University. In 2001 he was given the distinguished public service award by the Secretary of the Navy. He was awarded the presidential citizens medal award in 2008, for his distinguished career in public service. I have a little anecdote to share with you. My personal experience with Admiral Watkins was as a member of the Ocean Commission and, you know with a 630-page report, we obviously addressed a lot of issues. There was no way to cover all the issues, and we had to divide the labor from time to time. Admiral Watkins gave me one of these assignments to work through. When we reported back to him to review our recommendations, I said to him, "will this do, will this cover it?" He said, 'Yes, I will give you an A-." Well, I turned and walked away with my head turned a little bit wondering about the minus. I then heard this voice, "oh, by the way Paul, anyone you know in the Navy will tell you that the highest grade that I have ever given is A-."

Additional comments at end of panel

I am going to make a few brief comments of my own before we go into discussion. Professor Moore recognized Satya Nandan earlier, former Secretary-General of the International Seabed Authority (ISA). I also wanted to acknowledge the presence of Michael Lodge, the Legal Counsel of the ISA. We are glad to have you here Michael. I wanted to express my appreciation and let you know about two recent technical papers that were done by ISA. One is *Technical Study No. 4* that was a result of a conference/seminar held at Chatham House in London, last February [2009]. I was invited as a petroleum industry "expert" but there were no other Americans there and you can understand why. The group was gathered to begin thinking about the collection of fees – here in the United States we call them royalties – on production that would be occurring on extended continental shelves around the world. It will be some time before there will be production and collection of royalties, but ISA wants to think through how the whole system would work when the time comes, both in the terms of collection of royalties or fees and in terms of the disposition of the fees received for the activity.

I wanted to mention to you that I took along with me to the meeting an annex that is currently provided to operators of oil and gas leases offshore of the United States. For leases that are very close to the 200-mile limit and, indeed with careful measurement, could almost be on the line, MMS (Mineral Management Service) has given notice to operators that they may be subject to the payment of these royalty fees to ISA. I wanted to comment on this because this payment has often been referred to by the critics of US accession to the treaty as United Nations' taxation of American companies or the American government. By the way, MMS has given notice in its annex to the leases that it will be the companies' duty to pay the fee. The fee is determined thusly: first, someone who operates and has production on a lease has to pay one percent in the first year of production following a five-year grace period, in which no royalty or fee is taken. Then, following that, the royalty increases one percent every year up to a maximum of seven percent where it holds. So in effect, an oil company would not reach the maximum of seven percent until twelve years after the time it initiates production. No one in the private sector would call that a tax or an unreasonable fee. In fact, most companies would be delighted with royalties at those levels. This is another argument that can be addressed and countered in our debates later today on this program.

PowerPoint comments

Ambassador Balton talked earlier about the new numbers of submissions of claims under the treaty A second *Technical Study*, just issued by the ISA, *No. 5*, I refer to all of you. It is available on the ISA website now. Figure one from that paper is reproduced here. The red (dark) areas show where countries have filed their submissions for extended continental shelves. You can see the world is getting pretty crowded. Look at the coast of the United States on this map. There is nothing there. This is a map that can be used effectively in making the case for accession to UNCLOS.

I want to give you some additional information from *Technical Study No. 5*, some bullet points. The Commission on the Limits of the Continental Shelf has now completed consideration of nine out of the fifteen submissions that have been filed. Their work on those is finished as of January 31, 2010. As Ambassador Balton also said, we now have 159 States that have become party to the Convention and it is estimated by ISA that between 60 and 70 of those have continental shelves with the potential to extend their limits beyond 200 miles. Several states are filing partial submissions separately. This could increase total filings to 100 or more.

Difficulties in preparing submissions, especially for small countries, caused the Commission on the Limits of the Continental Shelf to declare that States Parties, for which the Convention entered into force before 13 May 1999, will have their ten year period for filing run from that date. You can see the details on the ISA website. In addition, a further 44 sets of preliminary indicative information describing the status of preparation and the intended date of submission by countries has been deemed to satisfy the period required.

The Chairman of the Commission, Mr. Alexandre Tagore Medeiros de Albuquerque, has estimated that at the present rate of progress, the latest submissions received would not be considered by sub-commissions of the full Commission before August of 2028. Recommendations could be issued to the respective states no earlier than March 2030. This is a long time from now. The United States needs to get in the queue.

A note to John Norton Moore and Myron Nordquist – you had better increase the number of young people going into oceans law and policy. The world is going to need them.

There is a comment in *Technical Study No. 8* which indicates that estimating which coastal States will be the first to exploit depends on their technical track record, burgeoning consumer demand for oil and natural gas, and the possibility of our reaching a point of low prospects on existing continental shelves around the world.

I thought you would be interested in those points. Do take a look at those ISA *Technical Studies* on its website.

The author's PowerPoint can be viewed at <http://www.virginia.edu/colp/pdf/Kelly-comments-presentation.pdf>.

PANEL II: ENERGY AND ECONOMIC DEVELOPMENT

*Admiral James D. Watkins, USN (Ret.)**

First, I would like to acknowledge John Norton Moore, a longtime friend and of course, now Director of the Center for Oceans Law and Policy at UVA. John has been a linchpin in keeping the Law of the Sea flame alive over all these years. We have worked hard in the trenches together for at least twenty years. So, I am hopeful now that the United States will start implementing some of our recommendations over the next few years. It takes about that long in this country to make a revolutionary change to the way we have governed what I consider to be the greatest resource that God gave us – the ocean – where life began and where life sometimes ends. The oceans are where we find so much of our beautiful biology. We all look to the oceans, but yet we need to give them the time of day, which heretofore we have not. Oceans are not just for snorkeling, swimming and so forth. Sure, they are lovely and wonderful, but they are not just tourist attractions. No, they are bigger than that, and we need to treat them with respect if the human race is to survive.

Paul Kelly, here today, was a member of my Commission. He is a highly respected voice in the oil and gas industry. I always found him to take a balanced view of the world when he represented the oil and gas industry.

Also with us is Bruce Josten, Executive VP for Government Affairs of the US Chamber of Commerce. The Chamber has been consistently supportive of our work on the oceans over all these years. They are absolutely vital now to help carry the day with necessary actions to help a new national policy. The Chamber is critical for achieving success of the Law of the Sea.

Randall Luthi, President of NOIA, an oil industry association, is also extremely supportive. NOIA reflects the full spectrum of offshore energy industries, conventional and renewable, and in a sensible way.

Brian Petty, VP for International Association of Drilling Contractors, is also heavily vested in seeing that the Law of the Sea comes to fruition to help protect this vital industry so key to our competitiveness.

As most of us here know, the United States has long been a leader in developing and supporting international initiatives vital to the health of the world's

* US Navy (Ret.); Co-Chair, Joint Ocean Commission Initiative; Chairman, US Commission on Ocean Policy; and former Secretary of Energy.

oceans and coasts. These include agreements to help protect the marine environment, conserve whales and other marine mammals, implement responsible fishing practices, preserve coral reefs and enhance port security. As such, this nation must continue to protect and advance its maritime interests by actively engaging in international policies, global scientific initiatives, and programs to build ocean management capacity in developing nations.

About internationalism: Americans, in general, don't think internationalism is here to stay. As a result, most don't think it important to pay much attention to what is going on in the world around us. We are owned by China, deeply in debt and beginning to be co-owned by other nations whom we have educated and then sent back home to compete against us. They are now winning. We have some real chores here to rectify this weakness since everything we do is internationally connected. If you don't think internationalism affects our nation, our states, our communities, and our local entities, you don't get it. Other nations get it, however, and they are beginning to worry as well about long-term outcomes. International policy, then, is much more than a bunch of multi-lateral treaties that are good or bad. It's now a fact of life and adversely affecting us as a nation. Do we want to look back fifteen years from now and confess that we are sorry we went bankrupt, for example, because we could not get Senate floor time? I mean come on! Let's get the Senate floor time or get a new Chairman of the Senate Foreign Relations Committee.

Yet, over the last several decades we have seen: creation of a comprehensive body of international oceans and law policy; renewed efforts in ocean and coastal management by many nations; enhanced scientific understanding of the marine environment; and a proliferation of new actors who participate in oceans governance at global, regional, and national levels. Despite this rise in activity and scrutiny, resource depletion has continued. Conflicts persist over management of ocean uses, and many countries in the developing world lack the means to manage effectively the marine area resources within their jurisdiction. Is there a higher priority international objective for this country than to solve some of these problems? I don't think so.

Other issues also continue to exert influence in the international ocean arena. Most obviously these include climate change, which has significant implications for polar regions, such as the startling rise of Arctic ice melt of 2007, as well as sea level rise and coastal erosion. Many Americans do not know that the Arctic is actually an ocean, many believe it is a continent. In reality, it is a very strange and wonderful place and we know so little about it. The history of the Arctic is fascinating and it is now coming to light as an amazing region that we have to deal with intelligently. Talk about a role for Law of the Sea to play – that is a big one. For example, who are the sovereign owners of the Arctic-connected territories that these ships from China are going to traverse en route to Europe in the future over that whole trade route? How do we handle this fast emerging challenge? How do we work with Canada, our closest ally in trade and ensure that they are fairly dealt with? So, I say there is no better convention to address all of the relevant issues involved here than are those contained in the Law of the Sea Convention. The United States can best influence ocean management globally by enacting and enforcing exemplary policies at home, even though domestic action alone will not be enough to deal with the many matters facing the world's oceans and coasts. Solutions at the international level will require broad participation and cooperation, particularly when taking into account the interests, rights, and responsibilities of all coastal nations. To this end, the United States must take a leading role in helping other nations develop institutions and mechanisms to improve all aspects of ocean governance.

Let's talk about governance for a minute. Poor governance is at the heart of so many of our problems today. If you went out on the streets of Washington and asked the casual observer to relate all he knew about the importance of good governance practices they would respond "are you some kind of kook?" What is the big deal with governance? Well for one thing, you have to manage the money and we don't know how to manage money right now. We have broken the good government system set up properly by our forefathers. Over time we have screwed it up and now we must get it straight again. We have to start dealing with oceans-related matters in a horizontally-integrated way since most of the pertinent issues are interconnected: oceans and human health; oceans and the environment; and ocean science and technology. The oceans are alive but sick and yet the oceans are everything to sustained human existence. So come on guys, let's get with it! These are the kind of thoughts that come to my mind as I listened to the wonderful testimony this morning at this program. Twenty years of lack of attention in this area are enough. All in this room or most of this room have been punching this bag now for all these years and more.

So, now is the time to push that rock over the top to start it rolling down the other side. As a former CNO of the Navy, former Secretary of Energy, leader of the Consortium for Ocean Research and Education (now the Consortium for Ocean Leadership), and chairman of several national commissions, my commitment to US accession to the Law of the Sea has only increased. Support for our oceans has been shared virtually across the board by every major organization and institution that has a vested interest in the long-term integrity of the US international policy: defense, intelligence, environmental, scientific communities and core economic sectors of energy, shipping, telecommunication and fishing. For example, as soon as we put out our National Ocean Policy report and as soon as the Pew Commission, under the chairmanship of Leon Panetta, put out their report, both Leon Panetta and I got together. We said we know nothing would be done, so let's get together right now and start an implementation strategy and put out an annual report card on the government's response to its recommendations. We have fiddled around the edges of our report and adopted a couple of little trinkets in there, but we really haven't done the required full job. While there is a list of some accomplishments – the Maritime Technology Society reminded us of this at a meeting here earlier in the week – while good, they are not good enough or big enough. But, our lack of success to date, while frustrating, cannot discourage us from continuing to pursue our goal. All in this room today firmly believe that US accession to the Law of the Sea is instrumental in re-asserting US foreign policy preeminence.

I stand ready to assist the participants of this conference in carrying the message to President Obama. Let's get him to sit down with the right advisors and for God's sake make a decision. Let's get the Secretary of the State, who has her head screwed on and knows what is going on in this area to take a lead role. Let's get her at the table with the Chairman of the Senate Foreign Relations Committee, and get such silly little questions as Senate floor time off the table. Let's set the floor time! This is high priority stuff, so let's get our priorities straightened out. Mr. President and Madam Secretary, let's get things going! You two need to get the message sent very clearly to the administration and to the other leadership on Capitol Hill. Now is the time to do it. The urgency is clear, so let's not get locked into saying that we are fighting two wars and can't get Senate floor time. Sure, we are also fighting a huge economic problem and we have a healthcare reform bill we are trying to get out. My answer is "so what, can't we do multiple things at the same time?" I think we can. This nation is big enough to do them all simultaneously. So, let's get on with it! While I am sympathetic for the poor staff people who have to put up with this one-thing-at-a-time nonsense, it should not override the urgency to prioritize oceans and get them up in the national interest where they belong.

That is the message to the President, which I hope this group will convey to him, perhaps about ten minutes after we adjourn. If this requires a more aggressive approach than we have pursued thus far, then so be it. Let the group gathered for this conference focus its energy on steps needed to see the strategy implemented this summer, not next year. Don't let them say "we will do it next year." We have been saying this for twenty years. So, let's stop doing it next year and let's do it this year, get it going now. I would like to leave you with the feeling that you are on an important mission so don't give up on it. Don't get discouraged. John Norton Moore and I are not discouraged. We labor alongside other members of my Commission and many of the good people here in the room today – all of us trying to get oceans on a front burner. Now is the time to do it. As a matter of fact, I hope we can all pull together and do just that, within the next few days. The urgency is now. Unfortunately a leadership vacuum is prevalent at all levels of government. I am sorry to say that, but the Lugars and others fighting along with us in past years are fast disappearing. We need to re-educate the new leadership. I tell those good staff people who are up here on The Hill this morning, "you have a real job to do, not only educating yourself but seeing that the youngsters coming up the line in both the House and Senate are inundated with a sense of urgency on this issue." We have got to ferret out new leaders because they probably won't be allowed by old naysayers to make a difference. For a few years outsiders like you and me have to make the difference. That is where organizations like NOIA, COLP, and others can come into play. We are going to have to work on Capitol Hill; we are going to have to work on the White House; and we are going to have to find the right contacts and keep oceans' issues alive and moving forward.

Due to the leadership vacuum, education, which we heard mentioned this morning, is critically important, not only to the people who are running the country, but also to the American people who must be educated on the urgency of the health of the oceans. As a related matter, we are also tired of hearing the sovereignty issue played to slow down progress. Isn't this a great time to take care of issues like that? I say on the sovereignty thing, get over it! We are a big nation and a great leader of the Western world and a great champion of the world-wide movement towards democracy now taking place. Let's spread the good news around by setting a good example ourselves. Let's start getting serious about oceans' issues. By doing that we will set an example and return to our proper role on the world's oceans law and policy that affects so many nations. We are the nation that has historically been sympathetic and sensitive to other nations' challenges, particularly in humanitarian assistance to the downtrodden and so forth. There isn't any other nation that is greater than we are. We are letting all of them down if we don't get in there and start showing that we know how to govern this whole system properly. We can't be on the one hand really worried about clean water and clean air in Africa, for example, but apologize because we can't get Senate floor time for the Convention. Let's get off of that kick and keep up the faith and keep up the hope and dedication to build a better and sustainable world.

PANEL II: US LOS RATIFICATION: A POTENTIAL RESOURCE BONANZA FOR US INDUSTRY

*R. Bruce Josten**

United States ratification of the Convention would:

- Establish international legal framework, allowing US industry to compete for strategic minerals and search for offshore energy sources;
- Create a fluid maritime and aircraft navigation system, and provide right-of-way for undersea cable, crucial to global communications;
- Secure sovereign rights over extensive marine areas;
- Provide certainty and stability (crucial) for investment in global marine enterprises; and
- Create a more effective and less costly way of preserving naval power and maritime commerce interests.

Failure to approve LOS (UN Convention on the Law of the Sea) will be a strategic disadvantage to US industry. LOS, unlike most other treaties, will form the basis of maritime law regardless of our participation. The cost of non-participation is too high. By ratifying the treaty, the US becomes a member of the Commission on the Limits of the Continental Shelf, the body that ultimately determines the validity of a country's claim to a natural extension of its continental shelf, ensuring exploration for natural resources.

It is imperative that the US accede to the treaty allowing our US economy, resource exploration, and commercial enterprises to sustain our economic position.

- The Law of the Sea Convention is an essential action to protect the interests of American industry in the development and use of the oceans and their sea beds;
- Internationally recognized rights of exclusive access and transfer of title to recovered resources and to lay and maintain cables in the Exclusive Economic Zones (EEZ) of other states are essential before such investments can be considered. The LOS Convention recognizes and protects these rights;

* Executive Vice President Government Affairs, US Chamber of Commerce.

- American business must depend upon legal means to protect its right in foreign EEZs and on foreign continental shelves;
- With the LOS treaty as a tool our competitors abide by the strict environmental regulations we follow in the United States;
- By ratifying the Law of the Sea Convention the United States will be able to obtain international recognition of our control of resources on the extended shelf beyond a US EEZ and of our freedom to sail the seas free of arbitrary foreign interference;
- Business will not invest in exploration of the extended shelf until it is clear that licenses to deposits will be recognized by all nations;
- In lieu of accession to the LOS Convention, American business is unable to obtain international recognition of exclusive rights to mine sites that it has claimed under US law, and without being party to the Convention;
- Secretary of State Hillary Clinton: "there's nothing that they can do because there's no protocol that they can feel comfortable that gives them the opportunity to pursue commercial interests";
- The United States needs to protect our security, economic and environmental interests in the Arctic from non-Arctic states; and
- American industry stands with environmental and conservation organizations in support of the Convention. While our specific concerns in ocean use may differ, we all recognize the benefits of the Law of the Sea Convention in managing ocean use and protecting the seas.

****

American Industry and the Law of the Sea Convention

US accession to the Law of the Sea Convention is an essential action to protect the interests of American industry in the development and use of the oceans and their sea beds. Action is needed now, before foreign states capitalize on the rights and resources that could benefit US industry for the next generation of Americans.

Business needs international recognition of rights to exploit that are exclusive against all others

Ocean development is expensive, whether in the capital required to explore and exploit oil and gas or hard minerals miles below the surface or in the laying of undersea cables thousands of miles along the ocean floor.

Internationally recognized rights of exclusive access and transfer of title to recovered resources and to lay and maintain cables in the Exclusive Economic Zones (EEZs) of other states are essential before such investments can be considered. The LOS Convention recognizes and protects these rights.

Business needs protection against erosion of rights in foreign EEZs

While the US Navy need not recognize foreign claims of jurisdiction beyond our understanding of international law, American business must depend upon legal means to protect its rights in foreign EEZs and on foreign continental shelves. We need to have the US active in defending our interpretations and understandings of the law of the sea and that must be done from within the Law of the Sea Convention.

Level the Playing Field and Protect the Environment

The Convention can be a tool to make our competitors abide by the strict environmental regulations we follow in the United States and give us the leverage to push other countries, from the smallest developing states to China and Russia, to protect the seas from pollution.

The Extended Continental Shelf and the Arctic Ocean will be the new American frontier for the next generation. We need to secure them now

By ratifying the Law of the Sea Convention the United States will be able to obtain international recognition of our control of resources on the extended continental shelf beyond a US EEZ and ensure freedom to sail the seas free of arbitrary foreign interference.

Renewed US leadership in international ocean law and policy will strengthen our influence in essential rule-making bodies and will give us the strength to defend our understandings of maritime law against foreign efforts to extend their authority seaward against our security and economic interest.

A Delay in Accession is a Delay in Developing New Domestic Oil and Gas Resources

Business will not invest in exploration of the extended shelf until it is clear that licenses to deposits will be recognized by all nations. Failure to join the Convention during this administration will deflect consideration of Arctic and other offshore development from the US shelf to that of other Arctic countries or away from the Arctic altogether, a cost to the US economy and to our energy security.

Resuscitate an American Deep Seabed Mining Industry

In lieu of ascension to the LOS Convention, American business is unable to obtain international recognition of exclusive rights to mine sites that it has claimed under US law. Without being party to the Convention, American business interests will lack the confidence that codification of law and boundaries would give them to search and mine for manganese nodules, which would yield commercially viable metals: manganese, iron, nickel, cooper and cobalt.

Quoting Secretary of State Hillary Clinton, who stated during her confirmation hearing while responding to a vehement supporter of the treaty, Senator Murkowski, "Our industrial interests, particularly with seabed mining, just shut up. I mean, there's nothing that they can do because there's no protocol that they can feel comfortable that gives them the opportunity to pursue commercial interests."

Our Allies Are Our Competitors and They Gain From Our Inaction

European and Asian nations are showing interest in use of the Arctic, and those interests are in competition with ours. Australia is trying to require US ships to use Australian pilots to pass through international straits; the EU is talking about actions to take their share of benefits from the Arctic and to impose their will on activities within their EEZ. The United States needs to protect our security, economic and environmental interests in the arctic from non-arctic states.

The LOS Coalition of Industries, Organizations and Associations has nearly 50 members

Bringing together hundreds of individual businesses and millions of active members. All of these groups support immediate approval of the Convention by the Senate and accession by the United States.

Industry Stands with the Ocean Community in Support of the LOS Convention

American industry stands with environmental and conservation organizations in support of the Convention. While our specific concerns in ocean use may differ, we all recognize the benefits of the Law of the Sea Convention in managing ocean use and protecting the seas.

PANEL II: ENERGY AND ECONOMIC DEVELOPMENT: POWERPOINT PRESENTATIONS

Note: Links to all PowerPoint presentations from this conference are available on the annual conference page of the COLP website: *http://www.virginia.edu/colp/annual-conference.html*

The National Ocean Industry and the Law of the Sea Treaty
http://www.virginia.edu/colp/pdf/Luthi-presentation.pdf
Randall Luthi

Law of the Sea Resource Frontiers
http://www.virginia.edu/colp/pdf/Petty-Presentation.pdf
Brian T. Petty

Non-Living Resources of the Continental Shelf Beyond 200 Nautical Miles: Speculations on the Implications of Article 82 of UNCLOS
http://www.virginia.edu/colp/pdf/Kelly-comments-presentation.pdf
Paul L. Kelly

Panel III: Submarine Cables – Critical Infrastructure

PANEL III: SUBMARINE CABLES – CRITICAL INFRASTRUCTURE: POWERPOINT PRESENTATIONS

Note: Links to all PowerPoint presentations from this conference are available on the annual conference page of the COLP website: *http://www.virginia.edu/colp/annual-conference.html*

Submarine Cables: Critical Infrastructure
http://www.virginia.edu/colp/pdf/Burnett-Presentation.pdf
Douglas R. Burnett

Undersea Cables and International Telecommunications Resiliency: Important to the Evolution of Global Financial Services
http://www.virginia.edu/colp/pdf/Malphrus-Presentation.pdf
Stephen R. Malphrus

Submarine Cables: Critical Infrastructure – Cable Owners' Perspective
http://www.virginia.edu/colp/pdf/Wargo-presentation.pdf
Robert Wargo

Submarine Cables: Critical Infrastructure – Cable Suppliers' Perspective
http://www.virginia.edu/colp/pdf/Rapp-Presentation.pdf
Ronald J. Rapp

Panel IV: Protecting and Enhancing US National Security

PANEL IV: PROTECTING AND ENHANCING US NATIONAL SECURITY

*Vice Admiral Bruce W. Clingan, USN**

I am delighted to be here and have an opportunity to address such an important issue. Before I begin I would like to thank Professors John Norton Moore and Myron Nordquist for organizing this event and giving us an opportunity to look hard at what is an important convention with regard to Navy operations. Critics have asserted on occasion that the dialogue and debate on the Law of the Sea Convention is a Pentagon lawyer's initiative. I am here to dispel that assertion. I don't have any illusions that I will add value to the panel's discussion regarding the interpretation, the language, and the content of the Convention. My two esteemed colleagues are obviously well prepared to do that, but I am eager to share with you the impacts on the Navy and particularly Naval operations that occur because we remain outside the Convention.

In October 2007, the sea services – the Marine Corps, the Navy, and the Coast Guard – signed what is formally titled *A Cooperative Strategy for 21st Century Seapower*. We affectionately call it our maritime strategy and since that time we have been on and about globally implementing that strategy. It identified six core capabilities for the sea services or Naval services, as we combine them: forward presence; deterrence; sea control; power projection; maritime security; and humanitarian assistance and disaster relief. Underpinning this strategy is the simple concept that the sea is our maneuver space. It is not my intent this morning to highlight the impact of remaining outside the Convention on each of those six core abilities, but I would like to very briefly touch on the impact with respect to three of them.

Today, we have about 286 ships in the United States Navy and today almost exactly one half of them are at sea. Moreover, 40% of those ships are forward deployed, undertaking those six core capabilities that I highlighted for you. One of them is forward presence. We are forward so we can deter regional adversaries; respond rapidly to crises and to engage with allies and partners in areas of mutual national interests. Clearly, the right of transit passage, innocent passage, and archipelagic transit passage are critical to our ability to get forward without impediments. It is important also to touch on the increasing importance of allies and partners and as we go forward to operate concurrently with them, for

* Deputy Chief of Naval Operations, Plans and Strategy, US Navy.

example, on such an important initiative as the Proliferation Security Initiative as we endeavor to interdict the proliferation of weapons of mass destruction.

We at times find that our overtures to parties or states not party to that initiative to be constrained and they say: "we have a difficult time generating domestic support to join that initiative while the United States remains outside the Convention." Moreover, the initiative itself specifies that parties will adhere to international law, which includes that Convention.

Deterrence is another thing we are moving forward in doing. It is a by-product of being forward, but is also a by-product of the operations that we conduct. We are just not deterring aggression, we are deterring cohersion and what is increasingly called Law Fare, or using various international laws to the individual benefit of the Nation as opposed to the corporate benefit of the 150+ signatories to the Convention in this case. Everybody is well aware of numerous disputed boundaries, the extent of EEZs and things, but we find at times that States party to the Convention assert that the rights in it are not afforded the United States or Coast Guard ships. That is particularly important to us as we endeavor to conduct operations in EEZs of States party to the Convention.

Moreover, as we work to resolve their assertions our opinion is marginized because we are outside the Convention. Therefore what does it matter what we think? One of the growing concerns we have with regard to naval operations is enhancing global maritime security. The importance of this endeavor is not surprising when we look at Somali-based piracy, for example, and the impacts it is having on commerce and transit of commodities and oil resources through that area, as well as the prices that get passed on to consumers globally in a depressed economic time because of the additional costs, ransoms, security costs and etc.

The fundamental premise that we use as we work with allies and partners regarding maritime security is that it's important to have good governance and the rule of law apply at sea. The question then becomes what rule, what law? For us, we can only say customary international law and that causes us to forgo the power of being able to cite the rules in the Convention, which has over 150 parties, as I mentioned. So we could have more effective impact as we enhance maritime security or undertake operations and initiatives to enhance maritime security if we could state the fundamental law that we are endeavoring to have applied globally is the Law of the Sea Convention.

Lastly, and I close with this, sometimes critics of the Convention will say "well aren't diplomatic efforts and the power of the United States Navy sufficient to guarantee the rights that are accorded under the Convention?" I would suggest they are insufficient and that we could be considerably more effective if we had the authority and the backing of that Convention to underpin our actions. We certainly can't ply the High Seas and exercise the right of transit passage, fighting our way through everyone of those choke points in the world, for example. We have a future characterized by an increasing number of diverse crises. Having our efforts enabled by the Convention would enable us to pay attention to the crises and not merely to our authority to use the sea as a maneuver space and to transit, to get to the place where we can apply and project power to influence the outcomes of these crises, would be of great benefit.

PANEL IV: PROTECTING AND ENHANCING US NATIONAL SECURITY: THE REALITY OF THE OPERATIONAL ASPECTS OF UNCLOS

*Rear Admiral William L. Schachte, Jr., JAGC, USN (Ret.)**

I very much thank my long-time good friends, Professors John Norton Moore and Myron Nordquist, for organizing this event and inviting me to speak. We never imagined when we began work on the Law of the Sea Convention back in the 1970s that the United States would still be on the outside five decades later. John and Myron have been steadfast supporters of the United States taking its rightful leadership role as a party to the Convention and we are in their debt.

I also appreciate the opportunity to share my views both from my background as a designated Surface Warfare Officer (SWO) with combat experience and from my extensive work with the Convention throughout most of my military career as a Navy JAG, serving as a member of the US delegation to the negotiations during President Reagan's administration and as the Defense Department Representative for Ocean Policy Affairs. As our military commanders are keenly aware, the national security benefits of the United States' joining the Convention remain essential as evidenced by the endorsement earlier this year by Secretary of Defense Gates in the 2010 Quadrennial Defense Review. I should stress that DOD support for the Convention is driven by recognition of its direct benefits to our operational forces. They know, and you should also, that this support is not from or about lawyers, but based squarely and solely on the recognized needs of our operating forces from a national security perspective. In spite of this, and unfortunately, misleading and inaccurate statements continue to be made by some of the opponents to the Convention.

From an operational perspective, it is very important to carefully and comprehensively study the LOS Convention together with President Reagan's 1983 Ocean Policy Statement and the 1994 Agreement whose provisions prevail on Seabed Mining. Our naval and air force operations have been complying with and benefiting from the navigational provisions of the Convention since

* Former Department of Defense Representative, Ocean Policy Affairs, and former Acting Judge Advocate General of the Navy.

President Reagan's order to do so in 1983. Joining the Convention will sharpen the focus of all government agencies in compliance with international law as a matter, not just of customary law, but of treaty obligations.

National Security Benefits of the Convention

Accession to the Law of the Sea Convention will enhance US national security and economic interests. Military planners have long sought international respect for the freedoms of navigation and over-flight that are set forth in the LOS Convention. The Convention guarantees our ships the right of innocent passage through foreign territorial seas.

It guarantees our warships, military aircraft and submarines the right of transit passage through straits used for international navigation, such as Gibraltar, Bab el Mandeb, Hormuz and Malacca. This right of transit passage is critical to maintain the mobility and flexibility of our armed forces. With the extension of the territorial sea from 3 to 12 nautical miles, more than 100 international straits, which previously had high seas corridors, became overlapped by territorial seas. The Convention guarantees our armed forces a non-suspendable right of transit passage in, over and under these straits in the "normal mode" of operation. That means that our submarines can transit submerged, military aircraft can overfly in combat formation with normal equipment operation, and warships can transit in a manner necessary for their security, including launching and recovering aircraft, formation steaming and other force protection measures.

Our operators know that the same guaranteed, non-suspendable rights apply to warships, military aircraft and submarines transiting through archipelagoes, such as Indonesia and the Philippines. The Convention recognizes the right of some island nations to claim archipelagic status if they meet the requirements of the Convention. But it also guarantees our armed forces the right of archipelagic sea lanes passage in the "normal mode" through all routes normally used for international navigation and overflight, regardless of whether sea lanes have been designated by the archipelagic nation.

The Convention guarantees our right to exercise high seas freedoms of navigation and overflight and all other internationally lawful uses of the seas related to those freedoms within the Exclusive Economic Zones (EEZ) of other nations. This includes the right to engage in military activities, such as:

- launching and recovery of aircraft, water-borne craft and other military devices;
- operating military devices;
- intelligence collection;

- surveillance and reconnaissance activities;
- military exercises and operations;
- conducting hydrographic surveys; and
- conducting military surveys (military marine data collection).

By codifying these important navigational rights and freedoms, the Convention provides our operators with an international recognition of essential maritime mobility rights used by our forces on a daily basis around the globe. It establishes a legal framework for the behavior of its 160 parties and provides the legal predicate that enables our armed forces to respond to crises expeditiously and at minimal diplomatic and political costs. Today, more than ever, it is essential that key sea and air lanes remain open as an international legal right, and not be contingent upon approval by nations along the route. Anything that might inhibit these inherent freedoms is something we must avoid. The stable legal regime for the world's oceans codified in the Convention will guarantee the legal basis for the global mobility needed by our armed forces. And I might add that the navigational provisions of the Convention must continue to be exercised by our operational forces, particularly in the maritime environment of the global commons, an environment that has traditionally been one of claim and counterclaim.

I'm not here to discuss the economic benefits of the Convention, but I would like to mention that the US EEZ is by far the largest and richest of any in the world. We have some of the richest and most abundant fisheries in the world – all of which are under our exclusive control. Moreover, the pot of gold in the seabed is the energy and mineral resources that were also placed under coastal nation control. With all due respect, the focus on deep seabed mining concerns an activity that has no market and is economically not feasible at this time because many of the same minerals are found on land or within the EEZ. In short, our national security and economic interests will be advanced if we join the Convention.

The connection of energy to security issues is highlighted in the 2008 Joint Forces Command report, "The Joint Operating Environment," which is not optimistic about the world's future energy needs. It observes that: "The implications for future conflict are ominous." And "One should not forget that the Great Depression spawned a number of ferocious totalitarian regimes that sought economic prosperity for their nations by ruthless conquest, while Japan went to war in 1941 to secure its energy supplies."

By becoming a party to the Law of the Sea Convention the United States could assert a claim to an extended continental shelf off its coasts, including into the Arctic where climate changes and technological advances are opening up the possibility of making available vast amounts of resources. However, as a non-party, we are not able to participate in the process of obtaining international recognition of legal title that is essential to industry investment in off-shore projects.

Inaccuracies About the Convention

I will now briefly address three areas where inaccurate statements have been made regarding the Convention: (1) the impact of US accession to ongoing intelligence gathering activities, including submerged transits by submarines; (2) reliance on customary international law to exercise our navigational freedoms; and (3) the impact of mandatory dispute resolution on US sovereignty, in particular, US military activities at sea.

Impact on Intelligence Gathering

Nothing in the Convention will affect the way we currently conduct surveillance and intelligence activities at sea. Opponents to the Convention argue that the Convention's provisions on innocent passage – Articles 19 and 20 – will prohibit or otherwise adversely affect US intelligence activities in foreign territorial seas at a time when such activity is vital to our national security. I can say without hesitation that nothing could be further from the truth.

While it is true that Article 19 provides that intelligence collection within the territorial sea is inconsistent with the innocent passage regime and that Article 20 provides that submarines must navigate on the surface when engaged in innocent passage, it's a far stretch to thus conclude that the Convention prohibits intelligence collection and requires submarines to navigate on the surface when transiting the territorial sea. Nothing in Article 19 has or would prohibit a US vessel from engaging in intelligence activities in a foreign territorial sea. If a vessel does engage in such activities, it simply cannot claim that it is engaged in innocent passage. The same rule has applied for the past seven decades. Similarly, Article 20 does not prohibit submerged transits through the territorial sea, *per se*. Article 20 merely repeats the rule from the 1958 Convention on the Territorial Sea, a convention to which the United States is a party. The rule concerning submerged transits from the 1958 Convention has been the consistent position of nations, including the United States, for more than 70 years and it has never been interpreted in theory or operational practice as prohibiting or otherwise restricting intelligence collection activities or submerged transits in the territorial sea. In short, if or when the need arises to collect intelligence in a foreign territorial sea, as was the case of the 1958 Geneva Convention on the Territorial Sea, nothing in the LOS Convention will prohibit that activity.

Reliance on Customary International Law

Some have argued that joining the Convention is not necessary because the navigational rights and freedoms codified in the Convention already exist as customary international law and are therefore binding on all nations. This premise is flawed for a number of reasons.

While it is true that many of the Convention's provisions are reflective of customary international law, others, such as the rights of transit passage and archipelagic sea lanes passage that I previously discussed, are creations of the Convention. Additionally, if you examine the evolution of customary international law in the 20th century, you'll find that it evolved the erosion, not the preservation, of navigational rights and freedoms. In the mid-1950s the major maritime powers concluded that the best way to stop that erosion was through the adoption of a universally recognized treaty that established limits on coastal nation jurisdiction and preserved traditional navigational rights and freedoms.

It is also important to note that not everyone agreed with our "customary international law" interpretation announced by President Reagan in his 1983 Ocean Policy Statement, including allies such as the United Kingdom. However, our ability to influence the development of customary law changed dramatically in 1994 when the Convention entered into force. As a non-Party, we no longer had a voice at the table when important decisions were being made on how to interpret and apply the provisions of the Convention. As a result, over the past 16 years, we have witnessed a resurgence of creeping jurisdiction around the world. Coastal States are increasingly attempting to exert greater control over waters off their coasts and a growing number of States have challenged US military activities at sea, particularly in their 200 nautical mile EEZ.

For example, Malaysia has closed the strategic Strait of Malacca, an international strait, to ships carrying nuclear cargo. Chile and Argentina have similarly ordered ships carrying nuclear cargo to stay clear of their EEZs. These actions are inconsistent with the Convention and customary law, but will other nations attempt to follow suit and establish a new customary norm that prohibits the transport of nuclear cargo? Will attempts be made to expand such a norm to include nuclear-powered ships?

China, India, North Korea, Iran, Pakistan, Brazil, Malaysia and others, have directly challenged US military operations in their EEZs as being inconsistent with the Law of the Sea Convention and customary international law. Again, the actions by those countries are inconsistent with the Convention and customary law, but will other nations follow suit and attempt to establish a new customary norm that prohibits military activities in the EEZ without coastal State consent?

If we are going to successfully curtail this disturbing trend of creeping jurisdiction, we must reassert our leadership role in the development of maritime law and join the Convention. It is short-sighted to argue that, if the customary law system somehow breaks down, the United States, as the world's pre-eminent naval power, wouldn't have any trouble enforcing it. Clearly, our Navy could engage in such an effort. However, enforcing our navigational rights against every coastal nation in the event the Convention and customary law systems collapse would be unsustainable, both politically and economically. Moreover, it would divert our forces from their primary missions, including the long-term global war on terrorism. Indeed, coastal nation claims that are not consistent with the LOS Convention are the primary threat to our navigational freedoms. Those claims can spread like a contagious virus, as they did in the 20th century. The added legal security we get from a binding treaty permits us to use our military forces and diminishing resources more efficiently and effectively by concentrating on their primary missions.

Loss of US Sovereignty?

Concerns have been raised that it is not in the best interests of the United States to have its maritime activities subject to the control of an international tribunal, like the International Tribunal for the Law of the Sea or the International Court of Justice (ICJ). That concern is clearly wrong. While the Convention does establish a Tribunal, parties are free to choose other methods of dispute resolution. The United States has already indicated that, if it becomes a party, it will elect two forms of arbitration rather than the Tribunal or the ICJ.

More importantly, this concern fails to recognize the reality that no country would subordinate its national security activities to an international tribunal. This is a point that everyone understood during the negotiations of the Convention, and that is why Article 286 of the Convention makes clear that the application of the compulsory dispute resolution procedures of section 2 of Part XV are subject to the provisions of section 3 of Part XV, which includes the provision that allows for military exemptions.

Some may try to argue that Article 288 allows a court or tribunal to make the final determination as to whether or not it has jurisdiction over a matter where there is a dispute between the parties as to the court's jurisdiction. They argue that Article 288 could be read to authorize a court or tribunal to make a threshold jurisdictional determination of whether an activity is a military activity or not and, therefore, subject to the jurisdiction of the court or tribunal. However, Article 288 is also found in section 2 of Part XV and therefore does not apply to disputes involving what the US Government has declared to be a military activity under section 3 of Part XV. I submit this is clearly supported by the negotiating history of the Convention, which reflects that certain disputes, including military activities, are considered to be so sensitive that they are best resolved diplomatically, rather than judicially. This interpretation is also supported by a plain reading of the Convention.

Of course it is very important, as has been previously recommended by the Senate Foreign Relations Committee, that while depositing an instrument of accession, the United States will reemphasize this point by making a declaration or an understanding that clearly states that military activities are exempt from the compulsory dispute resolution provisions of the Convention and that the decision regarding whether an activity is military in nature is not subject to review by any court or tribunal. Twenty-two parties to the Convention have deposited declarations invoking the military activities exemption. They are: Argentina, Belarus, Canada, Cape Verde, Chile, China, Cuba, Denmark, France, Gabon, Guinea-Bissau, Mexico, Nicaragua, Norway, Portugal, the Republic of Korea, the Republic of Palau, Russia, Slovenia, Tunisia, Ukraine, and the United Kingdom. Additionally, since the Convention permits States to opt out of dispute resolution procedures for military activities at any time after signing, ratifying or acceding to the Convention, Bangladesh, Brazil, India, Morocco, Pakistan, and South Africa have declared that they shall, at the appropriate time, make the declarations provided in Article 298.

One final point on dispute settlement, Mr. Chairman. The Convention itself tends to take disputes out of a bilateral context, with both parties directing their attention to the Convention and not necessarily at each other. As you will recall, that's how we resolved the 1988 Black Sea Bumping incident with the former Soviet Union, which resulted in the 1989 Joint Statement by the U.S.S.R. and the United States concerning a Uniform Interpretation of the Rules of Innocent Passage. The Convention's provisions on innocent passage provided the legal basis for the uniform interpretation.

While we remain on the outside in a small club that includes North Korea, Iran, Syria, Libya, and Venezuela, there is now almost universal adherence to the Convention, with 160 parties, including all of our major allies and important non-aligned nations. Except for the United States, all permanent members of the UN Security Council and all Arctic nations are members. The Convention establishes a stable and predictable legal framework for uses of the oceans that will benefit our armed forces. As a matter of substance, all of his successors have agreed with President Reagan that the Convention sets forth the appropriate balance between the rights of coastal nations and the rights of maritime nations. The United States is both and will benefit two-fold by becoming a party. The Convention is good for America – good for our economy, good for our well-being and, most importantly, good for our operating forces. It is time that we reassert our position as the pre-eminent maritime nation of the world and take our rightful place as a party to the Convention.

PANEL IV: PROTECTING AND ENHANCING US NATIONAL SECURITY

Rear Admiral Nanette DeRenzi, JAGC, USN

I am very happy to represent Vice Admiral Houck this morning who unfortunately could not be with us today. Vice Admiral Houck is participating in something that is equally vital to the Navy's interests and its freedom of navigation and that is the selection of our young officers for promotion. I can only hope that the young officers that are being selected for lieutenant commander this week, will be able to advise their operator clients in the future on operating within the Law of the Sea Convention, with the United States as a party, instead of as we have done throughout our careers, which is working with the United States to become a party to the Convention. Thank you Professor Moore and Professor Nordquist for organizing this event.

I will be echoing a lot of the comments by Admiral Clingan and Admiral Schachte, not because we don't have anything new to say, but because what we have said is very true, about how so important UNCLOS is to the freedom of navigation and to naval operations. It is essential to our Navy's mission and to the ability of our warships to go wherever and whenever needed, whether we are engaged in counter-proliferation, counter-piracy, counter-terrorism or humanitarian relief operations. The more restrictions there are on our freedom to navigate, the harder it is for the Navy to do its job. The Convention provides clear legal support for freedom of navigation. It sets forth a blueprint by which we can challenge illegal maritime claims and it underscores, among other things, our right to conduct military activities in the EEZ without the need to obtain prior permission from, or give advance notice to, the coastal State.

As you are no doubt aware, we are engaged in fighting piracy on a scale that we haven't encountered before. The risk of attack in the Gulf of Aden and the Indian Ocean has increased greatly since 2008. Our Navy, in conjunction with coalition partners and individual contributing states, is hard at work to address this threat. At this very moment Navy Judge Advocates are at sea providing critical advice on the law applicable to counter-piracy. While these attorneys are well versed in the relevant Security Council resolutions, they also look to the Law of the Sea Convention as the primary authority for counter-piracy operations. Article 100 mandates that all nations must cooperate in suppressing piracy. Article 110 provides clear legal authority to board vessels reasonably suspected of engaging in this crime. Fighting piracy is only one example of how UNCLOS supports continuing military operations.

Another example is the myriad maritime interdiction operations continuing around the globe today. In addition to piracy, Article 110 also allows warships to stop and board any private vessel suspected of being stateless. Using Article 110, coalition ships have conducted boardings to interdict terrorists and drug and weapon smugglers supporting terrorists. Pursuant to the Proliferation Security Initiative, United States and partner warships have used the rules under Articles 92 and 110 to board vessels in concert with our counter-proliferation efforts. Coalition operations are the new norm, the ever-increasing number in scope of threats to our national security and to world peace require that we form and leverage strong bonds with coalition partners and that those coalition operations are grounded in the rule of law.

It is critical that to the greatest extent possible we operate from the same set of rules. The Law of the Sea Convention, with 160 parties and used by the Navy around the world every day, is the obvious document to enhance mutual trust and cooperation and to provide continuing stability in the maritime domain. After almost 30 years after its negotiations, negotiations as you have heard and as you know, in which the United States paid a critical and significant role, we still haven't ratified it. The initial objections associated with deep seabed mining are no longer operative. They were resolved satisfactorily along time ago in the 1994 agreement. Yet we continue to remain outside the most widely subscribed to legal agreement in history, due to the efforts of a concerted opposition, which argues that ratification would somehow harm America's interests. As Admiral Schachte states, these arguments, though often repeated, are simply not true and a careful review grounded in international law – and frankly the plain text of the treaty itself – makes this clear.

For example, critics argue that we don't need UNCLOS because we already enjoy its protections and its benefits under customary international law. Well, while that is partly true, this argument ignores serious risks. As you know, back in 1983 President Reagan, despite his concerns with some of the deep seabed mining provisions, said the United States would accept and act in accordance with the provisions regarding the traditional uses of the oceans, so as long as the navigational freedoms that the United States enjoy were likewise recognized by other states. For nearly 30 years we have asserted our navigational rights based on customary usage, but customary usage is just that. It reflects the current customs and practices of navigation and as coastal States and maritime States alter their conduct and seek to change the customary law of the sea, we are at a distinct disadvantage and limited in our ability to engage them effectively by standing outside UNCLOS.

To prevent illegal and excessive claims from becoming the new norm, we right now only have two options, diplomatic protests and freedom of navigation operations or FONOPS, as we like to call them in the Navy. During FONOPS we send out ships and sailors into disputed areas to assert our persistent objections of excessive claims. This further tests our resources and frankly it risks escalating tensions unnecessarily. We run another risk by standing on the sidelines. While the Convention codifies maritime rights and freedoms, its written provisions are not static and parties to the Convention can agree to change it. The Law of the Sea Convention in its current form represents the best possible case for US national interests. Were the current parties to agree to amend the Convention, the results simply couldn't be more favorable to the United States and indeed they could be less favorable to United States. We need to be on the field when these matters are being discussed. Our participation in the Convention as a full partner will better position us to maintain our vital navigational and overflight freedoms and most importantly help shape the development of international law. Detractors, as Admiral Schachte discusses, also point to dispute resolutions, claiming that our service members would be somehow subject to international tribunals. I promise you, I wouldn't be sitting here today nor would Admiral Houck support the agreement, nor would any one of his living predecessors support UNCLOS if we thought for one minute that our service members could be subject to international tribunals.

You have heard the same points, at least from Admiral Clingan and me. This isn't some lawyer-driven position that the department takes. Military leaders across the services and the Joint Staff support the Convention because it is good for our national defense. In a 2007 letter to the Chairman of the Senate Committee on Foreign Relations, every service chief and the Chairman of the Joint Chiefs of Staff voiced clear and unequivocal support for the Convention. In the February 2010 Quadrennial Defense Review the Department of Defense strongly urged accession. Similar statements supporting the accession to the Convention have been made by Senior Cabinet officials, the current and prior Secretaries of State and as you know, both Presidents Clinton and George W. Bush expressed bi-partisan support for joining the Convention as a non-partisan matter, as does President Obama. The only thing about UNCLOS that could hurt our national interests is remaining a non-party. Joining the Law of the Sea Convention will lock in the rights and freedoms necessary for our Navy's success. Becoming a party will reassert, quite frankly, our rightful place as the leader in maritime law and ensure that we have a say in how that law involves. Participating in the Convention will provide clearly defined mechanisms for peacefully confronting excessive maritime claims. Affirming our commitment to international law will facilitate the partnerships that are so very critical to our current operations and acceding to the Convention will provide our men and women in uniform at sea the most solid legal footing possible as they execute their missions around the globe.

Panel V: DEBATE: Resolved: The Senate Should Give Prompt Advice and Consent to the Law of the Sea Convention

PANEL V – DEBATE: RESOLVED: THE SENATE SHOULD GIVE PROMPT ADVICE AND CONSENT TO THE LAW OF THE SEA CONVENTION

*Ambassador John Norton Moore v. Steven Groves, Esq.**

Introduction by the Honorable Thomas R. Pickering†

My name is Thomas Pickering and I am delighted to be here and very, very delighted that we have two excellent representatives to deal with this problem. Steven Groves is a Fellow at the Heritage Foundation where he focuses on international law. Before Heritage, he was senior counsel to the US Senate Permanent Subcommittee on Investigations and he played a lead role in the "oil-for-food" scandal. I am delighted he is here today. John Norton Moore is well known to all of you as well. John played a hugely instrumental role in the UNCLOS as a US Ambassador to UNCLOS and Chairman of the National Security Council Interagency Task Force on the Law of the Sea. For many years he has maintained a very strong interest in the Law of the Sea treaty, and indeed has been one of the primary progenitors of early ratification. Your success is not measured in timeliness, John, but in your persistence, if I can say it that way. We will hear from each of them for a little over twenty minutes, then they will each respond to each other for a little over eight minutes. I will keep the watch. Then the moderator, yours truly, will have an opportunity to ask a question or two, and then we will open the floor to you for questioning of each of them. We will try to allow a few minutes at the end for both of you, to do your summing up. Thank you again for being here and I look forward – as I know all of you do today – to the strength and importance of this debate, as we all look ahead with great anticipation to this question coming actually before the Senate once again. Thank you very much.

---

* John Norton Moore is Director of the Center for Oceans Law & Policy at UVA. He was US Ambassador and Deputy Special Representative of the President to the Law of the Sea Conference.

Steven Groves is the Bernard and Barbara Lomas Fellow in the Margaret Thatcher Center for Freedom at the Heritage Foundation.

† The Honorable Thomas R. Pickering retired from the US State Department in 2000 as Under Secretary of State for Political Affairs. He is currently Vice-Chairman of Hills and Company International Consultants.

PRO: Opening Remarks – Ambassador John Norton Moore

Greetings Ambassador Pickering, my distinguished opponent, Steven Groves, and ladies and gentlemen. My opening remarks will be in three parts: first, the background and importance of the Law of the Sea Convention for the United States; second, why the arguments of the opponents, though well-meaning, are simply misinformed; and third, something about the very real ongoing costs for the failure to move forward to adhere promptly to the Law of the Sea Convention.

Beginning first with the background and importance of the Convention, the United States during the early 1960s was a party to four Geneva Conventions of 1958 on the Law of the Sea. During the next few years we begin a process of trying to modernize the Law of the Sea, as a result of a number of critical problems facing the United States and the world. The first of those was a threat to navigational freedom including warship mobility and the mobility of commercial ships around the world as a result of illegal unilateral coastal State claims in the world's oceans. The second was related to heavy overfishing by foreign fishing fleets attacking the fish stocks off the coast of the United States and severely harming those stocks. Thirdly, following a global environmental awakening, we understood that we needed provisions dealing with protection of the marine environment. Finally, we understood that we needed a legal regime for the mining of manganese nodules in the deep ocean floor containing copper, nickel, cobalt, and manganese. We needed stable property rights for US industry to be able to go out and mine those sites. A site, by the way, is something about the size of the state of Rhode Island and since this was located beyond areas of national jurisdiction, we needed to create property rights to enable mining to go forward.

These needs resulted in a decades-long negotiation that was very successful for the United States leading to the 1982 Convention on the Law of the Sea. The Convention was extremely favorable to all of those interests we have just talked about with one exception at that time, which was deep seabed mining. The provisions in the 1982 Convention in Part XI concerning seabed mining were not consistent with American needs. Indeed, as one who had supervised the preparation of the instructions for the United States in these negotiations, but who was then outside the government, I sent a letter to then-President Reagan saying, "I think there are six changes that need to be made in Part XI on seabed mining before the United States should go forward." I am delighted to say that Reagan did a thorough review and came out of that review agreeing exactly as I did, that there were six changes that needed to be made in the deep seabed mining area, but only in the deep seabed mining area, and that the rest of the treaty was strongly in the interests of the United States. Now, Reagan at that time then put out a press statement indicating that there were these six changes that needed to be made for US adherence to the Convention. That became the official US policy. Happily in 1994 there was a successful re-negotiation of Part XI that resulted in achieving *all* of the Reagan conditions and additionally some other excellent changes we had not thought about at that time.

So the result is that this Convention, as it was re-negotiated on Part XI in 1994 was very favorable for US national interests. It included a 200-mile Exclusive Economic Zone so that we would have control over the economic activities, particularly the fisheries, of that area and it included control over the extended continental shelf of the United States in areas, for example, off of Alaska that probably even go out beyond 500 nautical miles and to a 200-nautical mile Exclusive Economic Zone (EEZ) in all of the coastal areas of the United States. That indeed was the largest Exclusive Economic Zone and continental shelf given to any nation in the world. You would think from that alone that the United States would be the first in the queue to be adhering to this Convention.

In addition, we achieved all of the defense goals of the United States. I worked very closely with the Office of the Chairman of the Joint Chiefs of Staff and we met all of our very important interests for the Navy, including straits transit passage and other fundamental security issues. In addition, we received the four best mine sites in the world's oceans for deep seabed mining that were basically set aside for the United States. We had an excellent environmental chapter that really reflected many of the environmental laws already put in place by the United States for the oceans at that time. We increased the protection for critical infrastructure of underwater cables and we had a powerful precedent for new international organizations in which the United States of America was singled out to be the only nation in the world given a permanent seat on the council of the International Seabed Authority that was going to facilitate seabed mining and create the needed property rights for mining to take place. This seat brought with it a veto over important issues.

Indeed, there is absolutely *no* US oceans or foreign policy interest which would be better off without the treaty than with the treaty. Now, that is highly unusual. Typically there are trade-offs in treaties. But in this case, there were no trade-offs of US oceans, foreign affairs or security interests. All are served by the Convention.

Not surprisingly there is a powerful base of support to move forward on the Convention. That support includes all Presidents of the United States of both parties since the re-negotiation in 1994. It includes all living Chiefs of Naval Operations, all living Commandants of the Coast Guard, all living Secretaries of States of the United States, the United States Chamber of Commerce, the Secretary of Homeland Security, the National Ocean Industries Association, the oil and gas industry, the environmental movement, and two overwhelming adoptions by the Senate Foreign Relations Committee. It was unanimously supported by the United States Oceans Policy Commission, a bi-partisan group appointed by Congress and the President to look at US Oceans Policy, and I am delighted to say there is also a very fine letter from then-Governor Sarah Palin on the letterhead of the National Governor's Association supporting the treaty on behalf of the National Governor's Association.

Well, you ask in that setting, why has the treaty not been approved when it has such overwhelming support and in which every single element basically serves the interests of the United States? I am sorry to say here there have been a handful of well meaning, but misinformed, critics of the Convention. In fact, let me give you someone else's view of this. This is a statement about what I just said made by Secretary Michael Chertoff, President Bush's Head of the Homeland Security Department. He said, "Let me briefly acknowledge that there is a small group of strident opponents who have raised a number of badly flawed arguments against the Convention." Well, I think Secretary Chertoff was absolutely right about these "badly flawed arguments" of the "strident opponents."

Let me give you some examples of why these arguments are not just wrong, they are upside down; they are a 180-degrees wrong. My opponent, Mr. Groves argues, "the treaty will undermine US sovereignty." False! There is not an ounce of American sovereignty lost by this Convention. To the contrary, there is the largest expansion of resource jurisdiction for the United States in the history of the nation. It is a larger expansion than we got from the Louisiana Purchase and the acquisition of Alaska combined. In addition, we secured very strong support for the sovereignty of US warships and US vessels on the high seas.

My opponent and those who make this argument should also go back and look at their US foreign relations law and understand that under the classic Supreme Court precedent of *Whitney v. Robertson* a treaty can *never* remove an ounce of sovereignty of the United States of America. That is, you can never violate the Constitution or remove the ability of the Congress of the United States to override a treaty and have a new policy. *We do not lose an ounce of sovereignty from this Convention.*

My opponent, Mr. Groves, argues that the Convention will create, "a new international bureaucracy with the power to regulate the oceans. It awards effective control of 70% of the earth's surface to an international treaty organization." Wrong! The only regulatory authority that is created by this Convention is the new International Seabed Authority (ISA), which has a small area of functional jurisdiction solely dealing with property rights and mining of resources from the deep ocean floor beyond national jurisdiction; that is, beyond these expanded areas of coastal State jurisdiction. There is no other jurisdiction, no other issue dealt with by the ISA. The ISA is strongly in the interest of the United States because we need stable property rights, a very conservative concept, in order to enable US industry to make the two billion dollar investment necessary to develop one of these sites. In addition, the ISA is a closely cabined small international organization similar to many of which the US is already party. The ISA is comparable to the Great Lakes Fisheries Commission between the United States and Canada that engages in fisheries management in the great lakes. After 25 years of operation the ISA has a staff of only 28, including secretaries and drivers, and a tiny budget of less than six million dollars for the entire agency. I don't believe, Mr. Groves, that the ISA is about ready to take over planet earth. In fact, an interesting contrast might be with the Heritage Foundation itself that you are from because it turns out that the Heritage Foundation has approximately ten times more employees than the International Seabed Authority and a budget that is approximately ten times larger than that of the International Seabed Authority!

Mr. Groves argues that Ronald Reagan would have opposed the treaty even as it was re-negotiated. Again, wrong! I participated very closely in watching the Reagan review and one of my students chaired the interagency task force for Reagan. President Reagan had a thorough review and came out saying we only need the six changes in relation to seabed mining. All of those six and more were achieved in these fundamental Reagan amendments to the Convention in 1994. In addition, in 1983 Ronald Reagan later issued a very important order that the Navy still follows to the effect that other traditional non-seabed portions of this treaty were provisions the United States would comply with and move forward. That is hardly the indication of someone objecting to a treaty.

But don't take my word for it, let's look at George P. Schulz, the Secretary of State for Ronald Reagan in this period and see what he has to say. He said "it surprises me to learn that opponents of the treaty are invoking President Reagan's name arguing that he would have opposed ratification despite having succeeded on this deep seabed issue. During his administration, with full support from President Reagan, we made it very clear that we would support ratification if our position on the seabed issue were accepted."

Most egregiously, my opponent Mr. Groves argues that, "American participation will undermine US military operations." Here ladies and gentlemen one might ask some questions about Mr. Grove's military credentials. He stands on this issue in opposition to all living Navy Chiefs of Naval Operations, the classic 24-star letter recently from the Chairman of the Joint Chiefs, the Deputy Chairman and all of the Chiefs, all of the former Commandants of the Coast Guard, the Head of Homeland Security, virtually all the Secretaries of State and many Secretaries of Defense and Heads of the CIA. You have quite an explanation Mr. Groves to indicate why you were right on the defense issues of the United States and that collective group of defense experts supporting the treaty is all wrong.

Further, just let me give you one of the specifics of the kinds of arguments where I believe I can properly use the term "uninformed" with respect to an argument made by Mr. Groves and others in relation to this issue. He argues, "that US submarines will be required to transit on the surface and show their flag while in the territorial sea." The problem with that argument is that this requirement is already binding on the United States and has been since 1958. The requirement comes from Article 14 of the 1958 Geneva Convention on the Territorial Sea and the Contiguous Zone. Mr. Groves also fails to understand on many of these issues that the law of the sea operates reciprocally and we are not eager to see North Korean or Iranian submarines submerged off New York City or San Diego. Finally, in this argument he neglects the most important point of all that one of the major reasons for the re-negotiation was to make sure this limitation was done away with in relation to submarines going through straits used for international navigation. We were quite successful in doing that. Once again we find an opponent making an argument 180 degrees from reality.

Now sadly, these kinds of misinformed arguments, and there are many others, have not been just of academic interest, they have done real damage to the national security of the United States of America and every day that we don't move forward is continuing that damage to our national security and our economic interests. However well-meaning these opponents are, and I believe they are as many are my friends, they are wrong on national security and they are harming this nation and our economic interests.

What are some of the specifics of that harm? Well, first they basically are, by keeping us outside the treaty, arming nations such as Iran and Syria to be able to make arguments opposed to the legality of US actions that are crucial, such as US warships going through the Strait of Hormuz. This is an essential ability of the United States to be using the rule of law. We won these issues in the Convention, and now to have them denied to us by Iran and others because we are not a party is extremely harmful. There is a potential for losing our seabed sites if we don't move forward. We have already lost one that has been essentially given away to the Germans. In addition we are in a setting in which we are about ready to have a very substantial delay in moving forward on the delimitation of our extended continental shelf, something Senator Murkowski was just talking to this group about.

We have lost US oceans leadership by failing to have a seat at the table. We do not participate, except as an observer in the meeting of States Parties every year. We do not have a US national as a representative on the International Seabed Authority or the International Law of the Sea Tribunal and that has had significant costs. Let me just give you one. By not having a participant on the Commission on the Limits of the Continental Shelf, we have never had access, for example, to the Russian submission about the Arctic. By not taking our permanent seat on the Council of the ISA, we would not be able to exercise our veto to block, for example, any effort to transfer funds to a national liberation group. Yet, if we are on the Council, we would have a veto on that and other important issues.

Let me conclude by way of summarizing some of the harm to the United States if one were to support my opponent's position.

- You should support my opponent's position if you favor a gradual loss of the United States sovereign rights over naval and commercial navigation on the world's oceans;
- You should support my opponent's position if you believe the United States should substitute the lives of service men and women for the stability of the rule of law;
- You should support my opponent's position if, at this time of high oil prices, you want to greatly delay the work of the oil and gas industry on the United States continental margin beyond 200 miles and its associated jobs in the United States;
- You should support my opponent's position if you want to kill the US seabed mining industry, permanently lose US mine sites staked out as the best in the world, and prevent the development of seabed mining jobs in the United States;
- You should support my opponent's position if you do not want the United States to participate in assessing continental margin claims such as that of Russia in the Arctic Ocean;
- You should support my opponent's position if you believe it is wrong for the Convention to confirm for the United States the most extensive EEZ and extended continental shelf in the world;
- You should support my opponent's position if you oppose stable expectations and the rule of law in the world's oceans;
- You should support my opponent's position if you believe the United States should have a diminished voice in protecting our oceans' interests worldwide; and
- Finally, you should support my opponent's position if you believe that advice from non-law of the sea experts on oceans, security, and military issues are more reliable than that from the Joint Chiefs of Staff, the Navy, Presidents of both parties and all the US oceans' industry, and the unanimous opinion of the congressionally-established Commission on Oceans Policy.

CON: Opening Remarks – Steven Groves, Esq.

Thank you Ambassador Pickering. A special thanks to Ambassador Moore for inviting me to the debate today. Congratulations for putting together another successful and informative conference. I have enjoyed it very much, but I must admit it is daunting after listening to two days of panels about the reasons to favor accession to the treaty to come and make arguments in opposition to it, and it is especially daunting to debate you, John, about this issue. I tried to come up with an analogy that would encapsulate that burden and this is the best I come up with: debating John Norton Moore about the meaning of the Law of the Sea treaty is like debating somebody about the meaning of the Bible who was at the Council of Nicaea.

So let me make one concession straight away, if I sufficiently lowered expectations that is, and that is that I don't have a problem and I don't believe that conservatives have a problem with the treaty provisions that the Navy is in favor of. It comes as no surprise that the Heritage Foundation rarely disagrees with the military or the Navy when it says repeatedly and forcefully that it needs something to better its operations. And the particular provisions that the Navy is in favor of are unobjectionable. Those are the important provisions relating to freedom of navigation, transit rights, transit rights through straits and archipelagic waters. While it is debatable, we have heard a couple of panels raise as a debate item whether the United States already enjoys the rights by way of customary international law, I will concede for the moment that if there was a way to secure those provisions for our Navy and support them in their operations, I think we should do that. To me the freedom of navigation provisions in the treaty are the proverbial "baby in the bathwater." If the US Senate could somehow manage to save that baby while tossing out some of the bath water I think there would be a way to ratify or accede to this treaty.

But before I go into one of those bath water provisions, I would like to first note that the argument in favor of the freedom of navigation provisions isn't airtight. That is to say that while the Navy contends that its operations would be greatly aided if the United States acceded to UNCLOS, there is evidence that when push comes to shove on the high seas, I mean that both figuratively and literally, that those conflicts are ultimately settled, not by citing treaty provisions. The evidence shows that those conflicts are settled by naval power or by bi-lateral diplomatic moves. This gets me to my first point about UNCLOS, which is that there is no guarantee that US interests will be advanced by acceding to the treaty and that is because of the unreliability of our prospective treaty partners. With UNCLOS, the United States is faced with a situation where part of its calculus as to whether it should accede to the treaty is a concern about the reliability of its prospective treaty partners, like every treaty. The United States must consider whether its treaty partners are going to hold up their end of the bargain.

The unreliability of treaty partners is common in other treaties, as well, we see this all the time. The Law of the Sea treaty is only one of a dozen or more treaties that I am responsible for at the Heritage. I have seen when brutal regimes signed international human rights treaties with no intention of following up on them. It even appears to be the case in the New START arms control treaty, recently signed with Russia, where the Russians are using the treaty to claim that they are going to have a great deal of say over our missile defense programs. When you have unreliable treaty partners you really don't have a treaty. When countries ratify a treaty, but have no intention of actually adhering to it you have a big problem. Just like when you enter a contract with someone who doesn't intend to perform their end of the deal. That is the case in my opinion with UNCLOS, unfortunately, and we see this not through argument, not through these panel discussions, but we see this with the evidence that we see on the high seas with our unreliable treaty partners, our unreliable prospective treaty partners.

After all, if UNCLOS members strictly follow the terms of the treaty, the Navy would have no need to prosecute its Freedom of Navigation Program, which is a program that has come up a couple of times over the past couple days. The Navy established that program back in 1979, but still utilizes it today in order to protest excessive coastal claims through diplomatic channels and to exercise navigation and over flight rights in disputed areas. In fiscal year 2007 alone, the United States conducted freedom of navigation challenges – I think these were called by RADM DeRenzi "FONOPS" – against China, India, Indonesia, Malaysia, the Maldives, Oman and the Philippines, all of whom are party to UNCLOS. Since the time UNCLOS came into force the United States has conducted hundreds of these freedom of navigation operations against scores of nations that are parties to UNCLOS.

In short, a significant number of current treaty members assert claims that already violate the treaty's terms, and you have to internalize this as part of your calculus whether we should become party to a treaty where the members of that treaty that have ratified that as part of their law. They claim that they are part of the international community and they are going to follow this treaty and they already don't. They didn't intend to when they signed the treaty, when they ratified it, and they are not doing it now. You have to ask yourself whether you want to be part of the treaty where those are your treaty partners. Some of these nations require prior permission or notification for innocent passage through their territorial sea or through their EEZ in violation of the treaty. Others make excessive claims regarding the breath of their territorial waters in violation of the treaty, and still others claim rights to impose improper security controls, all in violation of the black letter law of the treaty.

So it is bad enough that the Navy has to regularly conduct these freedom of navigation operations for the purpose of disputing these excessive claims. What is even more problematic is when Navy vessels are confronted with hostility on the high seas in the name of UNCLOS. I am speaking, of course, of the aggressive behavior of UNCLOS member China, which last year incited more than one confrontation with the United States in international waters.

There have been several high profile incidents. I am sure you have heard of these, they were with the US surveillance ships, the USNS *Impeccable* in March 2009 and the USS *Victorious* in May 2009. Now this isn't one of the Navy's standard freedom of navigation operations. This is the Navy conducting military surveillance against China, the rising military power in the East, the military that has a growing navy and a growing submarine fleet, including nuclear subs. The *Impeccable* and the *Victorious* were in the South China Sea to monitor the comings and goings of these subs from their new base on Hainan Island. The US ships weren't right off the coast of China; they weren't even in China's territorial sea. In the case of the *Impeccable*, it was 75 miles off of China's territory and *Victorious* was 120 miles away, well outside of China's territorial waters.

Now prior to the existence of UNCLOS, these actions by China would have been called what they are, which is naked aggression against unarmed US Navy ships operating in international waters, but now UNCLOS has muddied those waters. The Chinese used the provisions of the treaty as diplomatic cover for their aggression. They are behaving in the same way towards our close ally Japan in the East China Sea, but UNCLOS has been touted as the treaty that will draw the lines in the ocean and define the rights of coastal States and as the treaty that will be used to resolve these disputes on the high seas. But the treaty as I have said is only as good as its membership and that must go into your calculation about whether the United States should accede.

As I mentioned, for better or worse, when true national interests are at stake, naval power will prevail and not reliance on treaty language and not on the International Tribunal for the Law of the Sea. The best evidence for that is what? After the incident with the *Impeccable* the USS *Chung-Hoon*, an Aegis destroyer, was dispatched to serve as an escort for the surveillance mission.

So, it is legitimate to question, in my opinion, whether the existence of UNCLOS, or more to the point, whether UNCLOS membership in the treaty would really simplify things for our Navy. Now Ambassador Moore is right, I am not an admiral, but I have a brain. Logic dictates that you enter into a treaty with other countries that intend to live up to its terms. I don't think that is too much to ask, especially when it is black and white on the treaty. Yet, China has no intention of doing so. All these countries that we do these freedom of navigation flights against, they don't intend to, they never did. The United States follows its treaty obligations, for the most part. I think we are better than most countries in the world, but the parties to whom we are going to ensconce ourselves with this huge treaty, they don't have the same respect for it as we would if we were a party. You have to assess what is the actual blow back from that? We can't argue this treaty in a vacuum. The reality of what happens out on the high seas is different from what it says in basic terms of the treaty. I want to give admirals in the Navy operations the benefit of the doubt, obviously, but I am not sure the evidence substantiates their unqualified support for the treaty.

I would like to briefly address one of the "bathwater" provisions of UNCLOS. My favorite bath water provision of UNCLOS is Article 82. Now more than one panelist yesterday and I heard a couple people today speak pretty derisively or dismissively about the concept of the sovereignty. I heard something along the lines of "I am tired of hearing about this sovereignty issue." Well, you are entitled to your opinion on this of course, but if your goal is to convince skeptical conservatives or conservative senators about the benefits of this treaty, I submit this is not the way to go about it. Conservatives and conservative senators and I would say a lot of Americans, average Americans, care about the idea of sovereignty. It is something that is important to them and you even hear the Tea Parties talk about sovereignty. The bath water provision I would like to touch on my remaining time involves sovereignty. It is Article 82, which was discussed yesterday during the second panel. This is a problematic provision, and no I am not saying it is fatal. I am not saying this would be the end of the world if we ratify the treaty with this provision in it, but as proponents of the treaty, as fans of the treaty, you guys have to have a better answer to this. If you want to convince conservatives, then you had better come up with something better than implying they are wearing tin foil hats and you are flying around in black helicopters. That ain't gonna cut it.

This Article 82 is problematic because it changes the status quo regarding the continental shelf and it is up to the proponents of UNCLOS to convince people that Article 82 improves the status quo. That is another point, this burden is on you. There is a status quo and it is your job to convince senators or conservatives that this treaty will benefit and change because it is going to change the status quo. Will it benefit the United States and its interest? That is your burden, not mine. Article 82 is problematic because currently the United States has full and unqualified sovereign rights and exclusive jurisdiction over its own continental shelf, most importantly, for the purpose of exploiting its natural resources, including crucial commodities such as oil and natural gas. The United States holds these rights due to the actions of our government, not signing the treaty and not being part of the international conference, but acting as a sovereign state. As you know in 1945 President Truman signed Proclamation 2667 exercising jurisdiction control over the natural resources of the continental shelf. That proclamation was later codified by Congress and signed into law as the Outer Continental Shelf Lands Act of 1953. This is the traditional manner in which a government asserts sovereignty over its own land and own property. Truman in 1945 and Congress in 1953 declared that the United States continental shelf and all of its resources belong to the United States without qualification, without exception, and that is how sovereign nations should behave.

This is our property, not yours, and it is not a United Nations commission that will have final say about the extent of our continental shelf or whether any revenues that are generated from our continental shelf would be distributed. It should only be us – our President, Congress and most importantly the American people – where sovereignty truly resides. Now accession to UNCLOS will change the status quo and that is an important note to make. Accession would place conditions as to how the United States may use its own continental shelf because it places certain commercial conditions on certain commercial activities on the continental shelf beyond the 200 nautical mile mark, also known as the extended continental shelf, the ECS. Specifically, Article 82 would require the United States to make royalty payments for the exploitation of mineral resources on the ECS, up to seven percent of the value of the production of resources such as oil and natural gas would be paid by the United States to the International Seabed Authority, which would then redistribute the funds to other members of UNCLOS, particularly to developing countries and land-locked nations. Because, as we know, land-locked nations have a great deal to say about how the ocean should be regulated.

Essentially, the United States is transferring a portion of its wealth on its own continental shelf in the form of royalty payments to an international body, and power to redistribute it to a developing world. The first question that occurs to me is who is going to be paying these royalties? I am sure some of the oil and gas people in the audience have thought about this question too, because as it is written the treaty places the responsibility for payments of these royalties squarely on the States parties. Article 82, Section 1, specifies that the coastal State shall make payments. So, what is the coastal State? Well, it is me and it is all of you and it is the rest of the American taxpayers that will be required to pay up to seven percent of the total value of production on our own continental shelf. This is our own continental shelf. I am not talking about the deep seabed. This is our continental shelf beyond the 200 nautical mile mark. For every billion dollars of oil or natural gas recovered on the ECS, American taxpayers will be responsible for paying up to 70 million dollars to the ISA. The estimated size of the ECS is substantial. You see on the cover of the conference brochure the areas that are in red are ECS. The figure that is most regularly cited is twice the size of California. That is quite a bit of land, subsea land, and quite a bit of oil and natural gas on that land, and it may be even larger than that according to the State Department website on the ECS. So, we could be talking about real money here, for every billion dollars of oil and natural gas extracted, up to 70 million dollars for American taxpayers.

Another question is how will those dollars be spent? To which developing or land-locked nations will the ISA transfer those royalty payments? Would the US seat on the finance committee guarantee that the United States would be able to direct all of the royalty payments as it sees fit? These are legitimate questions to ask. These are the things you have to ask yourself if you are going to convince me and other conservatives that this treaty is in our best interest, because who is to say that royalties won't be transferred to countries that are hostile to the United States?

For example, Cuba, which is considered a state sponsor of terror, and Sudan, which is a genocidal regime, are both considered developing countries and both are party to UNCLOS. What happens to these royalties once they arrive in these developing or land-locked nations? Will the money be spent with transparency and accountability? Well, for better or for worse many parties to UNCLOS have a long history of corruption and misusing development funds. The misuse of development funds in difficult environments is all too common. You need only look to the problems that the United Nations Development Program has had in places like North Korea, Gambia, Thailand and Burma for recent examples. Gambia and Burma are both parties to UNCLOS, and the treaty counts among its members the most corrupt nations on the planet, according to Transparency International, including Chad, Somalia and dozens of other countries that are at the bottom of Transparency International's annual index.

So, I will repeat that I think Article 82 poses a problem for UNCLOS proponents. You have to explain to average Americans, and average senators for that matter, why the United States should have to make royalty payments to an international body that may then distribute the money to corrupt regimes and all for commercial activity that is occurring on our own continental shelf.

So, to wrap up, in some treaties you can keep the baby and throw out the bath water by entering reservations, understandings and declarations as a condition for ratification. But with the Law of the Sea treaty, I don't believe the United States would be able to enter the reservations necessary to keep just the baby without violating the object and purpose of the treaty. At bottom just like any treaty we are assessing, we need to do a cost-benefit analysis. Does accession advance US national interests, and if so at what cost? Ambassador Moore maintains that the cost-benefit analysis weighs heavily and irrefutably in favor of accession, and I think it is a closer call than that, and that is why we are debating here today. Thank you and I look forward to addressing some of the points raised by Ambassador Moore during the rebuttal time.

John Norton Moore Response

Thank you, Steven and thank you for coming here. I have offered to Steven to return this favor with any group of his choosing that he would like me to go and address. I would be eager, in fact, to take the message of support for the Convention to those opponents who simply seem not to understand it. I was also very pleased Steven that you said the navigational and defense issues, those that the Navy believes are extremely critical for the United States were good and you wish there was an easy way to get that, but Steven there is and on this I would like to start with a classic story about the importance of not overlooking the obvious because I am afraid you are overlooking the obvious here. That was the story with Sherlock Holmes and Dr. Watson, who went camping in their tent one evening under the stars and in the middle of the night, Holmes nudges Watson and says, "Watson, Watson look at all those stars. What do you deduce"? Watson, very sleepy, looks up and says, "I see millions and millions of stars, perhaps billions... we are a small and insignificant part of the universe. What does it tell you, Holmes?" "Watson, you idiot!" he exclaimed, "Someone has stolen our tent!"

Well, Steven the obvious is to support United States adherence to the Law of the Sea Convention, which unequivocally supports our security interests. I note that you don't make any kind of a case as to why your argument about Article 82 offsets – even if we accepted all that, which I don't – why that offsets everything else in all the important security and economic interests for the United States of America.

First, let me turn to Article 82, which is your first argument, and then turn to your second argument. Let's start with the Article 82 argument. The problem with your starting premise is you assume that the United States always had the continental shelf we get under the Convention. But it did not under the 1958 conventions. Instead, it only had a shelf going out to 200 meters plus a very vague and uncertain area beyond that depth related to "adjacency" from the coast. The question in an international negotiation was what is going to be the outer limit for the United States? We knew we had an extremely broad continental margin so we wanted to ensure that we got those sovereign rights on the full shelf. We believe in sovereignty. Sovereignty is important. This treaty *serves* sovereignty. By agreeing to a tiny price of two to four percent over the life of a well, Steven, we got the full extended margin beyond 200 meters. Not seven percent, that is the final payment. Two to four percent over the life of a well – a tiny payment in order to be able to get an additional area of the continental shelf and its resources for the United States of America, dramatically expanding our resource jurisdiction in areas, probably the size of two Californias, if we add them up off the coasts of the United States and its island possessions. I would suggest to you that this was the same kind of bargain as the acquisition of Alaska.

Secondly, you say that these funds go to the International Seabed Authority; maybe they can be given to corrupt nations. Well, I am so glad you have raised that point because that is precisely the point of getting the United States on the Council of the International Seabed Authority where we clearly have a veto over where any of these funds can go. So, yes Steven if we do not join the Convention and take our seat on the Council, the Council at some point in the future, when there are such funds will perhaps be able to send it to some corrupt regime, but not, emphatically *not* if the United States is a member of the Council where it has a clear veto over where those funds go.

By the way, also look at this wonderful way to assist the additional aid budget of things we really believe in and helping developing countries around the world because not just the two to four percent off the US continental shelf will go to that, but the two to four percent off of everybody else's extended continental shelf that the United States of America will then have a veto as to where those go, but only Steven, if the United States of America is a party. I might note that although you oppose this formula, the oil and gas industry, which will live under it, is actually the group that developed it for our delegation and is quite happy with the provision.

Let's go to the "member" argument you make because for me this is actually a little more shocking. There are 160 other members, plus the European Union that are parties to this treaty at this point [May, 2010]. There are only 193 countries in the world. This is an overwhelming participation of the international community, but Steven tells us, well wait a minute because there are some bad actors out there, we shouldn't join this treaty. That is, in fact, an argument that the United States should never be able to enter into any international agreements because there might be in any kind of multilateral agreement some bad party out there. That is a kind of crippling isolationism to be imposed on the United States of America that I don't think is going to be very appealing. In addition Steven, I think it dramatically understates the importance of the rule of the law of the treaty generally, and specifically it understates the effect of this treaty in working to support US interests. Thus we have seen a pattern of nations that have previously been taking the wrong position now adopting and following the Convention because of precisely the authority of the rule of law itself as embodied in the Convention.

I might also add that the problems you give, including particularly this very sad example with China is a very good example of precisely why the Navy particularly wants this because that provides an additional argument for the United States because we are correct in that interpretation, Steven. In order to go the other way you have to be assuming that China is correct in its extreme interpretation. But they are not and I am surprised that the Heritage Foundation effectively would be taking the position of China in that crucial security debate with the United States. This is an issue in which the majority of the international community is very clear that there is full freedom of intelligence gathering in the EEZ. I think that is an issue, by the way, that is also in the long-term interests of China and I would expect through time that China itself would adopt that position, which has been the effect of most of the Convention through time.

Finally, it does seem to me your position is an extraordinary position to take in relation to the rule of law generally. Are we going to say that in any setting in which there are violators that somehow we should not seek the rule of law? I would like to suggest to you, with all due respect, that controlling violators is a fundamental reason for supporting the rule of law, not undercutting it.

Steven Groves Response

You covered quite a bit of territory there. Let me see if I can catch up. First, on Article 82, you mentioned the 1958 convention and you accurately portrayed it, but the 1958 Convention post-dates the Proclamation 2667 and the Outer Continental Shelf Lands Act. The 1958 Convention was vague about what the continental margin was, as you know. This wasn't based on measuring the actual end of the continental margin, but they had this vague and poorly defined definition for the end of the continental margin based on accessibility.

While the 1958 definition was bad, the controlling definition is the one set by Truman and by Congress. They made it quite clear and anticipated your argument, sir. From the Truman Proclamation, this is how things used to be done: "The government of the United States regards the natural resources of the subsoil and the seabed of the continental shelf beneath the high seas, but continuous to the coast of the United States as appertaining to the United States subject to its jurisdiction and control." Thank you President Truman! Congress acted just a couple years later, defining the continental shelf in 43 U.S.C. Section 1331(a) means, all submerged lands lying seaward and outside the area of lands beneath navigable waters as defined in Section 1301 in which the subsoil and seabed appertained to the United States and are subject to its jurisdiction and control.

So, I don't find the 1958 Convention argument very persuasive. It was a weak definition and more importantly the provisions that are in the UNCLOS about the continental margin, while interesting, are not the final say over where our continental margin begins and where it ends and who draws those lines and who accepts them. The best that can be said about UNCLOS is that our continental margin, where it would be drawn, would only allow maximum recognition by the international community, but that is not a standard I am particularly happy with anyway. I think it is up to the Navy, the Congress, the President and most important, the American public, who put those people into office to decide where our continental margin ends. We do not need to seek the approval of an international organization; we do not need to sign the treaty with Chad and Somalia and France and Denmark to have our own continental margin defined. That is up to us. We decide that, it is our own continental margin. They cannot any more define that for us than they can define the margins on the moon to us.

In the deep seabed area, supposedly the "common heritage of all mankind," they have no more right to that and they can't call that the common heritage of all mankind any more than they can call the Moon or Mars the common heritage of all mankind. If we would all of a sudden find a way to Mars and there was some great new mineral on there that we could bring back and it is worth trillions of dollars, would we have to redistribute those funds through some international organization? After all, Mars doesn't belong to the United States and isn't it the common heritage of all mankind because it is just as accessible as the deep seabed right now? Will we have to set up a new international space authority to distribute these funds from Mars to countries that don't have a space program? Ed Williamson brought this up earlier, this 1970s construct of the New International Economic Order and this "common heritage of all mankind" silliness.

That is the type of thing that conservatives get upset about. Those are the types of arguments you need to bring to them, not that we have a seat on this international commission so we can't define our own continental margin. We don't buy that. Senator DeMint, Senator Inhofe, these guys aren't going to buy that, because at the end of the day we decide where our land ends and where it starts. That is up to us.

In terms of who pays in the Article 82 royalty payments, I do hope that there is ultimately an answer to this. I found out yesterday that there were two technical bulletins on the ISA website about Article 82, so I went last night to peruse them hoping to get a nice executive summary or something, but it turns out that each of these technical bulletins is about 85 to 150 pages long. This is on a single article of the treaty, by the way. A treaty that has over 400 articles and this one Article 82 has two bulletins that you could prop your table up with, but they didn't shed much light on it anyway, from what I could glean. I will tell you what the evidence shows. The treaty says the States parties will pay these royalties – that is you and me. When President Clinton transferred the treaty to the Senate for ratification, it noted also, it implied that it would be the United States that would be responsible for making the payments because the administration justified the revenue sharing as "modest" and "part of a package that establishes with clarity and legal certainty the control of the coastal States over the full extent of their geological continental margin." That is in treaty document 103–39. So, nowhere in that treaty document does it state or imply that any other entity but the United States, and therefore it is taxpayers who are responsible for the royalty payments. Now, some will say that it is going to be up to the industry and they are going to have to pay that. Well, is Paul Kelly here? I sat next to Paul at lunch. He testified back in 2004 that our understanding is that this royalty should not result in any additional cost to industry. Well, I agree. I don't think there should be any additional cost to industry and I don't think it should be an additional cost to the American taxpayers, either because I don't think the royalties should ever be paid because it is our continental shelf. I will have to move on from there because I am out of time.

Moderator Thomas Pickering

Thank you very much Steven Groves. I will now use my prerogative as moderator of the debate to ask questions of the panelists before we open the floor to the rest of you. My first question is to Steven Groves. I will take you in the reverse order of your original presentation. You have spoken about your support for those provisions of the treaty, which affect naval activities. You have spoken about your objections to Article 82. You have spoken about your concern about the unreliability of international partners in the treaty regime. What else would you – because this is a debate on the whole agreement – single out as areas of significant concern to you in the treaty regime?

Steven Groves Response

Well, the ones I talked about and I may someday reference this to the deep seabed mining provisions, but personally I should have noted in the beginning that I don't speak on behalf of the Heritage Foundation. These are my personal views. I came to Heritage in 2007 and inherited this issue along with all the papers that had been written about it before I arrived. Not that I necessarily disagree with anything in the papers, but I just have a different approach to this treaty. I think it is very debatable whether the 1994 Agreement made improvements or let's say made all the fixes or fixed it to the point where conservatives would be satisfied, but my approach is more systematic in that I made this my primary argument, which is that the treaty can't be great.

We hold treaties, the United States holds treaties and their language to be sacrosanct, like our own law. We believe in those words and try to follow them and we are not perfect and nobody is, but when we sign on to a treaty we sure as heck are going to do our best to live up to our treaty terms because we don't want to upset our treaty partners, but the rest of the world doesn't operate that way. I am not just talking about the Law of the Sea treaty. I monitor lots of other treaties, human rights treaties, arms control treaties, global warming treaties, and our treaty partners are, for the most part when national interests come into line, just not as reliable as we would like them to be. Now that becomes a problem in treaties that we are already party to, but so what if we are party to the International Convention on Civil and Political Rights and we respect the civil and political rights of our people, but China, Cuba and other countries who are party to that human rights treaty don't? That doesn't come as a cost to us because although we are not in favor of how they treat their people, what does that do to the American people or more to the point, what does that do to the American Navy? Nothing! Become a party to this treaty, I think it is fair to say – and I challenge anyone to argue with me on this point – is it fair to say when you enter into a treaty you should be able to rely on the good faith of your treaty partners? They are big boys and big girls. They signed on to these treaties with their eyes open, but they have signed on with no intention of following the treaty. How does that give you any certainty that we are going to be able to rely on these treaty provisions? If we were parties to UNCLOS, would we have not sent that Aegis destroyer to the South China Sea? What would we have done? Gone to the railing of the USNS *Impeccable* and waved the treaty in the air? Hey, China we are in the EEZ! It is ridiculous. It all comes down to reliability of our treaty partners. If it is not there, you don't have a treaty and you don't have a contract.

Moderator Thomas Pickering

My second question is to John Norton Moore. It is a different kind of a question and maybe not quite a kosher question, John, but if you were arguing this particular issue from the other side what would be the most forceful arguments you could muster?

John Norton Moore Response

There are none.

Steven Groves Response

This is the kind of approach that will never convince conservatives, Mr. Ambassador. It's absolutist. There is nothing wrong, no flaws...

John Norton Moore Response

I do think a response is needed to Steven Groves' point just made. For, I count myself as a conservative. We have also heard from a former Secretary of State, Lawrence Eagleburger, also strongly supporting the Convention. Lawrence is a strong supporter of the Convention and a solid conservative Republican. But from Steven we have heard from one particular viewpoint, so I will respond to that viewpoint, whether called conservative or something else. One of the problems I have generally with the opposition here, and I think it sad because I have great respect for people making these arguments as they are generally well meaning, but sadly they don't know a lot about law of the sea. Let me just start with the rebuttal that was made to me in relation to the Truman proclamation and the Outer Continental Shelf Lands Act. The Outer Continental Shelf Lands Act uses the language as Steven indicated of United States jurisdiction and control. That completely begs the question of what is the area of United States jurisdiction and control. Steven also ignores the notifications issued along with the Truman proclamation that claim only out to the 100 fathom isobath. But in the Convention we are not just talking about the 100 fathom curves but instead about the entire shelf beyond 200 nautical miles.

This was a major, major win for the United States to get this. It is hugely beyond anything contemplated by the Truman proclamation and I would suggest to you that it was an extraordinary bargain in order to be able to get an area the size of two Californias for nothing more than two to four percent of mineral revenues from the area.

Secondly, you're wrong about the function of the Commission on the Limits of the Continental Shelf. The Commission has no ability itself to decide on the outer edge of the continental margin for the United States or any other country. It is instead a mechanism in which you submit your national proposal in order to try to keep the various submissions honest. It is an initiative of the United States of America because we didn't want out of control unilateralism in the world's oceans on this. The Commission can only simply send things back to you as they have done with the Russians in the first Arctic submission. So, you have to finally get to the point where only the continental margin outer limit accepted by the United States would in the end be binding for the United States.

In addition to that your preferred option of simply unilateral claims and that the United States should be free unilaterally to decide whatever it wants – how about a straight baselines system from Southern California and Hawaii to the Aleutians and claim everything for the United States in between Steven? The Law of the Sea is reciprocal; it works the other way around. One of our core concerns in protecting our interests is to make sure there is a rule of law, a reasonable rule of law. Not only is it reasonable in this case, the United States of America is given the largest extended continental margin of any nation in the world. We really came out like gang busters in this. Finally, Steven, it seems to me your last argument is nothing more than once again an overly broad argument against the rule of law itself. Yes, there are going to be violators in the world, yes there are bad guys and one of the mechanisms that you use to try to control them is precisely the rule of law.

Audience Questions and Answers

Moderator Thomas Pickering: I am now going to ask the audience to participate. Each of the panelists will have a chance to respond, but you may direct your question to one of the panelists for the first response.

Edwin Williamson: First, just let me make a comment, John. I think two things; first I think your claim that there is not a concession of sovereignty is just wrong. Every treaty is a concession of sovereignty. The question is how good of a deal is it? In fact Congress can come back and pass us up with the law. That is true about every treaty. The fact that the ISA is currently a small bureaucracy as I said yesterday, and that royalties on drilling are not large is not the issue. The question is not the quantity it is the quality.

Steven, I think you got two things I sort of fundamentally disagree with and that is that you overlooked the fact that it is much better to take diplomatic and even military action with the law on your side. That happens and it is much better to go to court with the law on your side. The second is what you attribute to intentions to not abide by the law really sort of attempts to seek a better interpretation of what have you. It is just much better to argue the offending party is violating the agreement than to face up to the fact that they may be changing this customary international law that you have been relying on. My question is, in the Article 82 debate, do you know of any companies who are prepared to make the investment in that area on the basis of the Truman declaration and the congressional action and the 1958 Convention?

Steven Groves: Thanks, Ed. Yes, I agree that it is best to go into something with the law on your side. The problem here is China doesn't obey the law and doesn't have any intention to, despite the fact that they are the ones who signed on to this law. They are the ones who are party to UNCLOS, not us, and yet when we are in their EEZ, not conducting economic activity, not doing marine scientific research, but purely military surveillance activities trying to find nuclear subs, which is kind of an important mission, they are the ones who attack our ships with their fishing boats and other Chinese naval vessels. So it is great to go into court with the law on your side, but not if they are not the ones who are going to obey the law or recognize the law. They are not even in the courthouse.

What if this case did go to an arbitral panel? What if somehow China decided it was going to prosecute this case or the United States was foolish enough to try and go into one of these arbitral panels, or God forbid the International Tribunal for the Law of the Sea – no offence to anyone who is here from there – and try to come to a conclusion with China about whether our activities inside their EEZ are military or economic? We have not fared well in these tribunals in the past, folks. Consider the ICJ's decisions about the Nicaragua mining case, or the ICJ decision that led to the Medellin case down in Texas. The United States does not fare well so I don't think I would want to resolve this in a courthouse, anyway. Even with the law on our side.

Ed Williamson: I am sorry my reference to the courthouse was an attempt to be a private domestic contractual equivalent.

Steven Groves: I was just extending your analogy.

Ed Williamson: Mine was in the context of diplomatic and military force. I am just simply saying it is better to have the law on your side, than not.

Steven Groves: That is indisputable. The problem is we know what the law is and the Chinese aren't following it. On your actual question on the Article 82 debate, no, I don't know of any companies who are willing to go out on to the ECS based on the Truman Proclamation or the Outer Continental Shelf Lands Act. That is their problem. It is their problem and the government's problem. If the United States wants those companies out there, give them the assurances they need. We are still the US Government after all. It is still our extended continental shelf. Are you telling me that the Congress and the President…

Ed Williamson: Tell me what the assurances are. We have a law, a proclamation, we have a Navy and they are still not doing it. What else can you do?

Steven Groves: Well, if the law needs to be more specific about activities on the ECS by US companies, write the law, get it to the President to sign it. We are having a debate between ourselves here, now Ed, but I am trying to answer your question, which is you are telling me the US Government doesn't have the ability or the power to do something, to write something or do a regulation that will give assurances to US companies who want to go out on the ECS? Come on! Of course.

Thomas Pickering: Ed, I am going to ask that we pluralize this a little bit. Steven, thank you. I am going to ask John Norton Moore if he has a comment.

John Norton Moore: Well, very clearly there are no firms that are prepared to do that at this point based on the "Truman proclamation." Secondly, my understanding is there is already US legislation that recognized the ECS revenue sharing provision on the extended continental shelf. But, let me come to the point Ed raised with me even though I am always reluctant to take on a former senior partner of Sullivan and Cromwell, one of the finest law firms in the world.

I take sovereignty very, very seriously and I think you are wrong in your statement that all treaties basically do end part of the sovereignty of any country that enters into them. Specifically, under United States Foreign Relations Law, you can never violate the Constitution, you can never deal with a setting in which Congress would not have the ability to override the treaty obligation. What you are assuming as any international lawyer who works in this area of national and international interface understands is that you have a setting of international legal obligation that is important. But an international legal obligation is emphatically *not* a loss of sovereignty. The only way the United States of America could lose sovereignty would be to actually alter the Constitution. You can lose sovereignty if you become a member of the European Union in relation to certain kinds of issues governed by the Union. Our states did lose sovereignty in relation to the Constitution of the United States. You do *not* lose sovereignty in relation to entering into a treaty because we always retain the ability to violate the treaty as a matter of domestic law. That is what sovereignty is.

Helmet Tuerk: I am Judge and Vice-President of the International Tribunal for the Law of the Sea. I would like to make a few comments, but I will not speak in my capacity as a judge, but only as a former delegate in the UNCLOS conference and as a simple citizen of a land-locked country. Who profits the most from the Law of the Sea Convention? Certainly not land-locked countries, certainly not geographically disadvantaged countries. Those countries which profited most are the countries with very long coast lines and countries with big islands. There is a revolutionary concept in the Convention, the EEZ. But does the EEZ really benefit developing countries?

Thomas Pickering: Please ask your final question.

Helmet Tuerk: I was always surprised that the United States did not adhere to the Law of the Sea Convention because the United States as a country has much to gain. First, as far as resources are concerned, and second, as far as transit passage and overflight rights are concerned. If you were to renegotiate these provisions today we would not get them in the same manner. If the Law of the Sea is left to drift, it will drift in the direction of stricter coastal State control and coastal State limitation of global freedoms. It is up to you.

John Norton Moore: I couldn't agree more. We have a huge achievement for the United States of America in this Convention. We would not be able to negotiate a treaty that well today for the United States. It is astounding that the country in the world that was given the largest expansion of resource jurisdiction in the world has not, 15 years later, signed onto the Convention. One other very important point, we got all of these six points that we asked for in a renegotiation on Part XI dealing with seabed mining. The United States was accommodated by the other States in the renegotiation. Not, then, to move forward to accept the treaty is to dramatically undermine our ability in the future to be taken seriously in negotiations because here we have said make Reagan's changes, give us the Reagan conditions and the Reagan amendments and we can then accept. By the way Steven, President Reagan, a conservative surely, said that the six points were all he needed and he got those. Yet we have not moved forward on the agreement.

One last point and that is there is a mythology surrounding all this that I hear over and over in the rhetoric about the common heritage or the new international economic order. Yes, there was some of that in the early days, in the early 70s we had that around. What is the reality of this negotiation? It is precisely what Helmet Tuerk said. This is the greatest expansion of national resource jurisdiction in the history of the world. The winners are the coastal nations of the world and the rule of law in the interest of all nations. The coastal nations have dramatically expanded their sovereign rights over resources. That is the central thrust of the negotiations. We should take the Convention and move on.

Steven Groves: Two things. On the freedom of navigation provisions, I will accept for the sake of this debate that they couldn't have been negotiated better than that. Fine. It was their mistake not to end it there and have the treaty on the navigation provisions that is something that is separate and divorced from the deep seabed mining, from royalty payments on continental shelves, from dispute resolutions. Why couldn't they just have a treaty about the navigation provisions? That makes perfect sense to me. So what? So, I am glad they got the provisions they did, but they filled it with so much of this bathwater that we are not able to have that baby. Luckily, we got customary international law and we can have a separate debate about how effective it is.

Since Ambassador Moore has brought up Reagan for a second time, I wish I had brought my cite on this. I should have anticipated this, but in his biography they quoted his diary, where he said given my best quote from it, "Just had NSC meeting, National Security Council meeting, still would not push for ratification or support ratification of the UNCLOS regardless of the deep seabed provisions." I don't believe the treaty should rise or fall on what Reagan thought, but he was a conservative and since John brought him up for a second time I will assure you that in his diary he said he still wouldn't support it regardless of those six changes to Part 11. That's the fact!

Ronald Rapp: I am not sure, Steven if you were in yesterday's discussion on the importance of international telecommunications cables that carry traffic around the world and things like financial data. My question for the panel is those of us that operate ships, but not navies to enforce maritime boundaries without UNCLOS, what recourse do we have to help us negotiate the disputes or coastal States exerting greater rights in the EEZs that limit our ability to lay cables or route cables? We have no recourse at the moment except for a seat at the UNCLOS table, if you will, to try and pressure these coastal States to abide by what they signed up to. I couldn't agree with you more. Many states are not abiding by UNCLOS, but the only way we can push back is to have a seat at the table. The question is what other avenues are there if we do away with UNCLOS and what other recourses do we have?

Steven Groves: I was unable to be here for that panel so unfortunately I am not fully up to speed on what your presentation was. My first reaction is that I assume there have been underwater cables laid to date and those were negotiated through some forms of bilateral or small multilateral arrangements. I assume also that with regard to the destination where the cable is going, that you got a starting point for your cable and an ending point for your cable, so you have two countries that are already interested in making it successful. Are we talking about cables that transit through EEZs of non-compliant parties?

Ronald Rapp: I would say many of our national cables will transit, but not land, in probably a dozen countries, as an example: the Red Sea. Many of those cables transit but don't land and we are in a situation now where permits are required in some EEZs to operate ships in violation of UNCLOS. We have no way to fight that.

Steven Groves: You are telling me there are parties to UNCLOS who are not following its terms?

Ron Rapp: Yes.

Steven Groves: Oh shucks! I will tell you that there are some corrupt countries out there. In terms of solutions, you are a US company, you have the Chamber, you have the government. If this is important enough to the United States and its bilateral relations with these law-breaking countries, who are making excessive claims and violating the terms of UNCLOS, that we apparently want to be a party to that is a tough nut to crack. I guess we have to rely on our government to help ease those easements.

John Norton Moore: Well, I think your question is very good because it really is part of the response to Steven's question of why not simply ignore the law. The answer, Steven is the United States has many other oceans interests. We have an interest in securing the critical infrastructure of cables, which we have done in this Convention. We have a very substantial interest in protecting fish stocks, in protecting the marine environment, in relation to getting secured property rights from seabed mining and extending as we did the sovereign rights of the United States over the largest continental shelf recognized anywhere in the world. So, that is how I would answer that and you are absolutely right. We needed these strong provisions protecting cables. The Convention is very good for the cable industry. You do need the rule of law. Indeed, the rule of law is as important for the cable industry as it is for the US Navy.

Thomas Pickering: I am going to take one more question since we are running over time and then allow each of the panel members a couple of minutes for summing up.

Fred Tipson: I am a former member of the Senate staff, as I know you are [Steven Groves]. I would like to ask two quick questions. Since I now represent the United Nations Development Programme (UNDP) in Washington, I must ask you to suggest where in the report of the Permanent Subcommittee on Investigations, which you used to serve on, about UNDP's program in North Korea, it concludes that UNDP's money went for anything other than legitimate development purposes in North Korea?

But my main question has to do with the logic that you, yourself, use in advising either your current colleagues at Heritage or, more importantly, the Senators who might be asked to vote on this treaty. How do you decide the right calculus in concluding whether this treaty is in the national interest or not? Is it your contention that if you can find a single hypothetical that might be adverse to the United States, such as a possible ruling by a dispute settlement panel, or a single problematic provision, such as Article 82 – or any other single problem or set of problems – that you would advise a Senator not to approve the treaty, even though the rest of it is overwhelmingly in the interests of the United States?

I don't ask this question frivolously because, as I listen to the discussions in the Foreign Relations Committee over the last few years, it would appear that this is the assumption some members are making – namely, if there is anything they can find wrong with this treaty, then the entire thing should go down. If that is not your calculus, how do you weigh the overall interests of the United States in the Convention?

Steven Groves: Thanks, Fred. On the first question I will have to refer you to Mark Greenblatt and some of the people who are my successors on the Permanent Subcommittee on Investigations. I wasn't there for the beginning middle or end of the UNDP investigation into the DPKR case. I really don't know what the answer is to that question. On the treaty itself, different senators have different concerns, and often before we go brief a senator, their staff informs us that we want to hear what the treaty does with this, and we want to hear what the treaty does with that. Some have environmental concerns, some have military concerns and some have sovereignty concerns. It is kind of up to the senator and believe me, if there is just one little thing that bugs them, then that is enough for them to oppose it, they can and do that regardless of whether you or I find that to be a logical approach.

Some of that is because some senators are inclined to disagree with the treaty and are just looking for the right reason, others see a legitimate set of issues or even a single issue that they oppose and that is enough to outweigh any beneficial parts of the treaty including the freedom of navigation provisions. In terms of what I personally brief on, it is difficult to say because we got a very, very lengthy treaty and a complex 1994 Agreement and then we got behavior of the member States themselves that are party to the treaty, and I use hypotheticals, but only if I think I can back them up with fact and law. I just think right now my personal belief, I don't know how this extends to the members of the Senate, is that just in the grand scheme of things, I wish there was a way we could find to give the Navy the tools it needs on the freedom of navigation provisions, but the rest of the provisions for me just outweigh those.

John Norton Moore: I am delighted that Steven raised the question of the argument based on the "Reagan Diary." I have been looking for an opportunity to drive a stake through the heart of that specious argument. First, we take an obscure diary provision that we really don't know what he was talking about and we say that is going to trump the statement from his Secretary of State, emphatically to the opposite, and that it will trump all of Reagan's official statements that he made. It will trump the conclusions of his interagency task force that reviewed all of this very carefully and came out with an official view of the Reagan administration. I revere Ronald Reagan, maybe because I had four Presidential appointments from Ronald Reagan. I revere this man and I think it is very important that we not ascribe views to Reagan that would be very harmful to the national interests of the United States. I am confident from the review he undertook that his view was if we met those six Reagan conditions the treaty was acceptable. We met the six conditions, and then some. But finally, let me just indicate what I suspect. The actual meaning of that provision, if you look at the timeline in terms of a decision being made by Reagan that he is writing about, the decision is entirely different from what Steven is talking about. It is a decision as to whether the United States might consider going forward with a reservation on deep seabed mining, all of Part XI, but accept all the rest of the treaty, which was seriously being considered internally by the US Government at that time. Reagan on that issue was advised correctly by the State Department otherwise; that is that to do so would not be consistent with the Convention which did not permit reservations. Such a reservation would have been in complete violation of the treaty, but more importantly it was going to totally open a Pandora's Box counter to the interests of the United States and permit every other country in the world to be asserting a variety of reservations to issues the United States had won and that were very important to us, including all the navigational issues. So, Steven, I think that argument actually ought to be put aside, not gently, but with force.

Thomas Pickering: Now for the closing points. By tradition, John Norton Moore, arguing the affirmative began the discussion, and out of a sense of fairness, I will give Steven the opportunity to choose whether he has the first or last closing arguments.

Steven Groves: Actually, I am a gentleman and I will defer to my host.

John Norton Moore: I don't need to take very long. I think you know my views at this point and I think it is very important that we move forward with this treaty. This is not something that is simply of academic interest. This is enormously important as is attested by the fact that the CNO, the Deputy CNO and others in the Navy, and the Chairmen of the Joint Chiefs have been seeking to move this forward for a long time. This Convention is powerfully in the interests of the United States economically, and politically in terms of rejoining the international community and restoring United States leadership in the oceans area. It is too long that we have had to sit on the sidelines and not be able to take the US leadership role back that we played throughout the course of these negotiations. I would urge the US Senate and the Administration to move forward with this. I laud the statement of Secretary of State Clinton, it is a wonderful statement. She is absolutely right! I know that President Obama supports this, as has every other American President and I am very hopeful we will move forward quickly.

Steven Groves: I would like to thank Ambassador Moore again for inviting me to this debate and thank you all for sitting here this whole time. I thought it was a very spirited debate and I had fun and I hope you did too. I will end by just giving some advice, which is if you want the United States to ultimately accede to this treaty you have to approach the people who can make that happen for you and point out some of the weaknesses. If you are absolutist on this and are of the opinion that there is nothing wrong with this treaty, that there are no flaws and it is pure as the driven snow, that causes senators and their staff to raise eyebrows. So, I would be more realistic. Talk about some of these warts. Find how you can distinguish them or excise them through a reservation or understanding or a declaration. Take on the issue directly about treaty partners who are not going to be reliable with their excessive claims. Or, don't take my advice and continue what has been going on for the past couple of decades, which is coming forward and saying the treaty is awesome, and there are no problems, and everything is fixed, that Reagan is in favor, even though he is dead. Point out the warts, get some Compound W for them and make your best case to the senators. That is your best chance. Thank you very much.

PART II

"Globalization and the Law of the Sea"

OPENING REMARKS

Hak-So KIM[1]

Welcome, Ladies and Gentlemen. Thank you for taking your time to come to this conference on Globalization and the Law of the Sea. I especially want to thank José Luis Jesus, the President of the International Tribunal for the Law of the Sea, Dr. Bosworth from the Brookings Institution, Jin-Hyun Paik, Judge of the International Tribunal for the Law of the Sea, and Sergey Tarasenko, Director of the United Nations Division of Oceans Affairs.

I also want to thank John Norton Moore, the Director of the Center for Oceans Law and Policy at University of Virginia, and Alfred Soons, the Director of Netherlands Institute for the Law of the Sea at Utrecht University, for their commitment to this conference. Last but not least, I want to thank Myron Nordquist for organizing and arranging this conference in cooperation with the KMI people.

This conference's title, "Globalization and the Law of the Sea," has a crucial undertone.

The world is now moving on under the regime of the United Nations Convention on the Law of the Sea (UNCLOS). As you know, the United Nations Convention on the Law of the Sea was adopted on December 10, 1982 and came into force on November 16, 1994. The Convention currently has 161 countries directly involved including Malawi, which joined on September 28, 2010. I have heard that the United States may ratify the UN Convention on the Law of the Sea in the near future.

Also, most of UNCLOS is part of customary international law. Therefore, we can say that every country is bound to observe the UNCLOS regime regardless of whether a country has joined the Convention. The UNCLOS system expands costal States' jurisdiction while protecting its traditional rights such as freedom of navigation. Also it recognizes the resources of the deep-sea floor as the common heritage of mankind.

However, as you all know, there are many issues to be solved within today's UNCLOS system. This conference will probe deeply into issues regarding the increased use of commercial vessels, pirates' actions and terrorist activities in the oceans. We shall seek ways to justify the effect of the islands under the Law of the Sea, as well as look at safety issues and issues regarding marine scientific

---

[1] President, Korea Maritime Institute http://www.kmi.re.kr/english/index.asp.

research, coastal States' sovereignty, and global warming. Numerous scholars and conferences have considered these issues; however, individuals and the states have different perspectives and interests which cannot always be resolved.

Despite all the difficulties, I have a firm expectation and hope for this conference. We have the best experts in the Law of the Sea to discuss these issues who come from six continents and 15 countries. In this conference we will try to understand different views and also learn new facts.

I am really happy to have this conference in Washington DC which is the capital of the United States as well as the center for international discussions with numerous research institutions. We at KMI are trying our best to develop partnerships with related international research institutes. I hope we will have a successful conference and develop productive relationships among the institutes.

Lastly I want to conclude my opening remarks by introducing the classic Asian Analects of Confucius. It starts like this, "학이시습지불역열호." This means "isn't it happy to learn and familiarize often?" The Chinese character here, 습(習), is an ideograph meaning "flap the wings." It is used in the sense of how a baby bird keeps flapping its wings until it eventually flies high up into the sky. I hope you all have a great time learning and thinking about the issues regarding the Law of the Sea and take advantage of this conference as a step to fly high.

Finally, I would like to once again extend my gratitude to all the participants.

Keynote Addresses

POST-CRISIS GLOBAL REBALANCING

*Barry Bosworth**

Abstract
This presentation is directed at illustrating the growing importance of the Asian economies in the world economy and their recent elevated role in the governance of that system. The economic gains are evident in the growing share of Asian economies in global GDP (incomes) and trade. The G-20 replaced the G-8 as the primary forum for discussion and coordination of international economic policies after the global financial crisis, and it proved to be very effective in coordinating national programs for economic stimulus and avoiding significant increases in trade protectionism. However, there has also been an increasing amount of friction – largely between the United States and China – over trade and the need to rebalance the global economy to reduce the prevalence of large trade surpluses and deficits. The presentation will address questions of how the trans-pacific relationship will evolve in future years.

For two centuries after the industrial revolution, economic development was limited to a few countries of Western Europe and North America, while most of the rest of the world continued to live in abject poverty. After World War II, that began to slowly change as people in an increasing number of countries began to raise their incomes beyond the subsistence level. But progress was slow until the 1960s when a number of countries, concentrated in East Asia, began to grow at unprecedented rates. What began with economic reconstruction in Japan spread to the newly-industrializing economies of Korea, Taiwan, Singapore, and Hong Kong, then to Southeast Asia, China, and now India. Today, growth in income per worker in East Asia and India, shown in figure 1, is 4–5 times that of the high-income economies of the OECD. It is an unprecedented accomplishment in which more than half of the world's population is now experiencing gains in income that are moving them from low to middle-income level status, in which poverty is no longer their defining characteristic. However, it is important to balance that success with the recognition that incomes still remain far below those of the advanced economies of the OECD (figure 2).

---

* A former presidential advisor, Barry Bosworth is a Senior Fellow, Economic Studies and the Global Economy and Development, Brookings Institution, Washington, DC. The figures in this paper are based on the author's calculations from data of the World Bank, *World Development Indicators.* The tables are based on the author's calculations from the International Monetary Fund, *World Economic Outlook*. His PowerPoint can be viewed at http://www.virginia.edu/colp/pdf/kmi-bosworth.pdf.

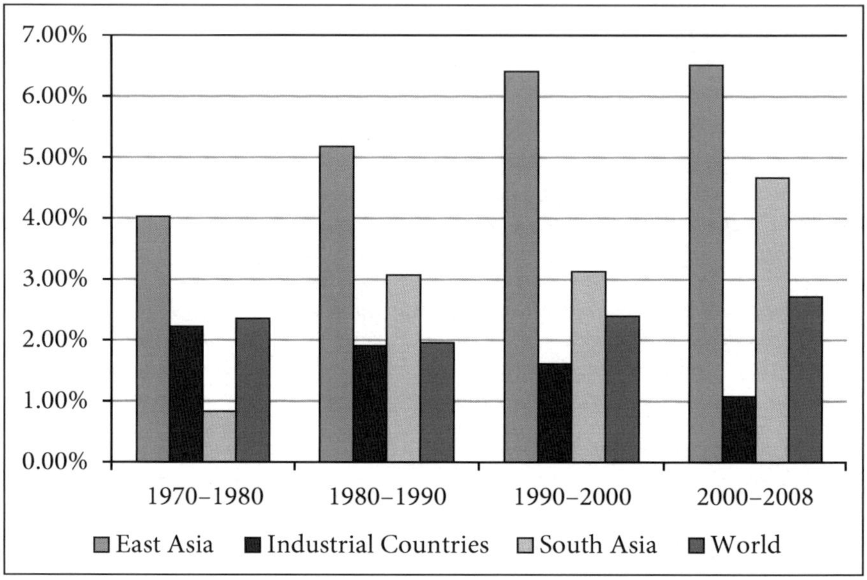

Fig. 1. Growth in Output per Worker

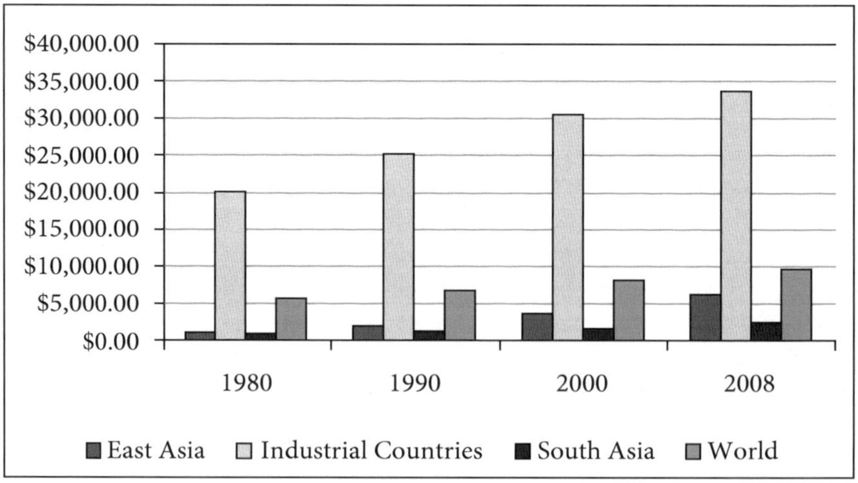

Fig. 2. GDP per capita, US$ PPP

The economic progress in Asia has been dramatic and sustained, but the region still has a long way to go to catch-up with the high-income countries.

The major innovation that has made this possible is the increased access of unskilled labor to the global market. The world has long been awash with unskilled workers, but until recently, they had no means of selling their services in a broader global market. That change can be credited to the opening of the global trading system, modern transport and communications technologies and the organizational contribution of multi-national companies. The process of economic development at this stage is largely driven by a simple formula: cheap wages make a low-income economy competitive in labor-intensive manufacturing (apparel, shoes and toys, for example). Factories sprout up, creating jobs and increasing incomes. Every rapid-growth economy in Asia jump-started its economy in this way, and China is just the biggest example – although I think there is much more to China's success than just cheap labor. And at some stage countries do exhaust their reserves of unskilled labor and they will have to broaden their approach to economic development if they are to keep growing. They need to innovate and use labor and capital more productively. That requires an entirely different way of doing business, and there is no single formula for success; but countries, such as Korea and Taiwan have managed that transition with great success.

Asia's success has also led to a major transformation of the structure of the global economy and its governance from a focus on the transatlantic region to a new order in which Asia has emerged as a primary source of future growth. In the United States, the discussion has clearly shifted from an old focus on a trans-Atlantic partnership to a much greater emphasis on expanding its trans-Pacific relationship.

Another dimension in which the changes are most marked is in the governance of the global economy. The G-8, a narrow club of transatlantic high-income countries, has been replaced by the G-20. While it is not perfect, the G-20 has greatly expanded the role of the large emerging-market economies, particularly those of Asia. It gives countries from all regions of the world a voice in the discussion of developments in the global economy and the coordination of national economic policies. The G-20 played an important role during the financial crisis of coordinating government pledges to not engage in the type of trade protectionism that had worsened the economic crisis of the 1930s, and it assisted in a similar process of joint stimulus to offset some of the depressive effects of the crisis. It also took the lead in efforts to expand the support programs of the World Bank and the IMF. Overall, the G-20 was a very effective forum for avoiding an outbreak of "beggar-thy-neighbor" policies in the aftermath of the crisis.

A third dimension in which East Asia has had a large impact is in the expansion of the global trading system. As shown in figures 3 and 4, the growth of

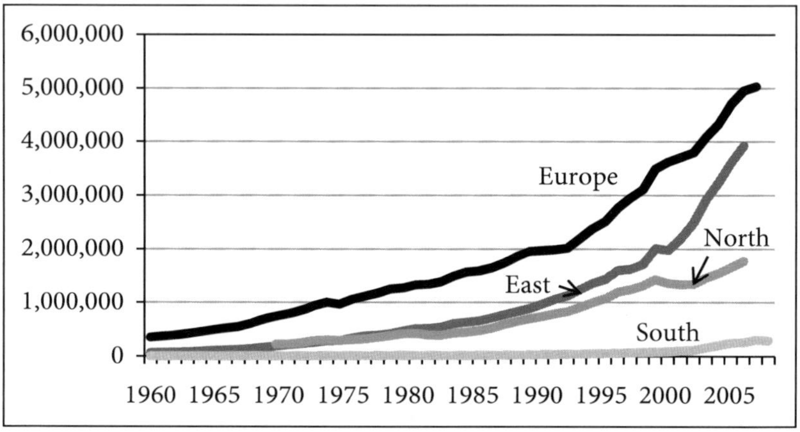

Fig. 3. Exports in Millions of Constant US$

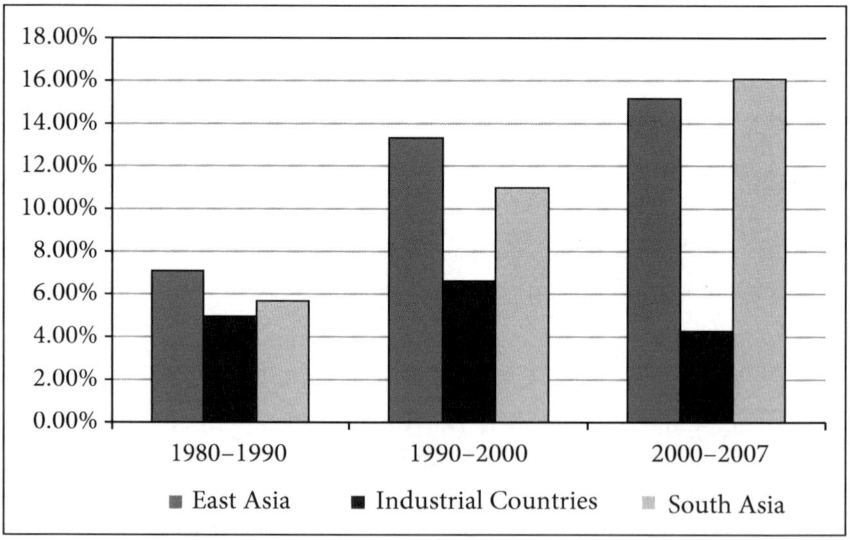

Fig. 4. Growth in Exports of Goods and Services

Table 1. World Economic Outlook

	2000–2008	2009	2010P	2011P
Advanced Economies	2.3	–3.2	2.7	2.2
United States	2.3	–2.6	2.6	2.3
Japan	1.4	–5.2	2.8	1.5
Euro Area	2.0	–4.1	1.7	1.5
Emerging Economies	6.5	2.5	7.1	6.4
Developing Asia	8.3	6.9	9.4	8.4
China	10.4	9.1	10.5	9.6
India	7.0	5.7	9.7	8.4

East Asia's trade has far exceeded that of other regions of the world economy, and it is on the verge of becoming the center of the global trading system. In the past decade, trade has begun to grow at a rapid pace in south Asia as well, though it starts from a very low level. The expansion of trade has played a central role in the development of the Asian economies, and the continuation of efforts to further reduce the barriers to cross-border trade is of particular importance in Asia.

The emerging markets of Asia also provide a striking contrast with the high-income economies in the aftermath of the financial crisis. They are fully recovered from the crisis and most countries have returned to the very high growth rates of the pre-crisis years. This contrasts with the near economic stagnation that continues to plague the United States, Europe and Japan. Admittedly, much of Asia's speedy recovery can be traced to the fact that most avoided significant financial problems. Having had their own crisis only 10 years earlier, they did not get caught up in the speculative excesses that proved so costly to the United States and Europe. Nearly all of their problems were induced by the collapse of the global trading system. And having previously experienced the slow response of the IMF, they had built up their own foreign exchange reserves that carried them through the crisis.

What has now emerged is a two-track global economy marked by a return to high growth in most of Asia and stagnation in the high-income economies. This is very evident in the projections of the IMF for the world economy shown in table 1. Growth in the high-income economies is projected at little more than two percent per year, not enough to significantly reduce current levels of high unemployment. Meanwhile, growth in emerging Asia is projected at 8–9 percent per year. This gives rise to a question of whether the economies of Asia have reached the point where their own growth is self-sustaining and no longer dependent on recovery in the United States and Europe.

In the 1997 crisis, each of the affected Asian economies sought to export their way out of the crisis: expanding exports offset much of the decline in

Table 2. Current Account as a Share of World GDP, Selected Regions and Years

Region	1990–99	2000–05	2006–08	2009	2010
U.S.	–0.43	–1.41	–1.37	–0.72	–0.79
Japan	0.36	0.35	0.33	0.24	0.24
Europe	0.08	0.23	0.16	0.11	0.18
Emerging Asia	0.06	0.38	0.87	0.81	0.78
Emerging Latin America	–0.14	–0.02	0.04	–0.02	–0.06
Middle East	–0.04	0.21	0.49	0.10	0.23
Other countries	–0.21	0.00	–0.11	–0.21	–0.18
Discrepancy	0.30	0.27	–0.41	–0.32	–0.41

domestic investment and consumption. And in large measure, they were successful because the United States and Europe kept their markets open and tolerated a substantial growth in their trade deficits as an offset to the Asian surpluses. Those deficits continued in the years after that crisis as the United States continued its emphasis on domestic consumption, and both the United States and Europe got caught up in a speculative bubble in real estate.

Now, with the end of the asset bubble, the United States, Japan and Europe will be looking to an expansion of exports to lead them out of the recession. The issue is particularly important for the United States because it is by far the world's largest debtor country, and its large trade deficit is matched by surpluses in most other countries, particularly Asia. This is most evident in the distribution of current account imbalances shown in table 2. Prior to the crisis, a consumption boom in the United States provided the engine for global economic growth: the boom led to an increase in imports, and countries in Asia used the large deficits of the United States to expand their own export sectors. However, with the financial crisis, the imbalances in the global trading system are no longer sustainable.

Moreover, it is evident that the issue of trade imbalance is largely an issue between the United States and Asia. Historically, most countries have fluctuated between small surpluses or deficits, but this was not true after the Asian financial crisis. The US trade deficit grew to exceed over six percent of its GDP, and it was offset by large surpluses in Asia and OPEC. For many years, the situation was attractive to both sides. With the boom in home prices and the stock market, many Americans thought they were rich and spent accordingly. Unemployment was very low and jobs were readily available. In effect, they embarked on a decade-long process of spending more than they earned, saving declined, and they imported the excess consumption from Asia.

The countries of Asia also approved of the emerging trade pattern, as they needed the trade surpluses to promote production and jobs in the face of a slump in domestic investment. China is a good example because during most

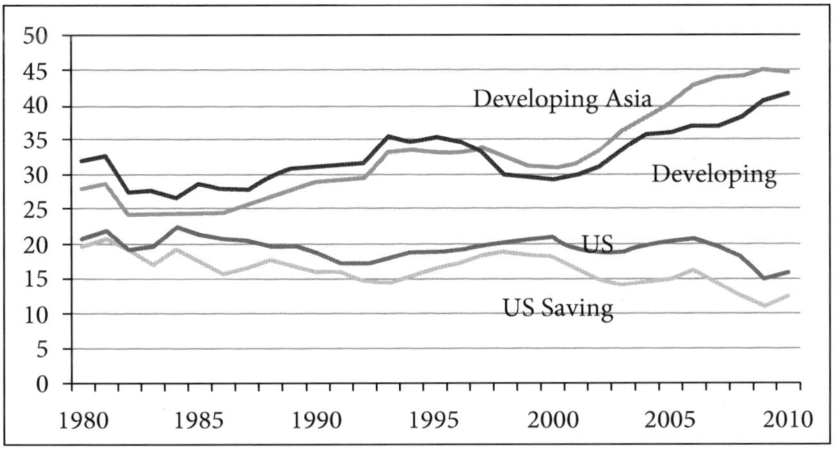

Fig. 5. Saving and Investment, US & Developing Asia 1980–2010

of its era of rapid growth, exports and imports remained in relative balance, and only after 2004 did a new pattern of trade emerge in which China generated large surpluses and became the primary offset to the American deficit.

The domestic counterparts of the trade imbalance are also illustrated in figure 5, which shows the high rates of saving and investment in Asia, but of greater significance, we can observe the growing excess of saving over investment. Meanwhile, the United States shows the opposite pattern, as its much lower rate of national saving has consistently fallen short of its investment needs. The magnitude of the shortfall also grew substantially after the late 1990s.

Economic theory suggests that the pattern of global imbalances should be self-correcting. The surplus countries will have strong aggregate demand, stimulating higher rates of domestic inflation and an appreciation of their real exchange rate; the opposite process would be at work in the deficit countries. Unfortunately, that adjustment does not seem operative in today's economy or is doing so very gradually. The United States expanded its fiscal deficit in the aftermath of the recession to the point that its national saving has turned negative, and the real exchange rate actually appreciated during the crisis as many investors fled to the safety of U.S. treasuries. In addition, American firms have been largely ineffective in expanding their exports, and as oil prices again rise, the US trade deficit will worsen. China's trade surplus fell sharply during the crisis, but with the recovery of world trade, it is again growing. The United States continues to consume too much and save too little, while Asia continues to save far in excess of its own investment. The United States expands its issues of debt and Asia buys it up.

Each side in the imbalance would like to blame the other, but it seems obvious that it was largely a symbiotic relationship that met the needs of both

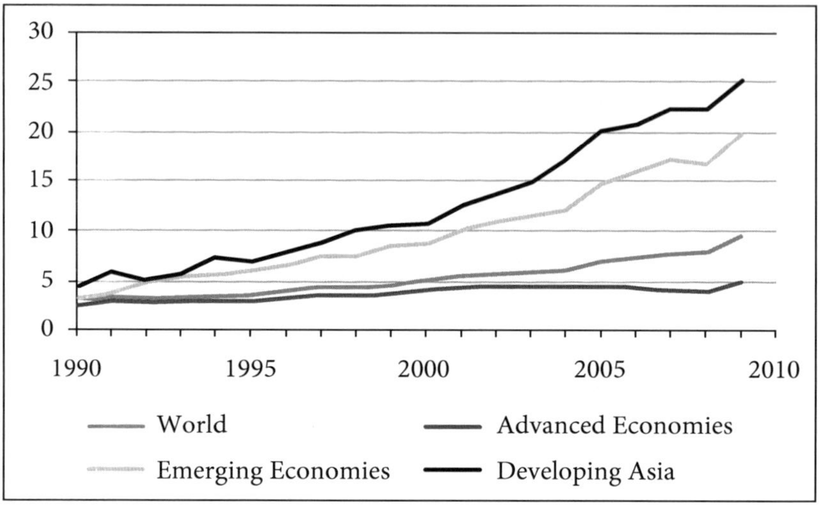

Fig. 6. International Reserves, 1990–2009

regions until the crisis. Americans are now far less wealthy than they thought, jobs are in short supply, and they will need to find a means of bringing their exports up to be more in line with their imports. They cannot afford the trade deficits of the past, even if they cannot generate surpluses as a means of recovery from the crisis. That means that Asia will need to find an alternative means of fueling its future economic growth. It implies that countries like China will need to revert back to a greater emphasis on the expansion of their own domestic economies.

Both sides in the debate over imbalances need to recognize that the current situation is not a sustainable process for either the United States or Asia. On the Asian side, they have neutralized the excess inflow of foreign exchange by simply adding to their own exchange reserves, and issuing domestic bonds to finance the purchases. They suppress any remaining pressure on exchange rates with capital controls. The result has been an extraordinary accumulation of foreign exchange reserves throughout Asia, but particularly in China. This change is highlighted in figure 6, which shows the rise in foreign exchange reserves as a share of GDP. For decades, countries maintained reserves near 5 percent of their GDP, despite the growing size of global trade. However, in the aftermath of the Asian financial crisis some countries began to accumulate an extraordinary amount of foreign exchange, and in developing Asia those reserves now exceed 25 percent of GDP, or 5 times the previous levels relative to GDP.

Initially, the increases might have been justifiable as a response to the IMF's policies during the 1997–98 crisis. It was very slow to provide assistance and tried to use the situation to force its own preferred changes in countries' economic policies. Countries in Asia have sought to respond to their experience with the IMF by self-insuring against future crises. However, such a policy has large inefficiencies as the reserves tie up funds that could go to meet domestic needs, and in recent years the earnings on those reserves have been negligible. They also expose the countries to large capital losses in the face of any future adjustment to a more sustainable pattern of trade and exchange rates.

On the US side, there is a growing realization that the United States needs to restructure its economy to move away from its excess domestic consumption toward the production of exportable products. At a minimum, it needs to achieve a level of exports sufficient to pay for its imports. The United States cannot afford to continue with ongoing trade deficits financed by debt issuance and asset sales to the rest of the world. It is already the world's largest debtor nation by a large margin. But, if it is to export more in the short-run, the only way to do so is to make its exports cheaper in world markets: in other words, the US dollar needs to fall in value. In addition, the magnitude of the change needs to be big. Historical research suggests that for every change in the trade balance of one percent of GDP, the exchange rate needs to fall by about 10 percent. Since the United States needs an adjustment of about 3 percent of GDP, the required change in the real trade-weighted exchange rate is about 30 percent.

Adding to the difficulties, the major competitors of the United States are Japan and Europe: the countries that make the same high-tech capital intensive products as the United States. We do not compete with emerging Asia, which specializes in relatively low-technology labor-intensive products. However, our major competitors are in nearly as much trouble as we, and cannot allow a realignment to be between the United States and Europe alone. Thus, they believe that the realignment needs to be at the global level.

The adjustment will be very painful for the United States because as a country living beyond its means, it will experience a considerable decline in standard of living. Americans will need to save more, and government budget deficits must be eliminated either with expenditure cuts or tax increases, if the public dissaving is to be reduced; but regardless, overall consumption must fall. The evidence that Americans are willing to accept those sacrifices is currently non-existent and it is the opposite of the message of US political leaders who continue to promote tax cuts and program expansions. However, there is at least some evidence of the beginning of a national discussion, even if specific actions seem several years away. The United States is still an extraordinarily rich country and the supply side of its economy is still very efficient and innovative. Thus, the current situation could continue for some time. However, continuing high levels of unemployment will create severe socio-economic strains, and those strains will ultimately spill over into the political arena and affect US foreign policy.

I believe that imbalances in global trade, while complex in origin, have the potential to create severe problems in the relationship between the United States and Asia. The United States, as a large relatively self-sufficient economy, has always had a very mixed attitude toward trade, and the support for an open-trading regime is weaker than in other countries. There is a concern that continued poor economic performance and the lack of job opportunities will lead to increased trade protection and a mentality of blaming foreigners, rather than a recognition that the United States has caused its own problems through over-consumption, financial excesses, and extraordinarily weak government decision-making. On the other side, Asia has become too dependent on what may become an unreliable United States. It needs to reduce its emphasis on trade with the United States and shift toward a broadening of intra-regional economic relations.

THE UNITED NATIONS' ROLE IN COMBATTING PIRACY AND TERRORISM AT SEA

Sergey Tarasenko[1]

Abstract

The presentation will describe the role of the United Nations in the efforts to combat, on the one hand piracy and, on the other hand, terrorist acts against shipping, offshore installations and other maritime interests both of which are of particular concern to the international community. It will start by setting out the clear distinction between these types of offences and the international legal regimes that apply to them including the relevant international conventions and other instruments, such as Security Council and General Assembly resolutions. The presentation will highlight the importance of international cooperation in combating both piracy and terrorist acts at sea, and describe the development of regional and international cooperation frameworks. It will also highlight some key capacity-building initiatives currently underway and address the role of the United Nations and other relevant actors in this regard. The presentation will conclude by assessing the current challenges facing the international community in addressing these offences.

Introduction

My presentation will seek to establish the fact that though piracy and terrorism are both serious crimes, they are distinct in nature and are governed by different legal regimes. I will also describe the measures that the United Nations has taken to address both crimes including through the establishment of legal frameworks, cooperation mechanisms and capacity building. In my conclusion, I will explore possible ways forward.

---

[1] Sergey Tarasenko is currently the Director of the Division for Ocean Affairs and the Law of the Sea, Office of Legal Affairs at the United Nations. From 1985 to present he has been at the United Nations Office of Legal Affairs: Treaty Section, Office of the Legal Counsel, Codification Division and the Division for Ocean Affairs and the Law of the Sea. During 1980–1985 he was at the U.S.S.R. Ministry of Foreign Affairs, Department of Law and Treaties. He earned his Ph.D. at the Institute of State and Law, Russian Academy of Sciences and graduated from the Moscow State Institute of International Affairs, Faculty of Public International Law. The views expressed in this presentation are solely my own and do not reflect the view of the United Nations.

I. *Piracy vs. Terrorism*

As just mentioned, piracy and terrorism are distinct crimes governed by different legal regimes. This is an important point that we all need to keep in mind because it has real policy implications. For this reason, it will be useful to go over some particularly relevant differences between the two types of offenses. In particular, we shall focus on five principal differences: the definition of the crimes, the animus for the crimes, the location of the crimes, the jurisdiction of states, and the requirement for international cooperation.

a. *No universally-accepted definition*

The first thing to point out is that while piracy is a well-defined crime under international law, there is still no universally accepted definition of terrorism. The definition of piracy is contained in Article 101 of the 1982 United Nations Convention on the Law of the Sea (UNCLOS). This definition is also considered to represent customary international law and has been incorporated into many international instruments, as well as into the national laws of a number of States.

On the other hand, the international community has thus far failed in its efforts to adopt a universally accepted definition of terrorism. A number of definitions have been put forward. For example, the General Assembly's definition in its 1994 Declaration on Measures to Eliminate International Terrorism (Resolution 49/60) was:

> *Criminal acts intended or calculated to provoke a state of terror in the general public, a group of persons or particular persons for political purposes are in any circumstance unjustifiable, whatever the considerations of a political, philosophical, ideological, racial, ethnic, religious or any other nature that may be invoked to justify them.*

The search for a consensually agreed definition and scope of the crime of piracy remains a major sticking point in the negotiations on a draft comprehensive convention on international terrorism in the Sixth Committee of the General Assembly. Instead, the international community has worked around the need for a definition by regulating specific "terrorist" acts in a series of sixteen global counter-terrorism instruments.

b. *Motivation: private ends vs. political purposes*

Piracy is defined in Article 101 of UNCLOS as a crime committed for private ends. On the other hand, although it is generally understood that terrorist acts are committed with a certain intent, such as political or ideological purposes, such an *animus* is not usually an element of the offences set forth in relevant counter-piracy instruments. As there is no valid justification for committing terrorist acts, the purpose for committing the crimes is generally not taken into account. There is, therefore, a clear difference in the element of intent for the two types of offenses.

c. Locus delicti: *high seas vs. anywhere*

Another important distinction relates to where the offenses are committed. Under UNCLOS, the crime of piracy can only be committed on the high seas, or, pursuant to Article 58(2), in the Exclusive Economic Zone (EEZ) of a State. Terrorism does not have such a geographical restriction. Generally, terrorist acts may be committed anywhere in the world, on land, on the seas or in the sky. This distinction is particularly important because of the next distinction highlighted, namely, the question of jurisdiction.

d. *Universal jurisdiction vs. other bases of jurisdiction*

Piracy under UNCLOS is subject to universal jurisdiction. This means that the warship of any State may take measures on the high seas or in the EEZ of a State to seize a pirate ship or aircraft and arrest the persons on board. The courts of the seizing State may prosecute the suspected offenders, regardless of whether there is any jurisdictional link between the State and the incident.

On the other hand, in the case of terrorist acts, a State may exercise its jurisdiction only subject to other bases of jurisdiction under international law, such as the territoriality principle, nationality principle, or the passive personality principle.

e. *Duty to cooperate v. prosecute or extradite*

A final, very important, distinction is that while States have a broad duty to cooperate to the fullest possible extent in the repression of piracy, pursuant to Article 100 of UNCLOS, the duty of States pursuant to relevant counter-terrorism instruments is far better defined. In particular, counter-terrorism instruments provide States with a duty to prosecute or extradite suspected offenders within a relevant jurisdiction. These instruments also contain other cooperation provisions, for example, with regard to information sharing, judicial cooperation and extradition.

f. *Legal and cooperation frameworks and capacity building*

Having described some of the differences between the two types of crimes, the paper will now highlight the way in which the United Nations has sought to address them. For both piracy and terrorism, the United Nations has participated in the establishment of an international legal framework, has developed cooperation frameworks and has undertaken substantial capacity-building.

II. *Piracy*

a. *Legal Framework*

i. *UNCLOS*

The legal framework for the repression of piracy under international law is set forth in UNCLOS, particularly in its Articles 100 to 107, and 110. As noted above, the provisions of UNCLOS relating to piracy are generally considered to reflect customary international law, binding on all States.

The definition of piracy is set out in Article 101 of UNCLOS and includes any illegal acts of violence, detention or depredation committed on the high seas or in the EEZ of a state for private ends by the crew or passengers of a private ship against another ship, or persons or property on board that ship. If similar acts are committed within the territorial sea of a State, they constitute armed robbery against ships and fall under the jurisdiction of the coastal State.

Article 105 of UNCLOS permits States to exercise universal jurisdiction over acts of piracy. This is the broadest possible jurisdiction under public international law and in this context means that the warship of any state may seize a pirate ship or a ship under the control of pirates, arrest the suspects and prosecute them. It is important, in this regard, to also be aware that under UNCLOS, universal jurisdiction is "permissive." That is, the exercise of such jurisdiction by States is not an obligation but a right.

ii. *Other instruments*

In addition to UNCLOS, a number of other international instruments may be relevant to combating piracy, as certain elements of the crime of piracy may also constitute offenses under these instruments.

At present, the incidence of piracy is particularly high off the coast of Somalia and in certain parts of Asia. The latest International Maritime Bureau report indicates that from January to June 2010 there were 127 incidents of piracy off the coast of Somalia. During the same period, there were 30 attacks in the South China Sea. Therefore, in recent years, a number of regional instruments have been concluded to strengthen regional cooperation in the repression of these crimes in these regions. These include the 2004 Regional Cooperation Agreement on Combating Piracy and Armed Robbery against Ships in Asia (ReCAAP) and the 2009 Djibouti Code of Conduct concerning the Repression of Piracy and Armed Robbery against Ships in the Western Indian Ocean and the Gulf of Aden (Djibouti Code) which was concluded under the auspices of the International Maritime Organization (IMO).

iii. *Security Council resolutions*

Furthermore, as regards the specific situation off the coast of Somalia where piracy has become particularly pervasive in the past few years, the Security

Council has adopted six resolutions under Chapter VII of the Charter of the United Nations, namely resolutions 1816 (2008), 1838 (2008), 1846 (2008), 1851 (2008), 1897 (2009), and 1950 (2010). These resolutions, *inter alia*, authorize States and regional organizations cooperating with the Transitional Federal Government of Somalia to take measures to repress piracy and armed robbery against ships in Somalia and within its territorial sea. Such measures must be consistent with the requirements set forth in these resolutions, as well as with international law, including international humanitarian and human rights law. These resolutions expressly provide that they apply only to the situation in Somalia and should not be considered as establishing customary international law. Pursuant to these resolutions there are currently three international naval counter-piracy coalitions patrolling off the coast of Somalia as well as a number of national navies.

b. *Cooperation framework (Duty to Cooperate)*

International cooperation against piracy is key for the effective implementation of the legal framework just described. Indeed, by virtue of Article 100 of UNCLOS, States are under a duty to "cooperate to the fullest extent possible in the repression of piracy on the high seas or in any other place outside the jurisdiction of any State."

The United Nations, through the work of the General Assembly and the IMO has provided a forum for such cooperation. The General Assembly, which is a principal organ of the United Nations comprising all 192 Member States of the Organization, discusses piracy every year in the context of its debates on the agenda item "Oceans and the law of the sea". It has, *inter alia*, urged states to cooperate to suppress this crime as well as to "take appropriate steps under their national law to facilitate the apprehension and prosecution of those who are alleged to have committed acts of piracy." It has also dedicated part of two meetings of the United Nations Open-ended Informal Consultative Process on Oceans and the Law of the Sea to the issue of piracy.

Piracy also is regularly discussed at the IMO's Legal Committee and its Maritime Safety Committee, which have developed a number of non-binding guidance instruments.

The specific case of piracy off the coast of Somalia has also been on the agenda of the Security Council since 2008. Resolution 1851 (2008) called for the establishment of "an international cooperation mechanism to act as a common point of contact between and among states, regional and international organizations on all aspects of combating piracy and armed robbery at sea off Somalia's coast."

Following this call, cooperation between States in relation to piracy off the coast of Somalia has also been taking place through the Contact Group on Piracy off the Coast of Somalia. Fifty-four states are now members of this Group which recently held its seventh plenary session in New York on 10 November 2010. The United Nations Secretariat actively participates in the work of the Contact Group and its four Working Groups which cover topics such as military and cooperation coordination and legal issues.

c. *Capacity-Building*

The United Nations has also taken steps to assist States in the implementation of the international legal framework to combat the crime of piracy, including in particular through capacity-building. Although there are a number of entities involved in capacity-building activities in relation to piracy, it is important to highlight, in particular, the work of the IMO and the United Nations Office on Drugs and Crime (UNODC).

i. *IMO*

The IMO has been implementing a long-term anti-piracy capacity-building project since 1998 aimed at fostering the development of regional agreements to implement counter piracy measures. Through its technical cooperation programme, IMO provides assistance to States around the world.

The IMO is currently undertaking a broad range of capacity-building activities to assist signatory States in implementing the Djibouti Code of Conduct. The code was concluded under IMO's auspices, including the development of three regional counter-piracy information sharing centres as well as a regional training facility in Djibouti. Also included was regional training on mechanisms for maritime law enforcement, communications and other issues of concern. This initiative assists Member States in bringing their national anti-piracy legislation in line with the Djibouti Code. In November 2010, the IMO organized a regional meeting of member States to the Code in Yemen.

ii. *UNODC*

Since its inception in 2008, UNODC's counter-piracy programme has remained focused on piracy off the coast of Somalia. It provides assistance to regional States to facilitate the prosecution and imprisonment of suspected pirates, particularly through legislative assistance, support and capacity-building for law enforcement, prosecutors and the judiciary as well as support for the trials of piracy suspects through the facilitation of witness attendance, and, the assurance of interpretation and defence counsel for unrepresented accused.

UNODC is also providing assistance to Somalia and has assisted legal experts from the Transitional Federal Government of Somalia, as well as regional authorities from Puntland and Somaliland, to jointly draft new anti-piracy legislation, which is currently pending adoption. Finally, UNODC is working with the United Nations Development Programme (UNDP) in building and overseeing the management of prisons in Somalia. This could enable those sentenced outside of Somalia to be repatriated to Somalia to serve their sentences there.

III. *Terrorist Acts Against Shipping, Offshore Installations and Other Maritime Interests*

a. *Legal framework*

Turning now to international efforts to combat terrorist acts at sea, the legal framework for combating terrorist acts at sea (as contrasted with piracy) is found in a wide range of international instruments, including UNCLOS.

i. *UNCLOS*

Although no provisions under UNCLOS relate specifically to terrorism, UNCLOS provides the overarching legal framework for combating terrorist acts at sea in particular because it sets forth the rights and obligations of States in the various maritime zones.

ii. *SUA Convention and Protocols*

For more detailed provisions relating specifically to terrorist offences, however, one needs to turn to the 16 global counter-terrorism instruments, of which four relate specifically to terrorist acts at sea. These four IMO instruments are: (1) the 1988 Convention for the Suppression of Unlawful Acts against the Safety of Maritime Navigation (SUA Convention); (2) the 1988 Protocol to the SUA Convention for the suppression of unlawful acts against the safety of fixed platforms located on the continental shelf; (3) the 2005 Protocol to the SUA Convention; and (4) the 2005 Protocol to the SUA Protocol for the suppression of unlawful acts against the safety of fixed platforms located on the continental shelf. The SUA Convention and its 1988 Protocol, which were negotiated in response to the terrorist hijacking of the *Achille Lauro* in 1985, are widely ratified, with 156 States parties and 145 States parties, respectively. The 2005 Protocols, on the other hand, just entered into force on 28 July 2010.

These instruments require States to criminalize a wide range of terrorist acts committed against shipping, offshore installations and other maritime interests. As with other counter-terrorism instruments, States parties to the SUA Convention and its protocols are required to extradite or prosecute suspected offenders. In addition, the 2005 Protocol to the SUA Convention includes a set of innovative high seas boarding provisions.

iii. *Other instruments*

In addition, although they do not address terrorist acts at sea directly, some of the other 12 global counter-terrorism instruments, such as the 1997 International

Convention for the Suppression of Terrorist Bombings and the 1999 International Convention for the Suppression of the Financing of Terrorism, may also be relevant depending on the circumstances. As these instruments do not have a restricted geographical scope, they apply regardless of where the relevant unlawful acts take place. There are also a number of other conventions which, although, not designed to combat terrorism, play an important role in combating terrorist acts at sea. These include the 1974 Convention for the Safety of Life at Sea (SOLAS), and the 2004 International Ship and Port Facilities Security (ISPS) Code.

In addition to the 16 global counter-terrorism instruments, 14 counter-terrorism instruments have been concluded at the regional level. Moreover, many important resolutions have been adopted by the Security Council, acting under Chapter VII of the Charter of the United Nations.

iv. *Security Council resolutions*

Since the early 1990s, the Security Council has been consistently dealing with terrorism issues. Security Council resolutions 1368 (2001), 1373 (2001) and 1624 (2005) note that all terrorist attacks irrespective of their motivation, may be considered to pose a threat to international peace and security, which may warrant action under Chapter VII of the UN Charter. These resolutions address issues such as co-operation including in connection with criminal investigations or criminal proceedings relating to the financing or support of terrorist attacks and the obligation on States to deny financial and all other forms of support and safe haven to terrorists and those supporting terrorism. The Security Council has also called upon States to prohibit by law incitement to commit a terrorist act or acts and to prevent such conduct.

b. *Cooperation Framework*

As with piracy, the United Nations has taken steps to develop an international cooperation framework for addressing international terrorism.

i. *United Nations Global Counter-Terrorism Strategy*

As is the case with piracy, both the Security Council and the General Assembly serve as important for a for discussions amongst States on this important issue. Indeed, five of the 16 global counter-terrorism instruments were adopted by the General Assembly, and discussions on a draft comprehensive convention on international terrorism remain ongoing. Most recently, the United Nations Global Counter-Terrorism Strategy was adopted by the General Assembly, in its resolution 60/288 of 8 September 2006. It provides a four pillar strategic framework and practical guidance on joint efforts for the international community to counter terrorism. This is the first time that all Member States have agreed to a common strategic approach to fight terrorism, not only by sending a clear message that terrorism is unacceptable in all its forms and manifestation but also in resolving to take practical steps individually and collectively to prevent and combat it.

Recently, on 8 September 2010, the General Assembly adopted resolution 64/297 which reaffirmed the UN Global Counter-Terrorism Strategy as well as the fact that it is the primary responsibility of member States to implement the strategy while recognizing the need to enhance the important role by the United Nations.

ii. *CTITF*

Cooperation within the United Nations takes place through the Counter-Terrorism Implementation Task Force (CTITF) which was established by the Secretary-General in 2005 to enhance coordination and coherence of counter-terrorism efforts of the United Nations system. Currently the Task Force consists of 30 international entities which work on issues related to international terrorism, including the UN Office of Legal Affairs.

c. *Capacity-building*

i. *CTED*

Many of the entities participating in the CTITF also provide capacity-building assistance to States in the implementation of the international legal framework set out above. With regard to terrorist acts at sea, examples include the work of three entities: the IMO, the UNODC and the Counter Terrorism Executive Directorate (CTED).

ii. *IMO*

IMO continues to develop guidance material and to encourage States to cooperate in addressing threats to maritime safety and security through bilateral and multilateral instruments and mechanisms aimed at monitoring, preventing and responding to such threats. In addition, through its Technical Cooperation Programme, IMO assists States to implement effectively relevant IMO instruments, such as the SUA Convention and the SOLAS Convention. Programme activities are delivered through regional, sub-regional and national seminars, workshops or training courses; regional and sub-regional meetings to promote co-operation at the regional and sub-regional level; needs assessment and technical advisory missions; and through the provision of training materials.

iii. *UNODC*

UNODC also provides capacity-building and technical assistance in the implementation of the global counter-terrorism instruments. It focuses on the provision of assistance to States, upon request, in the legal and related aspects of counter-terrorism, especially for ratifying and implementing the international legal instruments against terrorism and for strengthening the capacity of the national criminal justice systems to apply the provisions of these instruments in compliance with the principles of rule of law. The counter-terrorism technical assistance delivered by UNODC also helps countries to comply with the requirements of Security Council resolution 1373 (2001). In this regard, UNODC has developed guidance material, including legislative guides and model laws. In addition, it holds workshops and provides technical assistance at the national level. Recently, UNODC has also been focussing on the implementation of the international legal framework for maritime security, and has organized regional workshops in both Africa and Asia on this topic, in which DOALOS participated.

The Security Council's Counter-Terrorism Committee, through CTED, facilitates the provision of technical assistance to Member States by disseminating best practices through identifying existing technical, financial, regulatory and legislative assistance programmes; by promoting synergies between the assistance programmes of international, regional and sub-regional organizations; by serving as an intermediary for contacts between potential donors and recipients and by maintaining an online directory of assistance providers, all within the framework of Security Council resolution 1373 (2001). CTED also undertakes national assessment missions and provides technical assistance, at the request of States.

IV. *Conclusion*

Firstly, it is imperative to recall the important distinctions between piracy and terrorism at all times. Any effort to conflate such crimes should be carefully avoided. Secondly, the approach of the United Nations to address such crimes has revolved around three elements – the development of a strong international legal regime, the establishment of effective cooperation mechanisms, and the delivery of capacity-building.

In both the case of piracy and the case of international terrorism, the international community's focus has shifted to the second and third elements of this approach. Two important challenges, going forward, will be to ensure that cooperation mechanisms created to help combat piracy and terrorism crimes are as effective and efficient as possible, and to ensure that all States have the necessary capacity to effectively implement the international legal regimes. In both cases, the United Nations has an important role to play, and a responsibility to its Member States as well as to the broader international community to act both quickly and effectively. States, however, also have to take responsibility for fulfilling their international commitments and for assisting other States to do the same.

It is my hope that the international community will be successful in addressing these challenges.

THE ROLE OF ITLOS IN THE SETTLEMENT OF LAW OF THE SEA DISPUTES

José Luis Jesus[1]

Abstract

The International Tribunal for the Law of the Sea (ITLOS) has a core competence to deal with all disputes and all applications submitted to it in accordance with the 1982 UN Law of the Sea Convention. As an international judicial body with specialized jurisdiction, the Tribunal is particularly positioned to play a major role in the settlement of international law of the sea disputes. This role is enhanced by the fact that the Convention confers on the Tribunal certain functions which are indeed unique in international adjudication.

The Tribunal has both contentious and advisory jurisdiction. In particular, it has jurisdiction over (a) any dispute concerning the interpretation or application of the provisions of the Convention which is submitted to it in accordance with Part XV; (b) disputes concerning the interpretation or application of an international agreement related to the purposes of the Convention, which is submitted to it in accordance with the agreement; and (c) any dispute concerning the interpretation or application of a treaty already in force concerning the subject-matter covered by the Convention if all the parties to such a treaty so agree.

The Tribunal, as a full court, has also jurisdiction to entertain requests for advisory opinions, based on a procedure which has no parallel in previous adjudication practice, as we shall see later.

In addition, the Seabed Disputes Chamber, composed of 11 of the 21 judges of the Tribunal, has quasi-exclusive jurisdiction over any disputes related to activities in the Area and has also jurisdiction to entertain any request for advisory opinions related to the legal regime concerning the international seabed area, as embodied in Part XI and related annexes of the Convention and the 1994 New York Agreement on the implementation of Part XI of the Convention.

The jurisdiction of the Tribunal ratione personae *also represents an interesting development of procedural international law.*

It is with great pleasure that I address this gathering of distinguished scholars. I am honoured by the kind invitation addressed to me on behalf of the organizers and grateful for the opportunity to exchange views with you on the work of the International Tribunal for the Law of the Sea.

---

[1] Judge José Luis Jesus is President of the International Tribunal for the Law of the Sea. He kindly provided this keynote address at the Conference "Globalization and the Law of the Sea," co-sponsored by the Center for Oceans Law and Policy and the Korea Maritime Institute on 2 December, 2010.

I have chosen to speak today about the judicial work of the Tribunal. I will briefly describe that work with special emphasis on some of the procedural details of the new cases pending before it. I will also try to identify the reasons why the Tribunal has received more cases than any other court or tribunal referred to in Article 287 of the Convention. Lastly, I will make some observations concerning prospects for the future work of the Tribunal and its role in implementation of the Convention's dispute settlement system.

Cases handled by the Tribunal

A great deal has been written and said about the Tribunal's shortage of cases. Although it could have entertained more cases than it has, the fact is that States have made greater use of the Tribunal than is commonly believed. Since 1998, when it received its first case, a total of 18 cases have been filed. Of these, 13 have been resolved, two were discontinued and the last three cases, instituted in the past 12 months, are under way.

Of the 13 cases that have been resolved, eight were prompt release cases,[2] four involved provisional measures[3] pending the constitution of an Annex VII arbitral tribunal and one dealt with compensation for the illegal arrest of a vessel. The majority of these cases concerned prompt release of vessels and crews detained for alleged violation of coastal States' fisheries regulations in the exclusive economic zone. The Tribunal has developed a substantial *corpus* of jurisprudence in this regard.

The two discontinued cases were case No. 7 – *Conservation and Sustainable Exploitation of Swordfish Stocks in the South-Eastern Pacific Ocean* (Chile / the European Union) and Case No. 9 – *The "Chaisiri Reefer 2" Case* (Panama v. Yemen), Prompt Release.

Case No. 7 was submitted to an *ad hoc* Special Chamber of the Tribunal formed under article 15, paragraph 2, of the Statute of the Tribunal; to date, this is the only contentious case that has been submitted to a chamber of the Tribunal. In March 2001, the parties informed the Special Chamber that they had reached a provisional arrangement concerning the dispute and requested that the proceedings before the Chamber be suspended. The time limits in

2 The *M/V "Saiga"* case (Saint Vincent and the Grenadines v. Guinea); the "*Camouco*" case (Panama v. France); the "*Monte Confurco*" case (Seychelles v. France); the "*Grand Prince*" case (Belize v. France); the "*Volga*" case (Russian Federation v. Australia); the "*Juno Trader*" case (Saint Vincent and the Grenadines v. Guinea Bissau; the "*Hoshinmaru*" case (Japan v. Russian Federation); the "*Tomimaru*" case (Japan v. Russian Federation).

3 The *Bluefin Tuna* cases (Australia v. Japan; New Zealand v. Japan), the *MOX Plant* case (Ireland v. the United Kingdom) and the *Land Reclamation* case (Malaysia v. Singapore).

the proceedings were therefore extended by successive orders at the request of both parties. This case was ultimately discontinued in December 2009 at their request.

Although the Chamber did not deal with the substance of this case, the fact that it had been filed with the Tribunal may have helped the parties to reach an out of court agreement. As stated by the President of the Special Chamber, "[t]he Tribunal may assist the parties in more than one way. Adjudication is, of course, the main function of the Tribunal. It may also assist the parties, where appropriate, in reaching direct settlement of the dispute between them".[4]

The *"Chaisiri Reefer 2"* prompt release case was also discontinued at the request of the parties as the detaining State had released the vessel, cargo and crew before the Tribunal could begin to deal with it.

The three new cases currently pending before the Tribunal are Case No. 16 – *Dispute concerning delimitation of the maritime boundary between Bangladesh and Myanmar in the Bay of Bengal*; Case No. 17 – a request for an advisory opinion concerning *Responsibilities and obligations of States sponsoring persons and entities with respect to activities in the Area*; and Case No. 18 – *The M/V "Louisa" Case (Saint Vincent and the Grenadines v. Spain).*

Case No. 16 – On maritime delimitation

As I have mentioned, Case No. 16 relates to the dispute between the People's Republic of Bangladesh and the Union of Myanmar concerning the delimitation of their maritime boundary in the Bay of Bengal.

By letter dated 13 December 2009, the Minister of Foreign Affairs of Bangladesh notified the President of the Tribunal of declarations issued, under Article 287 of the Convention, by Myanmar on 4 November 2009 and by Bangladesh on 12 December 2009, in which both countries accepted the jurisdiction of the Tribunal as the forum for settlement of their maritime boundary dispute. In the same letter, the Minister of Foreign Affairs of Bangladesh invited the Tribunal to exercise jurisdiction over the dispute "[g]iven Bangladesh's and Myanmar's mutual consent to the jurisdiction of ITLOS". Accordingly, the case was entered in the list of cases on 14 December 2009.

Subsequently, the President of the Tribunal held consultations with the representatives of the parties in order to ascertain their views on issues concerning the conduct of the case.

As a result of these consultations, the President set the time limits for presentation of the memorial and the counter-memorial. The Tribunal subsequently

[4] See the protocol of the session during which the order of discontinuance was read out.

issued an order in which it set the time limits for the filing of the reply and the rejoinder. The written proceedings are now under way; Bangladesh submitted its memorial and Myanmar its counter-memorial on 1 July and 1 December 2010, respectively, as scheduled, and the written phase of the proceedings should conclude by 1 July 2011. Both parties have chosen judges *ad hoc* to sit in the case.

Case No. 17 – Request for an advisory opinion

In addition, in May 2010, the Tribunal's Seabed Disputes Chamber received a request for an advisory opinion from the International Seabed Authority. This case has been entered in the list as Case No. 17. The written and oral proceedings, in which a significant number of States parties and international organizations participated, have taken place. Twelve States and four international organizations made written submissions and, during the three-day hearing held before the Seabed Disputes Chamber in Hamburg, eight States and three international organizations made oral presentations.

The Chamber is now deliberating on the case. Since, under the Convention, advisory opinions are to be given as a matter of urgency, a decision is expected in early 2011.

This request for an advisory opinion is a significant development in our work, since it is the first case brought before the Seabed Disputes Chamber, which, as the body with exclusive competence over seabed-related disputes and requests for advisory opinions on matters concerning the work of the Council and the Assembly of the International Seabed Authority, has enormous potential. As seabed activities increase, the disputes that may be brought before the Chamber will, in all likelihood, also increase.

Case No. 18 – The M/V "Louisa" Case

Saint Vincent and the Grenadines last week instituted proceedings before the Tribunal against Spain in a dispute concerning the *MV Louisa,* flying its flag, which allegedly was arrested on 1 February 2006 by the Spanish authorities and held since that date.

According to the Applicant, the *MV Louisa* was involved in conducting sonar and cesium magnetic surveys of the sea floor of the Bay of Cadiz in order to locate and record indications of oil and methane gas. The Applicant stated that the vessel was arrested for alleged violations of Spain's historical patrimony or marine environment laws, that various members of the crew were also arrested but have since been released and that the vessel is being held in Spain without bond. The Applicant maintained that the vessel was involved in scientific research with a valid permit from the coastal State. The Applicant claimed that Spain violated several articles of the Convention and requests the Tribunal to award compensation for damages caused.

The Application instituting these proceedings before the Tribunal includes a request for provisional measures under Article 290, paragraph 1, of the Convention.

Hearings on the request for provisional measures are to take place on the 10th and 11th of the current month.

Both Saint Vincent and the Grenadines and Spain have made declarations under Article 287 of the Convention, recognizing the competence of the Tribunal as a means for the settlement of disputes concerning the interpretation or application of the Convention.

What do these cases indicate to us?

Based on an analysis of the cases that have come before the Tribunal, the following observations may be made:

(a) The Tribunal has received 18 cases[5] in 14 years, which is undoubtedly a good record, especially in light of the fact that it is a new institution and that, as a specialized court, it has limited jurisdiction *ratione materiae* for dealing only with disputes related to the law of the sea;
(b) These cases have involved both developed and developing countries from all regions of the world as disputant States; this shows that recourse to the Tribunal is a global trend rather than a regional proclivity;
(c) The cases submitted to the Tribunal have covered a wide range of law of the sea issues, such as protection of the marine environment, conservation of marine living resources, prompt release of vessels and crews, delimitation of maritime boundaries, compensation for illegal detention of vessels, and the responsibility and liability of sponsoring States. This confirms that this Tribunal is really the tribunal for the law of the sea; and
(d) Since it began its work in 1996, the Tribunal has received the highest number of cases of all the courts and tribunals listed in Article 287 of the Convention. This last point raises the question of why the Tribunal has

[5] After this article was written, another case, Case No. 19, was submitted to the Tribunal, Case 19, submitted on 4 July 2011 through Special Agreement, concerns proceedings instituted in a dispute between Panama and Guinea-Bissau regarding the oil tanker *Virginia G.*

received, during the same period, far more law of the sea related cases than the other dispute settlement mechanisms listed in Article 287.

Article 287 of the Convention

As you know, the Tribunal is one of four law of the sea dispute settlement mechanisms listed in Article 287 of the Convention. The parties to a dispute are in principle free to select any of these mechanisms. Though this article does not accord the Tribunal any special treatment as compared to the other dispute settlement mechanisms, I believe that the Tribunal is nonetheless accorded a relatively better position in this regard by certain provisions of the Convention.

This may come as a surprise to some people, for it is often stated that the Convention does not accord the Tribunal preferential treatment in relation to the other means of dispute settlement listed in Article 287. This is true as a general statement for, of the four listed mechanisms, Article 287 gives a prominent position only to Annex VII arbitration by granting it special status as the default procedure. If the parties to a law of the sea dispute have not made a common decision to choose the same mechanism as the forum for the settlement of their dispute, then one of them may, under compulsory jurisdiction, institute an Annex VII arbitration against the other, without prejudice of the exceptions set out in the Convention.[6]

While the Convention does not grant the Tribunal the privilege of being the default procedure, some of its provisions, however, accord it more favourable treatment in at least four circumstances. This may account for the fact that the Tribunal has received 18 cases in a relatively short period of time and may also explain why it has received, in the same period, more cases than the other courts or tribunals referred to in Article 287.

These four circumstances are: the exclusive jurisdiction of the Tribunal's Seabed Disputes Chamber regarding disputes and requests for advisory opinions related to the international seabed regime;[7] the residual jurisdiction of the Tribunal in prompt release cases;[8] the special and unique jurisdiction, conferred on the Tribunal by the Convention, to entertain requests for provisional measures pending the constitution of an arbitral tribunal under Annex VII of the Convention;[9] and the authority, granted to the President of the Tribunal by

[6] See Articles 297 and 298 of the United Nations Convention on the Law of the Sea.

[7] *Ibid.*, Arts. 187 and 191.

[8] *Ibid.*, Art. 292, para. 1.

[9] *Ibid.*, Art. 290, para. 5.

Annex VII, to appoint arbitrators to an arbitral tribunal at the request of a party and in consultation with both parties.[10]

Exclusive jurisdiction of the Tribunal's Seabed Disputes Chamber

The Convention recognizes the exclusive jurisdiction of the Tribunal's Seabed Disputes Chamber to entertain both disputes arising out of interpretation or application of the provisions of the Convention concerning activities in the Area, and requests for advisory opinions made by the Assembly or the Council of the Authority "on legal questions arising within the scope of their activities".[11] Thus, the framers of the Convention granted preferential treatment to the Tribunal, since none of the other "means of dispute settlement" referred to in Article 287 of the Convention has jurisdiction to deal with such disputes[12] or requests. There are, however, two narrow exceptions to this rule: first, the parties to a dispute between States concerning the interpretation or application of Part XI of the Convention and related annexes may choose a chamber of the Tribunal or refer the dispute to a three-member *ad hoc* chamber of the Seabed Disputes Chamber itself;[13] and, second, a party to a dispute concerning a contract or a plan of work may request that it be submitted to binding commercial arbitration.

Thus, a whole set of potential disputes concerning an important Part of the Convention is reserved for the Seabed Disputes Chamber's adjudication. Recently, this special treatment made it possible for Case No. 17 to be filed with the Chamber.

Prompt release of vessels and crews

The Convention confers on the Tribunal residual jurisdiction to entertain cases of prompt release of vessels from detention either for alleged non-compliance with laws and regulations concerning living resources in the exclusive economic zone that have been adopted by the coastal State in conformity with

[10] *Ibid.*, Annex VII, art. 3.

[11] See Art. 191 of the Convention.

[12] See Carl-August Fleischhauer, "The Relationship Between the International Court of Justice and the Newly Created International Tribunal for the Law of the Sea in Hamburg", *Max Planck Yearbook of United Nations Law*, vol. 1 (1997), p. 332. See also Dame Rosalyn Higgins' statement at the tenth anniversary of the International Tribunal for the Law of the Sea.

[13] Art. 188, para. 1 (a), of the Convention.

the Convention,[14] or for pollution of the marine environment.[15] Other courts and tribunals referred to in Article 287 may exercise jurisdiction in cases of prompt release of vessels and crews on the basis of an agreement between the parties. If, however, as is usually the case, no such agreement is reached within 10 days of the detention of the vessel, the flag State may institute the case before a court or tribunal accepted by the detaining State under Article 287 or, on a compulsory basis, before the Tribunal.[16] This residual jurisdiction gives the Tribunal an edge over other courts or tribunals referred to in Article 287. The flag State has thus the option of bringing a prompt release case before the Tribunal 10 days after the detention of the vessel, irrespective of whether the detaining State agrees with the choice of the Tribunal as the forum to entertain the prompt release case.

As a result of this residual jurisdiction, the Tribunal has received nine cases of prompt release of vessels and crews from detention for alleged violation of fisheries regulations in the exclusive economic zone. All these cases were introduced by the flag State, or on its behalf, on the basis of compulsory jurisdiction. No such cases have been instituted before the other courts and tribunals referred to in Article 287 of the Convention.

Provisional measures pending the constitution of an Annex VII arbitral tribunal

Provisional measures pending the constitution of an Annex VII arbitral tribunal is another example of preferential treatment accorded to the Tribunal by the Convention.[17] This procedure is an innovation in international adjudication; it allows a party to a case that has been instituted before an arbitral tribunal under Annex VII of the Convention to file for interim measures before the Tribunal, pending the constitution of the arbitral tribunal.

The request for provisional measures may also be made to any court or tribunal referred to in Article 287 on the basis of an agreement between the two parties to the dispute. If no such agreement is reached, either party may introduce the request for provisional measures to the Tribunal (and only to the Tribunal) two weeks after it has notified the other party of the request. Thus,

[14] *Ibid.*, Art. 73, para. 1.

[15] *Ibid.*, Arts. 220, para. 7, and 226, paras. 1 (b) and (c).

[16] *Ibid.*, Art. 292, para. 1.

[17] *Ibid.*, Art. 290, para. 5.

the Tribunal is the default procedure if the parties do not agree on a settlement mechanism.[18]

This special treatment explains why the Tribunal, and no other court or tribunal listed in Article 287, has received four such cases. The *Bluefin Tuna* cases, the *MOX Plant* case and the *Land Reclamation* case were all instituted before the Tribunal under this provision entailing compulsory jurisdiction.

Annex VII special authority

Another situation that may facilitate the institution of a case before the Tribunal has to do with the role granted to its President by Annex VII to the Convention.

Under Annex VII arbitration, the parties are to appoint three arbitrators and the President of the arbitral tribunal by agreement. If, within 60 days from the notification of institution of arbitral proceedings, they cannot agree on these appointments or on an entity to make them, either party may request the President of the Tribunal to do so[19] in consultation with the two parties.

This recourse to the President brings the parties to Annex VII arbitration closer to the Tribunal. In some instances, as a result of contacts made in the context of the appointment of arbitrators, the parties may end up shifting the case from arbitration to the Tribunal. Financial considerations may play a major role in this regard; the costs of arbitration are not negligible and can be substantially reduced if the case is transferred to the Tribunal.

Moreover, States parties to a dispute, after years of consultations and negotiations, are sometimes left with no alternative other than to institute Annex VII arbitral proceedings (for which the instituting party does not require the agreement of the other disputant party), as a first step towards possible referral of the dispute to another third party procedure. Once Annex VII arbitration has been instituted, considerations of costs reduction and time effectiveness may lead the parties into agreeing to refer the case to the Tribunal.

On three occasions, cases that were initially brought to Annex VII arbitration were later shifted to the Tribunal by agreement of the parties: This happened in the *"Saiga" 2* case, in the *Swordfish Stocks* case and in the case concerning the *Delimitation of the maritime boundary case in the Bay of Bengal*, now pending before us.

---

[18] *Ibid.*, Art. 290, para. 5.

[19] *Ibid.*, Annex VII, art. 3.

Prospects for the future work of the Tribunal

What are the prospects for the future judicial work of the Tribunal? The Tribunal is anew judicial institution that received its first case in 1998. Since then, it has been building its docket, case by case. Its pace has been comparable to that of other international courts in the early years of their work; as Judge Higgins put it, "[t]he experience of most international courts is to start slowly and steadily build their docket".[20]

Two important factors may condition the number of cases that the Tribunal receives in the future. The first has to do with the very slow progress of activities in the Area, as a result of which only one seabed-related case has been instituted to date. This is nonetheless an encouraging development for the Tribunal. The more exploration and exploitation activities take place in the Area, the likelier it is that disputes which can be brought only before the Seabed Disputes Chamber will arise.

The second factor has to do with familiarity with the Convention's dispute settlement system and the corresponding procedures of the Tribunal. The dispute settlement provisions of the Convention are not easily understood, and our procedures seem to reflect that uneasiness. Aware of this, the Tribunal has taken a number of initiatives to disseminate information on its work; we have prepared a guide to our procedures and have organized eight regional workshops for government legal officers. In addition, some of the Tribunal's judges have written a commentary to our Rules. It appears, however, that we need to do a better job in this regard.

As States become more involved with the law of the sea dispute settlement system established by the Convention and more familiar with our procedures and methods of work, the likelihood that more cases will be instituted with the Tribunal will increase. Judging from the number of cases that we have received thus far, the built-in preferential treatment granted to the Tribunal by the Convention, the prospect of increased seabed activities in the near future and the potential for increased numbers of disputes as the use of the oceans and the exploitation of its resources increase substantially to keep pace with development needs, there are solid prospects for our docket to grow much stronger. This makes me believe that the Tribunal is well positioned to be a very busy court in the near future and that it may therefore be able to play a major role in global ocean governance.

As intended by the framers of the Convention, "We are seeing the development of a multifaceted system for the settlement of law of the sea-related disputes

[20] Statement by Dame Rosalyn Higgins, President of the International Court of Justice, on the occasion of the tenth anniversary of the Tribunal.

with ITLOS as an important player".[21] I have no doubt that as time goes by and ocean uses increase exponentially, the Tribunal will be well placed to continue to play the "important role and authority...concerning the interpretation and application of the Convention and Part XI Agreement" that is stressed in the General Assembly's 2010 resolution on oceans and the law of the sea.[22]

I thank you for your attention.

[21] See footnote 18 above.

[22] A/Res/64/71, para. 29.

SOME REFLECTIONS ON THE FIRST REQUEST TO THE SEABED DISPUTES CHAMBER FOR AN ADVISORY OPINION

Michael W. Lodge[1]

Abstract

In September 2010, the advisory jurisdiction of the Seabed Disputes Chamber of the International Tribunal for the Law of the Sea was invoked for the first time since the Tribunal was established in 1996 with the issuance of a request to the Chamber from the Council of the International Seabed Authority. Oral hearings took place in Hamburg in September 2010 and the Chamber is expected to deliver its opinion early in 2011. The subject matter of the request – the responsibilities and liabilities of sponsoring States under Part XI of the Law of the Sea Convention and the 1994 Implementation Agreement – raises important issues of interpretation of the provisions of the Convention relating to environmental protection. This presentation will review some of the background to the request for an advisory opinion, which was initially proposed by Nauru, and will also reflect on some of the potential implications for the International Seabed Authority, governments and industry of the forthcoming advisory opinion. The presenter is the Legal Counsel for the Authority and also acted as agent and counsel for the Authority throughout the hearing of the Advisory Opinion.

Let me begin by thanking Professor John Norton Moore and the Center for Oceans Law and Policy, the Korea Maritime Institute and the Netherlands Institute for the Law of the Sea for inviting me to speak today and for their initiative in putting together this timely and important conference on the impacts of globalisation on the Law of the Sea.

The overall theme of globalisation feels particularly apt to me as I have just returned from the World Economic Forum's Summit on the Global Agenda in Dubai, where I had the privilege of participating as a member of the Global Agenda Council on Ocean Governance. As several hundred leading experts in a multiplicity of fields considered the impact of the challenges wrought by such issues as economic uncertainty, natural resource scarcity, climate change, failing states, an increase in regional confrontations, and a massive shift in the global balance of power, it became ever more apparent to many of us that, almost more than any other factor, it is the ocean – this 70 percent of our planet – that both divides us and connects us.

This, of course, comes as no surprise to most people in this room. Yet in Dubai I was struck by how, in a crowded global agenda dealing with a multitude

[1] Legal Counsel, International Seabed Authority.

of risks and challenges, good governance of the ocean appears to many people to be taken for granted. "So big it is invisible" – was the catchphrase adopted by our group.

The challenges for ocean governance in this globalised economy are numerous and severe. Some, such as the challenge of dealing with the threats posed by climate change and ocean acidification will require an unprecedented level of political will and commitment to overcome. However, there is one key prerequisite that is necessary before any of these challenges and issues can be addressed, and that is a durable and robust legal and jurisdictional framework for the rule of law in the global ocean. That framework is provided by the United Nations Convention on the Law of the Sea[2] – a fact that, again, probably does not come as news to most of the people in this room, but is largely taken for granted by many in the wider community.

Another thing that is largely taken for granted is how hard many of us – and by "us" I mean not only a select gathering such as this one, but all actors in the Law of the Sea community, including States parties, practitioners, NGOs and academics – work to ensure that the legal framework remains durable, robust and, most of all, resilient in the face of new challenges.

One of the most important ways in which resilience is built into a legal framework is through the medium of effective mechanisms for the avoidance and resolution of disputes. Today, I want to speak about the use of one such mechanism: the procedure under the Convention for the referral of a matter to the Seabed Disputes Chamber of the International Tribunal for the Law of the Sea for an advisory opinion. The recent use by the Council of the International Seabed Authority of this procedure – for the first time ever – is, I believe, an excellent demonstration of the innate resilience of the treaty to new and unexpected situations arising in part from the effects of increasing globalisation.

Before I go on let me first make something of a disclaimer. Although the oral proceedings in the advisory opinion have been concluded, the Chamber has not yet delivered its opinion. I want to make it clear that anyone who hoped that I might pre-empt the findings of the Chamber by predicting the outcome is going to be disappointed. As agent and counsel for the International Seabed Authority throughout the proceedings, I made it clear in both our written and oral submissions that the function of the Authority was not to take a position on any of the issues involved in the request, but to ensure that the Chamber had the benefit of all the information necessary to enable it to form an opinion.[3] What I am about to say today must also be understood in that light.

[2] United Nations Convention on the Law of the Sea of 10 December 1982, *UNTS*, vol. 1833, p. 3. As of 15 December 2010, 160 States and the European Union were parties to this Convention.

[3] Written statement of the International Seabed Authority, 19 August 2010, paragraph 3; oral statement of the International Seabed Authority, 14 September 2010, Verbatim Records,

So, for those of you who are not aware, let me briefly lay out the background that led to the request to the Chamber for an advisory opinion. Back in 2008, two applications for exploration licences were filed with the International Seabed Authority by private sector enterprises incorporated in and sponsored by the small island developing States of Nauru and Tonga. Sponsorship by a State party is one of the most important aspects of the legal regime for deep seabed mining and this was the first occasion on which an application for a deep seabed exploration licence had been sponsored by a developing State rather than an industrialised State or emerging economy. These applications were also firsts in the sense that they were the first applications to be filed by genuine private sector interests rather than state-funded operations and also the first such applications to be filed in respect of the so-called "reserved areas" which were originally intended to be taken up by the Enterprise with a capital "E" – the proposed commercial arm of the Authority that has been put in abeyance by the provisions of the 1994 Agreement.[4]

The applications having been filed, they were then considered by the Authority's Legal and Technical Commission in accordance with the procedures set out in the Convention and the 1994 Agreement.[5] Unfortunately, the global financial crisis then intervened and the applicants requested that the two applications be temporarily deferred.[6] At the same time, both Nauru and the corporate investors involved in the project began to consider further what the implications of the rather general language of the Convention and the Authority's Regulations might be with respect to the responsibility and liability of Nauru as a sponsoring State for one of the applications.

I should pause at this point to remind you that Nauru is one of the smallest countries in the world, with a population of around 2,000 people. It is located in the middle of the Central Pacific and has no natural resources to sustain itself beyond tuna in its exclusive economic zone that are fished by distant water fishing fleets. The reason it has no natural resources is that for more than 50 years the island was operated as an open-cast mine by the British Phosphate Commission, which resulted in the entire island, other than a narrow coastal strip,

---

ITLOS/PV.10/1/Rev.1, pp. 6–7. Both are available at the website of the International Tribunal for the Law of the Sea: http://www.itlos.org.

4 Annex, Section 2, Paragraphs 1 and 2 to the Agreement relating to the implementation of Part XI of the United Nations Convention on the Law of the Sea of 10 December 1982, UNTS, vol. 1836, p. 3. As of 15 December 2010, there were 140 parties to this Agreement.

5 ISBA/14/C/8, Summary report of the Chairman of the Legal and Technical Commission on the work of the Commission during the fourteenth session, paragraph 10; ISBA/14/C/11*, Statement of the President of the Council of the International Seabed Authority on the work of the Council during the fourteenth session, paragraphs 6 to 8. Available at the website of the Authority: http://www.isa.org.jm.

6 ISBA/15/C/5, Summary report of the Chairman of the Legal and Technical Commission on the work of the Commission during the fifteenth session, paragraph 6.

being completely devastated so that today nothing remains but pinnacles of limestone rock. For those who wish to read more I would strongly recommend Judge Weeramantry's excellent book on the extraordinary history of the British Phosphate Commission and Nauru's struggles to recover compensation from the governments of Australia, New Zealand and the United Kingdom.[7] Suffice to say that given its history, it is hardly surprising that the issue of responsibility and liability for the potential environmental damage caused by mining is an issue which the Government of Nauru takes extremely seriously.

It is against this background that in 2010 Nauru submitted a paper to the Council of the International Seabed Authority requesting the Council to use its power under Article 191 of the Convention to request the Seabed Disputes Chamber to render an advisory opinion on a number of issues relating to the responsibility and liability of Nauru as a sponsoring state.[8] This led to a lengthy debate in the Council and it is fair to say that there was quite a wide divergence of views. Some members of the Council felt that the request was premature and that the jurisdiction of the Chamber should not be invoked merely to resolve the problems of a single State. Others felt that the Council did not need to seek external legal advice from the Chamber and that a detailed analysis of the provisions of the Convention prepared or commissioned by the Secretariat would be sufficient to enable the Council itself to clarify the issues. Many more, however, felt that the request by Nauru should be supported and that Article 191 should be utilised in the manner envisaged by the framers of the Convention – that is, to request the Chamber to provide clarity on legal questions arising within the scope of activities of the Council. In this regard, there was a universal view in the Council that, whatever the political merits, the questions put by Nauru were far too specific, too complex and too detailed to go forward in the manner in which they were presented and that Article 191 should be applied in a manner similar to Article 65 of the Statute of the International Court of Justice.[9] This meant that the questions were to be reframed in a manner that was abstract, did not relate to the concerns of a single state and that reflected the concerns of the Council as a whole as the requesting organ of the Authority.

---

[7] Weeramantry, C., *Nauru: Environmental Damage under International Trusteeship*, Oxford University Press, 1992.

[8] ISBA/16/C/6, Proposal to seek an advisory opinion from the Seabed Disputes Chamber of the International Tribunal for the Law of the Sea on matters regarding sponsoring State responsibility and liability. Submitted by the delegation of Nauru.

[9] ISBA/16/C/14*, Statement of the President of the Council of the International Seabed Authority on the work of the Council during the sixteenth session, paragraph 7. See also the unofficial account of the records of the discussions (Dossier no. 3) in the Dossier submitted on behalf of the Secretary-General of the International Seabed Authority pursuant to Article 131 of the Rules of the Tribunal; like all the written and oral proceedings, the Dossier is available at the website of the Tribunal: http://www.itlos.org.org.

Once this was done, in three short paragraphs, it was an easy matter for the Council to adopt the request by consensus.[10]

In essence, the questions for the chamber were threefold. One, to define the legal responsibilities and obligations of States' Parties to the Convention with respect to the sponsorship of deep seabed mining. Two, to define the extent of liability of a State for any failure to comply with the provisions of the Convention by an entity that it has sponsored. And three, to elaborate what are the necessary and appropriate measures that a sponsoring State must take to fulfil its responsibility under the Convention.

The importance of these questions to the overall scheme set out in the Convention and the 1994 Agreement cannot be underestimated. Sponsorship provides the fundamental link between the Authority, States parties and deep seabed miners. In many ways it is akin to the genuine link that must exist between flag States and the vessels that fly their flag.[11] The clear intent of the Convention, the 1994 Agreement and the Regulations established by the Authority, is that State sponsorship exists to ensure that, whatever the nature and structure of the mining operation, there is a State party which takes responsibility in accordance with Article 139, Article 153, paragraph 4, and Annex III, Article 4, paragraph 4, of the Convention.

Under the excellent guidance of the President of the Chamber, Judge Treves, written and or oral statements were made by 15 States parties: Argentina, Australia, China, Chile, Fiji, Germany, Republic of Korea, Mexico, Nauru, Netherlands, Philippines, Mexico, Russian Federation, Romania and the United Kingdom. Statements were also made by the Authority and three intergovernmental observer organizations: IOC-UNESCO, UNEP and IUCN. I cannot help, of course, making the observation before this audience that the lack of participation in any part of the proceedings by the United States was very much to be regretted, especially given the long history of constructive participation by the United States in the development of the advisory jurisprudence of the International Court of Justice.

So, to come to the crux of the matter, what is the real significance of the request for an advisory opinion to the development of the law of the sea?

Of course, the full answer to that question will have to await the opinion of the Chamber. When that comes, I am sure that it will provide food for many analyses and panel discussions at gatherings like this. However, I would like to offer the following two immediate thoughts that I feel are valid regardless of the outcome of the Chamber's deliberations.

---

[10] ISBA/16/C/13, Decision of the Council of the International Seabed Authority requesting an advisory opinion pursuant to Article 191 of the United Nations Convention on the Law of the Sea (see Appendix).

[11] Article 91 of the Convention.

First, the making of the request, and the manner in which it was made, demonstrates that the system set out in the Convention works and that the sceptics have been proved wrong. A legitimate set of issues were raised. They were given anxious, urgent and transparent consideration by the Council. All views were taken into account, the list of issues was redacted into a set of manageable questions and a decision was adopted by consensus. This was not a case where the decision was delayed, obfuscated or blocked for political reasons. The fact that the Authority and its political organs are willing and able to react to concerns in a responsible and diligent manner should give great comfort to individual States parties as well as to the future seabed mining industry. Furthermore, the Chamber itself acted expeditiously, diligently and, if I may say so, judiciously in the manner in which it dealt with there quest, including the transparency with which the written and oral proceedings were conducted.

Second, the making of the request shows that whilst there are provisions in the Convention which are difficult to understand and apply in dynamically shifting circumstances, there is a strong willingness on the part of States parties and other actors to do what it takes to make the provisions work in practice. Let me remind you that 15 States parties and four intergovernmental organisations made extensive written and or oral submissions to the Chamber on a range of issues in which they did not necessarily have a direct national interest at stake. The strong interest and commitment of States parties to ensuring the resilience of the Convention in this manner is one of the most remarkable features of the Law of the Sea compared to almost any other global rule-making treaty and again should provide an important reassurance not only to the future seabed mining industry but also to the many other global ocean-related industries.

On the issues of substance, of course, it remains to be seen whether the Chamber's opinion will help or hinder the development of seabed mining. The mere fact that the questions were asked, however, shows a level of business interest in the development of seabed resources that has been lacking for many years. This is encouraging, but at the same time it is incumbent on the "system" to demonstrate to the business community that it is serious about doing business. In the nature of things, it is perhaps unlikely that the opinion of an international court will provide the same level of certainty as might be contained in the judgement of a domestic court. As long ago as 1948, Judge Alvarez in the International Court of Justice noted that "international law is not strictly juridical; it is also political, economic, social and psychological: hence, all the fundamental elements of traditional individualistic law are profoundly modified".[12] Having said that, however, I feel confident that authoritative and

[12] Admission of a State to the United Nations (Charter, Art. 4), Advisory Opinion: I.C.J. Reports 1948, 67 (individual opinion by M. Alvarez, J.) cited in Butcher, G. T. 'The Consonance of U.S. Positions with the International Court's Advisory Opinions', 423–446

clear answers to the questions posed in the advisory opinion will go a long way towards addressing some of the fundamental concerns of both Nauru and the mining industry.

I said at the beginning that I would not attempt to pre-empt the findings of the Chamber but nevertheless, having observed the proceedings closely throughout, I believe that there are at least three areas of commonality in the positions expressed by States parties and which we can expect the Chamber to deal with.

First, there does not seem to be much support for the view that there can be any distinction in the scope and content of the duty to protect and preserve the marine environment between developed and developing States. It seems to be widely agreed that there is nothing in Part XI or elsewhere in the Convention, or in the 1994 Agreement, to suggest that the obligations of sponsoring States vary in any way depending on their level of development. In several places Part XI does provide for special consideration to be given to the interests of developing States, but in every case where this occurs, it is qualified and limited by the words "as specifically provided for in this Part" (that is, Part XI).[13]

Second, it seems unlikely that the obligation of sponsoring States to take necessary and appropriate measures to ensure compliance by the entities that they sponsor can be satisfied merely by entering into a contract with the entity concerned. It is necessary that sponsoring States adopt and apply some form of regulatory measures within their legal systems to ensure compliance by the sponsored entity with Part XI, the rules, regulations and procedures of the Authority and the terms of the contract. In the absence of any such measures, sponsoring States Parties will fail to comply with their responsibility.

Third, it will likely be very difficult for the Chamber to lay down any hard and fast rules as to the limits of liability for sponsoring States. Some clarity would be useful, however, around the question of what exactly it is that sponsoring States are liable for. In this regard, there was considerable agreement that the liability of the sponsoring State will be for its failure to fulfil its obligations under the Convention and 1994 Agreement and not for the acts of the sponsored entity as such. There may in some circumstances be a causal link between damage caused by the entity and the State's failure to fulfil its obligations under the Convention, in which case the State may be liable for the full amount of the damage caused by the entity. In other cases, however, it may be demonstrated that all or part of any damage caused by the entity was not a consequence of the State's failure to fulfil its obligations under the Convention, and in that event the State may not be liable in full or even at all for the damage caused.

in Damrosch, L. F. (ed.), *The International Court of Justice at a Crossroads*, Transnational Publishers Inc., Dobbs Ferry, New York (1987).

[13] See, for example, Articles 148 and 152 of the Convention.

Let me conclude by saying that the making of the request for an advisory opinion is an example of the durability and maturity of the legal regime provided by the Convention. It is both a demonstration of confidence by States parties in the institutions created by the Convention, and a sign that these institutions are becoming sufficiently mature to deal with new and dynamic legal challenges to the Convention.

APPENDIX

Decision of the Council of the International Seabed Authority requesting an advisory opinion pursuant to Article 191 of the United Nations Convention on the Law of the Sea (ISBA/16/C/13)

The Council of the International Seabed Authority,

Considering the fact that developmental activities in the Area have already commenced,

Bearing in mind the exchange of views on legal questions arising within the scope of activities of the Council,

Decides, in accordance with Article 191 of the United Nations Convention on the Law of the Sea ("the Convention"), to request the Seabed Disputes Chamber of the International Tribunal for the Law of the Sea, pursuant to Article 131 of the Rules of the Tribunal, to render an advisory opinion on the following questions:

1. What are the legal responsibilities and obligations of States Parties to the Convention with respect to the sponsorship of activities in the Area in accordance with the Convention, in particular Part XI, and the 1994 Agreement relating to the Implementation of Part XI of the United Nations Convention on the Law of the Sea of 10 December 1982?
2. What is the extent of liability of a State Party for any failure to comply with the provisions of the Convention, in particular Part XI, and the 1994 Agreement, by an entity whom it has sponsored under Article 153, paragraph 2 (b), of the Convention?
3. What are the necessary and appropriate measures that a sponsoring State must take in order to fulfil its responsibility under the Convention, in particular Article 139 and Annex III, and the 1994 Agreement?

161st Meeting
6 May 2010

Panel I:
Global Trends in Commercial Shipping

IMPACT OF SURGING SHIP-OWNERS' LIABILITY AND COMPENSATION ON P&I INSURANCE

Beom Shik PARK[1]

Abstract

The marine insurance industry has expanded both in external quantum and internal complexity with the rapid growth and development of the global shipping industry. It is necessary to insure the losses for third party liabilities incidental to the owning and operation of ships with the P&I (Protection & Indemnity) industry, and the industry has significantly expanded thanks to the emergence of animated chartering activities, upsizing of ships and soaring of cargo and material value. However, the recent trend and development of anti-shipping regimes along with various international conventions and legal precedents are continuously evolving and adding their burden of liabilities on both the shipping and the P&I industry. These trends are reflected in the numerous newly emerging international maritime conventions and regimes together with the legal precedents and arbitrations from many sectors of the field. This will eventually result in the burden of the compensation level to the ship-owners and their liability insurers, i.e. P&I Clubs. In the past 10 years or so, the P&I insurance premium has soared three fold and eventually became a heavier burden on basic shipping operation costs. These recent developments around the shipping industry have led the ship-owners to pay more attention to P&I insurance to achieve a more competitive P&I cost and receive more satisfaction in P&I service quality. This trend will be further strengthened in the future as the cost of P&I is expected to continuously increase.

The speaker, Dr. B. S. Park reviews how the stream of liabilities on the ships/ship-owners/operators has recently developed, what impact has been given to the P&I insurance and how it will take shape in the future.

[Note: the author's PowerPoint presentation can be viewed online at http://www.virginia.edu/colp/pdf/kmi-park.pdf]

[1] Executive Senior M.D. and Chief Operating Officer, Korea Shipowners' Mutual Protection and Indemnity Association.

NEW DEVELOPMENTS IN THE ARCTIC: PROTECTING THE MARINE ENVIRONMENT FROM INCREASED SHIPPING

Erik Franckx and Laura Boone[1]

Abstract

It is generally accepted that the Arctic is warming at a rapid pace. Studies have shown that with this warming trend, sea ice and glaciers are melting and thus sea levels are rising. However, the situation might be more severe than originally anticipated. The ice is retreating a lot more quickly than was projected, with an absolute low point in 2007. A second low point occurred in 2008 and September 2010 provided us with the third lowest sea ice extent in the satellite record. Maybe even more important than the decline in sea ice extent, is the fact that the ice volume is decreasing with it. The ice pack is becoming more and more vulnerable to melting due to the decline in the amount of old, thick ice and it appears that five-year or older ice has nearly completely disappeared from the Arctic.

This Arctic melt opens up new possibilities for (trans) Arctic shipping. Of particular importance was key finding #6 of the Arctic Climate Impact Assessment (ACIA) report, which stated that "Reduced sea ice is very likely to increase marine transport and access to resources". Indeed, due to this warming trend, the Northwest Passage, the Northern Sea Route and maybe even the Central Arctic Route in the future, are opening up. In the fall of 2008 the first commercial ship transported cargo from the east through the Northwest Passage and in 2009 two German cargo vessels, the MV Beluga Fraternity and the MV Beluga Foresight were the first foreign flag ships to sail the entire Northern Sea Route. This year navigation has really picked up in the Northern Sea Route and therefore 2010 can be viewed as the breakthrough year for trans-Arctic commercial shipping, with more voyages planned for 2011.

These new developments are again raising questions concerning the outstanding maritime boundaries in the area, the legal status of the waters concerned, the efficiency of current solutions and the extent of national jurisdiction. As national legal regimes will need to adapt, substantial changes are to be expected to meet these new challenges. Meanwhile, as shipping increases, the stress on the already fragile environment increases with it, which results in great concerns regarding the preservation and protection of the environment. Environmentalists warn about the dangers of vessel-source pollution and emphasize that the lack of infrastructure, information and mandatory legislation, are issues that should urgently be addressed at an international level.

This paper will provide insights about recent developments in the Arctic in the abovementioned areas.

---

[1] Erik Franckx is a Professor of International Law at the Vrije Universiteit Brussel and Laura Boone is a Researcher at the Institute for European Studies, Brussels, Belgium.

Introduction

The predicted substantial growth in (trans-)Arctic shipping is expected to pose significant stress to the already fragile environment. An assessment report on Arctic marine shipping by the Arctic Council, published in 2009,[2] provides an overview of the actual and potential impacts on the environment and biodiversity in the Arctic from shipping. The 2009 Arctic Marine Shipping Assessment (AMSA) Report divides these environmental considerations into three groups, namely the "vulnerability of Arctic species and ecosystems", "ship based impacts" and "potential disturbances from shipping and shipping activity in the Arctic". Obviously the particularly sensitive Arctic environment will need a rather high level of protection for these risks, as they will become even more significant in view of the predicted increase in shipping activity.

From an international legal perspective, the shipping activities not limited to the waters over which one single Arctic rim country exercises sovereignty or jurisdiction with respect to navigation according to international law are of particular interest. In view of the expected increase in Arctic shipping, especially Canada and even more so the Russian Federation, as will be seen, will play an important role as gatekeepers to circumpolar navigational routes connecting the Atlantic and the Pacific Oceans.

Some Arctic coastal States have already adopted a mixture of mandatory and voluntary standards for navigation in their waters,[3] but global bodies primarily perform the international regulation of vessel-source pollution. This is consistent with the 1982 United Nations Law of the Sea Convention,[4] according to

---

[2] Arctic Council, *Arctic Marine Shipping Assessment Report*, 2nd printing 2009, available at <http: //www.pame.is/images/stories/PDF_Files/AMSA_2009_Report_2nd_print.pdf>, hereinafter 2009 AMSA Report. One of the present authors contributed to this 2009 AMSA Report (see *ibid.*, p. 188).

[3] For a good overview, see the study commissioned by the Marine Safety Division of Transport Canada, Ottawa, Canada part of Canada's contribution to the Arctic Council's Arctic Marine Shipping Assessment: D.L. Vander Zwaag and A. Chircop (eds.), *Governance of Arctic Marine Shipping* (Halifax: Marine & Environmental Law Institute, 2008), 108 p., available at <http: //arcticportal.org/uploads/vZ/6u/vZ6uVo9aTTQv45iwl93oFw/AMSA-Shipping-Governance-Final-Report—Revised-November-2008.pdf>. One of the present authors contributed to this study (see *ibid.*, p. i). The national legal frameworks of Canada and the Russian Federation received special attention in this study (see *ibid.*, p. 50–68). For a more elaborated analysis of the Canadian legislation, see for instance L. Clark, 'Canada's Oversight of Arctic Shipping: the Need For Reform', 33 *Tulane Maritime Law Journal*, No. 1, 2008, 79–110, and of the legal framework applicable in the Russian Federation, see for instance E. Franckx, 'The Legal Regime of Navigation in the Russian Arctic', 18 *Journal of Transnational Law and Policy*, No. 2, 2010, 327–342.

[4] United Nations Convention on the Law of the Sea (10 December 1982), 1833 *U.N.T.S.* 3.Hereinafter 1982 LOS Convention.

which, as a general rule, unilateral coastal State prescription is only allowed under certain conditions. Most of the 1982 LOS Convention's provisions on vessel-source pollution are laid down in Part XII, entitled Protection and Preservation of the Marine Environment and are principally aimed at flag and coastal States. Their prescriptive jurisdiction is linked to, and at the same time limited by the notion of "generally accepted international rules and standards" (GAIRAS) and relates to pollution of the marine environment by vessels. Flag State prescriptive jurisdiction is mandatory and must have at least the same level as GAIRAS.[5] This means that flag States can therefore order their vessels to adapt to more stringent standards than GAIRAS. On the other hand, coastal State prescriptive jurisdiction is optional and therefore, when exercised, cannot be more stringent than the level of GAIRAS.[6] There is however an exception, which provides the coastal States with a broader prescriptive and enforcement jurisdiction within their own Exclusive Economic Zone (EEZ) than is the case with the application of the above-mentioned general rule, namely Article 234 of the 1982 LOS Convention.[7] Consequently, this exception gives broad prescriptive and enforcement jurisdiction in ice-covered areas, and is worded as follows

> *Coastal States have the right to adopt and enforce non-discriminatory laws and regulations for the prevention, reduction and control of marine pollution from vessels in ice-covered areas within the limits of the exclusive economic zone, where particularly severe climatic conditions and the presence of ice covering such areas for most of the year create obstructions or exceptional hazards to navigation, and pollution of the marine environment could cause major harm to or irreversible disturbance of the ecological balance. Such laws and regulations shall have due regard to navigation and the protection and preservation of the marine environment based on the best available scientific evidence.*[8]

Therefore, Arctic coastal States are legally positioned to play a leading role in developing and enforcing appropriate rules and standards in their EEZ. At the same time it is clear that only the IMO can adopt global rules and standards for shipping. Indeed, there is a particular relationship between the global functionality of the IMO on the one hand and the special legislative and enforcement jurisdiction of the Arctic coastal States on the other hand.[9] Then again,

[5] *Ibid.*, Art. 211(2).

[6] *Ibid.*, Art. 211(5).

[7] K. Gustafson Juras, J.E. Noyes and E. Franckx, *Law of the Sea in a Nutshell* (St. Paul, Minnesota, West Publishing Company, 2010), p. 399, where it is stated: "This Article provides the only instance in the LOS Convention where national rules concerning vessel-source pollution do not have to conform to generally accepted international rules and standards".

[8] 1982 LOS Convention, *supra* note 4, Art. 234.

[9] A. Chircop 'International Arctic Shipping: Towards Strategic Scaling-up of Marine Environment Protection', in: Nordquist, Moore, Heidar (eds.), *Changes in the Arctic Environment and the Law of the Sea* (Leiden, Martinus Nijhoff Publishers, 2010), pp. 181–185.

as shipping activity in the Arctic increases, one should question the long-term effectiveness of these national rules and standards. Shipping is by its very nature an international activity and hence must be addressed as such, bearing in mind that shipping will likely traverse the maritime zones of more than one State and possibly high sea areas as well. Coastal regulations alone will not be able to adequately address the challenges presented by Arctic shipping. To assure that overall shipping is conducted in an environmentally sound fashion, a uniform and comprehensive system seems to be necessary. With the expected increase in navigation, new possibilities arise for the international community and the Arctic States in particular, to influence the next generation by setting out mandatory regulations[10] in view of the fact that at the moment very little mandatory international standards apply specifically to the Arctic. The IMO has taken cognizance of this need and is preparing a binding draft polar code for navigation in ice-covered waters as a follow-up to the recently revised non-binding polar guidelines. The draft is expected to be presented in 2012. However, this is not enough. The 2009 AMSA Report recommended that, next to mandatory regulations, identifying particularly sensitive sea areas and exploring the need for the designation of special areas be considered.[11]

The present contribution will first look into the facts before moving into the legal aspects of the increased shipping in the Arctic. Starting from an update on global warming in the Arctic, the most recent developments during the last Arctic shipping seasons (ending with the shipping season 2010) will first be briefly depicted. This will constitute the backdrop against which some legal developments aimed at the protection of the fragile Arctic marine environment against such increased shipping will subsequently be analyzed.

Likely increase in Arctic navigation

For a long time the Arctic ice-cover was a sufficient deterrent for international shipping companies tempted to plot their ship movements based on maps with a polar projection. Instead a more traditional Mercator projection was relied upon. Characterized by the fact that the scale increases from the equator to the Poles, where it becomes infinite, a Mercator projection of the World not only represents the North Pole as a long line, distorting all sense of distance in the area, but also makes it very hard to even imagine a transpolar voyage. This vision, however, is changing. Whether increased shipping will contribute

[10] I.G. Brosnan, 'The Diminishing Age Gap Between Polar Cruisers and Their Ships: A New Reason to Codify the IMO Guidelines for Ships Operating in Polar Waters and Make Them Mandatory?' 35 *Marine Policy*, No. 2, 2011, 262.

[11] 2009 AMSA Report, *supra* note 2, p. 7.

to the fact that the North Pole will become a new "spatial point center" of the world, as predicted by some,[12] obliging us all to look at the world rather from a polar azimuthal equidistant projection centered on the North Pole, as in the emblem of the United Nations, is maybe only a visionary long-term perspective at present. The fact remains, as will be seen next, that shipping companies might have good reasons to start seriously looking at such north polar projections of the world when determining the business plan of their companies for the years to come.

A. *Effect of global warming on Arctic shipping*

An appropriate starting point for the proper evaluation of the effect of global warming on Arctic shipping is most certainly the joint assessment effort of the Arctic Council and the International Arctic Science Committee undertaken at the beginning of the 21st century. This resulted in the Arctic Climate Impact Assessment of which a synthesis report was first published in November 2004,[13] followed by the full scientific report of more than 1,000 pages in 2005.[14] This assessment had been prepared over a period of five years with the involvement of more than 300 scientists, experts and members of the indigenous communities.[15] Of particular importance for this paper is key finding number six of the 2004 ACIA Synthesis Report, entitled "Reduced Sea Ice is Very Likely to Increase Marine Transport and Access to Resources".[16] In addition to a reduction in annual average sea-ice extent of 5–10 per cent, most prominent in summer, a reduction in average thickness over the past few decades of 10–15 per cent was highlighted, with a 40 per cent reduction in the central Arctic Ocean.[17] The report concluded on the basis of these findings that longer seasons with less severe ice conditions are to be expected with "improved ship accessibility around the margins of the Arctic Basin (although this will not be uniformly

[12] T. Valsson and G.F. Ulfarsson, 'Future Changes in Activity Structures of the Globe Under a Receding Arctic Ice Scenario', 43 *Futures*, No. 4, 2011, 455, where these authors argue: "As the Arctic has become free of ice, and hence with active shipping and resource exploitation, it becomes an important global area, with the North Pole as a spatial point center. In the far future, as the activity has reached a high degree, the new spatial point center of the Arctic can start to compete with the spatial linear center of the ribbon of today's world". With the "ribbon of today" these author refer to the fact that mankind is at present living on a ribbon that surrounds the globe at lower latitudes.

[13] S.J. Hassol (ed.), *Impacts of Warming Arctic: Arctic Climate Impact Assessment* (Cambridge: Cambridge University Press, 2004), 140 p. Hereinafter 2004 ACIA Synthesis Report.

[14] C. Symon, L. Arris and B. Heal (eds.), *Arctic Climate Impact Assessment* (Cambridge: Cambridge University Press, 2005), 1042 p. Hereinafter 2005 ACIA Scientific Report.

[15] *Ibid.*, p. iii.

[16] 2004 ACIA Synthesis Report, *supra* note 13, pp. 82–85.

[17] *Ibid.*, p. 82.

distributed)".[18] The latter parenthetical remark concerns the difference the 2004 ACIA Synthesis Report makes between the Northwest Passage,[19] where high year-to-year variability and the restricted nature of the waters inside the Canadian archipelago[20] result in "exceptionally complex sea ice conditions",[21] and the Northern Sea Route[22] where the number of navigable days will increase substantially over the next decades.[23] The 2004 ACIA Synthesis Report thus implies that international shipping will most probably pick up first in the Northern Sea Route. As will be demonstrated in the next part, this seems to be borne out by developments above the Eurasian continent during the most recent shipping seasons.

But before addressing these shipping developments, a few words need to be added on the time scale predicted by the 2004 ACIA Synthesis Report. Only one of the four models relied upon predicted an ice-free Arctic during the month of September by the middle of the 21st century. The other three did not predict that to happen during the present century.[24] A later study conducted by the Intergovernmental Panel on Climate Change (IPCC) concluded in early 2007 that in some projections the late-summer sea ice would disappear entirely

---

[18] *Ibid.*

[19] This is the Arctic shipping route between the Atlantic and Pacific Oceans along the northern coast of the North American continent.

[20] Resulting in an increased risk of icebergs, which are particularly dangerous for shipping.

[21] 2004 ACIA Synthesis Report, *supra* note 13, p. 85.

[22] This is what the Russians call part of the Northeast Passage, i.e. the Arctic shipping route between the Atlantic and Pacific Oceans along the northern coast of the Eurasian continent. The Russians distinguish between the Northeast Passage, which is the broader concept, and the Northern Sea Route, which starts in the West from the western entrances of Novaia Zemlia, thus normally excluding the Barents Sea and ends in the East at the Bering Strait, or vice versa. Besides this difference in lateral extent, the vertical extent also differs, implying once again that the Northeast Passage is the broader concept of the two: the Northeast Passage runs up to the North Pole whereas the Northern Sea Route is in principle limited to the 200 nautical-mile zone. It must nevertheless be noted that the practical application by the Russians of the just-mentioned distinction renders the difference between the two concepts much more blurred to the point one can even question its utility. For a discussion see E. Franckx 'Should the Law Governing Maritime Areas in the Arctic Adapt to Changing Climatic Circumstances?', in: Koivurova, Keskitalo and Bankes (eds.), *Climate Governance in the Arctic* (Berlin, Springer, 2009), pp. 131–133.

[23] 2004 ACIA Synthesis Report, *supra* note 13, p. 83. Confirming this general trend, while at the same time further distinguishing between the Barents, Kara and Laptev Seas, see I.I. Mokhov, V.C. Khon and E. Roeckner, 'Variations in the Ice Cover of the Arctic Basin in the 21st Century Based on Model Simulations: Estimates of the Perspectives of the Northern Sea Route', 415 *Doklady Earth Sciences*, No. 5, 2007, 759–763.

[24] 2005 ACIA Scientific Report, *supra* note 14, p. 193.

by the latter part of the 21st century,[25] allowing for an ice-free Northwest Passage and Northern Sea Route by 2080-2100.[26]

But 2007 was also the year of an exceptional summer melt in the Arctic during the month of September, the lowest ever since satellite measurements started in 1979,[27] making certain scientists wonder whether summer ice would make it until 2050,[28] or even earlier.[29] Even before this exceptional summer, some had already argued that the IPCC findings were thought to be "conservative",[30] predicting that an essentially ice-free summer Arctic was more likely to occur well within the present century.[31] The summers of 2008 and 2009 broke no new record, but were nevertheless the second and third lowest years of satellite recorded sea-ice extent during the month of September.[32] The summer of 2010, finally, dethroned the summer of 2009 from third place.[33] No wonder that scientists have since further downscaled the timing to the late 2020s.[34] Others

---

[25] S. Soloman, D. Qin, M. Manning, Z. Chen, K.B. Averyt, M.M. Tignor and H.L. Miller (eds.), *Contribution of Working Group I to the Fourth Assessment Report of the Intergovernmental Panel on Climate Change, 2007* (Cambridge: Cambridge University Press, 2007), p. 750. See also Core Writing Team, R. Pachauri and A. Reisinger (eds.), *Climate Change 2007: Synthesis Report. Contribution of Working Groups I, II and III to the Fourth Assessment Report of the Intergovernmental Panel on Climate Change* (Geneva: IPCC, 2008), p. 46.

[26] See the map and legend reproduced in M. Parry, O. Canziani, J. Palutikof, P. van der Linden and C. Hanson (eds.), *Contribution of Working Group II to the Fourth Assessment Report of the Intergovernmental Panel on Climate Change, 2007* (Cambridge: Cambridge University Press, 2007), p. 659.

[27] To give an indication of the extreme nature of the ice decline, see J.C. Comiso, C.L. Parkinson, R. Gersten and L. Stock, 'Accelerated Decline in the Arctic Sea Ice Cover', 35 *Geophysical Research Letters*, No. L01703, 2008, 6, where these authors indicate that the ice cover on 14 September 2007 was about 25 per cent less than the previous record low, which happened only two years before, namely on 21 September 2005, and almost 40 per cent less than the climatological averages.

[28] R.A. Kerr, 'Is Battered Arctic Sea Ice Down for the Count?', 318 *Science*, No. 5 October 2007, 2007, 33–34.

[29] D. Cressey, 'Arctic Melt Opens Northwest Passage', 449 *Nature*, 2007, 267, predicting summer free ice conditions could occur as soon as within the next 40 years.

[30] J. Stroeve, M.M. Holland, W. Meier, T. Scambos and M. Serreze, 'Arctic Sea Ice Decline: Faster than Forecast', 34 *Geophysical Research Letters*, No. L09501, 2007, 1.

[31] *Ibid.*, p. 5.

[32] L. Polyak, R.B. Alley, J.T. Andrews, J. Brigham-Grette, T.M. Cronin, D.A. Darby, A.S. Dyke, J.J. Fitzpatrick, S. Funder, M. Holland, A.E. Jennings, G.H. Miller, M. O'Regan, J. Savelle, M. Serreze, K. St. John, J.W.C. White and E. Wolff, 'History of Sea Ice in the Arctic', 29 *Quaternary Science Reviews*, No. 15/16, 2010, 1759.

[33] D. Perovich, W. Meier, J. Maslanik and J. Richter-Menge, 'Sea Ice Cover: Arctic Report Card, Update for 2010', available at <http://www.arctic.noaa.gov/reportcard/seaice.html>.

[34] M. Wang and J.E. Overland, 'A Sea Ice Free Summer Arctic Within 30 Years?', 36 *Geophysical Research Letters*, No. L07502, 2009, 4.

deny that a so-called tipping point has been reached,[35] since abrupt losses are often followed by equally abrupt recoveries during the following years.[36] But, these authors also predict ice-free summers well before the turn of the century, namely between 2060 and 2080.[37]

These recent extraordinary years of limited summer ice cover in the Arctic also have a direct impact on future shipping perspectives in the Northwest and Northeast Passages. In 2007, for instance, for the first time in history, the Northwest Passage completely opened up, making it possible for a standard ocean-going vessel to sail through.[38] In 2008 both the Northwest and Northeast Passages opened up at the same time, which was said, once again, to be the first recorded occurrence.[39] Finally, in 2010 the US National Ice Center declared both the Northwest and Northeast Passages open for a certain period during the month of September, making it possible for two sailing expeditions, one Norwegian[40] and one Russian,[41] to circumnavigate the Arctic using both passages during one and the same season.[42]

Finally of special importance for Arctic shipping is the fact that scientists have noted that the shrinking of the ice extent during summer goes hand in

[35] S. Tietsche, D. Notz, J.H. Jungclaus and J. Marotzke, 'Recovery Mechanisms of Arctic Summer Sea Ice', 38 *Geophysical Research Letters*, No. L02707, 2011, 4.

[36] *Ibid.*, p. 1.

[37] *Ibid.*, p. 2, Figure 1. This period is somewhat extended on the lower end of the scale by key finding 6 of a 2011 scientific assessment conducted under the auspices of the Arctic Monitoring and Assessment Programme, which projects "a nearly ice-free summer within this century, likely within the next thirty to forty years". Arctic Council, *SWIPA 2010 Executive Summary: Snow, Water, Ice and Permafrost in the Arctic* 2011), p. 7.

[38] Press release of the National Snow and Ice Data Center (University of Colorado at Boulder) (hereinafter NSIDC Press Release), 1 October 2007, 'Arctic Sea Ice Shatters All Previous Record Lows: Diminished Summer Sea Ice Leads to Opening of the Fabled Northwest Passage', available at <http://nsidc.org/news/press/2007_seaiceminimum/20071001_pressrelease.html>.

[39] NASA Earth Observatory, 9 September 2008, 'Both Routes Around Arctic Open at Summer's End', available at <http://earthobservatory.nasa.gov/IOTD/view.php?id=9078>.

[40] It concerns a light 9.5 meters Corsair 31 trimaran, called *Northern Passage*. See 'Around the North Pole in Less than Three Months', Barents Observer, 24 September 2010, available at <http://www.barentsobserver.com/around-the-north-pole-in-less-than-three-months.4822563-16334.html> and 'The Northern Passage 2010', available at <http://www.explorapoles.org/expeditions/detail/the_northern_passage_2010/>, where a map can be found showing the exact route followed.

[41] It concerns an 18 meters sailing boat, called *Peter 1*. See 'Arkticheskaiakrugosvetka' (Arctic voyage around the world), available at <http://new.rusarc.ru/?page_id=2141>, where the exact route followed can be consulted.

[42] NSIDC Press Release, 4 October 2010, 'Weather and Feedbacks Lead to Third-lowest Extent', available at <http://nsidc.org/arcticseaicenews/2010/100410.html>.

hand with an overall marked decrease in Arctic ice thickness.[43] At the end of the summer melt of 2010 less than 15 per cent of the remaining ice was more than two years old, which contrasts sharply with the 1980s where this percentage still ranged between 50 and 60 per cent.[44] From an estimated mean average ice draft of 2.9 meters at the end of the 1980s,[45] scientists today rather believe that figure to be less than two,[46] or a reduction by more than 30 per cent over a time period of exactly 20 years.

This brief overview of scientific findings with respect to summer ice cover extent and thickness in the Arctic may suffice to illustrate that trans-Arctic shipping is definitively looming on the horizon. With the restricted area inside the Canadian archipelago, as explained above, the Northern Sea Route will particularly profit from these improved ice conditions.[47]

---

43 Polyak *et al., supra* note 32, p. 1758. Within the central Arctic Ocean old ice of five years or more has declined by 88 per cent and ice of nine years or older has simply disappeared (*ibid.*, p. 1759). Arctic ice is thus becoming considerably younger, meaning thinner as well. J. Maslanik, J. Stroeve, C. Fowler and W. Emery, 'Distribution and Trends in Arctic Sea Ice Age Through Spring 2011', 38 *Geophysical Research Letters*, No. L13502, 2011, 5.

44 NSIDC Press Release, 4 October 2010, *supra* note 42.

45 R. Bourke and R. Garrett, 'Sea Ice Thickness Distribution in the Arctic Ocean', 13 *Cold Regions Science and Technology*, No. 3, 1987, 262.

46 J.A. Maslanik, C. Fowler, J. Stroeve, S. Drobot, J. Zwally, D. Yi and W. Emery, 'A Younger, Thinner Arctic Ice Cover: Increased Potential for Rapid, Extensive Sea-ice Loss', 34 *Geophysical Research Letters*, No. L24501, 2007, 1–5.

47 That the Northern Sea Route will most probably be opened first is generally supported by writers addressing this issue, either explicitly (see A. Chircop, 'The Growth of International Shipping in the Arctic: Is a Regulatory Review Timely?', 24 *International Journal of Marine and Coastal Law*, No. 2, 2009, 356) or implicitly (see for instance J. Ho, 'The Implications of Arctic Sea Ice Decline on Shipping', 34 *Marine Policy*, No. 3, 2010, 713–715, who only touches upon the Northern Sea Route or Northeast Passage without even mentioning the Northwest Passage. This author bases himself moreover on predictions made by the US National Intelligence Council to rely on the year 2013 as the starting date for a seasonally ice-free Arctic (*ibid.*, p. 714 and 715); see also C. Schofield and T. Potts, 'Across the Top of the World: Emerging Arctic Navigational Opportunities and Arctic Governance', 2009 *Carbon & Climate Law Review*, No. 4, 2009, 472–482. These authors distinguish between the Northwest Passage, the Northern Sea Route and a direct trans-Arctic route over the Pole as possible alternatives. Nevertheless, the ice conditions in the Northwest Passage are said to render navigation "considerably more hazardous" (*ibid.*, p. 476), whereas the trans-Arctic route "would potentially be competitive in the longer term" (*ibid.*, p. 477). Only with respect to the Northern Sea Route do these authors provide a practical example of its international commercial use (*ibid.*, p. 472 and 476–477)). That the Northern Sea Route will most probably be subject to increased international navigation before the Northwest Passage is moreover borne out by simulations of Arctic sea ice characteristics affecting the navigation along both routes performed by global climate models in comparison with observations. A prolongation of the shipping season at the end of the century, not requiring ice-breaker assistance, is estimated to be three to six months with respect to the Northern Sea Route and two to four months concerning the Northwest

B. *Recent ship movements along the Northern Sea Route*

Favorable ice conditions are of course one aspect facilitating shipping in the Arctic, but these have to be accompanied by favorable political conditions as well. This submission holds particularly true with respect to the Northern Sea Route, which for a long time simply remained off limits for foreign commercial ships, always in need of the infrastructure and ice-breaker assistance of the coastal State involved. Since the late 1960s the former Soviet Union has at times taken initiatives to open up the Northern Sea Route to foreign shipping, but these initiatives have never been very successful because no foreign commercial vessel ever took advantage of them: The first Soviet initiative in 1967 is thought to have been tacitly withdrawn because of the Suez canal crisis, and the Murmansk speech of Gorbachev 20 years later was short lived because of the dissolution of the Soviet Union in 1991.[48] Neither the *Tiksi* in 1989, a Soviet vessel chartered for hard currency,[49] nor the *Astrolabe* in 1991, a French ice class 1 super multipurpose offshore ship,[50] nor the *Uikku* in 1997, a Finnish flagged ice class 1A super oil tanker,[51] were foreign ships making use of the passage for international commercial purposes.

Passage. V.C. Khon, I.I. Mokhov, M. Latif, V.A. Semenov and W. Park, 'Perspectives of Northern Sea Route and Northwest Passage in the Twenty-first Century', 100 *Climate Change*, No. 3, 2010, 766. Moreover, the Northwest Passage will suffer from penetrating thick multi-year ice (*ibid.*, p. 764) and will be characterized by a slower start in becoming less ice-infested only after 2030 (*ibid.*, p. 763).

[48] For more details about these initiatives, see Franckx, *supra* note 3, pp. 328–330.

[49] For a more detailed account on the voyage of the *Tiksi*, see E. Franckx, 'New Developments in the North-east Passage', 6 *International Journal of Estuarine and Coastal Law*, No. 1, 1991, 38–40. Even though there was a clear international commercial interest here in making use of the Northern Sea Route for transit purposes only (goods were loaded in Hamburg and unloaded in Osaka), the former Soviet Union was not inclined at that time to convoy a foreign flagged vessel through this sea route, but rather required the goods to be transported on a Soviet flagged vessel instead. Since it had no proper interest in the goods, as for instance in the case of the voyage of the Russian flagged vessel MV *Monchegorsk* making a transit passage in 2010 (see *infra* notes 72–73 and accompanying text), this attitude by the former Soviet Union can be considered as having undermined the true international commercial use of the route in the case of the *Tiksi*.

[50] For a more detailed account on the voyage of the *Astrolabe*, see E. Franckx, 'The Soviet Maritime Arctic, Summer 1991: A Western Account', 1 *Journal of Transnational Law and Policy*, No. 1, 1992, 140–144.

[51] This vessel claims to be the first foreign flagged oil tanker to cross the whole Northern Sea Route. The purpose of the voyage was to transport diesel oil from Murmansk to Pevek. After having unloaded the cargo, the vessel continued its journey through the Bering Strait. See S. Lumminsivu, 'The M/t *Uikku* Navigated the Entire Northern Sea Route in 1997: The M/t *Uikku* was the First Western Oil Tanker to Navigate the Entire Northern Sea Route – World Records Also After Nordenskiöld, But for How Long?', available at <http://www.smu.fi/in_english/communication/the_m_t_uikku_navigated_the_enti/>. This vessel, however, had

One had to wait for the summer season of 2009 for the first crossing by a foreign flagged vessel of the Northern Sea Route for an international commercial purpose. It concerned the MV *Beluga Fraternity* and the MV *Beluga Foresight* two multi-purpose heavy lift carriers, both belonging to the German Beluga Group[52] but flying the flag of Antigua and Barbuda. The company at first tried to make the voyage during the summer of 2008 but was unable to obtain the necessary permission from the Russian authorities in time.[53] Apparently the Beluga Group intended to make the crossing without having to rely on Russian icebreakers or other assistance "the cost of which would wipe out any benefits" according to a spokesman of the Beluga Group.[54] When they did accomplish the voyage in 2009, however, the two vessels, after having left Uslan, South Korea, and stopping for inspection in Vladivostok,[55] met and convoyed with

been chartered since 1993 by a company, based in Murmansk, in which two Russian companies (the Murmansk Shipping Company and Primorsk Shipping Yards) and one Finnish company (Nemarc Shopping Oy) were a principal shareholder. Together with a sister ship, the M/t *Lunni*, they had been chartered to transport diesel oil and jet fuel to Russia's estuaries. See M. Voytenko, 'How Many Non-Russian Flagged Vessels Sailed Russian Northern Passage?', available at <http://www.odin.tc/eng/articles/617–How-many-non-Russian-flagged-vessels-sailed-Russian-Northern-Passage-.asp>. As such, even though being a foreign flagged vessel, the M/t *Uikku* was working for the Russian authorities at the time of the 1997 crossing and was clearly not engaged in international trade. In 1998 the same vessel took part in an Arctic Demonstration and Exploratory Voyage, a research project funded by the European Union, during which she sailed from Murmansk to the Ob river estuary to load a cargo of gas condensate and then sailed back to Europe. Information available at <http://www.transport-research.info/web/projects/project_details.cfm?ID=21>. See also L.W. Brigham, 'The Northern Sea Route, 1998', 36 *Polar Record*, No. 196, 1999, 21–22. This voyage may have been closer to international trade, but the vessel only sailed a small part of the Northern Sea Route on this occasion (for the exact route followed, see *ibid.*, p. 22, Fig. 2). Besides the M/t *Uikku*, also a tanker flying the Latvian flag has been reported to have completed a full transit in 1997. L.W. Brigham, 'The Northern Sea Route, 1997', 34 *Polar Record*, No. 190, 1998, 220, who bases this information on a personal communication with the Northern Sea Route Administration. Despite the fact that further information on this particular crossing is missing, one can assume that the purpose of that transit was similar to that of the M/t *Uikku*. Indeed the same author wrote in 2001 that no through transit was carried on the Northern Sea Route during the years 1997–1999. L.W. Brigham, 'The Northern Sea Route, 1999–2000', 37 *Polar Record*, No. 203, 2001, 329 and 330.

52 Technical details of these two ships are available at <http://www.beluga-group.com/en/flottendatenbank/mehrzweck-schwergutfrachter/f-series/>.

53 G. Garfield, 'Trailblazer Beluga: A German Player is Planning to Send a Ship Through the Northeast Passage – Without Assistance', 18 *Trade Winds*, 5 September 2008, available at <http://www.beluga-group.com/uploads/media/2008_09_08_TradeWinds_Trailblazer.pdf>.

54 Statement by Niels Stolberg, President and CEO of the Beluga Group, as quoted in *ibid.*

55 This inspection, together with the time required for obtaining the necessary clearances, took nearly a month. 'Successful Transit of Northeast Passage', Ships Monthly, December 2009,

Russian icebreakers as soon as they passed through the Bering Strait. When the vessels rounded the most northern and difficult part of their route, namely Vil'kitskii Strait,[56] they formed part of a convoy led by two Russian atomic icebreakers.[57] The ships first delivered 44 heavy modules to Novii Port, at the mouth of the Ob river, for a Russian power plant in Surgut upstream that river. From there they sailed to Archangelsk where they loaded 6,000 tons of steel pipe destined for Nigeria, and continued their trip to Rotterdam.[58] Even though the trip has been qualified as a success by the Beluga Group, the mandatory charges for the icebreaker escort were not disclosed.[59]

In 2010 the same German company used two of its vessels, the MV *Beluga Fortitude*[60] and the MV *Beluga Houston*,[61] two ice-hardened multipurpose heavy lift carriers sailing under the flag of Antigua and Barbuda, to deliver, once again, complex components destined for the Surgut power plant. Russian icebreakers escorted these vessels. But since the ships loaded in Norrkoping, Sweden, and Rotterdam, the Netherlands, respectively, and later discharged again in Novii Port, returning to Rotterdam, this was only a partial use of the Northern Sea Route.[62] At the end of the 2010 summer season, moreover, Rosmorport chartered the MV *Beluga Houston* to load two tugs built in the Leningrad region, one in the ship's hold and the other one on deck, and to deliver them to

available at <http://www.beluga-group.com/uploads/media/2009–12–01–Ships-Monthly-Succesful-Transit_01.pdf>.

56 About the difficult physical and legal nature of this strait, see E. Franckx, 'Non-Soviet Shipping in the Northeast Passage, and the Legal Status of ProlivVil'kitskogo', 24 *Polar Record*, No. 151, 1988, 269–276.

57 'Northeast Passage Journey Successful: Beluga Vessels Call Siberian Port', Breakbulk Magazine, 9 September 2009, available at <http://www.breakbulk.com/node/810>.

58 *Ibid.* See also 'Successful Transit of Northeast Passage', *supra* note 55.

59 'Successful Transit of Northeast Passage', *supra* note 55. As duly stressed by a privileged observer of the Northern Sea Route. See L.W. Brigham, 'The Fast-changing Maritime Arctic', 136 *U.S. Naval Institute Proceedings*, No. 5, 2010, 55, who moreover remarks that in the Northwest Passage during that same shipping season the only passages had been made by yachts and ice-strengthened tour vessels (*ibid.*, p. 56).

60 Technical details of this ship are available at <http://www.beluga-group.com/en/flottendatenbank/mehrzweck-schwergutfrachter/f-series/>.

61 The *MV Beluga Houston* was only delivered to the Beluga Group earlier that same year. It belongs to the H class of the company, meaning it is able to carry larger and heavier project cargoes than the other ships of the company mentioned earlier, which all belong to the F class. See J. Nodar, 'Beluga Shipping Takes Delivery of New Ship', The Journal of Commerce Online, 19 January 2010, available at <http://www.joc.com/maritime/beluga-shipping-takes-delivery-new-ship>.

62 'Safely Passing the Ice Floes on the Way to Siberia', 24 August 2010, as available at <http://www.beluga-group.com/en/search/?tx_indexedsearch[sword]=arctic2010#Press-Pressreview>.

Vladivostok.[63] But this operation missed an international component for it only used a foreign flag to move goods within Russian waters.[64]

A better example for present purposes is therefore the voyage during the summer of 2010 of the MV *Nordic Barents*, an ice-class 1A bulk carrier flying the flag of Hong Kong and owned by the Norway-based Tschudi Shipping Company. The ship left the port of Kirkeness, Norway, with a cargo of 41,000 tons of iron ore concentrate to be unloaded just twelve days later in China. Note that this ship did not stop at a Russian port to load or unload. It therefore represents the first instance that a true transit passage for international commercial purposes took place by a foreign flagged vessel using the Northern Sea Route merely as a shipping lane relying the Atlantic and Pacific Oceans.[65] The MV *Nordic Barents* was escorted by Russian nuclear icebreakers as well[66] and completed the entire passage of the Northern Sea Route in nine days.[67]

Only ten days earlier, the SCF *Baltica* had completed its voyage from Murmansk to Ningbo, China, where it delivered 70,000 tons of gas condensate. The ship is an ice-class 1A super tanker flying the Liberian flag and belonging to the Sovcomflot Group, one of Russia's largest infrastructure companies with headquarters in St. Petersburg. Novatek, the largest independent gas producer in Russia, ordered the transport. Three nuclear icebreakers escorted

---

[63] 'Rosmorport Sends Tugs to Its Vladivostok Branch', 186 Lekko International, November/December 2010, pp. 325–326, available at <http://www.pellaship.ru/pdf/lekko_international_186.pdf>; 'Opening the Northern Sea Route', Asia Maritime, September/October 2010, available at <http://www.thisisasiamaritime.com/ckfinder/userfiles/images/2010102195859400.pdf>.

[64] This is also part of the reason why the voyage of the *Georg Ots*, the first non-ice strengthened passenger ship ever to traverse the Northern Sea Route will not be listed here: it "only" sailed under icebreaker escort from Murmansk to Vladivostok, thus lacking an international commercial interest. '"Georg Ots" Passenger Ferry Made an Unprecedented Passage Through the NSR: Satellite Imagery Helped Optimizing the Route', ScanEx Newsletter, 1 October 2010, available at <http://www.scanex.ru/en/news/News_Preview.asp?id=n18316175>. Moreover, the ship flew a Russian flag. 'Passenger Ship Traverses the Northeast Passage', Maritime Arctic, 30 September 2010, available at <http://maritime-arctic.com/2010/09/30/passenger-ship-traverses-the-northeast-passage/>. With a capacity of 368 passengers and 107 cars, there might of course have been foreign passenger on board, but the international commercial context of interest here relates to the shipping aspect of the voyage. It completed the crossing of the Northern Sea Route in only seven days. See A. Rohlen, 'Tor Viking – A Late Return from Alaska to Europe – A New Possibility to Link Atlantic and Beaufort Sea Basins for the Offshore Industry?', Arctic Passion Seminar, Helsinki, 3 March 2011, PowerPoint presentation available at <http://www.akerarctic.fi/Arctic_Passion_2011–TransAtlantic-Tor_Viking_Trip_through_NSR-Rohlen.pdf>, slide 22.

[65] '"MV Nordic Barents" Makes Historic Voyage', Barents Observer, 26 August 2010, available at <www.barentsobserver.com/mv-nordic-barents-to-make-historic-voyage.4812338–16175.html>.

[66] '"MV Nordic" Gets Icebreaker Assistance', Barents Observer, 8 September 2010, available at <www.barentsobserver.com/index.php?id=4816926>.

[67] Rohlen, *supra* note 64, slide 22.

the ship.[68] This is so far the largest ship having made the passage.[69] Doubts can be raised as to whether it is appropriate to mention this voyage in the present list. Even though according to Russian terminology the SCF *Baltica* completed the Northern Sea Route during the summer of 2010,[70] it did not really use the Northeast Passage linking the Atlantic and Pacific Oceans because the Barents Sea, where it started its journey, is normally defined as a marginal sea of the Arctic Ocean.[71] On the other hand, of course, the ship is flying a foreign flag and an international commercial interest is clearly present.

Following the just-cited rule of thumb, mention should also be made of the summer 2010 voyage of the MV *Monchegorsk*,[72] running a commercial test voyage between the port of Murmansk and Shanghai. The vessel belongs to the Russian mining company Norilsk Nickel. It is an ice-strengthened container ship flying the Russian flag. After having started to ship its own products to Western Europe, the company now intends to start exporting its own products to the Far East as well by means of the Northern Sea Route. The vessel left Murmansk on September 15 loaded with metal, unloaded at Shanghai and returned with consumer goods for Norilsk. The importance of this trip is that it made history by sailing the Northern Sea Route without icebreaker assistance both on the out- and inbound voyages.[73]

Finally, a brief mention should be made of the passage of the Swedish vessel *Tor Viking II*, itself a class 10 icebreaker, whose work in US waters had been delayed and was urgently needed back in the Baltic Sea.[74] This was again an

---

[68] 'First High-tonnage Tanker Through Northeast Passage', Barents Observer, 17 August 2010, available at <http://www.barentsobserver.com/index.php?id=4809756>.

[69] It is a 100,000 ton tanker, with a length of 250 meters and a beam of 44 meters. By comparison, the MV *Nordic Barents* has a length of 189 meters and a beam of 30 meters. The tonnage of the SCF *Baltica* is double of what the International Northern Sea Route Program (1993–1999) had predicted to be the maximum cargo if a northerly route were to be followed without port calls. R.D. Brubaker and C.L. Ragner, 'A Review of the International Northern Sea Route Program (INSROP) – 10 Years On', 33 *Polar Geography*, No. 1–2, 2010, 19. As stated, the ship was only carrying 70,000 tons of gas condensate at that time, but it did make a so-called technical anchorage at the port of Pevek. Sovcomflot, 'SCF Baltica Completes Her Voyage from Murmansk to Ningbo (China)', Press Release of 8 September 2010, available at <http://www.scf-group.com/npage.aspx?anim=1&cs=5&cid=113&cs2=1&curDate=1-9-2010&did=72347>.

[70] It did so in nine and a half days. See Rohlen, *supra* note 64, slide 22.

[71] This also explains why ship movements between Norilsk and West-European ports have not been included in the present listing.

[72] The ship has a length of 168 meters and a beam of 26 meters.

[73] 'First Ever Round-trip Voyage Without Icebreaker', Barents Observer, 17 November 2010, available at <http://www.barentsobserver.com/first-ever-round-trip-voyage-without-icebreaker.4848358–116320.html>.

[74] Unlike the *Polar Sea* saga of 1985, which stirred a severe diplomatic row between the United States and Canada when this US icebreaker sailed through the Northwest Passage for very

historic voyage, since it was the first time in Russian history that the passage was made that late in the season. The *Tor Viking II* met a Russian nuclear icebreaker after passing the Bering Strait and it took both icebreakers nine days to make the crossing of the Northern Sea Route, rounding the northern tip of Novaia Zemlia on Christmas day.[75] Though the *Tor Viking II* is a foreign flagged vessel making use of the Northern Sea Route to sail from the Pacific to the Atlantic, the international commercial interest could be questioned, even though in this case the economic gain was directly related to the shipping aspects of the voyage.

This short overview shows that the summer of 2010 has been exceptional indeed as far as the use of the Northern Sea Route for international commercial purposes is concerned. A wide variety of crossings were made during that year. And even though many of them were "a first ever" when considering their specific characteristics, not all were directly relevant for present purposes. Nevertheless, the above-made analysis of the use of the Northern Sea Route during the shipping season 2010 confirms the somewhat prophetic words of one commentator: "When the future history of the Arctic will be written, 2010 will be marked as the breakthrough year for commercial shipping along the Northern Sea Route".[76]

At the same time, while this route is being mastered and prepared for international shipping,[77] it remains a harsh environment where the possibility of accidents cannot be totally excluded. Despite the assistance of nuclear icebreakers and despite the fact that the oil tankers have the highest ice-class, collision may still occur, as was painfully illustrated in this same exceptional year [2010]. Two tankers belonging to the Murmansk Shipping Company, the MT *Indiga*

---

similar reasons (as described in E. Franckx, *Maritime Claims in the Arctic: Canadian and Russian Perspectives* (Dordrecht, Martinus Nijhoff Publishers, 1993), pp. 89–101), here instead letters of mutual thanks were exchanged, praising the good cooperation between both vessels *en cours de route*. Rohlen, *supra* note 64, slide 31, where two letters, one in English and one in Russian, are reproduced.

[75] Rohlen, *supra* note 64, slide 31.

[76] T. Nilsen, 'The Future History of the Arctic is Now', Barents Observer, 2 September 2010, available at <http://www.barentsobserver.com/index.php?id=4814307>. Again, this sharply contrasts with the Northwest Passage where the first real transit transport of goods still has to take place. See G. Wilkman and M. Niini, 'Arctic Transit: The Northern Sea Route and the Northwest Passage Offer Enormous Opportunity While Posing Enormous Challenge', *Marine Technology*, 2011, 34–40.

[77] At present, for instance, the Russian Federation is considering the building of two hubs for the Northern Sea Route. In the west it concerns the construction of a new port in Murmansk Bay and in the east the further development of the port of Petropavlovsk for that specific purpose. 'Russians Plan Arctic Hub', Breakbulk Online, 10 December 2010, available at <http://www.breakbulk.com/ports-terminals/russians-plan-arctic-hub>.

and the MT *Varzuga*,[78] both A1 super ice-class oil tankers flying the Russian flag, collided on 16–17 July. At that time they were each transporting 13,300 tons of diesel fuel from Murmansk to Chukotka. At the time of the incident, two nuclear icebreakers accompanied them. The hull of the MT *Indiga* was damaged but no spill was reported.[79]

This factual background sets the stage for an analysis of the legal developments, discussed in the next part, which appear to be necessary in order to cope with this projected increase of shipping in the Arctic in the near future.

From voluntary Arctic guidelines to a mandatory polar code

A. *Pollution of the marine environment in Arctic waters*

Within the Arctic environment the 2009 AMSA Report highlights the following possible consequences of increased shipping in the area.[80] Arctic species are especially vulnerable to potential environmental stresses such as oil spills, accidental discharges, ship strikes and disturbances. The growing presence of ships in the areas where species gather and in migration corridors used by marine mammals and birds will most likely result in a particularly hazardous situation. With regard to "ship based impacts", a distinction can be made between accidental discharges and operational discharges into the water and ship emissions into the air. Oil spills and accidental discharges of other toxic chemicals will possibly constitute the most serious threat to the Arctic ecosystems as a result of increased shipping. Because of the particular environmental conditions of the Arctic, that is the presence of ice, the extreme weather conditions, the problem of visibility, exceptional hazards and little human infrastructure, an adequate response and cleanup of these possible spills form a major challenge for the region for which mankind remains essentially unprepared. At the same time one has to acknowledge that vessels do produce a range of substances in their natural mode of operation, such as oil, ballast water, grey water, bilge water, garbage, etc., which will eventually have to be discharged at some point. Such operational discharges are regulated through the International Convention for

[78] It is interesting to note that the MT *Indiga* and the MT *Varzaga* are the same vessel as the *Lenni* and the *Uikku*, which in the past had been chartered by the former Soviet Union for similar purposes (see *supra* note 51). They were both sold to the Murmansk Shipping Company after 25 years of service in 2003. At that time they also changed flag.

[79] 'Arctic Oil Tankers Collided', Barents Observer, 19 July 2010, available at <http://www.barentsobserver.com/index.php?id=4801363>.

[80] 2009 AMSA Report, *supra* note 2, p. 134–151. The following paragraph is based on this report.

the Prevention of Pollution by Ships (MARPOL).[81] In theory, these discharges should not pose a particular threat to the Arctic since they concern small amounts of legally discharged substances. Even though the MARPOL regulations have significantly reduced pollution in the marine environment, they have not eliminated discharges altogether. If these international rules and regulations are not strictly followed, even a small amount of illegally discharged oily sludge could cause substantial environmental damage. The last above-mentioned impact from shipping concerns the emission into the air of, among others, carbon dioxide, methane, nitrogen oxides, sulphur oxides and particulate matter. Because of these emissions resulting from shipping activity, increased shipping will most probably contribute to global climate change and to health impacts in the Arctic. Apart from these direct impacts, shipping activity also causes some potential disturbances to the marine environment. These potential disturbances consist of sound and noise produced by ships as a by-product of their operation, damage caused by ice-breakers, vessel strikes on mammals and the introduction of invasive species through ballast water discharge, hull fouling, cargo operations and casualties or shipwrecks.

B. *Development of a code for ships operating in polar waters*

The polar regions received little attention in the 1982 LOS Convention and thus only one article directs the future development of international maritime traffic in the Arctic.[82] As mentioned above, Article 234 of the 1982 LOS Convention provides coastal States with broader prescriptive and enforcement jurisdiction within their EEZ in ice-covered waters than is normally the case in more temperate waters. Unfortunately, this article does not excel in clarity.[83] Of particular interest is one of the fundamental questions regarding this article, namely whether the notion of "due regard" obliges coastal States to observe at least GAIRAS concerning the design, construction, manning or equipment

[81] International Convention for the Prevention of Pollution by Ships (Nov. 2, 1973), 1340 *U.N.T.S.* 184, amended by Protocol of 1978 Relating to the International Convention for the Prevention of Pollution from Ships, 1973 (Feb. 17, 1978), 1340 *U.N.T.S.* 61. Hereinafter MARPOL.

[82] B. Yeager and R. Huebert, *A New Sea: The Need for a Regional Agreement on Management and Conservation of the Arctic Marine Environment* (Oslo, WWF International Arctic Programme, 2008), p. 21.

[83] See for instance the presentation of Kristin Bartenstein at the 39th Annual Conference of the Canadian Council on International Law, Northern Exposure: International Law and the Challenge of the Arctic, October 28–30, 2010, Ottawa, Canada. On October 29 this author revisited Article 234. This contribution was based on an article which appeared shortly afterwards: K. Bartenstein, 'The 'Arctic Exception' in the Law of the Sea Convention: A Contribution to Safer Navigation in the Northwest Passage?', 42 *Ocean Development and International Law*, No. 1, 2011, 22–52.

of vessels, or not.[84] In the early 1990s, Canadian officials launched the idea of a polar code in anticipation of the expected future increase of shipping in the Arctic. The idea was to have a common set of rules and regulations for Arctic shipping before an increase in shipping would make such a harmonization impossible. This initiative led to a series of meetings held in the early 1990s under the auspices of the IMO.[85] The object of the polar code was "to provide that all ship operations in Polar Waters meet internationally acceptable standards".[86] Originally the idea was that a set of mandatory rules would be developed and that these rules would apply to both polar regions. This was however opposed by the United States in 1999 which stated that not only should the code be limited to the Arctic instead of trying to cover both polar regions, but also that it would be premature to develop a set of mandatory rules at that time. Instead, the United States insisted on the development of Arctic guidelines instead of a polar code.[87] These considerations were accepted by the Maritime Safety Committee (MSC), which decided to further develop the proposed regulations as recommendatory and therefore non-binding guidelines.[88] This can be viewed as regrettable because such a binding regime could be key in securing the ultimate objective of Article 234 by giving concrete content to the "due regard" notion to be found therein.[89]

These prolegomenae finally resulted in the development of the Guidelines for Ships Operating in Arctic Ice-covered Waters, approved in 2002.[90] The

[84] K. Hakapaa, E. Franckx, E.J. Molenaar 'International Law Association London Conference (2000). Committee on Coastal State Jurisdiction Relating to Marine Pollution. Final Report', in: Franckx (ed.), *Vessel-source Pollution and Coastal State Jurisdiction: The Work of the ILA Committee on Coastal State Jurisdiction Relating to Marine Pollution (1991–2000),* (The Hague, Kluwer Law International, 2001), p. 102.

[85] Yeager and Huebert, *supra* note 82, p. 22.

[86] O. Jensen, 'Arctic Shipping Guidelines: Towards a Legal Regime for Navigation Safety and Environmental Protection?', 44 *Polar Record,* No. 229, 2008, 108.

[87] MSC/71/20/11. Code on Polar Navigation. Submitted by the United States, 19 February 1999. In this document submitted to the Maritime Safety Committee, the United States pointed at the vast differences between the Arctic and the Antarctic, in particular the difference in ice conditions, geography and the fact that the Antarctica already has its Antarctic Treaty System, making it undesirable and unnecessary to capture both regions in one agreement. It further commented on some aspects of the draft code for some being too detailed at the moment while for others too vague to have substantial future importance. It also highlighted the ambiguity the code contains regarding the non-mandatory nature of some clauses. Lastly the US stressed that a mandatory code was not to be favored for the time being and that, as is the normal course of action, guidelines should be developed instead, to be reconsidered at a later time when experience is gained.

[88] Jensen, *supra* note 86, p. 109.

[89] Hakapaa, Franckx, Molenaar, *supra* note 84, p. 105.

[90] MSC/Circ.1056; MEPC/Circ.399 of 23 December 2002. Guidelines for Ships Operating in Arctic Ice-covered Waters. Adopted by the MSC at its seventy-sixth session (2–13 December

2002 Arctic Guidelines include, besides a general part, three other parts on construction, equipment and operation, each subdivided into chapters. The 2002 Arctic Guidelines were intended to address those provisions that were considered necessary beyond the existing requirements of other applicable conventions or codes and must be regarded as additional not only to the SOLAS Convention,[91] but also to the MARPOL Convention, STCW[92] and the ISM[93] code.[94] The 2002 Arctic Guidelines promote safety of navigation and the prevention of vessel-source pollution. They were heavily criticized for having substantial shortcomings.[95] Moreover, questions were raised regarding the impact of a non-binding legal regime. The 2002 Arctic Guidelines not only are recommendatory, but also they are to be interpreted "as providing recommendations rather than mandatory direction".[96] The document invites member governments to bring the regulations to the attention of all parties concerned with the operation of ships in Arctic ice-covered waters. They are thus by definition not legally binding. The effectiveness of these 2002 Arctic Guidelines depends on cooperation of all the parties involved. Actual application is only possible through state practice and compliance by the international shipping community. Meanwhile the 2002 Arctic Guidelines have been revised to also cover the Antarctic sea area. In addition, they have been updated to acknowledge the technical, technological and regulatory developments since their approval in 2002. This revision resulted in the Guidelines for Ships Operating in Polar Waters as first agreed upon by the Sub-Committee on Ship Design and Equipment (DE) when it met for its 52nd session in 2009.[97] The MSC later approved the Guidelines for Ships Operating in Polar Waters at its 86th session,[98] and the IMO Assembly subsequently adopted them on 2 December 2009.[99] The

2002) and by the MEPC at its forty-eight session (7–11 October 2002). Hereinafter 2002 Arctic Guidelines.

[91] International Convention for the Safety of Life at Sea (Nov. 1, 1974), 1184 *U.N.T.S.* 2.

[92] International Convention on Standards of Training, Certification and Watch keeping for Seafarers (July 7, 1978), 1361 *U.N.T.S.* 190.

[93] A/18/Res.741. The International Safety Management Code. Adopted on 4 November 1993.

[94] Jensen, *supra* note 86, p. 109.

[95] These shortcomings included, among others, the lack of clearly defined training qualifications for operating a vessel in ice-covered waters and insufficient regulations concerning the problems and risks associated with icing.

[96] 2002 Arctic Guidelines, *supra* note 90, P-1.3. This recommendatory nature is further stressed in the definition of the word "Guidelines" (*ibid.*, G-3.8) as well as in the introductory paragraphs of this MSC and MEPC circular.

[97] DE/52/21 of 14 April 2009, Report to the Maritime Safety Committee on its Fifty-second Session pp. 26–29.

[98] MSC/86/26/Add.2 of 12 June 2009, Report of the Maritime Safety Committee on its Eighty-sixth Session, p. 69.

[99] A/26/Res.1024 of 18 January 2010. Guidelines for Ships Operating in Polar Waters. Adopted on 2 December 2009.Hereinafter 2009 Polar Waters Guidelines. See also International

2009 Polar Waters Guidelines must still, as the title suggests, be considered as non-mandatory recommendations.[100]

Although both the 2002 Arctic Guidelines and the 2009 Polar Waters Guidelines provide important guidance, the fact remains that, because of their soft law nature, these guidelines' contribution is rather limited and their effect stays basically untested.[101] The 2009 AMSA Report acknowledged this situation and advised, in its recommendations, that:

> *The Arctic states, in recognition of the unique environmental and navigational conditions in the Arctic, decide to cooperatively support efforts at the International Maritime Organization to strengthen, harmonize and regularly update international standards for vessels operating in the Arctic. These efforts include:*
> *– Support the updating and the mandatory application of relevant parts of the Guidelines for Ships Operating in Arctic Ice-covered Waters (Arctic Guidelines); and,*
> *– Drawing from IMO instruments, in particular the Arctic Guidelines, augment global IMO ship safety and pollution prevention conventions with specific mandatory requirements or other provisions for ship construction, design, equipment, crewing, training and operations, aimed at safety and protection of the Arctic environment.*[102]

Despite the above-mentioned criticism, these guidelines provide a valuable tool when trying to achieve universal shipping standards in the Arctic. The revised 2009 Arctic Waters Guidelines are already adopted by the IMO Assembly thus guaranteeing that they do not violate existing international instruments. Also, much of the groundwork has already been accomplished by the IMO and by relying on these presently non-binding guidelines one would therefore save time and enhance the chances of a binding regime of becoming operational in the not too distant future. Moreover, the IMO is internationally accepted as the primary regulator of marine shipping and as such will be confronted with less opposition from the global shipping community.[103]

Together with the approval of the revised 2009 Polar Waters Guidelines, a proposal was set forward to develop mandatory requirements for their

---

Maritime Organization, *Ships operating in polar regions*, available at <http://www.imo.org/OurWork/Safety/SafetyTopics/Pages/PolarShippingSafety.aspx>.

100 The very restrictive language of the 2002 Arctic Guidelines (*supra* note 96) was simply retained. See 2009 Polar Waters Guidelines, *supra* note 99, P-1.4. Contrary to the 2002 Arctic Guidelines, the word "Guidelines", with its further emphasis on the recommendatory nature, no longer appears under the section definitions in the 2009 Polar Waters Guidelines (see *ibid.*, G-3). The IMO merely "recommends Governments to bring the annexed Guidelines to the attention of shipowners, ship operators, ship designers, shipbuilders, ship repairers, equipment manufacturers and installers and all other parties concerned with the operation of ships in polar waters" (*ibid.*, operational para. 4).

101 Jensen, *supra* note 86, p. 111.

102 2009 AMSA Report, *supra* note 2, p. 6.

103 S.J. Dresser, 'Safeguarding the Arctic from Accidental Oil Pollution: The Need for a Binding, Region-specific Shipping Regime', 16 *Southwestern Journal of International Law*, No. 2, 2010, 536.

application in the polar regions. A draft of the mandatory polar code is expected by 2012.

At the MSC 86th session in February 2009 a proposal was submitted by Denmark, Norway and the United States, upon adoption of the revisions to the 2002 Arctic Guidelines, to add a new work program item to the agendas of the DE Sub-Committee in order to develop mandatory requirements for application in the polar regions.[104] The proposal reads:

> *There are no international regulations in effect for ships operating in these locales that specifically address the safety and environmental concerns arising from operating in such remote and harsh locales and that the establishment of mandatory requirements would correct a significant gap in the existing regulations for ships operating in the Polar Regions.*

This proposal, together with the proposal by Argentina and Chile for the development of additional safety measures[105] and the justification prepared by DE 52 for the inclusion in the work program of a new item on "development of a code for ships operating in polar waters",[106] supported by the United Kingdom,[107] led the MSC to agree to include a high-priority item on "Development of a Mandatory Code for Ships Operating in Polar Waters" in the work program of the DE Sub-Committee, with a target completion date set for 2012. Subsequent to the MSC proposal, Denmark, Norway and the United States directed the same document to the 59th session of the MEPC where it found support in NGO quarters.[108] At the 60th session of the MEPC, Norway submitted a document, which provided an overview of environmental issues to be considered in relation to the development of a code for ships operating in polar waters.[109] Norway did not present a concrete proposal or draw conclusions, but simply offered an overview of possible questions that could warrant further consideration in

---

[104] MSC/86/23/9 of 24 February 2009. Mandatory Application of the Polar Guidelines. Submitted by Denmark, Norway and the United States. Hereinafter MSC/86/23/9.

[105] MSC/86/23/2 of 27 January 2009. Safety Measures for Navigation in the Antarctic Area. Submitted by Argentina and Chile.

[106] MSC/86/23/17 of 16 April 2009. Justification for New Work Programme Items Proposed by the DE Sub-Committee.

[107] MSC/86/12/4 of 8 April 2009. Comments on the Report of the Sub-Committee on Ship Design and Equipment. Submitted by the United Kingdom.

[108] MEPC/59/20/5 of 8 May 2009. Mandatory Polar Code. Submitted by Friends of the Earth International (FOEI), Greenpeace International, IFAW and WWF; MEPC/59/20/7 of 22 May 2009. Mandatory Requirements for Polar Shipping. Submitted by the World Wide Fund for Nature (WWF). In these proposals, FOEI, Greenpeace International, the International Fund for Animal Welfare (IFAW) and WWF expressed their support and provided additional observations on the submission by Denmark, Norway and the United States.

[109] MEPC/60/21/1 of 12 January 2010. Environmental Aspects of Polar Shipping. Submitted by Norway.

light of the development of a meaningful environmental chapter in the code. The submission was however only briefly discussed at the meeting and the MEPC decided to refer the document to DE 54. Norway used the comments received at the MEPC 60 to rework document MEPC 60/21/1[110] before submitting it to DE 54.[111] Together with the submission of the reworked document, Norway submitted a report prepared by Det Norske Veritas on "Regular operational emissions and discharges from shipping in polar areas", giving a clear and comprehensive overview of particular environmental aspects.[112] At the same time, two documents were submitted by NGOs providing their view on additional MARPOL provisions needed and wider environmental provisions to be included in the mandatory polar code.[113]

C. *Environmental and other considerations to be considered when drafting a polar code*

The idea is that, taking into account the existing conventions that already apply to the polar waters, the environmental chapter in the new code should address any additional requirements deemed necessary to ensure environmentally friendly operation in the polar areas. The following is an overview of the proposed environmental considerations put forward by Norway and the following NGOs: FOEI, IFAW, WWF, Greenpeace International, Pacific Environment and CSC.

Additional MARPOL provisions

Annex I, prevention of pollution (accidental and operational) by oil. As a normal consequence of ship operations, oil is routinely released into the marine environment. From a legal perspective these operational discharges of oil can be divided into two types: oil resulting from machinery spaces such as bilge oil, and oil resulting from cargo areas of oil tankers, slop oil. The MARPOL regulations foresee that small amounts of these operational discharges are allowed and do not pose a significant threat to the marine environment when released

[110] DE/54/INF.5 of 20 August 2010. Environmental Aspects of Emissions and Discharges from Shipping During Regular Operation in Polar Areas. Submitted by Norway. Hereinafter DE/54/INF.5.

[111] DE/54/13/7 of 20 August 2010. Environmental Aspects of the Code. Submitted by Norway. Hereinafter DE/54/13/7.

[112] DE/54/INF.5, *supra* note 110.

[113] DE/54/13/8 of 20 August 2010. Additional MARPOL Provisions for the Polar Code. Submitted by FOEI, IFAW, WWF, Pacific Environment and CSC [Clean Shipping Coalition]. Hereinafter DE/54/13/8; DE/54/13/9 of 20 August 2010. Wider Environmental Provisions for the Polar Code. Submitted by FOEI, IFAW, WWF, Pacific Environment and CSC,. Hereinafter DE/54/13/9.

from an appropriate distance from the shoreline.[114] However, due to the Arctic's sensitive waters and imperiled marine life and ecosystems, more stringent oil pollution discharge standards for ships operating in the area are desired. For that reason, a ban on vessel discharges of oil or oily mixtures into Arctic waters, as is already the case in Antarctic waters,[115] is proposed.[116] Next to these operational discharges, the risk of accidental discharge of oil will increasingly be present. If this already poses a great risk in temperate waters, accidental pollution causes even greater risks in polar waters due to the special circumstances of the area. Combating oil spills in polar waters would be complicated, time-consuming and moreover, practically nigh impossible.[117] The question has been raised whether the MARPOL regime regarding on board emergency plans and equipment is adequate for polar shipping. Due to the threat of substantial and irrevocable environmental harm, inserting a ban on the use and carriage of heavy fuel oil by vessels operating in polar waters might be needed.[118]

Annex II, control of pollution by noxious liquid substances in bulk. The discharge of noxious liquid substances poses the same risks, threats and problems for polar waters as is the case with oil spills. Even though the current transportation of these goods is quite marginal, due to the possibly severe consequences, it should be addressed in the code. Norway noticed that precautionary measures should be considered as necessary.[119] The NGOs go even further by proposing that vessel discharges of noxious liquid substances or mixtures be prohibited,[120] just as they are for Antarctic waters.[121]

Annex III, prevention of pollution by harmful substances carried by sea in packaged form. As a form of accidental discharge, loss of containers and goods during bad weather are considered a safety hazard and in addition a potential pollution problem depending on the content.[122] As shipping in the polar waters increases, losses will occur, especially considering the difficult weather conditions. Packages or their contents will float around or sink, making navigation in the polar waters more difficult. The presence of ice forms constitutes an additional complicating factor while open sea in these areas is scarce and often

---

[114] DE/54/INF.5, *supra* note 110, p. 15.

[115] Protocol on Environmental Protection to the Antarctic Treaty (4 October 1991), 30 *International Legal Materials* 1455, Annex IV, Art. 3.

[116] DE/54/13/8, *supra* note 113, p. 2.

[117] DE/54/13/7, *supra* note 111, p. 2.

[118] *Ibid.*

[119] *Ibid.*

[120] Protocol on Environmental Protection to the Antarctic Treaty, *supra* note 115, Annex IV, Art. 4.

[121] DE/54/13/8, *supra* note 113, p. 3.

[122] DE/54/INF.5, *supra* note 110, p. 20.

used by marine life for several purposes. The question to be answered here is whether the present design criteria should be adapted accordingly.[123]

Annex IV, prevention of pollution by sewage from ships. Vessels, when operating, produce several categories of waste regulated in MARPOL Annexes IV and V. Sewage or black water consists of body wastes and wastes from toilets and such. Grey water consists of waste water from sinks, baths, showers and laundry.[124] The problem of black and grey water is acute, in view of the fact that cruise activity is picking up rapidly and cruise ships, depending on their size, have the potential of discharging as much waste as a small town. Such discharges are very problematic for the vulnerable polar areas because, in comparison to other waters, the polar marine environment is less tolerant of rapid changes in the nutrient status of the water column or seabed. It also has a heightened vulnerability due to the presence of sensitive wildlife species and coastal communities that are dependent on marine ecosystems. It is therefore very probable that existing regulations will prove to be inadequate for the polar waters and must be strengthened. This could be mitigated through a banning of all discharges of treated or untreated sewage, the creation of "no discharge zones" or the requirement of advanced waste water treatment systems on board all vessels.[125]

Annex V, prevention of pollution by garbage from ships. Some categories of regular waste are allowed to be dumped into the sea depending on the distance to shore.[126] Stricter regulations are already applicable in the Arctic and Antarctic. However, food waste discharges still pose a certain threat. Arguments have been made in favor of a complete ban on garbage discharges or to identify mandatory discharge distances from more sensitive sites as an alternative. In addition, it has been proposed that Special Area status under MARPOL Annex V should be awarded to the Arctic through the polar code.[127]

---

123 DE/54/13/7, *supra* note 111, p. 3.

124 DE/54/INF.5, *supra* note 110, pp. 16–17.

125 DE/54/13/8, *supra* note 113, pp. 3–4. An example of such "no-discharge zones" and "advanced waste water treatment systems" can be found in the Clean Water Act of the United States; Water pollution prevention and control, 33. U.S.C. §1322. Also, when operating in the applicable waters of Alaska, each cruise vessel should maintain a legible Sewage and Greywater Discharge Record Book; 33 C.F.R. part 159.

126 The MEPC at its 61st session approved amendments to revise and update MARPOL Annex V regulations. One of the main changes concerns the inclusion of a new requirement specifying that discharge of all garbage into the sea is prohibited, except as expressly provided otherwise (food wastes discharges will remain permitted). Information available at <http://www.imo.org>.

127 DE/54/13/8, *supra* note 113, pp. 4–5. Special area designation under MAPROL Annex V has been granted to the Mediterranean Sea, the Baltic Sea, the Black Sea, the Red Sea, the "Gulfs" area, the North Sea, the Antarctic area (south of latitude 60 degrees south), and the wider Caribbean region including the Gulf of Mexico and the Caribbean Sea. These special areas

Annex VI, prevention of air pollution from ships. Soot and particles resulting from air emissions are regarded as a major pollutant because of their association with serious public health problems and their effects on ice melting.[128] The Arctic Council called attention to the accelerating effect on global climate change resulting from ship emissions of greenhouse gases and other pollutants in the 2009 Tromsø Declaration. This declaration notes

> *...that preserving the unique Arctic environment and protecting the Arctic against potentially irreversible impacts of anthropogenic climate change depends mainly on substantially reducing global emissions of CO_2 and other greenhouse gases...and recognize[s] that reductions of emissions have the potential to slow the rate of Arctic snow, sea ice and sheet ice melting in the near-term.*[129]

Here too the question needs to be raised whether or not existing regulations are sufficient, or whether additional regulations are needed.[130] Vessels operating in the fragile polar regions should take the lead by setting a precedent with respect to reducing air emissions that negatively impact health, the environment and climate.[131]

Other considerations

Noise pollution. Noise pollution is generally regulated neither in polar nor in any other maritime areas. Nonetheless, recent assessments address this issue as being a relevant particular challenge in polar waters. Underwater noise can interfere with the ability to communicate, to navigate, or to detect prey and predators. Noise can even result in permanent hearing loss, displacement from preferred habitat and death of marine species. The IMO has taken cognizance of the effects of underwater noise through an MEPC Correspondence Group, but so far the work has not focused on polar regions specifically.[132] Because of the

are operational in all mentioned areas, except for the Black Sea and the Red Sea where a lack of notifications on the existence of adequate reception facilities has to be noted of MARPOL parties whose coastlines border the relevant areas. Information available at <http://www.imo.org>.

128 *Ibid.*, pp. 5–7.

129 Arctic Council, *Tromsø Declaration*, 29 April 2009, available at <http://arctic-council.org/article/2009/4/the_tromso_declaration_ratified>. This statement has been supported by a number of studies, including: Core Writing Team, Pachauri and Reisinger, *supra* note 25; J.J. Corbett, D.A. Lack, J.J. Winebrake, S. Hardder, J.A. Silberman, M. Gold, 'Arctic Shipping Emissions Inventories and Future Scenarios', 10 *Atmos. Chem. Phys. Discuss*, No. 4, 2010, 10271-10311; S.C. Amsrup, E.T. DeWeaver, D.C. Douglas, B.G. Marcot, G.M. Durner, C.M. Bitz, D.A. Baily, 'Greenhouse Gas Mitigation Can Reduce Sea-ice Loss and Increase Polar Bear Persistence', *Nature*, No. 468 (16 December), 2010, 955–958.

130 DE/54/13/7, *supra* note 111, p. 4.

131 DE/54/13/8, *supra* note 113, p. 6.

132 MEPC/57/INF.4 of 17 December 2007. Shipping Noise and Marine Mammals. Submitted by the United States; MEPC/58/19 of 25 June 2008. Minimizing the Introduction of

particular environmental features of polar regions, measures need to be adopted which will decrease the risk of harm proposed to marine life. The methods for reducing the harmful effects by noise emissions can be divided into two groups. The first group dealing with active protection would attack noise pollution by addressing the source, while the second group with passive protection would shield the victims of emissions. When confronted with underwater noise, the most viable approach would be to address the source.[133] One possibility is to include rerouting measures to avoid certain areas in sensitive periods, lower speed, and alternative engine and hull designs to make ships more silent.[134]

Ballast water discharges. The threat posed by spreading alien species through ballast water to the marine ecosystems is generally accepted. In 2004 the IMO International Convention for the Control and Management of Ships' Ballast Water and Sediments (BWM Convention) was adopted in London.[135] The convention, which is expected to enter into force in 2016, sets out general requirements to control pollution through ballast water. The MEPC, at its 61st session in 2010 readdressed the need for countries to ratify the Convention to achieve its entry into force at the earliest opportunity. It is set to enter into force twelve months after not fewer than 30 States have become parties to the Convention. At the moment, 27 States have ratified this legal instrument.[136] The problem with respect to the polar waters is that not all states are parties to the convention and effective implementation is to be awaited. It has been recommended that the polar code should require that the provisions of the Convention be applied to all ships operating in polar waters and to consider necessary additional restrictions.[137]

Anti-fouling systems. The use of anti-fouling compounds is regulated by the IMO International Convention on the Control of Harmful Anti-fouling Systems on Ships (AFS Convention). The latter entered into force in 2008.[138]

Incidental Noise from Commercial Shipping Operations into the Marine Environment to Reduce Potential Adverse Impacts on Marine Life. Submitted by the United States; MEPC/58/INF.19 of 1 August 2008. Information on Noise from Commercial Shipping Operations and Marine Life. Submitted by Australia; Resolution 61/222 adopted by the General Assembly on 16 March 2007, UN Doc.A/RES/61/222 (2007), para. 107.

[133] N. Matz-Lück 'Underwater Pollution by Vessel Noise: A European Perspective', in: Franckx, Gautier (eds.), *The Exercise of Jurisdiction over Vessels: New Developments in the Fields of Pollution, Fisheries, Crimes at Sea and Trafficking of Weapons of Mass Destruction* (Brussels, Bruylant, 2010), p. 108.

[134] DE/54/13/9, *supra* note 113, pp. 3–4.

[135] International Convention for the Control and Management of Ships' Ballast Water and Sediments (13 February 2004), IMO Doc. BMW/CONF/36.

[136] MEPC/61/12/1 of 8 July 2010. Outcome of the One Hundred and Fourth Session of the Council (C 104). Note by the Secretariat, p. 6.

[137] DE/54/13/9, *supra* note 113, p. 4.

[138] International Convention on the Control of Harmful Anti-fouling Systems on Ships (5 October 2001), IMO Doc. AFS/CONF/26 (2001).

But, as is the case with the BWM Convention, not all states are parties to the AFS Convention and effective implementation is therefore not assured. Again it is recommended that the draft mandatory polar code require that the provisions of the AFS Convention are applied to all vessels operating in polar waters and the need for additional provisions be considered.[139]

Vessel strikes on marine mammals. Vessel strikes on marine mammals do not pose a significant risk for the marine ecosystem. They do, however, pose a severe threat to vulnerable species, particularly cetaceans.[140] The IMO has recently addressed this problem and issued voluntary guidelines on the subject of ship strikes.[141] To ensure adequate levels of marine mammal protection in polar waters, it is proposed that other measures or tools be considered for inclusion in the draft mandatory polar code.[142]

Conclusions

If the 2010 shipping season has been exceptional in many respects as far as international commercial use of the Northern Sea Route is concerned, the 2011 shipping season is expected to be more so. Not less than 15 orders for nuclear icebreaker assistance had already been received for 2011 before the end of the 2010 season.[143] A substantial increase in the tonnage of the transported goods is moreover predicted for the next shipping season: 150,000 tons of oil, 400,000 tons of gas condensate and 600,000 tons of iron ore are planned to be shipping through the Northern Sea Route.[144] By using different kinds of routes, it is also clear that the shallowness of certain areas is being avoided and that larger and larger ships are starting to make the transit. As specifically remarked during the above-mentioned overview of last year's passages, icebreaker assistance for non-Russian flagged vessels has so far been compulsory. The exact costs involved have up till now not really been part of the public domain. Nevertheless, their impact on the future commercial success of the use of the Northern Sea Route for international commercial purposes seems to be detrimental, as revealed by

139 DE/54/13/9, *supra* note 113, pp. 4–5.

140 DE/54/INF.5, *supra* note 110, p. 20.

141 MEPC/Circ. 674 of 31 July 2009. Guidance Document for Minimizing the Risk of Ship Strikes with Cetaceans.

142 DE/54/13/9, *supra* note 113, p. 5.

143 '15 Orders for Nuclear Icebreaker Assistance in 2011', Barents Observer, 11 September 2010, available at <http://barentsobserver.com/15–orders-for-nuclear-icebreaker-assistance-in-2011.4817937–16149.html>.

144 'More Oil and Ore along Northern Sea Route', Barents Observer, 11 February 2011, available at <http://barentsobserver.com/more-oil-and-ore-along-northern-sea-route.4884187–116320.html>.

a recent study.[145] The competitive advantage over the more traditional routes using either the Panama or the Suez Canal has been recently calculated; it will only be present if these ice-breaking fees can be reduced by 85, or even better, 100 per cent.[146] Only in the latter event will the route be truly competitive in all the scenarios envisaged by the authors.[147] The conclusion to be drawn therefore is that, despite the many uncertainties that surround the future use of the Northern Sea Route, the fact seems undeniable that its use will increase during the years to come. And in that, it does not differ much from the predictions with respect to the ice-situation along the Northern Sea Route for the shipping seasons to come: whether the ice will diminish, and eventually one day disappear in summer time appears not to be the question asked anymore, but rather the tricky question of when one can expect these changes to materialize. The trend towards better ice conditions and, consequently, to increased navigation in the Arctic is, in other words, clearly discernable at present.

As far as the legal framework is concerned, it should be clear, considering the number of environmental considerations proposed to the DE Sub-Committee working on the development of the draft mandatory polar code, that a comprehensive, adequate and uniform regime regarding pollution prevention is needed for the Arctic. The Arctic is already a fragile environment and will be particularly vulnerable to the actual and potential impacts from increased shipping activity. As mentioned above, a very high level of protection will be needed for the Arctic and should best be addressed on an international level. The contribution of the non-binding 2009 Polar Waters Guidelines has been limited to say the least and national legislation too will most likely prove insufficient to adequately address the dangers for the environment posed by increased (trans-) Arctic shipping. The lack of an international, binding and region-specific pollution prevention regime can therefore be viewed as an important gap in the legal framework governing the Arctic. The IMO has taken cognizance of this need and has, through the DE Sub-Committee, commenced work on a draft polar code, an initiative that surely should be encouraged to fulfill its objective of providing that "all ship operations in Polar Waters meet internationally acceptable standards".[148]

---

[145] M. Liu and J. Kronbak, 'The Potential Economic Viability of Using the Northern Sea Route (NSR) as an Alternative Route Between Asia and Europe', 18 *Journal of Transport Geography*, No. 3, 2010, 434–444.

[146] *Ibid.*, p. 443.

[147] The different scenarios concerned mainly the evolution of bunker prices and the number of days the Northern Sea Route would become navigable in the future. *Ibid.*, p. 441.

[148] As already quoted, *supra* note 86 and accompanying text.

CLIMATE CHANGE AND SHIPPING: PROBLEMS OF REGIME COMPATIBILITY

Nilufer Oral[1]

Abstract

Regulation of marine bunker fuel was not included in the Kyoto Protocol to the 1992 United Nations Framework Convention on Climate Change (UNFCCC). The Kyoto Protocol instead provided in Article 2.2 that Annex I countries were to pursue limitation of bunker fuel through the International Maritime Organization (IMO). In 1997 the IMO undertook its first study on greenhouse gas (GHG) emissions and shipping and in 2009 completed its second study. As part of its work in addressing climate change and international shipping, the IMO Marine Environment Protection Committee (MEPC), at its 60th session, established an Expert Group on Feasibility Study and Impact Assessment of Possible Market-based Measures (Expert Group). The Expert Group prepared a study that was introduced at MEPC 61. The Expert Group Study assessed ten market-based proposals for reduction of ship-based GHG emissions. These included establishing a Greenhouse Gas Fund, a Leveraged Incentive Scheme to promote increased energy efficiency of ships, establishing a Ship Efficiency and Credit Trading system, a Vessel Efficiency System, and an Emission Trading System for international shipping. The introduction of market-based systems for emission reduction from international shipping introduces a new role for the IMO. In addition, the linkage between the 1992 UNFCCC and IMO Conventions contains elements of inter-regime conflict, such as, for example, the applicability of the principle of "common but differentiated responsibilities" (CBDR) of the 1992 UNFCCC and the "no more favourable treatment" (NMFT) of the IMO Conventions.

This paper will critically assess the proposed market-based proposals for the reduction of GHG emissions from international shipping within the IMO legal structure and the problems of inter-regime linkage with the UNFCCC system.

I. *Introduction*

Shipping is heralded as one of the safest and cleanest modes of transport. International shipping is also a vital part of international commerce, providing a relatively low-cost mode of transport for billions of dollars worth of trade across the world. And in the overall big picture of climate change and "dirty" activities, shipping ranks as a modest contributor. Nonetheless, it has also come

[1] Nilufer Oral is a member of the Faculty of Law at Istanbul Bilgi University. The author's PowerPoint presentation can be viewed at http://www.virginia.edu/colp/pdf/kmi-oral.pdf.

under pressure to reduce greenhouse gas emissions. In response, the International Maritime Organization (IMO) conducted two studies on shipping and climate change. The first study was completed in 2000[2] and the second study in 2009.[3] According to the report of the first study, shipping accounted for approximately 1.8 percent of the world's anthropogenic emissions of CO_2. The 2009 study increased this amount to 3.3 percent for all shipping or 2.8 percent (870 million tones of CO_2 annually) for international shipping alone. The 2009 study also estimated that if no action were taken shipping emissions would increase to 1250 million tonnes annually or approximately 6 percent of global emissions by 2020 and by 150–200 percent over 2007 levels by the year 2050.[4] The report further recognized that GHG emissions from shipping were the most important source of CO_2 over other emissions. Adopting a positive outlook, the 2009 study concluded that very substantial reductions of shipping emissions were possible through increased efficiency by improved ship design (up to 50 percent) and improved operational standards (25 percent) for a total of 75 percent decrease in GHG emissions.[5]

The 1992 UNFCCC[6] is the principal global convention for addressing climate change. It is a framework instrument that sets out the overall objectives, obligations, principles, and operational mechanisms, financing structure and procedural matters for addressing climate change at the global level. The more technical and detailed regulations for implementation are to be provided by the implementing protocols and decisions of the conference of the parties. The first implementation protocol to the UNFCCC is the Kyoto Protocol, which was adopted in 1997 and entered into effect in 2005.[7] The Kyoto Protocol has a term limitation and will expire at the end of 2012.

The UNFCCC and the Kyoto Protocol are based on a bifurcated system between the developed countries and developing countries, formally identified in annexes to each respective instrument. Key principles such as the common but differentiated responsibilities and equity create the legal framework of relationship between the developed and developing Parties. The UNFCCC did

---

[2] Study of Greenhouse Gas Emissions from Ships, Final Report to the International Maritime Organization (31 March, 2000) available online at http://unfccc.int/files/methods_and_science/emissions_from_intl_transport/application/pdf/imoghgmain.pdf.

[3] Second IMO GHG Study (2009) Available online at http://www.imo.org/ourwork/environment/pollutionprevention/airpollution/pages/greenhouse-gas-study-2009.aspx.

[4] *Id.*

[5] Bunker fuels and the Kyoto Protocol: How ICAO and the IMO failed the climate change test (European Federation for Transport and Environment, 2009) available online at http://www.transportenvironment.org/.

[6] 1771 UNTS 107, adopted 9 May 1992, entered into force 21 March 1994.

[7] Kyoto Protocol to the United Nations Framework Convention on Climate Change adopted on 11 December 1997, entered into force on 16 February 2005, 2303 UNTS 14.

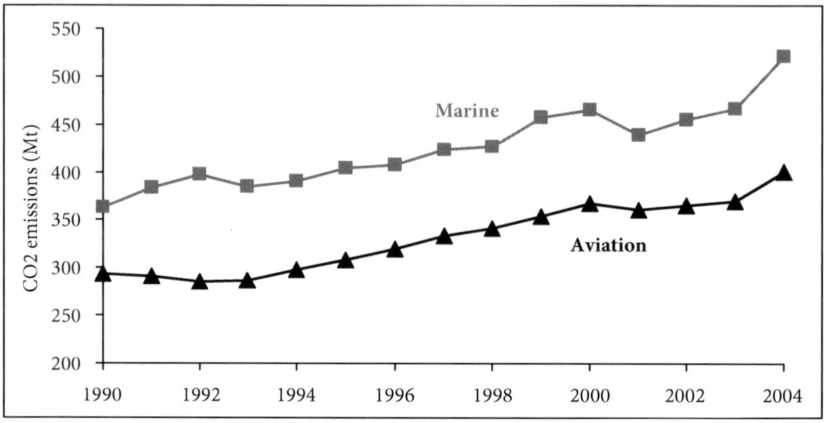

Source: International Energy Agency

Table 1. CO_2 World emissions from international aviation and maritime transport

not make specific reference to shipping activities. However, the Kyoto Protocol mandated that Parties listed in Annex I of the Convention were to pursue limitation of GHG emission from bunker fuels through the International Maritime Organization.[8] In order to fulfill the mandate given to the IMO to address vessel sources of GHG emissions an Expert Group was established to study the various options available. The outcome of this Expert Group was the Report of the Expert Group on Feasibility Study and Impact Assessment of possible Market-based Measures (Expert Report).[9] The report was submitted to the IMO 61st Marine Environment Protection Committee (MEPC) for further discussion and consideration. The Expert Report is a detailed analysis of the proposal submitted by governments and organizations to address ship-based sources of greenhouse gases through market-based mechanisms (MBM).

This article will review the existing international climate change regime under the UNFCCC and its relation to international shipping. The problems of inter-regime compatibility will be analyzed following a brief summary of market based mechanisms proposed to the IMO.

II. *International Framework for Climate Change*

The "ultimate" objective of the UNFCCC as provided in Article 2 is "to achieve... stabilization of greenhouse gas concentrations in the atmosphere at a

[8] Article 2(2).

[9] Available online at http://www.imo.org/OurWork/Environment/PollutionPrevention/AirPollution/Documents/INF-2.pdf See also MEPC 61/INF.2/Corr.1 and MEPC 61/INF.2/Corr.2

level that would prevent dangerous anthropogenic interference with the climate system "...within a time frame sufficient to allow ecosystems to adapt naturally to climate change, to ensure that food production is not threatened and to enable economic development to proceed in a sustainable manner." Principles that are important to the implementation of the Convention include the principle of common but differentiated responsibilities, equity,[10] the inter-generational principle, the precautionary approach, and that developed countries take the lead in combating climate change and its adverse effect.[11] Furthermore, a key principle and central theme to the entire regime is that of recognizing the specific needs and special circumstances of developing country Parties, especially those that are particularly vulnerable to the adverse effects of climate change.[12] In other words, the UNFCCC system is based on a purposeful discrimination in favor of the developing countries.

The UNFCCC was structured to focus primarily on the mitigation of anthropogenic GHG emissions by developed countries.[13] The developed countries were categorized in two separate annexes: Annex I countries includes those countries that in 1992 were members of the Organisation for Economic Co-operation and Development (OECD) as well as the economies in transition (EIT).[14] Annex II includes the rich industrialized countries. The remaining non-Annex countries were comprised of the developing countries, who assume additional obligations under the Convention that include providing financial support to the developing countries and the transfer of environmentally sound technologies and know-how to all Parties, presumably including non-Annex II Parties listed in Annex I.[15]

The UNFCCC did not provide quantified emission limitations for the Annex I and II Parties other than the overall objectives under Article 2. Quantified emissions commitments were provided by the Kyoto Protocol. According to Article 3 of the Protocol Annex I, Parties are obligated to:

> *[I]ndividually or jointly, ensure that their aggregate anthropogenic carbon dioxide equivalent emissions of the greenhouse gases listed in Annex A do not exceed their assigned amounts, calculated pursuant to their quantified emission limitation and reduction commitments inscribed in Annex B and in accordance with the*

[10] While not expressly articulated in the UNFCCC the underlying rationale of the equity principle is in recognition of the historical responsibility that the industrialized developed countries have in climate change and the adverse impact it will have on developing countries with little if any historical responsibility.

[11] Article 3 (1).

[12] Article 3 (2).

[13] See Article 4.2.a.

[14] The Convention recognized a degree of flexibility for the former Eastern bloc Communist countries whose economies were negatively impacted following the dissolution of the former USSR in 1990.

[15] These would comprise the EITs and Turkey.

> *provisions of this Article, with a view to reducing their overall emissions of such gases by at least 5 per cent below 1990 levels in the commitment period 2008 to 2012.*

As part of creating a cost-efficient method for Annex I countries to meet their commitments to mitigate their national GHG emissions the Kyoto Protocol adopted a set of "flexible mechanisms" to supplement national mitigation efforts. The three Kyoto flexible mechanisms are Emission Trading (ETS),[16] Joint Implementation (JI)[17] and the Clean Development Mechanism (CDM).[18] Each, however, is distinct from the others in scope. The ETS and the JI are specifically limited to Annex I countries with commitments under Annex B of the Kyoto Protocol. Only Annex I Parties with commitments under Annex B are eligible to trade GHG emissions under the ETS. Furthermore, the Conference of the Parties is the only authority that can determine the principles, modalities, rules and guidelines, in particular for verification, reporting and accountability for emissions. The CDM is the only flexible mechanism that allows Annex I Parties to meet their compliance requirements by investing in low-emission technologies in developing countries, or non-Annex countries, thereby generating "certified emission reductions" (CERs) that can be used as offsets against their own commitments, or can be traded.[19]

The issue of regulating GHG emissions from bunker fuels had been on the agenda of the UNFCCC for many years.[20] Allocation, control and guidelines for reporting bunker fuel emissions in national inventory reports as required under the Convention were adopted early on by the Intergovernmental Panel on Climate Change (IPCC.)[21] However, three issues remained problematic: allocation of allowable bunker fuel emissions, control options and reliability of

---

[16] Article 17.

[17] Article 6.

[18] Article 12.

[19] C. Streck and J. Lin, 'Making Markets Work: A Review of CDM Performance and the Need for Reform', 19 *European Journal of International Law* (2008) 409.

[20] Technical Workshop on Emissions from Aviation and Maritime Transport: 4–5 Oct. 2007 (available online at http://www.iisd.ca/download/pdf/sd/ymbvol146num1e.pdf). Examples of early decisions are: Decision 9/2 (INC, 1994): In providing information on emissions from international aviation and marine bunker fuels, Parties should include such data, in a separate category, in their inventories of emissions on the basis of fuel sold and should, as far as possible, not include them in total national emissions; and Decision 4/CP.1 (1995). The COP decided that the SBSTA and SBI, taking fully into account ongoing work in Governments and international organizations, including the IMO and the ICAO, address the issue of the allocation and control of emissions from international bunker fuels, and report on this work to the Conference of the Parties at its second session.

[21] 1996 IPCC Guidelines for National Greenhouse Gas Inventories, emissions based upon fuel sold to ships or aircraft engaged in international transport should not be included in national totals, but reported separately.

inventories. The Kyoto Protocol chose to delegate the responsibility of reducing GHG emissions from ships and aviation bunker fuels to the IMO and International Civil Aviation Organization (ICAO) by requiring the Annex I Parties to: "pursue limitation or reduction of emissions of greenhouse gases not controlled by the Montreal Protocol from aviation and marine bunker fuels, working through the International Civil Aviation Organization and the International Maritime Organization, respectively."[22] This relieved Parties individually from the obligation to regulate GHG emissions from bunker fuels nationally, consistent with the international framework of both shipping and aviation. Furthermore, bunker fuels were not made part of the Kyoto target.

III. *Post-Kyoto 2012 Period*

The commitment period for the Kyoto Protocol was limited to a five-year interval that ends at the end of 2012. Negotiations for a new "legally binding instrument" to either extend or succeed the Kyoto Protocol commenced in 2007 in Bali where the Parties adopted the Bali Road Map (BAP).[23] One of the pivotal objectives of the BAP was to create the framework for negotiation and adoption of a "legally binding agreement" in 2009 at the much anticipated COP 15 and CMP 5 meeting to be held in Copenhagen. Bunker fuels were made part of the negotiations of the *Ad Hoc* Working Group on Long-term Cooperation (AWG-LCA).[24] However, the COP 15 and CMP 5 failed to achieve the required consensus and no final agreement on the future of post-2012 climate commitments was reached in Copenhagen other than for the Parties to "take note" of the Copenhagen Climate Change Accord, a political agreement, which did not include provisions on bunker fuels.[25]

No doubt much of the underlying reason why Copenhagen failed to produce the much-anticipated new climate change agreement stemmed from the significant changes in the global economic balance since 1992 and the impact these have had on the relationship between the Annex I developed country Parties with emission reduction commitments and the non-Annex developing countries

---

[22] Article 2.2.

[23] Dec.1/CP13. Available online at http://unfccc.int/resource/docs/2007/cop13/eng/06a01.pdf#page=3.

[24] See paras. 135–138 in the draft negotiation text FCCC/AWGLCA/2009/17. Available online at http://maindb.unfccc.int/library/view_pdf.pl?url=http://unfccc.int/resource/docs/2009/awglca6/eng/08.pdf. See also para. 32 of FCCC/CP/2010/2 available online at http://unfccc.int/resource/docs/2010/cop16/eng/02.pdf.

[25] FCCC/CP/2009/L.7 18 December 2009 available online at http://unfccc.int/resource/docs/2009/cop15/eng/l07.pdf.

claiming differential right of emissions. In the nearly two decades since the 1992 UNFCCC was adopted, the global economy has witnessed the colossal economic growth of China and other emerging economies such as India and Brazil. Several countries that were kept outside the UNFCCC annex categories continue to benefit from the preferential treatment accorded to developing countries regardless of their actual level of economic development. This in turn has raised questions as to the validity of the continued classification of certain non-Annex countries as "developing." This underlying fracture between the demands for development without commitments by the non-Annex economies and the demand for commitments by the Annex I countries also has significant implications for the role the IMO will have in regulating GHG emissions from maritime bunker fuels and shipping.

In December of 2010, Governments reassembled in Cancun, Mexico for the UNFCCC COP16/MOP 6. However, this time expectations were kept low as Governments realized that there was little prospect for adopting a final binding agreement for climate change. Tempered expectations and strong leadership by the Mexican Government enabled COP 16 to end on a relatively positive note with consensus achieved for adoption of a package of decisions called the "Cancun Agreement".[26] However, missing from the package of decisions was any agreement on regulation of bunker fuels and greenhouse gases from shipping activities. The division between the developed and developing countries institutionalized under the UNFCCC blocked the Parties from making any advancement. In particular, as will be discussed further below, it was the principle of common but differentiated responsibilities that was the major reason underlying the inability to reach an agreement. The IMO objectives at COP 16 were to continue to be entrusted with the development and enactment of global regulation for the control of greenhouse gas emissions from ships, to apply such regulation based on the principle of non-discrimination and to take fully into account the interests of developing countries through IMO's Technical Cooperation Programme through the distribution of revenues obtained from market-based instruments for shipping under the aegis of the IMO.[27] The IMO further expressed concern that international shipping would be subject to

[26] Bolivia remained as the sole negative vote against the adoption of the COP 16 package of decisions.

[27] See "IMO and COP 16" available online at http://www.imo.org/OurWork/Environment/PollutionPrevention/AirPollution/Pages/IMO-at-COP-16.aspx (Last visited 13 March 2011). See also the IMO submission to the 16th Conference of the Parties to the UNFCCC on "Greenhouse Gas Emissions from Ships Engaged in International Shipping," (5 November 2010) available online at http://unfccc.int/resource/docs/2010/smsn/igo/094.pdf.

double taxation coming from the UNFCCC and the IMO instruments related to regulating greenhouse gas emissions from international shipping.[28]

IV. *IMO and Climate Change*

The IMO is recognized as the principal international organization for regulating international shipping. Without question international shipping and aviation are among the most internationally regulated activities. Most international regulations and standards applicable to international shipping relating to safety, security and the environmental protection are developed and adopted in the IMO. It is generally understood that references in the 1982 United Nations Convention on the Law of the Sea (LOS Convention)[29] to the "competent international organization" in the singular implicitly refers to the IMO. Over the years the IMO has adopted numerous international agreements for the marine environment.[30]

As will be examined in greater detail below, international shipping standards are based on principles of non-discrimination among the different flag States. This has been enshrined in the IMO Constitution, which in Article 1 of its Convention states that one of the purposes of the IMO is "to encourage the removal of discriminatory action and unnecessary restrictions by Governments affecting shipping engaged in international trade." Furthermore, virtually every major IMO agreement had adopted rule of "no-more favorable treatment."[31] One of the problems that international shipping has been trying to solve is that of "flags of convenience", where ship owners register their vessels under the flag of a State that does not adhere to the shipping standards required under IMO instruments. The corollary to this in the world of climate change is the risk of 'leakage", that is when an activity that is made subject to the climate change

[28] Statement by the IMO Secretariat on "Further progress made by the Marine Environment Protection Committee on technical, operational and market-based reduction measures" submitted to COP 16. Available online at http://www.imo.org/OurWork/Environment/PollutionPrevention/AirPollution/Documents/COP%2016%20Statements/IMO%20LCA%20statement.pdf.

[29] The United Nations Convention on the Law of the Sea, adopted in Montego Bay on 10.12 1982, entered into force on 16.11 1994; 1833 UNTS 3.

[30] L. de La Fayette, 'The Marine Environment Protection Committee: The Conjunction of the Law of the Sea and International Environmental Law', 16 *Int'l J. Marine & Coastal* L. 155 (2001).

[31] Pamborides, G.P. *International Shipping Law Legislation and Enforcement*, Athens 1990, 106–112.

regulation, such as capped emissions or levies, the individuals impacted simply relocate to a 'climate regulation-free' jurisdiction.

V. *IMO Expert of Expert Group on Feasibility Study and Impact Assessment of Possible Market-based Measures submitted to MEPC*

The IMO Expert Group on Feasibility Study and Impact Assessment ("Expert Group") prepared a report of the different options available for the reduction of GHG emissions from shipping. Ten market-based mechanisms (MBM) proposals from different governments and organizations were introduced to the MEPC for consideration.[32] The Terms of Reference for the Expert Group study was to review the practicability of implementing the proposed MBMs, identify the GHG reduction potential from international shipping and its impact on world trade, including the maritime sector, and to examine how the socioeconomic needs of developing countries can be addressed in each option.[33] A very brief summary of the ten proposals is provided below. It should be noted that the Expert Group report is a technical and detailed assessment of each option. The following is simply a selective highlight of some of the key aspects.

a. *An International Fund for Greenhouse Gas Emission From Ships (Cyprus, Denmark, The Marshall Islands, Nigeria and IPTA-MEPC 60/4/8)*

The proposal foresees the establishment of a GHG Fund and the adoption of a new IMO Convention. The proposed convention would require the registration of bunker fuel *suppliers* located within the territory of a State Party and provide for the voluntary registration for bunker fuel suppliers in the territory of non-State suppliers. Ships, when taking bunker, will be required to make a GHG contribution to the Fund from either the bunker supplier or the ship owner. The Fund administrator will be responsible for the allocation of revenues according to decisions of the Parties. Also the Fund administrator would keep a ship-specific registry or account and maintain a list of all registered bunker fuel suppliers and submit an annual report. Ships flying the flag of party States will be required to purchase bunker fuel from registered suppliers. Ships will be required to keep on board a Bunker Delivery Note that must be shown to PSC upon request. The responsibility for monitoring and enforcement will belong to the flag-State.

[32] MEPC 61/INF.2, 13 August 2010, Full Report of the work undertaken by the Expert Group on Feasibility Study and Impact Assessment of possible Market-based Measures.

[33] *Id.* at 20.

The global reduction target is to be set either by UNFCCC or the IMO. The revenues obtained are to be allocated consistent with UNFCCC objectives and be compatible with any future climate change agreement. Revenues are to be used to cover administration costs of the GHG Fund Administrator and R & D activities and for IMO Technical Cooperation within existing IMO framework. There is a strong emphasis in favor of the least developing countries (LDCs) and the Small Island Developing States (SIDS). The proposal allows for the use of offsets obtained from CDMs and allows for the trade of out-of-sector carbon market emissions.

b. *Leveraged Incentive Scheme to Improve the Energy Efficiency of Ships Based on the International GHG Fund-Japan (MEPC 60/4/37)*

This proposal aims to target "direct" reduction of CO_2 emission from the shipping sector through a positive incentive scheme. A GHG contribution is levied from marine bunker fuel but part of it is refunded to "good performance ships." This will promote GHG emission reduction through increased ship efficiency. The proposal actually creates a dual incentive: to reduce the use of fuel in order to reduce GHG contribution and secondly, to receive a refund. In essence, it creates a GHG Fund with an additional refund incentive. The criteria for "good performance ships" are those ships with the highest level of energy efficiency. The question is how at the technical level ships will be monitored and assessed.

The proposal is designed to apply to all ships, making no distinction between flags. The positive aspect of this according to the Expert Group is the minimum risk of leakage. The revenues raised through contributions to the GHG Fund could be used to provide assistance to LDC countries. This proposal would also require the adoption of a new IMO Convention.

c. *Achieving Reduction in Greenhouse Gas Emissions from Ships through Port State Arrangement Utilizing the Ship Traffic, Energy and Environment Model, STEEM-Jamaica (MEPC 60/4/40)*

This proposal also foresees the adoption of a new IMO Convention and a GHG fund. The system would levy a uniform emissions charge – Port State Levy – on all ships calling at the respective ports based on the amount of fuel consumed on that voyage. The charge would be levied on the ship (irrespective of owner, charterer or operator) and not on the bunker suppliers. The amount of fuel consumed on the ship is to be regularly monitored and recorded. The fee would be structured to reward good performance along the lines of the Japanese proposal. For example, the fee would be staggered, higher for heavier and dirtier fuels and lower for cleaner fuels such as natural gas. The proposal also expressly foresees using the revenues of the fund for mitigation and adaptation measures to aid developing countries such as Small Island Developing States (SIDS).

The Expert Group report, however, evinced some concerns, especially as to the potential for leakage and problems of verification of fuel use as well as the potential administrative burden and costs in having each vessel monitor and record fuel use for each port visited (port-to port).

d. *Ship Efficiency and Credit Trading [SECT]: The United States (MEPC 60/4/12)*

This proposal aims to promote increased ship efficiency through imposition of phased-in mandatory energy efficiency standards on ships rather than a cap-and-trade on fuel use or the imposition of surcharges. It builds on the IMO Energy Efficiency Design Index (EEDI) for design standards for new ships. SECT also creates an efficiency credit-trading programme for ships. Ships operating more efficiently than required for the compliance period will be able to earn efficiency credits based on current ship efficiency rate and activity, which can be traded in the maritime sector. Ships operating less efficiently than required would have the option of purchasing these efficiency credits, as one method of achieving compliance with the efficiency standards.

This proposal does not include establishing a fund or a new IMO instrument leaving open the possibility to include it in Annex VI of MARPOL.

e. *Vessel Efficiency System (VES)- World Shipping Council (WSC) (MEPC 60/4/39)*

The Vessel System is similar to a US proposal in that it imposes mandatory efficiency standards on new and existing ships. Ships that fail to meet the efficiency standards are assessed a cost per ton (non-compliance fee). The fees go into a fund. The revenues can be used for R&D, out-of-sector CO_2 reductions or however the Parties decide.

Port State Control would be limited to verification of certificates, record books and Bunker Delivery Notes. Ships that fail compliance must pay fees on a regular interval through the fuel supplier or directly by the ship.

f. *Global Emission Trading System for International Shipping (ETS): Norway*

This is a classic "cap and trade" system. A new mechanism would be created under the auspices of the IMO. There would be a cap on total ship emissions. A target year (commitment period) would be established as would an ETS Registry for shipping. Ships would have to provide an annual emission report and keep control of bunker consumption, A survey and certification regime by the Flag Administration/RO would ensure that ships comply with emission allowances allotted (that have to be periodically surrendered). The system would allow to other UN emission credits such as CDM credits. It also would make available an exemption clause for certain voyages to developing countries such as SIDS/LDCs.

A Fund would be established by auctioning of emission allowances. The Fund would be administered by an international entity that would be under the control of the Parties to the system. The GHG Fund can be used for climate change mitigation and adaptation purposes on developing countries as well as technical cooperation activities under the IMO framework.

g. *ETS–United Kingdom (MEPC 60/4/26)*

The UK proposed the creation of a Global Emissions Trading System. Ship operators would be responsible for compliance evidenced by a Greenhouse Gas Certificate they would be required to keep on board ship at all times. An overall global cap with fixed allowances for ship emissions would be determined and then allowances auctioned. To ensure certainty for the shipping industry, a long-term declining trajectory of emission reductions would be established.

Ship operators would be required to keep a record of fuel purchases by using a Bunker Delivery Note mechanism that is already part of MARPOL Annex VI. The ETS would be linked to the global carbon economy permitting allowances and project credits from other sectors could be purchased and used in the shipping sector.

h. *Further Elements for the Development of an Emissions Trading System for International Shipping-France (MEPC 60/4/41)*

This proposal seeks to supplement the Norwegian proposal. It foresees creating a global cap rather than a cap on specific parties or individual ships. Based on the cap a number of shipping units would be auctioned. It would also be based on an open market system that would allow ships to use credits from other regulated carbon markets, in particular CDM credits.

An administrative body under the control of the Parties (COP) would be created. The administrative body would have the responsibility of managing the shipping CO_2 registry. Each ship would be given an account in the registry identified by its IMO number. Ships would be required to have on board at all times a Bunker Delivery Note that indicates the amount of CO_2 units due by a ship for each bunkering action.

A GHG Fund would be established with the auctioned revenues and managed by the administrative body. The GHG Fund would be used for climate change mitigation and adaptation actions in developing countries as well as technical cooperation under the IMO.

i. *Market-based Instruments: A Penalty on Trade and Development – The Bahamas (MEPC 60/4/10)*

The Bahamas did not submit a proposal but drew attention to the problems associated with the market-based approaches and levies. As a developing island

State that is susceptible to the impacts of climate change, the Bahamas is also an important flag State and for this reason is sensitive to any additional financial burdens on shipping from either emission trading or levy schemes, especially for developing countries.

j. *A Rebate Mechanism for a Market-based Instrument for International Shipping-IUCN (MEPC 60/4/55)*

The IUCN proposal is a two-step process that seeks to reconcile the principle of CBDR with the impact of implementing market based instruments within the international shipping context on developing countries. On the one hand, the IUCN recognizes the problems that a differentiated system could create on international shipping, and on the other hand, the unfair burden of the costs of MBI to developing countries. The IUCN proposal entails the use of a rebate system to balance the costs of MBI between the developed and developing counties. Based on the view that all countries benefit from international shipping, the IUCN proposes that such benefit can be best calculated based on the imports of a country. Rather than using fuel consumed as the parameter for assessing any emission levy, the IUCN proposal would use import data instead. The principle of CBDR would be accomplished by a rebate where "[e]ach developing country Party to the UNFCCC would be entitled to obtain an unconditional payment (rebate) equal to the cost incurred due to the maritime MBI."[34] The amount of rebate would be calculated annually in proportion to the country's share of global imports by value.

The reliance on proportion of global imports would distribute the burden of the MBI more equitably between the developed countries and the developing countries. Moreover, the revenues generated from this levy would be used to assist developing countries in combating climate change. Furthermore, the funds would be managed by the UNFCCC and not the IMO.

VI. *Inter-regime Compatibility*

The linkage between the IMO and the UNFCCC raises fundamental questions of compatibility between the two regimes. This issue has been the source of heated debates at the IMO. The main points of this debate center on the legal compatibility between the "no more favorable treatment" principle key to IMO Conventions and the principles of 'common but differentiated responsibilities' dictate that the developed countries take the lead in combating climate change. Also, related is the question of whether the Annex-based system

[34] Paragraph 17.

under the UNFCCC is compatible with the "tonnage" based and flag State system that characterizes international shipping and the IMO conventions. Thirdly is the question of whether the IMO should be undertaking activities of a financial character. Other differences between the two regimes include the process by which decisions are taken: the IMO has adopted the tacit amendment mechanism[35] whereas the UNFCCC is structured on consensus-based decision-making.[36]

a. *No More Favorable Treatment vs. Common but Differentiated Responsibilities*

The "no more favorable treatment" principle is included in many of the major IMO Conventions such as the Safety of Life at Sea Convention 1974/1978 (SOLAS)[37] and MARPOL '73.[38] It aims to prevent "free-riders" and create an equal playing field by requiring that no more favorable treatment is shown to vessels flying the flag of a non-Party to the convention than those flying the flag of a Party. This is in turn closely linked to the problem of "flags of convenience" which creates a system of unfair competition. The objective is to promote safety of navigation and protection of the environment based on the standards adopted at the IMO. However, these involve costs and if certain ship owners can avoid these costs by registering under the flag of a non-Party State, not only will the objectives sought by the IMO through these Conventions be undermined but also the field of competition in a highly competitive sector would be skewed in favor of sub-standard shipping.

The principle of common but differentiated responsibilities adopted in the UNFCCC, on the other hand, purposefully seeks to alter the playing field in favor of developing countries in order to allow them to develop sustainably.[39] Article 3(1) of the Convention states that Parties the "should protect the climate

[35] The 'tacit amendment procedure' aims to facilitate the amendment procedure by giving effect to amendments against parties who do not file an objection within a specified time period. See Pamborides, *supra* note 31, at 108–109.

[36] Farhana Yamin and Joanna Depledge, *The International Climate Change Regime: A Guide to Rules Institutions and Procedures*, (Cambridge 2004), 432–434.

[37] Article II of the 1978 Protocol to SOLAS provides that "With respect to ships of non-Parties of the Convention and the present Protocol, the Parties shall apply the requirements of the Convention and the present Protocol as may be necessary to ensure that no more favourable treatment is given to such ships."

[38] Article 5(4) of MARPOL '73 provides: "With respect to the ship of non-Parties to the Convention, Parties shall apply the requirements of the present Convention as may be necessary to ensure that no more favourable treatment is given to such ships."

[39] C. Stone, 'Common but Differentiated Responsibilities under International Law', 98 *American Journal of International Law* (2004), 276–301; Yamin, F. and Depledge, J. *The International Climate Change Regime: A Guide to Rules Institutions and Procedures*, Cambridge 2004, 69–70.

system for the benefit of present and future generations in accordance with their common but differentiated responsibilities." Furthermore, developed countries are required to take the "lead" in combating climate change. Moreover, according to Article 4 of the UNFCCC, all Parties commit to undertaking certain obligations; however, this commitment is qualified by the language of "taking into account their common but differentiated responsibilities and their specific national and regional developmental priorities." The UNFCCC and the Kyoto Protocol are expressly structured to favor economically the developing and least developing countries. The Annex II countries are committed to providing financial, technological and capacity building support to the developing countries. This codified and institutionalized differentiated system of legal obligations and economic commitments has been carried over into the negotiation of the post-2012 period where the Bali Action Plan is structured around the principle of common but differentiated responsibilities.

b. *Mixing Flag States and Annex States*

There are different practical problems in trying to reconcile the purposeful discrimination pursued under the UNFCCC and the non-discrimination approach of the IMO. For example, the classification systems of the two regimes are based on different criteria and seek to achieve different objectives. The UNFCCC categorizes countries based on economic development whereas the IMO system is based principally on flag States. The question is whether these two different systems can be combined. For example, would this mean that vessels flying the flags of developing countries, or non-Annex countries would be accorded greater rights of GHG emissions to supposedly further their rights of sustainable development? Would such a system create a new set of "GHG emission" flags of convenience? In climate change jargon, would this create a "leakage" problem?[40]

To answer this question requires assessing how the Annex categories under the UNFCCC would interrelate with the current tonnage and flag registry of ships. The flag State is the key party in the international regime of shipping. Most IMO Conventions require a combination of a minimum number of State ratifications and cumulative vessel tonnage by the ratifying flag States to enter into effect. The importance of the flag State in prescriptive and enforcement functions is also codified international law. Applicable provisions of the 1982 LOS Convention provide that the flag State has the principal

[40] 'Leakage' is the consequence of when measures for reducing emissions in a certain sector or activity results in the relocation of that sector or activity to a jurisdiction where such measures are not imposed.

Table 2. Percentage of Annex I countries and flag State tonnage

Annex I Flag States
32.7% of global ships
25.46% GT
22.28% DW
Non-Annex I FS
67.3% of global ships
74.54% GT
77.72% DW

Source: Second IMO GHG Study (2009)

obligations for adopting the laws and regulations for shipping under its flag and for enforcement.[41]

Secondly, in the UNFCCC and climate change context, allocation of greenhouse gas emissions is attached to territorial activities, such as energy production or factory activities. Shipping, by contrast, is mobile and transboundary which in turn creates difficulty in determining how allocation of greenhouse emissions would be done and how they could be effectively monitored and calculated. Under the 1982 LOS Convention and customary international law, the flag State is accorded principal responsibility for adoption and enforcement of shipping standards. However, given the reality of shipping and the issue of a "genuine link" serious doubts emerge as to how a territorial system of emission allocation can be assessed and accounted for within the shipping system.[42] As shown in Table 2 much of the world tonnage sails under the flag of States that are not listed under the UNFCCC Annexes; in other words, they are flags of developing countries. There would be a great incentive for ship owners to register their vessels under the flags of non-Annex States in order to benefit from the emission advantages that would be accorded under the discriminatory system of the UNFCCC. This would in turn undermine the very objective of reducing GHG emissions from international shipping.

c. *Climate Change, Emissions Trading and the IMO Mandate*

The objectives and functions of the IMO are set out in its Constitution. Among the key purposes enumerated in Article 1 of the Convention are: first, "to provide

[41] Article 91 of the 1982 LOS Convention requires that there be a 'genuine link' between the State and the ship, and Article 94 enumerates the duties of the flag State.

[42] See C. Pisani, 'Fair at Sea: The Design of a Future Legal Instrument on Marine Bunker Fuels Emissions within the Climate Change Regime', 33 *Ocean Development & International Law*, (2002) 57–76, 68.

a machinery for co-operation among Governments in the field of governmental regulation and practices related to technical matters of all kinds affecting shipping. . . ." Second, "to encourage and facilitate the general adoption of the highest practicable standards in matters concerning maritime safety, efficiency of navigation and prevention and control of marine pollution. . . ." Third, "to encourage the removal of discriminatory action and unnecessary restrictions by Governments affecting shipping engaged in international trade. . . ."

The role of the IMO in removing discriminatory practices raised concerns among certain governments that the IMO would become involved in commercial activities. Governments were given assurances that the IMO would not be engaged in commercial or economic activities and in some cases this point was included in reservations during ratifications of the IMO Convention.[43] The responsibilities for addressing commercial aspects of shipping were delegated to the United Nations Conference on Trade and Development (UNCTAD).[44]

One of the fatal flaws in the ten MBM proposals is their requirement that the IMO would be involved in financial activities such as emission trading or administering a fund. While there is some argument that the International Oil Pollution Compensation Funds (IOPC Funds)[45] provide a precedent, in reality the two fund systems are quite different. The IOPC Fund has a narrowly drawn purpose which is to provide supplemental compensation in cases of oil pollution from tankers.[46] The IOPC Fund is part of the IMO liability and compensation legal framework for oil spill pollution established by the Civil Liability Convention. It is funded by levies collected by a State from entities that import oil carried by sea. The IOPC Funds, including the Supplementary Fund apply only if the insurance coverage under the CLC is inadequate to cover damage and losses arising from compensable claims from an oil spill coming within the scope of application of the liability and compensation instruments. The climate change GHG funds proposed to the IMO, on the other hand, have a broader purpose and involve commercial activities, such as trading of emissions.

---

43 Pamborides, *supra* note 31 at p. 83.

44 In 1983, UNCTAD and IMO signed a Memorandum of Understanding for cooperation.

45 International Convention on the Establishment of an International Fund for Compensation for Oil Pollution Damage 1971 (FUND 1992) Done at London, 27 November 1992, Entry into force, 30 May 1996, Protocol of 2000 to the International Convention on for Oil Pollution on the Establishment of an International Fund for Compensation of for Oil Pollution1 (FUND 2000) Done at London, 27 September 2000, Entry into force 27 June 2001.

46 There are three IOPC funds: the 1971 Fund, the 1992 Fund and the Supplementary Fund.

UNFCCC	IMO
• CBDR • Equity (HR) • More favorable treatment of developing countries	• No discrimination • NMFT • Flags/Ports of convenience
• Right of sustainable development of Developing Countries	• Non-commercial role of the IMO (UNCTAD)
• Duty of developed countries to take the lead	• Governance structures IMO Assembly and Council
• Annex/Non-Annex system • Role of the COP (Consensus)	• Tacit approval for IMO Conventions

VII. *Annex VI of MARPOL '73*

An alternative to the proposals for creating a market-based system for regulating GHG emissions from shipping is to develop legal regulations within the existing framework of international law under the 1982 LOS Convention and IMO Conventions, in particular Annex VI of the International Convention for the Prevention of Pollution, 1973/78 (MARPOL).[47] The 1982 LOS Convention lays out the overall regulatory framework for shipping, allocating prescriptive and enforcement competence on vessel source pollution, including vessel source atmospheric pollution,[48] among the coastal, flag and port States. The virtually exclusive role of the International Maritime Organization in regulating international shipping activities is implicitly recognized in UNCLOS by the reference in singular to the "competent international organization." And under the existing instruments adopted by the IMO, the MARPOL Convention is without doubt the principal instrument for regulating vessel-source pollution. There are six Annexes to the MARPOL Convention,[49] vessel source pollution being covered under Annex VI. The emissions covered by Annex VI are those of nitrogen oxides (NOx), sulphur oxides, volatile organic compounds, and ozone-depleting substances. However, notably absent are greenhouse gas emissions.

[47] International Convention for the Prevention of Pollution by Ships, 2 November 1973, reprinted in ILM 1319 (1973); Protocol of 1978 Relating to the International Convention for the Prevention of Pollution from Ships, 1973, 16 February 1978, reprinted in 17 ILM 546 (1978); *See* Pisani, "Fair at Sea: The Design of a Future Legal Instrument on Marine Bunker Fuels Emissions within the Climate Change Regime," *supra* note 42 at note 47.

[48] Article 212 provides that states are to adopt laws and regulations to prevent, reduce, and control such pollution from or through the atmosphere.

[49] The other five annexes are: Annex I for oil; Annex II for noxious substances (such as chemicals); Annex III for harmful substances in packaged form; Annex IV for sewage; and Annex V for garbage.

The MARPOL methodology is regulatory through command and control mechanisms and is not a market-based system. Specific activities are prohibited, such as the discharge of oil and oily substances into the marine environment, or regulated, such as the requirement for double hull tankers. Enforcement is entrusted principally to the flag State, with the additional supervisory control of port State control. Thus, Pisani favors developing an IMO instrument regulating bunker fuel emissions based on the framework for shipping under the 1982 LOS Convention. He states that:

> *Accordingly, a future legal instrument on bunker fuels emissions would oblige its parties to enforce these international policies and measures and stretch their applicability to all parties to UNCLOS, as is currently the case regarding MARPOL. States would be responsible, through port state control, to ensure compliance with bunker fuels emissions rules and standards by vessels that enter their territory. In this manner, the UNCLOS framework provides for a differentiated allocation of responsibility by requiring flag States and allowing port States and coastal States to enforce such international rules and standards. This allocation of responsibilities reflects a commitment to fairness. Thus, a future legal instrument for bunker fuels emissions based upon the framework of UNCLOS would be in compliance with the overarching principles of the climate change regime.*[50]

The adoption of a specific Annex to MARPOL regulating GHG would be consistent with the practice and legal framework of the IMO and avoid having the IMO engage in activities that could be challenged for falling outside its scope of competence, especially in relation to financial activities such as emission trading, levies and managing climate change funds. During the 62nd session of the Marine Environmental Protection Committee (MEPC 62) of the IMO, the Parties decided to amend Annex VI on air pollution by adding a new Chapter 4 regulating energy efficiency for ships by making Energy Efficiency Design Index (EEDI) mandatory for new ships 400 gross tons and above engaged in international voyages, and the Ship Energy Efficiency Management Plan (SEEMP) for all ships.[51] All ships will be required to keep on board a SEEMP, which can be part of the Ship Safety Management Plan.[52] However, the amendment was not adopted by consensus with a number of Parties disagreeing with it.[53] The MEPC will continue to further develop guidelines for both.

---

[50] Pisani, *supra* note 47, at p. 69.

[51] Res. MEPC 62/6/3, adopted 15 July 2011. The EEDI will enter into effect 1 January 2013 http://www.imo.org/MediaCentre/PressBriefings/Pages/42–mepc-ghg.aspx.

[52] Regulation 22. *Id.*

[53] See statements of Brazil, India and Peru at Annex 8 to Report of the Marine Environment Protection Committee on its Sixty-Second Session (MEPC 62/24, 26 July 2011).

Conclusions

The UNFCCC and IMO regimes are fundamentally different and any attempt to combine the two raises important legal questions. The UNFCCC framework is expressly based on discrimination between developed and developing countries as reflected in the principles of CBDR. By contrast the IMO operates on the principle of non-discrimination and NMFT. The underlying goal of CBDR is to remedy past inequities of causation for climate change attributed to the high-energy use of developing countries. The objective of non-discrimination and NMFT in shipping is to avoid market distortions and the problems of flags or ports of convenience where lower standard shipping threatens both safety of navigation and the protection of the environment. These two systems cannot easily be wed with one another.

An ancillary problem is the underlying financial activity associated with the UNFCCC, especially in implementation of its flexible mechanisms, which rely on market-based instruments. Early on, the IMO agreed to exclude financial aspects of shipping from its activities. If the IMO were to assume the role of a regulatory body for emission trading as well as for the management of funds of revenues levied from ships, it would be in clear breach of this commitment and of its practice since becoming operational over fifty years ago.

The alternative that would best meet the needs of the UNFCCC and Kyoto Protocol without compromising the legal and institutional framework of the IMO is either to adopt a new annex to MARPOL or to amend Annex VI. In July 2011, the Parties to MARPOL at the IMO chose to amend Annex VI by instituting mandatory Ship EEID for new vessels and SEEMP for all vessels. This is consistent with the practice of the IMO and aligns with its existing legal framework.

Panel II: Piracy and Terrorism

MARITIME TERRORISM AND THE LAW OF THE SEA: BASIC PRINCIPLES AND NEW CHALLENGES

Robert Beckman and Tara Davenport[1]

Abstract

General principles governing a State's jurisdiction over maritime activities are well established under the United Nations Convention on the Law of the Sea (UNCLOS) and under principles of customary international law. First, only the coastal State has enforcement jurisdiction in maritime zones subject to its sovereignty and second, ships on the high seas are subject to the exclusive jurisdiction of the flag State, with limited exceptions. However, after the terrorist attacks on the United States on 11th September 2001, concerns were raised that traditional principles governing jurisdiction over maritime activities could potentially hamper efforts to combat acts of maritime terrorism. This is amply illustrated by the debates that surrounded the negotiation and adoption of certain instruments to combat maritime terrorism such as the 2005 Protocol to the 1988 SUA Convention for the Suppression of Unlawful Acts Against the Safety of Maritime Navigation, the Security Council Resolutions on the Illicit Trafficking of Weapons of Mass Destruction (WMD) and the US-led Proliferation Security Initiative (PSI), with some States fearing that these instruments would go beyond general principles governing jurisdiction over maritime activities.

To this end, this paper first discusses the general principles governing a State's jurisdiction over maritime activities. It then examines the various instruments adopted both before and after 11th September 2001 that can be used to combat maritime terrorism, and the extent to which these instruments are consistent with general principles governing jurisdiction over maritime activities. It then explores the extent to which States have participated in and effectively implemented these measures. Last, the paper concludes that the measures adopted to deal with maritime terrorism are consistent with general principles governing a State's jurisdiction over maritime activities and argues that focus should now shift to how to encourage participation in such measures and ensure effective implementation of such measures by States.

I. *Introduction*

After the terrorist attacks on the United States on 11th September 2001, States and international organizations were forced to rethink the threat of maritime terrorism. They recognized that if terrorist groups could use commercial aircraft

---

[1] Robert Beckman is the Director of the Centre for International Law at the National University of Singapore. Tara Davenport is a Research Associate at the Centre for International Law. The authors' PowerPoint presentation can be viewed at http://www.virginia.edu/colp/pdf/kmi-beckman.pdf.

in attacks, they could also use commercial shipping in the same manner.[2] While there is no internationally accepted definition of maritime terrorism,[3] it can encompass a wide range of potential attack scenarios[4] including ships being hijacked, ships being used as weapons against other ships or port facilities; terrorists entering countries posing as seafarers; and weapons of mass destruction being shipped on merchant ships to terrorist organizations.[5]

The legal regime governing a State's jurisdiction over maritime activities are set out in the 1982 *United Nations Convention on the Law of the Sea* (UNCLOS)[6] as well as general principles of customary international law. To summarize briefly these principles, first, only the coastal State has enforcement jurisdiction in maritime zones subject to its sovereignty and second, ships on the high seas are subject to the exclusive jurisdiction of the flag State, with limited exceptions.

Maritime terrorism poses a particular challenge for the legal regime governing a State's jurisdiction over maritime activities. Prior to 11th September 2001, legal instruments that addressed maritime terrorism, such as the 1988 *Convention for the Suppression of Unlawful Acts against the Safety of Maritime Navigation*,[7] (1988 SUA Convention) focused on the prosecution and punishment of perpetrators of maritime terrorism after the attacks had occurred. As will be explained below, these instruments were consistent with principles governing jurisdiction over maritime activities.

After 11th September 2001, concerns were raised that the traditional principles governing jurisdiction over maritime activities could potentially hamper

---

[2] S.L. Hodgkinson, E. Cook, T. Fichter, C. Fleming, J. Shapiro, J. Mellis, B. Boutelle, S. Sarnoski and G. Noone, 'Challenges to Maritime Interception Operations in the War on Terror: Bridging the Gap', 22 *American University International Law Review* (2006–2007) 583 at 587.

[3] The Council for Security Cooperation in the Asia Pacific (CSCAP) has defined maritime terrorism as "the use of violence at sea or to a ship or fixed platform for political ends, including any use of violence for the purpose of putting the public or any section of the public in fear." See CSCAP Memorandum No. 5 on Cooperation for Law and Order at Sea, available online at <http://www.cscap.org/uploads/docs/Memorandums/CSCAP%20Memorandum%20No%205%20—%20Cooperation%20for%20Law%20and%20Order%20at%20Sea.pdf>.

[4] P. Parfomak and J. Frittelli, 'Maritime Security: Potential Terrorist Attacks and Protection Priorities', Congressional Research Service Report for Congress available at <http://www.fas.org/sgp/crs/homesec/RL33787.pdf>.

[5] R. Beckman 'International Responses to Combat Maritime Terrorism', in Ramraj, Hor, Roach (eds.), *Global Anti-Terrorism Law and Policy* (Cambridge University Press, 2005), pp. 248–269 at 248.

[6] *United Nations Convention on the Law of the Sea,* adopted 10 December 1982, 1833 UNTS 3 (entered into force 16 November 1994) (UNCLOS).

[7] *Convention for the Suppression of Unlawful Acts Against the Safety of Maritime Navigation,* adopted 10 March 1988, 1678 UNTS 221 (entered into force 1 March 1992) (1988 SUA Convention).

efforts to *prevent* acts of maritime terrorism. In maritime zones outside territorial sovereignty, only the flag State could board and arrest ships (or consent to such a boarding by another State) that were preparing to commit an act of maritime terrorism. To this end, this article examines the measures that have been taken, both before 2001 and after 2001, to prevent and suppress acts of maritime terrorism and discusses how these measures have presented challenges to the traditional principles governing jurisdiction over maritime activities.

Part II will examine the general principles of international law governing jurisdiction over maritime activities. Part III will examine how three of the UN counter-terrorism conventions adopted before 2001 can be utilized to combat maritime terrorism. Parts IV and V will examine the actions taken by the UN Security Council and the International Maritime Organization (IMO) in response to the terrorist attacks on the United States on 11th September 2001. Part VI will examine the actions taken by the UN Security Council in response to the threat of the proliferation of weapons of mass destruction from the Democratic People's Republic of Korea (DPRK). Part VII will examine the US-led Proliferation Security Initiative (PSI) and its provisions designed to counter the threat of the proliferation of weapons of mass destruction (WMD) and their delivery systems by sea. Part VIII will address the extent to which States have participated in and implemented the various measures adopted to combat maritime terrorism. In Part IX, this paper concludes that the measures adopted are consistent with principles governing jurisdiction over maritime activities, and that if States participate and effectively implement such measures, there will be a robust legal framework to address maritime terrorism.

II. *Principles Governing Jurisdiction over Maritime Activities*

Jurisdiction refers to the:

> *Power of a State under international law to govern persons and property by its municipal law. It includes both the power to prescribe rules (prescriptive jurisdiction) and the power to enforce them (enforcement jurisdiction). The latter includes both executive and judicial powers of enforcement.*[8]

"Prescriptive jurisdiction" generally refers to the authority of a State to *prescribe* laws and make them applicable to persons or circumstances.[9] "Enforcement jurisdiction" describes the "authority of a State to take action to enforce those

---

[8] D. Harris, *Cases and Materials on International Law,* 7th Edition (London, Sweet and Maxwell, 2010), p. 227.

[9] See International Bar Association, *Report of the Task Force on Extraterritorial Jurisdiction,* July 2008 available at <http://tinyurl.com/taskforce-etj-pdf> at pp. 7–8.

laws through, for example, arresting, detaining, prosecuting, convicting, sentencing and punishing persons for breaking those laws."[10]

The principles governing jurisdiction over maritime activities, as set out in customary international law and UNCLOS, depend on whether the act took place within maritime zones under the territorial sovereignty of a coastal State, or in maritime zones outside the territorial sovereignty of a coastal State.

In maritime zones under the territorial sovereignty of a coastal State, i.e. internal waters, archipelagic waters and territorial seas, coastal States have both prescriptive and enforcement jurisdiction.[11] No State may exercise enforcement jurisdiction in an area under the territorial sovereignty of another State without its express consent.[12]

In maritime zones outside the territorial sovereignty of a coastal State i.e. the Exclusive Economic Zone (EEZ) and highs seas, coastal States are permitted to exercise their prescriptive jurisdiction subject to any rules prohibiting such prescription.[13] However, only the flag State can exercise enforcement jurisdiction over vessels in the EEZ and on the high seas.[14] Such ships may not be boarded without the express consent of the flag State or the master.

There are limited exceptions to the principle of exclusive enforcement jurisdiction of the flag State in the EEZ and on the high seas. First, warships or ships on government service of all States[15] may board and arrest pirate ships in areas outside the territorial sovereignty of any State i.e. in the EEZ and on the high seas.[16] A ship is considered a pirate ship if it is intended by the persons in dominant control to be used for the purpose of committing any of the acts of piracy referred to in Article 101 of UNCLOS.[17]

---

[10] *Ibid.*

[11] See Articles 2 and 49 of UNCLOS, *supra* note 6.

[12] *SS Lotus (France v. Turkey)* 1927 PCIJ (ser A) No. 10 at 18–19.

[13] *SS Lotus (France v. Turkey), ibid.* However, it should be noted that there is an alternative view that a State is not able to extend its prescriptive jurisdiction outside its territory unless permissive rules support such an exercise: See V. Lowe, 'Jurisdiction', in M. Evans, (ed.) *International Law*, 2nd edition, (Oxford, Oxford University Press, 2006), p. 335.

[14] Article 89 of UNCLOS, *supra* note 6, provides that "(n)o State may validly purport to subject any part of the high seas to its sovereignty." Article 94 sets out the duties of the flag State over vessels flying its flag on the high seas. Articles 88 to 115 on the high seas apply to the exclusive economic zone in so far as they are not incompatible with Part V on the exclusive economic zone (Article 58 (2), UNCLOS).

[15] Article 107 of UNCLOS, *supra* note 6.

[16] See Article 105 of UNCLOS, *supra* note 6, which allows all States to seize a pirate ship or a ship taken by piracy and under the control of pirates (piracy is defined in Article 101), and arrest the persons and seize the property on board. Article 105 applies in the EEZ by virtue of Article 58 (2) of UNCLOS.

[17] See Article 103 of UNCLOS, *supra* note 6, for the definition of a "pirate ship."

Second, a warship may board another ship in the EEZ of another State or on the high seas if there are reasonable grounds for suspecting that the ship is engaged in piracy, the slave trade, or unauthorized broadcasting, the ship is without nationality or the ship is the same flag as the warship. This is known as the right of visit under UNCLOS.[18]

Third, UNCLOS also recognizes that additional reasons for exercising the right to board foreign flagged ships may be established by treaty.[19]

Fourth, it should also be mentioned that a State has enforcement jurisdiction under UNCLOS in relation to certain other matters. UNCLOS gives coastal States the power to enforce their fishing laws and regulations in their EEZs including the power to board, inspect and arrest ships violating its fisheries laws and regulations,[20] as well as limited enforcement jurisdiction to enforce their laws governing marine scientific research and pollution of the marine environment.[21]

These exceptions to the principle of exclusive flag State jurisdiction in areas outside the sovereignty of any State do not apply to warships and government ships owned and operated by States and used only on government non-commercial service. Such ships have complete immunity from the jurisdiction of any State other than the flag State.[22]

III. *Global Conventions relating to Maritime Terrorism Prior to 2001*

1. *Overview of the UN Counter-Terrorism Conventions*

Prior to 2001, the UN had not been able to agree on a general definition of terrorism. However, a series of global conventions were adopted to create a framework for cooperation among States Parties for specific offences. The first of these was the *Hague Convention for the Suppression of Unlawful Seizure of Aircraft*, 1970.[23] These conventions are often referred to as the UN

[18] See Article 110 of UNCLOS, *supra* note 6, on the Right of Visit. This would apply in the EEZ by virtue of Article 58 (2).

[19] Article 110 of UNCLOS, *supra* note 6, provides that "except where acts of interference derive from powers conferred by treaty."

[20] See Article 73 of UNCLOS, *supra* note 6.

[21] Article 56 (b) of UNCLOS, *supra* note 6, gives the coastal State jurisdiction over marine scientific research and the protection and preservation of the marine environment in the EEZ.

[22] See Articles 95 and 96, UNCLOS, *supra* note 6.

[23] *Hague Convention for the Suppression of Unlawful Seizure of Aircraft*, Adopted on 16 December 1970, 860 UNTS 105 (entered into force on 14 October 1971).

counter-terrorism conventions, even though the acts that are made offences in most of the conventions do not require a terrorist purpose or motive.[24]

The UN counter-terrorism convention that was specifically designed to address maritime terrorism was the 1988 SUA Convention and the 1988 *Protocol for the Suppression of Unlawful Acts against the Safety of Fixed Platforms located on the Continental Shelf*[25] (1988 Platforms Protocol). The 1988 SUA Convention and 1988 Platforms Protocol were adopted in response to the 1985 hijacking by extremists of the Italian-flag cruise ship *Achille Lauro* in the Mediterranean Sea.

Two more of the UN counter-terrorism conventions can also be used against certain acts of maritime terrorism. The 1979 *Convention against the Taking of Hostages*[26] (1979 Hostages Convention) applies whenever the passengers or crew of a ship are taken hostage for ransom. The 1999 *International Convention for the Suppression of the Financing of Terrorism*[27] (1999 Terrorist Financing Convention) provides that it is an offence for a person to finance offences under the 1988 SUA Convention or the 1979 Hostages Convention. We will first examine the general framework for each of these Conventions, and then examine the specific offences under each of them.

2. *Framework for Cooperation in the UN Counter-Terrorism Conventions*

The framework for cooperation among States Parties is the same in all of the UN counter-terrorism conventions. In essence, they establish universal jurisdiction among States Parties for the specific offences defined in the Conventions, and obligate States Parties to either prosecute or extradite any alleged offenders present in their territory. All of the UN counter-terrorist conventions have the following features:

First, they define specific acts which all States Parties are obliged to make criminal offences under their domestic law punishable by serious penalties.

---

[24] However, Article 2 (1) (b) of the *International Convention for the Suppression of the Financing of Terrorism,* unlike the previous counter-terrorism conventions, contains what has been described as a mini-definition of terrorism: See *Implementation Kits for the International Counter-Terrorism Conventions,* 2002 available at <http://www.thecommonwealth.org/shared_asp_files/uploadedfiles/%7B8AE4DB15–88A5–46F2–8037–357DFF7D3EC1%7D_Implementation%20Kits%20for%20Counter-Terrorism.pdf>.

[25] *Protocol for the Suppression of Unlawful Acts against the Safety of Fixed Platforms located on the Continental Shelf,* adopted 10 March 1988 1678 UNTS 304 (entered into force 1 March 1992) (1988 Platform Protocol).

[26] *Convention Against the Taking of Hostages,* adopted 17 December 1979, 1316 UNTS 205 (entered into force 3 June 1983) (1979 Hostages Convention).

[27] *International Convention for the Suppression of the Financing of Terrorism,* adopted 9 December 1999, 2178 UNTS 229 (entered into force 10 April 2002) (1999 Terrorism Financing Convention).

States Parties are also obliged to provide that it is an offence to be an accomplice or to abet the commission of the offence.

Second, they place an obligation on States Parties to establish jurisdiction over offences that take place in their territory, as well as offences that take place outside their territory provided that there is some jurisdictional nexus between the State Party and the offence, for example, when the alleged offender is a national of the State Party or the offence takes place on board a ship or aircraft registered in that State Party. This is consistent with general principles of criminal jurisdiction recognized under international law.[28] More importantly, the conventions also oblige States Parties to establish jurisdiction over offences where the alleged offender is present in its territory and the State does not extradite him to any of the States Parties having jurisdiction over the offence. This is a form of universal jurisdiction based on the presence of the offender, sometimes described as "subsidiary universal jurisdiction."[29]

Third, they place an obligation on all States Parties to take alleged offenders into custody if they are present in their territory, and to either extradite them to another State Party or submit the case to its competent authorities for the purpose of prosecution. This is referred to as the obligation to "extradite or prosecute."[30]

Fourth, all the counter-terrorism conventions contain measures to facilitate extradition of offenders found in the territory of a State Party. First, a convention offence is deemed to be included as an extraditable offence in any existing extradition treaty between States Parties. State Parties also undertake to include the convention offence as an extraditable offence in every future extradition treaty concluded between them. Second, State Parties which make extradition conditional on the existence of an extradition treaty, may, at their option, consider the convention as the legal basis for extradition in respect of the convention offence. Third, where States Parties do not make extradition conditional on the existence of a treaty, they are required to recognize the convention offence as an extraditable offence as between themselves.

Fifth, States Parties are obliged to afford one another the greatest measure of co-operation in connection with criminal proceedings to prosecute the offenders.

---

28 Under international law, there are five general principles under which criminal jurisdiction can be claimed: the territorial principle, the nationality principle, the protective principle, the universality principle and the passive personality principle. For further discussion on these principles, see D. Harris, *Cases and Materials on International Law,* 7th Edition (London, Sweet and Maxwell, 2010), pp. 228 to 258.

29 See Separate Opinion of President Guillaume in *The Arrest Warrant Case* ICJ Rep 2002.

30 Although it is described as an obligation to "extradite or prosecute," it is not strictly an obligation to prosecute but to submit the case to competent authorities which could decide, for example, that there is insufficient evidence to prosecute.

Sixth, they do not apply when there is no transnational element. For example, the 1979 Hostages Convention has no application "where the offence is committed within a single State, the hostage and the alleged offender are nationals of that State and the alleged offender is found in the territory of that State."[31]

The net effect of these provisions is that if all the States in a region are parties to the counter-terrorism conventions and fulfil their obligations in good faith, any alleged offenders will have no place of refuge. If they enter the territory of any State Party to the Convention, they will be taken into custody, and they will either be extradited to another State Party or the case will be submitted to the competent authorities for prosecution.

3. *1988 SUA Convention and the 1988 Platforms Protocol*

The offences defined in the 1988 SUA Convention involve acts which endanger the safety of international maritime navigation,[32] including:

1) The seizure of or exercise of control over a ship by any form of intimidation;
2) Violence against a person on board a ship;
3) Destruction of a ship or the causing of damage to a ship or to its cargo;
4) Placement on a ship of a device or substance which is likely to destroy or cause damage to that ship or its cargo; and
5) Destruction of, serious damaging of, or interference with maritime navigational facilities.

The 1988 Platforms Protocol has identical offences for fixed platforms.[33]

The 1988 SUA Convention applies to offences against ships committed in maritime zones under the territorial sovereignty of coastal States (territorial seas and archipelagic waters) provided that the ship was navigating or scheduled to navigate into, through or from waters beyond the territorial sea of a State[34] as well as in maritime zones outside the territorial sovereignty of coastal States (high seas or EEZ).

The 1988 SUA Convention and the 1988 Platforms Protocol do not contain any provisions giving powers to States Parties to board and arrest ships. Enforcement is dependent on States Parties arresting alleged offenders who enter their territory, including their territorial waters.

Under Article 8 (1) of the 1988 SUA Convention, the master of a ship of a State Party ("the flag State") may deliver to the authorities of any other State

[31] Article 13, 1979 Hostages Convention, *supra* note 26.
[32] Article 3, 1988 SUA Convention, *supra* note 7.
[33] Article 2, 1988 Platforms Protocol, *supra* note 25.
[34] Article 4, 1988 SUA Convention, *supra* note 7.

Party ("the receiving Party") any persons who he has reasonable grounds to believe has committed one of the offences set forth in Article 3, provided that the master whenever practicable and if possible gives notice of delivery of the suspect before entering the territorial sea of the receiving State[35] and the flag State furnishes the receiving State with any relevant evidence.[36] A receiving State is under a primary obligation to accept delivery of a suspect and can only refuse to accept delivery "*where it has grounds to consider that the Convention is not applicable to the acts giving rise to the delivery*" in which case it must give a statement of the reasons for the refusal.[37] Once a delivered suspect is received within its territory, the receiving State must exercise its option to either extradite or prosecute.[38]

4. *1979 Hostages Convention*

Although it is not designed specifically for maritime terrorism, the 1979 Hostages Convention would be applicable to acts of maritime terrorism when the passengers or crew of a ship are taken hostage. Article 1 states that:

> *Any person who seizes or detains and threatens to kill, to injure or to continue to detain another person ("the hostage") in order to compel a third party, namely a State, an international governmental organization, a natural or juridical person, or group of persons, to do or abstain from doing any act as an explicit or implicit condition for the release of the hostage commits the offence of taking of hostages ("hostage-taking") within the meaning of this Convention.*

5. *1999 Terrorism Financing Convention*

Article 2(a) of the 1999 Terrorism Financing Convention provides that:

> *Any person commits an offence within the meaning of this Convention if that person by any means, directly or indirectly, unlawfully and wilfully, provides or collects funds with the intention that they should be used or in the knowledge that they are to be used, in full or in part, in order to carry out:*
>
> (a) *An act which constitutes an offence within the scope of and as defined in one of the treaties listed in the annex.*

The treaties listed in the Annex are the UN counter-terrorism conventions,[39] including the 1979 Hostages Convention and the 1988 SUA Convention and

[35] Article 8 (2), 1988 SUA Convention, *ibid.*
[36] Article 8 (4), 1988 SUA Convention, *ibid.*
[37] Article 8 (3), 1988 SUA Convention, *ibid.*
[38] Article 7, 1988 SUA Convention, *ibid.*
[39] The Annex consists of the following conventions:
1. Convention for the Suppression of Unlawful Seizure of Aircraft, done at The Hague on 16 December 1970.

the 1988 Platforms Protocol. Therefore, any person who finances the hijacking of ships or other offences under the 1988 SUA Convention and 1988 Platforms Protocol has committed an offence under the 1999 Terrorist Financing Convention. Similarly, any person who finances the act of taking passengers or crew of a ship hostage for ransom has committed an offence under the 1999 Terrorist Financing Convention.

It should also be noted that the financing of offences under the 2005 SUA Convention or the 2005 SUA Protocol would also be offences under this convention (these Conventions will be dealt with in Part IV).

6. *Consistency of these Conventions with International Law*

As mentioned above, in areas under territorial sovereignty, States are prohibited from exercising enforcement jurisdiction without the coastal State's consent. In areas outside of territorial sovereignty, States are allowed to exercise extra-territorial prescriptive jurisdiction, subject to any rules prohibiting such prescription. Further, only flag States are permitted to exercise enforcement jurisdiction in areas outside of territorial sovereignty with limited exceptions.

The three counter-terrorism conventions discussed above do not address enforcement jurisdiction against vessels i.e. the boarding or arrest of ships suspected of engaging in acts of maritime terrorism and only require States Parties to exercise prescriptive jurisdiction. States Parties are obliged to establish jurisdiction over defined offences (consistent with general principles on criminal jurisdiction under international law), to take alleged offenders present in their territory into custody and to either extradite them or submit the case to its

2. Convention for the Suppression of Unlawful Acts against the Safety of Civil Aviation, done at Montreal on 23 September 1971.
3. Convention on the Prevention and Punishment of Crimes against Internationally Protected Persons, including Diplomatic Agents, adopted by the General Assembly of the United Nations on 14 December 1973.
4. International Convention against the Taking of Hostages, adopted by the General Assembly of the United Nations on 17 December 1979.
5. Convention on the Physical Protection of Nuclear Material, adopted at Vienna on 3 March 1980.
6. Protocol for the Suppression of Unlawful Acts of Violence at Airports Serving International Civil Aviation, supplementary to the Convention for the Suppression of Unlawful Acts against the Safety of Civil Aviation, done at Montreal on 24 February 1988.
7. Convention for the Suppression of Unlawful Acts against the Safety of Maritime Navigation, done at Rome on 10 March 1988.
8. Protocol for the Suppression of Unlawful Acts against the Safety of Fixed Platforms located on the Continental Shelf, done at Rome on 10 March 1988.
9. International Convention for the Suppression of Terrorist Bombings, adopted by the General Assembly of the United Nations on 15 December 1997.

competent authorities for prosecution. Accordingly, these conventions are consistent with principles governing jurisdiction over maritime activities.

IV. *Measures by the UN Organizations after 2001*

1. *2001 Security Council Resolution on Terrorism*

The UN Security Council responded almost immediately to attacks on the United States on 11th September 2001. It declared in Resolution 1373 of 28 September 2001[40] that the attacks on the United States, "like any act of international terrorism, constitute a threat to international peace and security." This enabled the Security Council to invoke its special powers under Chapter VII of the UN Charter to take collective action that is binding on all members of the UN. Resolution 1373 sets out a comprehensive set of measures that all member States of the UN must take in order to prevent and suppress the financing of terrorist acts. It establishes that States have a legal obligation to refrain from providing any form of support, active or passive, to entities or persons involved in terrorist acts. Further, it calls on all States to enhance coordination of efforts on national, sub-regional, regional and international levels in order to strengthen the global response to the challenge of international terrorism.

Although the Security Council Resolutions do not specifically mention maritime terrorism or threats to international shipping, the events of 11th September 2001 focused the attention of the international community on the threats posed by international terrorists to maritime security. Since the taking of passengers as hostages on the *Achille Lauro* in 1985, there have been a few incidents of maritime terrorism, both before and after 11th September 2001. These include the deliberate ramming of the US naval ship, *USS Cole* in Aden Harbour, Yemen in 2000 by a small suicide boat loaded with explosives and operated by Al-Qaeda,[41] a similar attack on a French oil tanker, *Limburg,* in the Gulf of Aden in 2002,[42] also allegedly by Al-Qaeda as well as the attack by the *Abu Sayyaf* terrorist group against the Philippine flagged ship, *SuperFerry 14*

[40] UN Security Council Resolution 1373, 28 September 2001, S/RES/1373 (2001) available at <http://daccess-dds-ny.un.org/doc/UNDOC/GEN/N01/557/43/PDF/N0155743.pdf?OpenElement>.

[41] See Michael Isikoff, "10 years later, still no trial for accused USS Cole attack mastermind," 10 December 2010, MSNBC available online at <http://www.msnbc.msn.com/id/39634317/ns/us_news-security/>.

[42] See "US kills Al-Qaeda suspects in Yemen," 5 November 2002, USA Today available online at <http://www.usatoday.com/news/world/2002–11–04–yemen-explosion_x.htm>.

in 2004.[43] It is said that while maritime terrorist attacks are more difficult to execute and as a result, less likely to occur than other types of attacks, they remain a significant possibility and States should continue to be vigilant.[44]

2. *2002 IMO Measures on Maritime Security*

As a result of the events of 11th September 2001, as mentioned above, States and international organizations were forced to completely rethink the threat of maritime terrorism. The United States initiated and led the drive at the IMO to adopt measures to strengthen maritime security on ships and in ports.[45]

The IMO adopted Assembly Resolution A.924(22)[46] calling for a review of the existing measures and procedures to prevent acts of terrorism which threaten the security of passengers, crew members and the safety of ships. At the 22nd Assembly meeting in November 2001, it was agreed to hold a Conference on Maritime Security in December 2002 to adopt new regulations to enhance ship and port security.

The 2002 Conference adopted resolutions containing a series of measures to strengthen maritime security and prevent and suppress acts of terrorism against international shipping. Many of the measures were adopted through amendments to the major IMO Convention governing the safety of ships, the 1974 *International Convention on the Safety of Life at Sea*[47] (SOLAS Convention). The 2002 amendments to SOLAS 1974 entered into force on 1 July 2004.

3. *New Chapter XI-2 to SOLAS Convention*

One of the most important measures taken at the 2002 Conference was to add a new Chapter on maritime security to the SOLAS Convention. The new

---

[43] J. Power, 'Maritime Terrorism: A New Challenge for National and International Security', 10 *Barry Law Review*, (2008), p. 111 at 124.

[44] See P. Parfomak and J. Frittelli, *supra* note 4.

[45] On 15 January 2002, the United States submitted a proposal to the 75th Session of the IMO Maritime Security Committee on measures to improve maritime security (IMO Doc MSC 75/ISWG/5/7) (text provided to author). The proposal covered the following areas: Automatic Identification Systems, Ship and Offshore Facility Security Plans, Port Facility Security Plans, Ship Security Officers, Company Security Officers, Seafarer Identification Verification and Background Check, Port Vulnerability Assessments, Port of Origin, Container Examinations, Cooperation with the World Customs Organization, Information on the Ship and its Cargo and People, Means of Ship Alerting and Ship Security Equipment.

[46] Assembly Resolution A.924 (22), Review of Measures and Procedures to Prevent Acts of Terrorism which Threaten the Security of Passengers and Crews and the Safety of Ships, adopted on 20 November 2001.

[47] *International Convention on the Safety of Life at Sea,* adopted 1 November 1974, 1184 UNTS 2 (entered into force 25 May 1980).

Chapter XI-2 is entitled "Special Measures to Enhance Maritime Security," and is applicable to ships engaged on international voyages, to companies operating ships on international voyages, and to port facilities serving ships engaged on international voyages. The special measures include the following: First, flag States are required to set security levels for their ships, and port States are required to set security levels for their port facilities. Second, the master is required to have information on board the ship concerning persons or organizations responsible for the appointment and employment of crew members of the ship. Third, ships constructed after 1st July 2004 are required to be provided with a Ship Security Alert System. Fourth, the master of a ship is given the overriding authority and the responsibility to make decisions and measures with respect to the safety and security of the ship.

4. *ISPS Code*

Supplementary to the new Chapter XI-2 is the *International Ship and Port Facility Security Code* (ISPS Code) adopted on 1st July 2004. As the title suggests, the ISPS Code contains measures designed to enhance the security of ships and the security of port facilities. The ISPS Code has two parts, A and B. Part A is mandatory for the purpose of compliance with Chapter XI-2. Part B is to be used as a guide and treated as recommendatory.

The ISPS Code contains various measures designed to enhance the security of ships. First, a ship is required to carry on board a Ship Security Plan approved by the flag State on the basis of a Ship Security Assessment. Second, a company operating a ship must designate a Company Security Officer (CSO) for every ship, and every ship is required to have a designated Ship Security Officer (SSO), both of whom are required to undergo training in maritime security in accordance with the guidance given in Part B of the ISPS Code. Third, drills and exercises with respect to the Ship Security Plan are required to be carried out at appropriate intervals by all parties concerned. Fourth, ships verified to be in compliance are issued with an International Ship Security Certificate (ISS Certificate). Fifth, a ship is required to act upon the security levels set by the port State or the flag State by carrying out the activities prescribed in the ISPS Code with the aim of identifying and taking preventive measures against security incidents. A security incident is defined in Chapter XI-2 as "any suspicious act or circumstance threatening the security of the ship, including a mobile offshore drilling unit and a high speed craft, or of a port facility or of any ship/port interface or any ship to ship activity".

The ISPS Code also contains measures to enhance the security of ports. Port Facilities to which Chapter XI-2 applies are required to develop and maintain a Port Facility Security Plan on the basis of a Port Facility Security Assessment. These facilities are required to designate Port Facility Security Officers who, together with appropriate port facility security personnel, are required to undergo training in maritime security in accordance with the guidance given in Part B of the ISPS Code. They are also required to conduct drills and exercises with respect to the Port Facility Security Plan.

Ships are subjected to Port State Control with respect to compliance with Chapter XI-2. The Port State Control inspection is limited to verifying that there is on board a valid International Ship Security Certificate (ISS Certificate) issued under the provisions of Part A of the ISPS Code. When a valid ISS Certificate cannot be produced or when there are clear grounds for believing that the ship is not in compliance with the requirements of Chapter XI-2 or Part A of the ISPS Code, certain control measures may be taken against the ship. Such control measures include inspection of the ship, delaying the ship, detention of the ship, restriction of operations including movement within the port, or expulsion of the ship from port. In addition, a port State may require that ships provide information to ensure compliance with Chapter XI-2 prior to entry into port, including information relating to the ISS Certificate, the security level of the ship, the security level at previous port calls, and security measures taken at previous port calls.

5. *Other Measures on Maritime Security*

The 2002 Amendments also included other measures to enhance maritime security. First, they brought forward the dates by which certain ships had to install an Automatic Identification System (AIS). The AIS system enables shore facilities to automatically identify ships and obtain basic information about them. Second, the regulations now require that a ship's Identification Number be permanently marked in two places on the ship, one of which must be clearly visible. Third, ships are required to carry on board a Continuous Synopsis Record, which is intended to provide an on-board record of the history of the ship with respect to the information recorded therein. This record will be issued by the Registry of Ships. The latter two measures will make it more difficult for hijackers or pirates to re-register and rename ships.

6. *Consistency of Measures with International Law*

The new maritime security measures described above did not pose any challenge to existing rules governing jurisdiction over maritime activities. They gave new obligations to both owners of ships as well as well as flag States but this is consistent with the principle that flag States have prescriptive jurisdiction over vessels which fly their flag. The new measures also gave new rights and responsibilities to port States, particularly the ISPS Code, but this is also consistent with customary international law and UNCLOS. Both customary international law and UNCLOS recognize that all States have jurisdiction over acts and events in their territory, which includes ports and internal waters.[48] A corollary of this is the principle that States have a wide right to prescribe conditions for access to their ports.[49]

The measures adopted by the IMO were very significant in two respects. First, they expanded the IMO's traditional responsibility for maritime safety to include maritime security. Second, they expanded the IMO's rule-making authority into port facilities, an area that had previously been considered a matter within the domestic jurisdiction of port States.

V. *2005 SUA Convention*

1. *Background to the 2005 SUA Convention*

As another of its measures to enhance maritime security after 11th September 2001, the IMO urged its members to become parties to the 1988 SUA Convention. Consequently, the number of States Parties to the 1988 SUA Convention almost tripled within five years, from 52 States on 31st January 2001 to 152 States on 31st October 2006.

In addition, in October 2001, the Legal Committee of the IMO also decided to review the 1988 SUA Convention (and the 1988 SUA Protocol). The Legal Committee agreed to include the review of the 1988 SUA Convention as a priority item in its work program.[50] In April 2002, the Legal Committee agreed to establish a Correspondence Group led by United States with the short-term aim of developing a working paper on the scope of possible amendments for consideration at the 85th session of the Legal Committee in October 2003. The longer aim was to draft the amendments and make a recommendation to the IMO Assembly to convene an international diplomatic conference to consider and adopt amendments to the 1988 SUA Convention.[51] All States and interested international organizations were invited to participate in the work of the Group.

The conclusion of the work of the Correspondence Group was that the offences in the existing conventions for maritime terrorism were too narrow and "would require expansion in order to cope with modern day terrorist threats,

---

[48] R.R. Churchill and A.V. Lowe, *The Law of the Sea* (United Kingdom, Manchester University Press, 1999) at 62.

[49] Churchill and Lowe, *ibid.* UNCLOS itself presupposes that States may set conditions for entry to their ports (See Articles 25 (2), 211 (3) and 255 of UNCLOS, *supra* note 6.

[50] IMO Legal Committee, 83rd Session, 8–12 October 2001. A summary of the work of the Legal Committee is available on the IMO Home Page under Committees. See www.imo.org.

[51] IMO Legal Committee, 84th Session, 22–26 April 2002, *ibid.*

including threats from biological, chemical and nuclear weapons or material."[52] Further, it was found that "these instruments did not include provisions that would allow law enforcement officials to board foreign flag ships on the high seas, either to search for alleged terrorists or their weapons, or to render assistance to a vessel suspected of being under attack."[53]

The Legal Committee worked on a revised draft protocol prepared by the Correspondence Group over the next three years. The Correspondence Group received comments and suggestions from numerous States and organizations which participate in the work of the IMO. Most delegations expressed support for the revision. However, concerns were expressed that the draft boarding provisions should not intrude into the principles of freedom of navigation on the high seas and the exclusive jurisdiction of flag States over their ships on the high seas.[54] Delegations also stated that the SUA Protocol must not impinge on the operation of international commercial shipping. The two articles which were the subject of major debate and disagreement were Article 3*bis*, which sets out new offences to be added to the Convention, and Article 8*bis*, which establishes new provisions for the boarding and search of ships suspected of committing an offence under the 1988 SUA Convention and the draft 2005 SUA Protocol.

After three years of study and deliberation, the Legal Committee completed its work at its 90th session in April 2005.[55] An International Conference on the Revision of the SUA Treaties (2005 Conference) was held in October 2005 to adopt amendments to the 1988 SUA Convention (and to the 1988 SUA Platforms Protocol). The 2005 SUA Protocol[56] was formally adopted at the 2005 Conference on 14th October 2005.[57]

2. *Entry into Force of 2005 SUA Convention*

The 2005 SUA Protocol entered into force on 28th July 2010, ninety days after the date on which 12 States formally ratified or accepted it by giving official notice to the IMO Secretary-General of their consent to be bound by its

[52] H. Tuerk, 'Combating Terrorism at Sea – The Suppression of Unlawful Acts Against the Safety of Maritime Navigation', 15 *University of Miami International and Comparative Law Review* (2007–2008) p. 337 at 356.

[53] *Ibid.*

[54] IMO Legal Committee, 88th Session, 19–23 April 2004, *supra* note 50.

[55] IMO Legal Committee, 90th Session, 18–29 April 2005, *ibid.*

[56] 2005 *Protocol to the Convention for the Suppression of Unlawful Acts against the Safety of Maritime Navigation,* adopted 14 October 2005, IMO Doc LEG/CONF. 15/21 (entered into force 28 July 2010) (2005 SUA Protocol).

[57] 2005 SUA Protocol, *ibid.*

provisions.[58] To become a Party to the 2005 SUA Protocol, a State must first become a Party to the 1988 SUA Convention.[59]

After the Protocol entered into force in July 2010, Articles 1–16 of the 1988 SUA Convention, as revised by the 2005 SUA Protocol, together with Articles 17 to 24 of the 2005 SUA Protocol and its Annex, are to constitute and be called the *Convention for the Suppression of Unlawful Acts against the Safety of Maritime Navigation*, 2005 (2005 SUA Convention).[60]

As of 31st October 2010, there are only 17 States Parties to the 2005 SUA Convention and 13 States Parties to the 2005 SUA Platforms Protocol.

3. *Offences under the 2005 SUA Convention*

One of the significant aspects of the 2005 SUA Convention is that it broadens the list of offences by adding three categories of new offences. The first category of new offences concerns acts of maritime terrorism such as using a ship as a weapon or as a means to carry out a terrorist attack.[61] These new offences require a specific knowledge and intent. They also require a "terrorist motive" – the purpose of the act must be to intimidate a population or compel a government to do or abstain from doing an act.[62] These new offences update the categories of acts that might endanger the safety of ships engaged in international maritime navigation.

The second category of new offences are non-proliferation offences that are intended to strengthen the international legal basis to impede and prosecute the trafficking by commercial ships on the high seas of WMD, their delivery systems and related materials. The non-proliferation provisions require States Parties to criminalize transport on the high seas of WMD and certain related materials, as well as nuclear material and equipment.[63] The offence for trafficking in WMD or related materials on the high seas requires certain "knowledge and intent". However, no "terrorist motive" is required because the proliferation offences are intended to cover the proliferation of WMD by sea for profit as well as for terrorist purposes. This category of new offences establishes a new tool to combat the proliferation of WMD. The United States justified the inclusion of this category of offences by pointing out that it was a response to

[58] 2005 SUA Protocol, *ibid.*

[59] Article 17(4), 2005 SUA Protocol, *ibid.*

[60] Article 15(2), 2005 SUA Protocol, *ibid.*

[61] Article 3*bis* (1)(a), 2005 SUA Protocol, *ibid.*

[62] *Ibid.*

[63] Article 3*bis* (1)(b), 2005 SUA Protocol, *ibid.*

the measures called for in UN Security Council Resolution 1540 on the non-proliferation of WMD.[64]

The third category of new offences in the 2005 SUA Convention makes it an offence to transport by sea any person who has committed an offence under the 2005 SUA Convention or its 2005 Protocol or any of the other UN counter-terrorism conventions when intending to assist that person to evade criminal prosecution. The counter-terrorism conventions concerned are listed in an Annex. This offence also requires specific "knowledge and intent" to ensure that innocent seafarers and masters are not made criminals.

4. *Boarding Provisions in the 2005 SUA Convention*

The most significant change in the 2005 SUA Convention is that it establishes a comprehensive set of procedures designed to facilitate the boarding of a vessel that is suspected of being involved in a SUA offence. Article 8*bis* of the 2005 SUA Convention allows States Parties to board the vessels of other States Parties outside the territorial sea of any State. If law enforcement or other authorized officials of a State Party ("the requesting Party") has reasonable grounds to suspect that the ship or a person on board the ship is involved or is about to be involved in the commission of SUA offences, it must ask the flag State of the ship to confirm the nationality of the ship and then for authorization to board and to take appropriate measures to determine if a SUA offence has been committed.

The 2005 SUA Convention envisages three mechanisms to allow States Parties to consent to the boarding of a vessel.[65] States Parties can either (a) consent on an *ad hoc* basis to requests for boarding, (b) consent implicitly by notifying the Secretary-General of the IMO that prior authorization to board is given if no response is received from the flag State after four hours of a request or (c) consent implicitly by notifying the Secretary-General of the IMO that prior authorization to board is given (no time limit is imposed).[66] Such notifications of implicit consent given by notifying the Secretary-General of the IMO can be withdrawn at any time.

For *ad hoc* requests to board, the flag State can either (a) authorize the boarding subject to any conditions it may impose, (b) conduct the boarding with its own law enforcement or other officials, (c) conduct the boarding with the

[64] See Security Council Resolution 1540 (2004), adopted by the Security Council at its 4956th Meeting on 28 April 2004, UN Doc No. S/Res/1540/2004 available at <http://daccess-dds ny.un.org/doc/UNDOC/GEN/N04/328/43/PDF/N0432843.pdf?OpenElement>.

[65] N. Klein, 'The Right of Visit and the 2005 Protocol on the Suppression of Unlawful Acts Against the Safety of Maritime Navigation', 35 *Denver Journal of International Law and Policy* (2006–2007) p. 288 at 319.

[66] *Ibid.* at 322.

requested party subject to any conditions it may impose, or (d) decline to authorize a boarding.

Many States and organizations argued that the new boarding provisions must not unduly interfere with the economic interests of flag States and ship owners or with the rights of seafarers. As a result, the new boarding provisions contain the most comprehensive set of "safeguards" ever included in any such convention. Among the safeguards are the following:

- Use of force must be avoided except when necessary to ensure the safety of its officials and persons on board or where the officials are obstructed in the execution of authorized actions, and any use of force must not exceed the minimum necessary and reasonable in the circumstances;
- The boarding State must take into account the dangers and difficulties involved in boarding a ship at sea;
- The boarding State must take due account of the need not to endanger the safety of life at sea and of the safety and security of the ship and its cargo, and must take reasonable steps to avoid a ship being unduly detained or delayed;
- The boarding State must take due account of the need not to prejudice the commercial and legal interests of the flag State, and must advise the master of its intention to board and afford him the opportunity to contact the owner and the flag State;
- The boarding State is liable for damage, harm or loss attributable to it when the grounds for the boarding prove to be unfounded or when the measures taken are unlawful or exceed those reasonably required in the circumstances.

5. *Consistency of the 2005 SUA Convention with International Law*

As mentioned in Part II, under UNCLOS, the flag State has exclusive jurisdiction on the high seas and other States have the right to board foreign flagged vessels in the limited circumstances set out in Article 110 (piracy, slavery, unlawful broadcasting and where suspicions as to the nationality of the vessel arise). Other States can also board foreign-flagged vessels if given express consent by the flag State. Article 110 also recognizes that additional reasons for exercising the right to board foreign flagged vessels may be established by treaty.[67] The 2005 SUA Convention creates a new treaty power to exercise the right to board foreign-flagged vessels. The boarding provisions were inevitably the subject of intense negotiations. As mentioned above, many States maintained that any new boarding provisions must be consistent with UNCLOS and must not interfere with the rights and jurisdiction of coastal States in their territorial sea,

[67] Article 110 states "except where acts of interference derive from powers conferred by treaty."

freedom of navigation or the principle that ships on the high seas are subject to the exclusive jurisdiction of the flag State.[68] The United States, on the other hand, insisted on the inclusion of a set of procedures to expedite the boarding of ships suspected of engaging in SUA offences.

The boarding provisions which were eventually agreed upon are consistent with UNCLOS. Boarding can only take place on ships under the flag of States Parties and only seaward of the outer limits of any State's territorial sea (on the high seas or in an EEZ). Boarding can only occur with the express consent of the flag State. The implicit consent procedures established under the Protocol are optional and States Parties can choose whether or not to participate in the implicit consent regime. If the flag State does decide to give its consent to the boarding, it may impose conditions on the boarding State. Further, given the comprehensive safeguards, there is little likelihood that the boarding provisions will be open to abuse.

VI. *Security Council Resolutions on Illicit Trafficking in WMD*

1. *UN Security Council Resolution 1540 of 28 April 2004*

In September 2003, President Bush asked the UN Security Council to adopt a new anti-proliferation resolution that called upon all members of the UN to criminalize the proliferation of WMD, to enact strict controls consistent with international standards, and to secure any and all such materials within their own borders.[69] On 28th April 2004, the UN Security Council unanimously adopted Resolution 1540 on preventing proliferation of WMD. Invoking its enforcement powers under Chapter VII of the UN Charter, it affirmed that the proliferation of nuclear, chemical and biological weapons constitute a threat to international peace and security.[70]

Under the Resolution, all members of the UN are legally bound to establish domestic controls including legislative measures to prevent the proliferation of WMD, in particular for terrorist purposes. With respect to the prevention of illicit trafficking by sea, no agreement could be reached on language concerning interdiction. The paragraph calling for cooperative action reads as follows:

---

[68] N. Klein, *supra* note 65 at 319.

[69] Statement by President George W. Bush at the 58th General Assembly Plenary on 23 September 2009: See Press Release GA 10156 at < http://www.un.org/News/Press/docs/2003/ga10156.doc.htm>.

[70] See Security Council Resolution 1540 (2004), adopted by the Security Council at its 4956th Meeting on 28 April 2004, UN Doc No. S/Res/1540/2004 available at <http://daccess-dds ny.un.org/doc/UNDOC/GEN/N04/328/43/PDF/N0432843.pdf?OpenElement>.

> *8. Further to counter that threat, calls upon all States, in accordance with their national legal authorities and legislation and consistent with international law, to take cooperative action to prevent illicit trafficking in nuclear, chemical or biological weapons, their means of delivery, and related materials.*[71]

2. *Security Council Resolutions on DPRK*

When the DPRK conducted a test of a nuclear weapon on 9th October 2006, it posed a danger to peace and stability in the region and presented a challenge to international efforts aimed at strengthening the global regime of non-proliferation of nuclear weapons. In response, the UN Security Council adopted Security Council Resolution 1718 (SCR 1718) on 14th October 2006 imposing binding economic sanctions on DPRK.[72]

Despite the fear of the proliferation of WMD by sea, SCR 1718 does not contain any express language authorizing the interdiction of ships suspected of carrying WMD or other military equipment prohibited by the resolution. The operative paragraph reads as follows:

> *(f) In order to ensure compliance with the requirements of this paragraph, and thereby preventing illicit trafficking in nuclear, chemical or biological weapons, their means of delivery and related materials, all Member States are called upon to take, in accordance with their national authorities and legislation, and consistent with international law, cooperative action including through inspection of cargo to and from the DPRK, as necessary.*

It was generally agreed that "through inspection of cargo" did not authorize the interdiction of ships exercising innocent passage rights in the territorial sea or the freedom of navigation beyond the limits of the territorial sea.

When DPRK conducted another nuclear test on 25th May 2009 in defiance of the UN and in violation of SCR 1718, the UN Security Council imposed additional economic sanctions in Security Council Resolution 1874 of 12th June 2009 (SCR 1874).[73] This Resolution contained stronger language than SCR 1718, and made it very difficult for DPRK to ship any prohibited items from its ports. The operative paragraphs read as follows:

> *11.* Calls upon *all States to inspect, in accordance with their national authorities and legislation, and consistent with international law, all cargo to and from the DPRK, in their territory, including seaports and airports, if the State concerned has information*

---

[71] *Ibid.*

[72] See Security Council Resolution 1718 (2006), adopted by the Security Council at its 5551st Meeting on 14 October 2006, UN Doc No. S/Res/1718/2006 available at <http://daccess-dds-ny.un.org/doc/UNDOC/GEN/N06/572/07/PDF/N0657207.pdf?OpenElement>.

[73] See Security Council Resolution 1874 (2009), adopted by the Security Council at its 6141st Meeting on 12 June 2009, available at <http://daccess-dds-ny.un.org/doc/UNDOC/GEN/N09/368/49/PDF/N0936849.pdf?OpenElement>.

that provides reasonable grounds to believe the cargo contains items the supply, sale, transfer, or export of which is prohibited by paragraph 8 (a), 8 (b), or 8 (c) of resolution 1718 or by paragraph 9 or 10 of this resolution, for the purpose of ensuring strict implementation of those provisions;

12. Calls upon *all Member States to inspect vessels, with the consent of the flag State, on the high seas, if they have information that provides reasonable grounds to believe that the cargo of such vessels contains items the supply, sale, transfer, or export of which is prohibited by paragraph 8 (a), 8 (b), or 8 (c) of resolution 1718 (2006) or by paragraph 9 or 10 of this resolution, for the purpose of ensuring strict implementation of those provisions;*

13. Calls upon *all States to cooperate with inspections pursuant to paragraphs 11 and 12, and, if the flag State does not consent to inspection on the high seas,* decides *that the flag State shall direct the vessel to proceed to an appropriate and convenient port for the required inspection by the local authorities pursuant to paragraph 11;*

3. *Consistency of Security Council Resolutions with International Law*

SCR 1874 calls for inspections in a manner that is consistent with UNCLOS. Paragraph 11 calls upon States to inspect suspect cargo "in their territory, including their seaports and airports." Paragraph 12 calls upon States to inspect ships on the high seas with the consent of the flag State. The key provision is paragraph 13, which provides that the Security Council "decides" that if the flag State does not consent to inspection on the high seas, the flag State shall direct the ship to proceed to an appropriate and convenient port for the required inspection by the local authorities. This reduces the possibility of a suspect ship flying the flag of the DPRK refusing to be inspected.

SCR 1874 is a very positive development because it in effect eliminates any legal loopholes but is at the same time completely consistent with UNCLOS. SCR 1874 places a clear obligation on the DPRK to either consent to inspection on the high seas or direct the vessel to proceed to a nearby port for the inspection.

VII. *US Proliferation Security Initiative*

1. *Background*

The Proliferation Security Initiative (PSI) is an initiative of the United States to establish a coalition of willing partners to respond to the growing challenge posed by the proliferation of WMD. It is an attempt by the United States to create a framework for international cooperation to deal with the threat posed by WMD outside the international organizations and international treaties that regulate the proliferation of WMD.

The PSI was announced by United States President George Bush in Poland on 31st May 2003, just prior to the G8 Summit. President Bush stated:

> *When weapons of mass destruction or their components are in transit, we must have the means and authority to seize them. So today I announce a new effort to fight proliferation called the Proliferation Security Initiative. The United States and a number of our close allies, including Poland, have begun working on new agreements to search planes and ships carrying suspect cargo and to seize illegal weapons or missile technologies. Over time, we will extend this partnership as broadly as possible to keep the world's most destructive weapons away from our shores and out of the hands of our common enemies.*[74]

The statement by President Bush implied that new international agreements would be created that would allow the United States and its allies to search planes and ships carrying suspect cargo and seize illegal weapons or missile technologies. However, as the PSI developed, it has not been based upon the development of new international agreements, but on the development of cooperative arrangements among participating States regarding the interdiction of ships suspected of carrying WMD.

The United States began working with ten other countries in 2003 to develop a set of principles that would identify practical steps to interdict shipments of WMD flowing to or from "state or non-state actors of proliferation concern." The ten countries were Australia, France, Germany, Italy, Japan, the Netherlands, Poland, Portugal, Spain and the United Kingdom. At a meeting in Brisbane in September 2003, the eleven participating countries agreed that North Korea and Iran were of particular proliferation concern and also agreed to a non-binding "Statement of Interdiction Principles"[75] (Interdiction Principles) There are presently ninety-eight (98) participating States as of October 2010.[76]

2. *Consistency of Interdiction Principles with International Law*

Questions have been raised as to whether some of the actions called for in the Interdiction Principles are consistent with existing rules of international law. Of particular concern was whether the provisions dealing with interdiction at sea were consistent with the provisions of UNCLOS.

The Interdiction Principles call upon participating States "to take specific action in support of interdiction... to the extent their national legal authorities permit and consistent with their obligations under international law."[77]

---

[74] President George W. Bush, Remarks at Wawel Royal Castle in Krakow, Poland on 31 May 2003, available at <http://www.whitehouse.gov.news/releases/2003/05/20030531–3.html>.

[75] Interdiction Principles for the Proliferation Security Initiative, Adopted in Washington, 4 September 2003 available at <http://www.state.gov/t/isn/c27726.htm> (Interdiction Principles).

[76] See Proliferation Security Initiative, US Department of State online available at <http://www.state.gov/t/isn/c27732.htm>.

[77] Principle 4, Interdiction Principles, *supra* note 75.

Generally speaking, some of the specific actions set out in the Interdiction Principles are consistent with international law as set out in UNCLOS. However, some of the specific actions required by the Interdiction Principles will be qualified by the provisions of UNCLOS.

The actions set out in the Interdiction Principles with respect to ships flying the flag of participating States are entirely consistent with the provisions in UNCLOS. States agree, on their own initiative, to board and search any suspect ships flying their flag in their internal waters or territorial seas or in areas beyond the territorial seas of any State.[78] This is consistent with the principles governing jurisdiction over maritime activities. States have a right to board and search ships flying their flag in their internal waters and territorial seas because the sovereignty of a State extends to these maritime zones and a State's laws apply to ships flying its flag. In areas beyond the territorial sea of any State, the flag State has exclusive jurisdiction over ships flying its flag.

The Interdiction Principles also provide that a participating State should seriously consider giving other States consent to board and search ships flying its flag under appropriate circumstances.[79] Given that the flag State has exclusive jurisdiction over ships flying its flag outside the territorial sea of any State, it is consistent with UNCLOS for flag States to give such consent. One of the goals of the United States under the PSI is to enter into bilateral agreements with major flag States which give the United States permission to board and search ships flying their flag when such ships are suspected of carrying WMD. The first such boarding agreement was signed by the United States and Liberia on 11th February 2004. The boarding agreement gives the United States authority, on a bilateral basis, to board ships flying the flag of Liberia if they are suspected of carrying illicit shipments of WMD. According to the United States, this boarding agreement was an important step in further operationalizing the PSI and strengthening the mechanisms that the United States has at its disposal to interdict suspect WMD-related cargoes. To date, the United States has signed eleven (11) of Ship-Boarding Agreements.[80]

The Interdiction Principles also provide that participating States should:

> *(T)ake appropriate actions to (1) stop and/or search in their* ***internal waters, territorial seas, or contiguous zones*** *(when declared) vessels that are reasonably suspected of carrying such cargoes to or from states or non-state actors of proliferation concern and to seize such cargoes that are identified; and (2) to enforce conditions on vessels entering or leaving* ***their ports, internal waters or territorial seas*** *that are reasonably suspected*

[78] Principle 4 (b), Interdiction Principles, *ibid.*

[79] Principle 4 (c), Interdiction Principles, *ibid.*

[80] See Proliferation Security Initiative, US Department of State available at < http://www.state.gov/t/isn/c27733.htm>.

> *of carrying such cargoes, such as requiring that such vessels be subject to boarding, search, and seizure of such cargoes prior to entry.*[81]

To the extent that these actions concern ships in a participating State's ports and internal waters as well as ships entering or leaving its ports or internal waters, this is consistent with customary international law and UNCLOS. Participating States agree to stop and/or search ships in their ports or internal waters when such ships are reasonably suspected of carrying such cargoes to or from States or non-State actors of proliferation concern. Participating States also agree to enforce conditions on suspect ships entering or leaving their ports and internal waters. Such conditions might include a requirement that such ships be subject to boarding and search prior to entry. As mentioned in Part IV (6), ports and internal waters are within the territorial sovereignty of a State, and States may impose conditions on ships in its ports and internal waters and on ships in its territorial sea that intend to enter its ports or internal waters.[82]

The most controversial actions set out in the Interdiction Principles concern actions of coastal States with regard to ships in their territorial sea or contiguous zone, and with regard to ships entering or leaving its territorial sea. These are controversial because under UNCLOS the ships of all States have a *right of innocent passage* through the territorial seas of all States.[83] Passage is innocent so long as it is not prejudicial to the peace, good order or security of the coastal state.[84] It is difficult to argue that the mere passage of a vessel containing WMD through the territorial sea of a coastal state is prejudicial to its peace, good order or security, given the fact that military vessels carrying nuclear weapons and foreign nuclear-powered ships and ships carrying nuclear substances[85] have a right of innocent passage through the territorial sea of a coastal State. Further, as acknowledged by many commentators, it is the intended use of the WMD at the point of destination that constitutes a threat to the coastal State and not the shipment of WMD itself.[86]

Furthermore, special passage rules for the ships of all States apply in straits used for international navigation which fall within the territorial sea of the littoral states.[87] The ships of all states have the right of transit passage through

---

81 Principle 4 (d), Interdiction Principles, *supra* note 75. Bold emphasis added.

82 See *supra* notes 48 and 49.

83 See Article 17, UNCLOS, *supra* note 6. Italic emphasis added.

84 See Article 19 (1), UNCLOS, *ibid.*

85 See Article 23 of UNCLOS which assumes that foreign nuclear-powered ships and ships carrying nuclear or other inherently dangerous or noxious substances have the right of innocent passage.

86 See, for example, J. Garvey, 'The International Institutional Imperative for Countering the Spread of Weapons of Mass Destruction: Assessing the Proliferation Security Initiative' 10 *Conflict and Security Law* (2005) p. 125 at 131.

87 See Part III, UNCLOS, *supra* note 6.

straits used for international navigation, and such a right cannot be impeded or suspended by the littoral states.[88] The right of transit passage is an even broader right than the right of innocent passage.

Therefore, some States Parties to UNCLOS are unlikely to interfere with ships exercising the right of transit passage through a strait used for international navigation or the right of innocent passage through the territorial sea. Instead, they are likely to take the position that any action taken with respect to such ships must be *consistent with their obligations under international law* as set out in UNCLOS. However, it would be legal for the coastal State to board and search a suspect ship passing through its territorial sea if the flag State of the suspect ship expressly authorized or requested such action by the coastal State.

There is one other circumstance in which it may be legal for a coastal State to board and search a suspect ship in its contiguous zone or territorial sea. If a suspect ship was on a route in which there was evidence indicating that it was intending to bring WMD into the territory of the coastal State in violation of its customs laws and regulations, such a ship would not have a right of innocent passage. It could be boarded and searched by the authorities of the coastal State in its territorial sea. Similarly, it could be boarded and searched in the contiguous zone, which is a zone adjacent to the territorial sea in which the coastal state has special powers to enforce its customs and immigration laws.[89]

3. *Relationship between PSI and 2005 SUA Convention*

The 2005 SUA Convention is consistent with the PSI and is complementary to it. The 2005 SUA Convention specifically provides that State Parties may conclude agreements or arrangements between them to facilitate law enforcement operations carried out under the boarding provisions.[90] The PSI would arguably be such an arrangement. In addition, the 2005 SUA Convention specifically provides that State Parties are encouraged to develop standard operating procedures (SOP) for joint operations and to consult with other States with a view to harmonizing SOP.[91]

The link between the PSI and the boarding provisions in the 2005 SUA Convention could be a very significant development. The Interdiction Principles are very general. As mentioned above, the United States has negotiated bilateral ship boarding agreements with most of the major flag States, but the safeguards in Article 8*bis* are much more extensive than in the bilateral agreements. Therefore, if States cooperating in the PSI used the procedures for boarding that are

[88] See Article 38 and 44, UNCLOS, *ibid.*

[89] See Article 33, UNCLOS, *ibid.*

[90] Article 8*bis*, paragraph 13, 2005 SUA Protocol, *supra* note 56.

[91] Article 8*bis*, paragraph 13, 2005 SUA Protocol, *supra* note 56.

set out in Article 8*bis* as their standard operating procedures, it would ensure that any interdictions and boardings under the PSI follow common procedures that contain extensive safeguards. This would alleviate some of the concerns in some States that interdictions and boardings under the PSI might be abused.

This link between the interdiction and boarding procedures in Article 8*bis* and the PSI could develop independent of the process of ratification or accession to the 2005 SUA Convention. If States participating in the PSI were to follow the procedures and safeguards in Article 8*bis* as standard operating procedures under PSI, the Article 8*bis* procedures could be incorporated into the PSI through practice. This would be a very positive development.

VIII. *Participation in and Implementation of Measures on Maritime Terrorism*

The success of the measures discussed above will depend on the extent to which States participate in such measures and where necessary, implement them within their national laws.

With respect to provisions to enhance maritime security that were adopted by the IMO in 2002, most States appear to have endorsed and implemented such provisions. The measures were adopted pursuant to the SOLAS Convention. Almost all States are parties to this Convention.[92] In addition, many of the IMO measures to enhance maritime security were implemented through port State measures.[93] Once major ports make compliance with the measures as a condition of entry into its port, the owners or operators of ships take the measures necessary to ensure that their ships meet the requirements necessary to obtain the certificates required for entry into ports. States were also diligent at meeting the requirements necessary to secure their port facilities, as they recognized that it was in their interests to do so for economic reasons. If they did not, ships carrying goods from their port would have difficulty entering major ports.

With regards to the UN counter-terrorism conventions such as the 1979 Hostages Convention, the 1988 SUA Convention, the 1999 Terrorism Financing Convention and the 2005 SUA Convention, the UN General Assembly and regional bodies have all called upon States to ratify and implement these conventions. States have been slow to ratify some of these conventions,

---

92 See Status of IMO Conventions, IMO Website available at <http://www.imo.org/About/Conventions/StatusOfConventions/Documents/Status%20of%20Conventions%202010.pdf>.

93 See discussion in E. Lobsinger, 'Post-9/11 Security in a Post WWII World: The Question of Compatibility of Maritime Security Efforts with Trade Rules and International Law' 32 *Tulane Maritime Law Journal* (2007–2008) p. 61 at 80–83.

particularly the 2005 SUA Convention. As of 31 October 2010, only 17 States are parties to the 2005 SUA Convention, and the list of parties does not include any major maritime States or major powers.[94] This may be due to the controversy caused by the boarding provisions in the initial drafts of the 2005 SUA Convention and the consequent misapprehension by States that the provisions are still contrary to UNCLOS. This is unfortunate because if acts of maritime terrorism take place, the international community will not have a legal framework in place to address the issues, and perpetrators of such acts will remain unpunished, a situation that is presently seen with the piracy off the Horn of Africa.

There are also problems in the implementation of such conventions within national law. First, States Parties which consider international conventions as automatically part of their national law often do not have implementing legislation for these conventions.[95] However, all of these conventions require States Parties to establish penalties for the offences that take into consideration the grave nature of the offences. While a national court could conceivably rely on the convention (rather than domestic legislation) for the elements of the offence, there would be no corresponding penalty within their domestic legislation.

Second, States Parties which do have implementing legislation some times do not incorporate all elements of the offence as set out in the relevant conventions. This may pose difficulties when it is time to frame the charges against an alleged offender and there is a danger such implementing legislation will not be available for use against the alleged offender.

Third, States Parties have often failed to give their courts universal jurisdiction over convention offences based on the presence of the offender within their territory and usually require some form of jurisdictional nexus between the offence and the State. This may result in a State Party being unable to prosecute foreign offenders found in its territory for offences committed outside its territory where there is no jurisdictional nexus with the offence. This goes against the whole purpose and spirit of the counter-terrorism conventions, which is to ensure that there are no safe havens for offenders.

Some States are also reported to have had problems implementing binding decisions of the UN Security Council in their national legal systems. This issue was recently raised by the President of the International Court of Justice during an address in Singapore. One State which has taken specific steps to implement its obligations under Security Council Resolutions is Singapore. The Singapore Parliament passed the United Nations Act (Cap 339, Singapore Statutes) in

---

[94] See Status of IMO Conventions, IMO Website available at <http://www.imo.org/About/Conventions/StatusOfConventions/Documents/Status%20of%20Conventions%202010.pdf>.

[95] This is often true of civil law countries whose systems of law are based on 'monism' whereby international conventions are considered self-executing.

2001 to enable the Singapore government effectively to carry out binding decisions of the UN Security Council.[96]

IX. *Conclusion*

It is evident that all of the measures taken to combat maritime terrorism, both before and after the terrorist attacks against the United States in 2001, are consistent with the principles governing jurisdiction over maritime activities. While some of the measures, such as the 2005 SUA Convention and the PSI, may have initially posed a challenge to such principles, they have ultimately been brought into conformity with international law or at the very least, be interpreted in a manner consistent with international law.

The importance of these measures being consistent with international law is undeniable. While the need to prevent and address maritime terrorism is imperative, the measures adopted must be defensible under international law to ensure their legitimacy and to ensure certainty in the international legal order. Further, the fact that they are consistent with international law will encourage States to participate in such measures.

The effectiveness of such measures depends on States participating in and implementing these measures. International and regional efforts should now focus on encouraging States to participate in such measures and on examining how States can effectively implement their obligations under the relevant conventions, the UN Security Council Resolutions and the PSI. This will help ensure that an effective legal framework is established to combat maritime terrorism.

[96] See United Nations Act 2001 (Cap 339), Singapore Statutes Online available at <http://statutes.agc.gov.sg/non_version/cgi-bin/cgi_getdata.pl?actno=2002–REVED-339&doctitle=UNITED%20NATIONS%20ACT%0a&date=latest&method=part&sl=1&segid=#1002272036–000004>.

BRANDISHING "LEGAL TOOLS" IN THE FIGHT AGAINST MARITIME PIRACY

Commander James Kraska, JAGC, US Navy[1]

Abstract

The Contact Group on Piracy off the Coast of Somalia (CGPCS) was established within the context of UN Security Council Resolution 1851 (2008). The CGPCS has four Working Groups (with a fifth focusing on piracy financing set to emerge), which are focused on developing better international cooperation among states and regional and international organizations to combat Somali piracy and armed robbery at sea. Working Group Two (Legal Issues) held a landmark meeting in Copenhagen on November 2–3, 2010, and the seventh plenary session of the CGPCS was held in New York on November 10, 2010.

The main purpose of Working Group Two has been to encourage the prosecution and imprisonment within national legal systems of piracy suspects. The Group Two discussions also have focused on a handful of critical issues that reside at the legal-policy divide: developing the international legal framework applicable to piracy, strengthening national laws on piracy and armed robbery at sea, overcoming legal and practical challenges to prosecution in domestic (municipal) courts, countering legal difficulties encountered in prosecution, ensuring rules governing the apprehension and detention of suspected pirates balance the interests of the accused and the interests of the international community, promote legal and administrative capacity-building, and synchronize approaches on the use of force in counter-piracy with human rights law, including non-refoulement of refugees.

In an effort to make Working Group Two as practical as possible, participants are developing a "legal toolbox" of relevant sources and precedents that states may use as models for strengthening their national capacity to combat piracy and armed robbery at sea. The "legal toolbox" contains, inter alia, three documents concerning the collection of evidence – the US Counter-Piracy Evidence Collection Guidance, which the author helped to write for operational forces, while he was serving with the US Joint Staff. The "toolkit" also includes the Kenya Transfer Guidance for piracy Suspects, and the Seychelles Transfer guide. (MSC 88/INF.10).Finally, the "legal toolkit" contains guidance for ensuring national decision-making frameworks are in place to enable states to make determinations of prosecution and extradition, best practices for post-trial transfer of pirates, criminalization of piracy and the

[1] Howard S. Levie Chair of Operational Law and member of the faculty of the International Law Department, US Naval War College. Commander Kraska also serves as a Guest Investigator, Marine Policy Center, Woods Hole Oceanographic Institution, Senior Fellow, Foreign Policy Research Institute, and recently published the study *Contemporary Maritime Piracy: International Law, Strategy, and Diplomacy at Sea* (Praeger, 2011). The views presented are those of the author and do not reflect the official policy or position of the Naval War College or the US Navy. This chapter is based on the author's PowerPoint presentation, which can be viewed at http://www.virginia.edu/colp/pdf/kmi-kraska.pdf.

possession of piracy-related equipment, improvements in data collection and processing of suspects, to include biometrics, and legal aspects of human rights and piracy financing.

The Threat of Piracy

On a crystal clear February 18 2011, Somali pirates, while sailing 240 miles west of Oman, hijacked the sailing vessel *Quest*. The boat was registered in Marina del Ray, California, and the four Americans on board were taken hostage as the tiny craft bobbed in the Arabian Sea. The next day US warships began to shadow the yacht as it headed toward the Somali Basin under an impossibly bright sky. The naval flotilla was comprised of the aircraft carrier USS *Enterprise*, the guided-missile cruiser USS *Leyte Gulf*, and the guided-missile destroyers USS *Sterett* and USS *Bulkeley*. After two weeks monitoring the sailing vessel, the standoff settled into a familiar routine. Thus, the sailors on watch on aboard USS *Sterett* on March 3, 2011 did not expect that the pirates would launch a rocket-propelled grenade (RPG) at their warship.

The *Sterett* had been trailing the *Quest* at 600 yards, but after a single RPG round from *Quest* went wide of its target, the sounds of gunfire from on board the yacht penetrated the early morning. Earlier, President Obama had authorized the use of deadly force by naval forces in the event that the lives of the hostages were believed to be in danger, so a team of U.S. Navy Sea/Air/Land (SEAL) commandos quickly left the *Sterett* in a rigid-hull inflatable boat and headed toward the sailing vessel.

Two pirates were killed during the boarding process, including one that was stabbed with a knife by a SEAL team member acting in self-defense. The remaining pirates surrendered. The boarding party detained 13 Somalis and one Yemeni national. The pirates were armed with AK-47 Kalashnikov and FN (Fabrique Nationale d'Herstal) automatic assault rifles.

The four American crew members were found dead or near death from close quarter gunshot wounds. The pirates were removed from the yacht and taken to the aircraft carrier, and later the suspects were flown with US Marshalls to Norfolk, Virginia. On March 10, 2011, the pirates appeared in federal district court for the first time. One minor involved in the attack was repatriated to Somalia without being charged. The remaining suspects sat before Magistrate Judge Tommy E. Miller in groups of five, and as one of the suspects began to speak to the judge, the Somali was cautioned to refrain from talking without counsel present.

Only two weeks before the attack on the *Quest*, a federal court sentenced Abduwali Abdukhadir Muse to 33 years and nine months in prison for attacking the US-flagged *Maersk Alabama* in 2009. Muse, who is imprisoned in New York, was convicted of two felony counts of hijacking maritime vessels, two

M/V *Maersk Alabama*
The surviving suspect in the April 2009 attack was convicted and is serving a sentence of 33 years and 9 months for two felony counts of hijacking maritime vessels, two felony counts of kidnapping, and two felony counts of hostage taking. He is incarcerated in New York.

USS *Nichols*
All five defendants charged in the April 2010 attack were convicted in November 2010 and received life sentences plus 80 years for piracy and additional charges including attack to plunder a vessel, assault with a dangerous weapon in the special maritime jurisdiction, conspiracy to use firearms during a crime of violence, and use of a firearm during a crime of violence. They are serving their sentences in Norfolk, VA.

USS *Ashland*
Six suspects were charged in the April 2010 nighttime attack against a U.S. warship, which occurred 330 nautical miles off the coast of Djibouti. The pirates had been at sea for a lengthy period of time, and were running low on food and fuel and were desperate to seize a mother ship. As a result of mistaking the *Ashland* for a commercial vessel, the pirates were taken and later arrested. In August 2010, one of the pirates, Jama idle Ibrahim, and five associates, plead guilty to attacking to plunder a vessel, engaging in an act of violence against people on a vessel, and use of a firearm in commission of a crime. The Somalis agreed to serve prison sentences of 30-years.

S/V *Quest*
The Americans on board *Quest* may have been murdered because they were Christian missionaries with boxes of bibles on board their vessel. Fourteen Somali men, thirteen from Somalia and one from Yemen, have been indicted on federal criminal charges for their suspected involvement in the S/V QUEST attack. One minor involved in this attack was repatriated to Somalia without being charged.

felony counts of kidnapping, and two felony counts of hostage taking. One week after the *Quest* standoff ended in tragedy with the cold-blooded murder of the crew and passengers, a group of five Somali pirates was sentenced to mandatory life in prison in the same Virginia district court for attacking the USS *Nichols*, in April 2010.

Nichols is a Norfolk-based warship that the pirates had mistaken as a merchant vessel. All five pirates were convicted in November 2010 and awarded life imprisonment, plus 80 years, for the crimes of maritime piracy, attack with intent to plunder a vessel, assault with a dangerous weapon in the special maritime jurisdiction, conspiracy to use firearms during a crime of violence, and use of a firearm during a crime of violence. The Somali men who attacked *Nichols* were the first to be convicted of maritime piracy by a US jury since 1820, and they are serving their sentences in Virginia.[2] These US criminal prosecutions

[2] *Convicted Somali Pirates Get Life Sentences in U.S. Court,* BBC News (United States and Canada), March 14, 2011.

underscore the challenge posed by Secretary of State Hillary Clinton: the international community needs to design 21st century solutions to defeat the reemergence of a 17th century crime.

The threat of piracy emanating from the Puntland region of Somalia has multiple dimensions, including a social element rooted in clan dynamics and East African culture, a political dimension arising from decades of internal Somali warfare and inter-militia combat, and a naval dimension, encompassing the efforts of a broad coalition of warships to repress piracy. Naval forces in the region are operating with the 24-nation Task Force 151, which also operates the Marine Liaison Office (MARLO) in Bahrain, the North Atlantic Treaty Organization, which is conducting Operation Ocean Shield, and the European Union, which is in its third year of conducting Operation Atalanta, and which also maintains the Maritime Safety Centre – Horn of Africa (MSCHOA) in Dubai. These operational dimensions of the international effort against piracy from Somalia represent the tip of the spear of the international community to address Somali piracy.

Economic Costs of Somali Piracy

The attack on the *Seabourn Spirit* on November 5, 2005 galvanized US attention toward the problem of maritime piracy.[3] The ship had 150 passengers on board, including American citizens. By employing a sonic Long-Range Acoustic Device (LRAD), the vessel was able to dissuade the pirates from actually boarding and the ship escaped.[4] The pirates fired automatic rifles and RPGs at the luxury cruise liner. After the ship escaped, a US Navy detachment from Explosive Ordnance Disposal Mobile Unit Eight (EODMU-8) removed portions of an RPG round from the superstructure of the ship. The piece was actually the remains of a rocket motor and not the warhead from the small rocket, which had not detonated on impact.[5]

Although no US citizens were injured in the attack, the event was a harbinger of surging piracy off the coast of Somalia. In the "early" years of the attacks, pirates rarely ventured beyond 50 nautical miles from the shore of Somalia; then it was 100 and for several years, 200 miles was deemed to be a safe distance for merchant shipping. By late 2008, however, Somali pirates were swarming throughout the Gulf of Aden. Gradually the shipping lanes of the

---

[3] Matt Cherry and Amanda Moyer, *Cruise Liner Outruns Armed Pirate Boats*, CNN.com, November 5, 2005.

[4] Adam Blenford, *Cruise Lines Turn to Sonic Weapon*, BBC News, Nov. 8, 2005.

[5] *Capture of Suspected Somali Pirates*, Embassy of the United States, Nairobi, Kenya, Media Press Release, February 2, 2006, *available at*, http://nairobi.usembassy.gov/pr_20060202.html.

Arabian Sea and the western Indian Ocean – virtually to the coast of India – were placed at risk.

Thirty thousand vessels annually ply the strategically important areas afflicted by Somali piracy – a vast maritime space that includes the Gulf of Aden, the Red Sea, the Arabian Sea and the western Indian Ocean. All stakeholders in the global marine transportation system are affected, including the flag States or registries, port States, coastal States, the countries of crew nationality, ship and cargo owners, and a constellation of insurance and re-insurance companies with policies on vessel hulls, war insurance, kidnapping and ransom (K&R) insurance, and related protection and indemnity clubs (P&I), which spread risk of loss among club members.

What vessels are at greatest risk of piracy? Vessels that are slower – transiting at 14 knots are less – and have a lower freeboard, are at greater risk. Ships that are not in conformity with Best Management Practices (BMP) for commercial shipping are also more vulnerable. Ships that stray outside well-patrolled routes are also at higher risk. In the Gulf of Aden, for example, the European Union and the United Kingdom Maritime Transportation Office (UKMTO) established a maritime security patrol area (MSPA) effective on February 1, 2009. The MSPA includes a 12-nautical mile wide internationally recognized transit corridor (IRTC) akin to a traffic separation scheme for traffic in the Gulf of Aden, and ships heading to or from the Strait of Bab el Mandeb.

The IRTC corridor has two lanes, each five miles wide, running parallel, separated by a two-mile wide buffer. The IRTC helps to reduce collision risk and provides standard grid geo-reference coordinates for warship zone coverage of the IRTC. Responsibility for patrolling the MSPA and IRTC is shared among NATO, EU and CTF 151, which is a multinational counter piracy task force with headquarters in Bahrain. Each command element cannot control units from other task forces, but recommendations may be made in order to coordinate deterrence and response. The task forces may communicate with each other over unclassified Mercury circuits and other communications systems. Beyond the efforts of the three multinational task forces, nearly every nation participating in counter piracy operations is willing to protect not just their own ships, but vessels of all nations.

By 2008, some merchant shipping firms began to route ships around South Africa rather than risk a Gulf of Aden transit. Going around the Cape of Good Hope rather than through the Gulf of Aden, the Red Sea and the Suez Canal, is considerably longer and more expensive. The route around the Cape of Good Hope is an extra 2,700 miles and takes an additional 10–14 days. As the cost of operating most ocean-going ships is between $50,000 and $1 million per day, rerouting is expensive. In an era of "just in time" manufacturing and clockwork shipping that reduced inventory costs and increased efficiency, the extra time required for the transit would have a market effect of raising the costs of doing business.

As attacks accelerated throughout 2009–2011, the commercial shipping industry and the seafarer's union threatened to boycott the dangerous northerly route in favor of the longer passage. But since pirates are operating so far east into the Indian Ocean and Arabian Sea, preying on cabotage shipping from the Indian subcontinent, it is not certain that bypassing the Gulf of Aden makes for a safer voyage. Pirates also have operated as far south as the Mozambique Channel. Still, the Baltic and International Maritime Council (BIMCO) and the International Transport Worker's Federation (ITF) have threatened to boycott the dangerous waters if governments cannot provide greater maritime security. The European Shipper's Council has warned that any such boycott would impose significant costs on the global supply chain, and further weaken an industry beset by rising fuel costs and uncertain world demand. Costs of re-routing ships around the Cape of Good Hope are estimated to be $2.4 to $3 billion per year.[6] At a time of fragile global economic growth, shifting sea lanes farther south and east to avoid piracy threats could further weaken maritime trade.

Now the costs of Somali piracy are ballooning. Ransoms are going up. During the first half of 2010, the number of attacks in the Gulf of Aden declined by 18 percent to 196, but the number of attacks in the Somali Basin increased by 14 percent to 51. But from 2009 to 2011, the average ransom paid to release a hijacked ship and captured crew has more than doubled, from $1 million to $3.5–4 million per year, and individual ransoms paid in excess of $10 million have been reported.

Despite the efforts to contain the threat, the costs of piracy are climbing, and now reach an estimated $7 to $12 billion per year. Ransoms, insurance (war risk, kidnap and ransom or "K&R," cargo and hull insurance) have increased steadily.[7] Security costs for ship owners and carriers have reached as much as $2.5 billion per year, and this figure does not include the cost of warship sorties and patrols.[8] If the macro-economic costs to world trade are considerable, the impact on African and regional states has been even greater. Secondary costs have been imposed on nations in the region, and include the government of Egypt losing revenue from Suez Canal operations ($642 million per year), a reduction in commercial trade by Kenya and Yemen ($564 million per year) and losses in fisheries and tourism for the tiny Seychelles ($6 million per year).[9] Even landlocked countries on the continent, such as Rwanda, are affected by Somali piracy through increased costs of regional trade.

---

[6] *Id.*

[7] See The Economic Costs of Piracy, Oceans Beyond Piracy, www.oceansbeyondpiracy.org (2010).

[8] *Id.*

[9] *Id.*

The pirates operating from Somalia are comprised of three types. The ex-militia men serve as the "muscle" for the seafaring gangs. These men are experienced fighters and generally own their weapons, which they bring to the enterprise. Militia enforcers generally would earn $100 per month, and the work is dangerous and dirty. Employment as a pirate offers the possibility of vastly higher rewards in a comparatively safer operating environment. "Techies" provide essential logistical and communications support, although they also may operate from a mother ship as much as from shore. The techies understand how to navigate and operate global positioning system (GPS) devices, and work and maintain radio communications and the automatic identification system (AIS) that can help to identify easy targets. Most importantly, techies supply ready access to Internet and cellular telephone communications, which are essential to the drawn out process of negotiating with ship owners. The third group of pirates consists of former fishermen who understand the sea and are able to operate on the oceans. These savvy mariners are accustomed to the vagaries of the monsoon cycle, and the pattern of currents and winds in the western Indian Ocean.

If pirates are captured, it is exceedingly difficult to establish their correct names (in fact, Somalis may use up to seven names, each for a different purpose or used to identify the Somali within a distinct hierarchical relationship), age (Somalis may not know exactly how old they are or their own birth date), or village or clan. False names are provided to investigators, and real names are virtually impossible to verify because of alternative spelling and lack of standard transliteration into English. Pirates do not carry identification. The clan-based Somali society, which is virtually impenetrable to outsiders, is a complex milieu of families, sub-clans, clans and shifting informal relationships, and adds another layer of confusion and complexity to the problem. Perhaps most worrisome, recent intelligence suggests that Somali pirates may be making payments to Al-Shabaab, the powerful Islamic extremist militia that seeks to impose Sharia law in the unstable nation.

Law of the Sea

The naval forces that are pursuing operational maritime security are complemented by international law and domestic legal systems designed to deter and punish pirates. The criminal law infrastructure for bringing pirates to justice was developed over centuries. Nations that capture suspected pirates must grapple with how to conduct criminal prosecutions against the lawless gangs. The jurisdiction in which the pirates are brought must have adequate substantive and procedural criminal laws against piracy, and have the administrative capacity and logistical capability to conduct the trial. But within this legal setting, the status and applicability of the international law is quite clear.

The legal aspects of counter piracy efforts constitute another important dimension of the problem. The law of nations recognizes that acts of maritime piracy include robbery, assault, murder, theft, destruction of property and hostage taking committed at sea. There are several models of contemporary maritime piracy: pure armed robbery at sea, robbery accompanied by cargo theft (typically occurring in port); and, the "phantom ship" phenomenon seen in Asia, in which a vessel is taken by pirates, the crew often murdered and the ship re-registered under a different name in a new flag state. Somali pirates, however, created yet another model of piracy – one that is centered on ship hijacking and hostage-taking for ransom. The Somali model has proved to be an immensely lucrative and low-risk approach to maritime piracy. Strengthening the legal response among the community of nations is one part of a comprehensive approach intended to raise the punitive costs to the pirates of doing business. Each of the forgoing models triggers the rule of universal jurisdiction for piracy, which is a hallmark of international law. Universal jurisdiction means that the law of nations recognizes that any nation may assert jurisdiction over the crime of piracy. This rule does not automatically create jurisdiction in domestic legal systems, however, and assertion of jurisdiction over a particular criminal act is determined by the jurisdiction in which the case is brought.

The United States is a typical criminal jurisdiction. As a nation of laws, the rules of society are fairly and clearly set forth by elected legislators. An independent judiciary sets limits on the law, which is enforced by an independent elected Executive branch under the leadership of the President of the United States. This structure, which is set forth in the U.S. Constitution, provides a framework for national governance. The scope of international law that undergirds coalition counter piracy efforts, in contrast, is derived from two millennia of jurisprudential philosophy, state practice and western development of positivist legal conventions.

There are five major strands of counter piracy law. First, the United Nations Convention on the Law of the Sea (UNCLOS) serves as the omnibus, umbrella treaty for essentially all activities occurring on the oceans. The treaty represents the fruition of four multilateral efforts over the past century to codify the laws applicable to the oceans. Major multilateral conferences in 1930, 1958 and 1960 were unsuccessful in adopting a major restatement of the international law of the sea The Third UN Conference on the Law of the Sea, however, which met from 1973–1982, codified the essential provisions of, *inter alia*, counter piracy law.

Under Article 100 of UNCLOS, all nations have a general duty to cooperate against maritime piracy, and other provisions immediately following Article 100 specify authority for nations to act against piracy. Second, the United Nations Security Council may act against piracy, declaring it a threat to international peace and security under Chapter VII of the UN Charter. Third, the 1988 Convention on the Suppression of Unlawful Acts against the Safety of Maritime Navigation (SUA) and the 2005 SUA Protocol provide an additional framework for states to extradite or prosecute persons suspected of ship hijacking. Since entry into force of the 2005 Protocol on July 28, 2010, the amended SUA Convention creates a broad set of additional rules that states can use to criminalize violent crimes at sea. Fourth, the UN Convention against Transnational Organized Crime (TOC) facilitates mutual legal assistance and law enforcement cooperation against international criminal networks. Finally, the International Maritime Organization (IMO) has adopted a series of guidelines against maritime piracy that form an essential source of soft law for governments and the shipping industry. Over the past decade, the IMO has served as a forum for a new menu of interlocking maritime security treaties and guidance, including major revisions to the Safety of Life at Sea Convention (SOLAS) and support to the development of Best Management Practices (BMP) by the world's civil shipping industry.

Piracy affects the entire international community, and therefore is a classic collective action problem that can be addressed through adoption and implementation of uniform rules. The international law of maritime piracy is reflected in the 1982 United Nations Convention on the Law of the Sea (UNCLOS). UNCLOS is recognized as the constitution for the world's oceans and it reflects customary international law binding on all nations. UN Security Council Resolution 1838 (2008) reaffirmed that UNCLOS sets forth the governing legal framework for suppressing piracy.

There are a variety of legal rationales that could support a compliant or noncompliant boarding of a hijacked vessel or pirate ship. During armed conflict, merchant vessels may be boarded by belligerents to a conflict in the exercise of the belligerent right of visit and search to determine the neutral character of the goods on board, but that rule of naval warfare does not apply to maritime piracy. In peacetime, boarding a vessel by the naval forces of a state other than the state of registry may be conducted with the consent of the flag State under articles 92 and 94 of the Law of the Sea Convention. The United States recognizes that the master of the vessel also may provide consent to a boarding of his vessel, since he is the agent of the flag State. Finally, under article 51 of the U.N. charter and customary international law, all nations may exercise of the right of individual or collective self-defense against a vessel committing a hostile act or demonstrating hostile intent. Measures short of the use of force, such as a noncompliant ship boarding of a suspect ship, are part of the tools available during the exercise of self-defense.

Naval forces also may board merchant vessels under the peacetime right of approach and visit pursuant to Article 110 of UNCLOS, if reasonable grounds exist to suspect the vessel is engaged in piracy. In some cases, the extension of port State control may be used to board a vessel that has declared its intention to enter port. Of course, port States exercise near plenary authority over ships moored at the pier, since those vessels are inside the internal waters of the port state and subject to port State regulations. The Security Council may authorize all states to take action against piracy under chapter VII of the UN charter, providing yet another potential authority for boarding pirate vessels.

It is typical of the vessels attacked by Somali pirates that the ships are registered in one state, such as Malta, owned by a corporation located in another state, such as the United Arab Emirates, and operated by a crew composed of nationals of several additional states, such as the Philippines, Romania, and Pakistan. Furthermore, the vessel is likely to be transporting either containerized cargo or bulk commodities owned by companies in one or more countries. For example, the very large crude carrier *Sirius Star*, which was hijacked in 2008, was registered in Liberia but owned by Aramco, a Saudi corporation. Moreover, a warship from a third state may interrupt a piracy attack, and each country with an important equity at stake is likely to have different tactics and distinct rules of engagement.

Articles 100–107 of UNCLOS contain both broad philosophy and specific mandate concerning repression of maritime piracy. First, naval warships or law enforcement vessels of any nation may interdict pirate ships. Ordinarily, jurisdiction may be asserted over a ship at sea only by the flag State, or in special cases, by a port or coastal State. There is no international law requirement for a jurisdictional link to the flag State – any nation may exercise jurisdiction over pirates, which are considered to be the "enemy of all mankind." Piracy may occur in any waters beyond the 12-nautical mile territorial sea; inside the territorial sea, the crime is termed "armed robbery at sea," and is the sole legal responsibility of the coastal State.

The generalized authority of all nations to assert universal jurisdiction over pirate ships is set forth in Article 105 of UNCLOS, which states: "On the high seas [or exclusive economic zone], or in any other place outside the jurisdiction of any state, every state may seize a pirate ship [or ship] taken by piracy and under the control of pirates, and arrest the persons and seize the property on board." In the case of Somalia, however, UN Security Council Resolution 1816 (2008) provides authority for warships from other nations to conduct counter piracy operations in Somalia's territorial sea.

Second, the crime of piracy is conducted for "private ends," meaning that pirates are not licensed to act on behalf of a government, but instead are private individuals. The "private ends" requirement, however, does mean that piracy may not be politically motivated, as is often the case with pirates operating against oil terminals located in the Gulf of Guinea. The intention to commit armed robbery or gain a pecuniary or monetary interest is also not required, since violence or acts of depredation fulfill the *actus reus* element of the crime of piracy. Acts of piracy may be prompted by feelings of greed, hatred or revenge, and not merely by the desire for gain. Third, two ships must be involved for a crime to constitute the act of piracy – a piracy craft (such as a skiff) and a victim ship. Mutiny of a single vessel is not piracy under the definition set forth in UNCLOS, which raises a "two state" problem when the pirates or hijackers come from the passengers or crew members. Fourth, the crime of piracy includes what are called "inchoate" or planning offenses, such as conspiracy to commit piracy or attempted piracy.

The definition of piracy is set forth in Article 101 of UNCLOS, which states that piracy is:

(a) Any illegal acts of violence or detention, or any act of depredation, committed for private ends by the crew or the passengers of a private ship or private aircraft, and directed –
   (i) On the high seas, against another ship or aircraft, or against persons or property on board such ship or aircraft;
   (ii) Against a ship, aircraft, persons or property in a place outside the jurisdiction of any state;
(b) Any act of voluntary participation in the operation of a ship or of an aircraft with knowledge of the facts making it a pirate ship or aircraft;
(c) Any act of inciting or intentionally facilitating an act described in subparagraph (a) or (b).

Pirate ships, however, may not be seized in the 12-nautical mile territorial seas, archipelagic waters (such as Indonesian or Philippine internal waters, set within the baseline forming the archipelago), and internal waters (such as harbors), without the consent of the coastal State, even for criminal acts of piracy that were committed on the high seas. In areas that have national waters in close proximity to other nations, fleeing pirate vessels can escape into the territorial sea of a neighboring state and avoid capture if the adjoining state is unable to act. A coastal State may lawfully pursue a ship from the territorial sea, archipelagic waters, or the contiguous zone onto the high seas, however, when it reasonably believes the vessel engaged in criminal activity that violated the law of that state.

If the pursuit begins within the contiguous zone, however, it may be conducted only for violations of the rules pertaining to the contiguous zone, such as customs-related offenses. Likewise, if a foreign ship violates the lawful regulations of the coastal State pertaining to the Exclusive Economic Zone, such as state fisheries laws, the coastal State may initiate pursuit of the vessel onto the high seas. The coastal State's right of hot pursuit does not extend into the territorial sea of another state, however, without the permission of the other coastal State.

Under the auspices of the International Maritime Organization (IMO), nations developed the 1988 Convention on the Suppression of Unlawful Acts against the Safety of Maritime Navigation (SUA) and the 2005 Protocol, which entered into force on July 28, 2010. These two treaties, which constitute a single protocol for States' parties to the later instrument, provide ample additional authority for interdicting piracy and collaborating in the detention, extradition and prosecution of piracy suspects.

The 1988 SUA Convention sets forth the rule that all nations have an obligation to prosecute or extradite individuals suspected of ship hijacking. UN Security Council resolution 1846 (2008) noted that the 1988 SUA Convention provides a comprehensive framework for cooperation in criminal prosecution of most types of piracy. The 2005 Protocol to the 1988 Convention criminalizes a wide range of offenses committed on a ship, including endangering a vessel, using a ship as a weapon, or seizing a vessel in order to compel government action.

Many commentators have focused on improving international law as a way to address the threat of piracy in the Horn of Africa. But the international law of maritime piracy is quite potent and clear – any nation may assert criminal jurisdiction over the crime of piracy. The courts of the state that carried out the seizure of suspected pirates may prosecute the detained individuals in criminal court. Most scholars also accept that the state seizing suspected pirates may transfer the suspects to other nations for legal disposition. Ultimately, the law of piracy is managed by each nation according to domestic laws, and the international law of maritime piracy is quite broad and derives largely from state practice in the law of the sea. Despite the disparate strands of law and the disorganized legal framework, the law against piracy has proved quite successful. Nonetheless, there is an attraction for creation of a tidy, top-down approach. The emergence of piracy as a contemporary maritime threat, and the fragmented nature of the law have enticed numerous proposals for legal reform. There is an elegant simplicity to the idea of a single multilateral institution to assume responsibility for counter piracy operations that has proved too tempting for a legion of scholars to resist.

Despite the pleasing symmetry and comforting notion of liberal globalism that is the foundation for most proposals, however, it is unlikely that the various national and regional counter piracy initiatives can be unified into a single program. Proposals to unify counter piracy efforts with the creation, for example of an international piracy court located in The Hague, generally suffer from a failure to appreciate logistical and practical difficulties, contending approaches and burden-sharing disparities inherent in such efforts. For the foreseeable future, counter piracy operations will be most commonly and effectively undertaken as a national effort, albeit one that is coordinated with partner nations. Because of this reality, national criminal law rather than international criminal law holds the key to bringing pirates to justice.

Djibouti Code of Conduct

There are three major international organizations that are involved in facilitating counter piracy activities in the western Indian Ocean. The United Nations Division of Ocean Affairs and Law of the Sea (DOALOS) and the United Nations Office of Drugs and Crime (UNODC) focus on developing international oceans law and international criminal law, and helping states to implement their international obligations within a domestic system. The International Maritime Organization (IMO) is focused on capacity building and ensuring that states in the region have national laws that address maritime piracy. The international organization is also working with both UNODC and the European Union (EU). Furthermore, the IMO is seeking ways to connect its efforts to the Eastern and Southern Africa and Indian Ocean (ESA-IO) initiative, which was devised at a meeting in Mauritius in October 2010.[10] At the tactical level, sea-going law-enforcement must be conducted within a domestic legal framework that has rules for arrest and detention of suspected pirates.

The Djibouti Code of Conduct is one of the most significant efforts of the IMO in recent years. The Code of Conduct concerning the Repression of Piracy and Armed Robbery against Ships in the Western Indian Ocean and the Gulf of Aden is the first regional agreement between Arab and African countries to address maritime piracy. The Code has its inception in groundwork laid by IMO. In November 2007 IMO Resolution A.1002(25) called upon regional states in East Africa to conclude an international agreement to prevent, deter and suppress piracy. Seeking to replicate the success of counter-piracy agreements in Asia, the IMO sponsored meetings from 2005–2008 in Yemen (Sana'a Seminar), Oman (the Oman Workshop), and Tanzania (Dar es Salaam), to facilitate negotiation of an anti-piracy agreement among regional states. Djibouti, Egypt, Eritrea, Jordan, Oman, Somalia, and Yemen endorsed the Sana'a-Muscat Memorandum of Understanding in January 2006 at the

[10] Joint Communiqué from the Eastern and Southern Africa – Indian Ocean Ministers and European Union High Representative at the 2nd Regional Ministerial Meeting on Piracy and Maritime Security in the Eastern and Southern Africa and Indian Ocean Region, October 7, 2010, Grand Bay, Republic of Mauritius.

Oman Workshop.[11] A final meeting in Djibouti in January 2009 produced an agreement among seventeen regional states to enhance cooperation in the prosecution and repatriation of captured Somali pirates.

Djibouti, Ethiopia, Kenya, Madagascar, Maldives, Seychelles, Somalia, the United Republic of Tanzania and Yemen signed the original agreement, which remains open for signature by other countries in the region. Comoros, Egypt, Eritrea, Jordan, Mauritius, Oman, Saudi Arabia, Sudan and United Arab Emirates have since signed the Code. Altogether, eighteen countries have signed the agreement out of 21 eligible states. Because of the limited capacity of the countries involved, however, the Code of Conduct is not legally binding. Participating nations are expected to act only in accordance with available resources, with international law, and within their respective national laws.

The signatories of the Code agree to cooperate in conducting a number of counter piracy activities, and the document is based on four broad pillars: information sharing, updating legislation, regional training and capacity building (particularly for maritime security). First, the states involved are establishing reliable maritime domain awareness networks in the region, including AIS and LRIT and radar networks, in order to be able to locate and track merchant shipping. The IMO is working with regional states to identify bilateral technical projects to fit AIS and radar sites along the periphery of the western Indian Ocean.

By capitalizing on existing infrastructure, the IMO is fusing information collection and sharing protocols and agreements to establish a common regional operating "picture." In Tanzania, for example, the IMO and the United States have improved the nation's national maritime domain awareness architecture by connecting an X-band radar at Tanga with AIS stations at Pemba, Kilwa, Ungujia and Mtwara and with a Maritime Center and base station in Dar es Salaam. The World Bank has funded a complementary effort to develop a data link from the Maritime Electronic Highway in the Mozambique Channel.

Second, states also are developing coastal security and naval forces, including boats, equipment, facilities, and maritime technical training, to be able to conduct constabulary patrols in the region. Finally, the states are establishing long-term infrastructure in the region to support maritime safely, security, and environmental resource management. The Republic of Korea is providing funds for linking Vessel Tracking Services (VTS) and AIS in the headquarters of the Yemen Coast Guard with the Information Sharing Centers in Sana'a, Djibouti and Oman. Once a common operating picture is established, the IMO is exploring the concept of creating an East Africa Standby Force Maritime

[11] IMO Doc. MSC 85/9, Draft Report of the Maritime Safety Committee on its Eighty-Fifth Session, Dec. 1, 2008, p. 89 and IMO Doc. C 105/12/Add.1, October 8, 2010.

Forces (EASF MARFOR) to maintain maritime security as a strategic regional objective under a single combined command structure.

Additional efforts include construction of new port facilities, aids to navigation and drafting regulatory codes that preserve freedom of navigation while also supporting port and coastal State authorities. The overall effort is comprehensive, and the Code provides the framework for assistance to regional states. Increasingly, donors are channelling funding for individual projects through the Djibouti Code framework, with the goal of enhancing the ability of states in the region to accomplish the range of anti-piracy tasks:

(a) the investigation, arrest and prosecution of persons, who are reasonably suspected of having committed acts of piracy and armed robbery against ships, including those inciting or intentionally facilitating such acts;
(b) the interdiction and seizure of suspect ships and property on board such ships;
(c) the rescue of ships, persons and property subject to piracy and armed robbery and the facilitation of proper care, treatment and repatriation of seafarers, fishermen, other shipboard personnel and passengers subject to such acts, particularly those who have been subjected to violence; and
(d) the conduct of shared operations – both among signatory States and with navies from countries outside the region – such as nominating law enforcement or other authorized officials to embark on patrol ships or aircraft of another signatory.

Participating states also agree to apprehend and prosecute persons. Pirates that are prosecuted and convicted at trial and imprisoned are entitled to proper care and treatment. The agreement also calls for states to repatriate seafarers, fishermen, and other shipboard passengers and victims of piracy. The signatory nations undertook to review their national legislation to ensure that there are laws in place to criminalize piracy and armed robbery against ships and to make adequate provision for the exercise of jurisdiction, conduct of investigations and prosecution of alleged offenders. Signatory states expressed a commitment to report relevant information through a system of national focal points and information centers, and to interdict ships suspected of engaging in acts of piracy or armed robbery against ships.

The Code provides for sharing information through creation of three tactical maritime security centers, which are being established in East Africa with the support of the IMO. In April 2010, the secretariat of the IMO in London developed a menu of projects to promote the Code of Conduct regionally. A new Project Implementation Unit (PIU) within the Maritime Safety Division of IMO is the lead institution for the effort. The PIU is funded through the Djibouti Code Trust Fund, and is helping to establish a training center

Figure 2: Djibouti Code of Conduct Information Sharing Network

Mombasa ISC,	Sana'a ISC,	Dar es Salaam ISC,
Kenya	Yemen	Kenya
Mauritius	Egypt	Tanzania
Maldives	U.A.E.	Comoros
Seychelles	Djibouti	Reunion (France)
Somalia (South Central)	Ethiopia	Madagascar
	Jordan	Mozambique
	Oman	South Africa
	Saudi Arabia	
	Somalia (Puntland)	
	Sudan	

in Djibouti (Regional Training Center Djibouti – DRTC) and three regional counter-piracy information-sharing centers (ISCs).

The infrastructure for information-sharing leverages existing facilities, such as the Regional Maritime Rescue Coordination Centre in Mombasa, Kenya and the Rescue Coordination Sub-Centre in Dar es Salaam, Tanzania. A new regional maritime information center also is being constructed in Sana'a, Yemen. The Sana'a ISC is studying the feasibility of using Vessel Traffic Services (VTS) and AIS in the Gulf of Aden. All three information-sharing centers are becoming operational as this chapter goes to press in October 2011. The information fusion centers will disseminate alerts regarding imminent threats or incidents to ships, and collect and analyze information, which can be transmitted as actionable intelligence, or be used to prepare statistics on threat trends.

The DRTC will be used to train staff watch officers in the three ISCs. The DRTC is intended to become the single point of contact for maritime training in the region, including maritime authorities and law enforcement agencies. The IMO has funded the construction of the DRTC with a grant to the government of Djibouti of up to $2.5 million. Djibouti is responsible for clearing the site, and providing services and road access to the site. Curriculum will be developed by the government of Djibouti, acting in conjunction with IMO and European Union.

As an initial step, all countries were asked to complete a needs assessment in order to establish a training matrix. The final workshop in Djibouti in May 2011 finalized the finalized training plan. Training in Djibouti will be developed in coordination with the European Commission (EC) team in Djibouti, and the EC team has devised early coursework. The first EC course is partially funded by IMO and was conducted in May 2011.

Each ISC also will integrate law enforcement agencies with the maritime industry and naval forces under a national focal point. The focal point should coordinate among the marine policy sector, port authorities, seafarers, ship owners, shipping agencies, ship registry, insurance companies and P&I clubs, fishery agency, coast guard and naval authorities. (In the United States, broad maritime security coordination is done through the Global Maritime Operational Threat Response (MOTR) Coordination Center, which is located in Washington, D.C.).

The ISCs should facilitate closer cooperation among states and build confidence in addressing the threat of piracy. By linking stakeholders and issuing warnings throughout a network of responders, the focal points can better alert national and coastal shipping to emergent threats. The focal points link tactical maritime law enforcement officials to ministry-level decision makers within each state. Developing these communications nodes is especially helpful in the Horn of Africa, where many countries have adequate laws on the books to deal with piracy, but find that the maritime coastal and naval forces work for a separate ministry and may not have a mandate or authority to take action or arrest pirates. Perhaps the best way to close this gap is to require that government patrol vessels carry on board law enforcement personnel who are authorized to make arrests in cases of piracy. This approach is essentially a domestic ship-riding concept, and it is used by a number of states.

Japan is a major contributor and leader in supporting the IMO's technical cooperation programs, and Tokyo pledged $13.5 million to initiate the Djibouti Code Trust Fund. A handful of prominent international organizations are involved in the effort. The European Commission (EC), Regional Agreement on Combating Piracy and Armed Robbery against ships in Asia (ReCAAP), United Nations Political Office for Somalia (UNPOS), the United Nations Office on Drugs and Crime (UNODC), and the International Criminal Police Organization (Interpol), are working to implement a broad maritime security capacity-building program for the states that have signed the Code. For example, counter-piracy officials from signatory states are receiving training by ReCAAP's Information Sharing Centre in Singapore, which promotes harmonization of counter piracy practices in Africa and Asia.[12]

Maritime and port authority officials from Djibouti, Egypt, Eritrea, Ethiopia, Jordan, Oman, Saudi Arabia, Somalia, Sudan, and Yemen have been trained at the ReCAAPISC.[13] A combined IMO/UNODC workshop was held in Djibouti from March 1 to 3, 2011 for regional ministries of transportation, police, and justice, to develop crime-scene methods and standardized protocols for arrest of suspected pirates. Further IMO/UNODC workshops for western Indian Ocean and Island States occurred in the summer of 2011 in Mombasa.

---

[12] IMO Doc. A.1002 (25) at ¶ 7.

[13] IMO Doc. C 102/14, April 3, 2009, Protection of Vital Shipping Lanes, Sub-regional meeting to conclude agreements on maritime security, piracy and armed robbery against ships for States from the Western Indian Ocean, Gulf of Aden and Red Sea areas. See also, IMO Doc. C/ES.25/12, November 5, 2009, C 102/14/1 5 May 2009, Protection of Vital Shipping Lanes, Project profile for the implementation of the Djibouti Code of conduct.

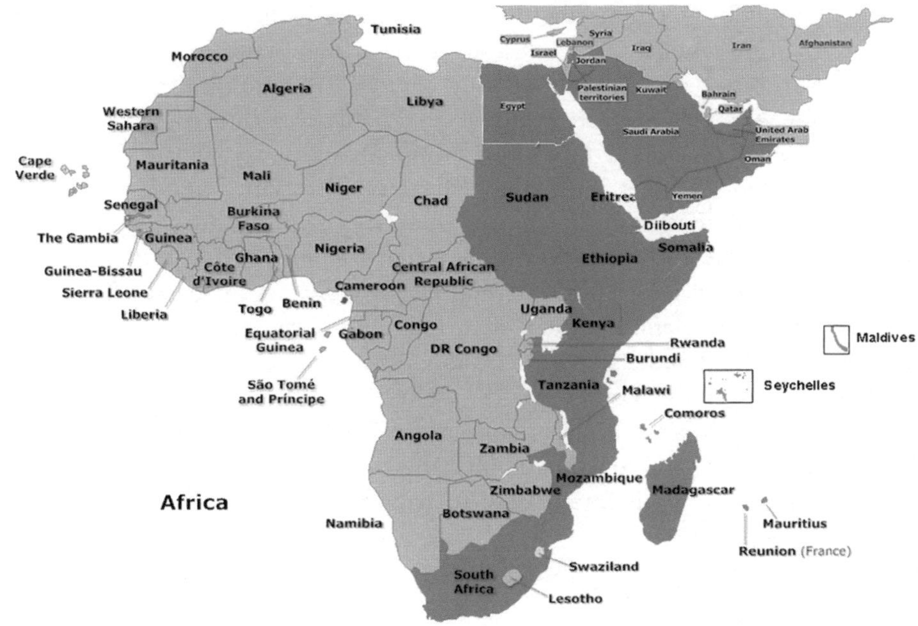

Graphic 1: Countries Eligible to Sign the Djibouti Code of Conduct

Figure 3: Countries prosecuting pirates in their national courts
(United Nations Office of Drugs and Crime, 2011)

State	Prosecutions	Convictions
Belgium	1	
France	15	
India	119	
Germany	10	
Japan	4	
Kenya	119	50
Madagascar	12	
Malaysia	7	
Maldives	34	
Netherlands	10	5
Oman	12	12
Republic of Korea	5	
Seychelles	58	41
Somalia – TFG	18	
Somalia – Puntland	>300	240
Somalia – Somaliland	94	68
Spain	2	
Tanzania	12	6
United States	26	8
Yemen	120	120
	968	

The legal difficulty in countering piracy arises in individual states implementing the international obligation to act against the crime. States may lack adequate domestic criminal laws for prosecuting pirates. In Resolution 1918 (2010), for example, the UN Security Council noted that the domestic criminal laws of a number of states lack provisions criminalizing piracy, or are deficient in criminal procedural rules needed to effectively prosecute pirates. States also face a dearth of the political will and resources required to conduct expensive criminal trials and to imprison convicted foreign pirates for long periods of time. In sum, although the international law against piracy is sufficient to provide a basis for nations to act, many states lack the practical criminal legislation, court and judicial resources and prison capacity to prosecute maritime piracy. Even the United States, which has a highly developed judicial system, has not had an entirely smooth experience in bringing pirates to justice. Consequently, the greatest effort is pivoting toward expanding the number of legal "tools" in the toolbox available to nations that are involved in fighting piracy.

The Contact Group on Piracy off the Coast of Somalia

The Contact Group on Piracy off the Coast of Somalia (CGPCS) is an *ad hoc* group established in the aftermath of a major increase in piracy in the fourth quarter of 2008. On December 16, 2008, the UN Security Council recommended in Resolution 1851 that states form a new coordinating group to counter maritime piracy. Less than one month later, a group of 24 countries formed the CGPCS, which reports to the UN Security Council. Now the Group has more than 60 participating countries, plus AU, EU, League of Arab States, IMO, INTERPOL and NATO.

The CGPCS should not be mistaken for the International Contact Group on Somalia, which focuses on bringing overall political stability to the fractured state. Instead, the CGPCS is a forum to share information and collaborate on issues relating to piracy, but the group has no funding or operational mandate and no decision-making authority or ability to task participating states or organizations. The arrangement is *ad hoc*, so it can adapt. The plenary body has a rotating chair headed by voluntary organizations, and the government of the United Kingdom, including the Foreign & Commonwealth Office and the Office of the Prime Minister, performs Secretariat functions for the group. Thus, the participants are driven by their own compelling national interest, either because they are affected by piracy off the coast of Somalia or they have contributed resources or naval forces to combat piracy.

Figure 4: Plenary Meetings of the Contact Group on Piracy off the Coast of Somalia

Location	Date
United States	January 14, 2009
Egypt	March 17, 2009
United States	May 29, 2009
Japan	September 10, 2010
Greece	June 10, 2010
Norway	January 28, 2011
Korea	November 10, 2010
Turkey	March 21, 2011
Singapore	July 14, 2011
The Netherlands	November 2011
Spain	2012

Divided into four Working Groups (WG) with a fifth on the way, the CGPCS has become the fulcrum of international counter piracy collaboration, largely displacing the IMO as the most important gathering for steering the multilateral effort. Working Group One (WG1) is dedicated to coordinating the disparate counter piracy naval operations being conducted in the Western Indian Ocean. The United Kingdom leads WG1, which has promoted Shared Awareness and Deconfliction (SHADE), an operational coordination process and forum in Bahrain. SHADE is co-chaired by Combined Maritime Forces and EUNAVFOR, and it is open to naval counter-piracy forces irrespective of mandate or affiliation. The group focusing on sharing operational information about suspected pirate vessels, and helps to deconflict force lay down to avoid duplication of effort. Naval forces from more than 24 nations participate in SHADE, benefiting merchant fleets and commercial, recreational, and naval ships.

States share information on criminal prosecution, extradition of suspects, post-trial transfer issues, ensuring production of seafarers at trial, and protection of basic human rights of suspected and convicted pirates. WG1 complements the work of WG2. Working Group Two has also explored creating a legal framework for the transfer of convicted pirates from states in the region, such Kenya and Seychelles, that have prosecuted pirates, back to Somalia, where the pirates can serve their confinement sentences in the newly constructed UN prison that opened in Hargeisa, Somaliland on November 22, 2010.

Working Group Two, chaired by Denmark, focuses on improving options for prosecution of pirates. WG2 is the source of most of the newer legal "tools" that are explained in this chapter, and relate to strengthening domestic policy and laws, creating new agreements and frameworks and building greater judicial capacity. Working Group Three is led by the United States, and is co-chaired by the US Maritime Administration and the US Coast Guard. WG3 is focused on enhancing shipping industry security, including development of the Best

Figure 5: Meetings of Working Group 2 (Legal) of the CGPCS

Location	Date
Vienna	March 5, 2009
Copenhagen	May 5–6, 2009
Copenhagen	August 26–27, 2009
Copenhagen	November 26–27, 2009
Copenhagen	May 17–18, 2010
Copenhagen	November 2–3, 2010
Copenhagen	March 3–4, 2011

Management Practices (BMP) in cooperation with the global shipping industry. The BMP promote shipping self-protection and support seafarers affected by piracy. The Group also enhances communication between commercial shipping and the IMO. Finally, WG4 is responsible for improving public diplomacy concerning the entire effort, and Egypt, which has been preoccupied with internal political upheaval, serves as the head of the effort. Communications strategies can raise awareness about the pernicious effect of piracy on regional stability and economic prosperity.

By influencing audiences in Somalia and regionally, WG4 hopes to reduce the social acceptance of maritime piracy inside Somalia as a viable or an alternative "business model." It remains to be seen whether suggestions to create a fifth WG dedicated to stemming the flow of piracy financing and ransom payments will be acted upon. Already, Italy coordinates an *ad hoc* working group on investigating financial flows. The first meeting was held in the United States in March 2011, and the second was held in Seoul, South Korea in June 2011. The *ad hoc* Work on Financial Flows seeks to disrupt illicit financial payments supporting piracy, including ransom payments (both before and after payment), money laundering (discerning where the money goes), dissecting formal and informal financial networks that finance piracy organizations, and targeting leaders, financiers and investors in the illicit enterprise.

Working Group Two of the CGPCS

Working Group Two (WG2) of the CGPCS was established to explore and implement more effective legal procedures to bring pirates to justice. From the time WG2 first met in January 2009 it has completed nearly ten sessions. The purpose of the meetings is to facilitate prosecution and the imprisonment of pirate suspects within domestic criminal law systems. States are sharing how they approach decision-making for prosecution and extradition of suspects, post-trial transfer issues, how to ensure that seafarer witnesses who may be traveling throughout the world are able to appear to testify at trial. WG2 is also involved in helping states implement basic human rights obligations for suspected and convicted pirates. States have shared their experiences regarding legal and practical challenges to national prosecutions, and the difficulty in apprehending and detaining suspects captured at sea.

In order to have practical value, the meetings developed a collection of legal resources and guidance that is called a "legal toolbox." The toolbox was constructed after discussions and written input to a UNODC questionnaire on the legal and practical challenges facing national piracy prosecutions. The findings of the UNODC report indicate how nations criminalize piracy and armed robbery at sea, the liability of persons for committing the offenses (or attempts to commit the offenses), rules concerning court jurisdiction and evidentiary and procedural requirements affect the outcome of trial.[14]

WG2 met for the sixth time in Copenhagen in November 2010, and participants focused on completing a number of tasks to facilitate prosecution of piracy. First, the participants explored the possibility of adopting a framework for transferring convicted pirates back to Somalia. A model bilateral prisoner transfer agreement could tie the criminal courts in neighboring nations to the prison facility in Somalia. One feature of such agreement is that the prisoners must accept the transfer to Somaliland. Post-trial transfer back to Somalia, however, still involves significant expense.

Initially, WG2 was able to clarify a number of the basic legal aspects of counter piracy activities. First, the group determined that there was a strong legal basis in UNCLOS as well as ample UN Security Council resolutions and the Convention for the Suppression of Unlawful Acts against the Safety of Maritime Navigation 1988 and Protocol 2005 for suppressing maritime piracy. The Law of the Sea reflects the historic right of all nations to assert universal jurisdiction over suspected pirates, although nations do not have an express obligation to prosecute suspects in criminal court. The WG determined, importantly, that there was a clear basis in international law for any state to prosecute suspected pirates – not merely the state which initially seized the suspects – resolving doubts about extradition.

Second, the group determined that the fight against piracy is a law enforcement activity – it is not the conduct of warfare. Consequently, the rules governing counter piracy operations are derived from human rights law and apply in a law enforcement paradigm, rather than international humanitarian law that would apply during times of armed conflict. This finding means that human rights legal issues are bound to arise. States may hold differing views on the rights of suspected pirates who are apprehended, detained or transferred. Pirates

---

[14] IMO Doc. LEG 97/9/1, September 30, 2010.

are protected from non-humane treatment in the same way as all people. Some interpretations of non-refoulement standards in refugee law also might apply to suspected pirates, potentially barring their return to Somalia. Non-refoulement is a term of art that means states have a duty not to return refugees to places from which they have fled if there is danger that they could be persecuted after return to their homeland. Third, the group determined that states are authorized to apprehend pirates in accordance with Article 105 of UNCLOS.

Designed to ensure national prosecution, the toolbox is also comprised of academic texts containing compilations of relevant international law, information sharing authorized by national counter piracy legislation, checklists on national approaches to prosecution of pirates in criminal court, templates for the transfer of suspected pirates, memorandums of understanding concerning foreign officers serving as ship riders on board patrol vessels, protocols for evidence gathering and chain of custody, and specific advice on how one nation may hand over a suspected or convicted pirate to another state.

The toolbox was designed to ensure nations have a package of essential rules and practices to enable criminal prosecution of piracy suspects. Upon interdicting pirates at sea, states are faced with a series of questions concerning legal disposition. The first question an apprehending state should address is whether it intends to prosecute the suspects in criminal court. If the nation does not intend to prosecute the suspects, then the flag State of the ship that was attacked may undertake criminal prosecution. If the flag State of the commercial ship declines to prosecute the case at trial, then a third state may be willing and able to do so. But the challenges of national criminal prosecution remain. Many states lack the political or logistical ability to successfully try suspected pirates in court. States also may lack national criminal procedure and laws to permit criminal prosecution under the concept of universal jurisdiction. Finally, nations may not have substantive criminal offenses of piracy in their current legislation.

Working Group Two seeks to remedy any of these shortcomings that can be found in national law. All affected states should have provisions for universal jurisdiction in the prosecution of pirates so that they may conduct trials of pirates seized by the naval forces of another nation. States also should have robust criminal justice systems that are capable of dealing with piracy cases. Finally, nations must make the decision to criminally prosecute suspected pirates. The responsibility for developing criminal laws and procedural rules for cases of universal jurisdiction falls particularly heavily on Somalia and neighboring nations.

Until such time as Somalia has the human capacity and the logistical capability to conduct criminal trials of piracy suspects, and confine those found guilty of the crime of piracy, other nations will continue to step into the breach. States should be prepared to prosecute or transfer suspected pirates to States that are willing to prosecute. Thus, either permanent or *ad hoc* arrangements should be made with other nations in order to facilitate transfer. States that are willing to prosecute suspected pirates should be supported, but currently there are only a handful of states that have shown the capability and willingness to criminally prosecute: Somalia, Kenya and the Seychelles. Finally, imprisoning pirates – often for years – creates a significant burden on many nations. Transferring pirates to one state, such as returning them to Somalia, after criminal prosecution and conviction in another state, is also a major challenge.

Working Group Two continues to develop the toolbox, which, by 2010, already included the following:

- Checklist of steps states might take to ensure that they are able to prosecute suspected pirates – closing possible gaps in national legislation, procedures etc.
- List of impediments to prosecution that have made prosecution efforts less effective than necessary
- UNODC report on legal and practical challenges with regard to prosecution in CGPCS States, including information on relevant national legal systems.
- Terms of reference for the International Trust Fund to help defray expenses associated with prosecution of suspected pirates as well as other activities related to implementing CGPCS objectives regarding combating piracy in all its aspects.
- A compilation of the international legal basis for prosecution of suspected pirates: *Treaty Jurisdiction Over Pirates: A Compilation of Legal Texts with Introductory Notes,* by Dr. Douglas Guilfoyle, University College London (August 26–27, 2009).
- A generic template on evidentiary standards, accompanied by an explanatory note.
- A generic template for and discussion paper on "ship rider" agreements.
- A general template for obtaining flag state consent when placing military personnel on commercial vessels flagged to other States.
- A generic template for drafting a Memorandum of Understanding on the conditions of transfer of suspected pirates and/or armed robbers as well as seized property.

Among these, three documents concerning the collection of evidence also are prominent instruments in the toolbox. The three documents are: the US Counter-Piracy Evidence Collection Guidance, which the author helped to develop while serving as Oceans Law & Policy Adviser with the US Joint Staff, the Kenya Transfer Guidance for piracy Suspects, and the Seychelles Transfer guide. The toolbox also contains guidance for ensuring national decision-making networks are in place to enable states to make rapid interagency-vetted decisions on criminal prosecution and extradition of suspected pirates. Best practices for post-trial transfer of pirates helps states accepting pirates that have been convicted at trial in another jurisdiction. Information on approaches to the criminalization of piracy and the possession of piracy-related equipment, such as boarding hooks and ladders and large horsepower outboard marine engines assists states in refining their criminal laws against maritime piracy. Finally, the toolbox contains suggestions on how states can make improvements in data collection and processing of suspects, to include biometrics, and legal aspects of human rights and piracy financing.[15]

US Counter-Piracy Evidence Collection Guidance

The US Counter-Piracy Evidence Collection Guidance, formerly called the US Disposition and Logistics Guidance, is useful as a guide for tactical processing of pirate suspects by commanding officers of warships patrolling off the Horn of Africa. The original version was coordinated among the Pentagon, the Department of State and the US Coast Guard, and subsequently released to commander, US Central Command by the Joint Staff in 2006.

The revised document states that law enforcement should be contacted to begin a criminal investigation and to initiate the gathering of intelligence as soon as the initial scene of the incident is secured. Warships conducting counter piracy maritime interdiction operations should prepare a summary report, indicating the location of the incident, the actions taken to disrupt the piracy activities, indicia of piracy during the interdiction (such as observing a display of weapons or other piracy paraphernalia by the suspects, including high horsepower outboard marine engines on board skiffs), the nature of the contact with the suspected pirates, and any other piracy incidents reported in the area over the previous 48 hours.

Investigators should try to identify accurately the suspects, including obtaining their name (and variations on the spelling of the name and family name), age, race, nationality, languages spoken, place of birth (identified by a parish, village, settlement, or landmark), and obtain photographs of the suspect. Diagrams and documentation outlining the piracy attack often are helpful to a criminal court trying to piece together the facts long after they occurred. Statements should be obtained from victim witnesses and government witnesses, all who must be made available and produced at trial in order to conduct a successful prosecution. All evidence must be secured to ensure a proper and unbroken chain of custody, including documentation of the communications equipment,

[15] IMO Doc. MSC 88/INF.10, September 20, 2010.

list of boarding equipment, such as ladders and hooks, and a list of weapons used in the attack – all supplemented by photographs.

Kenya Transfer Guidance

At the Copenhagen meeting in November 2010, WG2 focused on completing a number of tasks to facilitate prosecution of piracy. First, the participants explored the possibility of creating a legal framework for the transfer of convicted pirates from prosecuting states in the region, such Kenya and Seychelles, to Somalia to serve their sentences in the newly-constructed UN prison that opened in Somaliland, on November 22, 2010. A model bilateral prisoner transfer agreement could tie the more developed criminal courts in neighboring nations to the prison facility in Somalia. One feature of such agreement is that the prisoners must voluntarily accept the transfer to Somaliland. Post-trial transfer back to Somalia, however, still involves significant expense. A long-term solution to the problem of transferring convicted Somali pirates is to develop the criminal law infrastructure inside Somalia to handle the entire criminal law process, from indictment through pre-detention trial detention and arraignment to post-trial imprisonment of those suspects found guilty of piracy. The cost of developing such an independent penal and judicial capacity in Somaliland and Puntland is about $20 million.

The nation of Kenya has borne a disproportionate amount of the burden of criminally prosecuting Somali pirates. In 2006, Kenya conducted its first piracy prosecution by taking to trial 10 pirates that were picked up by the USS *Churchill.* All defendants were convicted in court and were awarded seven years confinement. In December 2008, the United Kingdom and Kenya signed a memorandum of agreement to facilitate the disposition and prosecution of Somali pirates seized by the British Navy. The United States and Kenya signed a similar agreement in January 2009. In March 2009, the EU and Kenya also signed an MOU. Although since the time of signature the memorandums of agreement have expired, Kenya has continued to accept suspected Somali pirates from other countries on a case-by-case basis, citing the general duty of states to cooperate to repress piracy. By November 2010, Kenya had accepted 17 cases, which included 142 suspected pirates. The primary challenge in these cases has been overcoming the logistical and practical difficulty of ensuring the appearance of seafarer witnesses at trial.

Kenya has criminally prosecuted more Somali pirates than all other nations combined. Under the Penal Code of Kenya, the crime of piracy is proscribed, as "any person who, in territorial waters or upon the high seas, commits any act of piracy *jure gentium* is guilty of the offence of piracy." The statute does not contain a more complete definition, but since Kenya became a party to

UNCLOS in 1989, the nation imports the definition of piracy reflected in Article 101 of the treaty, which is regarded as reflective of customary international law and binding on all nations.

Kenya released the Transfer Guidance for Piracy Suspects to facilitate coordination between Kenya and foreign maritime security forces. Under Kenyan criminal law, prosecutors must show that suspected pirates participated in the commission of the criminal offense of piracy as either a principal or joint offender. Article 20(1) of the Penal Code indicates that every person who actually does an act which constitutes an offense, or who does an act that enables another to do an act that constitutes an offense, or who aids, abets or counsels another committing such act, may be charged either with offense of the commission of the crime of piracy or the offense of an attempted commission of the crime of piracy.

In July 2009,UNODC issued guidance for countries requesting transfer of piracy suspects to Kenya. The guidance was developed during a workshop held on June 25, 2009 in conjunction with Kenya Department of Public Prosecutors, the EU/Kenya liaison officer for EU Naval Force Operation Atalanta, the legal advisor to the US-led Combined Maritime Forces in Bahrain, and a representative from the US Naval Criminal Investigative Service. The guidance includes a communication checklist specifying information to be provided to Kenyan prosecutors, as well as evidentiary standards to ensure successful criminal prosecution. The guidance sets forth appropriate points of contact in Kenya and evidence handling procedures required by Kenya for the associated with the transfer of piracy suspects to Kenyan authorities.

Months after the adoption of the IMO Code of Practice, UNODC issued additional guidelines for transferring suspected pirates from foreign warships to Mombasa, Kenya. Commanding officers of naval vessels should, if possible, ensure that all exhibits are bagged, labeled, and photographed; witness statements prepared and translated into English; the pirates are identified (to the extent feasible); and food and basic emergency medical care are provided to the pirates. UNODC also recommends that pirates not be brought topside of a ship transporting them into port or be visible on the ship as it approaches the jetty. Kenyan officials meet the warships carrying piracy suspects at the pier with a team of prosecutors and up to 10 police officers. The suspected pirates and evidence are taken to the Port Police Station.

As the warship transfers the pirates and evidentiary exhibits, it also may deliver a presentation to Kenyan authorities of the facts surrounding the case, and the legal theory for seizing the suspects. Based on the evidence and presentation, Kenya may decide to accept or decline jurisdiction over the pirates. Acceptance of the pirates is contingent upon successful interviews of the suspects by Kenyan authorities to ascertain that the pirates have not been mistreated. If Kenya accepts the suspects, the physical and demonstrative evidence will be removed from the warship by a local police exhibit handling team. The pirate suspects are formally arrested on the wharf, not on the foreign warship. Since the warship is protected by sovereign immunity in customary international law and Article 32, UNCLOS, Kenyan authorities may not exercise legal jurisdiction on board the ship.

In order to facilitate Kenya's role in piracy law enforcement, UNODC has provided funds for Kenyan police training, for the installation of secure exhibit rooms and for the reconditioning of police vehicles and information technology systems. Likewise, Kenyan courts have received aid from UNODC in how to transport witnesses to trial, how to conduct reviews of cases on remand, how to maintain courtroom security during trial, the provision of online legal resources and judicial training for conducting criminal trials, and interpreters and office equipment and assistance in acquiring experienced defense legal counsel.

The UNODC strategic plan for piracy is to support regional centers for criminal prosecution in Kenya and in the Seychelles as a means to ensure fair and efficient trials and imprisonment. That piece already is in place. But the organization also plans on expanding the effort by creating a third and fourth regional center for piracy prosecution in other nations in order to spread the burden. Meanwhile, a Somalia criminal confinement and corrections program is being pursued in order to ensure humane and secure imprisonment of Somali pirates inside Somalia. This effort entails raising the capabilities of Somali prosecutors, judges and legal defense counsel and pursuing substantive legal reform in the country, all with the objective of developing the organic capacity to conduct fair and efficient trials in Somalia.

Seychelles Transfer Guide

Under Section 65 of the Penal Code of Seychelles, piracy and armed robbery at sea are criminal offenses. The law states: "Any person who is guilty of piracy or any crime connected or relating or alleging to piracy shall be liable to be tried and punished accordingly to the law of England for the time being in force." Like US and Kenyan law, the criminal provision concerning piracy in the Seychelles Penal Code does not define precisely what actions constitute the crime of piracy. Instead, the Penal Code adopts the definition contained in UNCLOS, which is more of a broad framework imbued with custom and state practice.

Nations seeking to transfer captured piracy suspects should alert the Seychelles Attorney General and the Seychelles Ministry of Foreign Affairs as soon as possible. The detaining power should convey the number of persons to be transferred to Seychelles, including specific identifying information such as names (including alternate spellings), dates of birth, nationality and residence of suspected pirates, if known. A brief synopsis of the facts of the case should accompany the notification, including the location of incident; evidence supporting allegations of the crime of piracy; and, any specific evidence against each piracy suspect.

Seychelles recommends that nations that would like to hand over suspected pirates to the government of Seychelles should limit the potential number of witnesses that would have to be produced at criminal trial. The entire process of evidence collection should be tailored to reduce the likelihood that a large number of persons or critical personnel might be required to testify in court in Seychelles, reducing the logistical costs of the trial. Toward this end, the Seychelles guidance suggests that states should take the following steps in anticipation of turning over a suspect to authorities for criminal prosecution:

- Appointment of an Exhibit Custodian who is responsible for seizing all exhibits at the scene of the crime (including any dhows or skiffs), handling the exhibits, storing the exhibits and transferring exhibits to the Kenyan Police. Other persons should avoid handling evidentiary exhibits.
- Appointment of a Photography and Video Manager, who can take all the video and photographic evidence to be handed to Kenya. This ensures that only one person has to adduce the evidence in court, particularly for exhibits, such as dhows, that are too large to be physically produced.
- Appointment of an Operational Witness, who serves as the key observer or witness to the piracy incident.
- Appointment of a Primary Boarding Witness (PBW) – a single member of the boarding team that can serve as the key witness to events that occurred during the boarding of the pirated ship or pirate mother ship.

The Seychelles organizes a counter piracy case into three stages, and all evidence should be maintained with this in mind. Stage one constitutes the piracy alert and securing of a suspect vessel by a boarding party constituted of law enforcement or naval teams. Stage one should be recorded through:

- A chronology that provides a backdrop to the narrative of the witness statements. The chronology is a timeline, reporting the grounds for the reasonable suspicion that the vessel is suspected of being engaged in piracy. The chronology should include positional evidence and latitude and longitude data, as well as course and speed of relevant vessels. The evidence is important for proving where the incident took place (e.g. on the high seas or within territorial waters).
- Proof as to how the pirates' mother ship and/or skiffs were involved in an attack against another ship – evidence of the "two ship" requirement.
- Video and photographic evidence obtained once the warship is within visual range of the pirates. The graphic evidence captures the images and behavior of the pirates, and may focus closely on individuals suspected of piracy to confirm in-court identification of the accused.

Stage two includes evidence seized during the task of securing of the suspect pirate vessel. Evidence for stage two includes the actions of the boarding team to preserve the crime scene until the evidence collection team can be transferred from the warship to the skiff or mother ship. Consequently, the boarding team should ensure the Primary Boarding Witness (PBW) is able during trial, so far as possible, to make a note of the original positions of person on the vessel (particularly on a skiff), capture interaction among the suspects and between the suspects and the victims, and between the suspects and the boarding team. In order to track all of the people involved, every victim and suspect should be assigned a unique identifying reference number by the PBW.

Furthermore, the boarding team should not handle or move any pirate weapons or ammunition, unless dictated by safety. Evidence should remain *in situ* until the arrival of the evidence team. If any suspect possesses weapons or piratical paraphernalia, the PBW should make a note for the record. The boarding team also should keep suspects from talking to each other as much as possible. All suspects and victims should be photographed (front and profile), and images of the vessel hull and internal structure should be captured, with particular attention to any fishing nets or gear. The images should be maintained in a photographic log.

The evidence team should conduct a basic interview to question the suspects and victims, and basic information should be obtained, such as name(s), age, nationality, city of residence, clan (if relevant) role of the vessel, languages spoken, and next of kin. Statements from foreign witnesses and crew are particularly valuable, and the information should be forwarded with future contact details. If the statements are translated into English, they ideally should be accompanied by a testament of their truthfulness, signed by the translator.

Stage three involves the actual transfer of suspects to the Seychelles Police. Upon such transfer to Seychelles authorities, the pirate suspects must be accompanied by:

- Original copies of all statements of witness.
- A copy of detention records, including medical information.
- Original copy of photograph log, with a description of each image.
- Original copy of statements and copies of the evidence log.

Options for Criminal Prosecution

In Resolution 1918, the UN Security Council requested the UN Secretary-General to report on the options available for prosecuting the crime of maritime piracy, including an assessment of the option of creating special domestic chambers in a country in the region, possibly with international components, standing up a regional tribunal or creation of an international tribunal and corresponding imprisonment arrangements. In reply to this tasking, in July 2010, the Secretary-General issued a report that identified seven options for consideration for approaching the question of how to best criminally prosecute pirates: (1) build regional capacity; (2) create a Somali court in a regional state; (3) create a special tribunal in a regional state without UN support; (4) create a special tribunal in a regional state with UN support; (5) create a regional tribunal; (6) establish an international tribunal; and, (7) create an UN Security Council piracy court.[16]

The July 2010 report does not advocate any single approach over the other possibilities, but rather is a neutral compendium of the options available and a discussion of the advantages and disadvantages of each approach. The extraordinary time and costs of establishing and operating international courts, however, and the small volume of suspects they would prosecute, augurs in favor of national courts as a more efficient option.

Previously, at the Fourth meeting of WG2 in Copenhagen in November 2009, the WG2 Chair recorded that the group supported a regional approach:

> *The subsequent discussion in the Working Group showed that the most feasible model would be a specialized/dedicated piracy chamber established within the existing domestic criminal justice system of one or more States and located in one or more States willing and able to undertake prosecution, including Somalia when this becomes possible. It was furthermore the understanding that international elements – if required – could be added both through international financial support and/or through technical assistance (*inter alia *secondment of international personnel).*

At the sixth meeting of WG2, states determined that the most feasible model for criminal prosecution was creation of a dedicated piracy chamber in one or more states in the region. National prosecution by courts of national jurisdiction has

---

[16] S/2010/394, Report of the Secretary-General on possible options to further the aim of prosecuting and imprisoning persons responsible for acts of piracy and armed robbery at sea off the coast of Somalia, including, in particular, options for creating special domestic chambers possibly with international components, a regional tribunal or an international tribunal and corresponding imprisonment arrangements, taking into account the work of the Contact Group on Piracy off the Coast of Somalia, the existing practice in establishing international and mixed tribunals, and the time and resources necessary to achieve and sustain substantive results, July 26, 2010.The Secretary-General's seven options were:

1. Build regional capacity
2. Create a Somali court in a regional state
3. Create a special tribunal in a regional state *without* UN support
4. Create a special tribunal in a regional state *with* UN support
5. Create a regional tribunal
6. Establish an international tribunal
7. Create an UN Security Council piracy court.

proved to be a successful approach for taking individual pirates off the seas, but the lack of general deterrence that it generates has been appalling. But without better options, the criminal trials continue, and East African states that have conducted trials are receiving assistance from the international community. The principal difficulty with a regional piracy chamber is that it leaves open the question of where convicted pirates would be imprisoned, or how they would be transferred back to Somalia to serve a sentence.

At the Seventh meeting of WG2 on March 3–4, 2011, states discussed the report prepared by the UN Secretary-General's Special Adviser on Legal Issues related to Piracy off the Coast of Somalia, submitted by Jack Lang. The report was well received by states, and a number of the 25 proposals contained in the report were discussed and supported by the working group. Lang's proposals to establish a committee to investigate illegal fishing in Somalia's Exclusive Economic Zone (EEZ) and to encourage witnesses to provide testimony by video teleconference were endorsed by WG2.

Discussions at the Seventh meeting also focused in detail on the proposal to establish by the end of 2011, two specialized courts, one in Somalia and another possibly in Tanzania, to try suspected Somali pirates. The UN Office of Legal Affairs (UNOLA) provided information on the legal issues that would arise with the establishment of a Somali court located outside of the territory of Somalia. This recommendation can be acted upon by the CGPCS, which can refer the plan to the UN Security Council. The source of funding for the proposed courts is uncertain, however.

Conclusion – Improving Municipal Law

The toolbox is gaining wider traction, facilitating closer cooperation to ensure that pirates are brought to justice. In February 2011, for example, the Transitional Federal Government of Somalia and the Seychelles signed a post trial transfer agreement. Puntland and Somaliland signed similar memorandums of understanding with Seychelles on April 21, 2011 at a counter piracy conference sponsored by the government of the United Arab Emirates and the Dubai School of Government.[17] Under these arrangements, the receiving state is obliged to continue to enforce the sentence of the sending state to the same extent as if it had been imposed in that state and in accordance with international humanitarian law. Somali piracy has become rampant in waters off the coast of Seychelles, but despite a new wing being added to the national prison (with the

[17] Seychelles Finalizes Agreements on Transfer of Pirates to Puntland and Somaliland, April 2011, Seychelles Nation Online, http://www.nation.sc/index.php?art=23226.

help of foreign aid), the tiny island state cannot feasibly imprison large numbers of convicted Somali pirates for lengthy sentences of confinement.

Piracy is the quintessential crime of universal jurisdiction, which means that any nation may assert criminal law enforcement jurisdiction over piracy. Piracy is not, however, a "universal crime." A universal crime is one that is unlawful in every jurisdiction, such as the crime of genocide. Furthermore, there is no international piracy court, such as the International Criminal Court in The Hague that could assert jurisdiction over the crime of piracy. Creation of an international piracy court would be prohibitively expensive and politically contentious. Consequently, pirates must be brought to justice within a domestic criminal court system. Although there is ample authority in international law for all nations to bring pirates to trial, many states still lack sufficient domestic legislative authority, law enforcement capability, or judicial institutions and prison facilities. The best approach is for nations with greater resources – and a stake in freedom of navigation and global trade – to provide technical, legal and financial resources to expand the capability of justice systems in developing states in the Middle East and East Africa to be able to better repress Somali piracy.

PREDICTING PIRACY: CAN WE ANTICIPATE THE FUTURE OF MARITIME CRIME?

Samuel Pyeatt Menefee[1]

Abstract

This paper examines the possibility of predicting future piracies. Consideration is given to five major factors, viz. (1) patterns of geography, (2) patterns of transportation and trade, (3) patterns of instability, (4) patterns of anti-piracy enforcement activity, and (5) patterns of piracy. Discussing each of these areas in turn, the author provides historical examples of its relationship to the general problem and suggests why each is an important factor for divining where future attacks might occur. Taken together, these factors provide a useful paradigm for assessing maritime risk, albeit one still capable of further refinement. Based on these, the author ventures to make several predictions about the crime in the near, and the more distant, future.

Let me quickly make fifteen *predictions* about piracy. They are predictions about maritime piracy in the near, and the more distant, future. They may be right or wrong, but if you hold onto these remarks, or look them up in the *Proceedings* of this Conference, you can see to what degree they're on the mark. And they are *important* beyond their content, because they indicate to what extent we can truly "foresee" problems at sea.

- The United States will generally remain free of piracy in the near future, as will Australia and Northern Europe.
- Expect to see some increase in piracy in the Mediterranean.
- Latin America will continue to experience low to mid-range levels of maritime crime…
- …while Mexico may be a candidate for future piratical developments.
- Indonesia, Malaysia, and the Straits of Malacca will remain areas of piratical concern.
- The Bay of Bengal region will see an increase in reported low-level piracies.
- We are *unlikely* to see a repeat of the surge of piracies in Iraqi waters which occurred in 2005.
- But a new candidate for an area in which piracy will develop is…Pakistan.

[1] Samuel Pyeatt Menefee is the Maury Fellow at the Center for Oceans Law and Policy and an Adjunct Professor at the World Maritime University.

- Oil-related piracies and incidents involving drilling platforms will continue in Nigerian waters.
- In the absence of a transnational campaign to eradicate pirates, piracies off Somalia and in the Red Sea and the Gulf of Aden will continue to present a major problem.
- and if patrols continue in the Gulf and Red Sea, it is probable that Somali pirates will *further* expand their activities beyond the zone of present attacks.
- Piracy off the Horn of Africa will increasingly find common cause with Islamic extremism.
- There will be more piratical attacks in areas suffering from environmental degradation and sea-level rise.
- The discrepancy between piracy "on the water" and what counts as a piracy for international statistical purposes will continue to widen. Nations will generally avoid their responsibility to report such crimes, and more efforts will be made to limit "informal reporting."
- Piracy will evolve to avoid existing anti-piracy laws and activities. Expect more claims of political and environmental relevance and an increased number of juvenile, and perhaps female, pirates.

OK, that was the *easy* part. But how were those conclusions reached? That's a bit *harder*, and because it is, the rest of this paper will provide some support for these conclusions. Whether you agree or disagree, it is hoped that this will begin a general conversation which will enable us to get out *in front* of the problem of piracy, to wisely allocate our resources, and to start planning for what may occur at sea rather than simply *reacting* to it.

I. *Introduction*

Let us start with one of the *worst* "predictions" ever about piracy. What's the problem with it? It's easily accessible, allegedly authoritative, and dead *wrong*. No less an expert than Philip Gosse had this to say about the crime: "The end of piracy, after centuries, was brought about by public feeling, backed up by the steam-engine and telegraph. The last relic exists to-day in China, where a nest of troublesome pirates still carries on the old trade..."[2] So what are the problems with this "prognostication"? First, it is *logically inconsistent*; piracy can't be ended if there is still a "nest of troublesome pirates." Second, there is the

[2] P[hilip] Go[sse], "Pirate and Piracy," 17 ENCYCLOPAEDIA BRITANNICA (1964), 951 at 952. Compare this to PHILIP GOSSE, HISTORY OF PIRACY (1946) at vii ("...and finally to show how national organisation, backed by the steamship and the telegraph, brought it to an end").

lack of hedging. Had Gosse merely suggested that piracy had been *diminished*, it would have been harder to argue with him. Saying that it had *ended* is a bit too clear cut – and *easily* disprovable. Finally, there is the verbally satisfying, but ultimately empty "brought about by public feeling, backed up by the steam engine and telegraph." What does *that* mean? That being noted, this paper will attempt to follow Gosse by at least sketching "what conditions, geographical and social, preceded the rise of piracy, to trace its periodical rises and declines, its forms and fortunes...."[3]

Writing much later, but still slightly over twenty years ago, Professor M.J. Peterson has noted:

> *[H]istorical records show that... [piracy's] incidence differs from locality to locality and from time to time. This suggests that some conditions or clusters of conditions favour piracy while others discourage it. An understanding of the circumstances which favour piracy is useful to law enforcement authorities, seamen, and shippers alike since this permits concentrating attention on those areas at those times when it seems most likely to occur.*[4]

Peterson not only understands the potential *predictive* nature of such an understanding, but she goes on to argue that piracy flourished "when there are plentiful sources of booty, ready markets for the booty, and secure bases where pirates can rest and resupply between voyages."[5] Unfortunately, this trilogy appears to mix the obtaining and disposal of loot (which is fair enough) with the unrelated question of pirate security.

Today, the time appears right for a different, expanded, formulation of the problem, using factors which may allow us to more accurately predict where future maritime crimes may occur. This study will consider piracy by discussing five sorts of patterns which may provide such clues. These patterns are:

- Geography;
- Transportation and trade;
- Instability;
- Anti-piracy enforcement activities; and
- Prior piracies.

II. *Patterns of Geography*

Consider the influence of geography on maritime attacks. In Homeric times, "Cretan" was synonymous with pirate, in part because of that island's protected

[3] Gosse, *supra* note 2, at vii.

[4] M.J. Peterson, "An Historical Perspective on the Incidence of Piracy," in Eric Ellen Ed., PIRACY AT SEA (1989), 41, at 41.

[5] *Id.*

natural harbors.[6] Captain Henry Kepple, a noted pirate hunter in Asian waters in the 19th century, noted that, "[a]s surely as spiders abound where there are nooks and crannies...so have pirates sprung up wherever there is a nest of islands offering creeks and shallows, headlands, rocks and reefs – facilities in short for lurking, for surprise, for attack, for escape."[7] Speaking of the other side of the world, the author of *The Pirates Own Book* says that the Bahamas, "cut up into numerous intricate passages and channels, full of sunken rocks and coral reefs...afforded a sure retreat to desperadoes,"[8] noting that "[o]ther islands are full of mountain fastnesses, where all pursuit can be eluded,"[9] and that the roots of the mangrove "offer secure hiding places for those who are suddenly pursued."[10] This assessment was echoed by Gardner W. Allen, author of *Our Navy and the West Indian Pirates.*

> *The shores of the mainland surrounding the Gulf of Mexico and the Caribbean Sea and of the islands, many parts of which were uninhabited, abounded in secluded harbors, coves, and passages among dangerous reefs, inaccessible to vessels of size. The dense growth of mangroves at the water's edge made concealment and escape easy.*[11]

Such geographic features enhance the practice of piracy in a number of ways. River mouths and straits funnel potential targets into a more confined area creating a richer mix of potential victims. Shallows and labyrinthine waterways discourage pursuit. Impenetrable mangrove thickets and other undeveloped areas make it easier for criminals to operate and survive undetected. While these latter points may appear dated in an era of hydrofoils and aircraft, they still apply to low level attacks against more local targets.

III. *Patterns of Transportation and Trade*

Willie Sutton, when asked why he robbed banks replied, "Because that's where the money is!" In a similar way, the record of historical piracy has paralleled the development of maritime trade. In his *History of Piracy*, Gosse noted that, "[t]rade follows the flag, and robbery whether by land or sea follows trade."[12] A quick summary of several examples is illustrative.

---

[6] Angus Konstam, The World Atlas of Pirates: Treasures and Treachery on the Seven Seas, in Maps, Tall Tales, and Pictures, (2009), at 21–22.

[7] Gosse, *supra* note 2, at 1.

[8] The Pirates Own Book: Authentic Narratives of the Most Celebrated Sea Robbers (1993), at 358 (original edition 1837).

[9] *Id.*, at 538–39.

[10] *Id.*, at 359.

[11] Gardner W. Allen, Our Navy and the West Indian Pirates (1929), at 1.

[12] Gosse, *supra* note 2, at 1.

Perhaps the best-known piracies of the sixteenth and seventeenth centuries involved the riches of Spain's colonial empire, whether these were being gathered in ports to be shipped to Spain or had already been embarked as cargo in one of the Spanish plate fleets – convoys which operated from 1526 to protect against pirates.[13] In the late seventeenth century, the so-called "Pirate Round" had pirates fit out in New England, travel to the Red Sea, Persian Gulf, or coast of Malabar, where local shipping was raided, and return to sell their ill-gotten plunder in colonial markets. The West Indies and the pirate haven of Madagascar provided opportunities to rest and resupply along the way.[14] Eighteenth century attacks were often based on the triangular trade of goods, slaves, and rum between Europe, West Africa, and the Caribbean and North American colonies.[15] Raids on the Grand Banks fisheries provided a source of supplies and recruits.

More recently, piratical activities have been directed against fishermen to expropriate their catch and hold their boats to ransom, as is the case in Bangladesh,[16] or to enforce "no fishing areas," as has occurred off West Africa, with the activities of Polisario.[17]

Bottlenecks, whether these are due to geographical features such as straits, or to problems with port facilities, can slow the delivery of goods and expose ships and cargo to an increased risk of attack. In the 1970's Nigeria's "Cement Armada," according to that nation's UN Defence Attache, "is considered largely responsible for the increased number of attacks on vessels waiting in the roadsteads to berth. The shortage of berthing space in the few ports which were operational during this period created long queues and thus made the waiting vessels easy prey for robbers."[18] Captain Roger Villar, author of *Piracy Today*, agreed that West African piracy had

> *been encouraged in recent years by an enormous expansion of trade, largely founded on Nigerian oil production, which began in the mid-1970s.... [I]n Nigeria up to 40 ships were queuing at any one time to enter Lagos, which was then incapable of handling*

[13] Konstam, *supra* note 6, at 61.

[14] Gosse, *supra* note 2, at 177–78. *See also* Konstam, *supra* note 6, at 106.

[15] *See* "Golden Age of Piracy," <http://en.wikipedia.org/wiki/Golden_Age_of_Piracy>.

[16] *See generally* Samuel Pyeatt Menefee, "Under-reporting of the problems of maritime piracy and terrorism: are we viewing the tip of the iceberg?" in Maximo Q. Mejia Jr., Ed., Contemporary Issues In Maritime Security (2005), 245–63; Samuel Pyeatt Menefee, "Piracy in Bangladesh: What Lies Beneath?" in Bruce A. Ellman, Andrew Forbes, and David Rosenberg, Eds., Piracy and Maritime Crime: Historical and Modern Case Studies (2010), at 121–36.

[17] *See generally* S.P. Menefee, "Terrorist threat to fishing industry set to continue?," 6 *I.C.C. Commercial Crime International* (Mar. 1989) at 7.

[18] Office of the Defence Attache, Permanent Mission of Nigeria to the United Nations, "Piracy Control in Nigeria's Territorial Seas," in Ellen, Ed., *supra* note 4, 219, at 220.

> *such numbers. These vessels were obvious and easy targets. Pirates went for cargo... and there was a ready market ashore for everything.*[19]

There is also a long history of pirates receiving "protection money" in return for allowing the free passage of ships through areas they control. This was done by the Carian pirates of Julius Caesar's time,[20] and by Barbary corsairs in the Mediterranean and pirates along the Chinese coast during the early 19th century.[21] Today, some of the operators off Somalia, "claimed they were coast guards, protecting ships passing through their waters in return for the right to demand payment for their services."[22]

IV. *Patterns of Instability*

What is meant by a pattern of instability? On a meta level it can be a politically or economically weak entity, a so-called failed state. Peterson notes that "[a]ny time it becomes obvious that a particular government lacks the will or the resources to take piracy very seriously, pirates will congregate in places within or near its territorial jurisdiction."[23] More locally, it can be an area with higher crime rates, less policing, or one that has been subjected to some natural disaster with social ramification. Here are a few examples.

The Caribbean was a cockpit of colonial struggles from the first days of exploration, so it is hardly surprising to find that, over the centuries, pirates took advantage of the competing national interests of Spain, France, and England, to name but a few of the major players.

Some of the early eighteenth century attacks of the "Golden Age of Piracy" can be tied to the after-effects of the English Civil War and the Glorious Revolution. Not only was Royalist Prince Rupert branded a pirate,[24] but Stede Bonnet's crew when they captured a vessel in August of 1718, "made Bowls of Punch, and went to Drinking of the Pretender's Health,"[25] while Captain Walter Kennedy cursed King George, and stated "[w]e have 32 sail of ships and

---

[19] Captain Roger Villar, Piracy Today: Robbery and Violence at Sea Since 1980 (1985), at 16.

[20] Gosse, *supra* note 2, at 4–8.

[21] Konstam, *supra* note 6, at 12.

[22] *Id.*

[23] Peterson, *supra* note 4, at 59.

[24] *See generally* George Edinger, Rupert of the Rhine: the Pirate Prince (1936).

[25] Joel H. Baer, 2 British Piracy in the Golden Age: History and Interpretation, 1660–1730 (2007), at 343 (from *The Tryals of Major Stede Bonnet, and Other Pirates* (1719)).

will endeavour to place James III upon the throne."[26] George Roberts, captured by Captain Low in 1721, describes many of the pirates as vocal Jacobites.[27]

Many Caribbean piracies of the early nineteenth century were laid at the door of the privateers of revolted Spanish colonies. In 1815, one American officer wrote the Secretary of the Navy "'soliciting instructions relative to Vessels sailing under Carthagenian Colors, for 'tis under this Flag that most of the Piracies are committed and there is now added to that the Flag of the patriots of Mexico, which will, I have no doubt, be also used as a cloak for every species of violence, Plunder and Piracy.'"[28] Spanish (basically Cuban and Porto Rican) piracies, which often targeted United States vessels, were blamed by some on American participation in the depredations of the "Patriots,"[29] by others on the American take-over of Florida,[30] or the suppression of the Atlantic slave trade.[31]

More recently, several piracies in Southeast Asia in the early 1960s can be linked to Indonesian President Sukarno's *Konfrontasi* with Malaysia.[32] Continuing attacks in Nigeria are tied to a perceived inequitable sharing of oil revenues and to underlying tribal conflicts in the region.[33] Somalia is in a sense the "poster boy" of political instability, and its current association with piracy is too well known to require elaboration here.[34]

---

[26] Samuel Pyeatt Menefee, "Jacobite Pirates," in *Maritime Piracy: A Companion* (ms.). *See also* O. Anderson, "British Governments and Rebellion at Sea," 3 HISTORICAL JOURNAL (1960), at 56–84.

[27] *See* "I Waited to Have My Doom Determined," in John Richard Stephens, Ed., CAPTURED BY PIRATES: TWENTY-TWO FIRSTHAND ACCOUNTS OF MURDER AND MAYHEM ON THE HIGH SEAS (2006), 149 at 180.

[28] ALLEN, *supra* note 11, at 9.

[29] *See* CONNECTICUT GAZETTE [New Haven, Conn.] (November 14, 1821), at 2, cols. 4–5; FRANCIS B.C. BRADLEE, PIRACY IN THE WEST INDIES AND ITS SUPPRESSION (1923), at 13–14; NILES WEEKLY REGISTER (April 20, 1822), at 114, col. 1, NILES WEEKLY REGISTER (June 22, 1822), at 264, col. 2.

[30] BASIL LUBBOCK, CRUISERS, CORSAIRS & SLAVERS: AN ACCOUNT OF THE SUPPRESSION OF THE PICAROON, PIRATE & SLAVER BY THE ROYAL NAVY DURING THE 19TH CENTURY (1993), at 71.

[31] ALLEN, *supra* note 11, at 27–28 ("'The committee are induced to believe that this system of piracy is now spreading itself to a vast extent, attracting to it the idle, vicious, and desperate of all nations and more particularly those who have heretofore been engaged in the slave trade, from which the vigilance of the American cruisers has driven them ....'"; BRADLEE, *supra* note 29, at 13–14.

[32] Information from conversation of S.P. Menefee with Rear-Admiral J.R. Hill, circa Fall, 1998. *See also* <http://www.ask.com/wiki/Military_history_of_Australia_during_the_Indonesia-Malaysia_Confrontation>.

[33] Samuel Pyeatt Menefee, "Delta blues: maritime and riverine crime in the Nigerian Delta," in Maximo Q. Mejia and Jingjing Xu, Eds., COASTAL ZONE PIRACY AND OTHER UNLAWFUL ACTS AT SEA (2007) 199–236. *See also* KONSTAM, *supra* note 6, at 231–32.

[34] *See generally* Bibi Van Ginkel, and Frans-Paul Van Der Putten, Eds., THE INTERNATIONAL RESPONSE TO SOMALI PIRACY (2010); MARTIN N. MURPHY, SOMALIA: THE NEW BARBARY?:

Angus Konstam has summarized some of these economic underpinnings in comparing today's piracy to earlier iterations of the crime. Reflecting that many 18th century pirates were driven to the crime by circumstances, he notes:

> *If captured, these men often railed against the injustices of society and the way seamen were treated by ship owners and captains....*
>
> *This is strongly similar to accounts of modern pirates. Those who attack oil rigs off the coast of West Africa claim they are protesting against the harsh conditions of life in the region, where oil companies are seen as all-powerful, exploitative, and unsympathetic. In the waters of Indonesia and the Philippines, pirates often claim they attack passing ships in order to steal the food, weapons, and money they need to survive. For them, piracy is seen as a necessary means to an end. Then there are the Somali pirates, who capture ships and their crews and hold them for ransom. In interviews, they speak of themselves as coast guards, protecting their coasts and fishing stocks from rapacious interlopers. In all these cases, the excuses are pretty similar to those given in the early 18th century.*[35]

V. *Patterns of Anti-Piracy Enforcement Activities*

The presence of anti-piracy activity in an area often shifts piratical operations to one with fewer hindrances. This concept seems to have been recognized as early as Classical times. When Pompey the Great was given command over Roman resources to eliminate piracy in the Mediterranean, he divided that sea into thirteen districts, having his military commanders launch coordinated operations. Known bases were blockaded while Roman vessels searched for pirates at sea or in other unanticipated locations. The survivors of these attacks were driven east toward Cilicia, which had deliberately been left untouched. Here a double cordon of Roman vessels blockaded the coast as forces were sent ashore to destroy all vessels and strongholds, ending with the siege and conquest of Coracesium, the last hold-out. Konstam notes that during this "three-month campaign, the Romans had destroyed 120 pirate bases, killed or executed over 10,000 pirates, and destroyed over 500 of their ships.'[36]

> *Once piracy has reached large dimensions, rooting out of pirate bases is the only way to assure its suppression. The ending of the "Golden Age" of European pirates in the early eighteenth century demonstrates just how difficult this can be. The British campaign against these pirates began with clearing Madagascar in 1698–1701. The pirates then*

Piracy and Islam in the Horn of Africa (2010); Peter Eichstaedt, Pirate State: Inside Somalia's Terrorism at Sea (2010); Robin Geiss and Anna Petrig, Piracy and Armed Robbery at Sea: the Legal Framework for Counter-Piracy Operations in Somalia and the Gulf of Aden (2011).

35 Konstam, *supra* note 6, at 9.

36 *Id.*, at 27.

> *shifted activity to the Caribbean and western Atlantic, where the British had to replace many colonial officials and dispatch squadrons of small, fast naval ships... to deal with the problem. A number of pirates then shifted operations to the West African coast until the Royal Navy chased them down there.*[37]

By attacking or forcing the removal of depots for pirated goods at Barataria, Amelia Island, and Galveston, the fledgling United States was not able to eradicate piracy, but did generally succeed in moving attacks away from its coasts. Cuban-based piracies of the early 19th century were countered by an Anglo-American response, particularly during the period 1824–25, British and American cruisers worked in tandem in their anti-piracy patrols.[38]

More recently, Singapore saw a precipitous drop in reported attacks within its waters. Maps drawn for Roger Villar's *Piracy Today* showing annual Singapore Strait piracies from 1981–84 indicate the profound difference a national boundary can make; almost all of the attacks in this strait occurred just outside Singapore waters.[39] Today, the effort of Coalition forces to patrol the Gulf of Aden and Horn of Africa area to protect ships has resulted in a *scattering* of piratical attacks beyond the area being patrolled.

In addition to this *geographic* displacement, attention should be paid to the movement of pirates *between various sorts of criminal activities*. Many of the 19th century Cuban pirates had been forced out of the slave trade by the British and Americans.[40] The piracies committed against the Vietnamese Boat People by various fishermen appear to have been founded in robbery, but, at least in some cases, to have morphed into forced prostitution and the sex trade.[41] The Chinese "Snakeheads," who are primarily known for the illegal importation of immigrants have, on occasion, behaved in what appears to be a piratical manner.[42]

VI. *Patterns of Prior Piracies*

While this might seem like a no-brainer, several rules and caveats apply. First, predictive ability can be no better than the quality of the data provided. Major

37 Peterson, *supra* note 4, at 57.
38 Lubbock, *supra* note 30, at 83.
39 *See* Villar, *supra,* note 19, at 80–81.
40 *See supra* text at note 31.
41 *See generally* Samuel Pyeatt Menefee, "Piracy and the Vietnamese Boat People: a retrospective," in Maximo Q. Mejia, Jr., Ed., Maritime Security and Crime (2010), at 49–104.
42 *See* Samuel Pyeatt Menefee, "Revising Our Laws on the Maritime Slave Trade," 14 Tulane J. Int'l and Comp. L., no. 2, at 421–34 (Spring, 2006).

sources of piracy data include the IMO's quarterly and annual bulletins,[43] the ICC-International Maritime Bureau's quarterly and annual reports,[44] RECAAP's monthly reports (including semi-annual and annual summaries),[45] and the United States government's ASAMs.[46] Unfortunately, each of these leaves something to be desired in so far as inclusivity is concerned. In at least *some* cases, this seems due to political pressure applied by states who do not wish to be considered piracy hotbeds. In response to complaints, for example, the International Maritime Bureau first began to break attacks down into actual and attempted (an arguably positive development, as it more accurately reflected the seriousness of an incident), but then quietly dropped noting all those incidents which were not "officially" reported. While bringing their practice more in line with that employed by the IMO and RECAAP, this has cut off a source of information about piracy from the local press, both distorting and underplaying the effect of regional piracy. To give but one example, piracy reports for the waters of Bangladesh from January through October of 2003 show 57 attacks noted by the IMO (244, if we count attacks on each vessel as a *separate* incident) and 58 by the IMB (with an amplified figure of 213). A review of reports in the *Bangladesh Observer* for this period is instructive. "Conservatively stated, and that includes leaving out all the piratical estimates given (and only counting two ships where the plural is used without a specific number), 138 more cases have been added to the reported total of incidents from Bangladesh for 2003."[47] There has been an almost universal State tendency *not* to report piracies occurring in national waters or affecting flag vessels, placing the burden on NGOs.[48] Any discussion of patterns based on prior piracies should therefore acknowledge up front just how *faulty* and *patchy* the available data is. It should be keep in mind that most of the piracies reported to have taken place against international shipping do not "spring full-blown from the head of Zeus," but rather develop from a pattern of "lesser" crimes directed against country boats.

---

[43] These reports began in 1995. *See* <http://www.imo.org/OurWork/Security/PiracyArmedRobbery/Pages/PirateReports.aspx>.

[44] While the I.M.B. issued some reports in the early 1980's, the most recent iteration of reports began about 1992. *See* <http://www.icc-ccs.org/home/piracy-reporting-centre>.

[45] Reports began in December 2006 and are available at the ReCAAP website, <http://www.recaap.org>. *See also* Samuel Pyeatt Menefee, "A recap of ReCAAP," in Mejia, Jr., *supra* note 41, at 187–99.

[46] These reports began in November of 1985. *See* <http://www.fas.org/irp/world/para/docs/ASAM-1985.htm> etc.; <http://msi.nga.mil/NGAPortal/MSI.portal?_nfpb=true&_pageLabel=msi_portal_page_6>.

[47] Samuel Pyeatt Menefee (2005), *supra* note 16, at 257.

[48] *See id.*, at 247.

COUNTRY	2000	2001	2002	2003	2004	2005	2006	2007	2008	2009
Indonesia	119	91	103	121	94	79	50	43	28	15
Malacca Straits	75	17	16	28	38	12	11	7	2	2
Malaysia	21	19	14	5	9	3	10	9	10	16
Philippines	9	8	10	12	4	0	6	6	7	1
South China Sea	9	4	0	2	8	6	1	3	0	13
Vietnam	6	8	12	15	4	10	3	5	11	9
Bangladesh	55	25	32	58	17	21	47	15	12	17
India	35	27	18	27	15	15	5	11	10	12
Colombia	1	1	7	10	5	2	2	0	1	5
Ecuador	15	8	12	2	1	0	1	0	2	2
Guyana	1	0	12	6	2	1	1	5	0	0
Peru	4	1	6	7	5	6	9	6	5	13
Venezuela	3	1	8	13	7	2	4	1	3	5
Gulf of Aden/ Red Sea	13	11	11	18	8	10	10	13	92	131
Somalia	9	8	6	3	2	35	10	31	19	80
Nigeria	9	19	14	39	28	16	12	42	40	28
Tanzania	2	7	3	5	2	7	9	11	14	5
Iraq	0	2	0	0	1	10	2	2	0	0

Using the International Maritime Bureau's figures, consider the "major" areas of piracy since 2000 (any nation or area where there are ten or more attacks in any one of the years being considered has been included):

Based on these figures, which are open to some question, and which represent only a snippet of much more extended trends, there are piracy "hot spots" in Asia in the Malacca Strait area, the South China Sea region, and around India and Bangladesh. In Latin America, Guyana, Venezuela, Colombia, Ecuador and Peru all have noticeable problems, while North America, Europe, and Australia are largely free of concentrations. Nigeria and Tanzania both have outbreaks, but the worst area for attacks has undoubtedly been the Red Sea, Gulf of Aden, Somalia region.

VII. *Using these Factors to Make Predictions*

Having reviewed these factors, it remains to briefly consider how they may help predict the course of future piracies. Keeping in mind the fifteen initial predictions, one can see how one or more of the following makes each a possible, even a logical, outcome.

A. *Geography*

As indicated, features such as straits, which funnel potential targets into a confined space, and mangrove forests or other labyrinthine aquatic environments, tend to favor piratical practices. One should not expect to see piracy eradicated from the Red Sea, the Singapore Strait, or the coastal wetlands of Bangladesh any time soon. While geographical features change more slowly than other variables, *overtime* there will be a territorial evolution which *may* make a difference to the areas in which piracies occur. Environmental degradation due to sea level rise in areas such as Bangladesh or the Maldives could cause elements of the population to turn to piracy as an economic mainstay. Similarly, while attacks in the region do seem unlikely, the opening of the Arctic with the melting of the polar ice cap could provide another geographical area of concern. But as noted, such geographical changes are *well* in the future.

B. *Transportation and Trade*

In general, two factors would appear to be paramount in predicting *near-term* piracies, utilizing transportation and trade. The first is the transport of oil and oil-related products. As prices rise and the supplies of some nations run low, cargoes will become more valuable, and in some cases a blind eye may be turned toward *sources* of this bounty. (To a lesser extent, this may become the case for other resources.) The second is the transport of desirable consumer goods through or to economically depressed areas, whose populations cannot expect to legitimately acquire them or where "thieves' markets" operate with some tolerance. Much of coastal Africa and parts of Latin America, the Caribbean, and Asia would appear to qualify.

C. *Instability*

Instability in the Gulf of Aden and Horn of Africa, and in Nigeria's Rivers Region, will continue to make both these areas major targets for piracy. The same is true, to a lesser extent, for Bangladesh, and possibly other third world countries such as Indonesia, Malaysia, and India. Such events may not always be due to civil wars, insurgencies, or even political dysfunction; natural disasters such as tsunamis, volcanic eruptions, or even sea level rise might cause the sort of social dislocation in which piracy thrives. Asked to suggest a country *without* current major problems which might be a good candidate for future piracies, one choice would be Pakistan.

D. *Prior Piracies*

Use of prior piracies is perhaps the best predictive tool which we have, as long as it is remembered that this depends on high-quality data. The Red Sea/Gulf of Aden/Somalia region is clearly the region in which most attacks will be taking place in the short run. Nigeria is an area of secondary intensity, followed by Bangladesh and India and the Indonesia/Malaysia region.

E. *Anti-Piracy Enforcement Activities*

The effect of the anti-piracy patrols off the Horn of Africa and in the Gulf of Aden has already been noted; pirates have simply moved further offshore. There is no reason not to think that, as long as unstable conditions in Somalia continue to exist, the "ripple effect" of its piracies will move further and further into the Indian Ocean, causing problems for several island nations and, eventually, potentially for India. As there will be a tendency for piracy to congregate and grow in places where it is not opposed, wherever piracy is attacked in future, a concerted *regional effort* must be planned to prevent the criminals from moving into nearby waters or related fields of crime.

VIII. *The Evolution of Piracy: Conclusion*

While piracy is not an organic creation, it *is* the manifestation of organic conditions, and will thus continue to grow and evolve to meet new challenges. The very efforts to fight and curtail maritime crime will perforce contribute to its future *evolution*. Take, for example, the increased use of *justifications* involving the environment. These are but the most recent manifestation of political defenses, such as those utilized by Confederate sympathizers and "maritime border ruffians" during the American Civil War, or by Palestinian sympathizers in actions such as the *Achille Lauro* take over. Whatever can be used to confuse the issue *will* be used to confuse the issue in those cases which come to court. Similarly, to the degree that juveniles, or even women, are perceived as receiving "softer" sanctions, they will increasingly become preferred "foot sailors" to be used in future piracies.

The five patterns discussed herein: (1) geography, (2) transportation and trade, (3) instability; (4) prior piracies; and (5) anti-piracy enforcement activities, are all useful in helping predict the occurrence of future piracies. Other influences such as weather (e.g. monsoons) or time of day (moonlit nights) could be added to this mix. Further discussions and an increase in the amount and validity of available data could fine-tune all these into a series of formulas which could predict the possibility of future attacks with increasing accuracy.

Panel III: Islands and Rocks

ISLANDS AND ROCKS IN THE MODERN LAW OF THE SEA

*David Anderson**

Outline

1. Some legislative history
2. Roles of islands and rocks in establishing baselines
3. Roles of islands and rocks in generating entitlements to maritime spaces
   (1) Article 121 (1)
   (2) Article 121 (2)
   (3) Article 121 (3)
4. Roles of islands and rocks in delimitation between neighbouring States
   (1) Rocks which are low-tide elevations
   (2) Discounting islands and rocks in delimiting maritime boundaries
   (3) Archipelagic baselines drawn to islands, rocks and drying reefs
5. Disputes over the maritime spaces around islands and rocks
   The question of standing
6. Concluding remarks

In more than one decision, the International Court of Justice (ICJ) has laid down the proposition that "the land dominates the sea."[1] Given that the seas and oceans cover more than 70% of the Earth's surface and control many aspects of life on land through their effects on the global climate, at first sight this is a questionable proposition. The land dominates in the particular sense that sovereignty over the coast of land territory generates legal rights over adjacent parts of the sea. As well as mainland coasts, those of islands also generate maritime rights. Leaving aside the special case of archipelagic States, island States are treated in law like other coastal States.[2] Issues to do with islands and rocks are dealt with in several parts of the UN Convention on the Law of the Sea (Convention or LOS Convention).

After noting some legislative history, this paper reviews some of the many issues concerning islands and rocks. The paper examines in turn the roles of

---

* Member of the International Tribunal for the Law of the Sea 1996–2005. All views are personal.

[1] A recent example is afforded by *Nicaragua v Honduras*, ICJ Reports 2007, para. 113.

[2] *Libya/Malta* case: ICJ Reports 1985, p. 15, at p. 42.

islands and rocks in establishing baselines, in measuring maritime spaces and zones, and in delimitation. The final part discusses some aspects of the settlement of disputes concerning claims to maritime spaces around islands and rocks.

1. *Some Legislative History*

The first intergovernmental discussion of the regime of islands in the law of the sea took place at the Conference called by the League of Nations in 1930. There was general agreement that every island was entitled to a belt of territorial sea and that low-tide elevations within such a belt would be taken into account in drawing the outer limit of the territorial sea. Although it proved impossible to conclude a convention at that time, the outcome of the discussions informed the later work of the International Law Commission (ILC) during the 1950s, in preparation for the First UN Conference on the Law of the Sea in 1958. In both the discussions in The Hague of 1930 and the early discussions in the ILC, a proposition was considered (and rejected each time) to the effect that the definition of the term "island" should include the qualification that a feature should be "capable of effective occupation and control."[3] The Geneva Convention on the Territorial Sea and the Contiguous Zone (TSCZ Convention) of 1958 defined the term "island" to mean "a naturally-formed area of land, surrounded by water, which is above water at high tide."[4] The substantive rule was that the territorial sea of an island was to be measured in accordance with the provisions of the Convention. Other articles also made provision for islands, notably Article 4 concerning straight baselines and Article 11 concerning low-tide elevations. The term "island" also appeared in the Convention on the Continental Shelf (CS Convention), this time undefined but no doubt bearing the same meaning as in the TSCZ Convention. The CS Convention defined the concept of the continental shelf to include submarine areas adjacent to the coasts of islands.

During the period between 1964 (when the CS Convention entered into force) and 1974 (when the Third UN Conference on the Law of the Sea (LOS Conference) began its substantive work), some bilateral negotiations for conti-

[3] For example, the proposal of Prof Hersch Lauterpacht (I Yearbook of the ILC 1954, at p. 92). The proposal was rejected on the grounds that any rock could be made to serve as an automatic weather station, etc.

[4] Convention on the Territorial Sea and the Contiguous Zone, Article 10(1). The term appeared in the articles about straight baselines, inspired by the decision of the International Court of Justice (Court or ICJ) in *UK v. Norway* that Norway's system of straight baselines drawn to and from islands and rocks was not contrary to international law: ICJ Reports 1951, p. 3.

nental shelf boundaries had become deadlocked over the weight to be attached to islands. Some States wished to benefit in terms of maritime space from their ownership of small islands, while not surprisingly their neighbours opposed these claims. At the Conference, many delegations supported the retention of the Geneva wording in any new Convention.[5] Many other delegations wished to see change. To that end, several different proposals were submitted by Romania, Turkey and Ireland, mostly designed to divide islands into categories depending on size, population and economic activity, and no doubt inspired by particular issues over small islands in on-going bilateral negotiations.[6] The discussions covered two related issues: first, the regime of islands and, secondly, maritime boundary delimitation, in the context of accepting new and very extensive limits for the Exclusive Economic Zone (EEZ) and the continental shelf. The lengthy discussions were marked by a lack of consensus. In the final outcome, the Geneva regime was continued, but with the addition of a new exception applicable to certain rocks.

2. *Roles of Islands and Rocks in Establishing Baselines*

Article 7 of the LOS Convention allows the coastal State to draw straight baselines to and from islands and rocks which are islands where they are part of a fringe of islands. In the case of low-tide elevations (many of which are drying rocks), straight baselines may be drawn solely to and from those which have a lighthouse or similar installation on them. Especially in the days of 3 M limits of the territorial sea, many lighthouses were built on drying rocks beyond the outer limit of the territorial sea: in such cases, the lighthouses do not generate a territorial sea of their own although the lighthouse itself is under the jurisdiction of the coastal State.[7] In instances where the coast of a large island has some smaller islands forming a fringe or where a large island's coast is deeply indented, straight baselines may be drawn off the large island, in accordance with Article 7 read together with Article 121 (2). For instance, this was done, on the basis of the Geneva regime, to the west of Scotland in 1964, to parts of the Turks and Caicos Islands in 1989 and most of the Falkland Islands

[5] Proposals to that effect were in A/CONF.62/C.2/L.3, – /L. 30, and – /L.50.

[6] The various proposals are set out in the UN publication *The Law of the Sea – Regime of Islands* (1988), as well as in the commentary on Article 121 in vol. III of the Virginia *Commentary*, at p. 324.

[7] This was stated in the Commentary to the ILC's draft article 10: vol. II YBILC (1956), at p. 156.

in 1989.[8] Such straight baselines should not be confused with archipelagic baselines.

3. *Roles of Islands and Rocks in Generating Entitlements to Maritime Spaces and Zones*

Part VIII consists of a single article with three short paragraphs, yet it is not always easy to interpret and apply. At the outset, it is worth recalling that Part VIII should be interpreted, like the remainder of the Convention, in a reasonable manner, in accordance with the rules in the Vienna Convention on the Law of Treaties.[9] The need for reasonableness and restraint is greatest in those articles which attempt to describe in words some very varied geographical conditions and especially in the case of those which define or regulate the limits of national jurisdiction.

Part VIII contains provisions about islands, including those rocks which are accorded treatment similar to that of islands, and those other rocks which are accorded only part of that treatment. Rocks which are awash, sometimes called drying rocks, are not islands. Rather, they are low-tide elevations to which Article 13 applies.

(1) *Article 121(1)*

Paragraph 1 repeats the definition of the term "island" in the TSCZ Convention of 1958. The requirement that an "area of land" must be "naturally formed" means that the artificial enhancement of low-tide elevations, whether by means of dredging or the building or emplacement of artificial structures, does not turn them into islands for the purposes of the law of the sea. It may well turn them into *artificial* islands.

In order to qualify as an "island," the area of land must be surrounded by the sea at high tide. This test serves to exclude drying rocks and other low-tide elevations. The concept of high tide depends upon the coastal State's choice of tidal datum, such as mean high water spring tide or highest astronomical tide. State practice varies and some States have changed their choice of datum over

[8] The baselines were drawn under the similar provisions in the Convention on the Territorial Sea and the Contiguous Zone of 1958 by the Territorial Waters Order 1964 (1965 III, p. 6452A); Turks & Caicos Islands (Territorial Sea) Order 1989 (S.I. 1989, No. 1996, as amended in 1998); Falkland Islands (Territorial Sea) Order 1989 (S.I. 1989, No. 1993). For more details, see Anderson, *Modern Law of the Sea* (2008), chapter 26.

[9] Following paragraph 58 of the Advisory Opinion of the Sea-bed Disputes Chamber of the International Tribunal for the Law of the Sea on the Responsibilities and Obligations of States, 1 February 2011.

the years. The law allows for these variations in State practice. Peter Beazley's suggestion, to the effect that a State's high tide should be the one depicted on the charts it recognises officially, appears to be sound.[10] Baselines around islands are subject to Article 16's requirements concerning charts and geographical co-ordinates.

(2) *Article 121(2)*

Subject to the exception in paragraph 3, Article 121(2) provides for the measurement of the territorial sea, contiguous zone, EEZ and continental shelf from islands, just as from mainlands. This general rule is the same as Article 10 (2) of the TSCZ Convention of 1958, but now applied more widely to the exclusive economic zone and continental shelf. In principle, all coasts, whether mainland or insular, have baselines from which the territorial sea, contiguous zone, exclusive economic zone and continental shelf are measured. There are no additional requirements of habitability or economic life in the case of the exclusive economic zone and continental shelf, similar to those in Article 121(3). As a result, inhospitable islands that are uninhabited or even uninhabitable are still capable of generating a full EEZ and continental shelf, just like barren mainland coasts such as those facing the Arctic Ocean. Similarly, there being no minimum size for an area of land to qualify as an island, some small islands, including barren ones, are capable of generating a full set of zones, provided they are not "rocks" within the meaning of paragraph 3.

The Conciliation Commission between Iceland and Norway considered whether Jan Mayen fell under paragraph 2 or 3 before concluding that it was not a rock.[11] This conclusion was accepted by the two Governments. In the *Jan Mayen* case before the ICJ, Denmark and Norway were agreed that Jan Mayen was an island which generated an exclusive economic zone and continental shelf.[12] Jan Mayen is a substantial island with a high mountain and some resident officials, even though it has no indigenous population. There are several similar inhospitable islands in other parts of the world which generate maritime zones. In his Declaration in the "*Monte Confurco*" case before the International Tribunal for the Law of the Sea, Judge Vukas expressed doubts about the establishment of an EEZ around the Kerguelen Islands in the Southern Ocean.[13] Yet, looking at the map of the Southern Ocean, this group of features clearly includes some islands which are not rocks.

---

[10] P.B. Beazley, *Maritime Limits and Baselines: A Guide to their Delineation*, 3rd ed. (1987).

[11] XXVII RIAA, p. 1: Report No. 9–4, in Charney and Alexander (eds.), *International Maritime Boundaries*, vol. II, at p. 1755.

[12] ICJ Reports 1993, p. 38. The late Keith Highet visited the island and noted that it had an enormous mountain.

[13] ITLOS Reports 2000, p. 86, at p. 122.

(3) *Article 121 (3)*

Article 121(3) provides that "Rocks which cannot sustain human life or economic life of their own shall have no exclusive economic zone or continental shelf." By implication, rocks may have a territorial sea and a contiguous zone around them. The exclusion of the EEZ and continental shelf reflected the concern of many delegations to avoid according small rocks disproportionately large maritime zones which could diminish the size of neighbouring zones or the international seabed Area. Paragraph 3, which finds no equivalent in the Geneva Convention on the Territorial Sea and the Contiguous Zone of 1958, is especially difficult to interpret and apply in practice, and there is an ever-growing literature.[14] Uncertainty attaches to the term "rocks" and to the test of an inability to "sustain human habitation or economic life of their own." This latter test is somewhat similar to the test ("capable of effective occupation and control") which was considered at the Hague Conference of 1930 and in the early work of the ILC only to be rejected on each occasion.

Looking first at the context, paragraph 3 represents an exception to paragraph 2. The rocks referred to in paragraph 3 are solely those which meet the definition of islands in paragraph 1. Paragraph 3 does not apply to drying rocks: they are subject to Article 13 (low-tide elevations). The paragraph does not apply to those rocks which are included in a system of straight baselines drawn in accordance with Article 7.

In a maritime context, the word "rock" is defined by the Concise Oxford Dictionary as a "solid part of earth's crust…standing up…out of the sea…" Such features are simply the aerial summits of submarine plateaux, mountains, banks or ridges at today's sea levels. The term "rock" in the context of paragraph 3 suggests a relatively small feature. Circumstances vary from case to case, as well as from time to time. Thus, some small islands which are today rock-like and devoid of vegetation have had a surface layer of guano removed by mining operations in the past. Some features include "rock" in their names. In the practice of States, rock-like features known as Rockall, Shag Rocks and Mexico's Alijos Rocks have been accepted as rocks within the meaning of Article 121 (3). However, the name of a feature does not determine its legal status: a feature called an island may nonetheless qualify as a "rock." What is the status of islands that are no more than sand spits or mud flats? Many small

[14] Studies have been made by many authors including Symmons, in *Boundary and Security Bulletin* 6(1) (1998) 78; Kwiatkowska and Soons, in XXI Netherlands YBIL (1990) 139; Prescott and Schofield, *Maritime Political Boundaries of the World* (2nd Ed, 2005); Jon Charney in 93 AJIL (1999) 863; Prescott and Triggs, in IMB vol. V (2005), p. 3245; Bowett in vol. I of IMB (1993), at p. 131 and in Bernhardt (Ed), *Max Planck Encyclopedia of Public International Law;* Dipla, *Le Régime juridique des Iles* (1984) and "Islands" in *Max Planck Encyclopedia of Public International Law* (online); and Kolb in vol. XL AFDI (1994) 876.

cays and "desert islands" are uninhabited because they lack water or vegetation, but they are not normally considered to be rocks and some of them may be used as logistic bases by local fishermen. In the old case of *The Anna*, Lord Stowell considered the status of mud islands forming a "portico" in the mouths of the Mississippi when measuring the US 3 mile limit. The learned judge held that "whether they are composed of earth or solid rock will not vary the right of dominion, for the right of dominion does not depend upon the texture of the soil."[15] It is not clear whether what goes for the right of dominion applies similarly to the status of those diminutive, isolated features that are composed of mud, coral or sand, or whether the inclusion of the word "rock" means that solely solid features, that is to say, only those with hard surfaces, are covered. The texture of the surface materials may be hard in the cases of granite, basalt, coral and sandstone or soft in the cases of mud or sand. The surface materials may be not be a good guide if they constitute no more than a thin layer on top of something else. This question may have to be answered by an international court or tribunal on the facts of a particular case. So far, courts have managed to dispose of maritime boundary cases coming before them without making a ruling under Article 121 (3), even though the parties in some recent cases have argued the issue in their pleadings.

Paragraph 3 differs from the many proposals submitted to the LOS Conference that sought to qualify or reduce the effects of islands. The *travaux préparatoires* record disagreements which were not resolved by the main protagonists across the table. For this reason, the records are not a reliable guide to the provision's interpretation.

In short, paragraph 3 appears to have created a narrow exception, applying to those very small islands which can be characterised as amounting to no more than rocks and which are isolated from a mainland or a larger island. If a small area of land has been inhabited at any time in the past by a settled population or has a regular economic use by a mainland population (e.g. for seasonal grazing of animals or collecting fruit or birds eggs or as a base for fishing), then the feature appears to qualify as an island under paragraphs 1 and 2, and does not appear to fall within the exception contained in paragraph 3. The introduction on to a small feature, such as a rock or sand spit, of an official or military presence, serviced from outside, does not establish that the feature is capable of sustaining human habitation or has an economic life of its own.

[15] Quoted in Higgins and Colombos, *International Law of the Sea* (1943) at p. 75. The reference in article 47(1) of the LOS Convention to "limestone islands" is clearly a negotiated formula, not a general test.

In their excellent study, Professors Prescott and Schofield have produced a list of six rocks which they consider to be covered by Article 121 (3).[16] This number may prove to be too low.

4. *Roles of Islands and Rocks in Delimitation between Neighbouring States*

Several recent decisions by international courts and tribunals have raised issues concerned with the question of the effects, if any, to be accorded in maritime delimitation to islands and rocks. Three issues are considered below.

(1) *Rocks which are low-tide elevations*

A low-tide elevation within 12 M of the coast of a single State is under the sovereignty of that State as part of the seabed. Such a rock can be used as a base point for measuring the breadth of the territorial sea. What is the position where such a rock is within 12 M of two neighbouring States and they have not established a maritime boundary?

This question arose in the *Bahrain/Qatar* case. The ICJ considered an argument by Bahrain that some rocks which were low-tide elevations (LTEs) and situated in the area of overlapping 12 M limits should be used as Bahraini base points because Bahrain had exercised authority over these rocks, even though they were LTEs. The Court considered that "Whether this claim of Bahrain is well founded depends upon the answer to the question whether low-tide elevations are territory and can be appropriated in conformity with the rules and principles of territorial acquisition."[17] The Court reviewed the terms of Articles 7(4), 13 and 121(2) of the Convention and concluded that LTEs could not be equated to islands: indeed, LTEs had their own rules in the Convention. Such LTEs in areas of overlapping claims could not be appropriated by one State. The Court decided that "for the purposes of drawing the equidistance line, such low-tide elevations must be disregarded."[18] However, as a general proposition, this ruling may be thought to go too far. The facts that LTEs are not territory and are not subject to appropriation by occupation and administration may not always be determinative factors in the process of delimitation. There may still

[16] J.R.V. Prescott & C. Schofield, *Maritime Political Boundaries of the World*, at p. 89.

[17] ICJ Reports 2001, p. 40, at p. 101, paragraph 204.

[18] *Ibid.*, at p. 102, paragraph 209. See also the discussion of South Ledge in the *Pedra Branca/Pulau Batu Puteh* case (Malaysia/Singapore), ICJ Reports 2008, at pp. 100–101, leading to the ruling that "sovereignty over South Ledge, as a low-tide elevation, belongs to the State in the territorial waters of which it is located."

room for adopting pragmatic solutions which take appropriate account of the facts of the situation.

In 1977, the Court of Arbitration charged with resolving the delimitation dispute between France and the United Kingdom about the continental shelf held that it had no jurisdiction over the boundaries between the French coasts and those of the Channel Islands since the waters in question were territorial sea rather than high seas above the continental shelf. The Court found that "In narrow waters such as these, strewn with islands and rocks, coastal States have a certain liberty in their choice of base points..."[19] In the subsequent negotiations between France and the UK for a territorial sea boundary between the French coasts and those of Jersey, it was apparent that, because the tides are very high in the Bay of Granville, there were many LTEs in areas of overlapping 12 mile arcs. Prompted, no doubt, by the Court of Arbitration's finding that the two coastal States had some liberty of choice, these LTEs were treated pragmatically and none was disregarded simply for the reason that it was within 12 miles of both sides. Indeed, every turning point of the line eventually agreed involved at least one LTE and sometimes three.[20] LTEs vary in position, size and characteristics. A pragmatic approach, such as that indicated by the Court of Arbitration, may be needed in other delimitations in order to avoid unnecessarily disturbing an existing state of affairs.

(2) *Discounting islands and rocks in delimiting maritime boundaries*

In the recent case-law, the normal first step in the process of delimitation has been to draw a provisional equidistance line.[21] This is a line drawn between the nearest points on the respective baselines on the coasts, whether mainland and insular, of two neighbouring States. However, in some cases, courts and tribunals have selected "appropriate" base points in such a way as to give no effect to small islands, creating in effect a modified equidistance line from the outset. The most recent example is the ICJ's decision in *Romania v. Ukraine* where no point on Serpents' Island belonging to Ukraine was selected as a base point for drawing the provisional modified equidistance line beyond the 12M limit of the territorial sea.[22] The Court made no finding as to the status of the feature

[19] Paragraph 22 of the decision of 1977: 54 ILR (1979) 5.

[20] Agreement of St. Helier, 2000. See Report 9–24, in International Maritime Boundaries, vol. IV, p. 2979.

[21] Anderson, "Developments in Maritime Boundary Practice," in Colson & Smith, *International Maritime Boundaries*, vol. V (2005), p. 3197.

[22] ICJ Reports 2009 p. 61. For comment, see Anderson, 8 Law & Practice of International Courts and Tribunals (2009) 305. An earlier example was the *Libya/Malta* case: ICJ Reports 1985, p. 15 where the Maltese island of Filfla was discounted at the outset before drawing a provisional equidistance line.

in terms of Article 121, even though Romania had contended it was a rock within the meaning of Article 121 (3). Instead, Serpents' Island was accepted as having a 12M enclave.[23]

In the earlier case of *Nicaragua v. Honduras*, the Court decided exceptionally to draw two coastal fronts on the two mainlands and then to bisect the reflex angle between them.[24] The Court departed from its normal first step because of the presence of small, unstable mud islands in the mouth of the border river. The Court's bisector line was interrupted by five small offshore islands (one found by the Court to be Nicaraguan and four Honduran) which were each given a 12 mile enclave, subject to equidistance lines drawn between opposite islands. The mainlands bisector continued seaward of the small islands as if they did not exist.

These cases demonstrate a tendency to give primary attention to mainlands over small islands in delimitation. However, in some instances, islands are the equivalent of mainlands and accordingly in every case an island must be looked at on its merits in its geographical context.

(3) *Archipelagic baselines drawn to islands, rocks and drying reefs*

Part IV of the Convention introduced the concept of the archipelagic State which is entitled, in accordance with Article 47(1) of the Convention to draw archipelagic baselines, as long as 100M or even 125M, to and from "the outermost islands and drying reefs." It appears that such outermost islands could include those which are also rocks as defined in Article 121 (3). The drying reefs are low-tide elevations and as such are subject to the qualifications set out in Article 47(4), but there are no analogous qualifications there for the outermost islands. It may be recalled that Parts IV and VIII do not cross-refer. However, where an archipelagic State has an island or rock lying outside the archipelagic baselines, Part VIII would apply to the feature.

The question of maritime delimitation between archipelagic States and their non-archipelagic neighbours is not addressed specifically in Part IV. The LOS Conference included Article 47(6) in order to protect certain rights and interests, e.g. traditional fishing rights, of an "immediately adjacent neighbouring State" of an archipelagic State. However, the drawing of maritime boundaries in that type of geographical setting was not mentioned. As a result, the general provisions in Articles 15, 74 and 83 are applicable. Judicial practice varies concerning the role to be accorded in delimitation to straight baselines

[23] Similarly, in the *Eritrea/ Yemen* case concerning the boundary in the southern Red Sea where there are many small islands, the arbitral tribunal decided as a first step to construct an equidistance line based as far as practicable on the mainland coasts and then to examine the provisional line in the light of the islands. 40 ILM (2001) 983.

[24] ICJ Reports 2007, p. 659.

and archipelagic baselines. For instance, Malta's straight baselines were ignored by the ICJ in deciding the *Libya/Malta* case,[25] as were those of both parties in *Romania v Ukraine*.[26] In contrast, in the arbitration between Barbados and Trinidad and Tobago, Barbados claimed that the boundary should in part be the "territorial sea limit of Trinidad and Tobago" measured from the latter's baselines.[27] In rejecting this claim in favour of an equidistance line, the arbitral tribunal used the archipelagic baselines drawn to and from small islands to the north of Tobago and the low-water line on Barbados.[28] Archipelagic States benefit from the rules on drawing archipelagic baselines in order to safeguard national unity. The intention at the LOS Conference had to do with strengthening the national identity of such States, not conferring maritime advantages on archipelagic States over their neighbours. It would appear that features such as small islands, rocks and drying reefs used in the drawing of archipelagic baselines and the baselines themselves should not thereby be accorded any special weight in delimitation. In appropriate circumstances, such islands, rocks and reefs could be given reduced weight in order to achieve an equitable solution without impugning in any way the status of the archipelagic State or its archipelagic baselines.

5. *Disputes over the Maritime Spaces around Islands and Rocks*

Quite apart from sovereignty disputes, there exist some controversial claims and unresolved disputes concerning maritime zones around islands and rocks. Some of these disputes arise in the context of maritime boundary negotiations. Issues to do with islands and rocks may also arise incidentally in the work of the Commission on the Limits of the Continental Shelf. The Commission has an important task in considering scientific information for the purposes of Article 76, but its competence does not extend to questions of delimitation or the interpretation of other articles in the Convention such as Article 121.

Such questions could form the basis of a case between States Parties before an international court or tribunal brought in accordance with Part XV of the LOS Convention. Article 286 relates to "any dispute concerning the interpretation or application" of the Convention, subject to some qualifications contained in sections 1 and 3 of Part XV. Disputes about maritime boundaries arising under Articles 15, 74 or 83 can be submitted to one of the procedures specified in Article 287, unless a declaration has been made under Article 298 (1) (a) (i).

[25] ICJ Reports 1985, p. 13.

[26] ICJ Reports 2009, p. 61.

[27] XXVII RIAA, p. 147: 45 ILM (2006) 798, at p. 807.

[28] *Id.*, at p. 858 and p. 866.

A difference about the interpretation of Article 121 may form an element in a wider bilateral maritime boundary dispute or it may amount to a self-contained dispute between two States Parties. If, in the latter case, the dispute were to be submitted by means of an Application to a court or tribunal under Part XV, the question of the Applicant State's standing to bring the case could well be raised, in the context of considering the jurisdiction of the court or tribunal and the admissibility of the Application.

The question of standing

The question of standing to institute proceedings under Part XV has been examined primarily in the context of disputes concerning claims to the continental shelf, but it could arise in other instances including disputes concerning Article 121.[29] Commentators have recalled that in 1966, the ICJ stated in its judgment in the second phase of the *South West Africa cases* that "a right resident in any member of a community to take legal action in vindication of a public interest" – sometimes described as an *'actio popularis'* – was "not known to international law as it stands at present."[30] This finding would clearly tell against an applicant in those circumstances. Judge Nelson, writing in his private capacity, has expressed doubts over the success of such an application, while noting the trend towards acceptance of the *actio popularis*.[31] Similarly, Professor Noyes has concluded that "the doctrine of *actio popularis* has not yet been generally recognized in practice, at least when a treaty does not specifically authorize its use…"[32]

The decision in the *South West Africa* cases has other aspects. First, the decision turned upon the terms and nature of the former League of Nations Mandate, taken over by the UN. The two Applicant States were not parties to a treaty with the Respondent State; and, in reaching its decision, the Court took account of the existence of the supervisory functions of the Council of the League of Nations in regard to the Mandate. Secondly, the judgment also stated that "rights and interests…must be clearly vested in those who claim them by some

---

[29] There is a growing literature on an analogous situation concerning controversial claims to the continental shelf beyond 200 M, most recently E. Franckx, "The International Seabed Authority and the Common Heritage of Mankind" (25 IJMCL (2010) 543) and the literature there cited.

[30] ICJ Reports 1966, p. 6, at p. 45, para 88. For a discussion, see C. Gray, *Judicial Remedies in International Law* (1987), chapter 6.

[31] See L.D.M. Nelson, in Götz, Selmer & Wolfrum (eds), *Liber Amicorum Günther Jaenicke zum 85. Geburtstag*, p. 573, at pp. 581–2.

[32] J. Noyes, "Judicial and Arbitral Proceedings and the Outer Limits of the Continental Shelf," 42 *Vanderbilt Journal of Transnational Law* (2009) 1211 at p. 1248.

text or instrument, or rule of law."[33] In the circumstances under examination, it is not clear whether the Applicant State would in fact be taking action to vindicate a public interest or, rather, to enforce in its own interest a rule contained in the text of a treaty instrument, namely the Convention, to which both States had established their consent to be bound. Something would turn on the particular facts of the case and the contentions of the parties, in particular the applicant's explanation of its motives in instituting the proceedings.

There are some other considerations which could be relevant. First, the preamble to the Convention notes that "the problems of ocean space are closely interrelated and need to be considered as a whole." In particular, the Convention defined the maximum limits of national jurisdiction, in what was described at the time of its adoption as a "package deal." Articles 74, 76, 83 and 121 are some of the inter-related provisions that have to do with the limits of national jurisdiction.

Secondly, in the S.S. *Wimbledon* case, the PCIJ considered whether the proceedings against Germany could be instituted by the four applicant States, one of which (Japan) had not been directly affected by the denial of the vessel's passage through the Kiel Canal.[34] Article 386 (1) of the Treaty of Versailles provided that "In the event of violation of ... Articles 380 to 386, or of disputes as to the interpretation of these articles, any interested Power can appeal ..." to the PCIJ. The Court held that "... each of the four Applicant Powers has a clear interest in the execution of the provisions relating to the Kiel Canal, since they all possess fleets and merchant vessels ..." It followed that they were covered by the terms of Article 386(1) "even though they may be unable to adduce a prejudice to any pecuniary interest ..."[35] The Court went on to declare that the German denial of access was wrong and to order that Germany must make good the prejudice sustained by the private interests (French) in the vessel. This decision may have turned upon its own facts and the terms of Article 386(1): nonetheless, there is a parallel between the reference in that paragraph to "disputes as to the interpretation" of certain provisions in the Treaty of Versailles and the reference to "any dispute concerning the interpretation or application of this Convention" in Article 286 of the LOS Convention.

Thirdly, there is the doctrine of obligations owed by a State towards all other States, a doctrine which is clearly relevant to the law of the sea. In 1970, the ICJ's judgment in the *Barcelona Traction case* stated that "all States can be held to have a legal interest" in the protection of obligations that are owed *erga omnes*.[36] While the Court's examples of such obligations did not include any

---

[33] ICJ Reports 1966, p. 6, at p. 30, para 44.
[34] Judgment of 17 August 1923, Series A, No. 1.
[35] *Id.*, at p. 20.
[36] ICJ Reports 1970, p. 3, at p. 32.

parts of the law of the sea, nonetheless the obligations of each State Party in Article 89 (Invalidity of claims to sovereignty over the high seas) and Article 137 (Legal status of the Area and its resources), for instance, may be thought to be owed to all the other States Parties.

Following this important *dictum* of the Court, the International Law Commission included in its Articles on State Responsibility two articles that appear to be particularly relevant in the present discussion.[37] First, Article 42 (Invocation of responsibility by an injured State) recognised that a State which was specially affected by the breach of an obligation owed to the international community as a whole could invoke the responsibility of the violator. Secondly, Article 48 (Invocation of responsibility by a State other than an injured State) recognised that if a State breaches obligations protecting the interests of the international community as a whole, its responsibility may be invoked by another State without the latter having to show an injury or direct prejudice to its interests. Instituting legal proceedings represents a way of invoking State responsibility, even if the applicant requests no more than a declaration.[38] These articles are part of a considered text on State responsibility and different considerations may well be relevant in determining in a particular case before a court or tribunal questions of jurisdiction, admissibility and standing.

Before leaving the topic of obligations *erga omnes*, it may be recalled that the *Institut de Droit International* adopted a Resolution on obligations *erga omnes*, including those arising for States Parties to multilateral treaties, which contains the following Article 3:

> In the event of there being a jurisdictional link between a State alleged to have committed a breach of an obligation *erga omnes* and a State to which the obligation is owed, the latter State has standing to bring a claim to the International Court of Justice or other international judicial institution in relation to a dispute concerning compliance with that obligation.[39]

This proposition appears to be consistent with the *S.S. Wimbledon* case and the statement in the *South West Africa* cases about rights and interests vested by a treaty instrument.

To conclude, the question of an applicant's standing to bring legal proceedings in respect of a dispute concerning the status of a feature under Article 121 may have to be determined by the court or tribunal seized of a case, particularly if the Applicant State does not claim to have been especially affected by the

[37] J. Crawford, *The International Law Commission's Articles on State Responsibility* (2002).

[38] A point made by Judge Wolfrum: R. Wolfrum, "The Role of International Dispute Settlement Institutions in the Delimitation of the Outer Continental Shelf," in Lagoni & Vignes (Eds), *Maritime Delimitation* (2006), 19, at p. 30.

[39] Resolutions of the Krakow Session 2005: posted on the website of the *Institut de Droit International*: http://www.idi-iil.org.

contested claim, for example as a neighbouring State. A similar question of standing could arise in regard to disputes about a State Party's baselines or the outer limits of its EEZ or continental shelf. The answer in each instance would turn upon the facts of the particular case. However, the trend of development in the law may now have reached the stage where the judgment in the *South West Africa* cases about the issue of standing would have to be re-examined by the court or tribunal seised of the case in the light of the developments on international law and the terms of the Convention.

6. *Concluding Remarks*

The Convention on the Law of the Sea was a major achievement of diplomacy in the late 20th century. Its adoption has enhanced the rule of law in international affairs. The Convention and its institutions should be supported and all its provisions should be interpreted and applied in good faith.

Courts and tribunals are naturally prudent, and so reluctant to decide an issue unless it is necessary to do so in order to dispose of the case before it. Nonetheless, some authoritative rulings about the meaning of Article 121 could be helpful not only to the parties but also the wider international community.

ISLANDS OR ROCKS – IS THAT THE REAL QUESTION? THE TREATMENT OF ISLANDS IN THE DELIMITATION OF MARITIME BOUNDARIES

*Clive Schofield**

Abstract

Islands remain a key ingredient in maritime disputes, especially in the context of the delimitation of maritime boundaries between neighbouring States. Such disputes frequently revolve around the question of whether the island in question has the capacity to generate extensive claims to maritime jurisdiction and therefore influence the course of a maritime boundary line, or whether the feature is a mere "rock", incapable of generating extensive maritime claims. The importance of islands to the maritime claims of coastal States and in maritime delimitation is highlighted. The salient elements of the regime of islands are then outlined. The role of islands in the delimitation of maritime boundaries is then reviewed. On the basis of this assessment it is suggested that although a clear means of distinguishing between types of island remains out of reach, this debate is not necessarily the critical issue as a clear trend is emerging in terms of how small islands are dealt with in the delimitation of maritime boundaries.

Introduction: The Trouble with Islands

Islands represent a perennial source of discord between neighbouring coastal States. Such disputes frequently relate to small, remote and, at first glance at least, apparently intrinsically worthless, features. Disputes relate both to sovereignty over certain islands and also to their insular status, and thus their capacity to generate claims to maritime jurisdiction (though it is recognized that these issues are frequently intertwined). Discussions relating to the latter type of dispute often tend to be framed in the following manner: is the feature in question an island or a rock?

Whether a feature is an island capable of generating extended zones of jurisdiction (exclusive economic zone (EEZ) and continental shelf rights) or is, in fact, a "rock" which cannot, is a crucial one in terms of the capacity of the island in question to generate claims to maritime jurisdiction. However, distinguishing between these two types of insular feature remains a conundrum. This

* Professor and Director of Research, Australian National Centre for Ocean Resources and Security (ANCORS), University of Wollongong, Wollongong, NSW 2522, Australia. E-mail: clives@uow.edu.au.

question has been the subject of intense scholarly investigation but without a conclusive outcome being achieved.

This paper suggests that the question "island or rock" is, a misleading one. This is the case firstly because rocks are dealt with within under the same article of the United Nations Convention on the Law of the Sea (LOSC),[1] Article 121 dealing with the *Regime of Islands*. It is therefore more appropriate to regard rocks as a disadvantaged subcategory of island. Moreover, near forensic examination of the drafting history of Article 121 of LOSC merely reveals the opposing interests and positions of the States involved leading to a deliberately ambiguous outcome. Further, the subsequent practice of States and international courts and tribunals has thus far failed to provide an adequate route to clarifying the distinction between 'full' or 'fully-fledged' islands capable of generating EEZ and continental shelf rights and mere rocks which are restricted from doing so.

It is suggested that the more profitable avenue for discussion focuses on the treatment of islands in the delimitation of maritime boundaries and the generation of claims to maritime jurisdiction. A review of the treatment of islands drawn from relevant State practice and the jurisprudence of international judicial and arbitral courts suggests that, although practice remains somewhat diverse, there are signs of a consistent trend emerging and, at the least, numerous examples exist which indicate how disputes related to islands can be equitably resolved.

The Importance of Islands

Islands are the focus of numerous maritime boundary disputes. Such disputes tend to fall into two broad categories: those relating to sovereignty over islands themselves, their land territories and their related maritime space; and those concerned with the role of particular insular features in the delimitation of maritime boundaries. These factors are, however, often inextricably entangled with the potential role of islands in delimitation and the generation of claims to maritime jurisdiction also proving to be a key factor influencing and informing any dispute over sovereignty.

In many cases such sovereignty disputes relate to title over a few remote, barren, small and often uninhabited islands, rocks, low-tide elevations and reefs. Nonetheless, such features have proved to be a long-standing source of discord

[1] United Nations, *United Nations Convention on the Law of the Sea*, Publication no. E97.V10, (United Nations, New York, 1983). See 1833 UNTS 3, opened for signature 10 December 1982, Montego Bay, Jamaica (entered into force 16 November 1994). Also available at: <http://www.un.org/Depts/los/convention_agreements/convention_overview_convention.htm> (hereinafter "LOSC").

between States which, at the least, can exert a negative influence on bilateral relations and, at the worst, can provide the trigger (or excuse) for military confrontation. Salient examples in the latter category include the Falkland Islands (Islas Malvinas) and South Georgia in the southern Atlantic Ocean,[2] and the Paracel and Spratly Island groups in the South China Sea.[3] The underlying historical and geopolitical dimensions of disputes over islands are frequently highly influential, however. Despite the considerable impacts and influences of globalisation, sovereignty and territory remain powerful forces and States are inextricably linked to their territory. Any potential loss of claimed territory, however slight, can therefore be construed as a threat to a State's sovereignty, security and integrity, especially for domestic political audiences and gain. Profound reserves of patriotism and nationalism are consequently often invested in boundary and territorial disputes. Furthermore, while the territory at stake may be relatively insignificant, possession of it can be invested with significance out of proportion to its apparent intrinsic merits, especially in the context of a historically acrimonious relationship between the parties. Arguably Greece and Turkey's 1996 confrontation over the small islets of Imia (to Greece) or Kardak Rocks (to Turkey) can be seen in this light.[4] A further notable feature of sovereignty disputes over islands is for one (or more) of the parties to a given dispute (often the State in possession of the disputed feature itself) to simply deny that the grounds for a dispute exist and thus, any basis to engage in negotiations on the issue. Frequent assertions that a claimant State's sovereignty over a disputed feature or features is "indisputable" in the context of exchanges over the disputed islands in the South China Sea fits this pattern. For example, in 2009, in response to submissions related to the outer limits of the continental shelf in the South China Sea made to the relevant United Nations body, the Commission on the Limits of the Continental Shelf (CLCS)[5] by Vietnam and

---

[2] The military conflict between Argentina and the United Kingdom over the Falkland Islands (Islas Malvinas) and South Georgia in 1982 cost the lives of 655 Argentine and 236 British troops. See, for example, P. Armstrong and V. Forbes, *The Falkland Islands and their Adjacent Maritime Area*, Maritime Briefing, Volume 2, no. 3, (Durham, International Boundaries Research Unit, 1997), pp. 4–12.

[3] Similarly, in the "Battle of Fiery Cross Reef" between China and Vietnam in March 1988. In this engagement over possession of one of the disputed Spratly Islands 75 Vietnamese personnel were reported to have lost their lives and three Vietnamese ships were set ablaze. Chinese casualties were reported to be slight. See, D.J. Dzurek, *The Spratly Islands: Who's On First?*, Maritime Briefing, Vol. 2, no. 1, (Durham, International Boundaries Research Unit, 1996), p. 23.

[4] See, M.A. Pratt and C.H. Schofield, 'The Imia/Kardak Rocks Dispute in the Aegean Sea', 4 *Boundary and Security Bulletin*, No. 1 (Spring 1996), 62–69.

[5] The Commission is a body consisting of 21 scientists tasked with evaluating whether coastal States through their submissions have fulfilled the requirements of Article 76 of LOSC. On the basis of this assessment the CLCS makes "recommendations" to the coastal State on the

jointly by Malaysia and Vietnam, China issued a protest note in which it stated that it had "indisputable sovereignty over the islands in the South China Sea." Vietnam responded with a diplomatic note of its own stating that it similarly possessed "indisputable sovereignty" over both the Paracel (Hoang Sa) and Spratly (Truong Sa) Islands.[6]

In respect of the disputes concerning the maritime jurisdictional zones associated with islands, crucially, the second paragraph of Article 121 of LOSC dealing with the regime of islands provides that islands, in an identical fashion to mainland coasts, are capable of generating a full suite of maritime zones (see below). Consequently, even small islands potentially have the capacity to generate huge claims to maritime jurisdictional zones with significant resource/security implications. Critically, if an island had no maritime neighbours within 400nm, it could generate 125,664 sq.nm [431,014km^2] of territorial sea, EEZ and continental shelf rights. In contrast, if deemed a mere "rock" incapable of generating EEZ and continental shelf rights, a territorial sea of 452 sq. nautical miles (1,550km^2) could be claimed.[7]

The vexed issue of distinguishing between types of island is explored below. However, the potential capacity of insular features to act as base points for the claiming of extensive maritime zones goes a long way to explaining both the significance attached to islands and the rise in the number of international disputes involving islands. This is primarily because of the marine resource, both living and non-living that are, or, importantly, are perceived to be, present within the maritime areas that can potentially be claimed from islands. While such living resources tend to be associated with fisheries, and these certainly continue to play a significant food security role for many coastal States (despite increasing rates of stock depletion), other living resource opportunities include those derived from marine genetic resources and these are of increasing importance to coastal States.[8] With regard to non-living resources, focus has traditionally been on seabed hydrocarbon resources (oil and natural gas) and it

basis of which the coastal State can establish limits that are "final and binding" (LOSC, Article 76(8)). See, <http://www.un.org/Depts/los/clcs_new/clcs_home.htm>.

6 See, Note from the Permanent Mission of the People's Republic of China addressed to the Secretary General of the United Nations, CML/17/2009, 7 May 2009, available at, <http://www.un.org/Depts/los/clcs_new/submissions_files/submission_mysvnm_33_2009.htm>; and, Note from the Permanent Mission of the Socialist Republic of Vietnam to the United Nations addressed to the Secretary General of the United Nations, 86/HC-2009,<http://www.un.org/Depts/los/clcs_new/submissions_files/submission_mysvnm_33_2009.htm>.

7 It should be noted that these theoretical calculations assume that the island or rock in question has no area. As such features inevitably comprise some territory and therefore area, the potential maritime claims that can be generated from them are likely to be greater.

8 For example, it has been estimated that marine biotechnology related products were estimated to be worth USD$100 billion in 2000 alone. See, S. Arico and C. Salpin, 'Bioprospecting

is notable in this context that oil production has increasingly shifted offshore.[9] Additionally, disputes concerning and control over certain islands have strategic and security dimensions. For example, the proximity of the contested Spratly Islands in the South China Sea to a strategic waterway of global significance, providing the key maritime link between the Indian Ocean and East Asia, is often cited as an example of this consideration.[10]

The Regime of Islands under International Law

As noted above, the question of the definition of islands is a complex and crucially important one to many coastal States, essentially because of the impact of island status on the capacity of insular features to generate maritime claims and influence the course of maritime boundary delimitation lines. A key consideration is the Regime of Islands outlined in Article 121 of LOSC:

Article 121
Regime of islands

1. *An island is a naturally formed area of land, surrounded by water, which is above water at high tide.*
2. *Except as provided for in paragraph 3, the territorial sea, the contiguous zone, the exclusive economic zone and the continental shelf of an island are determined in accordance with the provisions of this convention applicable to other land territory.*
3. *Rocks which cannot sustain human habitation or economic life of their own shall have no exclusive economic zone or continental shelf.*

Although the question of the definition of islands has provoked fierce debate over the years, particularly during the drafting of LOSC, the four requirements for a feature to legally qualify as an island under LOSC Article 121(1) are relatively uncontroversial.[11] These insular criteria are that an island must be "naturally formed", be an "area of land", be "surrounded by water" and, critically, must be "above water at high tide".

of Genetic Resources in the Deep Seabed: Scientific, Legal and Policy Aspects', UNU-IAS Report, (United Nations University, 2005), p. 17.

[9] It has been estimated that around 60 per cent of global oil production is now derived from offshore exploration operations. See, "Offshore oil and gas around the World", Ministry of Energy, Mines and Petroleum Resources, Government of British Columbia, available at, <http://www.empr.gov.bc.ca/OG/offshoreoilandgas/Pages/OffshoreOilandGasAroundtheWorld.aspx>.

[10] See, for example, R. Emmers, *Maritime Disputes in the South China Sea: Strategic and Diplomatic Status Quo*, (Institute for Defence and Strategic Studies (IISS) Working Paper No. 87, Singapore, September 2005): pp. 7–9.

[11] J.R.V. Prescott and C.H. Schofield, *The Maritime Political Boundaries of the World* (Leiden/Boston: Martinus Nijhoff Publishers, 2005), pp. 58–61.

However, one of the key issues under debate prior to and during the drafting of LOSC related to island size and habitability. Many proposed that there should be some size limit coupled with the definition of what constitutes an island, such as to prevent each tiny isolated islet, even if permanently above water, from generating maritime claims. Malta, Ireland, a group of 14 African States and Romania all advanced proposals essentially aimed at denying or restricting small insular features from the maritime zones to be accorded to 'full' islands.[12] Contrary views on the part of States such as China, Greece, the United Kingdom and a group of Pacific island States were, however, also strongly voiced.[13] The then-Geographer at the United States Department of State also published a notable study suggesting a categorisation of insular features into rocks (less than .001 square mile in area), islets (.001 and 1 square mile), isles (greater than 1 square mile but not more than 1,000 square miles) and islands (larger than 1,000 square miles).[14]

Ultimately, no size criteria for defining islands were included in LOSC. Concerns over size and habitability were included in the form of Article 121(3) of LOSC states that: "Rocks which cannot sustain human habitation or economic life of their own shall have no exclusive economic zone or continental shelf." Rocks therefore represent a disadvantaged sub-category of island whose zone-generative capacity, and thus value to a potential claimant, is significantly reduced. Distinguishing between islands capable of generating EEZ and continental shelf rights and rocks which cannot remains hazardous (see below).

It is worth noting that the regime of islands does not include either artificial islands or low-tide elevations. Artificial islands are dealt with under Article 60 of LOSC, paragraph 8 of which states clearly that artificial islands, together with artificial installations and structures, "do not possess the status of islands," and "have no territorial sea of their own." Artificial islands are also specifically excluded from affecting maritime boundary delimitation.[15] Low-tide elevations, that is, features that are inundated at high tide but emerge above water at low tide, are dealt with under Article 13 of LOSC. Low-tide elevations are not

[12] See, United Nations, *United Nations Conferences on the Law of the Sea, Official Records, Third Conference*, (Buffalo, New York: William s. Hein & Co., 1980, reprinted 2000). See also, United Nations, Division for Ocean Affairs and the Law of the Sea, *Régime of islands: Legislative history of Part VIII (Article 121) of the United Nations Convention on the Law of the Sea*, (United Nations: New York, 1988); and, S.N. Nandan and S. Rosenne (eds.) *United Nations Convention on the Law of the Sea 1982: A Commentary*, Volume II (Dordrecht: Kluwer Law International, 1993), pp. 321–339.

[13] *Ibid.*

[14] D. Hodgson, *Islands: Normal and Special Circumstances*, (U.S. Department of State, Bureau of Intelligence and Research, Research Study, 1973).

[15] LOSC, Article 60(5) does, however, provide that safety zones of not more than 500 metres may be declared around such artificial islands or installations.

capable of generating claims to maritime space independently. However, if a low-tide elevation falls wholly or partially within the breadth of the territorial sea measured from the normal baseline of a State's mainland or island coasts, it can be used as a territorial sea base point.[16] Incidentally, it remains unclear whether low-tide elevations constitute territory as such and therefore questionable whether they can be subject to a claim to sovereignty.[17]

Distinguishing between Types of Island

Distinguishing between islands capable of generating extended maritime claims and rocks which cannot remains highly problematic. Article 121(3) provokes questions not only as to what constitutes a "rock" but also how to ascertain whether a feature "cannot sustain human habitation" or what constitutes the "economic life" of its own as no definition for these terms is offered in LOSC. The text of Article 121 of LOSC therefore remains opaque and essentially of little help on this issue. There exists no objective way to achieve this based on Article 121 and its supporting drafting history alone. Indeed, rather than providing a useful aid in clarifying interpretation of these provisions, the drafting history of Article 121 instead reveals the scope and depth of the disagreements that were evident during the negotiations on the regime of islands during the Third United Nations Conference on the Law of the Sea (UNCLOS III). States adopted widely divergent views on the issue of islands. These distinct positions led States to propose substantively differing and frequently directly conflicting proposals which tended to reflect particular and opposing national interests.[18]

A review of the considerable scholarly literature that has evolved on this question[19] indicates that no consensus has been reached on key interpretational

---

16 LOSC, Article 13(1).

17 See, *Case Concerning Maritime Delimitation and Territorial Questions between Qatar and Bahrain* (Qatar v. Bahrain) (Merits) [2001] ICJ Rep 40, available at <http://www.icj-cij.org/docket/files/87/7027.pdf>, paras. 205–206; and, *Case concerning Sovereignty over Pedra Branca/Pulau Batu Puteh, Middle Rocks and South Ledge* (Malaysia/Singapore), Judgment of 23 May 2008, available at <www.icj-cij.org/docket/files/130/14492.pdf> (hereinafter, the *Pedra Branca Case*), paras. 295–296. See also, R. Beckman and C.H. Schofield, 'Moving Beyond Disputes over Island Sovereignty: ICJ Decision Sets Stage for Maritime Boundary Delimitation in the Singapore Strait', *Ocean Development and International Law*, 40, 2009, 1, 4.

18 C.H. Schofield, 'The Trouble with Islands: The Definition and Role of Islands and Rocks in Maritime Boundary Delimitation', in S.-Y. Hong and J.M. Van Dyke (eds.) *Maritime Boundary Disputes, Settlement Processes, and the Law of the Sea*, Publications on Ocean Development, Volume 65 (The Hague: Martinus Nijhoff, 2009), pp. 19–37, at pp. 27–28.

19 See, for example, J.I. Charney, 'Rocks that cannot sustain human habitation', *American Journal of International Law*, 93, no. 4, 1999 863–78; A.G.O. Elferink, (1998) 'Clarifying Article 121 (3) of the Law of the Sea Convention: the limits set by the nature of international legal

questions, notably regarding the question of distinguishing between islands within the meaning of Article 121(1) and rocks in keeping with Article 121(3). Divergent views linger on despite exhaustive analysis of both the text of LOSC and its associated drafting history. This scenario is a direct consequence of the regime of islands having been drafted in an intentionally vague and ambiguous fashion.[20]

Some limited guidance can be gleaned from subsequent practice and jurisprudence. However, this experience is somewhat contradictory and therefore does not offer conclusive guidance. With regard to State practice, the picture is mixed. On one hand Mexico has opted to ignore a group of small and remote features, Roca Alijos, for the purposes of generating continental shelf and EEZ claims in the Pacific Ocean. The United Kingdom has gone a step further and unilaterally reclassified a similarly small and remote feature, Rockall, from the status of an island within the meaning of LOSC Article 121(1) to an Article 121(3) rock and consequently executed a 'roll-back' in its maritime jurisdictional claims from that feature.[21] Other States have, however, taken contrary views and opted to make full 200nm claims (and, in some cases, beyond the 200nm limit in respect of outer continental shelf rights) from frequently remote, uninhabited and small islands. Japan's Okinotorishima represents only one of the more extreme examples of this type of practice.[22] State practice on this issue can therefore be considered confused and conflicting. That said, it can be observed that States in possession of small islands have generally sought to maximise their maritime jurisdiction by advancing expansive maritime claims from such features.

---

processes', *Boundary and Security Bulletin*, 6, no. 2, 1998 58–68; B. Kwaitkowska and A.H.A. Soons, 'Entitlement to maritime areas of rocks which cannot sustain human habitation or economic life of their own', *Netherlands Yearbook of International Law*, XXI, 1990, 139–81; Prescott and Schofield, *supra* note 11, pp. 61–75; J.M. Van Dyke and R.A. Brooks, 'Uninhabited islands: their impact on the ownership of the oceans' resources', *Ocean Development International Law Journal*, 12, 1983, 265–84; and, J.M. Van Dyke, J. Morgan and J. Gurish, 'The exclusive economic zone of the northwestern Hawaiian Islands: when do uninhabited islands generate an EEZ?, *San Diego Law Review*, 25, no. 3, 1988, 425–494.

20 Prescott and Schofield, *supra* note 11, p. 58.

21 House of Commons (HC) *Hansard, Written Answers*, 21 July 1997, cols. 397–398. An identical statement was made in the House of Lords a day later on July 22, 1997 (*Hansard* (HL) *Written Answers*, 22 July 1997, cols. 155–156). Quoted in D.H. Anderson, 'British Accession to the UN Convention on the Law of the Sea', *International and Comparative Law Quarterly*, 46, 1997 761–786, at 778. See also, C.R. Symmons, 'Ireland and the Rockall dispute: an analysis of recent developments', 6 *Boundary and Security Bulletin*, no. 1, 1998, 78–93.

22 See, for example, Y.H. Song, 'Okinotorishima: A "Rock" or an "Island"? Recent Maritime Boundary Controversy between Japan and Taiwan/China', in: S.Y. Hong and J.M. Van Dyke (eds.) *Maritime Boundary Disputes, Settlement Processes, and the Law of the Sea*, Publications on Ocean Development, Volume 65 (The Hague: Martinus Nijhoff, 2009), pp. 145–176.

With regard to the jurisprudence of international courts and tribunals, unfortunately an authoritative interpretation of Article 121 from a body such as the International Court of Justice (ICJ) remains lacking, not least because the ICJ has opted to effectively sidestep the issue. While there were hopes, based on the pleadings of the parties to the *Black Sea Case*, which featured detailed arguments on the interpretation of Article 121 of LOSC, that the ICJ would provide an authoritative ruling on this problematic provision of the UN Convention on the Law of the Sea, this did not eventuate. Rather than addressing the interpretation of Article 121 the Court contented itself with the specific role of the problematic island in question, Serpent's Island,[23] with respect to the delimitation of a maritime boundary between the States involved, Romania and the Ukraine (see below).[24]

Despite this, coastal States and international adjudicative bodies have and continue to be faced with problematic issues related to islands, especially in the context of the delimitation of maritime boundaries. Practical ways in which to deal with islands in the context of the delimitation of maritime boundaries are examined below. It is suggested that this is the 'real' question: what role should islands have in the context of the delimitation of maritime boundaries and what mechanisms are there to overcome the presence of islands in the maritime delimitation scenario. Such an approach arguably offers a more profitable line of inquiry than the sterile debates over whether a particular feature is "an island or a rock" that tend to characterise many maritime disputes involving islands as the latter question is itself an inappropriate and unhelpful one.

The Delimitation of Maritime Boundaries

What, then, are the international law rules applicable to the delimitation of maritime boundaries involving islands, rocks and low-tide elevations? Fundamentally, the LOSC rules, such as they are, that apply to the delimitation of maritime boundaries generally also apply where islands are involved in the delimitation equation.

Wherever the maritime claims of neighbouring States overlap, a potential maritime boundary situation exists. In the context of a maritime boundary

[23] Ostrov Zmeinyy (Serpents' Island or Insular Serpilor in Romanian) is a small (0.135km^2) Ukrainian island, located approximately 19 nautical miles from the terminus of the land boundary between the two States on the Black Sea coast. The location of Serpents' Island is such that it could substantially influence a maritime boundary delimitation between the two States on the basis of equidistance.

[24] *Case Concerning Maritime Delimitation in the Black Sea* (Romania v. Ukraine), Judgment of 3 February 2009, available at <http://www.icj-cij.org/docket/files/132/14987.pdf>, para. 187 (hereinafter, "*Black Sea Case*").

determined by an international court or tribunal, delimitation depends on applicable international legal principles. These same legal principles are frequently influential in where a maritime boundary is delimited through negotiations between States. However, the States involved have considerable discretion to take into consideration any factor deemed relevant to the negotiation and agree on any boundary line mutually acceptable to the parties involved, so long as the rights of third States are not jeopardised. Accordingly, therefore, it is worth emphasizing that maritime boundary delimitation through negotiations is essentially a political act. While there are clear and essential legal and technical components to the delimitation of maritime boundaries, it is the political component that is crucial.

The provisions of LOSC governing the delimitation of maritime boundaries provide only limited guidance as to how such disputes may be resolved. In relation to the delimitation of the territorial sea, Article 15 of LOSC does offer a clear preference for the use of an equidistance or median line. This does not apply, however, if the States concerned agree to the contrary or there exists an "historic title or other special circumstances" in the area to be delimited which justify a departure from the equidistance line. Under the 1958 Conventions, delimitation of the continental shelf was also to be effected by the use of median lines unless, similarly, an agreement to the contrary or "special circumstances" existed that justified an alternative approach. However, under LOSC there was a distinct shift away from equidistance as a preferred method of maritime delimitation. Articles 74 and 83 of LOSC, dealing with delimitation of the continental shelf and EEZ respectively, merely provide, in identical general terms, that agreements should be reached on the basis of international law in order to achieve "an equitable solution". No preferred method of delimitation is indicated and thus the LOSC's 'rules' on delimitation, such as they are, can be viewed as being open to conflicting interpretation and thus dispute. Indeed, as the Arbitral Tribunal in the Eritrea-Yemen Arbitration stated in reference to the drafting of Article 83, this was "a last minute endeavour... to get agreement on a very controversial matter", and therefore, "consciously designed to decide as little as possible".[25]

In order to achieve delimitation of the continental shelf and/or EEZ in accordance with LOSC, therefore, a theoretically limitless list of potentially relevant circumstances needs to be taken into consideration in the delimitation equation in order to reach the goal of an equitable result. Nonetheless, it has become abundantly clear from the practice of coastal States, allied to the rulings of international courts and tribunals that geography, and particularly

[25] *Eritrea/Yemen Arbitration, Award of the Arbitral Tribunal in the Second Stage of the Proceedings (Maritime Delimitation)*, Award of 17 December 1999, available at, <http://www.pca-cpa.org/showpage.asp?pag_id=1160>, para. 116 (hereinafter, "*Eritrea/Yemen Arbitration*").

coastal geography, has a critical role in the delimitation of maritime boundaries. Aspects of coastal geography that have proved especially influential include the configuration of the coasts under consideration, the relative coastal length and the potential impact of outstanding geographical features, notably islands.[26]

The salient role of coastal geography in maritime boundary delimitation is linked to the widespread use of equidistance lines. While, as noted, there has been a shift away from equidistance as a preferred method of delimitation over time in the law of the sea, not least because in certain circumstances the application of strict equidistance can lead to clearly inequitable results,[27] equidistance has nonetheless proved extremely popular as a basis for maritime boundary delimitation in practice. The construction of equidistance lines offer considerable advantages – if there is agreement on the baselines to be used, there is only one strict equidistance line and this provides the appeal of mathematical certainty and objectivity as well as affording coastal States with the not inconsiderable attraction of jurisdiction over those maritime areas closest to their own coasts. Equidistance lines can also be flexibly applied and may be simplified, adjusted or modified to take specific geographical circumstances into account.[28]

In practice the equidistance method has proved more popular than any alternative method by far and most agreed maritime boundaries are based on some form of equidistance.[29] Consequently, equidistance lines are often constructed at least as a means of assessing a maritime boundary situation or as the starting point for discussions in the context of maritime boundary negotiations. Such lines have also frequently been adopted as the basis for the final delimitation line. Furthermore, it is the case that in recent cases the ICJ's approach has been to construct an equidistance line as a provisional delimitation line in the first instance. Indeed, in its, at the time of writing, most recent judgment, that in the *Black Sea Case* between Romania and Ukraine, the Court was explicit in stating that "[i]n keeping with its settled jurisprudence on maritime delimitation", a provisional delimitation line should be established consisting of an equidistance line "unless there are compelling reasons that make this unfeasible

[26] Prescott and Schofield *supra* note 11, pp. 221–2.

[27] Notable as a consequence of the North Sea Continental Shelf Cases. See, *North Sea Continental Shelf (Federal Republic of Germany/Denmark; Federal Republic of Germany/Netherlands) (1967–1969)*, Judgment of 20 February 1969, [1969] ICJ Reports, 3, at para. 89 and 101.

[28] C.M. Carleton and C.H. Schofield, *Developments in the Technical Determination of Maritime Space: Delimitation, Dispute Resolution, Geographical Information Systems and the Role of the Technical Expert*, Maritime Briefing, Volume 3, no. 4 (Durham: International Boundaries Research Unit, 2002), pp. 7–31; L. Legault and B. Hankey, (1993) 'Method, Oppositeness and Adjacency, and Proportionality in Maritime Boundary Delimitation', in: J.I. Charney and L.M. Alexander (eds.), *International Maritime Boundaries*, Vol. I (Dordrecht: Martinus Nijhoff, 1993), pp. 203–242; Prescott and Schofield, *supra* note 11, p. 236.

[29] Legault and Hankey *supra* note 18, p. 205; and, Prescott and Schofield *supra* note 11, p. 239.

in the particular case".[30] The ICJ's practice has then been to determine whether there exist any reasons to modify the provisional equidistance line in order to achieve an equitable result.[31]

The Role of Islands in Maritime Boundary Delimitation

The treatment of islands in the context of maritime boundary delimitation inevitably represents a developing area in terms of the practice of States given that less than half of potential maritime boundaries globally have been even partially delimited.[32] Nonetheless, there exists abundant experience regarding the treatment of islands in the delimitation of maritime boundaries. Contentious and seemingly intractable island-related disputes are often why coastal States seek third-party means of dispute settlement. This has, in turn, led international courts and tribunals to develop a number of mechanisms to deal with this scenario, even if an authoritative ruling on the interpretation of Article 121(3) has been lacking. Similarly, in negotiating bilateral maritime boundary agreements, States have faced analogous challenges and adopted numerous and diverse solutions to the potential problems posed by the presence of islands in the area to be delimited. Such approaches include, for example, affording islands reduced weight in the construction of equidistance lines or partially or wholly enclaving them.

A review of both State practice and the rulings of international courts and tribunals suggests several key means of addressing the challenge of dealing with islands in maritime delimitation. These approaches range from awarding all features, including small offshore islands, full effect on the maritime boundary delimitation line, applying partial effect to islands, enclaving or partially enclaving islands or, alternatively to wholly ignoring islands in the selection of base points relevant to the construction of the delimitation line.

Although definitive conclusions regarding the treatment of islands in the delimitation of maritime boundaries remain elusive, there has been a sustained trend in international jurisprudence towards awarding small islands a reduced effect in maritime boundary delimitation. This has proved to be especially the case where such islands are located at a considerable distance offshore and opposed to mainland coasts such that a great disparity in relevant coastlines is evident. Such features would tend to have a disproportionate impact on the construction of an equidistance-based boundary line. Consequently, the potential influence of such exceptional features on maritime boundary delimitation

---

[30] *Black Sea Case Case*, para. 116.

[31] Prescott and Schofield *supra* note 11, pp. 240–241.

[32] *Ibid.*, pp. 217–218.

lines has generally been discounted. Thus islands were awarded a reduced effect in the *Libya/Malta*[33] and *Jan Mayen*[34] *Cases*, half effect was accorded to the Isles of Scilly in the *Channel Arbitration*,[35] to the Kerkennah Islands in the *Libya/Tunisia Case*[36] and to Seal Island in the *Gulf of Maine Case*.[37] Moreover, the Channel Islands were enclaved in the *Anglo-French Arbitration*,[38] while the Hanish Islands were in effect semi-enclaved in the *Eritrea/Yemen Arbitration*[39] and arguably St Pierre and Miquelon were semi-enclaved in the *Canada/France Case*.[40] Furthermore, islands have, on occasion, been entirely ignored for the purpose of constructing the maritime boundary delimitation line, for instance in the context of the *Gulf of Maine Case* where numerous small islets and low-tide elevations were ignored,[41] in the *Eritrea/Yemen Arbitration* where isolated islands had no influence on the delimitation line[42] and in the *Qatar/Bahrain Case* where a potentially influential small island, Qit'at Jaradah, was discounted.[43] Similarly, Serpents' Island was deemed inappropriate for use as a base point in the construction of a provisional equidistance-based boundary line in the *Black Sea Case*.[44]

In contrast, where numerous islands which in combination have a long coastal front are located in relatively close proximity to a mainland coast such that they can be considered to be representative of the general configuration of the mainland coast or effectively geographically integrated with it, there is a tendency to accord such islands full weight in maritime delimitation. A salient

---

33 *Case Concerning the Continental Shelf* (Libyan Arab Jamahiriya/Malta), [1985] *ICJ Reports* 13, para. 73.

34 *Case Concerning Maritime Delimitation in the Area between Greenland and Jan Mayen (Denmark v. Norway)*, [1993] *ICJ Reports* 38, paras. 61–69.

35 *Arbitration between the United Kingdom and France on the Delimitation of the Continental Shelf*, Decision of 30 June 1977, *International Legal Materials*, Volume XVIII (1979): 3–129 (hereinafter, "*Anglo-French Arbitration*").

36 *Case Concerning the Continental Shelf* (Libyan Arab Jamahiriya/Tunisia), [1982] *ICJ Reports* 18, para. 129.

37 *Delimitation of the Maritime Boundary in the Gulf of Maine Area* (Canada v. United States), [1984] *ICJ Reports* 246 (hereinafter, "*Gulf of Maine Case*"), para 218.

38 *Anglo-French Arbitration*, para. 199.

39 *Eritrea/Yemen Arbitration*, paras. 154–162.

40 *Delimitation of the Maritime Areas between France and Canada*, Decision of 10 June 1992, 31 *International Legal Materials*, Volume 31 (1992): 1149. See also, T. McDorman, 'The Canada-France Maritime Boundary Case: Drawing a Line around St. Pierre and Miquelon', *American Journal of International Law*, 84, 1990, 157–189.

41 *Gulf of Maine Case*, para. 210.

42 *Eritrea/Yemen Arbitration*, paras. 147–148.

43 *Case concerning Maritime Delimitation and Territorial Questions between Qatar and Bahrain* (Qatar v. Bahrain), [2001] *ICJ Reports* 40, para. 219.

44 *Black Sea Case*, para. 149.

example of this type of scenario is provided by the Tribunal's treatment of the Dahlak archipelago in the Eritrea/Yemen Arbitration.[45]

As noted above, there are therefore numerous examples of islands being accorded a reduced effect, being partially or wholly enclaved or even being ignored altogether. State practice is diverse, and there have been cases of even extremely small features being accorded considerable effect in the delimitation of maritime boundaries. Nonetheless, these examples in State practice appear to be more the exception than the rule and the general trend in State practice in the treatment of islands appears to be toward giving islands a reduced effect. This is especially the case in respect of smaller, less significant (in terms of coastal front, area and population for instance) islands located at considerable distances offshore mainland coasts, as these features would be likely to have the most excessive and disproportionate impacts on potential delimitation lines were they to be granted full effect.

Implications for Insular Status

International courts and tribunals have tended to address the potentially disproportionate effect of particular, outstanding coastal geographical features, frequently islands, by according them reduced effect on the final delimitation line. This is often achieved by constructing strict equidistance lines and then modifying the line so as to give the feature concerned only partial effect. Alternatively, outstanding geographical features such as islands that would unduly influence an equidistance line may be ignored and not used as base points for construction of the equidistance-based boundary line, as was the case for Serpents' Island in the *Black Sea Case*.

Where these maritime delimitations involve the continental shelf and EEZ, this necessarily implies that the court or tribunal concerned has taken the view that the feature in question is an island within the meaning of LOSC, Article 121(1) rather than a rock in accordance with LOSC, Article 121(3). Islands that fall into this category include the Isles of Scilly belonging to the United Kingdom, Tunisia's Kerkennah Islands, Canada's Seal Island, France's St. Pierre and Miquelon Islands, Norway's Jan Mayen Island, and the islands of the Dahlak archipelago. Perhaps of particular significance in this context are those islands located at a considerable distance offshore such as the Isles of Scilly, St. Pierre and Miquelon and Jan Mayen. Whilst the Isles of Scilly and St. Pierre and Miquelon have fairly substantial populations (numbering in the thousands of people) of longstanding, it can be observed that Jan Mayen does

[45] *Eritrea/Yemen Arbitration*, paras. 139–146.

not, boasting only personnel stationed there to man a scientific research station. It is also notable that Jan Mayen is a mere 377km^2 in area as compared with Greenland's area of 2,166,086km^2.[46] The disparity between the lengths of the relevant coastal fronts of the two islands was also significant (9.2:1 in Greenland's favour).[47] This decision seems to run somewhat counter to the trend, even if Jan Mayen was accorded a reduced effect, largely on the basis of the great disparity in relevant coasts, in delimiting the maritime boundary line between Denmark (Greenland) and Norway (Jan Mayen).

In the context of the above-mentioned cases a number of insular features have also been accorded no weight in maritime delimitation beyond the territorial sea. It is, however, less easy to draw clear implications and conclusions from these findings, at least as far as Article 121 of LOSC is concerned. This is because the islands in question may have been given no weight in the construction of the relevant continental shelf or EEZ delimitation line for reasons other than their not qualifying as islands capable of continental shelf or EEZ claims. For example, islands are frequently discounted or ignored in the delimitation of maritime boundaries where their geographical position is such that taking them into account in the construction of a strict equidistance line-based boundary would lead to an inequitable result, rather than because such features are mere rocks within the meaning of LOSC, Article 121(3). It is the case that an international court or tribunal has yet to specifically discount an island on the basis that it is a "rock" within the meaning of Article 121(3) of LOSC.

The Value of Precedents from Case Law and State Practice

The value of the above experience in terms of precedents for yet to be delimited maritime boundaries and the treatment of islands is questionable. Strictly speaking, the arbitral and judicial decisions are only binding on the parties to the particular case and each case features its own particular facts and circumstances. Nonetheless, the decisions of the ICJ and *ad hoc* international arbitration tribunals are clearly influential – as demonstrated by the written and oral pleadings which are replete with references to past cases and judgments in support of either side's arguments. According to one eminent commentator, the rulings of such international courts and tribunals "carry special weight in international maritime boundary law" largely because of the "relative scarcity

[46] Area figures according to the CIA World Factbook, 2011. See <https://www.cia.gov/library/publications/the-world-factbook/geos/gl.html>. and <https://www.cia.gov/library/publications/the-world-factbook/geos/jn.html>.

[47] *Jan Mayen Case*, para. 61.

of authoritative pronouncements."[48] The same author goes on to observe that there are two key reasons for this: first, the existence of "a unique line of jurisprudence" stemming from a continuing series of decisions and, second, "the absence of clearer guidance from codification efforts, *opinion juris* and state practice,"[49] such that:

> *Even though there is no doctrine of stare decisis in international adjudication, it is not inaccurate to consider the impressive line of maritime boundary decisions as forming a common law in the classic sense.*[50]

The decisions of international courts and tribunals are capable of comparison and are likely to hold more value as potential precedents. In contrast, negotiated maritime boundary agreements frequently do not indicate the rules or principles on which they are based and, therefore, it is often unclear whether other factors, such as, for example, political or economic considerations unrelated to the delimitation question may have come into play: "While the Court and arbitration tribunals are required to apply the law, coastal states have greater latitude when fashioning voluntary settlements."[51] Consequently, State practice should be treated with caution with regard to its precedential value. While this is the case, State practice can, nonetheless, be helpful in providing examples of what the parties to a particular agreement have deemed to be an equitable result and this can be useful in the context of maritime boundary delimitation negotiations.

Practical Implications

What, then, are the implications arising from the foregoing analysis? That is, what are coastal States to do when faced with the prospect of delimiting maritime boundaries with neighbouring States where islands are present in the delimitation equation?

The practice in the delimitation of maritime boundaries generally indicates that application of the equidistance method has proved significantly more popular as the basis for international maritime boundary agreements over time.[52] As geometrically exact expressions of the midline concept, equidistance lines

48 J.I. Charney, 'Progress in International Maritime Boundary Delimitation Law', *American Journal of International Law*, 88 (1994), p. 227.

49 *Ibid.*: 227–228.

50 *Ibid.*: 228.

51 *Ibid.*

52 Prescott and Schofield, *supra* note 11, p. 238.

offer objectivity, mathematical precision and, assuming agreement exists with regard to relevant baselines, lack of ambiguity.[53] This is especially the case for delimitations between opposite coasts where equidistance-based solutions represent the dominant approach to an overwhelming degree.[54]

Inevitably, in the construction of equidistance lines issues related to baselines, base points and thus coastal geography, including islands, become critical in the delimitation equation.[55] In this context, the question of how outstanding geographical features, such as islands significantly far offshore, are treated is one of the most contentious issues in maritime boundary delimitation and has given rise to numerous maritime boundary disputes. As previously discussed, a 'fully-fledged' island may generate the full suite of maritime zones known to the international law of the sea, and consequently such a feature may be crucial to a State's claims to maritime jurisdiction and position regarding maritime boundary delimitation with neighbouring States.

However, even if a feature can be categorised as a fully-fledged island under law of the sea rules, it must be borne in mind that islands are not always accorded 'full effect' in maritime boundary delimitations – achieved either through negotiations or with third-party assistance. Equidistance lines can, therefore, be flexibly applied to deal with the disproportionate effect of particular geographical features. Indeed, as demonstrated, there are numerous examples of State practice and case precedents where islands have received a substantially discounted or reduced effect, been partially or wholly enclaved or even completely ignored.

With regard to the role of insular features of differing types in maritime boundary delimitation it is, however, worth emphasising that lack of certainty over the interpretation of LOSC Article 121 has led to diverse and, on occasion, contradictory State practice. Thus, in some instances extremely small insular features have been accorded a full role in the delimitation of continental shelf and EEZ rights, whilst in others substantial, populated islands have been given a partial or reduced effect.

---

[53] *Ibid.*, at 236.

[54] Equidistance based delimitation lines provide 89 percent of delimited maritime boundaries with an opposite coastal relationship. *Ibid.*, at 238. See also Legault and Hankey, *supra* note 18, pp. 203–242.

[55] Prescott and Schofield, *supra* note 11, pp. 215–244 and 248–252. See also Legault and Hankey, *supra* note 18, pp. 203–242.

In a number of instances relatively large islands home to substantial populations (for instance the UK's Channel Islands[56] and Isles of Scilly)[57] have been accorded a reduced effect in the delimitation of the maritime boundaries. This variety in the treatment of islands could be considered unhelpfully inconsistent. Alternatively, this can be viewed as illustrating the flexibility with which the equidistance methodology can be applied.

Of particular note is the fact that islands are often accorded a reduced effect in maritime boundary delimitation in recognition of a disparity in the relevant coastal lengths of the coastlines involved, for example between a small island and a mainland coastline, and the consequent disproportionate impact an island may have on the construction of a strict equidistance line. In light of this considerable experience in terms of maritime boundary delimitation and the general but not comprehensive trend towards according islands a reduced impact on determining the course of maritime boundary delimitation lines, there are therefore strong reasons to doubt that small, isolated insular features, with restricted coastal fronts, would be awarded full effect in a delimitation against large island or mainland coastlines. It follows therefore, that the maritime jurisdictional claims often associated with small islands, frequently according these features full effect in the definition of strict equidistance lines, are often significantly overstated.

Concluding Thoughts

The practice of international courts and tribunals, when reviewed, suggests that a sustained trend is emerging towards awarding islands a significantly reduced effect with respect to maritime delimitation. This has proved to be especially the case where such islands are located at a considerable distance offshore and opposed to mainland coasts such that a great disparity in relevant coastlines is evident. Such features would tend to have a disproportionate impact on the construction of an equidistance-based boundary line. Consequently, the potential influence of such exceptional features on maritime boundary delimitation lines has generally been discounted. These decisions arguably offer more value

[56] Taken as a whole, the Channel Islands total area is approximately 130,000km^2 with a combined total population of approximately 150,000 people. The populations of the inhabited islands are approximately as follows: Jersey (87,000), Guernsey (60,000), Alderney (2,400), and Sark (600). See <www.jersey.com>; <www.gov.gg/ccm/portal>; <www.alderney.gov.gg>; and, <www.sark.gov.gg>.

[57] The Isles of Scilly comprise five inhabited islands and around 140 small rocky islets totalling approximately 16km^2, with a total population of around 2,000 people. See, <www.scillyonline.co.uk>.

as precedents applicable to yet to be delimited maritime boundaries since they base their rulings squarely on the relevant international law.

State practice is more diverse and it is worth noting that in the context of negotiations the States concerned are merely required under international law to negotiate in good faith and may give weight to any factor and decide on any line they choose between them as long as third State rights are not infringed and this may lead to political trade-offs impacting on the delimitation line.[58] State practice regarding islands includes cases of even extremely small features being accorded considerable effect in the delimitation of maritime boundaries. Nonetheless, these examples in State practice are the exception than the rule and the general trend in State practice in the treatment of islands appears to be toward giving islands a reduced effect.

Overall the above review and assessment of international jurisprudence and State practice on the issue of the treatment of islands in the delimitation of maritime boundaries demonstrates that past practice is replete with examples of how islands can be effectively dealt with in the delimitation of maritime boundaries between neighbouring States. Ultimately, however, political will is crucial, especially in the context of maritime boundary delimitation negotiations. Unless one or more of the parties to a dispute over the insular status of a particular feature possesses the political will to compromise in the course of negotiations, deadlock will inevitably occur.

Arguably, therefore, the frequent preoccupation of disputing States with the island/rock conundrum represents a misleading distraction from the critical issue, that is, the role of islands in the delimitation of maritime boundaries. In practice, the concerns that States expressed at UNCLOS III on the potential disproportionate and inequitable effects of small islands on maritime boundary delimitations have been addressed both in the decisions of international courts and tribunals and in the practice of States. These developments offer the enticing prospect of the emergence of increasingly clear trends and approaches regarding the treatment of islands in maritime boundary delimitation. This, in turn, has the potential to assist in the resolution of multiple maritime disputes between States.

[58] B.H. Oxman, 'Political, Strategic, and Historical Considerations', in: J.I. Charney and L.M. Alexander (eds.) *International Maritime Boundaries*, Vol. I (Dordrecht: Martinus Nijhoff, 1993), pp. 2–40, at pp. 11–12; Prescott and Schofield, *supra* note 11, p. 223.

HOW MUCH CAN A ROCK GET? A REFLECTION FROM THE OKINOTORISHIMA ROCKS

Guifang (Julia) Xue[1]

Abstract

The paper examines the Okinotorishima Rocks and their entitlement in generating extended jurisdictional zones, together with issues aggravated by Japan's excessive national claims. Based on the Okinotorishima Rocks, Japan claims a 200-nautical mile Exclusive Economic Zone (EEZ) and an extended continental shelf (ECS). The practice has caused disagreement and concerns from the international community.

The paper starts with a brief introduction on the Okinotorishima Rocks and the maritime zone claims composed by Japan based on the tiny rocks against the island regime envisaged in the United Nations Convention on the Law of the Sea (UNCLOS). This is followed by a general review of the Japanese attempts to promote the Okinotorishima Rocks into legal islands (simplified as "islandisation") so as to support its national claims of multiple purposes. The paper continues with an illustration of the Japanese views and arguments in maintaining its claim and islandisation practice over the Okinotorishima Rocks. The paper raises some of the key questions associated with the Japanese islandisation attempts. These include whether or not rocks are distinguishable from islands based on the existing international law. How should UNCLOS be implemented and how should the concerns of international community be respected? How will the Commission on the Limits of the Continental Shelf accomplish its role with an applicable decision? After years of heavy, deliberate expansion, are the Okinotorishima Rocks still natural rocks or man-made artificial structures?

The paper concludes that the Okinotorishima Rocks do not qualify as legal islands, and are not entitled to extended jurisdictional zones. Moreover, what Japan has constructed around the rocks has changed their natural status and the expanded concrete structures have turned the rocks into artificial islands or artificial structures which deserve only a 500-meter safety zone.

Meanwhile, the paper points out the profound implications and far-reaching impact reflected from the Japanese claims based on the Okinotorishima Rocks. The rush by states to make ECS submissions has created a real crisis for international law and the deep seabed regime. The international community as a whole should work together to deal with this crisis.

Keywords: rocks, islands, Okinotorishima, Japan, extended continental shelf

---

[1] Director/Professor/Ph.D., Institute for the Law of the Sea, Ocean University of China. The opinions expressed in this paper are not representing the views of any government agencies. The author can be reached via email: <juliaxue@ouc.edu.cn>. Her PowerPoint presentation can be viewed at http://www.virginia.edu/colp/pdf/kmi-xue.pdf.

1. *Introduction: Japan's Claims on Okinotorishima Rocks and the Regime of Islands*

Japan signed the United Nations Convention on the Law of the Sea (UNCLOS) on 7 February 1983 and ratified it on 20 June 1996.[2] After years of preparation, Japan made a submission (the Submission) on 12 November 2008 to the Commission on the Limits of the Continental Shelf (hereinafter referred to as CLCS) regarding the outer limit of its continental shelves, which were calculated as 740,000 square kilometers, or about twice the size of its land territory (378,000).[3]

According to the Japanese Executive Summary containing all charts and coordinates, seven regions are included, namely, Southern Kyushu-Palau Ridge Region (KPR), Minami-Io To Island Region (MIT), Minami-Tori Shima (MTS), Mogi Seamount Region (MGS), Ogasawara Plateau Region (OGP), Southern Oki-Daito Ridge Region (ODR), and Shikoku Basin Region (SKB).[4] The extended continental shelf (ECS) claims of KPR, MIT, and SKB are based on a couple of rocks called Okinotorishima, or more precisely, the Okinotorishima Rocks.[5] This submission has intensified discussions and concerns from the international community.

Since the early 1980s, Japan has been putting enormous efforts into the islandisation of the Okinotorishima Rocks, and has claimed an Exclusive Economic Zone (EEZ) around these rocks up to 200 nm from all directions and even recently claimed an extended continental shelf beyond 200 nm.[6] Through this Submission, Japan expects to confirm its EEZ claims of 430,000 square kilometers in addition to 1550 square kilometers of territorial sea, and an

---

2 The UNCLOS was signed on December 10, 1982 and entered into force on November 16, 1994. For a list of ratifications, see <http://www.un.org/Depts/los/reference_files/chronological_lists_of_ratifications.htm#>. As of 30 December 2010, 160 States and the European Union had ratified or acceded to the UNCLOS. The Convention entered into force for Japan on 20 July 1996.

3 Regarding the work of the CLCS, see its website at <http://www.un.org/Depts/los/clcs_new/clcs_home.htm>. Japan was the 13th country to submit the data and information to the CLCS in November 2008. The Commission began its examination of Japan's submission at the meeting in August 2009. See <http://www.sof.or.jp/en/activities/index1.php>.

4 See <http://www.un.org/Depts/los/clcs_new/submissions_files/jpn08/jpn_execsummary.pdf> for the Executive Summary of Japan's Submission.

5 "Shima" in Japanese means "island", but Japan called it "Okinotorishima Islands" in its Submission. To match this expression, "Okinotorishima rocks" is adopted in this paper.

6 For details, see OPRF, Research Report on the Okinotorishima Revival and Related Issues (in Japanese), 2008. A pdf version is available from: <http://www.sof.or.jp/jp/report/pdf/200903_ISBN978-4-88404-216-5.pdf>.

ECS in three regions based on the Okinotorishima Rocks.[7] The farthest areas based on the Okinotorishima Rocks extend up to 550 nautical miles, together with rights to enforce on maritime activities and resources within the claimed zones.

The regime of islands is established by Article 121 of UNCLOS.[8] In this article, Paragraph 1 repeated the definition of an island provided in Article 10 of the 1958 Convention on the Territorial Sea and Contiguous Zone. It also sets forth the primary criteria of an "island", namely, it must be a natural feature, an area of land, surrounded by water, and above water at high tide. It also disqualifies artificial islands and low-tide elevations.[9]

Paragraph 2 reflects the "land dominates the sea" principle and confirms the same treatment of island as continental land territory regarding its maritime zones, namely, territorial sea, contiguous zone, EEZ, and continental shelf. These zones are to be determined in accordance with the UNCLOS and in the same manner as applicable to land territory.

Paragraph 3 is a critical part of the Article. It excludes "rocks" which "cannot sustain human habitation or economic life of their own" from application in the determination of EEZ and ECS jurisdiction. The main purpose of Article 121 (3) is to guarantee that the regime of islands in paragraphs 1 and 2 is not applicable to tiny rocks and islets on the basis that they are essentially different in terms of the natural conditions necessary for supporting normal human life. In this respect, UNCLOS differentiates between "islands" and "rocks".[10]

Having understood the provision and its connotations, Japan tried in vain to delete Article 121 (3) during the negotiation of the UNCLOS.[11] To adjust the disadvantaged status of Okinotorishima as rocks, Japan has ventured to work over decades in turning them into islands. What Japan has achieved from these tiny rocks is beyond evaluation at the present stage. However, it is worth noting the impact of its islandisation and excessive EEZ and ECS claims on State Practice.

---

[7] Yukie Yoshikawa, "Okinotorishima: Just the Tip of the Iceberg", *Harvard Asian Quarterly*, Vol. 9, No. 4, 2005. <http://asiaquarterly.com/2006/02/03/ii-131/>.

[8] Article 121 reads in full: (1) An island is a naturally formed area of land, surrounded by water, which is above water at high tide. (2) Except as provided for in paragraph 3, the territorial sea, the contiguous zone, the exclusive economic zone and the continental shelf of an island are determined in accordance with the provisions of this Convention applicable to other land territory. (3) Rocks which cannot sustain human habitation or economic life of their own shall have no exclusive economic zone or continental shelf. See *The United Nations Convention on the Law of the Sea*, 10 December 1982, 1833 U.N.T.S. 3.

[9] See Center for Ocean Law and Policy, University of Virginia School of Law, *United Nations Convention on the Law of the Sea 1982, a Commentary*, volume III, p. 338.

[10] *Ibid.*

[11] *Ibid.*, p. 337.

2. *Okinotorishima Rocks and the Japanese Islandisation Attempts*

The Okinotorishima Rocks have come to international notice since the 1980s, and discussions have focused on the subject of legal status and the weight accorded to maritime zones. A brief introduction is provided below.

2.1. *The Okinotorishima Rocks*

Okinotorishima ("沖ノ鳥島;おきのとりしま" in Japanese), located in the western Pacific Ocean, 1,740 kilometers from the Japanese mainland, consists of 5 atoll reefs that were originally called "Parece Vela" by a Spanish sailor in 1565, as "it looks like a sail".[12] It was later called "Douglas Reef" after a British navigator William Douglas in 1789.[13] It is located on the Kyushu-Palau Ridge in the Philippine Sea at the coordinates of 20°25'N 136°05'E /20.417, 136.083.[14] It is 534 kilometers SE of Oki Daitō, 567 kilometers WSW of Minami Iwo Jima of the Ogasawara Islands or 1740 kilometers south of Tokyo, Japan.[15]

No official record exists in Japan about Okinotorishima prior to 1888. In 1922 and 1925, Japan investigated the area and confirmed in 1931 that no other countries had claims and thus declared the reefs its territory.[16] Administratively, Japan placed it under the jurisdiction of the Tokyo Metropolis as part of the Ogasawara Islands, and gave it a new Japanese name Okinotorishima ("remote bird islands" or "the southernmost islands of Japan").[17]

The rocks are in the western part of a 3 to 4.6 meter-deep lagoon surrounded by a submerged coral reef, and extend 4.5 kilometers east-west and 1.7 kilometers

---

[12] See Wikipedia, the free encyclopedia: <http://en.wikipedia.org/wiki/Okinotorishima>.

[13] *Ibid.* Both "Parece Vela" and "Douglass Reef" are still used today.

[14] For relevant papers on this account, see Yann-huei Song, "Okinotorishima: A 'Rock' or an 'Island'? Recent Maritime boundary Controversy between Japan and Taiwan/China" in *Maritime Boundary Disputes, Settlement Processes, and the Law of the Sea*, ed. by Seoug-Yong Hong and Jon M. Van Dyke, Leiden, Martinus Nijhoff Publishers, 2009; J.I. Charney, "Rocks that cannot Sustain Human Habitation", *American Journal of International Law*, Vol. 93, 1999, 863–878.

[15] See Wikipedia, *supra* note 12.

[16] Song is of the view that it was debatable Japan claimed the Okinotorishima coral reefs under its sovereignty from the international law viewpoint in early 1930s. See Yann-Huei Song, *supra* note 14. Moreover, according to Paragraph 8 of the Potsdam Proclamation, Japan's sovereignty was limited to the islands of Honshu, Hokkaido, Kyushu, and Shikoku. Thus, Japanese sovereignty over the Okinotorishima is controversial and questionable. For details, see 'Potsdam Declaration: (United States, China, United Kingdom) A statement of Terms for the Unconditional Surrender of Japan, 26 July 1945, available from: <http://pwencycl.kgbudge.com/P/o/Potsdam_Declaration.htm>.

[17] See Yukie Yoshikawa, *supra* note 7.

north-south, with an area of roughly 5 square kilometers within the rim of the reef, most of which are submerged even at low tide.[18] The fringing reef is pear-shaped in an east-west direction with its greatest width at the eastern end. A small boat channel into the lagoon was made in the southwest, about 15 meters wide and 6 meters deep, 250 meters southeast of the rocks.

Typhoons and erosion are constant threats to the reef's existence. A few decades ago, there were about five visible protrusions. Nowadays, only two tiny individual rocks may be traceable, namely: Higashikojima (Eastern Exposed Rock, Japan calls it "Eastern Islet") and Kitakojima (Northern Exposed Rock, Japan calls it "Northern Islet") located somewhat to the West.[19] At high tide, the Eastern Exposed Rock is roughly the size of a twin bed and pokes just 16 centimeters out of the ocean, and the Northern Exposed Rock is less than a small bedroom only 6 centimeters above water.[20] From satellite images, the two original rocks appear completely artificial, with no trace of the two natural rocks that still appeared on photographs of 1987.

2.2. *Japan's Islandisation Attempts*

To stop the rocks from disappearing and to keep them above water at all times and to use them to extend to the maximum of its EEZ and continental shelf, Japan has tried with great effort to make the Okinotorishima Rocks meet the minimum criteria of an "island" in legal terms. The Japanese attempts in this account can be divided into three periods (for specific details, see the attached Annex 1: Okinotorishima: History and Events).

Starting from the discovery of the rocks to late 1970s, Japan claimed its sovereignty over the rocks and made some initial exploration on the nature and potential utilization of the rocks, including the construction of a Naval Base.[21] In post-World War II, Japan lost its sovereignty over the rocks to the United

[18] See Wikipedia, *supra* note 12.

[19] See Yann-Huei Song, *supra* note 14. See also Martin Fackler. "A Reef or a Rock? Question Puts Japan In a Hard Place To Claim Disputed Waters, Charity Tries to Find Use For Okinotori Shima", *Wall Street Journal.* 16 February 2005, p. A1. It is not clear when Japan changed the name of those rocks: in the "Portrait of Okinotorishima" (http://www.nodaland.com/okitori/okitori.php) updated the last time in 2003, the "Eastern Exposed Rock" *and* "Northern Exposed Rock" were still used, but since 2005, the "Eastern Islet" and "Northern Islet" have been used in relevant discussions and documents. It is assumed that the names have been changed in 2004.

[20] See Yann-Huei Song, *supra* note 14.

[21] The construction of the Naval Base started in 1939, but was interrupted in 1941 by the outbreak of World War II. As it seemed inappropriate to openly build a military facility in the international climate at that time, the government decided to refer to the base externally as "a lighthouse and a meteorological observation site." See Wikipedia, *supra* note 7.

States but regained it in the late 1960s.[22] This enabled Japan to continue its investigation of the rocks.

The rocks did not attract much attention in the Japanese government until the late 1970s when coastal States started to claim their EEZs. Japan extended its fisheries jurisdiction in the surrounding waters of the rocks up to 200 nm from the territorial sea baselines in accordance with its Law on Provisional Measures Relating to the Fishing Zone that went into force on 1 July 1977.[23] The fishing zone covers an area of approximately 400,000 square kilometers, an area considerably larger than the total land of the country.[24] This stimulated Japanese enthusiasm over the gain generated by the little rocks. The action also signified the second period of Japan's islandisation actions till 2004.

In 1983, Japan signed the UNCLOS, concluded in the previous year, which established the EEZ regime. Based on its possession of Okinotorishima, Japan could transfer its former fishing zone to an EEZ of the same size. However, the most serious issue the Japanese government feared was that the rocks could submerge and not lie above sea level. This would defeat exclusive jurisdiction related not only to a 200 nm EEZ in waters around them, but also a continental shelf claim beyond 200 nm. Since 1987, the Japanese government, represented by various governmental agencies and scientific institutions, undertook emergency measures leading to particularly noticeable islandisation movements.

In 1987, the sea level rise theory was employed and evidence was sought, and a proposal was raised to build constructions to prevent the physical erosion of the rock from submersion thereby keeping the rocks above water for making maritime claims. In the same year, the Japanese government launched an embankment building project.

During 1987–1993, the government of Tokyo and later the Central Government built steel breakwaters and concrete walls of 50 meters in diameter, and the original rocks (Higashikojima and Kitakojima) were completely covered by artificial concrete structures to stop the erosion.[25] In 1998, a covering costing eight billion yen was placed on the eastern exposed rock.

In 1988, Japan's Marine Science and Technology Center erected a marine investigation facility, a platform on stilts located in the shallow part of the lagoon, which appeared as a rectangle of 100 meters by 50 meters.[26] The platform

---

[22] Andrew L. Silverstein, "Okinotorishima: Artificial Preservation of a Speck of Sovereignty", *Brooklyn Journal of International Law*, Vol. 12, No. 1 (April 2009), pp. 409–432, 410.

[23] See Kiyofumi Nakauchi and Law of the Sea Institute, Japan, 'Emergy(sic) Measures for Protecting the "Oki-no-tori-Shima" Island from Waves' in *Japan's Ocean Affairs – Ocean Regime, Policy and Development*, September 1989.

[24] *Ibid.*

[25] In 1925, there were still five above-water rocks, which have eroded since. See Wikipedia, *supra* note 7.

[26] *Ibid.*

supports a helicopter landing pad and a large, three-story building for marine investigations as well as a meteorological station.

On 8 February 2002, Japan modified its Coast Law adopted on 12 May 1956.[27] According to Article 37(2), the Central Government took over the administration tasks for the artificial structure. From 2004 onward, the third period of national islandisation efforts started in a much enhanced manner with more comprehensive efforts. Repair work on the embankment was approved with significant funding and a series of research and observation projects began on the rocks and their surrounding waters.[28]

In 2004, the 22nd Ocean Forum organized by the Ocean Policy Research Foundation (OPRF) was held focusing on the status and regeneration of Okinotorishima.[29] A report was subsequently issued on the rehabilitation of the rocks and an electronic baseline coordinate was set up.[30] Since 2004, conferences on Okinotorishima related issues have been arranged by the OPRF as regular forums.[31]

In November 2004 and March 2005, the Nippon Foundation dispatched a mission to investigate how to utilize Okinotorishima and the surrounding EEZ, and mission members included experts in the fields of international law, coral reef ecology and construction.[32] The suggestions in the report include: to build a lighthouse so as to add the name Okinotorishima in the charts around the globe and to enhance its presence; to expand the size of the rocks by coral breeding and various other ways to develop an artificial reef; to build an ocean-thermal energy conservation power plant to attract fish, which was said to be the first such experiment in the world;[33] to explore mineral resources in the adjacent seabed; to build social infrastructure such as a port and houses for human habitation, marine studies, and development; and to promote sightseeing.[34] In 2005, a second mission was conducted by the Nippon Foundation

[27] See <http://law.e-gov.go.jp/htmldata/S31/S31HO101.html> (in Japanese).

[28] Yukie Yoshikawa. *supra* note 7.

[29] See <http://www.sof.org.jp/jp/forum/22/php>.

[30] See Hajime Kayane, "Submerged atolls and their regeneration-Territorial preservation of island states in the Pacific Ocean and islands along the Japanese border", in *Newsletter* No. 99, September 2004, OPRF, available from: <http://www.sof.or.jp/en/news/51-100/99_1.php#01>.

[31] For more details on OPRF, see http://www.sof.or.jp/en/index.php; for activity reports, see OPRF: http://www.sof.or.jp/en/report/index.php.

[32] Nippon Foundation, The Report on Promoting economic activities in Okinotorishima (in Japanese), 2005, available from: <http://nippon.zaidan.info/seikabutsu/2004/00009/contents/0001.htm>.

[33] Shintaro Ishihara's website: <http://www.citymayors.com/mayors/tokyo_mayor.html>.

[34] Nippon Foundation, The Report on Utilization of Okinotorishima (in Japanese), 2005, available from: <http://nippon.zaidan.info/seikabutsu/2004/00004/mokuji.htm>.

focusing on feasibility studies to the most promising fields of marine engineering, power generation, and lighthouse building.[35]

Stimulated by the efforts and research outcomes of the Nippon Foundation and OPRF, Japanese officials and politicians have successfully attracted more attention from the Central Governmental to the rocks.[36] In 2005, the Central Government decided to build a lighthouse,[37] installed a 330 million yen radar system for round-the-clock surveillance to detect vessels approaching Okinotorishima,[38] repaired the heliport, and set up an official address plate at the "island" reading "1 Okinotori, Ogasawara Village, Tokyo".[39] Despite protests by environmentalists, Governor Ishihara of Tokyo decided to build a power station.[40] Fishing expeditions were also sent to demonstrate the existence of "economic life" on the rocks.[41] On 16 March 2007, a light beacon was installed by Japan's Coast Guard and started operation; later, the beacon was plotted on a hydrographic chart. Okinotorishima has become an intermittent rallying point for Japanese nationalists and a hot-button political issue in Japan.[42]

In addition to the concrete protection actions, Japan launched a series of campaigns to raise public awareness on the significance of Okinortorishima.[43] Such efforts include the production of a public-oriented movie "Okinotorishima: Miraculous Islands".[44] The 70–minute movie was released in December 2007 and was made widely available in cinemas, libraries, information centers etc.

In January 2010, the Japanese government during a regular Diet session submitted a new bill for the protection of Japan's southernmost Okinotori coastline to preserve their EEZ claims and interests. In May 2010, Japan adopted the Law for the Reservation of Low Tide Line and Maintenance of Foothold

[35] Nippon Foundation, *supra* note 32.

[36] "A Reef or a Rock? Question Puts Japan In a Hard Place; To Claim Disputed Waters, Charity Tries to Find Use For Okinotori Shima", *Wall Street Journal*, 16 February 2005.

[37] "Japan plans to put lighthouse on disputed Pacific isle", *Kyodo News*, 24 August 2005.

[38] "Japan to establish surveillance system on Okinotori Island", *British Broadcasting Corporation*, 16 May 2005.

[39] "Japan sets up address plate on controversial reef in Pacific", *Xinhua News Agency*, 20 Jun 2005.

[40] 'May 2005 Governor Visits Okinotori Islands', available from: <http://www.sensenfukoku.net/mailmagazine/no36.html>, see also the paper written by Governor Ishihara, 'Strategic Significance of Okinotorishima', available from: <http://www.sankei.co.jp/>, 6 June 2005.

[41] "Boat returns after fishing near disputed Okinotori Island", *Kyodo News*, 19 April 2005.

[42] Yukie Yoshikawa, *supra* note 7.

[43] See PRF ocean forums and relevant activities: <http://www.sof.or.jp/en/index.php>.

[44] See <http://www.metro.tokyo.jp/ENGLISH/TOPICS/2005/index.htm>. The movie consists of six parts covering basically every aspect of Okinotorishima, such as location, history, weather, marine environment, resources, significance, and protection efforts.

Facilities.[45] Through this piece of national legislation, the protection of the Okinotorishima rocks is expected to be further enhanced to new record levels.

2.3. *Incentives of Japan's Okinotorishima Islandisation*

Japan has been investing money in the development of the Okinotorishima Rocks since 1932 with some intervals, including 85 billion yen (approximately 740 million US dollars) in building and maintaining a residence at the observation site. In 1987, Japan encased the reefs with $280 million worth of concrete to prevent them from being completely washed away and covered the smaller one with a $50 million USD titanium net to shield it from debris thrown up by the ocean waves.

In 2005, Japan allocated 10 million yen for the lighthouse and observation site. The following year another $7.55 million dollars was invested for the regeneration of coral reefs and 340 million yen for Japan's Coast Guard to install a solar-powered beacon. Since 2007, Japan has expanded the large scale regeneration of coral reefs and used sand-creating electrodes to save Okinotorishima.[46] According to a media report on 9 April 2008, the Japanese Government planned to invest 770 million yen over three years to farm the coral reef around Okinotorishima. A long-term plan is being carried out to make full use of the rocks.

In 2010, the Japanese government developed a plan for Okinotorishima reef management and maintenance. This plan aims to upgrade the bank maintenance from annual visual inspection to more effective measures to ensure the survival of the concrete structures from harsh natural conditions such as erosion, typhoons and waves.[47]

Most recently, Japan announced in January 2011 a new plan to allocate 750 billion yen over six years to build a port to further reinforce its maritime claims on the Okinotorishima Rocks. They also plan to use the rocks as a base to conduct marine resource surveys and to engage in other economic activities.[48]

---

[45] This is an abbreviated name of the Law. Its full name is: "Law concerning preservation of low tide line and maintenance and others of foothold facilities for protection and promotion of utilization of the exclusive economic zone and the continental shelf", See 'Japan enacts law to preserve Japan's EEZ' (Japan Today, Kyodo, 26 May 2010); OPRF MARINT Monthly Report (May 2010), Diet enacts law to preserve Japan's EEZ, <http://www.japantoday.com/category/politics/view/diet-enacts-law-to-preserve-japans-eez>, p. 12.

[46] 'Government will use sand-creating electrodes to save Okinotorishima', <http://www.japanprobe.com/2008/09/21/government-will-use-sand-creating-electrodes-to-save-okinotorishima/>.

[47] See <http://news.sina.com.cn/w/2010-05-19/082117532724s.shtml>.

[48] See Gus Lubin, 'China Stunned as Japan Makes Shock Island Announcement in Key Economic Zone', 7 January 2010, available from <http://www.businessinsider.com/chinese-angered-by

The question that might be asked is: what are the incentives for Japan to invest such heavy funding on these remote and tiny rocks? The answer may lie in the fact that the Okinotorishima Rocks carry enormous significance to Japan in many aspects. For example, the most obvious benefit to Japan is that these rocks are a major boost to Japan's offshore resource potential. In the resource field, Japan possesses state-of-art technology, and has a good reason to expect resources from its ocean and seas, especially marine natural resources, living and non-living, to sustain its national economic development. The seabed around the Okinotorishima Rocks is said to be potentially rich in oil and has already been found to be rich in manganese nodules and rare minerals.

From a national security point of view, Okinotorishima also has great weight. Sitting in the mid-central Pacific Ocean with a perfect geographical location, these tiny rocks may serve as an unsinkable aircraft carrier. This function highlights their strategic value and military potential as a vital enhancement to Japan's ability to control the Pacific Ocean and the navigational activities.[49]

The most significant and fundamental of the roles Okinotorishima could play falls into the category of generating substantial jurisdictional waters under sovereignty, sovereign rights and jurisdiction stemming from establishing an EEZ and ECS around the rocks.[50] In the age of UNCLOS, small solitary islands in the seas distant from the mainland can make states into major sea powers due to the entitlement of maritime zones.[51] This is particularly the case with Japan and the Okinotorishima Rocks. Without these rocks, Japan would have to retreat its territorial sea to its southern-most tip of Minami-Io To-shima, and suffer a loss of 1550 square kilometers of territorial sea and sovereignty over the water column, seabed and airspace. Japan's EEZ would be pushed back to either Minami-Iwo Jima, an island almost 400 miles to the NE, or to Oki Daitojima, another island about the same distance to the NW, and suffer a loss of 430,000 square kilometers of EEZ,[52] plus an ECS claim in three regions.

From economic, political, and social perspectives, it is also apparent that Japan could benefit immensely from such an "islandisation" effort. To achieve the benefits, Japan is determined to hold the Okinotorishima Rocks and to establish effective control over the surrounding waters through economic activities.

-japan-island-grab-2010-1>. See also 'Japan is to build base at the Okinotorishima' (in Chinese), <http://junshi.daqi.com/slide/2735790.html#t>.

49 Martin Fackler, *supra* note 19.

50 See Articles 55 and 77 of the UNCLOS.

51 Yasuhiko Kagami, "Environmental Policy for Desert Islands: Beyond "Island or Rock?", *OPRF, Research Report on the Okinotorishima Revival and Related Issues*, 2008, p. 109.

52 Yukie Yoshikawa, *supra* note 7.

3. *Japanese Views on the Okinotorishima Claims and Islandisation Practice*

Japan has maintained its claims based on the Okinotorishima rocks and islandisation practice. On one hand, it claims firmly the island status of the rocks; on the other hand, it paves its way with concrete actions toward enabling the rocks to satisfy the criteria of a legal island. Meanwhile, Japanese scholars have conducted thorough and comprehensive research on Okinotorishima in the recent decades to justify national claims and practices. Some evolving views represent theoretical support and reflect Japan's motivation and determination over its islandisation effort.

3.1. *To Assert "Island" Status of the Okinotorishima Rocks*

Regarding the legal status of Okinotorishima, the Japanese views are by and large concentrated on a "self-constructed belief" that these rocks are "islands" under Article 121 (1) and fit in the island criteria in Article 121 (1), that is, "a naturally formed area of land", "surrounded by water", "above water at high tide".[53] Moreover, Japan holds the position that as an Article 121 (1) island, it should not be restricted by Article 121 (3). Based on such logic, Okinotorishima is therefore "qualified" and "entitled" to its extended maritime zones including EEZ and continental shelf.[54]

Still, views are divided within this panel regarding the "island" status of Okinotorishima. Tadao Kuribayashi, a law professor of Toyoeiwa University in Tokyo, argues in part that rocks and reefs differ in composition and structure. He believes that only rocks that cannot be inhabited or have no economic life have no claims for EEZ or continental shelf, and that the intent of the Article 121 (3) was geared toward the former.[55] He adds that coral reefs and rocks (objects consisting of hard continental soil) are different,[56] thus the claim that

---

[53] *The Open Report to the Construction Committee of the House of Representatives of Japan* by Oshima Shotaro, Director of the Economic Bureau, Ministry of Foreign Affairs on 16 April 1999, available online at: <http://www.shugiin.go.jp/index.nsf/htm/index_kaigiroku.htm>, cited from Akesato Nakayama, Island Definition and related Issues in International Law p. 34, in OPRF, Research Report on the Okinotorishima Revival and Related Issues, 2008, pp. 26–38.

[54] *Ibid.*

[55] Yukie Yoshikawa, *supra* note 7.

[56] According to Kazuhiko Fujita, University of the Ryukyus, "Reef islands, generally low-lying, flat, small islands formed on reef flats of atolls, are largely composed of unconsolidated bioclastic sands and gravels. Thus, the islands are highly subject to inundation, coastal erosion, catastrophic storms, and other coastal hazards. See Kazuhiko Fujita, Enhancing foraminiferal sand productivity for the maintenance of reef islands, in *OPRF, Research Report on the Okinotorishima Revival and Related Issues*, 2008, p. 97.

Okinotorishima is not an islet but rocks does not make sense. Professor Kuribayashi insists that the Japanese claim is justifiable as there is no definition of a "rock" in international law, and a country can claim its own EEZ or continental shelf based on its possession of coral reefs.[57]

Another Japanese scholar, Kentaro Serita, argues that according to the Preamble of the UNCLOS, matters not regulated by the Convention continue to be governed by the rules and principles of general international law. He believes that the 200 nm fishing zone is part of customary international law,and thus Okinotorishima is entitled to have a 200 nm fishing zone.[58] He adds that the actions Japan adopted towards Okinotorishima through its national legislation since the entry into force of UNCLOS have never been protested by any country. He concludes that this fact supports the Japanese position that the EEZ of Okinotorishima should be maintained.[59]

Based on the two Okinotorishima rocks, Japan has claimed not only an EEZ up to 200 nm to all directions, but also an ECS at the SKB, MIT, and KPR regions based on the natural prolongation principle. According to the provision of UNCLOS Art. 76.1, "[t]he continental shelf of a coastal State comprises the seabed and subsoil of the submarine areas that extend beyond its territorial sea throughout the natural prolongation of its *land territory* (emphasis added) to the outer edge of the continental margin…".

In a similar fashion to its argument about its EEZ claim on Okinotorishima, Japan asserts the natural prolongation principle to claim its outermost ECS based on the rocks. This is reflected in Paragraph 2 of Section 6.2 of the Executive Summary of Japan's Submission that the Kyushu-Palau Ridge forms part of the natural prolongation of Japan's *land mass* (emphasis added) "represented by Okinotorishima Island" (so-called!).[60] Instead of admitting the fact that the submission areas extending down the ridge towards Palau was on the basis of the natural prolongation of Okinotorishima itself, Japan is trying to give the impression that it is the natural prolongation of Japan as a whole. Such a contention is associated with obvious problems, most notably, the remote nature of the seabed in question from the nearest Japanese mainland/main island territory.

---

[57] Tadao Kuribayashi "The position of Okinotorishima in international law" in Nippon Foundation, *Report on Promoting Economic Activities in Okinotorishima*, available from: <http://www.nippon-foundation.or.jp/eng/maritime/programsseas.html>.

[58] Kentaro Serita, *Japan's Territory* (in Japanese), C HUOKORON-SHINSYA, INC, 2002, pp. 182–189; 224–245.

[59] *Ibid.*

[60] See the Executive Summary of Japan's Submission, *supra* note 4.

3.2. *To Facilitate the Condition of the Okinotorishima Rocks to Sustain Human Habitation or Economic Life*

In addition to the arguments made over the legal status and geographical position of the Okinotorishima Rocks to support its claim to EEZ and ECS, Japan asserts the rocks maintain an economic life of their own.

A Japanese scholar believes the interpretation and application of Article 121(3) is problematic and criticized it as follows:

> If "rocks which can sustain human habitation or economic life of their own" is set as the condition for designation of an island without actually requiring such habitation in practice, then there are grounds for the interpretation that the possibility of meeting the condition alone is sufficient. If such is the case, the condition itself will evolve along with progress in science and technology, leading to uncertainty in the requirements to be met.[61]

This paragraph actually indicates the unsaid truth of how Japan has been creating the condition through evolving science and technology to keep Okinotorishima from being regarded as Article 121 (3) rocks.

To provide support for its claims and national islandisation attempts, Japanese scholars have also searched globally for relevant practices as evidence. One observation reports about other countries sending signals to show that scattered desert islands are (or will be) able to "sustain human habitation or economic life of their own."[62] These signals include permanent posting of small military forces or meteorological observation station staff, etc., construction of lighthouses and other navigational aids, fishing activities, and in recent years, an establishment of protected areas to reserve ecosystems or biodiversity in the oceans surrounding islands.[63] Recent examples employed by this scholar were the US establishment in 2006 of the then world's largest marine protected area (Papahānaumokuākea Marine National Monument) around the northwestern Hawaiian Islands where the US has had an EEZ around 10 uninhabited islands since the 1970s.[64] A second example cited was a new Marine National Monument established in January 2009 around remote islands in the Pacific Ocean.[65]

This Japanese scholar observed that environmental measures such as establishing marine protected areas around desert islands are implemented not only

[61] Hiroshi Terashima, "The Need for a Comprehensive Study on the Problems of Islands and Management of their Surrounding Waters", in *OPRF, Research Report on the Okinotorishima Revival and Related Issues*, 2008, p. 113.

[62] Yasuhiko Kagami, *supra* note 51.

[63] *Ibid.*

[64] According to an American expert in the law of the sea those "should not have EEZ" in light of UNCLOS Article 121, See Yasuhiko Kagami, *supra* note 51.

[65] See Yasuhiko Kagami, *supra* note 51.

by the US, but also by France, Australia, Kiribati, and other countries. He believes that these practices would have a positive significance or impact on the "Island or Rock" dispute, in that "desert islands will not be positioned as a basis for enclosing the sea, but as bases for positive ocean management for sustainable development."[66]

These practices may be expected to cast new light on management of desert islands. However, the key point this scholar forgot to mention is that Japan is indeed a foremost pioneer with practices that have set an example of claiming extended maritime zones over rocks.

Aside from looking for evidence from other countries, other Japanese scholars have tried to justify Japan's claims and national practice by new developments of international laws and State Practice. Hiroshi Terashima, the Executive Director of OPRF, argued to approach the Article 121(3) and Okinotorishima issue from the overall framework and spirit of the UNCLOS for comprehensive management of the ocean.[67] He indicated that discussions on the EEZ and the continental shelf focus primarily on coastal States' rights, rather than on their responsibilities and obligations to manage coastal areas in EEZs and continental shelves. Recent years have seen a large shift from the emphasis given to marine pollution responses at the time the UNCLOS was drafted, i.e. to conservation of marine biodiversity and other issues, such as to promote ecosystem-based management and marine spatial management of ocean areas around islands.

Professor Kuribayashi recommended not to talk about whether or not small islands are to be accorded EEZs and continental shelves, but to consider the problem from the perspective of who should manage the ocean areas around islands and how the management should be carried out. Further, he argued that it is advisable to clarify and reevaluate thinking about islands and the management of their surrounding waters. He called on States not only to address the question of how far the exercise of jurisdictional rights by small islands over resources in their surrounding waters is appropriate in distributing the common heritage of mankind, but also to answer the question of who is the most appropriate entity to fulfill the obligations and responsibilities for protecting the resources in the ocean areas around small islands, e.g. in protecting and conserving the marine environment.[68] He also hopes for Japan to make its contribution to the adaptive development of the UNCLOS regime of islands.[69]

---

[66] *Ibid.*

[67] See Hiroshi Terashima, *supra* note 61, p. 114.

[68] *Ibid.*

[69] See Tadao Kuribayashi," Concluding Remarks: The Present Implications regarding "'Island' Regime from the Perspective of International Law of the Sea Order", in *OPRF, Research Report on the Okinotorishima Revival and Related Issues*, 2008, pp. 83–84.

Such views and arguments confirm the Japanese islandisation actions towards the Okinotorishima Rocks and its generation of jurisdictional zones. At the same time, these views have also encouraged Japan to stray further away from the UNCLOS regime.

4. *Questions to Ponder*

The aforementioned Japanese views suggest that what Japan has done is to promote the conservation and protection of marine resources and environment through ecosystem-based management around these rocks. But questions have to be asked, including: will these arguments justify the Japanese claim and its islandisation attempts? May other States "do as the Romans do" with similar insular features? What are the implications for supporting excessive national claims? As States move forward with excessive claims and islandsation initiatives, what should be the guiding principle in interpretation and implementation of the UNCLOS? Will there be a potential danger of undermining UNCLOS and further encroachment on the common heritage of mankind? Who should defend the interests of international community, and how? These questions will be dealt with in this session.

4.1. *Are rocks distinguishable from islands?*

What Japan calls Okinotorishima Island, some 1,740 kilometers south of Tokyo, is merely an atoll that cannot sustain human habitation or economic life of its own. Japan argues Okinotorishima are islands, not rocks. Is this because the differences between rocks and islands are not distinguishable? The truth is, despite the fact that no objective standard was established on how to distinguish Article 121(1) islands from Article 121(3) rocks, the provisions of UNCLOS Article 121 are clear and explicit.

In comparison with the "island" definition provided in Article 121(1), a "rock" may be simplified as a "naturally formed" "area of land", "surrounded by water", "above water at high tide"; that "cannot sustain human habitation or economic life of its own". This implies the following features: a "rock" is a disadvantaged type of island; the size (refers to "area of the land" above water at high tide) of a "rock" is usually small;[70] and lastly, a "rock" is generally not able

[70] Dr. Hodgson, a geographer of the US State Department proposed that a "rock" is an area of land less than 0.001 square miles, the area of land for an "islet" is between 0.001–1 square miles, the area of land for an "island" is larger than one square mile. See Robert. D. Hodgson. "Island's: Normal and Special Circumstances", in John King Gamble, Jr. and Giulio Pontecorvo eds., *Law of the Sea: The. Emerging Regime of the Oceans*, 1974, Cambridge; Massachusetts: Ballinger Publishing, p. 148.

to provide the natural conditions necessary for supporting normal human life. In fact, the last feature is the determiner that differentiates rocks from islands. If an insular feature cannot fulfill this condition, it is only entitled to a territorial sea and a contiguous zone, but not an EEZ or continental shelf.

International law experts universally believe that an island must: sustain and maintain fresh water, be able to grow vegetation that can sustain human habitation, produce some material that can be used for human shelter, and be able to sustain a human community.[71] Some experts suggest that an island must be able to sustain at least fifty people.[72] Indeed, food, fresh water, and living space constitute the very fundamental criteria for human habitation on an island. With these three criteria, the island may be considered as being able to sustain human habitation, no matter how long it can "sustain", or if the "sustaining" of habitation is on a permanent or temporary basis.

To make these criteria more comprehensible, the Indonesian Ambassador and leading law of the sea expert, Hasjim Djalal, proposed three specific criteria: first, whether there is fresh water on the island or rocks; second, whether it is possible to grow food; third, whether there is material to build houses. Should all three criteria be met, the insular feature shall not only be a rock, but also an island able to "sustain" human habitation and reproduction; that is, it is entitled to its own jurisdiction no matter its size. If the three conditions are not met, the feature is only entitled to a 12 nm territorial sea.[73]

"The economic life of their own" criterion seems to appeal to the idea of the rock having the capacity or potential of bearing an independent, though not necessarily self-sufficient, economic life. This might imply the potential or capacity to develop its own sources of production, distribution and exchange in a way that, if it were to have human habitation, it would constitute a material basis that would justify the existence and development of a stable human habitation or community on the rock.[74] It would seem that the criterion of economic life of their own is more than the existence of a given resource or the presence of a given installation of an economic nature, however important it might be.[75]

If an area of "land" above water at high tide (no matter what it is called by tradition) satisfies either one of the two criteria to "sustain human habitation"

[71] For relevant discussions on this account, see José Luis Jesus, "Rocks, New-born Islands, Sea Level Rise and Maritime Space", in J. Frowein, *et al.*, eds. *Verhandeln für den Frieden. Negotiating for Peace*, 2003, pp. 587–592; Charney, Jonathan, "Rocks That Cannot Sustain Human Habitation", 93 *American Journal of International Law* (1999), 864–871.

[72] See International Seabed Authority Press Release, SB/15/10, p. 3, para. l8.

[73] Ian Townsend-Gault, "Preventive Diplomacy and Pro-activity in the South China Sea", *Contemporary Southeast Asia*, Vol. 20, no. 2, August 1998, p. 179.

[74] See José Luis Jesus, *supra* note 71, p. 590.

[75] *Ibid.*

or an "economic life of its own", it is entitled to its own EEZ and continental shelf. In the case of Okinotorishima, none of the reefs is larger than one square meter and the total area is less than 10 square meters.[76] Okinotorishima has no fresh water, nor soil; neither does it have any vegetation. More importantly, its size is too small to "sustain human habitation". Based on its natural conditions, it cannot be regarded as an island.

It is true that no consensus has been reached on the interpretation and application of Article 121. The treatment of islands/rocks has long generated international legal debates, and State Practice has remained somewhat diverse. Nonetheless, the understanding of international law experts on the text of the UNCLOS provisions, relevant jurisprudence by international judicial and arbitral courts and State Practices are consistent and identical. There are signs of a consistent trend emerging and, at the least, numerous examples exist which indicate how islands/rocks should be treated. No matter how Article 121 is interpreted, given its size and uninhabitable natural conditions, the Okinotorishima cannot be recognized as an island of legal nature. Japan's efforts confirm that it is trying to turn rocks into islands.

4.2. *How should UNCLOS be implemented and international community concerns be respected?*

Article 121 (3) of the UNCLOS expressly denies the right of a rock to support an EEZ and a continental shelf. However, Japan still claimed an EEZ to 200 nm and an adjoining continental shelf region beyond 200 nm using the Okinotorishima Rocks as a base-point in its submission. Japan's unilateral assertion is widely out of conformity with the intention and purpose of UNCLOS's "common heritage of mankind" concept. As the foremost advocate of "the Principle of the Common Heritage of Mankind", Ambassador Arvid Pardo of Malta pointed out, "[i]f a 200 mile limit of jurisdiction could be founded on the possession of uninhabited, remote or very small islands, the effectiveness of international administration of ocean space beyond national jurisdiction would be gravely impaired."[77]

In 1988, having noticed the Japanese construction over the rocks, Professor Jon Von Dyke of the University of Hawaii expressed his view in the following terms: "Okinotorishima – which consists of two eroding protrusions no larger than king-size beds – certainly meets the description of an uninhabitable rock that cannot sustain economic life of its own. It is not, therefore, entitled to generate a 200 [nautical]-mile exclusive economic zone."[78] He has further

[76] See <http://news.xinhuanet.com/world/2005-03/11/content_2681137.htm>.

[77] United Nations Sea-Bed Committee, Doc. A/AC. 138/SR. 57, p. 167.

[78] See Martin Fackler, *supra* note 19.

asserted that it is impossible to make "a plausible claim that Okinotori should be able to generate a 200 [nautical]-mile zone".[79] Professor Von Dyke made himself clear again in 2005.[80]

Professor Von Dyke has also suggested that the situation is similar to the failed British attempt to claim an EEZ around Rockall. Rockall is a small, uninhabited, rocky islet within the EEZ of the United Kingdom (UK) in the North Atlantic Ocean.[81] Rockall is almost 200 nm from the Scottish coast, 25 meters above sea level and measures 624 square meters.[82] In 1977, the UK established a fishing zone using Rockall as a base point for an extension of 200 nm beyond the islet. The British claim was protested by Denmark, Iceland and Ireland.[83] The UK eventually abandoned its claim after its accession to the UNCLOS in 1997.[84]

No doubt, the case of Rockall has the closest similarity to the Okinotorishima situation but the UK rationale was presented on a different footing. Article 121 (3) denies the capacity of tiny rocks to generate unfairly and inequitably huge maritime entitlements e.g. an EEZ or a continental shelf, which could, in most cases, impinge upon other States maritime space or on the International Seabed Area which is reserved for the Common Heritage of Mankind.[85]

Since 2004, as Japan's maritime neighbor, China has constantly objected to Japanese jurisdiction over marine scientific research around the Okinotorishima Rocks where Japan has claimed that it has the right to prescribe and enforce jurisdiction over the two rocks and surrounding waters up to 200 nm.[86] China's position is that the legal status of these waters is high seas and traditional fishing grounds for the fishers from the mainland of China, Taiwan, and Korea.

---

[79] "Speck in the Ocean Meets Law of the Sea", *New York Times*, 21 January 1988.

[80] "A Reef or a Rock? Question Puts Japan In a Hard Place; To Claim Disputed Waters, Charity Tries to Find Use For Okinotori Shima", *Wall Street Journal*, 16 February 2005.

[81] See EEZ of the UK and Ireland at: <http://www.seaaroundus.org/eez/eez.aspx>.

[82] For details on Rockall, see <http://en.wikipedia.org/wiki/Rockall>. See also James Fisher, 1956. *Rockall*. London: Geoffrey Bles. pp. 12–13.

[83] See <http://www.opsi.gov.uk/SI/si1997/19971750.htm> for the Fishery Limits Order 1997, Statutory Instrument 1997 No. 1750.

[84] The Foreign and Commonwealth Secretary of the United Kingdom expressed in a statement that "Rockall is not a valid base point for such limits under article 121(3)", and then the limit of the fishery zone was redefined accordingly through the Fishery Limits Order 1997. See Alex G. Oude Elferink, Clarifying Article 121(3) of the Law of the Sea Convention: the Limits Set by the Nature of International Legal Process, *IBRU Boundary and Security Bulletin* Summer 1998, p. 59; p. 66. Editors' note: see also D. Anderson, "Islands and Rocks in the Modern Law of the Sea" in the present volume.

[85] UN Doc. A/CONF. 62/122, 7 October 1982.

[86] *Xinhua News* on August 25, 2005, "Japan hopes to build lighthouse on atoll disputed with China".

China firmly opposed the Japanese unilateral actions and considers such actions a serious violation of the rights of other countries.[87]

The dispute regarding whether Okinotorishima is a rock or an island has escalated and intensified. The issue has caught the attention of the rest of the world because of the Japanese submission of its proposed outer limit of the continental shelf to the CLCS, which stimulated a public reaction from China and Korea.

In February 2009, China and South Korea respectively submitted to the Secretary-General of the United Nations Note Verbales commenting on the issue of the Okinotorishima in the Japanese Submission.[88] Both China and South Korea objected to Japan's claim to an EEZ and ECS based on the Okinotorishima Rocks.[89]

The international community has, for the most part, avoided involvement in the dispute. However, the Submission intensified the disagreement and raised concerns in the international community sparking varied comments. Concerns were articulated about Japan's duty not to infringe on the common space of the international community. On one occasion, Japan seemed to remember its duty and denied New Zealand's claims to the Antarctic. When New Zealand made its ECS submission to the CLCS,[90] Japan sent a Note Verbale to the UN concerning New Zealand's claims to the Antarctic region.[91] Japan emphasized that it does not recognize any State's "claim to territorial sovereignty in the Antarctic and consequently does not recognize any State's rights over or claims

---

[87] See Jia Yu, Li Mingjie, 'Not to accept the artificially constructed Okinotori', available from: <http://news.sina.com.cn/c/2004-05-24/12103317063.shtml>.

[88] For China's Note, see <http://www.un.org/Depts/los/clcs_new/submissions_files/jpn08/chn_6feb09_e.pdf>; for Korea's, see <http://www.un.org/Depts/los/clcs_new/submissions_files/jpn08/kor_27feb09.pdf>.

[89] *Ibid.*

[90] See <http://www.un.org/Depts/los/clcs_new/submissions_files/submission_nzl.htm> for New Zealand's submission.

[91] For Japan's note, see <http://www.un.org/Depts/los/clcs_new/submissions_files/submission_nzl.htm>. On 28 June 2006, the Permanent Mission of Japan to the United Nations presented its compliments to the Secretariat of the UN with reference to the circular CLCS.05.2006. LOS (Continental Shelf Notification) dated 21 April 2006, concerning the receipt of the submission made by New Zealand to the CLCS. Japan confirms the importance of keeping harmony between the Antarctic Treaty and the UNCLOS and thereby ensuring the continuing peaceful cooperation, security and stability in the Antarctic area. Recalling Article IV of the Antarctic Treaty, Japan does not recognize any State's right of or claim to territorial sovereignty in the Antarctic, and consequently does not recognize any State's rights over or claims to the water, seabed and subsoil of the submarine areas adjacent to the continent of Antarctica.

to the water, seabed and subsoil of the submarine areas adjacent to the continent of Antarctica."[92]

Views have also been expressed that the Okinotorishima Rocks are not entitled to any continental shelf, and that no entitlement should be granted on the portions related to the Okinotorishima Rocks in Japan's Submission. After Japan made its Submission to the CLCS concerning its extended continental shelf, at the l5th Session of the International Seabed Authority and at the 19th Meeting of the States Parties to the UNCLOS a thorough discussion ensued on relevant issues.[93] At these meetings, serious concerns were expressed by many countries regarding the possible encroachment on the international seabed area by using a rock as the base point for an extended continental shelf.[94] In addition to relevant discussions under current items in the agenda, it was also decided at the 19th meeting to consider the inclusion of a supplementary item entitled "International Seabed Area as the common heritage of the mankind and Article 121 of the United Nations Convention on the Law of the Sea" in a future meeting.

The EEZ and ECS policies and State practice are important for the future. It is not only a matter of economics and how ocean resources can be exploited from the continental shelf, but also the legal existence of the sovereign rights of a maritime nation. Japan's bid to extend its continental shelf based on rocks will not be supported. As a State party to UNCLOS, Japan is obligated not to violate the legal regime of the UNCLOS, and to respect the disagreement of its maritime neighbors as well as the concerns of the international community.

4.3. *How will CLCS accomplish its role with an applicable decision?*

Japan submitted the information on the limits of its ECS to the CLCS on 12 November 2008.[95] Through this Submission, Japan set an example of claiming an EEZ and an excessive continental shelf based on rocks in the vast Pacific Ocean. Concerns have been voiced about Japan using the CLCS as a forum to strengthen, maintain, or defend its claims concerning legal titles of rocks/ islands, and EEZs, continental shelf and extended continental shelf thereof. Should Japan's submission be confirmed by the CLCS about the location of the outer limit of Japan's continental shelf in Okinotorishima and Japan's entitlement to large areas of continental shelf beyond 200 nm, Japan would have

---

[92] *Ibid.*

[93] The 19th Meeting of the States Parties to the UNCLOS, SPLOS/L.60, 22 may 2009 <http: //daccess-dds-ny.un.org/doc/UNDOC/LTD/N09/346/55/PDF/N0934655.pdf?>; see also Yu Jia, 'Legal Issues Concerning the Oki-no-Tori', *Ocean Development and Management* (in Chinese), Vol. 8 (130), 2009, Beijing, August 2009.

[94] *Ibid.*

[95] <http://www.un.org/Depts/los/clcs_new/submissions_files/submission_jpn.htm>.

jurisdiction over an extra 740,000 square kilometers, which is about twice the size of its land territory.

Discussions have also been voiced about the applicable decisions of the CLCS. As an international body established by the UNCLOS, the CLCS is neither a judicial nor a political body.[96] It gives technical advice and guidance to States, and offers opinions on the data and analyses submitted by coastal States on the basis of the technical and objective criteria set out in the UNCLOS. As of 7 December 2010, there have been 54 Submissions delivered to the United Nations for the CLCS to consider.[97] Meanwhile, as of 30 November 2010, the CLCS has also received 61 Preliminary Information submissions indicative of the outer limits of the extended continental shelf.[98] The job of the CLCS is to consider the documentation submitted by the coastal State and to recommend where the outer limits of the continental shelf should lie.

Japan's Submission complicates the clear provision about island regimes and the authorization of the CLCS in the UNCLOS. This may lead to an infringement of the completeness of the UNCLOS and an encroachment on the International Seabed Area.[99] The CLCS will have to deal with Japan's Submission and also third party notifications.[100] As mentioned earlier, the Note Verbales of China and South Korea suggested that the CLCS should take no action on the portions related to the Okinotorishima Rocks in Japan's Submission.[101] How the CLCS will handle Japan's Submission regarding the regions generated based on the Okinotorishima Rocks continues to be an issue of general interest as well as a source of concern for many.

To consider Japan's Submission requires defining the legal status of Okinotorishima, but the CLCS is not in a position with authority to decide its legal

---

[96] For discussions on CLCS, see Ted L. McDorman, "The Entry into Force of the 1982 LOS Convention and the Article 76 Outer Continental Shelf Regime", *International Journal of Marine and Coastal Law*, 1995, Vol. 10, pp. 165–187; Ted L. McDorman, "The Role of the Commission on the Limits of the Continental Shelf: A Technical Body in a Political World", *International Journal of Marine and Coastal Law*, Vol. 17, 2002, pp. 301–324.

[97] For submissions, see <http://www.un.org/Depts/los/clcs_new/commission_submissions.htm>.

[98] See <http://www.un.org/Depts/los/clcs_new/commission_preliminary.htm>.

[99] The CLCS has seen many different kinds of Submissions and third party notifications, coping with different situations that the coastal States face. Among the 54 Submissions, 22 Submissions have already encountered the comments, oppositions, disapproval, or approvals expressed by as many as 58 third party notifications. Among 61 Preliminary Information submissions, four pieces have met communications from third States, expressing different ideas. See <http://www.un.org/Depts/los/clcs_new/commission_submissions.htm>.

[100] For relevant discussions, see Michael Sheng-ti Gau, "Third Party Intervention in the Commission on the Limits of the Continental Shelf Regarding a Submission Involving a Dispute", *Ocean Development and International Law*, Vol. 40, 2009, pp. 61–79.

[101] See Paragraphs 3–5 of the communication of China, Paragraphs 4–6 of the Korean communication to respond to the Japanese Submission. *Supra* note 88.

status. To comply with UNCLOS and to safeguard the Common Heritage of Mankind, it is advisable for the CLCS not to consider the controversial parts in Japan's Submission. The Okinotorishima situation will be an entrée to a broader discussion on the role of the CLCS as regards the submissions and information presented to it. One thing that is clear is that the CLCS shall not be used to infringe upon UNCLOS, or to abuse its own responsibility.

4.4. *Whether Okinotorishima are still natural rocks or artificial structures?*

The heart of this Okinotorishima rock/island issue is whether the feature can be used as a base point to claim an extended jurisdictional zone. According to Article 121, both islands and rocks have to be "naturally formed". Concerning what is "naturally formed", two views exist: the first view counts on whether or not there is deliberate construction, and insists that "naturally formed" means "no deliberate construction".[102] This view may seem a bit extreme. The second view tolerates "deliberate construction" but differentiates the decision depending upon the purpose:[103] if the deliberate construction is for the protection of the area of the "land", the legal status of the "land" remains unaffected;[104] if the deliberate construction is to expand the land mass of the area, the legal status of the original and additional new "land" will lose its legal status collectively with its territorial sea.[105] International law scholars mainly hold this view.[106] In particular, Diaz, Dubner, and Parent pointed out in their paper that to protect the island by using coral and other marine biotechnology to build it up creates an artificial island that is not entitled to its own maritime zone.[107]

In the case of the Okinotorishima Rocks, if the action Japan has taken is solely for the protection of the rocks, they will continue to be natural rocks with

---

[102] Clive R. Symmons, *The Maritime Zones of Islands in International Law*, The Hague: Martinus Nijhoff, 1979, p. 36.

[103] <http://www.seastead.org/localres>.

[104] See Andrew L. Silverstein, *supra* note 22, pp. 409–432.

[105] See Derek.W. Bowett, *The Legal Regime of Islands in International Law*, 1979, Dubbs Ferry; New York: Oceana Publications, p. 122.

[106] See Leticia Diaz, Barry Hart Dubner, and Jason Parent, "When is a 'Rock' an 'Island?': Another Unilateral Declaration Defies 'Norms' of International Law" *Michigan State Journal of International Law*, Vol. 15, 2007, p. 547. See also Yasuhiko Kagami, *supra* note 51.

[107] Bin Bin Jia is of the view that if an island cannot continue its existence without a concrete structure or artificial installation, it is no longer a natural island, but an artificial island, not entitled to a maritime zone but to a 500-meter safety zone. See Bin Bin Jia, "A Preliminary Study of the Problem of the Isle of Kolbeinsey", *Nordic Journal of International Law*, 66, 1997, p. 313. See also Diaz, Dubner and Parent, *supra* note 106.

an entitlement to territorial sea and contiguous zone, but if Japan's purpose is to expand the physical size of the rocks, the situation will be different.[108]

Japan rescued Okinotorishima with great efforts to make sure the rocks were not completely washed away. This was for the purpose of enabling them to generate vast maritime zones. To keep the rocks afloat and to fulfill the criteria of a legal "island", Japan has carried out ambitious projects to expand the "landmass" by artificially producing economic life there and planning to create a place that is actually liveable. The "national construction" increased the rocks much beyond their original shapes. Its purpose is not for the protection of the rocks, but for "expansion of its territory". Given the size of the rocks, years of heavy, deliberate expansion, concrete encasing and building facilities have changed the character of the rocks. On detailed satellite images, each of the rocks appears as a circle with a diameter of 50 meters, but these are mostly artificial structures. The Okinotorishima Rocks have lost their natural character. Instead, they are an "artificially formed area of land" or "artificially constructed area of land".[109]

Following Japan's logic, the rescuing construction was meant to "expand" the rocks to enable them to "sustain human habitation or economic life of [their] own" as an Article 121(1) island, and subsequently to generate extra maritime jurisdictional zones. Actually, this is an abusive interpretation of the UNLCOS, which aims at the conformity of the rights and interests of State parties based on the existing ocean order. The Japanese practice is contrary to international law and to the UNCLOS regime, as it tries to modify the natural features for the purpose of enhancing claims to jurisdictional zones that should not be legitimately granted.

Should such logic and practice be permitted and encouraged to any extent, States could rely on their national capacity to "transform" any insular features such as submerged rocks and sand bars into islands, and then claim large areas of waters and resources to which they are not entitled. This trend would lead to irreversible damage to the authority of the UNCLOS, and certainly would result in a new round of competing claims and chaos in the world's oceans.[110] UNCLOS endeavors to avoid situations of this kind by creating a framework based on customary international law and accepted State Practice.

Judging by what Japan has been doing with great determination, it is unfortunate that the result has turned out to be that Japan's islandisation attempts

[108] Silverstein agrees that artificial island is not entitled to a territorial sea, but he excluded the Okinotorishima as a special circumstance. See Andrew L. Silverstein, *supra* note 22, pp. 429–430.

[109] See Leticia Diaz etc., *supra* note 106, p. 519.

[110] *Ibid.*, pp. 519–555.

have transformed the legal status of Okinotorishima from Article 121 (3) rocks into artificial structures to which the law in Article 60 applies.[111] Japan has lost the very basic feature of rocks and has transformed them into the "Okinotorishima artificial islands" or "Okinotorishima artificial structures". Thus from an international law viewpoint, Japan is not entitled to any maritime zones but merely a 500-meter safety zone. Japan's expensive efforts have been counterproductive from an UNCLOS point of view.

5. *Concluding Remarks*

It can be argued that the vagueness of UNCLOS's island regime has resulted in enduring complexities for maritime claims, sovereignty disputes over islands, disputes over the legal weight accorded to insular features, and aggressive extended continental shelf submissions. However, no country has so vigorously taken advantage of the weakness of UNCLOS as Japan has to the extreme in attempting to claim large areas of jurisdictional zones based on rocks.

The legal effect of rocks in international law is clear and explicit. Maritime features can be accorded maritime zones, but not all features are entitled to an EEZ and beyond. The Okinotorishima, which are indeed uninhabted, isolated rocks located in the western Pacific Ocean, cannot sustain human habitation or economic life of their own at all. At high tide, the two rocks composing the Okinotorishima are barely above water and its total area is less than one sixtieth of Rockall. This is the clearest example of the rock provided for in Article 121(3) of UNCLOS which does not to generate an EEZ or continental shelf, not to mention an extended continental shelf.

Tempted by the vast ocean space and abundant resources therein, Japan has tried to use such small reef rocks to claim a huge 200 nm EEZ in all directions and even a continental shelf beyond 200 nm. Japan has also put into practice a series of manmade measures to enable the Okinotorishima Rocks to sustain human habitation or an economic life of its own obviously to increase the possibility for expanding otherwise unqualified maritime jurisdictional zones. From satellite images, the two original rocks now appear completely artificial, with no trace of the two natural rocks.

No matter how hard the Japanese have tried, it is doubtful that the Japanese effort can be successful due to the following factors: first, the Japanese islandisation campaign has violated the standards and undermined the authority of the UNCLOS framework; second, its excessive claims encroach on the International Seabed Area that is set aside for the international community as a whole; third,

[111] See UNCLOS Article 60(4); (5); (8); (11); (147), Subpara. 2 (e); and 259.

Japan has changed the legal status of the Okinotorishima Rocks from natural rocks into artificial structures. No matter how Japan tries to stretch the word "rock" or how it tries to twist the word "island", the history of the provision, the writings of various scholars, and the opinion of international community squarely place the Japanese on the wrong side, legally and morally.

A questionable "island" may rate a 12 nm territorial sea but a full entitlement is not consistent with the object and purpose of UNCLOS to limit excessive claims. With regard to the questionable natural status of Okinotorishima "artificial island, installation or structure", a 500-meter safety zone and exclusive jurisdiction is sufficient.

The problem with Japan's assertion over vast areas of waters based on the national building-up of artificial islands around rocks is rather obvious. It would be an example of greed, and constitutes a precedent on expanded maritime jurisdiction and of abusing UNCLOS and would seriously encroach upon the international seabed area. Yet, the profound implications and far-reaching impact reflected from the Japanese claims is worth noting. If every state decided to make the same type of expansion as the Japanese have, there would be no use for international rule of law and the legal system of order set forth in the UNCLOS would be meaningless. There will be a real crisis brought along by the submission rush of ECS to the international law and International Seabed Area. The international community as a whole should work together to deal with this crisis.

Annex 1: Okinotorishima: History and Events

Year	Events
1543	Unconfirmed reports claimed that the atoll was first sighted by the Spanish ship San Juan and named Abre Ojos ("Open your eyes, look!" in Spanish).
1565	Its name was recorded as "Parece Vela" ("looks like a sail" in Spanish) by Spanish ship San Pedro. After that, it was named "Engels Rocks" by Dutch ship Engels and "Douglass Reef" by British ship Iphigenia. Douglass Reef and Parece Vela are still used as alternative names for Okinotorishima.
1922	The Japanese Navy surveillance ship "MANSHU" made an investigation of the atoll, and reported the status of it.
1929	Okinotorishima was marked on hydrographic charts published by Hydrographic Department.
1931	The Cabinet declared it Japanese territory under the jurisdiction of the Ogasawara-shicho of Tokyo Prefecture, and named it Okinotorishima.
1933	Surveillance ship "KOSHU" investigated the islands and found 4 islets in addition to the Eastern Islet (Higashikojima) and Northern Islet (Kitakojima). A hydrographic chart was made by Hydrographic Department (Nagaoka, 1987).
1938	Surveillance ship "SHINSHO MARU" investigated the area.
1939–1941	The southwest reefs of the atoll were blasted to open new sea routes. A lighthouse and a meteorological observation site were built using 900 concrete columns. The construction was interrupted by the start of the Pacific War.
1952.4	The United States took over the Ogasawara islands.
1968.6	The United States returned the islands to Japan.
1969	Surveillance ship "MEIYO" investigated the area.
1976	Japan Amateur Radio League (JARL) "DX Pedition" set up an amateur radio station based on the observation site and directed radio waves around the globe from Okinotorishima. Within 78 hours, they made communications with about 9000 other radio stations.
1978	Tokyo Metropolis fisheries research ship "Metropolis" investigated the area.
1982	Survey ship AA "TAKUYO" investigated the area.
1984	Two islets were marked in the topographical map published by Geographical Survey Institute (GSI) (Nagaoka, 1987).
1987.9	The Agricultural Aquatic Committee of Japanese Diet held the first meeting on Okinotorishima and the rising sea levels.
1987.10	It was designated as a coastal protected area by Tokyo Metropolis.
1988	Japan Marine Science and Technology Center (JAMSTEC) built an unmanned marine investigation facility which had maintained following meteorological observation until 1991.
1988–1989	The former Ministry of Construction started the protection project for the Eastern Islet and Northern Islet.
1990–1993	The former Ministry of Construction started a base project for the observation station.
1993	JAMSTEC performed meteorological and marine meteorological observations at the working site (Continuing now).

Year	Events
1998	The former Ministry of Construction installed titanium metallic net to cover the Eastern Islet.
1999	According to the amended Coastal Act, the management was put under the National Government: former Ministry of Construction: responsible for bank protection; Coast Office of River Bureau of Ministry of Land, Infrastructure, Transport and Tourism and Keihin Department of Engineering Affairs: responsible for protective measures; the degree of general concern is not high.
2004.9	"Eco-engineering regeneration technology helps improve the regeneration capacity of the degraded coral reef ecosystem, contributes to the territory protection of island states in the Pacific Ocean, and avoids the flooding issues." Hajime Kayanne (Newsletter No. 99, Sep. 2004, OPRF)
2004.10	"Association for Okinotorishima Research" was set up by OPRF and held its first meeting.
2004.11	"Observation Group for Effective Utilization of Okinotorishima" established by the Nippon Foundation to centralise experts of different fields to investigate the status of the area from different perspectives, and discuss the possibility of effective utilization of the island and its surrounding waters.
2004.12	The 22nd Ocean Forum was held by OPRF with the theme "Current status and regeneration of Okinotorishima", speakers: Terashima Hiroshi and Hajime Kayanne.
2004	The Ministry of Land, Infrastructure, Transport and Tourism (MLITT) installed video cameras on surveillance facilities.
2005.3	"Investigation Group for Promoting Economic Activities of Okinotorishima" founded by Nippon Foundation to strengthen and improve economic activities of Okinotorishima, investigate aquatic organisms' proliferation status that can help the island regeneration such as coral, and the status of island building and expansion, set up beacon to insure marine traffic, and to investigate the feasibility of power generation by using ocean thermal energy conversion technology. Also, according to the contract between MLITT and Ministry of Agriculture, Forestry and Fisheries of Japan, some proposals were made such as assumption that coral proliferation promotes expansion of island, and protection strategies and utilization programs of Okinotorishima were discussed from various perspectives.
2005.3	The 25th Ocean Forum was held by OPRF with the theme as "Wise Use of Japan's exclusive economic zones, submarine mineral resources, and Okinotorishima", speakers: Yasuhiko Kakami, Takatoshi Matsuzawa, Tomohiko Fukushima.
2005.4	"Regeneration Plan of Okinotorishima" was announced by OPRF.
2005.6	Geographical Survey Institute (GSI) set up electronic reference point
2005	OPRF released "Regeneration Investigation and Research on Okinotorishima": Analysis of boring core technology; Basic ecological investigation of Foraminifera; Discussion of the legal status.
2005	Fisheries Association of Ogasawara-Shoto, Tokyo Metropolis provided operational support to Okinotorishima, released striped mackerel fish fries, and investigated fishing grounds in surrounding sea area.
2005	The MLITT set up ocean observation radar.

Table (*cont.*)

Year	Events
2005–2006	Tokyo Metropolis built the Instructional Ship for Fisheries Survey "KOYO".
2006–2008	OPRF carried out "Investigation and research on maintenance and regeneration of Okinotorishima": reorganized and analyzed the investigations on maintenance and regeneration of Okinotorishima; International comparative studies about islands status and management methods; Outreach investigations; Ecological investigations of Pacific island nations; Investigations on management implementation of different countries; and Others.
2006–2008	The Ministry of Agriculture, Forestry and Fisheries carried out research on "The Development of the Proliferation Methods under Abominable Natural Conditions" and the development of the coral proliferation technology.
2006–	Tokyo Metropolis carried out "Project to improve the utilization of Okinotorishima": to investigate fishing ground; to construct artificial floating fish reef in mid-layer of deepwater; and a public-oriented movie "Okinotorishima: Miraculous Islands" (2008) was made.
2007.3	The light beacon built by the MLITT started to work.
2007.7	The "Basic Ocean Law" was put into force: Article 26 regulates offshore island protection.
2007.11	"Okinotorishima Forum 2007" was held in Tokyo Metropolis.
2008	White Paper II of the MLITT: Chapter 6 "Construct a safe and peaceful society", Section 4: Crisis management and safety guarantee countermeasure: Para. 4 Marine rights protection of Japan "(4) The protection of Okinotorishima: Okinotorishima is located at the south most of our country's territory, and is the most important island, based on which we can establish over 400,000 km^2 exclusive economic zone. It is important to territory protection and utilization, and it is necessary to discuss whether it should be directly managed by the national government and to take complete measures to make the best use of it".
*2008.11	"Okinotorishima Forum 2008" was held in Tokyo Metropolis.
*2010.5	Japan adopted Law for Reservation of the Low Tide Line and Maintenance of Foothold Facilities.
*2011.1	A plan was announced to build a deep water port over 6 years with $10 billion US Dollars.

Source: Translated from OPRF, Research Report on the Okinotorishima Revival and Related Issues, 2008: <http://www.sof.or.jp/jp/report/pdf/200903_ISBN978-4-88404-216-5.pdf>.
Note: "*": updates of this author from other sources cited in this paper.

Panel IV: Safety and Navigational Freedom

POLICING THE SEA AND THE PROPORTIONALITY PRINCIPLE

Kuen-chen FU[1]

Abstract

In the name of national security and sovereign dignity, coastal States' law enforcement officials tend to use force against foreign vessels whenever they abruptly decide that their moves can be justified. Various incidents in recent years indicate that there is a real need for a more practical multilateral treaty to control state law enforcers at sea and to secure international navigational freedom.

Based on the UN Charter, the 1979 Code of Conduct for Law Enforcement Officials, the 1990 Basic Principles on the Use of Force and Firearms by Law Enforcement Officials, the UNCLOS and some other law of the sea agreements, this paper emphasizes the proportionality principle as the basic legal principle for policing the sea with force. While the needed new international statutory law is not yet available, this principle should be applicable as customary law in the international community.

From several classic cases, we can distill three factors of the proportionality principle: the principle of relevance, the principle of necessity and the principle of balance of interests. Coastal States are supposed to be familiar with the application of these principles in their constitutional law and administrative law arenas; but should be urged to apply these same principles to international marine incidents.

Key Words: law enforcement at sea, use of force, proportionality principle

I. *Incidents*

For many navigators in the world, the most dangerous threats to their safety at sea have come not from criminal pirates, but uniformed coastal State law enforcement officials.

On 15 January 2009, the *New Star*, a Chinese-owned cargo vessel flying the flag of Sierra Leone was attacked forcibly by the Russian Coast Guard and sunk in international navigable waters in Peter the Great Bay out of Vladivostok. According to the Xinhua News Agency, the vessel arrived earlier at Nakhodka, 65 miles east-western to Vladivostok, Russia, to unload 4,978 tons of packed eggs. Because of disputes between the carrier and the receiver, for days, the ship

[1] KoGuan Chair Professor of Law and Ph.D. supervisor at Shanghai Jiao Tong University. The author's PowerPoint presentation can be viewed at http://www.virginia.edu/colp/pdf/kmi-fu .pdf.

was not allowed to leave the harbor, and the captain decided to leave without finishing the administrative procedures. On 12 February, shortly before midnight at about 23:30 p.m., the ship quietly lifted her anchor and sailed out of the harbor. Irritated, the Russian Coast Guard caught up with the vessel the next morning and fired 515 shots at the *New Star*, sinking the ship. Among the 16 crew members, eight were rescued, and the other eight disappeared in the sea.[2]

As some commentators indicated, the Russian Coast Guard's use of firearms against the unarmed cargo vessel obviously exceeded their right of legitimate use of armed force, and violated contemporary international law.[3] As to which international law they might have violated, allow me to discuss this later.

In some other cases, coastal States' law enforcement authorities might not have used any firearms against foreign vessels, but nevertheless possibly violated their international legal duties and caused real damages against the foreign vessels.

One such possible violation is unreasonable extended detention.

On 24 November, 2010, Saint Vincent and the Grenadines instituted proceedings with the ITLOS (International Tribunal for the Law of the Sea) against Spain in a dispute concerning the MV *Louisa*, flying the flag of Saint Vincent and the Grenadines, which had been arrested on 1 February, 2006 by the Spanish authorities and held since that date.[4]

According to the Applicant, the MV *Louisa* was involved in conducting some marine scientific research at the Bay of Cadiz in order to locate and record indications of oil and gas. The vessel was arrested for alleged violations of Spain's historical patrimony or marine environment laws, but has already been held without bond in the port of El Puerto de Santa Maria for 5 years. The Applicant maintains that the vessel was involved in scientific research with a valid permit from the coastal State. The Applicant claims that Spain has violated Articles 73, 87, 226, 245 and 303 of the United Nations Convention on the Law of the Sea and requests that the Tribunal award damages in the amount of "not less than $10,000,000". The application instituting proceedings before the Tribunal includes a request for provisional measures under article 290, paragraph 1 of the Convention, in which the Tribunal is requested, *inter alia*, to order the Respondent to release the MV *Louisa* and return the property seized.[5]

---

[2] See: http://news.sina.com.cn/c/2009-02-25/115617285956.shtml, visited on Nov. 22, 2010.

[3] Zhang Zhao-zhong, *Three Unresolved Issues of the New Star Incident*, Bing-qi-zhi-shi (Weapon Knowledge), Preface, issue 4A, 2009.

[4] *Saint Vincent and the Grenadines Institutes Proceedings Against Spain Regarding the Vessel MV Louisa Tribunal Also Seized of a Request for Provisional Measures*, ITLOS/Press 154 – 24.11.2010, see: http://www.itlos.org visited on 24 November 2010.

[5] *Ibid.*

Another possible violation of international law without the illegal use of force by the coastal States is the "illegal, unreported and unregulated" ("IUU") law enforcement practice against foreign vessels.

This author has served on the Overseas Fishery Development Council (OFDC) in Taiwan for more than 22 years. At the risk of exaggerating a bit, I would say that the most frightening danger for the Taiwanese fishermen sailing around the world's oceans, are not pirates, but "IUU" law enforcement by foreign officials. To say the least, the number of piracy incidents encountered by Taiwanese fishing vessels is much smaller than that of incidents involving foreign law enforcement attacks or detention. From 2001 to 2010, a total of 204 Taiwanese fishing vessels were reported attacked or arrested by various coastal States' law enforcement officials, while only about a dozen were attacked or kidnapped by pirates in the Indian Ocean or other waters around the world.[6] We may not believe that all these arrested ships were innocent and should not have been arrested, but surely many of them should not have been so forcibly mistreated at sea, forced into positions that present the risk of collisions, attacked with firearms, or robbed by some of the coastal States' law enforcement officials.

Recently, a similar case occurred near the politically sensitive Diao-yu-tai Islands. A Chinese fishing boat, Min-jin-yu No. 5179, was arrested by the Japanese Coast Guard on 7 September 2010. The Japanese alleged that the damaged fishing boat tried to collide against the Japanese patrolling ship twice when the latter was trying to stop it from entering the Japanese claimed territorial sea around the small islands.[7] The Chinese side insisted, on the contrary, that it was the Japanese Coast Guard vessels which intentionally caused the collision, and caused serious damage to the Chinese fishing boat before arresting the latter in the Chinese claimed territorial sea around the small islands.[8] Under very unusual circumstances, the Prime Ministers of China and Japan exchanged harsh remarks over the incident.[9] This immediately made the incident widely noticed in the region.

Some news readers may find it hard to tell which side was telling the truth, but for me, the facts cannot be clearer. There is no fishing boat in the world that would dare collide against a coast guard armed ship made of steel – unless

[6] In the past ten years, from 2001 to 2010, a total of 204 Taiwanese fishing vessels were arrested around the world. According to the OFDC statistics, in 2001, 16 ships were arrested; 2002, 17 ships; 2003, 12 ships; 2004, 31 ships; 2005, 25 ships; 2006, 29 ships; 2007, 15 ships; 2008, 22 ships; 2009, 25 ships; and in 2010, 12 ships have already reportedly been arrested to date.

[7] The case of Min-jin-yu No. 5179 (闽晋渔 5179 号) occurred on 7 September 2010 near the Diao-yu-tai Islands. See: http://news.qq.com/zt2010/diaoyudaozc/ visited on 22 November 2010.

[8] See: http://news.qq.com/a/20100907/001316.htm, visited on 22 November 2010.

[9] See: http://news.qq.com/a/20100922/000071.htm, visited on 22 November 2010.

they were forced to do so. Later on, the Japanese released video footage proving that the Japanese patrol ship was making quick turns closely in front of the Chinese fishing vessel, attempting to force it to either stop or make immediate turns. This has actually been a very common method used by Japanese law enforcement vessels to stop or intercept Taiwanese fishing vessels in the waters near Diao-yu-tai Islands. I have personally been involved with negotiations over several such incidents, and know this tactic quite well. As a matter of fact, more Taiwanese than mainland Chinese fishing vessels have been arrested by the Japanese Coast Guard in this area. In the first eight months of 2010, a total of seven Taiwanese fishing vessels have already been arrested by the Japanese Coast Guard. These seven cases all involved Taiwanese fishing boats sailing through the overlapping EEZs between Taiwan and Japan, in the vicinity of the Diao-yu-tai Islands, which has been a traditional fishing ground for the Chinese and Taiwanese fishermen.[10]

To sum up, it is safe to say that, for the sake of navigational safety, coastal States' law enforcement practices deserve more attention than piracy issues in the international community, because they have actually caused much more danger and damages to the international navigators than have criminal pirates. And I believe the key to a possible solution is a more practical international norm for policing the sea under the proportionality principle.

II. *What Is the Proportionality Principle?*

In the field of legal studies, the proportionality principle can generally be understood as the requirement that measures adopted in statutes, regulations, court decisions or administrative adjudications should be purpose-oriented, and that there must be a proper, justifiable and balanced relationship between the measure and its intended purposes.[11] This principle has been applied repeatedly in the administrative and constitutional laws of countries such as Germany, and through such application, the substance of the proportionality principle has been gradually molded and solidified. Today, when we talk about the principle of proportionality, we are actually emphasizing three collaborating principles:

[10] The names and registered numbers of these seven arrested Taiwanese fishing boats are: (1) The Quan-sheng 36(泉盛 36 號, CT4-1592); (2) The Lian-sheng-fa (聯勝發號, CT3-4260); (3) The Yu-jin (漁津 136 號, CT3-5048); (4) The Yi-sheng 6 (益昇 6 號, CT4-2087); (5) The Shun-fu-yu 86 (順福漁 86 號, CT4-2848); (6) The Xin-de-yi 186 (新德益 186 號, CT4-2787); and (7) The Feng-rong 106 (豐榮 106 號, CT3-5587).

[11] Xu Yu-zhen, *A Jurisprudential Study of the Proportionality Principle*, China Social Science Press, 2009, p. 68.

the principle of relevancy, the principle of necessity and the principle of the balance of interests. [12]

1. The Principle of Relevancy

This principle emphasizes the purpose of the public authority. Whenever the government wishes to take any measure, that measure must be relevant to the purposes of the government agency's authority. In other words, the measure must be purpose-oriented.[13] However, this principle has limited utility in limiting the governmental agencies' authority.

2. The Principle of Necessity

This principle can sometimes be called "the least intrusive principle" or "the mildest measure principle." For example, if suspending driver's licenses satisfied the need for curbing traffic accidents, there would be no need to imprison offending drivers. In other words, government officials may not adopt unnecessary measures that would increase the possible harm to the people. The authorities' actions shall not exceed the necessary limits of the law. The opposite party's rights and interests shall be protected so to avoid any unnecessary intrusion.[14]

3. The Principle of the Balance of Interests

This principle can be regarded as the strictly defined proportionality principle. It is sometimes known as "the interests-balancing principle."[15] Whenever a new rule or new decision is adopted or a governmental action is taken, there are always two or more legitimate interests that are affected. A comparison of the interests involved shall be carefully made and the weightier interest shall prevail.

In 1963, the German Constitutional Court handed down a seminal decision,[16] nullifying a lower court's judgment which required the extraction of a union member's bone marrow by spinal tap in order to decide his civil liability. The union member rejected the union's demand, and refused to fill in a public opinion investigation form. This caused the company to be fined a sum of $1000 DM. In its opinion, the Constitutional Court wisely emphasized that

---

[12] Chen Xin-min, *De-guo-gong-fa-ji-chu-li-lun* (Basic Theories of German Public Law), vol. 2, Ji-nan: Shandong Peoples Publishers, 2001, p. 368.

[13] Xie Shi-xian, *On Proportionality Principle in the Public Law*, in Chen Zhong-mou ed., Xing-zheng-fa-zhi-yi-ban-fa-lv-yuan-ze (General Legal Principles of Administrative Law), vol. 1, 1999, Taipei: San-min Books Company, p. 123. See also, Jiang Xi, *A Study on Proportionality Principle – From the Perspective of Constitutional Law*, Beijing: Law Publishing Company, 2008, p. 33.

[14] Jiang Xi, *ibid.*, p. 34.

[15] Chen Xin-min, *supra*, note 11, p. 370.

[16] Die Entscheidung des Bundesverfassungsgerichts zur Liquorentnahme gegen den Willen des Betroffenen, BVerfGE 16, 194, BVerfGE 16, 194 = NJW 1963, 1597.

the interest involved were not balanced. Compared with the minor damage of a fine, or monetary punishment by the union, the medical risk of a spinal tap was simply too high. In other words, to protect the rather minor monetary interest of the union, the lower court's judgment sacrificed too much of the individual's human rights, and could not be regarded as proper and proportional.[17]

III. *Application of the Proportionality Principle in Contemporary International Law*

Other than the application of the proportionality principle to domestic administrative law and constitutional law, the principle has also often been applied in the field of the international law of treaties, human rights law, international humanitarian law and maritime boundary delimitations.[18]

In the field of law enforcement at sea, this principle has also been utilized in the following major statutory or customary international laws, within the context of the use of force.

(1) The United Nations Charter, as signed on 26 June 1945:
- **Article 2(4):** "All members shall refrain in their international relations from the threat or use of force against the territorial or political independence of any state, or in any other manner inconsistent with the purposes of the United Nations."[19]

(2) The 1979 Code of Conduct for Law Enforcement Officials, as adopted by the UN General Assembly on 17 December 1979:
- **Article 3:** Law enforcement officials may use force only when strictly necessary and to the extent required for the performance of their duty.
- **Commentary:** (a) This provision emphasizes that the use of force by law enforcement officials should be exceptional; while it implies that law enforcement officials may be authorized to use force as is reasonably necessary under the circumstances for the prevention of crime or in effecting or assisting in the lawful arrest of offenders or suspected offenders, no force going beyond that may be used. (b) National law ordinarily restricts the use of force by law enforcement officials in accordance with a principle of proportionality.

[17] Kuen-chen Fu, *The Citizens' Senses to Be Established by the Media in a Constitutional Society*, National Taiwan University Forum of Journalism, No. 1, April 1994, pp. 15–16.

[18] Judith Gardam, *Necessity, Proportionality and the Use of Force by States*, Cambridge: Cambridge University Press, 2004, p. 2.

[19] See: http://www.un.org/en/documents/charter/index.shtml, visited 24 November 2010.

It is to be understood that such national principles of proportionality are to be respected in the interpretation of this provision. In no case should this provision be interpreted to authorize the use of force which is disproportionate to the legitimate objective to be achieved. (c) The use of firearms is considered an extreme measure. Every effort should be made to exclude the use of firearms, especially against children. In general, firearms should not be used except when a suspected offender offers armed resistance or otherwise jeopardizes the lives of others and less extreme measures are not sufficient to restrain or apprehend the suspected offender. In every instance in which a firearm is discharged, a report should be made promptly to the competent authorities.[20]

(3) The 1982 UNCLOS:

- **Article 301:** "In exercising their rights and performing their duties under this Convention, States Parties shall refrain from any threat or use of force against the territorial integrity or political independence of any State, or in any other manner inconsistent with the principles of international law embodied in the Charter of the United Nations."
- **Article 225:** (Duty to avoid adverse consequences in the exercise of the powers of enforcement): "In the exercise under this Convention of their powers of enforcement against foreign vessels, States <u>shall not endanger the safety of navigation or otherwise create any hazard to a vessel</u>, or bring to an unsafe port or anchorage, or expose the marine environment to an unreasonable risk."[21] [emphasis added]

(4) The 1990 Basic Principles on the Use of Force and Firearms by Law Enforcement Officials, as adopted by the Eighth United Nations Congress on the Prevention of Crime and the Treatment of Offenders, 27 August to 7 September 1990:

- **Points 4** (non-violent means), **5** (restraint, minimize, medical aids), **9** (defense of imminent threat), **10** (pre-warning), **11** (appropriate use and reporting), **13** (non-violent assemblies – no use), **14** (violent assemblies – necessary use), **15** (persons in custody – no use) and **16** (persons in custody – strictly necessary) are all relevant to the restriction on the use of force by the law enforcement officials.[22]

---

20 See: http://daccess-dds-ny.un.org/doc/RESOLUTION/GEN/NR0/377/96/IMG/NR037796.pdf?OpenElement, visited 22 November 2010.

21 Kuen-chen Fu, ed., *UNCLOS and Pertaining Conventions with Chinese and English Index*, Xiamen University Press, 2005, p. 85.

22 See: http://www2.ohchr.org/english/law/pdf/firearms.pdf, visited 21 November 2010.

(5) The 1995 Straddling Stock Agreement (The Agreement for the Implementation of the Provisions of the United Nations Convention on the Law of the Sea of 10 December 1982 Relating to the Conservation and Management of Straddling Fish Stocks and Highly Migratory Fish Stocks):

– **Article 22-1-(f):** "...avoid the use of force except when and to the degree necessary to ensure the safety of the inspectors and where the inspectors are obstructed in the execution of their duties. The degree of force used shall not exceed that reasonably required in the circumstances."[23] [emphasis added]

(6) The 2005 Protocol To SUA Convention (The Protocol of 2005 To The 1988 Convention For The Suppression Of Unlawful Acts Against The Safety Of Maritime Navigation):

– **Article 8bis–9:** "When carrying out the authorized actions under this article, the use of force shall be avoided except when necessary to ensure the safety of its officials and persons on board, or where the officials are obstructed in the execution of the authorized actions. Any use of force pursuant to this article shall not exceed the minimum degree of force which is necessary and reasonable in the circumstances."[24] [emphasis added]

These provisions apply the proportionality principle to regulating law enforcement officials, and create a legal basis for judicial review on the necessity of their use of force, and decide whether a forceful response is warranted in any particular situation.[25] After all, the use of force can be expected to bring serious damage to the opposite party.

Some classical judicial precedents are also noteworthy. Among them, the 1937 case of the *Caroline* clearly described the Principle of Necessity and the Principle of Balance of Interests by stating that "...a necessity of self-defence, instant, overwhelming, leaving no choice of means, and no moment for deliberation, did nothing unreasonable or excessive, since the act, justified by the necessity of self-defence, must be limited by the necessity, kept clearly within it."[26]

The M/V *Saiga* (No.2) Case, 1999, is another landmark precedent which has laid down a modern criterion for use of force with the Proportionality Principle.

On the issue of use of force during hot pursuit, the Court interpreted the text of the UNCLOS and stated that "although the convention does not contain

[23] Kuen-chen Fu, *supra*, note 19.

[24] See: http://www.likumi.lv/doc.php?id=203435, visited 25 Nov. 2010.

[25] Judith Gardam, *Necessity, Proportionality and the Use of Force by States*, Cambridge: Cambridge University Press, 2004, p. xv.

[26] R.Y. Jennings, The *Caroline* and *McLeod* Cases, *AJIL*, vol. 32, 1938, pp. 82–99.

express provisions on the use of force in the arrest of ships, international law, which is applicable by virtue of Article 293 of the convention, requires that the use of force must be avoided as far as possible and, where force is unavoidable, it must not go beyond what is reasonable and necessary in the circumstances. Considerations of humanity must apply in the law of the sea, as they do in other areas of international law...."

It is commonly acknowledged that the normal practice used to stop a ship at sea is first to give an auditory or visual signal to stop, using internationally recognized signals. Where this does not succeed, a variety of actions may be taken, including the firing of shots across the bow of the ship. It is only after the appropriate actions fail that the pursuing vessel may, as a last resort, use force. Even then, appropriate warning must be issued to the ship and all efforts should be made to ensure that life is not endangered.

However, in the present case, "...the *Saiga* was almost fully laden and was low in the water at the time it was approached by the patrol vessel. Its maximum speed was 10 knots. Therefore it could be boarded without much difficulty by the Guinean officers.... Having boarded the ship without resistance, and although there is no evidence of the use or threat of force from the crew, they fired indiscriminately while on the deck and used gunfire to stop the engine of the ship. In the process, considerable damage was done to the ship and to vital equipment in the engine and radio rooms. And, more seriously, the indiscriminate use of gunfire caused severe injuries to two of the persons on board.... For these reasons, the Tribunal finds that Guinea used excessive force and endangered human life before and after boarding the *Saiga*, and thereby violated the rights of Saint Vincent and the Grenadines under international law."[27] [emphasis added]

The International Tribunal for the Law of the Sea (ITLOS) judges also cited the above mentioned 1995 Straddling Stock Agreement Article 22 (1) (f), and re-emphasized: "These principles have been followed over the years in law enforcement operations at sea.... The basic principle concerning the use of force in the arrest of a ship at sea has been reaffirmed by the Agreement for the Implementation of the Provisions of the United Nations Convention on the Law of the Sea of 10 December 1982 Relating to the Conservation and Management of Straddling Fish Stocks and Highly Migratory Fish Stocks, Article 22, paragraph1(f)...."[28]

Having reviewed the above cases and materials, the principle of proportionality is already part of the statutory and customary law for both domestic and international practice of use of force, on the land or at the sea. To satisfy the

[27] ITLOS, M/V"SAIGA" (No. 2) Case, Judgement, 1 July, 1999, paras. 155–159, 183.

[28] ITLOS, M/V"SAIGA" (No. 2) Case, Judgement, 1 July, 1999, para. 156.

requirement of the Principle, the following three points are essential: (1) the use of force must be compatible with its purpose; (2) the use of force must be compatible with the seriousness of the crimes/violations committed by the foreign vessel; and (3) a balanced choice must be made between the action to be taken and the value of life on board. Even if all these three factors are met, sufficiently proper warning is required before the actual use of force; otherwise it will still be regarded as violating international law.

Back to the previously mentioned 2009 Case of the *New Star*, with the foregoing explanation it should be clear now that the Russian Coast Guard violated international law, statutory and customary, when it exceedingly fired 515 shots against the escaping cargo vessel, and the government is liable for compensation to the victims.

IV. *What Is Needed for a Safer Navigational Environment?*

1. **To urge various coastal States to improve their law enforcement practice by applying seriously the Proportionality Principle defined in statutory and customary international law.**
   Most states are already familiar with the Proportionality Principle in the areas of their domestic administrative law and constitutional law. Yet, they are not seriously practicing it in the international law area, particularly when the law enforcement actions are taken at the sea with nobody else around, and the objects are foreigners and foreign vessels.
2. **To create a new marine law enforcement convention on the basis of the 1990 Basic Principles on the Use of Force and Firearms by Law Enforcement Officials, and make this new convention an enforceable, comprehensive statutory law for every state in the world.**
   The 1990 Basic Principles is not a strictly defined treaty in the eyes of the international law of treaties. Promoting its legal status may bring to the international community a better environment for serious treatment of the current issue.
3. **To include in the new convention a set of detailed practicable rules on measures to be taken by coastal States' law enforcers when they are policing the sea.**
   To achieve this goal, we may need to refer to the US Coast Guard (USCG) rules on actions with potential use of force. Under the basic guidelines of the Proportionality Principle, the USCG rules classify the subjects, the weapons to be used, the different levels of situations; and create a rather reasonable schedule of levels of force for the law enforcers to follow step by step against non-compliant vessels. Exceptional rules of restraint are also made for the USCG to deal with fishing vessels and vessels with migrants on board.

4. **To improve training of the law enforcement officials of various coastal States.**
   It is possible that some law enforcement officials of some countries are not very well aware of the law. We should bring to their attention all the currently applicable statutory and customary international law.
5. **Encouraging litigation to help establish sufficient applicable precedents on the proportional use of force and proportional law enforcement at sea.**
   For example, the ship owners, the victims of the *New Star* and other relevant parties should initiate litigation against the Russian Coast Guard to pursue remedies in appropriate forums. Their quietness is not helpful at all for the final solution of the current issue.

RECENT DEVELOPMENTS IN ENHANCING SAFE NAVIGATION IN THE ARCTIC

Captain J. Ashley Roach, JAGC, USN (Ret.)[1]

Abstract

During the 2010 summer season portions of the Arctic Ocean were sufficiently ice-free to permit a limited number of commercial transits of the Arctic Ocean. Guided in part by the 2009 Arctic Marine Shipping Assessment, this paper reviews the steps currently being taken by the international community to enhance the safety of navigation in the Arctic. It builds upon portions of the author's paper 'Arctic Maritime Transport: Navigation Issues' presented at the May 2009 COLP 33rd Annual Conference held in Seward, Alaska, and published in the report of that conference entitled Changes in the Arctic Environment and the Law of the Sea.

At the May 2009 Annual Conference of the Center for Oceans Law and Policy at Seward, Alaska, the author was privileged to present a paper on navigation issues posed by the potential for Arctic marine transport. At that time the Arctic Council Ministers had just approved and published the Arctic Marine Shipping Assessment,[2] which provided, *inter alia*, a road map for enhancing the safety of navigation for future shipping in the Arctic. The Assessment framed that paper, and will do so again for this appreciation of the developments in Arctic safety of navigation since the paper as published was updated through December 2009.[3]

Arctic Marine Shipping Assessment (AMSA)

The Assessment made seventeen recommendations in three broad and inter-related themes: Enhancing Arctic Marine Safety, Protecting Arctic People and

---

[1] The views expressed in this paper are those of the author alone and are not intended to reflect the positions of any department or agency of the US Government. The author's PowerPoint presentation can be viewed at http://www.virginia.edu/colp/pdf/kmi-roach.pdf.

[2] Arctic Council, *Arctic Marine Shipping Assessment 2009 Report* [hereinafter AMSA], *available at* http://pame.is/amsa/amsa-2009-report.

[3] This paper is current through January 2011. It does not address the impacts of Arctic marine shipping on the protection and preservation of the marine environment and on the marine biodiversity of the Arctic ocean area. In that regard *see* E.J. Molenaar, 'Arctic Marine Shipping:

the Arctic Environment, and Building Arctic Marine Infrastructure.[4] This paper will focus primarily on implementation over the past year of those recommendations that are within the purview of the IMO. There were further developments at the meeting of the Maritime Safety Committee that occurredin London (MSC 88) 24 November–3 December 2010.

The focus is on trans-Arctic shipping, the Bering Strait, development of the Polar Code, seafarer training, Arctic nautical mapping, new Arctic navigation warning areas and maritime safety information services, and negotiation of the new Arctic search and rescue (SAR) agreement. It closes by raising concerns concerning the continuing – and counterproductive – propensity for unilateral regulation of shipping in the Arctic.

Recent Shipping Through the Arctic

Arctic sea routes – Northern Sea Route and Northwest Passage

Sea routes along the edges of the Arctic ocean, or rather along the coasts of Northern Canada and Russia, hold potential for decreasing the number of days in shipping goods from the Pacific to Atlantic coasts in Europe and North America, and vice versa. In addition, this could provide a means to transport natural resources, such as oil and gas, extracted in the Arctic. Currently these routes have not been possible to use due to the ice conditions, but with decreases in ice this could provide a new possibility. In addition, this would

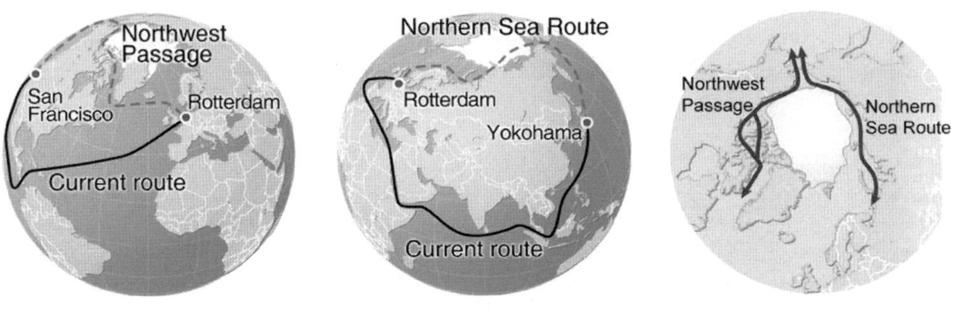

Fig. 1a–1b. Arctic Sea Routes

Overview of the International Legal Framework, Gaps, and Options,' *J. Transnat'l L. & Pol'y* 18, No. 2 (Spring 2009), 239, *available at* http://www.law.fsu.edu/journals/transnational/vol18_2/molenaar.pdf.

[4] The AMSA's recommendations are collated in Appendix I to L. Brigham and M. Sfrage (eds.), *Considering a Roadmap Forward: The Arctic Marine Shipping Assessment* (Fairbanks, Univ. of Alaska and Univ. of the Arctic Inst. for Applied Circumpolar Pol'y, 2010), available at *www.uarctic.org/AMSA_workshop_report_final_09.2010_-3FYy.pdf.file*

mean increased risk for the sensitive wilderness areas along these coasts, with oil spills and pollution.[5]

Climate models project that summer sea ice in the Arctic Basin will retreat farther and farther away from most Arctic landmasses, opening new shipping routes and extending the navigation season in the Northern Sea Route by between two and four months. Previously frozen areas in the Arctic may therefore become seasonally or permanently navigable, increasing the prospects for marine transport through the Arctic and providing greater access to Arctic resources such as fish, oil and gas. In addition to increased cargo shipping, opening of sea routes such as the Northern Sea Route and Northwest Passage will likely increase the number of tourist cruises and passenger vessels in Arctic waters. Although tourism is expected to experience a longer season in the Arctic, the industry is highly dependent upon weather conditions. A more unpredictable and rainier climate might reduce the attractiveness of some areas.[6] Via the Northern Sea Route, the navigational distance between Hamburg and Yokohama, for instance, is only 6,900 miles, compared with 11,430 miles via the Suez Canal.[7]

Transits of Northern Sea Route

During the 2010 summer season, there were at least seven notable commercial transits of the Arctic via the Northern Sea Route:

- The Russian ferry *Georg Ots* navigated between St. Petersburg and Vladivostok 28 August–October 2010 via the Northeast Passage (Northern Sea Route).[8]
- The Russian ore carrier *Monchegorsk* sailed from Dudinka to Shanghai in September–October 2010 via the Northern Sea Route.[9]

[5] UNEP GRID Arendal, 'Arctic Sea Routes – Northern Sea Route and Northwest Passage,' *available at* http://maps.grida.no/go/graphic/arctic-sea-routes-northern-sea-route-and-northwest-passage see also http://maps.grida.no/go/graphic/northern-sea-route-and-the-northwest-passage-compared-with-currently-used-shipping-routes.

The Northern Sea Route is the Russian domestic component of the Northeast Passage. Fig. 1a–1b cartographer: Hugo Ahlenius, UNEP/GRID-Arendal).

[6] UNEP GRID Arendal, 'Northern Sea Route and the Northwest Passage compared with currently used shipping routes,' *available at* http://maps.grida.no/go/graphic/northern-sea-route-and-the-northwest-passage-compared-with-currently-used-shipping-routes.

[7] Marine Log, 'Marine Industry: Getting ready for new ice age,' *Marine Log* (undated), *available at* http://www.marinelog.com/DOCS/PRINTMMV/MMVjularc1.html.

[8] 'Another ship successfully through Northeast Passage,' *Barents Observer*, 30 Sep. 2010, *available at* http://www.barentsobserver.com.

[9] 'Norilsk-Nickel sails to Asia via Arctic,' *Barents Observer*, 16 Sep. 2010, *available at* http://www.barentsobserver.com; 'Russia's Norilsk Nickel open new shipping route to Asia,' *Platts*,

- The Liberian flag-Cyprus managed oil tanker *SCF Baltica*, 117,000 dwt, ice class 1A-Super (Arc5), sailed from Murmansk to Ninbo, China carrying 70,000 tons of gas concentrate along the Northern Sea Route between 14 August and 6 September 2010.[10]
- The Hong Kong flag MV *Nordic Barents*, a 43,731 dwt bulk carrier, ice-class 1A, transported 40,000 tons of iron ore from Norway to China via the Northern Sea Route in September 2010.[11]
- The Gibraltar-flag German-owned *Beluga Houston* loaded equipment for the construction of an electric power station in Surgut, Russia, in early August 2010 in Rotterdam. The *Beluga Fortitude* (Antigua and Barbuda flag) loaded similar equipment in Noorkoping, Sweden, in mid-July 2010. Both ships delivered their cargo to Novy Port, Yamburg, Russia, for delivery by barge. On her return journey, the *Beluga Fortitude* delivered cargo from Arkhangelsk port to Rotterdam.[12]
- The Russian yacht *Peter the First* circumnavigated the Arctic Ocean through the Northeast and Northwest Passages for 109 days in the summer of 2010, sailing from St Petersburg, around Scandinavia to Murmansk to Novaya Zemlya and on back to St Petersburg.[13]

The first non-Russian commercial transit of the Northeast Passage occurred during the 2009 summer when the German-owned multi-purpose heavy-lift

---

16 Sep. 2010, *available at* http://www.platts.com/RSSFeedDetailedNews/RSSFeed/HeadlineNews/Metals/8960296.

[10] 'SCF Baltica Completes Her Voyage from Murmansk to Ningbo (China),' *Russian Daily Transport*, 9 Oct. 2010, *available at* http://rtdr.org/news/maritime/scf_baltica_completes_her_voyage_from_murmansk_to_ningbo_china.html; 'First high-tonnage tanker through Northeast Passage,' *Barents Observer*, 17 Aug. 2010, *available at* http://www.barentsobserver.com/first-high-tonnage-tanker-through-northeast-passage.4809756-16149.html; "SCF Baltica' makes good progress,' *Tanker Operator*, 27 Aug. 2010, *available at* http://www.tankeroperator.com/news/todisplaynews.asp?NewsID=2174.

[11] 'Faster than expected,' *Barents Observer*, 16 Sep. 2010, *available at* http://barentsobserver.com/faster-than-expected.4819400-116321.html; 'Cargo ship embarks on historic Arctic passage,' *Reuters*, 4 Sep. 2010, *available at* http://af.reuters.com/article/idAFLDE68308Q20100904; 'Bulker set for historic Northern Sea Route voyage,' *Marine Log*, 26 Aug. 2010, *available at* http://www.marinelog.com/DOCS/NEWSMMIX/2010aug00262.html. See also A.C. Rivkin, 'Arctic Shipping Gets Boring,' *N.Y. Times*, 16 Sep. 2010, *available at* http://dotearth.blogs.nytimes.com/2010/09/16/arctic-shipping-gets-boring/.

[12] 'Beluga Shipping Provides New Voyage via Northern Sea Route,' *Russian Transport Daily Report*, 10 Sep. 2010, *available at* http://rtdr.org/news/maritime/beluga_shipping_provides_new_voyage_via_northern_sea_route.html; " 'Beluga Houston' to Deliver Equipment for Nyaganskaya GRES in July–September 2010," *id.*, 1 Feb. 2010, *available at* http://rtdr.org/news/logistics/beluga_houston_to_deliver_equipment_for_nyaganskaya_gres_in_july-september_2010.html.

[13] 'Around the Arctic in 109 days,' *The Voice of Russia*, 14 Nov. 2010, *available at* http://english.ruvr.ru/2010/11/14/34232385.html.

cargo ships MV *Beluga Fraternity* and *Foresight* (both Antigua and Barbuda flag) sailed from Ulsan, Korea in late July 2009, received clearance in Vladivostok, transited the Bering Strait and the Northeast Passage, off loaded their cargo in Novy Port, Yamburg, Siberia between 7 and 14 September 2009, and departed the Northeast Passage for Rotterdam via Murmansk. This was also the first foreign commercial west-to-east transit of the Northeast Passage.[14]

Transits of Northwest Passage

During the 2010 summer season, there were at least eighteen transits of the Northwest Passage.[15] There are at least 135 full transits of the Northwest Passage documented to have occurred during the ten decades between 1903 and 2009.[16] Given these statistics, to deny, as Canada continues to do, that the Northwest Passage is not a strait used for international navigation,[17] as that term is used in Part III of the Law of the Sea Convention, is simply not credible.[18] The Northwest Passage is demonstrably a strait "used for international navigation between one part of the high seas or exclusive economic zone and another part of the high seas or exclusive economic zone."[19]

[14] *See* various Beluga-Group news archive articles *available at* http://www.beluga-group.com.

[15] 'Northwest Passage traffic up in 2010,' *CBC News*, 20 Sep. 2010 ("The Canada Border Services Agency says 18 ships have cleared customs in Inuvik, N.W.T. – at the western end of the Northwest Passage – so far this year, and the navigation season is not even over yet. By comparison, only seven ships cleared customs there in 2009, according to the agency."), *available at* http://www.cbc.ca/canada/north/story/2010/09/20/northwest-passage-ships-inuvik.html.

[16] R.K. Headland, 'Ten decades of transits of the Northwest Passage,' 33 *Polar Geography*, Nos. 1–2, (March–June 2010), 1–13. *See also* H. Stern, 'Record Number of Yachts Traverse Northwest Passage in Summer 2009,' *The Polar Times*, Jan. 2010, 7.

[17] The most recent Canadian assertion is contained in an address by Foreign Minister Cannon on 15 November 2010, 'Address by Minister Cannon to Third Annual Arctic Shipping North America Conference,' Montreal, Quebec, *Canada News Center*, No. 2010/89 ("All waters within the Arctic archipelago, including the waters of the Northwest Passage, are internal waters of Canada by virtue of historic title. Canada has an unfettered right to regulate them, as it would its land territory. Although some contend otherwise, we believe that no strait used for international navigation exists through these waters.", *available at* http://news.gc.ca/web/article-eng.do?m=/index&nid=574359.

[18] See D. Pharand, 'The Arctic Waters and the Northwest Passage: A Final Revisit,' 38 *Ocean Dev. Int'l L.*, 2007, 3–69; J. Kraska, 'A Diplomatic Solution for the Northwest Passage,' 19 *Nat'l Strategy Forum Rev.*, No. 3 (Summer 2010), *available at* http://www.nationalstrategy.com/Portals/0/documents/Summer%202010%20NSFR/James%20Kraska%20-%20Summer%202010%20NSFR.pdf.

[19] Article 37, Law of the Sea Convention.

Forecast for 2011

More transits of the Arctic are expected in 2011, particularly by Russian oil and gas tankers.[20]

The Bering Strait

The Arctic Marine Shipping Assessment noted that:

> *There are currently no established vessel routing measures in the Bering Strait region. A Traffic Separation Scheme (TSS) may need to be established in the region as vessel traffic increases. There is currently no active Vessel Traffic Service (VTS) or other traffic management system in place in the waters of the Bering Strait. Shipboard Automated Identification System (AIS) capability is currently limited.*[21]

The Bering Strait is approximately 51 nautical miles wide, between Cape Dezhnev, Chukotka Autonomous Okrug, Russia, the easternmost point (169°43' W) of the Asian continent and Cape Prince of Wales, Alaska, US, the westernmost point (168°05' W) of the North American continent, with latitude of about 65°40' north, slightly south of the polar circle. Its average depth is 98–160 feet.[22] Located in the middle of the strait are the Diomede Islands: Big Diomede is on the Russian side, and Little Diomede is on the US side of the International Date Line and maritime boundary.[23] The two islands are about 2.4 nm apart.[24] Accordingly, ships will normally pass to the east of Little Diomede and west of Big Diomede. The eastern strait between Little Diomede and Cape Prince of Wales, and the western strait between Big Diomede and Cape Dezhnev, are each about 22.5 miles wide.[25] As noted above, there are presently no routing measures in place for the Bering Strait, although there are some navigation lights.

On 8 November 2010, the US Coast Guard announced it is conducting a Port Access Route Study (PARS) to evaluate the "continued applicability of and the need for modifications to current vessel routing measures; and the need for

[20] 'Russia looks north for oil transit routes,' *UPI*, 22 Oct. 2010, *available at* http://www.upi.com/Science_News/Resource-Wars/2010/10/22/Russia-looks-north-for-oil-transit-routes/UPI-40961287760273; 'Russia's Novatek to ship 6–8 cargoes via Arctic to Asia in 2010,' *Platts*, 26 Aug. 2010, *available at* http://www.platts.com/RSSFeedDetailedNews/RSSFeed/HeadlineNews/NaturalGas/8909460.

[21] AMSA, *supra* note 2, at 109.

[22] http://en.wikipedia.org/wiki/Bering_Strait.

[23] Agreement between the United States of America and the Union of Soviet Socialist Republics on the Maritime Boundary, 1 June 1990, *available at* http://www.un.org/Depts/los/LEGISLATIONANDTREATIES/PDFFILES/TREATIES/USA-RUS1990MB.PDF.

[24] http://en.wikipedia.org/wiki/Diomede_Islands.

[25] Google Earth measurements.

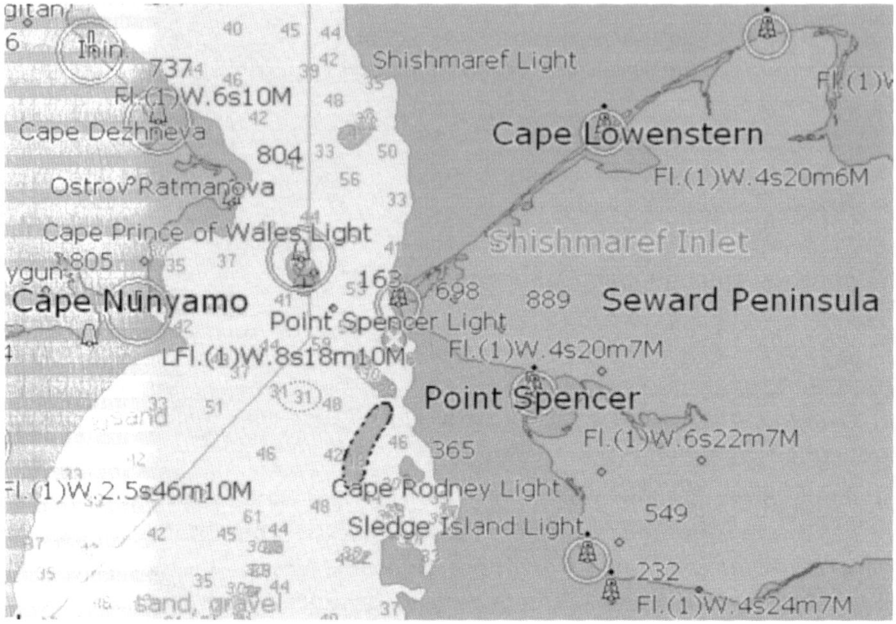

Fig. 2. Source: http://en.wikipedia.org/wiki/File:US_NOAA_nautical_chart_of_Bering_Strait.png

creation of new vessel routing measures in the Bering Strait." The announcement stated that the "recommendations of the study may lead to future rule making action or appropriate international agreements." Comments are due by 9 May 2011. The study is expected to take at least 24 months to complete.[26]

The study area is bounded by the line connecting the following geographical positions:

- 62°30'N, 173°00'W;
- 62°30'N, 167°30'W;
- 67°30'N, 167°30'W;
- 67°30'N, 168°58'37"W; thence following the Russian Federation/United States maritime boundary line to position
- 63°40'N, 173°00'W; thence to the first geographical position.[27]

An illustration of these coordinates shows that the area of the PARS is entirely on the U.S. side of the maritime boundary line, and does not extend very far

[26] U.S. Coast Guard, Notice of study and request for comments, 75 Fed. Reg., No. 215, 8 Nov. 2010, pp. 68568–68570, *available at* http://edocket.access.gpo.gov/2010/pdf/2010-28115.pdf.

[27] *Id.* at 68570.

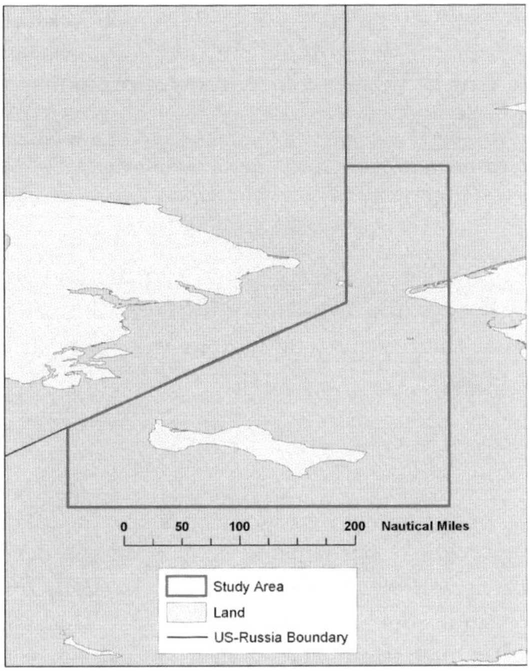

Fig. 3. Source: US State Department (OES/OPA)

north into the Arctic Ocean. So the study area will not provide full information on north-bound ships deciding whether to head to the trans-polar route or the Northwest Passage. But it is a start!

It is a statement of the obvious that the Russian Federation and the United States, as states bordering the Bering Strait, have a common interest in the safety of navigation through the Bering Strait. Nevertheless, the PARS announcement makes no direct reference to the requirement of SOLAS regulation V/10, paragraph 5, that:

> *Where two or more Governments have a common interest in a particular area, they should formulate joint proposals for the delineation and use of a routeing system therein on the basis of an agreement between them. Upon receipt of such proposal and before proceeding with consideration of it for adoption, the Organization shall ensure details of the proposal are disseminated to the Governments which have a common interest in the area, including countries in the vicinity of the proposed ships' routeing system.*

One obvious routing system would be to recommend or require northbound traffic to use the eastern strait and southbound traffic to use the western strait. This would require IMO approval.[28]

[28] Guidance on obtaining IMO approval for routeing measures is contained in the IMO's publication *Ships' Routeing* now in its 10th edition (2010). The publication defines various types of

As the eastern and western passages are each less than 24 nm wide, the regime of transit passage applies in those straits (and their approaches). Consequently, article 41(5) of the Law of the Sea Convention also requires that:

> *In respect of a strait where sea lanes or traffic separation schemes through the waters of two or more States bordering the strait are being proposed, the States concerned shall cooperate in formulating proposals in consultation with the competent international organization.*

It is still not yet known if the United States, Canada and Russia will develop appropriate submissions to the IMO for the Bering Strait/Chukchi Sea/Beaufort Sea area, or what the other Arctic nations will do regarding the other sea areas in the Arctic Ocean.[29]

Polar Code

The United States previously participated actively in the development of, and supported, the IMO *Guidelines for Ships Operating in Arctic Ice-Covered Waters*[30] that were developed under the leadership of Canada.[31] They addressed construction, equipment, ship operation, and environmental protection and damage control. The 2009 IMO Assembly adopted a revised version of these non-binding Guidelines for application in Antarctic as well as Arctic waters, *Guidelines for Ships Operating in Polar Waters.*[32]

On the initiative of Denmark, Norway and the United States, MSC 86 and MEPC 59 agreed to add to the agenda of the Sub-Committee on Ship Design and Equipment (DE), a new high-priority work program item on "Development

---

routing measures: A "recommended route" is a route of undefined width, for the convenience of ships in transit, which is often marked by center line buoys. A "recommended track" is a route which has been specially examined to ensure so far as possible that it is free of dangers and along which vessels are advised to navigate. A "traffic separation scheme" is a routeing measure aimed at the separation of opposing streams of traffic by appropriate means and by the establishment of traffic lanes. *See* 75 Fed. Reg. at 68569.

[29] International law permits a mandatory ship reporting scheme to be imposed in only two circumstances: unilaterally as a condition of port entry, and pursuant to IMO approval in accordance with SOLAS regulation V/11, the General Provisions on Ships' Routeing, IMO resolutions A.826(19), MSC.43(64) as amended by resolutions MSC.111(73) and MSC.189(79), and MSC circular 1060 and Add.1 of 26 May 2006, Guidance Note on the Preparation of Proposals on Ships' Routeing Systems and Ship Reporting Systems, the latter *available at* http://www.imo.org/OurWork/Safety/Navigation/Pages/ShipsRouteing.aspx. *See infra* text following note 83 for a discussion of article 234 of the Law of the Sea Convention in this context.

[30] IMO joint circular MSC/Circ.1056-MEPC/Circ.399, 23 Dec. 2002.

[31] IMO documents MSC 68/20/2, 27 Feb. 1997 and DE 39/31, para. 30.17.

[32] IMO Assembly Resolution A.1024(26), 2 Dec. 2009.

of a mandatory Code for ships operating in polar waters," with a target completion date of 2012.

The DE subcommittee began work during its 53rd session in February 2010 by establishing a correspondence group to develop the draft mandatory *International Code of Safety for Ships Operating in Polar Waters (Polar Code).*[33] At its session in October 2010, DE 54 decided to proceed with the development of a stand-alone mandatory Polar Code in order to provide an unambiguous, enforceable set of requirements for polar shipping.[34] The subcommittee then reviewed the work of the correspondence group, further developed the code in a working group, and re-established the correspondence group to continue its work and report to DE 55, tentatively scheduled to meet March 21–25, 2011.[35]

At DE 54, the Subcommittee agreed that the Code would be structured in three Parts:

- Part A – mandatory requirements;
- Part B – additional guidance in applying the requirements of Part A; and
- Part C – additional information on the methodology used to develop the requirements (Part A) and guidance (Part B) which could serve as institutional memory when further work would be undertaken in the future.[36]

The working group also developed a hazard matrix (annex 1), listed goals and functional requirements (annex 2), and began drafting the code (annex 3).[37] Because of the short deadline (17 December 2010) for submission of papers to DE 55, the correspondence group focused on further developing the hazard matrix.[38]

Following submission of its report to the plenary, the DE 54 Working Group on the development of a mandatory Polar Code continued its discussions on 28 October 2010, and the Chairman has submitted a summary of those discussions to DE 55.[39]

One of the issues discussed was how to mandate the Code under existing IMO conventions, SOLAS and MARPOL. Amendment of SOLAS could be accomplished through the tacit acceptance procedure for an amendment to Chapter V, Safety of Navigation, Regulation 34, Safe navigation and avoidance

---

33 Report to the Maritime Safety Committee, DE 53/26, 15 Mar. 2010, p. 38, para. 18.11.

34 Draft Report to the Maritime Safety Committee, DE 54/WP.8, para. 13.5.

35 *Id.*, paras. 13, 17 and 20.6.

36 Report of the Working Group, DE 54/WP.3, para. 23.

37 *Ibid.* annexes.

38 DE 55/12/1, 17 Dec. 2010.

39 DE 55/12, 10 Nov. 2010.

GEOGRAPHIC AREA FOR POLAR CODE

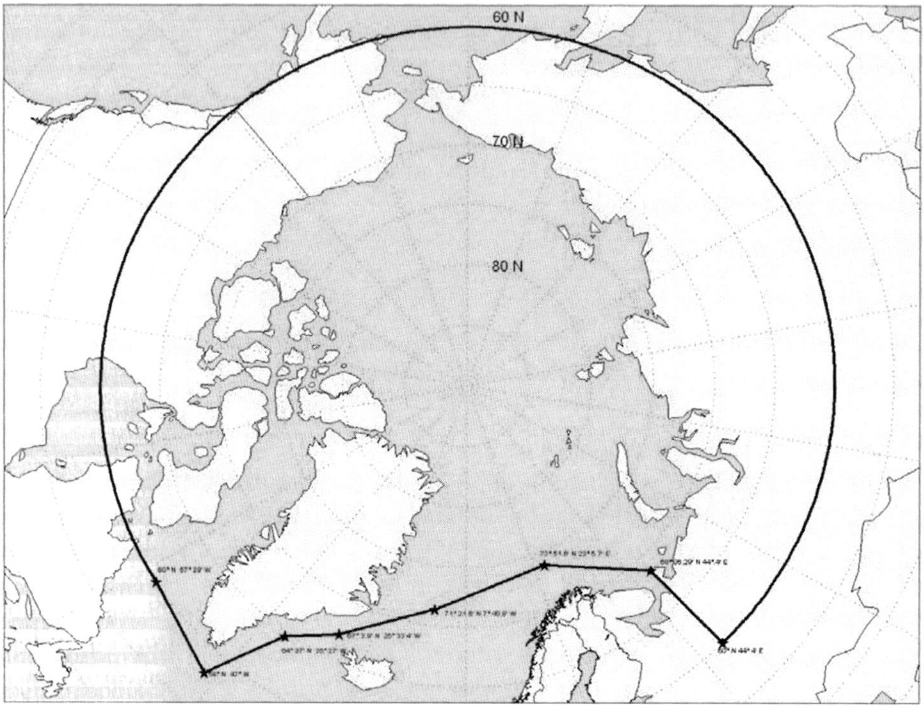

Fig. 4. Source: Guidelines for Ships Operating in Polar Waters, IMO Resolution A.1024(26), 2 Dec. 2009, page 9, fig. 1.

of dangerous situations, that, depending on the ultimate content of the Polar Code, could add another sentence to its first paragraph, following the guidance in Assembly resolution A.911(22), as follows:

1. *Amend SOLAS regulation V/34, Safe navigation and avoidance of dangerous situations, by revising paragraph 1 to read as follows (new text underlined)*:

> *1 Prior to proceeding to sea, the master shall ensure that the intended voyage has been planned using the appropriate nautical charts and nautical publications for the area concerned, taking into account the guidelines and recommendations developed by the Organization. For voyages intended to be in the Arctic or Southern Oceans, the master shall also comply with the applicable [mandatory] provisions of the Polar Code, adopted by the Maritime Safety Committee of the Organization by resolution MSC…(..), as may be amended by the Organization, provided that such amendments are adopted, brought into force and take effect in accordance with the provisions of*

article VIII of the present Convention concerning the amendment procedures applicable to the Annex other than chapter I.[40]

During these discussions the Working Group noted that "mandating the Polar Code through MARPOL is not a straightforward issue, given the different number of Parties to the various annexes to MARPOL."[41] An issue is which of the MARPOL Annexes would be appropriate to amend for this purpose, since none of them fit this situation. However, given that SOLAS regulation V/34.2.4 already refers to "marine environmental protection measures," it is not entirely clear now to this author that any amendment of MARPOL would be necessary to make the Code mandatory.

Seafarer Training

At present there still are no *requirements* for training and certification standards and crew qualifications for ships operating in the Arctic or Southern Oceans.

At the meeting of the Sub-committee on Standards of Training and Watch-keeping (STW) in early February 2009 (STW 40), Norway, supported by the Russian Federation and Chile, proposed a new regulation for the STCW Convention and a new section for the STCW Code with a view to introduce mandatory minimum requirements for the training and qualifications of navigators serving on board ships operating in areas where ice or ice floes are likely to be present. However, in light of the on-going work to revise the Guidelines by DE that began in March 2007, the STW Sub-committee agreed to establish a correspondence group coordinated by Norway to develop a preliminary proposed text for training guidance for personnel operating in ice-covered waters and submit its report for consideration by the next meeting of the Sub-committee in January 2010.[42]

The Maritime Safety Committee, at its 86th meeting in May–June 2009 approved the holding of an intersessional working group on the comprehensive review of the STCW Convention and Code (ISWG 2). The correspondence group submitted its report to ISWG 2. The intersessional working group agreed that the correspondence group should concentrate on guidance for inclusion in Part B of the Code. In November 2009, the correspondence group submitted

[40] The new text follows the provisions of resolution A.911(22) Annex paragraph 3, Guidelines on methods for making reference to IMO and other instruments in IMO Conventions and other mandatory instruments, using the 2000 amendments to SOLAS chapter X (HSC Code) as a model. If construction or other requirements are set out in the Polar Code, other similar amendments may need to be made.

[41] *Id.* at para. 3.

[42] The report of the correspondence group is IMO document STW 41/7/39, 6 Nov. 2009.

its report to STW 41, including draft guidance regarding training of officers on ships operating in Polar waters.[43] STW 41, meeting in January 2010, approved both the draft guidance[44] and a draft conference resolution.[45] At the Manila STCW Conference in June 2010, the conference adopted, without substantive change, the training guidance and resolution developed at STW 41.[46] The guidance notes that "there are no corresponding regulations in the Convention or sections in part A of the Code" for this guidance.[47] As these guidelines and recommendations were adopted well before the yet-to-be-drafted mandatory Polar Code, all recognize "the need for mandatory training requirements when the Polar Code under development by the International Maritime Organization is adopted."[48]

The conference resolution:

> *RECOMMENDS that governments adopt measures conducive to ensuring that masters and officers of ships, which operate in polar waters, have appropriate training and experience, so that they are able to:*
>
> 1. *plan voyages to polar waters, taking into account glaciological, hydrographic, oceanographic and meteorological factors;*
> 2. *navigate safely in polar waters, in particular in restricted ice-covered areas under adverse conditions of wind and visibility; and*
> 3. *supervise and ensure compliance with the requirements deriving from inter-governmental agreements and with those relating to safety of life at sea and protection of the marine environment.*[49]

So it is apparent that there will be no mandatory requirements for the training of seafarers operating in the Arctic until after the Polar Code is adopted. Hopefully, the implementation dates for the Polar Code and the training requirements will be compatible, if not identical.

Nautical Charting of the Arctic Ocean

The final AMSA recommendation states that "the Arctic states should significantly improve, where appropriate, the level of and access to data and information

---

43 *Ibid.*

44 STW 41/16/Add.1, Annex 3, pp. 90–92.

45 STW 41/16, page 40, para. 7.11.24.13; STW 41/WP.4, Annex 4, p. 14.

46 DE 54/13, Annexes 1 and 2; STCW/CONF.2/34, Annex, pages 330–332; STCW/CONF.2/32, p. 15.

47 DE 54/13, Annex 1, page 1 note; STCW/CONF.2/34, Annex, p. 330 note.

48 '2010 Manila Conference Resolution 11, Measures to ensure the competence of masters and officers of ships operating in polar waters,' STCW/CONF.2/32 p. 15.

49 *Id.*

in support of safe navigation and voyage planning in Arctic waters." The Assessment notes that this "would entail increased efforts for: hydrographic surveys to bring Arctic navigation charts up to a level acceptable to support current and future safe navigation; and systems to support real-time acquisition, analysis and transfer of meteorological, oceanographic, sea ice and iceberg information."[50]

Less than ten per cent of Arctic waters is charted to modern standards. The preparation of nautical charts is normally the responsibility of national hydrographic offices. Perhaps the results of the various Arctic nations' bathymetric surveys for the extended continental shelf will provide useful data to those offices.[51]

To facilitate the exchange of knowledge and information among, and the provision of quality assured data to, the national hydrographic offices, the five Arctic coastal States, on 6 October 2010, represented by their Hydrographic Offices, established the Arctic Regional Hydrographic Commission.

Since the establishment of the International Hydrographic Organization in 1921, fifteen Regional Hydrographic Commissions have been established worldwide. The Arctic Ocean remained without such a Commission until now.[52]

Regional Hydrographic Commissions

The 15 Regional Hydrographic Commissions (RHCs) and the Hydrographic Commission on Antarctica are important elements in the continuous review, co-ordination and delivery of official hydrographic and nautical charting services across the globe. The first RHC was, in effect, founded in 1929 when the Nordic Cooperation Agreement was signed – to establish periodic conferences of nations bordering the North Sea and the Skagerrak. This is now the Nordic Hydrographic Commission.

The RHCs complement the work of the International Hydrographic Organization (IHO) through the regional co-ordination of nautical information,

---

50 AMSA, *supra* note 2, at 7.

51 Title XII, Oceans, Subtitle A – Ocean Exploration and Subtitle B – Ocean and Coastal Mapping Integration Act, of the Omnibus Public Land Management Act of 2009, Pub. L. 111-11, 30 Mar. 2009, 123 Stat. 991 *et seq.*, provide a basis for NOAA National Ocean Service to include the bathymetric data collected by the US Extended Continental Shelf task force. Arctic-specific hydrographic services was the subject of H.R. 2864, Authorization of Funds for Arctic Hydrographic Activities, that was reported out by the Committee on Natural Resources on 13 July 2010. House Rep. 111-532. It remains to be seen if, unlike during the 110th Congress, it is enacted by the 111th Congress.

52 'Statement of the Arctic Regional Hydrographic Commission Drafted for Approval October 5, 2010,' *available at* http://www.iho-ohi.net/mtg_docs/rhc/ArHC/ArHC_Misc/ArHC_Statement_ 05Oct10.pdf.

hydrographic surveys, production of nautical charts and documents, training, and technical co-operation and hydrographic capacity building projects to be co-ordinated within each region. The RHCs are an important way of facilitating the exchange of information and consultation between hydrographic services, particularly those that are not presently members of the IHO. Geographically adjacent RHCs also liase with each other.

Co-ordination

The NAVAREA regions jointly established by the IHO, International Maritime Organization (IMO) and World Meteorological Organization (WMO) for the dissemination of maritime safety information (MSI) have been closely aligned with the RHCs for the obvious reason of better co-ordination. For the same reason, the co-ordination of both INT paper charts and electronic navigational chart (ENC) production is also based primarily on RHC areas.[53]

The Fifteen Regional Hydrographic Commissions and the Hydrographic Commission on Antarctica[54]

Acronym	Name of Regional Hydrographic Commission	Established
NSHC	North Sea Hydrographic Commission	1963
EAHC	East Asia Hydrographic Commission	1971
USCHC	US/Canada Hydrographic Commission	1977
MBSHC	Mediterranean and Black Seas Hydrographic Commission	1978
BSHC	Baltic Sea Hydrographic Commission	1983
EAtHC	East Atlantic Hydrographic Commission	1984
SEPHC	South East Pacific Hydrographic Commission	1991
SWPHC	South West Pacific Hydrographic Commission	1993
MACHC	MesoAmerican-Caribbean Sea Hydrographic Commission	1994
SAIHC	Southern Africa and Islands Hydrographic Commission	1996
HCA	Hydrographic Commission on Antarctica	1997
RSAHC	ROPME Sea Area Hydrographic Commission	2000
NIOHC	North Indian Ocean Hydrographic Commission	2002
SWAtHC	South West Atlantic Hydrographic Commission	2006
ArHC	Arctic Hydrographic Commission	2010

[53] 'Regional Hydrographic Commissions,' 13 *Hydro-International*, No. 7, Sep. 2009, *available at* http://www.hydro-international.com/issues/articles/id1112-Regional_Hydrographic_Commissions.html.

[54] Table adapted from *id.*

Arctic Search and Rescue

With increased melting of sea ice in the Arctic and more attention being paid to the Arctic, human activity has started to increase in the region. This has already led to increases in ship-borne tourism and will lead to more shipping of many types. The Assessment recommended that the Arctic States decide to support developing and implementing a comprehensive, multi-national Arctic Search and Rescue instrument, including aeronautical and maritime SAR, among the eight Arctic nations and, if appropriate, with other interested parties in recognition of the remoteness and limited resources in the region.[55]

As a result, the United States and the seven other Arctic Council (AC) Member States (Canada, Denmark, Finland, Iceland, Norway, Russian Federation, Sweden) adopted a Ministerial Declaration in April 2009 in Tromsø, Norway, which established a Task Force with the mandate of developing a search and rescue (SAR) agreement for the Arctic. The United States hosted the first meeting of the Arctic SAR Task Force during 9–11 December 2009, in Washington, D.C. The second round of negotiations was held 25–26 February 2010, in Moscow, Russian Federation. The final round of negotiations was held in mid-December 2010. The Arctic SAR Task Force has been asked to finalize the Arctic SAR agreement such that it can be presented for adoption by the AC at its Ministerial meeting in Nuuk, Greenland, 12 May 2011.[56]

Background

By way of background, the LOS Convention requires every coastal State to "promote the establishment, operation and maintenance of an adequate and effective search and rescue service regarding safety on and over the sea and, where circumstances so require, by way of mutual regional arrangements cooperate with neighboring States for this purpose."[57]

The Arctic nations are all party to the IMO's International Convention on Maritime Search and Rescue (1979).[58] The SOLAS Convention requires each party to provide search and rescue (SAR) services for the rescue of persons in

---

[55] AMSA, *supra* note 2, at 6.

[56] http://www.state.gov/g/oes/ocns/opa/arc/c29382.htm; http://arctic-council.org/meeting/ministerial_meeting%2C_2011.

[57] LOS Convention, article 98(2).

[58] International Convention on Maritime Search and Rescue, 1979, with annex, done at Hamburg 27 April 1979, entered into force 22 June 1985, as amended, *available at* http://www.admiraltylawguide.com/conven/searchrescue1979.htm *and at* http://www.admiraltylawguide.com/conven/amendsearch1998.html.

distress at sea around its coasts.[59] The Arctic nations are also party to the Convention on International Civil Aviation (ICAO), Annex 12 of which addresses aeronautical SAR.[60] The Arctic nations are also all party to the LOS Convention, or in the case of the United States to the 1958 Convention on the High Seas, that set out the customary international law duty "to render assistance to any person found at sea in danger of being lost."[61]

Both SAR Conventions require parties to establish SAR Regions (SRRs) and call on parties to cooperate in the establishment and provision of SAR services.[62] The United States has a number of bilateral SAR agreements and memoranda of understanding (MOUs) with other countries, including a maritime SAR agreement with Russia (1988)[63] and an aeronautical and maritime SAR MOU with Canada and the UK (1999).[64] The United States is also developing a multilateral SAR MOU for the North Atlantic SRR region.

In the US Coast Guard's experience, the nature of SAR cooperation does not require multilateral (or bilateral) SAR instruments to be binding international agreements. They have found that non-binding memoranda of understanding are quite sufficient to lay out the expectations of the cooperating countries. What has often been harder in reaching agreement on the texts is identifying the relevant national agencies that will be identified in the MOU. This is particularly difficult when the cooperation contemplates both maritime and aeronautical cooperation, as well as a potential for terrestrial cooperation in the Arctic, where the responsibilities lie with different governmental agencies in each country.

---

59 SOLAS Convention, regulation V/7.

60 Convention on International Civil Aviation, done at Chicago 7 December 1944, entered into force 4 April 1947, 61 Stat. 1180, TIAS 1591, 3 Bevans 944, 15 UNTS 295; *available at* http://www.icao.int/icaonet/arch/doc/7300/7300_9ed.pdf. *See also* http://www.icao.int/eshop/annexes_list.htm and http://www.icao.int/icao/en/ro/apac/2005/ATM_AIS_SAR_SG15/ip04.pdf.

61 LOS Convention, art. 98; Convention on the High Seas, art. 12.

62 IMO SAR Convention, annex para. 2.1.1; ICAO Annex 12, paras. 2.2.1, 3.1.1.

63 US-USSR Agreement on Maritime Search and Rescue, with exchange of letters, signed at Moscow 31 May 1988, entered into force 3 July 1989, TIAS 11440, 2191 UNTS 115.

64 Memorandum of Understanding for Co-operation among the Department of National Defence of Canada, the Department of Fisheries and Oceans of Canada, the United States Coast Guard, the United States Air Force, the United Kingdom Maritime and Coastguard Agency, the United Kingdom Civil Aviation Division of the Department of Environment, Transport and the Regions, and the United Kingdom Ministry of Defence Concerning Search and Rescue, signed at Ottawa, Washington and London 1 February–14 September 1999.

In the Alaska region, the US Coast Guard has been operating SAR aircraft from forward operating bases in Nome and Barrow since the summer of 2008[65] and conducting patrols in the Arctic Ocean.[66]

Arctic SAR Agreement

The current text has not yet been made publicly available. However, the author understands that agreement has been reached on the following points:

- The agreement will apply both to maritime and aeronautical SAR services and be designed to enhance cooperation and coordination in the provision of SAR services in the Arctic.
- The agreement will set out the boundaries of the national Search and Rescue Regions, and identify the Competent Authorities, SAR Agencies and Rescue Coordination Centers of each Party.
- The agreement will provide guidance on the conduct of SAR operations and cooperation between the SAR agencies.
- At the insistence of the Russian Federation, the agreement will be legally binding once it enters into force, as Russia desires to submit the agreement to the Duma. The United States will conclude the agreement as an executive agreement, in implementation of the IMO SAR and ICAO Chicago Conventions.

---

[65] R. Boswell, 'U.S. waking up to Arctic competition: Coast Guard chief,' *available at* http://www.canada.com/topics/news/story.html?id=9e1b3f2b-513a-4335-9be4-f3907adae7d7; M. Baldino, 'Coast Guard warmly welcomed in Alaska's Arctic,' *available at* http://www.ktuu.com/Global/story.asp?S=8816794; USCG Press Release, 'Coast Guard Conducts First SAREX in the Arctic Ocean,' 27 Aug. 2008, *available at* http://www.uscgalaska.com/go/doc/780/222426; A. Bailey, 'Barrow welcomes Coast Guard presence,' 13 *Petroleum News*, No. 33, week of 17 Aug. 2008, *available at* http://petroleumnews.com/pnarchpop/080815-15.html; 'Coast Guard continues Arctic Domain Awareness flights,' *Coast Guard News*, 16 Oct. 2008, *available at* http://coastguardnews.com/coast-guard-continues-arctic-domain-awareness-flights/2008/10/16/; USCG Press Release, 'Coast Guard conducts Arctic Domain Awareness flight to assess safety of Russian researchers 560 miles from Point Barrow,' 19 May 2010, *available at* http://www.piersystem.com/go/doc/780/555551.

[66] USCG press releases, 'Coast Guard Continues Operation Salliq Above Arctic Circle,' 8 Aug. 2008, *available at* http://www.uscgalaska.com/go/doc/780/220111/USCG press release; 'U.S. to Commence Homeland Security Patrols in the Arctic,' 21 Aug. 2008, *available at* http://www.uscgalaska.com/go/doc/780/221596. For more information and imagery regarding the U.S. Coast Guard in the Arctic, *see* 'Arctic Awareness,' *available at* www.uscgalaska.com/go/page/780/40903. *See also* A. McCullough, Assessing the polar problem,' *Navy Times*, 25 Aug. 2008 and S. Gvozdas, 'Allen takes steps to prepare for open Arctic waters,' *Navy Times*, 7 Sep. 2009, 25.

Draft Lines of Delimitation and National Application

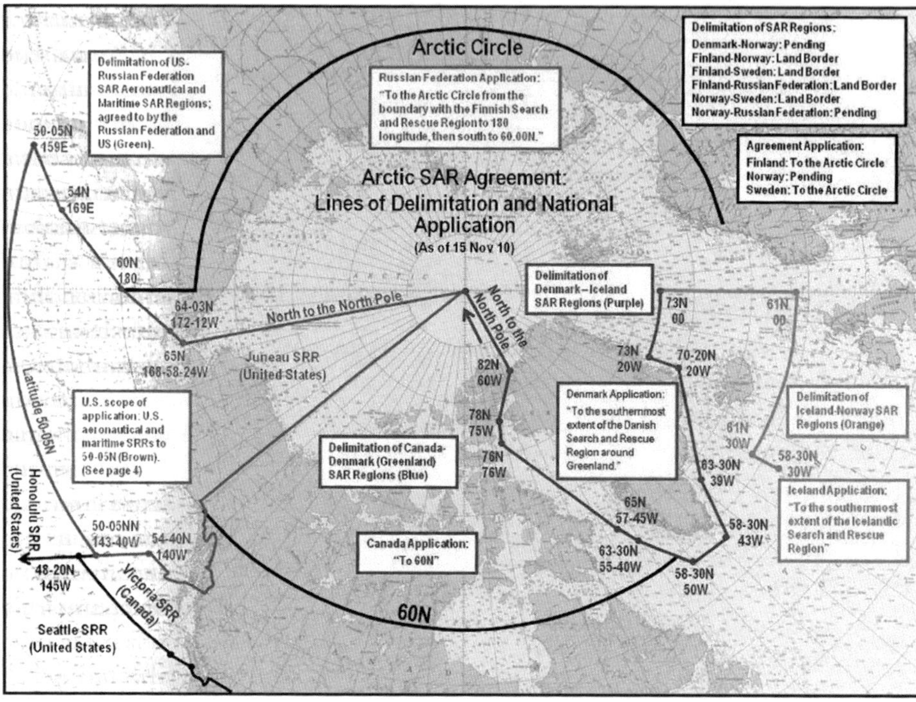

Fig. 5. Source: U.S. Department of State (L/OES)

- While the agreement will not enter into force until 30 days after the last of the eight Arctic Council Member States consent to be bound, they may individually choose to provisionally apply the agreement until that time.

Like all maritime SAR agreements, it should be forwarded to the IMO for publication in a SAR circular.[67]

Arctic Maritime Safety Information Services

The IMO's Sub-committee on Radio communications and Search and Rescue (COMSAR), in liaison with the IHO and WMO, have developed new areas in Arctic waters for expansion of the World-Wide Navigational Warning Service (WWNWS) to provide navigational, meteorological and other (including SAR) information. This is being done through the establishment of a common Maritime

[67] IMO SAR Convention, annex para. 2.1.4.

Safety Information (MSI) broadcast system for the Arctic.[68] The principal work has been done through a joint IMO/IHO/WMO Correspondence Group on Arctic MSI Services.[69] The system was tested in the 2009–2010 timeframe with a view to it becoming fully operational in 2011.[70]

Previously in 2010, the IMO, the IHO, and the WMO announced the establishment of five new Arctic NAVAREAs/METAREAs as part of the expansion of the IMO/IHO WWNWS into Arctic waters. The limits of the new Arctic NAVAREA/METAREAs are identified below. Effective 1 July 2010, an International SafetyNET Service for broadcasting navigational warnings and meteorological warnings and forecasts in the English language was declared to be in an "Initial Operational Capability" (IOC) for these waters with a transition to "Full Operational Capability" (FOC) on 1 June 2011.[71]

During the IOC period, these Arctic NAVAREA/METAREAs will be providing navigational warnings and meteorological warnings and forecasts on an intermittent and test basis. The broadcasting of SafetyNET messages to the new Arctic NAVAREA/METAREAs will be addressed to rectangular area(s) until the SafetyNET receiver modifications with the inclusion of the NAVAREA/ METAREAs boundary limits and its identification are in place. Reception of rectangular addressed messages should be automatic providing the ship's position is inside the addressed area. However, mariners are advised to check their manufacturer's operation manuals to obtain information on the setting of their EGC receivers to receive relevant SafetyNET messages.

The Arctic NAVAREA Co-ordinators and METAREA Issuing Services are:

NAVAREA/METAREA XVII – Canada
NAVAREA/METAREA XVIII – Canada
NAVAREA/METAREA XIX – Norway
NAVAREA/METAREA XX – Russian Federation
NAVAREA/METAREA XXI – Russian Federation.

In May 2010, the IMO published the third revision of the International Safety NET Manual, as prepared by the IHO, WMO and International Maritime

[68] *See* 'Updates agreed on MSI and navigational warning services,' *IMO News*, No. 2, 2008, at 19–20 (reporting results of the 12th meeting of the Sub-Committee on Radio-communications and Search and Rescue (COMSAR 12)), *available at* http://www.imo.org.

[69] *See* IMO documents COMSAR 13/3/4, COMSAR 13/WP.3 Section 3, COMSAR 13/14, paras. 3.13–3.22, COMSAR 14/3/7.

[70] IMO document COMSAR 13/14, para. 3.21.7; COMSAR 14/3/7.

[71] IHO, 'Establishment of Arctic Marine Safety Information Services: 5 new Arctic NAVAREAs/ METAREAs,' 19 Aug. 2010, *available at* http://www.iho-ohi.net/mtg_docs/com_wg/CPRNW/ CPRNW_Misc/Arctic_Announcement.pdf.

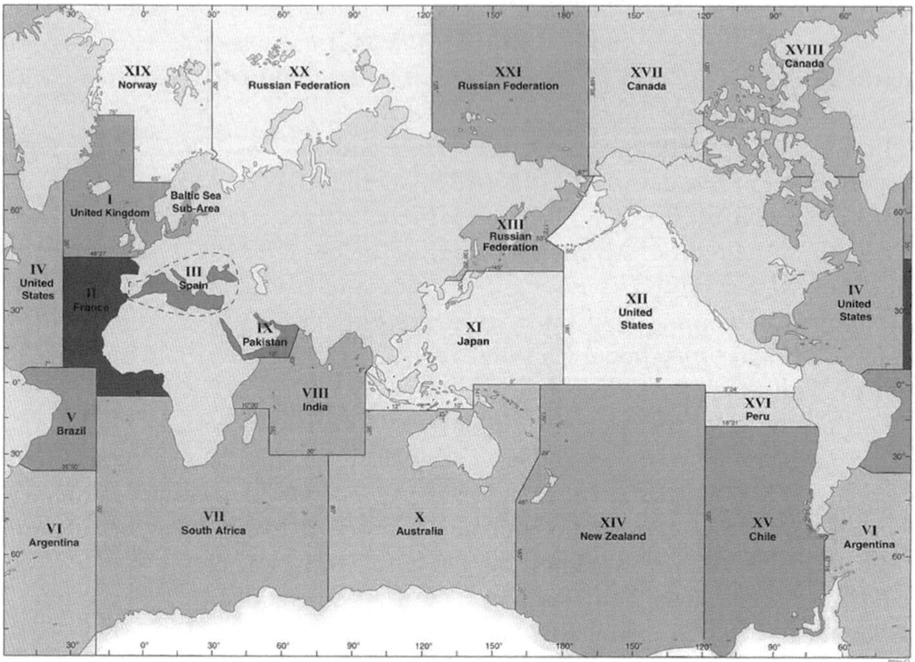

Fig. 6. NAVAREAS for coordinating and promulgating radio navigational warnings under the World-Wide Navigational Warning Service. Source: IMO doc. MSC.1/Circ. 1310, Annex page 9, 8 June 2009. The delimitation of such areas is not related to and shall not prejudice the delimitation of any boundaries between States.

Satellite Organization (IMSO),[72] and published the revised Joint IHO/IMO/WMO Manual on Maritime Safety Information on 8 June 2010.[73]

Unilateral Regulation: NORDREG and the Northern Sea Route

Both Canada and Russia have enacted domestic legislation and adopted regulations governing navigation through their waters, without seeking international approval. Many of these regulations are inconsistent with the provisions of the Law of the Sea Convention and IMO requirements.[74]

---

[72] IMO, *Revised International SafetyNET Manual*, 3rd rev., MSC.1/Circ. 1364, 24 May 2010, *available at* https://www.bimco.org/~/media/2010/BIMCO_News/Technical/MSC1-Circ1364-SafetyNET_manual.ashx.

[73] IMO, *Revised Joint IMPO/IHO/WMO Manual on Maritime Safety Information (MSI)*, MSC.1/Circ.1310, 8 June 2010, *available at* http://www.jcomm.info/index.php?option=com_oe&task=viewDocumentRecord&docID=6062.

[74] *See* the comparison by V.M. Santos-Pedro, 'Arctic Legal Landscape: Canada/Russia/International,' IMO World Maritime Day, Halifax, Nova Scotia, Canada, Nov. 2008, *available*

Canada

Canadian legislation in the Arctic began in 1970 with enactment of the Arctic Waters Pollution Prevention Act, and adoption of its implementing regulations, and adoption of straight baselines around the arctic archipelago. International reaction to these unilateral actions is well documented and need not be repeated here.[75] Rather, the focus here is on the most recent unilateral Canadian action to impose mandatory ship reporting on all ships seeking to navigate through Canadian arctic waters and its implications for the Polar Code.

NORDREG

On 27 August 2008, Canadian Prime Minister Harper announced plans to make the existing voluntary Arctic Ship Reporting System (NORDREG)[76] mandatory, and extend the geographic scope of its application to Canada's full Arctic 200-nautical mile EEZ.[77] The amendments contained in Bill C-3 received royal assent on 11 June 2009, and came into force on 1 August 2009.[78] The implementing regulations, and thus the mandatory requirements, came into force 1 July 2010. The geographic area of the NORDREG Zone, in which mandatory ship reporting is now required, includes not only the Canadian EEZ in the Arctic, but also the waters of Canada's Arctic archipelago, including the seven routes of the Northwest Passage.[79]

---

at http://www.tc.gc.ca/media/documents/marinesafety/santos-pedro_e.ppt, and criticisms by J. Kraska, 'International Law and National Strategy: Anti-Access and Area Denial,' in: L.D. Simmons (ed.), *Climate & Energy Symposium Proceedings on Climate & Energy: Imperatives for Future Naval Forces 23–24 Mar. 2010*, (John Hopkins Applied Physics Laboratory, 2010), pp. 223–238, *available at* http://www.jhuapl.edu/ClimateAndEnergy/Book/Author/Kraska.pdf.

75 J.A. Roach and R.W. Smith, *United States Responses to Excessive Maritime Claims* (2d ed., The Hague, Martinus Nijhoff, 1996), pp. 117–121.

76 'Canada Annual Notice to Mariners 2008,' section 6.1, *available at* http://www.notmar.gc.ca/eng/services/2008-annual/section-a/notice-6.pdf; Canadian Coast Guard, Radio Aids to Marine Navigation (Atlantic, St. Lawrence, Great Lakes, Lake Winnipeg and Eastern Arctic), 'Annual Edition 2006,' Part 3, *available at* http://dsp-psd.pwgsc.gc.ca/Collection/T51-4-2006E-3.pdf; *Arctic Ice Regime Shipping System Standards*, Transport Canada publication TP 12259E (1988), *available at* http://www.tc.gc.ca/MarineSafety/TP/tp12259.htm.

77 Prime Minister of Canada, 'PM Announces Government of Canada Will Extend Jurisdiction over Arctic Waters,' Press Release, 27 Aug. 2008, *available at* http://www.conservative.ca/EN/1091/101728 *and* http://www.pm.gc.ca.

78 Transport Canada, 'The Government of Canada takes action to protect Canada's Arctic waters and enhance northern sovereignty,' News Release No. H 088/09, 17 June 2009, *available at* http://www.tc.gc.ca/mediaroom/releases/nat/2009/09-h088e.htm, *and* 'Legislation to protect Canada's Arctic waters comes into force,' News Release No. H 110/09, 6 Aug. 2009, *available at* http://www.tc.gc.ca/mediaroom/releases/nat/2009/09-h110e.htm.

79 Transport Canada, 'Government of Canada Takes Action to Protect Canadian Arctic Waters,' Press Release No. H078/10, 22 June 2010, *available at* http://www.tc.gc.ca/eng/mediaroom/releases-2010-h078e-6019.htm.

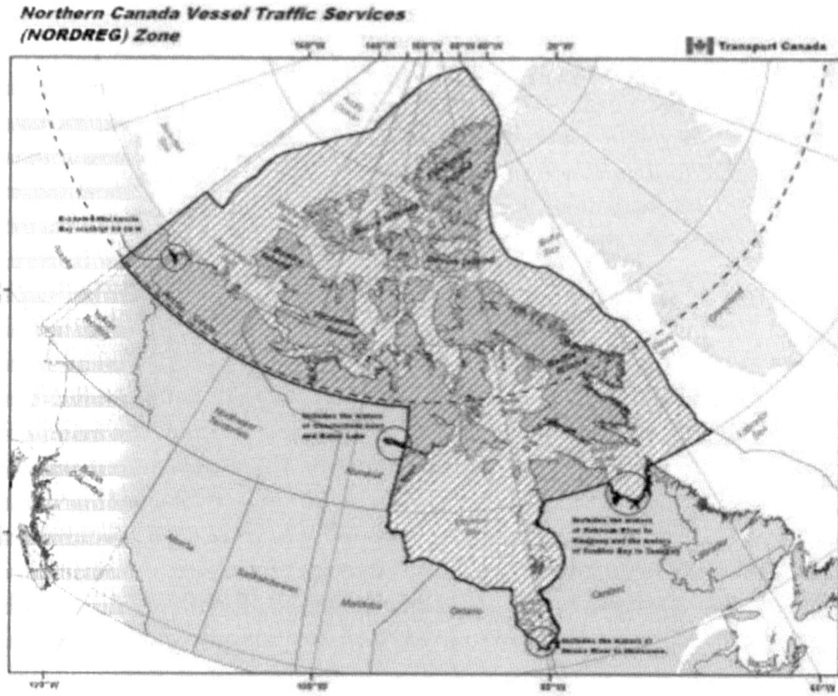

Fig. 7. Source: Transport Canada Press Release No. H078/10 Backgrounder, 22 June 2010.<http://www.tc.gc.ca/eng/mediaroom/releases-2010-h078e-6019.htm>

This unilateral action by the Government of Canada has been criticized by the United States, other Member States and industry, and was the subject of discussion at recent meetings of the IMO's Sub-committee on the Safety of Navigation[80] and the Maritime Safety Committee.[81] The criticism is grounded in Canada's failure to follow the requirements of SOLAS, particularly regulation V/11, Ship-reporting systems, and regulation V/12, Vessel traffic services, and the IMO and IALA implementing guidance.[82]

Canada has justified its unilateral action on the basis of article 234, Ice-covered areas, of the Law of the Sea Convention, which provides:[83]

[80] Report of the 56th Meeting, NAV 56/20, paras. 19.21–19.24, 31 Aug. 2010.

[81] INTERTANKO and U.S. joint submission, MSC 88/11/2, 22 Sep. 2010, and Report of the 88th session, MSC 88/26, paras. 11.28–11.39 and Annexes 27 (statement of Canada) and 29 (statement of Singapore). At MSC 88 Canada sought but did not receive the Committee's recognition of the mandatory system. MSC 88/26, para. 11.39.

[82] IMO resolution A.851(20) and MSC/Circ.1060; IALA Guideline No. 1071; and IALA, *VTS Manual* (2008 ed.).

[83] NAV 56/20, para. 19.22; MSC 88/11/3, Oct. 5, 2010; SN.1/Circ. 291, 5 Oct. 2010, Information on the Mandatory Canadian Ship Reporting System in Canada's Northern Waters (NORDREG).

> *Coastal States have the right to adopt and enforce non-discriminatory laws and regulations for the prevention, reduction and control of marine pollution from vessels in ice-covered areas within the limits of the exclusive economic zone, where particularly severe climatic conditions and the presence of ice covering such areas for most of the year create obstructions or exceptional hazards to navigation, and pollution of the marine environment could cause major harm to or irreversible disturbance of the ecological balance. Such laws and regulations shall have due regard to navigation and the protection and preservation of the marine environment based on the best available scientific evidence.*

Whether article 234 provides sufficient justification is the subject of Professor McDorman's paper which follows. At one level of analysis, article 234 seems to apply only in the EEZ, which Canada claims is seaward of its straight baselines enclosing its arctic archipelago, and only in "ice-covered areas within the limits of the exclusive economic zone, where particularly severe climatic conditions and the presence of ice covering such areas for most of the year create obstructions or exceptional hazards to navigation…". Query whether those climatic requirements for ice-covered areas are now met in the NORDREG Zone.

Regardless of the geographic and climatic scope of application of article 234 of the Law of the Sea Convention, the relationship between that article and SOLAS regulations V/8-1 (now V/11) and V/12 needs to be examined under the law of treaties, reflected in the Vienna Convention on the Law of Treaties.[84] Canada is a party to both the Law of the Sea Convention and SOLAS. Under article 30(3) of the Vienna Convention, "the earlier treaty applies only to the extent that its provisions are compatible with those of the later treaty."

A former deputy legal adviser of the UK Foreign and Commonwealth Office, and author of a book on modern treaty law and practice, has written, "indetermining which treaty is the earlier and which is the later, the relevant date is the date of adoption, not entry into force.… The obligations under Article 30 apply to a state only as from the date is becomes a party to the treaty."[85]

In this context, the Law of the Sea Convention is the earlier treaty, as it was adopted on 10 December 1982, while SOLAS regulation V/8-1 was adopted on 23 May 1994[86] and regulations V/11 and V/12 were adopted on 5 December 2000.[87] Canada became a party to the Law of the Sea Convention on

[84] Vienna Convention on the Law of Treaties, Vienna, 23 May 1969, 1115 UNTS 331, *available at* http://untreaty.un.org/ilc/texts/instruments/english/conventions/1_1_1969.pdf.

[85] A. Aust, *Modern Treaty Law and Practice* (2d ed., Cambridge, Cambridge University Press, 2007), p. 229.

[86] IMO resolution MSC.31(63), MSC 63/23/Add.1 Annex 2, pp. 2–3, *available at* http://www5.imo.org/SharePoint/blastDataHelper.asp/data_id%3D15391/31%2863%29.pdf.

[87] IMO resolution MSC.99(73), MSC 73/21/Add.2 Annex 7, pp. 128–130, *available at* http://www.navcen.uscg.gov/pdf/marcomms/imo/msc_resolutions/MSC73-21a2-7.pdf.

17 November 2003.[88] If and when the Polar Code is adopted in a mandatory form, it too will be the later treaty.

Since SOLAS regulations V/8-1, V/11 and V/12, and the Polar Code, are setting international rules and standards, and as they are *lex specialis*, "a special rule prevails over a general rule,"[89] article 234 would not permit Canada to enact exceptions to them.

However, SOLAS regulations V/8-1(j)(V/11(9)) and V/12(5) also provide that "[n]othing in this regulation . . . shall prejudice the rights and duties of Governments under international law". Aust states that this provision means that "[t]he treaty is subordinate to an earlier one".[90] If his analysis is correct, then article 234 still lives! But then the geographic and climatic scope of application of article 234 becomes important to resolve.

Russian Federation – Northern Sea Route

Russia has an extensive regulatory system for navigation of the waterways of the Northern Sea Route. These include the Regulations for Navigation on the Seaways of the Northern Sea Route;[91] Regulations for Icebreaker-Assisted Pilotage of Vessels on the Northern Sea Route, 1996;[92] and the Requirements for Design, Equipment, and Supply of Vessels Navigating the Northern Sea Route;[93] as well as a Guide to Navigation through the Northern Sea Route, 1996.[94] The compatibility of the Russian unilateral actions with international law has similarly been the subject of international attention[95] and need not be

---

88 http://www.un.org/Depts/los/reference_files/status2010.pdf.

89 Aust, *supra* note 85, p. 249.

90 *Id.* at 220, quoting article 4 of the 1995 Fish Stocks Agreement.

91 USSR Minister of Merchant Marine, 'Rules of Navigation: Regulations for Navigation on the Seaways of the Northern Sea Route,' 14 Sep. 1990, *available at* http://www.morflot.ru/about/sevmorput/en/RULES OF NAVIGATION.doc.

92 Summarized in *The Northern Sea Route: The Shortest sea route linking East Asia and Europe* (Tokyo, Ship and Ocean Foundation, 2001), pp. 84–85, *available at* http://www.sof.or.jp/en/report/pdf/200103_rp_ar0103e.pdf.

93 'Requirements for the Design, Equipment and Supply of Vessels Navigating the Northern Sea Route,' in: Mulherin, Sodhi, Smallidge, *Northern Sea Route and Icebreaking Technology: An Overview of Current Conditions*, (U.S. Army Corps of Engineers Cold Regions Research & Engineering Laboratory, June 1994), Appendix C, pp. 140–149, *available at* http://www.crrel.usace.army.mil/library/crrelreports/NSR.pdf. These requirements are summarized in *The Northern Sea Route: The Shortest sea route linking East Asia and Europe*, pp. 81–84, *supra* note 92.

94 The table of contents is listed in *The Northern Sea Route: The Shortest sea route linking East Asia and Europe*, p. 226, *supra* note 92.

95 *See passim* R.D. Brubaker, *The Russian Arctic Straits* (The Hague, Nijhoff, 2005); Erik Franckx, *The Legal Regime of Navigation in the Russian Arctic*, 18 J. Transnat'l L. & Pol'y 327 (2009), *available at* http://www.law.fsu.edu/journals/transnational/vol 18_2/franckx.pdf; and

repeated here. Like Canada, Russia has also adopted an extensive system of straight baselines along its Arctic coast (and elsewhere), which has attracted international objections.[96]

What is perhaps most worth following is what effect on these regulations results from adoption in 1998 of the Federal Act on the international maritime waters, territorial sea and contiguous zone of the Russian Federation.[97] Article 14 of this act, entitled Navigation along the waterways of the Northern Sea Route, provides:

> *Navigation on the waterways of the Northern Sea Route, the historical national unified transport line of communication of the Russian Federation in the Arctic, including the Vilkitsky, Shokalshy, Dmitry Laptev and Sannikov straits, shall be carried out in accordance with this Federal Act, other federal laws and* ***the international treaties to which the Russian Federation is a party*** *and the regulations on navigation on the watercourses of the Northern Sea Route approved by the Government of the Russian Federation and published in* Notices to Mariners. (Emphasis added.)

The relevant international treaties to which Russia is a party are, of course, the Law of the Sea Convention, and the various IMO Conventions and Codes, and when adopted, the mandatory Polar Code. It was reported in 2009 that these regulations were being revised by the Duma.[98] It is to be hoped that the revisions of the 1990 Regulations will bring them into conformity with these international agreements.

Conclusions

While there have been considerable developments over the past year in enhancing the safety of navigation in Arctic waters, the increasing pace of transpolar shipping raises questions as to whether these developments are occurring fast

---

summarized in The Northern Sea Route: The Shortest sea route linking East Asia and Europe, pp. 85–86, *supra* note 92.

[96] W.M. Reismanand G.S. Westerman, *Straight Baselines in International Maritime Boundary Delimitation* (New York, St. Martin's Press, 1992), pp. 150–151; Roach and Smith, *supra* note 75, at 100.

[97] 'Federal Act on the internal maritime waters, territorial sea and contiguous zone of the Russian Federation,' adopted by the State Duma on 16 July 1998 and approved by the Federation Council on 17 July 1998, *available at* http://www.un.org/Depts/los/LEGISLATIONANDTREATIES/PDFFILES/RUS_1998_Act_TS.pdf. The Act closely follows the relevant provisions of the Law of the Sea Convention, including the provisions on baselines contained in article 4 of the Act.

[98] *Barents Observer*, 'Russia prepared law on Northern Sea Route,' 13 Feb. 2009, *available at* http://www.barentsobserver.com/index.php?id=4557561. The author has located no further information on this effort.

enough. Since speeding up the pace of international regulatory developments does not seem feasible, industry should restrain its use of Arctic waters in the short term and take increased actions to minimize the risk of harm to the Arctic waters. The four groundings during the 2010 summer in the Arctic should be sufficient warning.[99]

[99] On 8 August 2010, a Canadian-flag tanker ran aground in a harbor near Pangnirtung, Baffin Island. 'Third vessel in less than a month to run aground in northern Canada Arctic region,' *Merco Press*, 4 Sep. 2010, *available at* http://en.mercopress.com/2010/09/04/third-vessel-in-less-than-a-month-to-run-aground-in-north-canada-arctic-region. The Bahamian-flag cruise ship *Clipper Adventurer* grounded in Canadian waters near Coppermine, Nunavut on 29 August 2010. J. Walker, 'Clipper Adventurer Cruise Ship Runs Aground in the Arctic,' *Cruise Law News*, *available at* http://www.cruiselawnews.com/2010/08/articles/sinking/clipper-adventurer-cruise-ship-runs-aground-in-the-arctic/. On 1 September 2010, the Canadian-flag loaded fuel tanker *Nanny* ran aground on a sand bar southwest of Gjoa Haven, Nunavut. J. Jones, 'Fuel tanker runs aground in Canadian Arctic,' *Reuters*, 2 Sep. 2010, *available at* http://www.reuters.com/article/idUSTRE68164I20100902. On 30 June 2010, the Barbados-flag cruise ship *Polar Star* ran aground off Hormsund, southern Spitsbergen. 'Cruise vessel aground in Arctic with passengers aboard,' *Maritime Bulletin*, 1 July 2010, *available at* http://www.odin.tc/eng/articles/417-Cruise-vessel-aground-in-Arctic-with-passengers-on-board.asp.

NATIONAL MEASURES FOR THE SAFETY OF NAVIGATION IN ARCTIC WATERS: NORDREG, ARTICLE 234 AND CANADA

Ted L. McDorman[1]

Abstract

In August 2008, Canada's Prime Minister announced the intention to extend the reach of the Arctic Waters Pollution Prevention Act (AWPPA) from 100-n. miles to 200-n. miles (consistent with Canada's Arctic Exclusive Economic Zone (EEZ)) and to make it mandatory (rather than voluntary as the system then was) that commercial vessels about to enter the shipping safety control zones in the Arctic (the Northern Canada Vessel Traffic Services (NORDREG) Zone) report to and receive clearance from Canadian authorities.

The amendment to the AWPPA came into force in August 2009. The regulations making NORDREG mandatory came into effect on 1 July 2010.

The mandatory reporting of commercial vessels part of the revisions to the NORDREG regime attracted some attention. The United States and others, while generally supportive of enhanced protection of the Arctic marine environment, have raised some questions about the necessity of having the new measures dealt with by the International Maritime Organization (IMO). Canada has indicated that the new measures are both consistent with the relevant IMO instruments and supported by Article 234 of the U.N. Convention on the Law of the Sea (the Arctic waters provision) such that the NORDREG measures need not be dealt with by the IMO.

Setting the Stage

In August 2008, Canada's Prime Minister announced the intention to extend the reach of the Arctic Waters Pollution Prevention Act (AWPPA)[2] from 100-n. miles to 200-n. miles (consistent with Canada's Arctic Exclusive Economic Zone (EEZ).[3] It was also announced that Canada intended to make it mandatory for most non-government vessels about to enter into Canada's

---

[1] Faculty of Law, University of Victoria, Victoria, B.C., Canada.

[2] Arctic Waters Pollution Prevention Act, *Revised Statutes of Canada 1985*, ch. A-12, as amended.

[3] Canada, "PM Announces Government of Canada Will Extend Jurisdiction over Arctic Waters," 27 August 2008, Press Release from Prime Minister of Canada, available at <pm .gc.ca/eng/media.asp?id=2248> (23 January 2011) and "Backgrounder – Extending the Jurisdiction of Canadian Environment and Shipping Laws in the Arctic," 27 August 2008, Prime Minister of Canada, available at <pm.gc.ca/eng/media.asp?id=2246> (23 January 2011).

shipping safety control zones in the Arctic area, which include all the waters covered by the AWPPA, to report and receive clearance from Canadian authorities. The amendment to the AWPPA came into force in August 2009.[4] The regulations making vessel reporting in the Arctic mandatory came into effect on 1 July 2010.[5]

Canada had long had in place a voluntary system of ship-reporting and vessel services covering Canada's Arctic waters, known as NORDREG, which applied to vessels over 300 gross tones and vessels carrying pollutants or dangerous goods as cargo.[6] It was claimed that there existed a near 100% vessel compliance rate with the voluntary NORDREG system.[7] Nevertheless, there had been numerous calls within Canada for making NORDREG mandatory.[8] The announcement of the shift from the voluntary NORDREG ship reporting system to the mandatory NORDREG ship reporting system was embedded as part of Canada's Northern Strategy:[9]

- to acquire better knowledge of shipping activity in Canada's Arctic waters;
- to enhance protection of Canada's Arctic waters from vessels inappropriately prepared for Arctic conditions;

[4] An Act to amend the Arctic Waters Pollution Prevention Act, *Statutes of Canada 2009*, ch. 11, sec. 1.

[5] Northern Canada Vessel Traffic Services Zone Regulations, *Canada Gazette Part II*, Vol. 144, No. 13, 23 June 2010 and Order Amending the Shipping Safety Control Zones Order, *Canada Gazette Part II*, Vol. 144, No. 13, 23 June 2010.

[6] Since 1977 Canada has had a voluntary ship reporting system in place for its Arctic waters up to 100-n. miles. See: Northern Canada Vessel Traffic Services Zone Regulations, *supra* note 5, "Regulatory Impact Analysis Statement;" Transport Canada, *User Assistance Package for the Implementation of Arctic Ice Regime Shipping System – AIRSS*, (TP 12819 E, 1998), section 4; and D. Pharand, 'The Arctic Waters and the Northwest Passage: A Final Revisit', 38 *Ocean Development and International Law* (2007), 49–50.

[7] As reported in Canada, "Rising to the Arctic Challenge: Report on the Canadian Coast Guard," Report of the Standing Senate Committee on Fisheries and Oceans, (40th Parliament, 2nd Session, 2009), at 58 citing directly statements from Transport Canada officials and Pharand, *supra* note 6, at 49 based on officials from Transport Canada.

[8] See: Canada, "The Coast Guard in Canada's Arctic: Interim Report," Report of the Standing Senate Committee on Fisheries and Oceans, (39th Parliament, 2nd Session, 2008), at 40 and the Committee's Final Report, "Rising to the Arctic Challenge," *supra* note 7, at 67 and 69; Pharand, *supra* note 6, at 49–50; F. Griffiths, 'The Shipping News: Canada's Arctic is Not on Thinning Ice', 58 *International Journal* (2003), 272; and S. Lalonde, 'Increased Traffic through Canadian Arctic Waters: Canada's State of Readiness', 38 *Revue Juridique Themis* (2008), 121–123.

[9] See: Canada, Minister of Indian Affairs and Northern Development, *Canada's Northern Strategy: Our North, Our Heritage, Our Future* (Ottawa, 2009), at 12 and Canada, "Statement on Canada's Arctic Foreign Policy: Exercising Sovereignty and Promoting Canada's Northern Strategy Abroad" (Ottawa, 2010), at 15.

- to enhance protection of Canada's Arctic waters from marine environmental pollution; and
- as part of a policy to assert "sovereignty" over Canada's Arctic waters.

An important feature of the NORDREG vessel reporting and traffic management system is that it applies to all Canadian Arctic waters, which includes:

- the waters within the Canadian Arctic archipelago, asserted by Canada as being historic internal waters;[10]
- the territorial sea adjacent to the baselines which delineate Canada's historic internal waters;[11] and
- the waters adjacent to the territorial sea out to 200-n. miles from the baselines which delineate Canada's historic internal waters.

The waters covered include the various routes that together are considered the Northwest Passage. A dispute exists, primarily between the United States and Canada, respecting the international legal status of the Northwest Passage as being either a strait used for international navigation (the US view) or historic internal waters through which no passage right exists (the Canadian view).[12] The "trigger" of this dispute has always been whether permission is (the Canadian view) or is not (the US view) required for vessels to utilize the waters of the Northwest Passage.[13] Further, neither the United States nor the European Union accept the international legal validity of Canada's Arctic baselines or the legal effect of the baselines as delineating historic internal waters.[14] Thus, the making of the NORDREG vessel reporting and traffic system mandatory came with baggage and an expectation of concern being raised internationally.[15]

---

[10] Canada, Department of External Affairs, Letter, 17 December 1973, reproduced in 12 *Canadian Yearbook of International Law* (1974), 279.

[11] The Arctic baselines were established by Canada, Territorial Sea Geographical Coordinates (Area 7) Order, *Canada Gazette Part II*, Vol. 119, 10 September 1985, 3996–4002.

[12] See generally: T.L. McDorman, *Salt Water Neighbors: International Ocean Law Relations between the United States and Canada* (New York: Oxford University Press, 2009), 225–228 and 233–244 and T.L. McDorman, 'The Northwest Passage: International Law, Politics and Cooperation', in M.H. Nordquist, J.N. Moore and T.H. Heidar (eds.), *Changes in the Arctic Environment and the Law of the Sea* (Leiden: Martinus Nijhoff, 2010), at 227–250.

[13] McDorman, *Salt Water Neighbors*, *supra* note 12, at 225.

[14] United States, "Letter from J.W. Dyer, Acting Assistant Secretary of State, Legislative and Intergovernmental Affairs to Senator C. McC. Mathias, Jr.," 26 February 1986, in J.A. Roach and R.W. Smith (eds.), *United States Responses to Excessive Maritime Claims* (The Hague: Martinus Nijhoff, 2nd ed., 1996), at 118 and British High Commission, Note No. 90/86, 9 July 1986 reprinted in part in Roach and Smith, at 121.

[15] See the comments attributed to Transport Canada officials in 2008 in "The Coast Guard in Canada's Arctic: Interim Report," *supra* note 8, at 32 and the comments of Prime Minister

At the time of Canada's announcement of the intention to make the NORDREG mandatory, the United States made little public comment with the US reaction described by a Canadian official as being "lukewarm" with the concern being that the stricter regulations might unnecessarily impede vessel traffic.[16]

As part of the domestic process of receiving comments on a proposed regulatory change, at least one shipping organization, the Baltic and International Maritime Council (BIMCO),[17] informed the Government of Canada of concerns that the proposed changes could be seen as interfering with innocent passage rights and that the proposed changes could raise issues under various provisions of the International Convention on the Safety of Life at Sea (SOLAS).[18] It was BIMCO's view that the proposed NORDREG regulations should go through the sub-committee for Safety of Navigation of the International Maritime Organization (IMO) as was normally the case for such vessel traffic management and routeing measures.[19]

At the 56th meeting of the IMO sub-committee on Safety and Navigation in the summer of 2010, the United States and BIMCO directly raised questions about Canada's NORDREG vessel reporting system. The United States is reported to have said:

> *The United States did not believe that the new Canadian northern zone regulations were consistent with key law of the sea principles related to freedom of navigation, including the right of innocent passage and the right of transit passage through straits used for navigation.*[20]

Stephen Harper reported in Randy Boswell and Andrew Mayeda, "U.S. concerned with new Canadian shipping rules in Arctic," 28 August 2008, Canwest News Service (no longer available online).

16 Randy Boswell, "Marine shippers pan tough new Arctic vessel regulations," 9 July 2010, Canwest News Service, available at www.canada.com/story_print.html?id=3257058&sponso= (accessed on 27 January 2011). See also: Randy Boswell and Andrew Mayeda, "U.S. concerned with new Canadian shipping rules in Arctic," 28 August 2008, Canwest News Service (no longer available online).

17 See the BIMCO website at www.bimco.org.

18 International Convention for the Safety of Life at Sea (SOLAS), London 1 November 1974, entered into force 25 May 1980, 1184 *U.N.T.S.* 2.

19 Baltic and International Maritime Council (BIMCO), "New Mandatory reporting of ships passing through Canada's Arctic waters," 23 June 2010, available at www.bimco.org/en/Members/News/2010/2010/06/23_New_mandatory_reporting (accessed on 27 January 2011) and Randy Boswell, "Marine shippers pan tough new Arctic vessel regulations," 9 July 2010, Canwest News Service, available at www.canada.com/story_print.html?id=3257058&sponso= (accessed on 27 January 2011).

20 IMO, Sub-Committee on Safety of Navigation, "Report to the Maritime Safety Committee," Doc. NAV/56/20, 31 August 2010 (Report of the 56th session of the Sub-Committee), para. 19.21.

These concerns were brought before the 88th meeting of the IMO Maritime Safety Committee (MSC) held in November/December 2010.

The United States (together with INTERTANKO)[21] made a submission to the MSC which included the comment that at the earlier sub-committee meeting: "concerns were expressed that the provisions on mandatory ship reporting and regulation on transiting vessels raised some critical issues with respect to consistency with international law."[22] The United States proposed that the MSC should:

- "determine" that Canada's NORDREG system has not been established in a manner consistent with the applicable IMO requirements for a "mandatory ship reporting and vessel traffic services system;"
- recommend that ships comply with the NORDREG system on a voluntary basis; and
- "request" Canada to submit an appropriate proposal to IMO if it wishes to make "its ship reporting and vessel traffic services systems mandatory."[23]

It is important to note that the United States expressly supported "Canada's intention to provide for the safety of navigation" in the Arctic area.[24]

In its formal submission to the MSC, Canada asserted that Article 234 of the 1982 UN Convention on the Law of the Sea,[25] the so-called Arctic exception, provided "a complete legal justification in international law for NORDREG,"[26] such that Canada was under no obligation to bring the NORDREG system before the IMO for assessment or approval. It was noted, however, that in October 2010 Canada had provided detailed information to the IMO on the NORDREG ship reporting system and in this document Canada formally sought the "recognition" of the system by the IMO.[27] Canada requested the MSC to "support" the NORDREG initiative.[28]

---

[21] INTERTANKO is the International Association of Independent Tanker Owners. See the organization's website at www.intertanko.com.

[22] United States and INTERTANKO, "Northern Canada Vessel Traffic Services Zone Regulations," IMO Doc. MSC/88/11/2, 22 September 2010, para. 1.

[23] *Ibid.*, para. 10.

[24] *Ibid.*, para. 2.

[25] United Nations Convention on the Law of the Sea, Montego Bay, Jamaica, 10 December 1982, entered into force 16 November 1994, 1833 *U.N.T.S.* 397. The United States is not a party to this Convention. Canada became a party in 2003.

[26] Canada, "Comments on Document MSC 88/11/2," IMO Doc. MSC/88/11/3, 5 October 2010, para. 5.

[27] Canada, "Information on the Mandatory Canadian Ship Reporting System in Canada's Northern Waters (NORDREG)," IMO Doc SN.1/Circ.291, 5 October 2010. See further below at note 45.

[28] Canada, "Comments," *supra* note 26, para. 12.

At the 88th session of the MSC, the submitted documents and the issues therein were discussed. The United States summarized that "it was their opinion that the majority of those who spoke had favoured…" its position "…that the Canadian NORDREG system had not been established in accordance with the IMO requirements…".[29] The meeting report indicates that Germany, while supporting Canada's intentions, "shared the views and concerns expressed by the United States…," in particular, that mandatory ship reporting systems and vessel traffic services had to be assessed through the IMO processes as the IMO was "the only competent organization" to deal with such matters.[30] Singapore indicated that Canada's NORDREG measures had to be consistent with international law and that as a "best practice" ship reporting systems should go through the relevant IMO processes.[31] Singapore further stated:

> *…it was important to ensure that any measures taken did not compromise the freedom of navigation and that it was not clear how NORDREG's proposed requirement for clearance would adequately give "due regard to navigation", as provided for in UNCLOS.*[32]

The Chair of the MSC summarized that "a majority of delegations had expressed appreciation for Canada's efforts while a number expressed the view that Canada should have submitted its proposal to the Organization."[33] On the substance of the discussions, the Chair:

- indicated it was "a legal issue" that was not under the purview of the MSC;
- encouraged the following of the relevant IMO guidelines; and
- noted that the documents highlighted "'ongoing' bilateral discussions."[34]

The invocation by Canada of Article 234 as a "complete legal justification in international law for NORDREG"[35] marks the first time that Canada has directly relied upon Article 234 to support a new initiative in Canada's Arctic waters. It is the application of Article 234 to the NORDREG vessel traffic system that is the central focus of this presentation. Nevertheless, the following section looks at the vessel reporting and traffic measures and the relevant IMO instruments.

29 IMO, "Report of the Maritime Safety Committee on its Eighty-Eighth Session," IMO Doc MSC/88/26, 15 December 2010, para. 11.38.

30 *Ibid.*, para. 11.35.

31 *Ibid.*, para. 11.36.

32 *Ibid.*, para. 11.36. The full text of Singapore's statement is at Annex 28 of IMO, "Report of the 88th Session of the MSC," *supra* note 29.

33 *Ibid.*, para. 11.39.

34 *Ibid.*, para. 11.39.

35 Canada, "Comments," *supra* note 26, para. 5.

Vessel Traffic Measures and the IMO

Not surprisingly, most of the discussion within the IMO forums was about the application or non-application of various provisions of SOLAS that involve ship reporting systems (SOLAS, Chapter V, Regulation 11)[36] and vessel traffic services (SOLAS, Chapter V, Regulation 12).[37]

It is not necessary or the intent here to be exhaustive on these matters.

Canada's view is that the NORDREG scheme is both a ship reporting system and a vessel traffic services regime and that Canada is acting consistent with the relevant SOLAS regulations.[38]

The United States (with INTERTANKO) took the view that since the NORDREG ship reporting system was not submitted to the IMO, the system has not been adopted or recognized by the IMO and thus Canada has not acted consistent with SOLAS, Chapter V, Regulation 11.[39]

In its submission to the MSC, the United States raised many questions about whether the NORDREG system met the criteria and understanding of what is a vessel traffic service or traffic organization system and the uncertainty of the application of the NORDREG system.[40] The United States noted that pursuant to SOLAS, Chapter V, Regulation 12.3, vessel traffic systems can be made mandatory only within the territorial sea of a State and that the NORDREG regime, which clearly applies beyond Canada's territorial sea, appears to be inconsistent with this provision.[41] More generally, it was noted that as regards waters beyond the territorial sea and within an international strait, vessel traffic services (including reporting) can only be made mandatory through approval under SOLAS, Chapter V, Regulation 11 or 12.[42]

Canada in its submission sought to answer some of the technical issues raised respecting the operation of NORDREG.[43] On the issue of bringing NORDREG to the IMO, Canada noted that SOLAS, Chapter V, Regulation 11.4 specifically states that: "Ship reporting systems not submitted to the Organization for adoption do not necessarily need to comply with this regulation" and that "Contracting Governments may submit systems to the Organization for recognition."[44] This explains the language of Canada's October 2010 submission to the IMO respecting NORDREG, which requested IMO "recognition"

---

36 SOLAS, *supra* note 17, Chapter V, Regulation 11 is entitled "Ship Reporting Systems."

37 SOLAS, *supra* note 17, Chapter V, Regulation 11 is entitled "Vessel Traffic Services."

38 Canada, "Comments", *supra* note 26, paras. 5 and 6.

39 United States, "Northern Canada VTS Regulations," *supra* note 22, paras. 3 and 10.

40 *Ibid.*, paras. 7–9.

41 *Ibid.*, para. 4.

42 *Ibid.*, para. 5.

43 Canada, "Comments," *supra* note 26, paras. 5–9.

44 *Ibid.*, paras. 4 and 5.

of NORDREG.[45] The United States made it clear that this "recognition" was not an assessment by the IMO of the legitimacy or the legal validity of the NORDREG system.[46] Canada also pointed out that in both Regulations 11 and 12 is the identical paragraph:

> *Nothing in this regulation...shall prejudice the rights and duties of Governments under international law....*"[47]

Canada's view was that its rights under Article 234 of the LOS Convention take precedence over the relevant provisions of the SOLAS Regulations and that nothing in the SOLAS Chapter V, Regulations "prejudice" its rights under Article 234.[48] The result being, according to Canada, that the NORDREG system is exempt from SOLAS Chapter V, Regulations 11 and 12 and that Canada is under no obligation to submit the NORDREG system to the IMO.

According to the meeting record, the United States did not engage in a discussion of the role of Article 234. Only Singapore made direct reference to Article 234. In its statement, Singapore commented:

> *[I]t is not readily apparent how the mandatory ship reporting and VTS system established under NORDREG ties in with the fundamental purpose of Article 234..., which is to allow for the prevention, reduction and control of marine pollution. The need for such a mandatory system should be supported by the best available evidence.*
> ...
> *Even though Article 234 allows the coastal State to impose measures that would prevent, reduce and control marine pollution, these are to be done with "due regard to navigation." It is, however, not clear to my delegation how the proposed requirement for clearance would adequately give "due regard to navigation."*[49]

It is reasonable to assess that for the United States and the others having the NORDREG system go through the IMO process, even if it were unchanged during the process, could provide comfort based on the same 'shall nor prejudice' provision in SOLAS Chapter V, Regulations 11 and 12[50] that Canada relied upon to apply Article 234. The NORDREG system going through the IMO process, for example, would not prejudice the international legal issue

[45] Canada, "Information on NORDREG," *supra* note 27. See also: Canada, "Comments", *supra* note 26, para. 4.

[46] IMO, "Report of the 88th Session of the MSC," *supra* note 29, para. 11.38 and see *supra* note 27.

[47] SOLAS, *supra* note 18, Regulation 11.9 and Regulation 12.5. Canada, "Comments", *supra* note 26, para. 5.

[48] Canada, "Comments," *supra* note 26, para. 5.

[49] Singapore, "Statement to MSC," *supra* note 32 and IMO, "Report of the 88th Session of the MSC," *supra* note 29, para. 11. 36.

[50] SOLAS, *supra* note 18, Regulation 11.9 and Regulation 12.5.

regarding the status of the Northwest Passage. It is less clear or certain that the same "without prejudice" results arise if the NORDREG system does not go through the IMO process.

Article 234

Article 234 provides:

> *Coastal States have the right to adopt and enforce non-discriminatory laws and regulations for the prevention, reduction and control of marine pollution from vessels in ice-covered areas within the limits of the exclusive economic zone, where particularly severe climatic conditions and the presence of ice covering such areas for most of the year create obstructions or exceptional hazards to navigation, and pollution of the marine environment could cause major harm to or irreversible disturbance of the ecological balance. Such laws and regulations shall have due regard to navigation and the protection and preservation of the marine environment based on the best available scientific evidence.*

As already stated, Canada's position was that "Article 234 provides a complete legal justification in international law for NORDREG."[51] Canada set out an explanation of the link between the mandatory NORDREG system and the "prevention, reduction and control of marine pollution from vessels in ice-covered areas... where particularly severe climatic conditions and the presence of ice covering... create obstructions or exceptional hazards to navigation" stating that "The probability of an incident and the associated risk of environmental damage increases with traffic."[52]

The negotiation of Article 234 during the Third United Nations Convention on the Law of the Sea (UNCLOS III) has been meticulously examined and studied by other (mostly Canadian) authors.[53] There is general accord that from a coastal State perspective there are two critical elements of the provision:

- a coastal State <u>can</u> adopt and enforce within its 200-nautical mile zone laws containing more stringent standards than the existing internationally accepted rules;[54] and

[51] Canada, "Comments," *supra* note 26, para. 5.

[52] *Ibid.*, para. 2.

[53] See, in particular, D. McRae, 'The Negotiation of Article 234,' in F. Griffiths (ed.), *Politics of the Northwest Passage* (Montreal: McGill-Queen's University Press, 1987), 98–114 and K. Bartenstein, 'The "Arctic Exception" in the Law of the Sea Convention: A Contribution to Safer Navigation in the Northwest Passage?' 42 *Ocean Development and International Law* (2011) (in press), galley proof pages 2–6.

[54] S. Rosenne and A. Yankov, *United Nations Convention on the Law of the Sea 1982: A Commentary*, Vol. IV (Martinus Nijhoff, Dordrecht 1991), 393 and 396.

- this is a unilateral right of the coastal State and not subject to pre-approval or review by the IMO.[55]

The latter point in particular was clearly asserted by Canada in its submission to the MSC.[56]

It is the non-role of the IMO that appears to have been the main concern of the United States INTERTANKO, BIMCO, Germany and unnamed others who expressed views at the 88th session of the MSC. Embedded in the concern about the role of the IMO is also the concern about the NORDREG regime being different from and more stringent than the existing internationally accepted rules. As already highlighted, the United States in its submission to the MSC expressed support for the Canadian initiative regarding enhanced navigational safety in the Arctic, but commented that "Arctic coastal States should propose such measures to the Organization [IMO] to receive the most solid foundation for them, rather than act unilaterally."[57] BIMCO at the earlier sub-committee meeting made a similar comment: "it would have been desirable if the regulation [NORDREG] had been brought forward for evaluation to the Sub-Committee [of IMO]."[58] Germany and Singapore in slightly different ways echoed these comments[59] as did other States at the 88th session of the MSC.[60]

The view here is that the core international legal question regarding NORDREG and Article 234 is not the engagement of the IMO *per se*. The wording and negotiating history of Article 234 strongly supports the view that review or pre-approval by the IMO is not required for a measure that fits the wording of Article 234 and that a coastal State may rely on Article 234 for unilateral action involving standards and measures more stringent than the existing internationally accepted rules. Thus, the central question is whether the NORDREG mandatory ship reporting system and/or vessel traffic services regime is, as set out in Article 234, a law or regulation for "the prevention, reduction and control of marine pollution from vessels in ice-covered…, where particularly severe climatic conditions and the presence of ice covering…create obstructions or exceptional hazards to navigation…". For the purposes herein, whatever the current and future ice conditions may be in Canadian Arctic waters, within 200-n. miles of Canada's Arctic shore there are and will continue to be for the

[55] See: McRae, *supra* note 53, at 108–109 and Bartenstein, *supra* note 53, at 15–16. Bartenstein at 16 comments: "The absence of an international review process is one of the few certitudes in Article 234."

[56] Canada, "Comments", *supra* note 26, para. 5.

[57] United States, "Northern Canada VTS Regulations," *supra* note 22, para. 2.

[58] IMO, "Sub-Committee Report to the MSC," *supra* note 20, para. 19.23.

[59] IMO, "Report of the 88th Session of the MSC," *supra* note 29, paras. 11.35 and 11.36.

[60] *Ibid.*, para. 11.39.

immediate future severe climatic conditions and significant ice-covering and, as a consequence "obstructions or exceptional hazards to navigation." Thus, the question is narrowed to whether the NORDREG mandatory ship reporting system and/or vessel traffic services regime is a law or regulation for "the prevention, reduction and control of marine pollution from vessels" given the physical reality of Arctic navigation.

- If the NORDREG system is such a law or regulation, then it is supported by Article 234 and there is no obligation on Canada to approach the IMO.
- If the NORDREG system is not such a law or regulation, then the NORDREG system, at least to extent that it is a vessel traffic system under SOLAS, Chapter V, Regulation 12, would need to be presented and approved by the IMO.[61]

There is no intention here to descend into a detail discourse on treaty interpretation rules and approaches. The general contours of dealing with the technical matter of the possible meaning of laws and regulations in the context of Article 234 is informed by a number of considerations.

First and foremost, there is the purpose of Article 234, which is to allow adjacent coastal States on Arctic waters to adopt unilaterally laws and regulations to enhance protection of the marine environment from potentially catastrophic vessel-source pollution.[62] Arguably, this purpose leads to a broad understanding of "laws and regulations" covered or permitted in order for the accomplishment of the goal. There is no qualifier in the first sentence of Article 234 on "laws and regulations," thus it is uncertain whether a law or regulation must be necessary, important or simply useful to accomplishing the purpose of Article 234. A broad understanding of "laws and regulations" to accomplish the goal of environmental protection would suggest that as long as the law or regulation in question is useful to this goal that the law or regulation is one that can be adopted by a coastal State under Article 234. One can add to this the argument that protection of the marine environment has attained a high degree of global acceptance such that a broad interpretation of any provision that enhances protection of the environment is to be favoured based on international public policy.

The flip-side of the above argument is that Article 234 was clearly intended to be, and is, an exception to the international legal rules set out in the LOS Convention respecting protection and preservation of the marine environment and in particular as regards vessel-source pollution and thus, as an exception,

[61] There is ambiguity regarding SOLAS, Chapter V, Regulation 11.4 and whether a proposed mandatory reporting system must be approved by the IMO.

[62] See generally: Bartenstein, *supra* note 53, at 2–4 and 11–12.

should be read narrowly and against the coastal State seeking to rely upon it. This perspective would suggest that a law or regulation captured by Article 234 must be more than just useful, but necessary, for the enhancement of protection of the marine environment.

Another consideration respecting the meaning of "laws and regulations" may be derived from the history of Article 234 and its direct link to Canada's 1970 Arctic Waters Pollution Prevention Act (AWPPA) and the regulations adopted under the Act in 1972.[63] The United States, for example, has made this direct link:

> *The purpose of article 234…is to provide the basis for implementing the provisions applicable to commercial and private vessels found in the 1970 Canadian Arctic Waters Pollution Prevention Act….*[64]

It can be argued that the "laws and regulations" envisioned by Article 234 are or should be restricted to those of a character similar to those that gave rise to the provision. The dominant characteristic of Canada's 1970s AWWPA regime concerned vessel construction, design, equipment, crewing and liability respecting pollution from a vessel. Less obvious within the 1970s AWPPA regime are measures respecting vessel traffic management. However, the 1970s was early days for vessel traffic and ship routeing systems, which only fully blossomed in the 1990s.[65] Supporting the argument that the reach of the wording "laws and regulations" in Article 234 is restricted to vessel construction, design, equipment, crewing and liability is that these were the matters that were in contention during UNCLOS III as regards freedom of navigation in coastal State waters, in particular as regards the territorial sea,[66] and would have been in the contemplation of the negotiators.

"Laws and regulations" in Article 234 has two qualifiers in the last sentence of the provision. To be noted first is the qualifier that "laws and regulations

[63] Canada, Arctic Waters Pollution Prevention Regulations, *Canada Gazette Part II*, Vol. 106, 2 August 1972, 1453.

[64] United States, President Clinton, "Message from the President of the United States transmitting United Nations Convention on the Law of the Sea, with Annexes, done at Montego Bay, December 10, 1982 (the Convention) and the Agreement Relating to the Implementation of Part XI of the United Nations Convention on the Law of the Sea of 10 December 1982, adopted at New York, July 28, 1994 (the Agreement) and signed by the United States, subject to ratification, on July 29, 1994," U.S. Senate, Treaty Document 39, 103d Congress, 2d Session IV (1994), at 40.

No attempt is made here to examine the Russian legislation and regulations that were in place at the time of the negotiation of Article 234.

[65] For a brief note on the vessel traffic services and the engagement of the IMO, see: Captain T. Hughes, 'When is a VTS not a NTS?' 62 *Journal of Navigation* (2009), 439–442.

[66] See generally: R.R. Churchill and A.V. Lowe, *The Law of the Sea*, 3rd ed., (Manchester: Manchester University Press, 1999), 94–95 and 346–348.

shall have due regard to...the protection and preservation of the marine environment based on the best available scientific evidence." This wording strongly suggests that "laws and regulations" are to be understood in a dynamic and not a static sense as information changes.[67] It can be argued that the wording does not support a change of the character of the laws and regulations (e.g., vessel construction, design, equipment, crewing, and liability) that can be adopted, although new "scientific evidence" can result in improvements and updating of vessel-related laws and regulations. Alternatively, it can be argued that "the best available scientific evidence" on dealing with protection of the marine environment reasonably leads to an expansion of the character of laws and regulations that can be adopted. This perspective can also be supported by the underlying purpose of Article 234, protection of Polar marine environment.

A further point respecting "the best available scientific evidence" is the perspective that a coastal State seeking to rely upon Article 234 has to establish a link between the measure and the scientific evidence. Singapore, it its MSC Statement noted this and indicated that "it would be useful" if Canada could provide "empirical data" linking the mandatory status of NORDREG to achieving the prevention, reduction and control of marine pollution.[68] Canada did put forward an explanation of the link between the NORDREG measures and the enhancement of protection of the marine environment.[69] While it is the case that the scientific evidence wording can be seen as "a bulwark against arbitrary restrictions on international navigation,"[70] it is not clear what level of relationship between the law and regulation and the scientific evidence has to be met by the coastal State, Singapore suggested that the relationship was one of "materially help,"[71] or to whom or where such evidence is to be presented or demonstrated.

The second qualifier on "laws and regulations" in the last sentence of Article 234 is the wording that "laws and regulations shall have due regard to navigation." This wording indicates a degree of limitation on what "laws and regulations" a coastal State may adopt under Article 234,[72] but the ambiguity is ponderous. It can be argued that "due regard to navigation" means regard to navigational rights, such as innocent passage, transit passage or navigational high seas rights in the 200-n. mile zone. If this was the case, navigational rights would trump or completely circumscribe coastal State rights under Article 234

[67] Bartenstein, *supra* note 53, at 19.

[68] Singapore, "Statement to MSC," *supra* note 32.

[69] Canada, "Comments," *supra* note 26, paras. 2 and 3.

[70] Bartenstein, *supra* note 53, at 19.

[71] Singapore, "Statement to MSC," *supra* note 32.

[72] See, in detail, Bartenstein, *supra* note 53, at 21, generally at 20–24 and R.D. Brubaker, *The Russian Arctic Straits* (Leiden: Martinus Nijhoff, 2005), 56–57.

and the purpose of Article 234 would be gutted. It is to be noted that unlike in other "due regard" provisions in the LOS Convention,[73] the "due regard" wording does not explicitly use the term "rights". Bartenstein has looked at the "due regard" clause in Article 234 in detail and concluded that there is neither express nor implied support for the view that "due regard to navigation" in Article 234 refers to any of the navigational rights regimes found in the LOS Convention and comments that such an interpretation has major flaws and that, if applied, would "deprive Article 234 of its intended meaning."[74] At the other extreme, if due regard to navigation was more of a procedural matter – a coastal State only having to indicate that it took into account navigational matters in the development of "laws and regulations" – this would give to the coastal State extensive powers limited only by a loose relationship to protection of the marine environment. This would lead to a broader understanding of "laws and regulations" covered by Article 234 and what they may encompass, but would deprive "due regard to navigation" of any real effect which is inconsistent with how "due regard" is understood in other parts of the LOS Convention.

Regarding the overall balance in Article 234, Singapore commented:

> *While we acknowledge the importance of protecting the marine environment and enhancing navigational safety within the Arctic region, it is also important to ensure that any measures taken do not compromise the freedom of navigation.*[75]

In the context of "due regard to navigation," Singapore's Statement tends to the view that navigation considerations create a major or significant constraint on an Arctic coastal State as laws or regulations adopted should "not compromise" the freedom of navigation. Bartenstein argues that "due regard" refers to "the reasonableness of the coastal state's measures with respect to the needs of international navigation"[76] and that the "due regard" phrase suggests that what was envisioned was a *sui generis* navigational regime for Arctic waters.[77] She describes the coastal State – navigation in balance in Article 234 as follows:

> *Due regard has to be paid to the navigation as well as to the protection and preservation of the marine environment. Hence, linking navigational and environment considerations in this clause seems to indicate that the balance struck can, and even should, be different from the balance struck in the innocent passage and the transit passage regimes, giving relatively greater weight to environmental considerations.*[78]

Along similar lines, it is suggested that the "due regard" wording arguably suggests a practical, on-the-water sense of navigation. Based on this, it can be argued

[73] LOS Convention, *supra* note 25, Articles 56(2) and 58(3).
[74] Bartenstein, *supra* note 53, at 21 and see 20–24.
[75] Singapore, "Statement to MSC," *supra* note 32.
[76] Bartenstein, *supra* note 53, at 20.
[77] *Ibid.*, at 24.
[78] *Ibid.*, at 24.

that the global proliferation of vessel traffic routeing and management systems suggests that the NORDREG system meets the Article 234 "due regard to navigation" as it interferes with navigation in a manner that has been accepted. Canada asserted that as NORDREG promoted safe and efficient navigation that the system was not problematic under "due regard to navigation."[79] On the other hand, with or without the term rights, it can be argued that the context of "due regard to navigation" in Article 234 must be to constrain coastal State rights from venturing into areas which are well understood to constitute interference with navigation. Arguably, this would include mandatory vessel reporting and the necessity of obtaining clearance from a coastal State, long a sensitive issue and one that was clearly in evidence during the negotiations of the LOS Convention,[80] and in particular, where such a reporting system applies beyond the territorial sea in the 200-n. mile zone.

The last sentence of Article 234 with the two qualifiers on "laws and regulations" engage a balance between "due regard to navigation" and protection of the marine environment based on the best available scientific evidence. This takes the discussion back to the beginning and the relationship between the adopted "laws and regulations" and the "prevention, reduction and control of marine pollution from vessels" and whether "laws and regulations" involves an interpretation that is broad, narrow, or somewhere in between.

Concluding Comments

As already referenced, the Chair of the MSC noted stated that the MSC (and also the IMO) is without jurisdiction to deal with the "legal matters" that arose respecting the mandatory NORDREG vessel traffic management and routeing system in Canada's Arctic waters that came into effect in July 2010.[81] It is unclear whether the international legal questions surrounding NORDREG, in particular, the understanding and application of Article 234, will arise in other multilateral forums, although it does not appear that there is an obvious stage for such discussions beyond the bilateral. It is worth noting that discussions are taking place within the IMO on the development of a mandatory code for ships operating in Polar waters.[82]

---

[79] Canada, "Comments", *supra* note 26, para. 5.

[80] The context at UNCLOS III was primarily authorization and permission for naval vessels and innocent passage in the territorial sea. See: Churchill and Lowe, *supra* note 66, at 89–90. As already noted, *supra* note 13, the issue of "permission" has been the principal issue between Canada and the United States respecting the Northwest Passage.

[81] IMO, "Report of the 88th Session of the MSC," *supra* note 29, para. 11.39.

[82] See: IMO, Sub-Committee on Ship Design and Equipment, "Report to the Maritime Safety Committee," Doc. DE/54/23, 17 November 2010 (Report of the 54th session of the sub-committee), at paras. DE 54/23, paras. 13.1–13.20.

In section 9 of the information sent by Canada in October 2010 to the IMO entitled "Mandatory Ship Reporting System in Canada's Northern Waters (NORDREG)," it is indicated that if the required vessel reports are not submitted, the offending vessel may be requested to leave Canadian waters "consistent with international law," or prosecution may take place "in accordance with Canadian law and consistent with international law."[83] This wording may be seen as demonstrating that Canada will apply the NORDREG system in a manner that takes into account to a certain extent the international legal rights of flag States and "due regard to navigation" in an operational manner. Given the high degree of compliance that existed with the voluntary NORDREG[84] and thus can reasonably be expected with the mandatory NORDREG, the above assurances may help avoid an "on the water" incident that flares the international legal dispute.

Further, Canada's information sent in October 2010 for "recognition" under SOLAS, Chapter V, Regulation 11.4[85] may placate the concerns of many States about NORDREG being devoid of IMO engagement. However, as referenced previously, the United States made it clear that the above-noted "recognition" was not an assessment by the IMO of the legitimacy or the legal validity of the NORDREG system.[86]

There is no attempt here to answer fully or provide an assessment of the central question raised – does the NORDREG mandatory ship reporting system and/or vessel traffic services regime fit the wording of Article 234 as being a law or regulation for the prevention, reduction and control of marine pollution from vessels. *Prima facie*, the proliferation of ship reporting and vessel traffic management systems is an indication that such measures are a significant enhancer of shipping safety and, thus, also for the prevention, reduction and control of marine pollution from vessels. It can also be noted that the high degree of compliance with the voluntary NORDREG vessel reporting system strongly suggests that operationally vessel reporting in Canada's Arctic waters has not been seen as an undue interference with navigation.[87] Equally evident, however, is the long-time resistance by many States to requirements in coastal State law that mandate reporting and clearance of vessels engaged in transit rights through international straits, innocent passage rights in territorial waters or high seas navigational freedoms in the 200–n. mile EEZ.

[83] Canada, "Information on NORDREG," *supra* note 27, Appendix, section 9.

[84] See *supra* note 7.

[85] Canada, "Information on NORDREG," *supra* note 27.

[86] IMO, "Report of the 88th Session of the MSC," *supra* note 29, para. 11.38.

[87] A point noted by Canada regarding the assertion that NORDREG "does not unduly restrict navigation." Canada, "Comments," *supra* note 26, para. 5.

Panel V: Marine Scientific Research

MARINE SCIENTIFIC RESEARCH

Captain Javier A. Valladares (Ret.)[1]

Abstract

The dramatic evolution of technologies from the middle of the twentieth century allowed the development of a new era of oceanographic instruments. The real time and the research in the most remote areas of the ocean plus the condition of expendable or remote sensors for many of them increase the capacities of research, developing a new category called operational oceanography.

The United Nations Convention on the Law of the Sea mentions Marine Scientific Research and until present it has not been clear what the border line is with operational oceanography. The Intergovernmental Oceanographic Commission of UNESCO is the organism in the UN system specialized in marine sciences and services.

If we can integrate scientific and operational research in a common objective we can increase the knowledge of the ocean, and with them no doubt we can go towards a better future for society. Observations and science can help to integrate multiple initiatives with the idea of One Ocean and One Planet.

[Note: the author's PowerPoint presentation can be viewed online at http://www.virginia.edu/colp/pdf/kmi-valladares.pdf]

[1] Chairman of the Intergovernmental Oceanographic Commission.

REGULATING MARINE SCIENTIFIC RESEARCH IN THE EUROPEAN UNION: IT TAKES MORE THAN TWO TO TANGO

*Ronán Long**

Abstract

The EU and the Member States are party to the 1982 United Nations Convention on the Law of the Sea. The EU has been a long-standing proponent of the conceptual underpinnings of the 1982 Convention as a "package deal" that balances conflicting interests in an equitable manner. Among the provisions of the package which are particularly germane to achieving this objective are those that are in Part XIII which facilitate and encourage the conduct of marine scientific research (MSR). These provisions are increasingly important in attaining the overall objectives of the EU's Integrated Maritime Policy and its environmental pillar, the Marine Strategy Framework Directive, which among other matters aims to promote new approaches to marine resource management including the ecosystem approach.

With a view to investigating the legal constraints and opportunities at an EU level for improving the implementation of this new normative concept in marine environmental management, this paper traces the progressive development of EU policy in relation to MSR and undertakes a brief review of current Member State practice in relation to implementation of Part XIII of the 1982 Convention. This is followed by a short account of EU regulatory instruments, which are relevant to improving access to data, samples and the results of scientific research on marine ecosystems.

The paper concludes by suggesting a number of steps that could be taken by the EU to streamline the current consent regime that applies to foreign vessel MSR with a view to facilitating the practical implementation of ecosystem approach at a pan-European level. A brief analysis of a number of policy and legal options is undertaken with a view to improving the collection and provision of scientific information and data across the maritime boundaries of the Member States. The paper suggests that the proposed course of action will facilitate a gradual transition from the current fragmented approach to the authorisation of ship-based MSR towards a fully integrated governance system in line with the requirements of a range of EU and international legal instruments. The proposed harmonisation measures sit com-

---

* Jean Monnet Chair of European Law at the School of Law, National University of Ireland, Galway. He is participating in the ODEMM Project on an *extramural* basis by means of MLOPRS Ltd. which is examining various management options for implementing the ecosystem-based approach in the European marine environment. Supported by the European Commission's 7th Framework Research Programme, Theme ENV.2009.2.2.1.1, Project No 244273. Further information is available at: www.liv.ac.uk/odemm/. The author wishes to acknowledge the contribution of Margaret Armstrong MSc in compiling data for Table 1 and Erin McVeigh for proof reading an earlier draft of this paper.

fortably with the 1982 Convention which places express obligations on States and competent international organisations to create favourable conditions for the conduct of MSR and requires them to adopt reasonable procedures that promote and facilitate MSR. The author contends that the proposed governance structure and harmonisation instrument will support the sustainable and integrated management of marine ecosystems. The identification of such structures and the streamlining of administrative procedures is one of the core objectives of the EU funded ODEMM project which is examining various options for ecosystem-based management in the European marine environment.

> The path to long term recovery from the current economic crisis; the path to tackling key societal challenges; the path to ensuring a prosperous and secure Europe, lie in research and innovation.[1]

1. *Introduction*

As is evident from the quotation above, the European Union (EU) is placing considerable emphasis on research, innovation and education as a means to stimulate recovery from the current economic crises. In this era of globalisation, there are several other factors which contribute to economic prosperity as is evident from the thought provoking paper delivered by Dr. Bosworth at the opening session of this conference where he articulates the arguments for rebalancing the global economy in the post crises period.[2] Although not specifically mentioned by Dr. Bosworth, one such factor is clarity and certainty in the rule of law as it applies to economic and maritime activities undertaken at sea. The history of the law of the sea teaches us this can often be achieved by seeking global solutions to global problems and by compromise and "accommodations" on the part of nations with respect to uses of the sea.[3] Few can argue with this approach as it has paid a handsome dividend in the form of economic prosperity, the strengthening of peace, security, co-operation and friendly relations among all nations in accordance with general principles of the United Nations Charter.[4]

---

[1] European Commissioner for Research, Innovation and Science, Máire Geoghegan-Quinn, speech delivered to the EurOcean Conference 2010. 09.09.2010. Available at: http://europa.eu/rapid/pressReleasesAction.do?reference=SPEECH/10/415&format=HTML&aged=0&language=EN&guiLanguage=en

[2] B. Bosworth, "Post-Crisis Global Rebalancing" *infra.*

[3] D.P. O'Connell, *The International Law of the Sea* (Oxford, Clarendon Press, 1982), p. 29.

[4] On the stability that the 1982 Convention has engendered in the international legal order as it applies to the sea, see, *inter alia*: A. Oude Elferink (Ed.) *Stability and Change in the Law of the Sea: The Role of the LOS Convention* (Leiden/Boston, Martinus Nijhoff Publishers, 2005) *passim.*

The EU is fully committed to achieving these ideals and in view of the general theme of this conference, globalisation and the law of the sea, it may be pertinent to recall that the European Economic Community (EEC), as it was then known, was the only intergovernmental organisation to sign the Final Act of the 1982 United Nations Convention on the Law of the Sea on 10 December 1982 (hereinafter "the 1982 Convention").[5] As we now approach the thirtieth anniversary of this momentous date, it is also instructive to note that the 27 Member States that make up the EU today, and the EU as a supra-national regional economic integration organisation with legal personality and capacity in its own right, are all party to the 1982 Convention.[6] Moreover, in the words of the European Court of Justice, the 1982 Convention now form an "integral part" of the European legal order.[7] This finding of the Court marks an important milestone in the progressive implementation of the 1982 Convention because the Member States of the EU represent a broad spectrum of interests in relation to the law of the sea. Judge Treves has previously noted

---

5 The EEC (as it was then) did not formally participate at UNCLOS III but had observer status at certain sessions. Indeed the only issue that the Member States were able to achieve consensus on at UNCLOS III was in pursuing the right of the EEC to become party to the 1982 Convention, see M. Nordquist *et al.*, *United Nations Convention on the Law of the Sea 1982: A Commentary* (Dordrecht/Boston/Lancaster, Martinus Nijhoff Publishers, 1985) Vol. 1, at 84. On the EEC and the 1982 Convention, see, *inter alia*: T. Treves, "The United Nations Law of the Sea Convention of 1982: Prospects for Europe", *Conference Papers Greenwich Forum IX, Britain and the Sea*, (Edinburgh, Scottish Academic Press, 1984) 166–182; K. Simmonds, "The Community's Participation in the U.N. Law of the Sea Convention", in D. O'Keefe and H. Schermers (eds.), *Essays in European Law and Integration*, (Deventer, Kluwer, 1982) 179–191; J.F. Buhl, "The European Economic Community and the Law of the Sea" (1982) 2 *ODIL* 188–200; K. Simmonds, "The Community's Declaration upon Signature of the UN Convention on the Law of the Sea" (1986) 23 *Common Market Law Review* 521–544; C. Nordmann, "Regional Organisations: The European Community and the Law of the Sea Convention" in D. Vidas, W. Østreng (Ed.) *Order for the Oceans at the Turn of the Century* (The Hague, Kluwer Law International, 1999) 355–363.

6 The Council approved the 1982 Convention and the Agreement relating to the implementation of Part XI by Council Decision 98/392 of 23 March 1998. OJ L 179/0001, 23.06.1998.

7 See, *inter alia*: Case C-459/03 *Commission v Ireland* [2006] ECR I-4635, paragraph 82 citing *inter alia*: Case C-344/04 *IATA and ELFAA* [2006] ECR I-403, paragraph 36. The law is well settled in so far as international agreements ratified by the EU such as the 1982 Convention are binding on both the European institutions and the Member States pursuant to Art 216(2) of the TFEU. This has important consequences for 'mixed' agreements such as the 1982 LOS Convention where the EU and the Member States are severally liable with Member States for the performance of all obligations arising under the agreement, even in cases where the obligation is within the exclusive competence of the Member States. C-316/91, *Parliament v. Council*, Judgment of 2 March 1994 [1994] ECR I-625, para. 29. However, Art 6 of Annex IX appears to preclude joint and several liability as noted by S. Boelaert-Suominen, "The European Community, the European Court of Justice and the Law of the Sea, 23 (2008) *The International Journal of Marine and Coastal Law* 643–713 at 672–673.

that these include: major and minor maritime powers (the United Kingdom, France, Spain and Portugal); twenty-two coastal States (Belgium, Bulgaria, Cyprus, Denmark, Estonia, Finland, France, Germany, Greece, Ireland, Italy, Latvia, Lithuania, Malta, Netherlands, Poland, Portugal, Romania, Slovenia, Spain, Sweden, United Kingdom); five land-locked States (Luxembourg, Austria, Hungary, Slovakia, and the Czech Republic); States on the Atlantic Ocean and on semi-enclosed seas such as the Mediterranean Sea and the Baltic Sea; States on the enclosed Black Sea (Romania and Bulgaria); States which border international straits (Spain, France, the United Kingdom, Denmark and Sweden, to name but a few); States with global fishing interests (Spain, Portugal and France); and States that have an active interest in the legal regime that applies to deep seabed mining.[8] This picture is further complicated if one takes into account the maritime concerns of Croatia, Turkey, and Iceland who are at the time of writing are negotiating to become future Member States of the EU.[9] A central argument made in this paper is that all of these States have an active interest in protecting marine ecosystems and the resources that they support.

At a practical level, one consequence of this broad spectrum of interests is that there is often little scope for absolutism in the EU's position regarding contentious issues in the law of the sea. Furthermore, this diversity of Member State interests goes a long way to explaining why the EU has been a long-standing proponent and beneficiary of the conceptual underpinnings of the 1982 Convention as a "package deal" that balances conflicting interests in an

[8] This range of interests has previously been noted in the introduction of the excellent compendium of Member State practice in relation to the law of the sea by T. Treves, L. Pineschi (Ed.) *The Law of the Sea, The European Union and its Member States* (The Hague, Kluwer Law International, 1997) at p. 2. Member States interests change with the passage of time and this can be seen in relation to the legal regime that applies to deep seabed mining. In the sense of having an active interest in mine-sites, the reality appears to be that no EU Members have an interest except for Germany and France, which are both contractors with ISA. Having said that, none of the EU Members listed as 'major investors' eligible for election to Group B of the Council in 1994 have been willing to surrender that status (http://www.isa.org.jm/files/documents/EN/16Sess/Assembly/ISBA-16A-CRP1.pdf). In light of this, they would probably not accept that they have no active interest. As a side note, Korea has been arguing for years that the Group B list should be updated and people should reveal their true investments, but others, particularly the Netherlands and Belgium, have blocked any such development. The UK, on the other hand, is part of Group E in a bilateral deal with Korea. Furthermore, it is clearly likely that the old, state-based model of deep sea mining as envisaged in the 1980s is redundant. Interests will likely be revealed in many other ways. For example, Nautilus is sourcing its mining support vessel from Belgium, and its mining equipment from the UK. Finance is being raised in both UK and Canada. These are not 'interests' in the sense discussed at UNCLOS, but are clearly real national interests that EU Members could be expected to defend.

[9] The former Yugoslav Republic of Macedonia is also a candidate Member State and is land-locked. For further information on the accession of new Member States to the EU, see: http://ec.europa.eu/enlargement/candidate-countries/index_en.htm.

equitable manner. Indeed, experience in the international arena over the past three decades has shown that the concept of "reasonable use" and the "balancing of rights and duties" enshrined in the 1982 Convention has served and continues to serve the EU well.[10] From a European law perspective, there is nothing unusual in this outcome as the principle of interdependence and the pragmatic reconciliation of conflicting interests reflected in the substantive text of the 1982 Convention are also mirrored in the general architecture and functioning of the EU on a day-to-day basis under the EU Treaties. Rather surprisingly, however, little concerted effort was made by the European institutions to harmonise the regulation and administration of the various maritime activities undertaken by the Member States outside of the domain of commercial sea-fisheries up until relatively recently.[11] Somewhat belatedly, this omission is now being addressed through a broad range of ocean governance initiatives which have been launched under the rubric of the EU's Integrated Maritime Policy and by means of its so-called environmental pillar, the Marine Strategy Framework Directive (MSFD), which requires all Member States to achieve and maintain good environmental status of marine waters by 2020 at the latest.[12] All of these initiatives are influenced, to a greater or lesser degree, by the 1982 Convention and its associated agreements.[13] Moreover, all of these initiatives are aimed at promoting sustainable uses of the seas and conserving marine ecosystems.

In spite of this progress, many aspects of the 1982 Convention remain dormant within the European legal order and little effort has been made to date to explore the legal constraints and opportunities under the Convention which facilitate the implementation of ecosystem-based management in practice. With this in mind, this paper aims to show that much remains to be done at a European level regarding the implementation of Part XIII of the Convention, which deals with marine scientific research (MSR) and provides safeguards for the various stakeholders concerned with scientific enquiry into the "phenomena and processes occurring in the marine environment and the interrelationship

[10] On the concept of reasonable use, see D.P. O'Connell, *The International Law of the Sea* (Oxford, Clarendon Press, 1982), pp. 57–58.

[11] See, *inter alios*: R.R. Churchill, D. Owen, *The EU Common Fisheries Policy* (Oxford: Oxford University Press, 2010); R. Long, P. Curran, *Enforcing the Common Fishery Policy* (Oxford: Blackwell Science, 2000).

[12] Directive 2008/56/EC of the European Parliament and of the Council of 17 June 2008 establishing a framework for community action in the field of marine environmental policy (Marine Strategy Framework Directive) OJ L 164/19, 25.06.2008. On the Integrated Maritime Policy see note 18 *infra*.

[13] *Op. cit.* note 6.

between them".[14] On a similar vein, as will be seen later, there is considerable scope for improving the way the EU and the Member States discharge the specific obligations placed on States and competent international organisations to create favourable conditions for the conduct of MSR through the conclusion of bilateral and multilateral agreements.[15] Likewise, Member States could do a lot more in discharging their duty to adopt reasonable rules and procedures that promote and facilitate MSR in accordance with the general scheme set down in Part XIII.[16] Although these provisions of the Convention are not free from controversy at a global level,[17] they are increasingly important to the attainment of the overall objectives of the EU's Integrated Maritime Policy including the implementation of new approaches to marine resource management such as the ecosystems approach which is based on science and knowledge of the marine environment, as well as knowledge about the interrelationships of the processes that occur therein.[18] They are also central to the fulfilment of the EU's

[14] For commentary on international law as it applies to MSR, see A. Soons, *Marine Scientific Research and the Law of the Sea* (Kluwer Law and Taxation Publishers, Deventer, 1982); M. Gorina-Ysern, *Marine Scientific Research* (Transnational Publishers, Inc., Ardsley, 2003); F.H. Wegelein, *Marine Scientific Research, The Operation and Status of Research Vessels and Other Platforms in International Law* (Martinus Nijhoff Publishers, Leiden/Boston, 2005); United Nations, *Guide for the Implementation of the Relevant Provisions of the UN Convention on the Law of the Sea* (United Nations, Office for Ocean Affairs and the Law of the Sea, New York, 1991); and D.R. Rothwell, T. Stephens, *The International Law of the Sea* (Oxford, Hart Publishing, 2010) pp. 320–337. Art 243 of the 1982 Convention.

[15] Art 243 of the 1982 Convention.

[16] Art. 255 of the 1982 Convention.

[17] There is, for example, no consensus regarding the precise meaning of a number of the terms and expressions in the 1980 Convention pertaining to MSR and survey activities. See *inter alia*: A. Soons, *Marine Scientific Research Provisions in the Convention on the Law of the Sea: Issues of Interpretation* (Law of the Sea Institute, William S. Richardson School of Law, Honolulu, 1989), pp. 365–372; as well as the authorities cited by P. Birnie, "Law of the Sea and Ocean Resources: Implications for Marine Scientific Research" (1995) 10 *International Journal of Marine and Coastal Law* 229. On the meaning of both "scientific research" and "scientific research", see F.H. Wegelein, *Marine Scientific Research, The Operation and Status of Research Vessels and Other Platforms in International Law* (Martinus Nijhoff Publishers, Leiden/Boston, 2005), pp. 77–80. For an alternative view, see J.A. Roach, "Marine Scientific Research and the New Law of the Sea" (1996) 27 *Ocean Development and International Law* 59 (especially at pp. 60–61).

[18] The policy also aims to: promote the integration of maritime governance structures in the Member States; improve the quality of sector policies such as the transport, energy and fisheries policy; implement tailor-made solutions for specific problems taking into account the Regional Seas Convention. The Integrated maritime Policy was endorsed by the General Affairs Council of 16 November 2009. The European Commission has published a number of documents on the policy including: Green Paper, Towards a future Maritime Policy for the Union: A European vision for the oceans and seas, COM(2006) 275, 5.6.2006; Communication from

commitment to protect and preserve marine environment under an ever-expanding array of international agreements.[19]

With a view to improving the way ecosystem-based management of the marine environment is undertaken at a pan-European level, this paper reviews how the law and policy on MSR is functioning in practice in the Member States and identifies where there is scope for improving the implementation of Part XIII on a regional basis. The paper commences by examining a number of provisions in the European Treaties that are applicable to scientific research and describes the rather cumbersome division of legal competence between the EU and Member States regarding the adoption of measures that promote and facilitate MSR. The paper goes on to identify a range of European secondary legislation that may be relied upon by interested parties to access and use data and information derived from MSR and held by public bodies in the Member States. This is followed by a brief review of Member State practice regarding the implementation of Part XIII of the 1982 Convention generally and the procedural requirements that apply to foreign vessel MSR in sea areas under their sovereignty and jurisdiction more specifically. This paper concludes by suggesting a number of measures that could be taken by the EU to streamline the current consent regime that applies to foreign vessel MSR with a view to facilitating the practical implementation of the ecosystem approach in line with the requirements of the EU's Integrated Maritime Policy, the MSFD and the Habitats Directive at a regional level.

Before pressing ahead, two further preliminary points can be made. Firstly, it needs to be emphasised that Professor Soons first advocated the introduction of simplified MSR procedures for European Member States in the early 1990s.[20] His recommendations were well received but few practical steps were undertaken to follow-up on his prescient and incisive views on the subject. In the intervening years, European law and policy has moved on and there now appears to be a cogent case for reopening the discussion on this matter as the significance of Part XIII takes on a new meaning with the pressing need to advance study of the role of the ocean in the functioning of marine ecosystems and in influencing climate change. In other words, ecosystem-based manage-

---

the Commission, An Integrated Maritime Policy for the European Union, COM(2007) 575 final, Brussels, 10.10.2007; Commission Staff Working Document, SEC(2007) 1278, Brussels, 10.10.2007; Report from the Commission to the Council, the European Parliament, the European Economic and Social Committee and the Committee of the Regions, Progress Report on the EU's Integrated Maritime Policy, COM (2009) 540, Brussels, 15.10.2009.

[19] For a discussion of the EU's international obligations see V. Frank, *The European Community and Marine Environmental Protection in the International Law of the Sea: Implementing Global Obligations at the Regional Level* (Leiden, Martinus Nijhoff, 2007) *passim*.

[20] See A. Soons, "Regulation of Marine Scientific Research by the European Community and its Member States" (1992) 23 *Ocean Development and International Law* 259.

ment may act as a catalyst that improves the way European Member States implement Part XIII of the Convention at a regional level.

The second is a more general point and relates to the important term "competent international organisation" which is used in Part XIII but remains undefined in the 1982 Convention.[21] One UN sponsored study that sheds considerable light on this subject concluded that this term "may generally be considered to mean intergovernmental organisations which are empowered by their constituent instrument or other rules of the organisation to undertake, to co-ordinate, or to promote and facilitate the development of MSR".[22] Following this interpretation, the EU appears to be one such organisation as it has a clear legal mandate to encourage and advance scientific research with a view to implementing, amongst other matters, eco-system based management by the Member States in line with the objectives of the MSFD. On this basis, it may be appropriate to commence our discussion by taking a brief look at the relevant EU Treaty provisions on scientific research and their applicability to MSR.

PART I
EU Law and Policy on MSR

2. *EU Treaties and MSR*

The EU Treaties establish a unique legal order under which the Member States have limited their sovereignty in a number of fields with a view to achieving greater economic, social and political integration. For understandable reasons relating to the political and economic nature of the EU, the European Treaties do not have specific provisions on MSR *simpliciter.*[23] Indeed, the provisions in the foundation Treaties with their emphasis on economic matters had very

---

[21] See, *inter alia*: M. Gorina-Ysern, *Marine Scientific Research* (Transnational Publishers, Inc., Ardsley, 2003); F.H. Wegelein, *Marine Scientific Research, The Operation and Status of Research Vessels and Other Platforms in International Law* (Martinus Nijhoff Publishers, Leiden/Boston, 2005).

[22] United Nations, *Guide for the Implementation of the Relevant Provisions of the UN Convention on the Law of the Sea* (United Nations, Office for Ocean Affairs and the Law of the Sea, New York, 1991), p. 1.

[23] The Treaty on European Union (TEU) and the Treaty on the Functioning of the EU came into force on 1 December 2009 as a result of the ratification of the Lisbon Treaty by the 27 Member States. A copy of the Consolidated Treaties is published in the Official Journal of the European Union at OJ C 306/50, 17.12.2007. An electronic copy is available at: http://europa.eu/lisbon_treaty/full_text/index_en.htm

little to say about maritime matters.[24] Thus it is unsurprising to see that much of the initial policy on scientific research was focused on more mundane matters such as the liberalization of public procurement rules and the removal of fiscal and trade barriers to intra Community trade.[25] A major step forward was taken in 1986, however, when the earlier treaty provisions were consolidated and elaborated upon by the Single European Act which provided, for the first time, a specific legal basis for the adoption of pan-European measures which encouraged and facilitated research across a broad range of scientific disciplines including MSR.[26]

Today the treaty position is far more prescriptive as there is a solid normative basis for EU action in the fields of scientific research and technological development in the Treaty of European Union (TEU) and the Treaty on the Functioning of the European Union (TFEU).[27]

For those unfamiliar with the European legal order it may be appropriate to point out that the TEU sets out the broad political, economic and social objectives of the EU. This may be contrasted with the TFEU which is concerned with the role, policies and functioning of the EU including the law-making process that has to be followed by the European institutions when adopting secondary legislation. As such, both of these Treaties mark "a new stage in the process of creating an ever closer union among the peoples of Europe, in which decisions are taken as openly as possible and as closely as possible to the citizen."[28] Importantly, the TEU clearly states that one of the specific objectives of the EU is to promote scientific and technological advancement.[29] As will be seen below, these wide-ranging treaty provisions provide the framework for the

[24] These include: Article 55 of the European Coal and Steel Community Treaty; Articles 4 to 11 of the European Atomic Energy Community Treaty which deal with nuclear research; and Articles 35 and 308 of the European Community (EC) Treaty Community Research and Technological Development (RTD) policy which was originally based on Article 55 of the European Coal and Steel Community Treaty (expired in 2002); Articles 4 to 11 of the European Atomic Energy Community (EAEC) Treaty (Euratom: nuclear research); and Articles 35 and 308 of the European Community (EC) Treaty. See J. Elizade, "Legal Aspects of Community Policy on Research and Technological Development" (1992) 29 *Common Market Law Review* pp. 309–346.

[25] See *inter alia*: P. Kapteyn, The Law of the European Union and the European Communities p. 1263; W. Sauter, *Competition Law and Industrial Policy in the EU* (Oxford, OUP, 2003) p. 84.

[26] Arts 130f–130q of the Single European Act 1986.

[27] See, in particular, Title XIX, Treaty on the Functioning of the European Union.

[28] Art 1 of the TFEU. Art 2 of the TEU codifies core values in the European legal order such as respect for human dignity, freedom, democracy, equality, the rule of law, and respect for human rights.

[29] Art 3(3) of the TEU.

adoption of *lex specialis* on topics such as MSR in general and ship-based MSR more specifically.

The importance of freedom of scientific research is underscored by the Charter of Fundamental Rights, which has the same legal value as a treaty in the European legal order.[30] Article 13 of the Charter provides that "... scientific research must be free of constraint and academic freedom must be respected".[31] Considerable care ought to be taken with this provision as the Charter is addressed to the EU and Member States when they are implementing EU law and it needs to be emphasised that it does not extend the scope of EU law, or indeed create any new competences or tasks for the EU.[32] Furthermore, the House of Lords in the United Kingdom has suggested that "the language of Article 13 is vague and one could conclude ... that the right is limited to freedom of ... scientific expression".[33] This suggests that the right of freedom of scientific research enunciated in the Charter is not absolute or enforceable and may therefore be of little practical use in advancing the concept of freedom of MSR as understood by international lawyers. Despite this shortcoming, the importance of this provision in the Charter should not be underestimated as it is very similar to the protection afforded to scientific research in the constitutions of several Member States.[34] Furthermore, it supports the view that any putative EU harmonisation which facilitates freedom to undertake scientific research at sea must be viewed through the combined prism of the rights and duties set down in the European Treaties, the Charter on Fundamental Freedoms, and in the constitutional law of several EU Member States.

In contrast to the TEU and the Charter, there are elaborate provisions in Title XIX of the TFEU dealing specifically with research, technological development and space.[35] Most importantly, this Title provides a solid legal plinth for the establishment and operation of a European Research Area in which researchers, scientific knowledge and technology circulate freely.[36] Again, the TFEU is very

---

[30] Art 6(1) of the TEU.

[31] Art 13 of the Charter of Fundamental Rights.

[32] Art 6(1) of the TEU and Art 51(2) of the Charter. See *inter alia*: F. Van den Berghe "The EU and Issues of Human Rights Protection: Some Solutions to More Acute Problems?" (2010) 16 *ELJ* p. 112; G. Harpaz "The European Court of Justice and its relations with the European Court of Human Rights: the quest for Enhanced Reliance, Coherence and Legitimacy" (2009) 46 *CMLRev* p. 105.

[33] House of Lords, 10th Report of Session 2007–08, THE TREATY OF LISBON: AN IMPACT ASSESSMENT, p. 93.

[34] For instances, the constitutions of Germany, Greece Italy, Austria, Portugal, Spain are cited by H. Wagner, *Gibt es ein Grundrecht der Wissenschaftsfreiheit im Europäischen Gemeinschaftsrecht?* in DÖV [1999], pp. 129–137.

[35] Arts 179 through to 190 of the TFEU.

[36] Art 179(1) of the TFEU.

specific in this regard in so far as it states that this to be achieved by "permitting researchers to cooperate freely across borders" and by "enabling undertakings to exploit the internal market potential to the full, in particular through the opening-up of national public contracts, the definition of common standards and the removal of legal and fiscal obstacles to that cooperation."[37] In pursuing these objectives, and with a view to complementing the activities carried out in the Member States, the EU is mandated with four specific responsibilities under the Treaty, namely: (1) the implementation of research, technological development and demonstration programmes by promoting cooperation with and between undertakings, research centres and universities; (2) the promotion of cooperation with third countries and international organisations; (3) the dissemination and optimisation of the results of research, technological development and demonstration; and (4) the stimulation of the training and mobility of researchers in the EU.[38]

One should keep in mind that the activities undertaken by the EU in the domain of scientific research are complementary to the activities of the Member States. Indeed, the TFEU goes as far as to require the EU and Member States to coordinate their research and technological development activities so as to ensure that national policies and EU policy are mutually consistent.[39] Much of the burden in this regard is placed on the European Commission which is obliged to take initiatives aimed at the establishment of guidelines and indicators, the exchange of best practice, and to put in place the necessary elements for periodic monitoring and evaluation.[40] The European Parliament must be kept fully informed of such activities. Apart from the coordination of national policies in the Member States, the Treaty clearly provides the Commission with a very wide remit with regard to the taking of initiatives that promote research and technological development. In practice, this is mainly achieved by means of the multiannual framework programmes which are examined in further detail below. Suffice to note here that the overall aim of these programmes is to strengthen the scientific and technological bases of industry, develop their international competitiveness, and to support the broad range of research activities that are considered necessary by virtue of the Treaties.[41]

Apart from the provisions on scientific research mentioned above, there are many other provisions in the Treaties which are relevant to MSR, and some of these are examined towards the end of this paper as they provide a legal justification for the adoption of EU harmonisation measures. Suffice to note here

---

[37] Art 179(2) of the TFEU.
[38] Art 180 of the TFEU.
[39] Art 181(1) of the TFEU.
[40] Art 181(2) of the TFEU.
[41] Art 179(1) of the TFEU.

that the general spirit of the EU Treaties is to oppose discrimination in the Member States on the grounds of nationality.[42] Other Treaty provisions that are relevant to MSR are those that facilitate the free movement of persons and services.[43] This extends to persons employed on a ship flying the flag of a Member State.[44] These rights are also enjoyed by European citizens who are members of the marine scientific community subject to certain limitations set down by the Treaties and secondary legislation.[45] Elsewhere, the TFEU provides that the EU and the Member States are obliged to take action aimed at "fostering better exploitation of the industrial potential of policies of innovation, research and technological development."[46] There are many instances where MSR serves the industrial competiveness of the Member States in areas such as biotechnology and the life sciences.[47] Other provisions in the Treaties that are relevant to MSR are those that aim to protect and preserve the environment.[48] Significantly, in preparing a policy for the environment, the EU must take into account: available scientific and technical data; environmental conditions in the various regions of the Union; the potential benefits and costs of action or lack of action; the economic and social development of the Union as a whole and the balanced development of its regions.[49] In some instances, the EU makes policy decisions in the absence of definitive scientific data by relying on the precautionary principles which has a clear legal basis in the TFEU.[50] This does not detract from the firm obligation that is placed on Member States to collect and share scientific data in relation to the status of the marine environment and to implement ecosystem based management under a whole range of secondary

---

[42] See, for example, Arts 2 and 3 TEU, and Arts 10, 18, 36, 37 40(2), 45(2), 65(3), 95(1), 107 (2) (a) of the TFEU.

[43] Art 26(2) of the TFEU. Arts 45 through to 48 of the TFEU concerns workers. Arts 49 to 55 concerns establishment and Arts 56 to 62 concerns services.

[44] See, *inter alia*: Case 167/73, *Commission v. France* [1974] ECR 359; Case 9/88, *Mario Lopes da Veiga v. Staatssecretaris v. Justitie* [1989] ECR 2989.

[45] Exceptions are set down in inter alia: Arts 45(3), 45(4) and 51 of the TFEU and in Directive 2004/38/EC of the European Parliament and of the Council of 29 April 2004 on the right of citizens of the Union and their family members to move and reside freely within the territory of the Member States amending Regulation (EEC) No 1612/68 and repealing Directives 64/221/EEC, 68/360/EEC, 72/194/EEC, 73/148/EEC, 75/34/EEC, 75/35/EEC, 90/364/EEC, 90/365/EEC and 93/96/EEC OJ L 158, 30.4.2004, pp. 77–123.

[46] Art 173(1) of the TFEU.

[47] Art 173(1) of the TFEU.

[48] Arts 4, 11, 191–193 of the TFEU.

[49] Art 191(3) of the TFEU.

[50] Art 191(2) of the TFEU. On the requirements of using available scientific data see L. Kramer, *EC Environmental Law*, 6th Edition, (London, Sweet and Maxwell, 2007) 29–30.

legal instruments including the MSFD and the Water Framework Directive as will be seen below.[51]

In summary, there is a solid normative basis in the EU Treaties aimed at advancing scientific research and technological development. From a law of the sea perspective, it is interesting to note that the various provisions on scientific research in the Treaties are very general in ambit and make no attempt to define what constitutes MSR or indeed any other form of scientific research. Significantly, neither the Treaties nor the European framework research programmes distinguish basic from applied research.[52] Indeed, as a matter of practice European funded research often entails undertaking applied research projects at sea which allows one to conclude that the EU Treaty provisions on scientific research apply to the various types of research apart from those that are aimed at increasing knowledge of the marine environment for the benefit of science. Moreover, many of the core provisions in the Treaties aimed at fostering greater European integration are also clearly applicable to creating more favourable conditions for the conduct of MSR in sea areas under the sovereignty and jurisdiction of the Member States. These include: the provisions which prohibit discrimination on the grounds of nationality; the articles that provide the pan-European right to provide and receive a service; as well as the elaborate provisions which advance the EU policy on the environment. We will return to these provisions towards the end of this paper as they all are clearly relevant to the adoption of EU harmonisation measures governing ship-based MSR and therefore deserve closer consideration. First however it is necessary to discuss the competence of the EU to legislate or to act in relation to MSR.

3. *EU competence to regulate MSR*

The EU operates under the principle of conferral in so far as it can "only act within the limited competences conferred upon it by the Member States in the Treaties to attain the objectives set out therein".[53] For those unfamiliar with the unique parlance of the EU, the term "competence" which is derived from

---

[51] Directive 2008/56/EC of the European Parliament and of the Council of 17 June 2008 establishing a framework for community action in the field of marine environmental policy (Marine Strategy Framework Directive) OJ L 164/19, 25 June 2008. Directive 2000/60/EC of the European Parliament and of the Council of 23 October 2000 establishing a framework for Community action in the field of water policy, OJ L 327, 22 December 2000, 1. Directive as last amended by Directive 2008/32/EC (OJ L 81, 20 March 2008, p. 60).

[52] See A. Von Bogdandy, D. Westphal, "The Legal Framework for an Autonomous European Research Council" (2004) 29(6) *European Law Review* 788–807, at 790.

[53] Art 5(2) of the TEU.

the French term *competencé*, may be understood as denoting the powers of the European institutions to legislate in a particular area or to enter into international agreements with third parties on a particular subject matter. The corollary of this principle is that competence not conferred on the EU by Treaty remains with the Member States.[54] In the context of the law of the sea, a good example of the latter is the power of the Member States to determine their maritime boundaries in accordance with international law.[55]

The precise division of legal competence between the EU and the Member States is a complex matter and has fundamental implications for the implementation of the 1982 Convention. Generally speaking, it falls into three broad categories: exclusive, shared, or exercised by the EU in the form of supporting actions in areas such as administrative cooperation.[56] If we start with exclusive competence, in such instances, the EU is vested with the power to adopt legally binding acts in a particular policy area or to enter into an international agreement with a third party.[57] One longstanding example is the power of the EU to exercise exclusive competence in the conservation of marine biological resources under the common fisheries policy.[58] This is now codified in the TFEU but traces its origins back to some decisive judgements of the European Court of

[54] Art 4(1) of the TEU.

[55] In exercising such competence, however, a Member State must respect the interests of other Member States as protected by EU law, see Case C-146/89, *Commission v. United Kingdom* [1991] ECR I-03533. Furthermore, the extension of a Member State's maritime boundaries automatically entails the extension of the geographical area where the EU can exercise its legislative competence, insofar as the EU is internally competent to regulate the subject matter in question see Case C-6/04 *Commission v. UK* [2005] ECR I-9017. As a general rule, the geographical and material scope of application of EU law can extend to all areas where Member States exercise their sovereignty and jurisdiction under public international law.

[56] Arts 2 through to 6 of the TFEU.

[57] Joined Cases 3, 4. and 6/76, *Kramer and Others* (1976) ECR 127; Case C-405/92, *Ets. Armand Mondiet SA v. Armement Islais SARL*, [1993] ECR I-6133: Case C-25/94, *Commission v. Council*, [1996] ECR I-01469.

[58] The exclusive power of the EU extends to adopting the relevant rules on the management, structural and marketing aspects of the policy, as well as the power to enter into external undertakings with third States or competent international organisation in relation to fisheries. This competence applies to taking measures which apply to activities undertaken in sea areas under national jurisdiction and to the high seas. Subject to EU law, however, Member States retain power to exercise jurisdiction over vessels flying their flag, the registration of vessels, as well as to invoke penal and administrative sanctions for non-compliance with EU measures. In such instances, they must exercise their jurisdiction in conformity with EU law. See *inter alia*: Case C-221/89 *The Queen v. Secretary of State for Transport, ex parte Factortame Ltd and others*, [1991] ECR I-03905; Case 57/86, *Hellenic Republic v. Commission* [1988] ECR 2855; and Case C-127/87, *Commission v. Hellenic Republic* [1988] ECR 3333.

Justice in the late 1970s.[59] Exclusive competence must be distinguished very carefully from the position where a competence is shared between the EU and the Member States. This means that both the EU and the Member States are empowered to legislate and adopt legally binding acts.[60] This is subject to the important caveat that Member States must exercise their competence only to the extent that the EU has not exercised its competence.[61] Also, competence may revert to the Member States to the extent that the EU has decided to cease exercising its competence.[62]

The scope and arrangements for the exercising of EU competence, whether exclusive, shared or otherwise, are determined by the provisions of the Treaty that are applicable to the particular subject matter.[63] Previously, ascertaining the division of legal competence between the EU and the Member States in any given area demanded a forensic examination of the substantive provisions of the Treaties. The Treaty of Lisbon has simplified this process considerably as the categories and areas of EU competence are set down in Title I of Part One of the TFEU.[64] A brief perusal of these provisions reveals that one of the areas where competences are *shared* between the EU and the Member States is to carry out activities and implement programmes in the areas of research and technological development, in particular to define and implement [research] programmes (emphasis added).[65] The TFEU goes on to provide that the exercise of such competences by the EU must not result in Member States being prevented from exercising their competences.[66] The latter is an important caveat because the Member States can only legislate and adopt legally binding acts in areas of shared competence as matter of law if the EU has not exercised its competence to act or if the EU has ceased to act.[67] Furthermore, one of the protocols appended to the Treaties provides that when the EU has taken action

---

59 Arts 2(1) and 3(1)(d) of the TFEU. Joined Cases 3, 4 and 6/76, *Kramer and Others* (1976) ECR 1279; Case 61/77, *Commission* v. *Ireland* [1978] ECR 417.

60 Arts 2(2) and 4 of the TFEU.

61 Art 2(2) of the TFEU. See also Protocol (No 25) which provides that where the EU has taken action in a certain area, the scope of this exercise of competence only covers those elements governed by the Union act in question and therefore does not cover the whole area.

62 Art 2(2) of the TFEU.

63 Art 2(6) of the TFEU. Under the TFEU, there are three categories of EU powers, namely, areas of exclusive competence where the EU has the exclusive right to legislative (Art 3 of the TFEU); areas of shared competence where both the EU and the Member States may legislate (Art 4 of the TFEU); and areas where the EU has competence to carry out actions to support, coordinate or supplement the actions of the Member States (Art 5 of the TFEU).

64 Arts 2 through to 6 of the TFEU.

65 Art 4(3) of the TFEU. This extends to research in space.

66 *Ibid.*

67 Art 2(2) of the TFEU.

in a certain area where there is shared competence, the scope of the Union act in question only covers those elements governed by the EU act in question.[68] In other words, it does not extend to or cover the whole area.

Apart from the implementation of research programmes, there are several ways that the EU institutions can choose to exercise its shared competence, the most obvious ones being through the adoption of secondary legislation which are applicable to the Member States such as directives and regulations, or where necessary by entering into binding agreements with third countries and international organisations. The exercise of EU competences is also governed by the principles of proportionality and subsidiarity and these are considered separately at the end of the paper as they have implications for the regulation of ship-based MSR in sea areas under the sovereignty and jurisdiction of the Member States.[69]

The division of competence between the EEC (the predecessor of the EU) and the Member States was the subject of a Declaration at the UNCLOS III. Appended to the Declaration was the list of matters where competence was shared with the Member States and this included "marine environment research and scientific and technological cooperation".[70] More recently, when the EEC deposited the instrument of formal confirmation with the United Nations Secretary-General in 1998, it also deposited a Declaration specifying the matters governed by the Convention and the Fish Stocks Agreement in respect of which competence has been transferred to it by its Member States. This Declaration provides, *inter alia*, that:

> *. . . with regard to the provisions of Parts XIII and XIV of the Convention, the Community's competence relates mainly to the promotion of cooperation on research and technological development with non-member countries and international organisations. The activities carried out by the Community here complement the activities of the Member States. Competence in this instance is implemented by the adoption of the programmes listed in the appendix.*

The said appendix goes on to list the following programmes: the marine science and technology programme; the environment and climate programme; cooperation with non-member countries and international organisations: as well as scientific and technological cooperation with developing countries programme. The Declaration also notes that the scope and the exercise of EU competences

[68] TFEU, Protocol No 25 on the Exercise of Shared Competence.

[69] Art 5(1) of the TEU.

[70] Declaration concerning the Competence of the European Community with regard to Matters governed by the United Nations Convention on the Law of the Sea of 10 December 1982 and the Agreement of 28 July 1994 relating to the Implementation of Part XI of the Convention, 1 April 1998, OJ L 179, 23 June 1998, p. 130, point 1.

are, by their nature, subject to continuous development. This is a theme that frequently recurs in the jurisprudence of the European Court of Justice when the existence or exercise of competence by the EU and its predecessor the European Community is disputed by the Member States.[71] Instructively, in the *Mox Plant* case, the Court held that the question whether a provision of a mixed agreement such as the 1982 Convention comes within the competence of the EU is "one which relates to the attribution and, thus, the very existence of that competence, and not to its exclusive or shared nature".[72] Furthermore, within the specific context of the 1982 Convention, a finding that there has been a transfer to the EU of areas of shared competence is contingent on the existence of EU rules within the areas covered by the Convention provisions in issue, irrespective of what may otherwise be the scope and nature of those rules.[73] In this regard, the Court held that the appendix to the Declaration of Community competence, while not exhaustive, constitutes a useful reference base. Crucially, the Court went on to find that the Member States could not rely on an international agreement such as the 1982 Convention (and the appended Declaration) to contest the internal division of competence or to "affect the allocation of responsibilities defined in the Treaties and, consequently, the autonomy of the Community legal system".[74] As a result, Ireland was censured by the Court for seeking a remedy to the dispute with the United Kingdom outside the European legal order as it concerned a matter concerning marine environmental protection where competence was shared between the EU and the Member States.

As a matter of practice, the exercise of EU competence on a particular subject matter where competence is shared with the Member States tends to be evolutionary in nature. There is nothing unusual in this process within the broader scheme of EU law. Indeed, when considering the ambulatory nature of EU law generally, it may be useful to recall Lord Denning's illustrative analogy that described the EEC Treaty (now the TFEU) as like "an incoming tide. It flows into the estuaries and up the rivers. It cannot be held back."[75] This of course has the practical effect of shrinking Member States' scope for regulatory intervention and placing limits on their sovereignty. On the other hand, it has allowed the European institutions to respond to new challenges and to develop

[71] The exercise of shared competence between the Member States and the EU in the international arena as it applies to maritime matters (fisheries in particular) has been the subject of litigation in the European Court of Justice, see Case C-25/94, *Commission v. Council*, Judgment of 19 March 1996 [1996] ECR I-01469.

[72] Case C-459/03 *Commission v. Ireland*, [2006] ECR I-4635, para. 93.

[73] Case C-459/03 para. 108.

[74] Case C-459/03 para. 123.

[75] *Bulmer v Bollinger* [1974] Ch. 401 at 418.

the *acquis communautaire* (the settled law of the EU) through the creative interpretation of the European Treaties.

For the purpose of this paper, this discussion allows us to make two key points about the implementation of Part XIII on MSR of the 1982 Convention. One is that in areas of shared competence, such as the adoption of new measures that encourage and facilitate MSR, it is open to the EU to act internally by adopting a secondary legal instrument and/or a common policy, or to exercise its competence externally by entering into a binding international agreement with third countries or international organisations as it sees fit.[76] Secondly, insofar as Member States can legislate for vessels flying their flag under public international law, the EU has similar powers provided it is competent to legislate on such matters internally within the EU.[77] There thus appears to be no legal impediment to the adoption of EU measures that encourage and facilitate MSR apart from satisfying the relevant requirements of the EU Treaties regarding the adoption of such measures. We will return to a number of procedural matters in this regard concerning the principles of subsidiarity and proportionality towards the end of the paper.[78] We turn now to the area where the EU has been particularly active in exercising its competence: the domain of the framework research programmes.

4. *EU Framework Research Programmes*

The Framework Research Programmes for Research and Technological Development (commonly referred to by the abbreviation "FP") are the principal mechanism by which the EU manages and funds research and related activities. As seen above, these programmes have a solid legal basis in the TFEU and their nature and content have evolved steadily since the mid 1980s.[79] Much of the administrative burden associated with designing, delivering and implementing the programmes is borne by the European Commission which brings forward proposals regarding their objectives and content, as well as the administrative and financial rules governing their implementation. The final say regarding their adoption, however, rests with the European Parliament and the Council who

[76] See D. Verwey, *The European Community, The European Union and the International Law of Treaties* (The Hague, TMC Asser Press, 2004) at 180.

[77] Para 6 of the EC's Declaration of Competence concerning the 1994 Implementation Agreement and the 1995 UN Fish Stocks Agreement notes that the "Community enjoys the regulatory competence granted under international law to the flag State of a vessel, OJ L 189, 03.07.98, p. 39.

[78] See the discussion *infra* on the principles of proportionality and subsidiarity.

[79] Art 179(1) of the TFEU.

act in accordance with the ordinary legislative procedure in the EU institutions after consulting with the Economic and Social Committee.[80] This procedure puts the Parliament on an equal footing with the Council in making decisions on matters such as the duration, objectives, priorities and the amount of EU financial support for the various components of the programme. In practice, this also means that the programmes are subject to a considerable amount of parliamentary scrutiny and debate prior to their ultimate adoption. In 2005, the Parliament adopted a resolution on science and technology, which sets down Guidelines for future EU policy to support research and development, and this informs the shape and content of the framework programmes.[81]

Since their inception, there have been seven framework programmes.[82] The current programme, referred to as the 7th Framework Programme, is scheduled to run for seven years from 2007 to 2013 and is divided into five thematic areas, namely: cooperation, ideas, people and capacities.[83] The overall regulatory regime governing this programme is set down in Regulation (EC) No 1906/2006 and the overall strategic goal is to make the EU the "most competitive and dynamic knowledge-based economy in the world, capable of sustainable economic growth with more and better jobs and greater social cohesion.[84] The programme is strongly focused on promoting and investing in "world-class state-of-the-art research" and supporting "trans-national cooperation at every scale across the EU".[85] Similar to previous programmes, the overall aim of the 7th Framework Programme is to advance the European research agenda by enhancing research and innovation capacity in the Member States, improving

[80] Art 182(1) of the TFEU. This used to be referred to as the co-decision procedure under the EC Treaty.

[81] OJ C 320 E, 15.12.2005, p. 259.

[82] The division of the framework programme into specific sub-programmes for particular activities is facilitated by the Treaty which only affords the European Parliament a consultative role regarding their adoption under Art 182(3) and 182(4) of the TFEU. This may be contrasted with the wider role enjoyed by the Parliament in the adoption of the overall framework programme, as seen above, where it has a full say regarding the objectives, content and financial rules of the programme.

[83] For further information on the 7th Framework Programme see: http://cordis.europa.eu/fp7 For a history of the early programmes see European Parliament Fact Sheet: Policy for Research and Development. Available at: http://www.europarl.europa.eu/factsheets/4_13_0_en.htm

[84] Regulation (EC) No 1906/2006 of the European Parliament and of the Council of 18 December 2006 laying down the rules for the participation of undertakings, research centres and universities in actions under the Seventh Framework Programme and for the dissemination of research results (2007–2013), OJ L 391/1, 30.12.2006. See Recital 2, Preamble, Decision No 1982/2006/EC of the European Parliament and of the Council of 18 December 2006 concerning the Seventh Framework Programme of the European Community for research, technological development and demonstration activities (2007–2013), L 412/1, 30.12.2006.

[85] Recital 4, Preamble, Decision No 1982/2006/EC.

the mobility of researchers throughout Europe, and creating a solid scientific basis for EU policy-making. A broad range of public and private entities participate in the programmes, which for obvious reasons tend to be highly competitive. These include: universities, government institutes, public agencies, research centres, businesses, as well as individual researchers.[86] There are different rules for different categories of participants and the EU retains discretion under the Treaty to lay down the rules governing dissemination of the results of the research.[87] Over the past decade, the European Commission has sought to involve the less industrialised Member States in the framework research programmes with a view to strengthening economic and social cohesion across the EU. There is also scope for participation by international organisations that are made-up of Member States or countries associated with the EU. Indeed, the Treaty provides a specific legal basis for cooperation with third countries and international organisations in research and development matters.[88] A key feature of framework research programmes is the transnational element in so far as many of the projects are undertaken by scientists from different European and third countries. Importantly, the 7th Framework Programme is open to all researchers irrespective of their country of origin and participants from Russia, Eastern European and Central Asian countries, developing countries and Mediterranean partner countries, are entitled to funding under the same conditions that apply to researchers from European partner countries provided that they are willing to work with scientific groups from the European Research Area.

The research undertaken under the framework programme should not be viewed in isolation as it is intended to complement the research activities undertaken in and by the Member States. In this regard, the TFEU has a number of miscellaneous provisions which provide for, *inter alia*: the adoption of supplementary programmes which involve the participation of a limited number of Member States;[89] EU participation in research and development programmes

---

[86] Responsibility rests with the Commission to implement the framework programme including its financial aspects. Although frequently the subject of criticism within the scientific community, the administrative burden associated with project participation has lessened considerably in recent years. The procedure is relatively straight forward in so far as research consortia involving partners from more than one Member State come together and submit project proposals in response to research call made by the European Commission. The process is highly competitive and successful projects are selected by the Commission who are assisted by panels of experts who are especially convened for the purpose of evaluating the proposals submitted by various consortia.

[87] Art 183 of the TFEU.

[88] Art 186 of the TFEU.

[89] Supplementary programmes must be financed by the Member States. EU participation requires the agreement of the Member States concerned. The EU however retains discretion to adopt

undertaken by Member States subject to their agreement;[90] and the establishment of joint undertakings to undertake specific projects.[91]

Since their inception, the EU framework research programmes have served the EU extremely well and command a significant proportion of the EU's central budget. This investment was discussed at the Barcelona European Council meeting in 2002, where it was agreed by the European heads of state that overall spending on research, development and innovation in the EU should be increased with the aim of achieving 3% of GDP by 2010. In recent framework programmes, there has been a concerted effort to marshal research infrastructure, platforms and facilities in the Member States with a view to making them available to European researchers. The current research budget under the 7th Framework Programme is in the order of €52 billion and a sizeable proportion is allocated to marine-related research projects.

4.1 *EU funded marine research projects*

The history of marine related research within the framework programmes is somewhat disjointed and it is difficult to identify a central "marine theme" linking the various programmes together since their first commencement in the early 1980s. The first Marine, Science and Technology Programmes were referred to by the acronyms MAST I, II and III and formed component parts of the 2nd, 3rd and 4th Framework Programmes during the period 1986 to 1998. In the main, the marine projects were focused on providing a scientific and technological plinth for the sustainable exploitation of marine resources and enhancing our understanding of the role of marine ecological systems in global change. This allows to say that origins of ecosystem-based research may be traced back to a number of projects funded under MAST I. Conspicuously, these projects had sizeable budgets for vessel based MSR in the North-east Atlantic Ocean, the Baltic Sea and the Mediterranean Sea. After 1998, there were no specific marine science and technology research programmes and these topics were largely funded under the Environment and Sustainable Action component of the 5th Framework Research Programme (1998–2002). Once again, much of the focus of the research was on improving scientific knowledge of marine processes, ecosystems and their interactions with the wider marine environment. During this period, there were specific projects within other aspects of the programme on topics which are clearly germane to ecosystem-based management such as fisheries, CO2 exchange processes in the context of global

rules applicable to supplementary programmes including rules regarding the dissemination of knowledge and access by other Member States. Art 184 and 188 of the TFEU.

[90] Art 185 of the TFEU.

[91] Arts 187–188 of the TFEU.

climate change and biodiversity, global observing systems, as well as the development of marine research infrastructure in the Member States.

The 6th Framework Programme which ran from 2002 to 2006 had no dedicated programme for marine research and technological development but nevertheless funded 245 marine related projects in areas such as: global change, ecosystems research, and sustainable surface transport, food quality and safety, biotechnology, international cooperation and research for policy support. The levels of EU funding for marine related research in this programme were fairly impressive and amounted to over €600 million. Moreover, one recent statistical analysis of this programme reveals some interesting data, which demonstrate that this was truly a global programme in so far as 83 countries participated in marine related projects. [92] This was made-up of the 27 EU Member States, 10 other European countries and 46 non-European countries including Russia, Argentina, Israel and the United States.[93] Perhaps reflecting the size and expertise of their respective research communities, the United Kingdom, France, Germany and Italy participated in the largest number of marine projects followed by Norway, which was involved in 76 projects. Surprisingly, this placed Norway on a par with the Netherlands and well ahead of 21 EU Member States. This is strong reflection of the importance of marine related research in Norway. Although the budget for marine related research projects grew by three fold between 1986 and 2006, it still remained less than 4% of the overall EU budget for research under the framework programmes.[94]

Similar to the 6th Programme, the 7th Framework Programme has no specific marine programme but funded marine and maritime-related research topics under a number of thematic areas including: Food, Agriculture and Biotechnology", "Energy", "Environment", and "Transport". At the time of writing the estimated EU contribution to marine research is in the order of €735 million for 345 marine related projects.[95] Many of these projects, such as CORALFISH, have a significant budget for ship time much of which is co-funded by the marine research agencies in the Member States. Most importantly, the 7th Framework Programme has a whole range of projects examining various options on how to improve ecosystem-based management of the marine environment including the ODEMM project.

---

[92] R. Santos, T. Carvalho, L. d'Ozouville, "Marine Science and Technology Projects Funded under the Sixth Framework Programme of the European Commission: A Statistical Overview". Available at: http://www.eurocean.org/np4/file/65/FP6_20statistics_20Paper_2024_01_07.pdf

[93] *Ibid.*

[94] *Ibid.*, at p. 4.

[95] European Commission Press Release, 12 October 2010. Available at: http://europa.eu/rapid/pressReleasesAction.do?reference=IP/10/1317&

5. *EU policy and MSR*

At the time of writing, neither the EU nor the Member States have concluded any bilateral or multilateral agreements to give specific effect to the MSR provisions in the 1982 Convention. There have however been a number of important policy initiatives at an EU level that accord with the spirit and central thrust of Part XIII. From a European law perspective, these initiatives have sought to promote excellence in MSR as a means to support the development and implementation of the EU's Integrated Maritime Policy and a range of legal instruments pertaining to the conservation and management of offshore resources and the protection of the marine environment generally. These policy initiatives include: the European Marine and Maritime Research Strategy; Marine Knowledge 2020; and the European Marine Observation and Data Network. Before examining these in greater detail, it is relevant to our discussion to note that these initiatives have received additional impetus from the European scientific research community through a number of declarations adopted by scientists attending the Euro Oceans Conferences at Galway, Aberdeen, Bremen and Ostend.[96] One of the central themes in the Declarations is the need for the scientific community to actively foster working relationships with their colleagues in neighbouring countries with whom Europe shares regional seas including, the Baltic Sea, the Black Sea and the Mediterranean Sea.[97] Although the Declarations are hortatory in content and lack legal substance they nonetheless provide us with an excellent indicator of the views of the broader scientific community on what should be the underlying philosophy of EU policy as it pertains to MSR. Thus, for example, the Ostend Declaration calls for the development of an integrated research framework at a European level which combines the assets available under the European programmes with those of Member States, as well as the development of the European Ocean Observing System, and the "establishment of an appropriate mechanisms to keep under review current marine and maritime research programmes and projects with a view to enhancing their impact".[98] A central theme in the Declarations is the strengthening of international cooperation on MSR both within and beyond the EU. The Declarations are fully consistent with central thrust of Part XIII of the 1982 Convention and convey precisely the same message that is evident in the more formalised policy initiatives taken by the Commission and it is to these that we must now turn as they give us a clear understanding of the

[96] Galway Declaration, 4 May 2004. Available at: http://www.eurocean2004.com/pdf/galway_declaration.pdf

[97] Aberdeen Declaration, 22 June 2007. Available at: http://www.crpm.org/pub/agenda/340_aberdeen_declaration_packaged_rev2.pdf

[98] Ostend Declaration, 13 October 2010. Available at: http://www.eurocean2010.eu/declaration/

importance of maximising the infrastructural resources available at a European level to undertake research at sea into the functioning of marine ecosystems and the processes that take in the wider marine environment.

5.1 *European Marine and Maritime Research Strategy*

The EU's integrated maritime policy is very much science driven and is founded on a number of policy initiatives including the European Marine and Maritime Research Strategy (the "Strategy").[99] Within the wider landscape of the EU's research and educational policies, the Strategy is a blueprint and part of the so-called Ljubljana Process which is focused on widening and deepening of the European Research Area.[100] In line with this process, the Strategy places considerable emphasis on the development of infrastructure, education, capacity building and the implementation of a new cross-thematic approach to marine research. One of the principal aims of the Strategy is to enhance integration between marine research and maritime research. Although the Strategy does not define MSR, the Commission in the accompanying memorandum distinguish marine research from maritime research as follows:

> *Marine research addresses a branch of earth science that studies the oceans and seas including their flora and fauna as well as their interaction with coastal territories and with the atmosphere. It covers a wide spectrum of scientific knowledge and phenomena such as marine organisms, ecosystems dynamics, ocean currents, plate tectonics and geology. These diverse topics involve multiple disciplines to understand the underlying processes and the complexity of their interaction. Nowadays, one of the major concerns of marine research is the preservation of marine ecosystems.*
>
> *Maritime research aims at technologies and innovative solutions for a better exploitation of sea and ocean resources such as the design, building and operation of vessels, harbours, oil platforms and more widely any kind of human related activity centred around sea and ocean resources (e.g. tourism).*[101]

Apart from consolidating the linkage between marine research and maritime research, the Commission believes that the EU must identify the means with which it can strengthen its capacity to carry out all aspects of marine research if it is to remain at the forefront of advances in world research. In the words of the Strategy:

---

[99] Communication from the Commission, European Strategy for Marine and Maritime Research a coherent European Research Area framework in support of a sustainable use of oceans and seas. Brussels 3.9.2008, COM(2008) 534 final.

[100] Council Conclusions on the launch of the "Ljubljana Process" – towards full realisation of ERA adopted on 30 May 2008. Council Document 10231/08. Available at: http://register.consilium.europa.eu/pdf/en/08/st10/st10231.en08.pdf

[101] Memo 08/553, Brussels, 3 September 2008. Available at: http://europa.eu/rapid/pressReleasesAction.do?reference=MEMO/08/553&format=HTML.%C2%A0

> *World-class marine science requires specialised and sophisticated research infrastructures, which are costly. Today, most infrastructures are operated to take account of national priorities. To optimise their use it will be essential to build lasting and complementary relationships between infrastructure holders based on joint plans for future investments and* ***standardisation*** *in measurement, observation and reporting methodologies.*[102] (emphasis added)

In the context of the subject matter of this paper, it is significant that the Strategy calls for greater integration in the use of European marine research infrastructure and the harmonisation of procedures relating to research.[103] There is considerable emphasis in the Strategy on the promotion of inter-disciplinary research on cross-cutting issues such as climate change, the impact of human activities on coastal and marine ecosystems, continental margin research, operational oceanography and marine technology, as well as the protection and exploitation of marine biodiversity. Similar to the framework programmes discussed above, the Strategy aims to promote synergies between the EU, the Member States, and non-EU countries regarding access to research infrastructure. For understandable reasons which accords with the regional approach adopted in a number of legal instruments such as the MSFD, the Strategy has a strong regional seas focus and calls for the strengthening of research partnerships with third countries that share sea basins with the EU.

One of the interesting proposals in the Strategy is the call for the establishment of new forms of governance including the creation of a stable partnership of various stakeholders including scientists, policy-makers, industry and civil society with a view to setting research priorities and fostering greater cooperation between concerned parties. In line with long-standing policy on research in the EU, the Commission foresee its own role curtailed to that of a facilitator with the Member States responsible for the implementation of national and EU policy on research. One of the themes that run through the Strategy is the need to identify ways of providing better scientific evidence to policy makers. Regrettably, the Strategy does not present any concrete proposals on how to achieve this objective apart from the establishment aforementioned stakeholder consultation forum.

Since its publication, the Commissioner with responsibility for research and innovation at a European level has pointed out in the intensive and competitive environment of global research, "The best infrastructure also helps to attract and keep the best researchers".[104] Moreover, in her view the Member States

---

[102] COM(2008) 534 final, 3.9.2008, at p. 8.

[103] *Ibid.*

[104] Commissioner Máire Geoghegan-Quinn, SPEECH/10/415 09.09.2010. Available at: http://europa.eu/rapid/pressReleasesAction.do?reference=SPEECH/10/415&format=HTML&aged=0&language=EN&guiLanguage=en

could achieve greater added value by "pooling resources or coordinating initiatives at the EU level, such as in observation of the seas or in research on marine biodiversity".[105] Accordingly, the Commissioner has called for the harnessing of the synergies between the Member States on the grounds that "marine ecosystems do not stop at maritime borders and actions taken in one Member State have consequences in regional waters."[106] This is an interesting argument and appears to support the view the practical implementation of the ecosystems approach by the EU will require a greater effort and a more harmonious approach by the Member States in implementing Part XIII of the 1982 Convention with a view to creating more favourable conditions for the conduct of MSR in sea areas under their sovereignty and jurisdiction.[107]

5.2 *Marine Knowledge 2020*

In 2010, the Commission published the *Marine Knowledge 2020: A better understanding of our seas and oceans to boost competitiveness and growth.*[108] This policy initiative may have far reaching implications for the future development of EU policy on MSR as it focuses on improving knowledge of the status of the European marine environment, facilitating greater access to marine data, and enhancing cooperation between the providers of marine data and end users in the Member States.

In order to understand the background to this initiative, it is first necessary to recall that the collection of marine data is primarily undertaken by public and private entities in the Member States.[109] The financial contribution made by the EU to the collection of marine data is nevertheless considerable and recent estimates suggest that it is in the region of €110 million per annum, much of which is invested by means of the framework programmes discussed above.[110] In addition, the Commission estimates that public bodies in the Member

[105] *Ibid.*

[106] *Id.*

[107] Arts 242, 243 and 255 of the 1982 Convention.

[108] Communication from the Commission, Marine Knowledge 2020 marine data and observation for smart and sustainable growth, COM(2010) 461 final, Brussels, 8.9.2010.

[109] Communication from the Commission to the European Parliament and the Council, Marine Knowledge 2020, Marine data and observation for smart and sustainable growth, COM(2010) 461 final, Brussels, 8.9.2010, p. 3.

[110] COM(2010) 461 final, Brussels, 8.9.2010. This figure is made-up of two component parts, €40 million for fisheries data and €70 million for marine spatial data. The EU has augmented this spending by an additional €18.5 million per year for the period 2011–2013 through the Global Monitoring for Environment and Security initiative and under the Integrated Maritime Policy. See, Proposal for a Regulation of the European Parliament and of the Council establishing a Programme to support the further development of an Integrated Maritime Policy, COM (2010) 494 final, Brussels, 29.9.2010.

States are spending about €1.5 billion a year in marine observation and data collection.[111] The scale of this investment is all the more remarkable in view of the fact that it does not take into account the collection of marine data by private companies for other purposes.[112] Despite the large amounts of money spent on the collection of data, a survey conducted on behalf of the Commission found that there was "widespread dissatisfaction with the European marine data infrastructure amongst professionals who need to process marine data in both the public and private sector."[113] Instructively, many of those consulted in the survey sought an enhanced role for the EU in improving matters.

There are several restrictions on data access and use including "fragmented standards, formats and nomenclature, lack of information on precision and accuracy, the pricing policy of some providers and insufficient temporal or spatial resolution".[114] In response to these shortcomings, the Commission has suggested nine different actions to improve access to marine data as well as the setting-up of a unique electronic architecture for as a focal point for the collection and dissemination of marine data. The Marine Knowledge 2020 initiative applies to all marine data held by bodies within the EU irrespective of where the data originates although in the initial phase of rolling-out the initiative there is an emphasise on improving access to data sets that are applicable to the regional seas adjacent to the European continent with a view to helping Member States meet the requirements of the MSFD for monitoring environmental status. Significantly, the Commission has acknowledged that data are normally collected for specific purposes such as to improve the safety of navigation or to facilitate fisheries management. Conversely, the aim of the new European marine data architecture is to provide for multi-purpose uses including ecosystem-based management of the marine environment under the MSFD. This objective is facilitated by the establishment of the European Marine Observation and Data Network.

5.3 *European Marine Observation and Data Network*

As is evident from the discussion in this paper, the EU has a diffuse range of policies and legal instruments which are aimed at facilitating greater access and use of data that is collected and held by public bodies in the interest of the

---

[111] Speech by Commissioner Maria Damanaki, European Commissioner for Maritime Affairs and Fisheries, Marine research as pillar of the Integrated Maritime Policy of the European Union, Oostende, 12.10.2010. Available at: http://europa.eu/rapid/pressReleasesAction.do?reference=SPEECH/10/542&format=HTML&aged=0&language=EN&guiLanguage=en

[112] *Ibid.*

[113] Commission Staff Working Document, "Marine Data Infrastructure Outcome of Public Consultation", 22.1.2010, SEC(2010)73 final.

[114] COM(2010) 461 final, Brussels, 8.9.2010, p. 4.

common good. Many of these instruments do not, however, apply to data held by scientific institutions or other bodies that have no formal role in government or public administration. Such data are nonetheless essential to undertaking ecosystem-based management of the marine environment. This problem is often compounded by the fact that different teams often process physical and biological data collected during the same research cruise and this information is frequently stored in different databases.[115] As a result, is not possible to assess the spatial and temporal coverage of scientific research programmes across the maritime boundaries of the Member States.

The EU is not unique in this respect as a report published in 2004 by the United States National Research Council on *A Geospatial Framework for the Coastal Zone* pointed out that at least 15 federal agencies are involved in the collection of coastal geospatial data and this resulted in "a chaotic collection of potentially overlapping, and often uncoordinated, coastal mapping and charting products that can frustrate the efforts of users to take advantage of existing data sets and build on past studies".[116] The Committee chaired by a contributor to this conference, Professor Larry Mayer, produced the report and recommended the establishment of a seamless geodetic framework for all US coastal regions, easier access to timely data, and improved coordination and collaboration between federal, state, local agencies, academic researchers, and the private sector in the collection and sharing of data.[117] In 2010, the United States Congress responded to this challenge by enacting a law which provides for the establishment of a program to develop a coordinated and comprehensive Federal ocean and coastal mapping plan for the Great Lakes and sea areas under the sovereignty and jurisdiction of the United States with a view to enhancing "ecosystem approaches in decision-making for conservation and management of marine resources and habitats, establishes research and mapping priorities, ... and advances ocean and coastal science".[118] The outer continental shelf of the United States comes within the scope of the program.

The response to the difficulties encountered with collecting and accessing marine data in the EU shares some similarities with the one adopted in the United States described above. In 2008, the European Commission established of a new European Marine Observation and Data Network (EMODNET).[119]

[115] Commission Staff Working Document. Building a European marine knowledge infrastructure: Roadmap for a European Marine Observation and Data Network. SEC (2009) 499 final. Brussels, 7.4.2009, at p. 10.

[116] See, National Research Council, *A Geospatial Framework for the Coastal Zone* (Washington, National Academy of Sciences, 2004) at p. 4.

[117] Chapter 7 *ibid.*

[118] 3 USC Chapter 48 – Ocean and Coastal Mapping Integration.

[119] Commission Staff Working Document, European Marine Observation and Data Network Impact Assessment, SEC (2010) 998 final, Brussels, 8.9.2010.

Essentially the Network has eight objectives, namely: (1) the collection of data once and its subsequent re-use many times; (2) the development of standards across disciplines as well as within them; (3) the processing and validating of data at different levels. Structures are already developing at national level but infrastructure at sea-basin and European level is needed; (4) the provision of sustainable financing at an EU level so as to extract maximum value from the efforts of individual Member States; (5) building on existing efforts where data communities have already organised themselves; (6) the development of a decision-making process for priorities that is user-driven; (7) the accompaniment of data with statements on ownership, accuracy and precision, and; (8) recognise that marine data is a public good and discourage cost-recovery pricing from public bodies.[120]

EMODNET and its associated Web-based tool facilitate access to bathymetric, geological, physical, chemical, biological and habitat data for selected sea basins.[121] Additional impetus for the Network is derived from the work of the Data Expert Group which is made up of scientific, technical and operational experts who will oversee the marine knowledge projects and meet a number of times a year. Ultimately, it is foreseen that EMODNET will become one of the component systems of the Global Earth Observation System of Systems as a complement to the Global Monitoring for Environment and Security which went into operation in 2009.

The importance of the Network cannot be overstated and it is anticipated that it will become a vital tool for scientists and public officials who are working at the science-policy interface and who are responsible for implementing ecosystem-based management of the European marine environment under the MSFD and related instruments.

6. *EU legal instruments on data discovery, access and use*

The discussion so far has focused on a number of soft law initiatives and the establishment of EMODNET. The central thrust of these measures is to foster greater collaboration and coordination in relation to MSR at a regional level. This approach has considerable merit and complements a number of regulatory instruments governing public access to environmental data and information. Some of these instruments are applicable to MSR data, samples and the results of research obtained during the course of ship-based MSR and that is subsequently held or acquired by public bodies. They include the INSPIRE Directive,

[120] SEC(2009) 499 final. Brussels, 7.4.2009, at p. 11.

[121] http://www.emodnet-chemistry.eu/portal/portal/emodnet/Home.

the Environmental Information Directive, the Public Sector Information Directive, and the Fisheries Data Collection Regulation.

Little has been published on how effective these measures are in practice and it is therefore difficult to comment on their utility as instruments that can be relied upon by interested parties to ensure greater access to MSR data, samples and the results of ship-based MSR. Broadly speaking, these instruments seek to improve public access to information on the environment as well as access to justice in environmental matters. Undoubtedly, they are aimed at bringing many benefits including greater transparency in the environmental decision-making process in the Member States. From a law of the sea viewpoint, it is interesting to note that the general trend in EU law is towards the enhancement of greater public access to environmental data and information held by public bodies. Some of the principal features in these instruments are highlighted here with a view to showing their utility in facilitating ecosystem-based management of the marine environment. Mention is also made of the data sharing requirements that arise under the framework research programme.

6.1 *INSPIRE Directive*

The so called "INSPIRE Directive" establishes an infrastructure for sharing data in the EU which requires Member States to establish networks allowing their spatial data holdings to be searched and displayed.[122] The Directive came into force in 2007 and aims to assist public authorities in exercising their functions in support of EU policies that protect the environment. The scope of the instrument applies to spatial data held in electronic form by public authorities including hydrographical, geologic, oceanographic, and habitat data, as well as aggregate data on species distributions. Significantly, the INSPIRE Directive does not set down requirements for the collection of new data, or for reporting such information to the Commission. Nor does it set down any requirements regarding the sharing of samples acquired during the course of ship-based MSR. Nonetheless, the Directive will assist policy makers in making decisions regarding the implementation of the ecosystems approach which have cross boundary implications. Overall, the Directive accords with general spirit of Part XIII in providing greater access to scientific knowledge of the marine environment and data acquired during the course of scientific research projects including those undertaken at sea. Again, however, the Directive only applies to data held by public authorities.

[122] Directive 2007/2/EC of the European Parliament and of the Council of 14 March 2007 establishing an Infrastructure for Spatial Information in the European Community (INSPIRE), OJ L 108/1, 25.4.2007.

6.2 *Environmental Information Directive*

The "Environmental Information Directive" provides for public access to environmental information in line with the requirements of the United Nations/ECE Convention on Access to Information, Public Participation in Decision-Making and Access to Justice in Environmental Matters ('the Aarhus Convention').[123] This instrument has facilitated greater public access to environmental data and information in the Member States on a day-to-day basis. The applicant does not require any particular *locus standi* to gain access to information that is held by public bodies or by persons that perform public functions. This includes information and data held by public research institutes and agencies. There are a number of significant limitations on the application of the Directive stemming from the fact that Member States may restrict access to such data on a number of grounds including, *inter alia*: intellectual property grounds, or with a view to protecting international relations, public security or national defence. In the context of MSR, for instance, access to bathymetric data may be restricted on military security grounds in some European Member States, either for all sea areas under national jurisdiction such as in Finland, or in some restricted areas such is the case in France.[124] In such instances, these data do not come within the scope of the Directive. Once again, this Directive does not set down any specific requirements regarding the collection or dissemination of new data or information concerning the marine environment. Accordingly, as a legal instrument it can only play a very limited role in the implementation of the ecosystem approach at an operational level. There is however an underlying rationale underpinning this Directive, which is also evident in Part XIII of the 1982 Convention,[125] and that is the belief that information on the state of the environment and its biological diversity should be publically available.

[123] Directive 2003/4/EC of the European Parliament and of the Council of 28 January 2003 on public access to environmental information and repealing Council Directive 90/313/EEC. OJ L L 41/26, 14.2.2003. As well as Regulation (EC) No 1367/2006 of the European Parliament and of the Council of 6 September 2006 on the application of the provisions of the Aarhus Convention on Access to Information, Public Participation in Decision-making and Access to Justice in Environmental Matters to Community institutions and bodies. OJ L 264/13, 25.9.2006.

[124] Commission Staff Working Document. Building a European marine knowledge infrastructure: Roadmap for a European Marine Observation and Data Network. SEC(2009) 499 final. Brussels, 7.4.2009, at p. 19.

[125] See, for example, Art 249(1)(e) of the 1982 Convention which requires that the research results are made internationally available through appropriate national or international channels, as soon as practicable.

6.3 *Public Sector Information Directive*

Another legal instrument which has limited utility in the context of MSR, is the "Public Sector Information Directive" which aims to remove the barriers which individuals or companies encounter while developing new cross-border information services and products based on public data resources.[126] The Directive establishes a minimum set of rules governing the re-use and the practical means of facilitating reuse of existing documents, whatever its medium, held by public sector bodies of the Member States.[127] The type of information that comes within the scope of the Directive includes social, economic, geographical, weather, tourist, business, patent and educational information.[128] Similar to the Environmental Information Directive described above, there are a number of exceptions which remove certain categories of documents from the scope of the Directive including information pertaining to the protection of national security (i.e. State security), defence, or public security.[129] Although marine data could ostensibly come within its scope, the Directive does not apply to "documents held by educational and research establishments, such as schools, universities, archives, libraries and research facilities including, where relevant, organisations established for the transfer of research results."[130] This restriction appears to curtail the utility of this instrument in widening public access to MSR data, samples and the results of scientific research projects undertaken at sea.

6.4 *Fisheries Data Collection Regulation*

In many ways, the approach taken by fisheries managers within the framework of the common fisheries policy sets the European standard of "best practice" regarding the collection and sharing of MSR data and related information. In 2008, a sophisticated instrument, the Fisheries Data Collection Regulation, was adopted by the Council in order to establish a scheme for the collection, management and use of data in the fisheries sector and to provide support for scientific advice.[131] This instrument greatly facilitates the implementation of the ecosystem approach to fisheries management by the EU. This is achieved through the establishment of a multi-annual EU programme for the collection,

[126] Directive 2003/98/EC of the European Parliament and of the Council of 17 November 2003 on the re-use of public sector information. OJ L 345/90, 31.12.2003.

[127] Art 1 of Directive 2003/98/EC.

[128] Recital 4 of the Preamble, Directive 2003/98/EC.

[129] Exceptions are set out in Art 1(2) of Directive 2003/98/EC.

[130] Art 1(2)(e) of Directive 2003/98/EC.

[131] Council Regulation No 199/2008 of 25 February 2008 concerning the establishment of a Community framework for the collection, management and use of data in the fisheries sector and support for scientific advice regarding the Common Fisheries Policy. OJ L 60/1, 5.3.2008.

management and use of biological, technical, environmental, and socio-economic data concerning: commercial fisheries carried out by fishing vessels flying the flag of a Member State both within and beyond EU waters.[132] National programmes must be drawn up in accordance with EU programmes and these must include schemes for *inter alia*: monitoring of commercial and recreational fisheries where necessary; research surveys-at-sea; the management and use of the data for scientific purposes.[133] Crucially, Member States must make detailed and aggregated data available to end-users in three instances: firstly, as a basis for advice to fisheries management, including to Regional Advisory Councils; secondly, in the interest of public debate and stakeholder participation in policy development; thirdly, for scientific publication.[134] 'End-users' are defined in the regulation to mean: "bodies with a research or management interest in the scientific analysis of data in the fisheries sector".[135] Although the regulation sets down specific guidance on the timeline for the provision of such data, the Commission may withhold data transmission to the end-users for a period of three years in order to protect the professional interests of the data collectors.[136] In line with the general trends in European law, the regulation provides certain safeguards and restrictions regarding access to personal data and the use of data derived from satellite vessel monitoring systems.[137]

This Regulation sets an important standard but does not establish a free-for-all approach to fishery data in so far as it clearly circumscribes the obligations of the end-users in relation to the data by providing that they: use the data only for the purpose stated in their request; are responsible for correct and appropriate use of the data with regard to scientific ethics; inform the Commission and the Member States concerned of any suspected problems with the data; provide the Member States concerned and the Commission with references to the results of the use of the data; not to forward the requested data to third parties without the consent of the Member State concerned; not to sell the data to any third party.[138] Albeit it comes within an area where the EU exercises exclusive competence under the CFP and thus cannot be compared to other forms of MSR data, the Regulation nonetheless sets an important precedent

[132] This includes commercial fisheries for eels and salmon in inland waters. The EU Programme also extends to: recreational fisheries carried out within EU waters including recreational fisheries for eels and salmon in inland waters; aquaculture activities related to marine species, including eels and salmon, carried out within the Member States and EU waters; industries processing fisheries products.

[133] Art 3(1)(a) of Council Regulation No 199/2008.

[134] Art 18 of Council Regulation No 199/2008.

[135] Art 1(1)(i) of Council Regulation No 199/2008.

[136] Art 18(3)(a) of Council Regulation No 199/2008.

[137] Arts 1(3) and 18(2) of Council Regulation No 199/2008.

[138] Art 22 of Council Regulation No 199/2008.

regarding the sharing of European MSR data with a view to implementing ecosystem-based management in accordance with the requirements set down by a range of regulatory instruments such as the MSFD and the Water Framework Directive.

6.5 *Data acquired under the Framework Research Programmes*

As seen previously, a considerable amount of research concerning the practical aspects of undertaking ecosystem-based management is undertaken under the European framework research programmes. The Regulation governing the 7th Framework Programme has specific rules concerning the sharing and dissemination of "background" and "foreground" information.[139] The former relates to information which is held by participants prior to their participation in a European research project and the latter relates to "the results, including information, whether or not they can be protected," which are generated by the research. Such rights are also governed by the Grant Agreement which is concluded between the Commission and the various parties participating in the research programme. Again the central thrust of these measures is to ensure that scientific information and data are made available to the scientists working on specific projects where appropriate.

PART II
Ship-based MSR in EU Member States

7. *Member State practice in relation to MSR*

The practice of the EU Member States regarding the implementation of the MSR provisions in the 1982 Convention varies considerably. This divergence of practice has its origins the different positions taken by the EEC Member States at UNCLOS III and their inability to adopt a common position regarding the legal regime that ought to apply to MSR in sea areas under coastal State sovereignty and jurisdiction.[140] At the Conference, some Member States such as France, the Netherlands, and United Kingdom were strong advocates of the freedom of scientific research. The Netherlands made considerable efforts to

---

139 Arts 49 and 50, Regulation No 1906/2006. OJ L 391/1, 30.12.2006.

140 See, *inter alia*: M. Nordquist (*et al.*) *United Nations Convention on the Law of the Sea 1982: A Commentary* (Dordrecht/Boston/Lancaster, Martinus Nijhoff Publishers, 1985) Vol. 1, p. 84; J.F. Buhl, "The European Economic Community and the Law of the Sea" (1982) 2 *ODIL* 188–200 at 186.

ensure that the development of the concept of the EEZs would not result in an unjustifiable restriction on MSR.[141] Other Member States such as Ireland were interested in the establishment of a practicable regime that reflected the principles of qualified coastal State consent in relation to research conducted within the EEZ and on the continental shelf.[142] Moreover, the views expressed by 9 Member States at the time of the Conference do not reflect the position of the 27 Member States that make-up the EU today.[143] In the absence of harmonisation measures at an EU level, ascertaining what the precise nature of Member State practice in relation to the implementation of Part XIII of the Convention presents its own challenges as little has been published on the subject since Professor Soons completed his incisive study in the mid 1990s.[144]

One of the most comprehensive primary sources of information on state practice is the IOC survey on the practice of IOC Member States with respect to Parts XIII and XIV (which deals with the Transfer of Marine Technology (TMT)) of the 1982 Convention for the period 1998–2002.[145] The results of the survey have to be treated with care in view of the transient nature of state

[141] See A. Soons, *Marine Scientific Research and the Law of the Sea* (Kluwer Law and Taxation Publishers, Deventer, 1982) at pp. 63–66.

[142] Official Records of UNCLOS III, Vol. VI, Summary Record of Meetings, Third Committee, 30th Meeting, Para 20. For a comprehensive insight into the Irish position on MSR and related matters, see M. Hayes, *The Law of the Sea: The role of the Irish delegation at the Third UN Conference* (Dublin, Royal Irish Academy, 2011).

[143] The nine EEC Member States which participated at the conference were: Belgium, Denmark, Germany, France, Ireland, Italy, the Netherlands, Luxembourg and the United Kingdom.

[144] A. Soons, "Regulation of Marine Scientific Research by the European Community and its Member States" (1992) 23 *Ocean Development and International Law* 259.

[145] Further, to a request from the United Nations General Assembly and the IOC Executive Council, the IOC drafted and issued a Questionnaire to survey the practice of IOC Member States with respect to Parts XIII and XIV (which deals with the Transfer of Marine Technology (TMT)) of the 1982 Convention for the period 1998–2002. See Paragraph 23 of United Nations General Assembly Resolution A/RES/56/12 and the International Oceanographic Commission Executive Council Resolution EC-XXXV-7. The purpose of the survey was threefold: firstly, to assess the problems encountered in the implementation of Part XIII; secondly, to assist States in establishing generally accepted guidelines, criteria and standards for the transfer of marine technology in accordance with Article 271 of the 1982 Convention; and thirdly, to inform the international community as to the status of MSR and TMT and the practical issues raised in the implementation of Part XIII and XIV of the 1982 Convention. Although there were a relatively high number of non-respondents with only 82 of the 136 IOC Member States had responded to core components of the survey by 2008 which amounts to a 60% response rate, the results of the survey make interesting reading as it provides us with an excellent overview of the general thrust of international state practice on this important aspect of the Convention. In addition, a concise and useful analysis of the data compiled from the survey was undertaken by experts on behalf of the IOC in 2003 and 2005, with an update in 2008. One core component of this analysis which was undertaken by an expert from the United States State Department, Ms. Elizabeth Tirpak, and is cited

practice both within and beyond the EU. Regardless of this shortcoming, the IOC survey provides us with a useful yardstick with which to measure progress by Member States in discharging their obligations under Part XIII. Out of a total of 22 coastal Member States, 16 completed the IOC Questionnaire.[146] Somewhat surprisingly, the results of the survey demonstrate that Member State practice in the EU does not appear to have changed to any great extent since

here in full as it clearly outlines a number of emerging trends regarding state practice in this evolving field of law. This passage reads as follows:

- "There are a considerable number of countries interested in receiving guidance/assistance in updating or creating legislation for marine scientific research.
- Very few of the respondents that acknowledged national legislation for MSR provided copies of the relevant national legislation as requested per Section I Question IA.3.
- Of the 25 countries that have specified an MSR application form, fewer than half were based on ICES or the UN Standard Form A.
- Most countries listed security as the rationale for not employing the implied consent regime.
- The implied consent regime has been employed – in general – by governments lacking resources to conduct the same research in their EEZs.
- Data indicate that there are very few instances of misrepresentation on behalf of the researching State, which would likely trigger the suspension or cessation of research.
- IOC Member States show very high approval rates for MSR applications.
- Researchers need to be acutely aware of the coastal State's perspectives on such specifics as "start dates" when applying for clearance.
- Observers, when employed by the coastal State, typically serve multiple purposes.
- Researching States are sharing their data – however half of those countries are apparently *not* conducting research in waters outside their jurisdiction."

Since 2008, five additional IOC Member States (Croatia, Fiji, Ireland, Samoa, and South Africa) have completed the Questionnaire. Overall, the results of the IOC Survey suggest that the practical implementation of Parts XIII appears to be far from satisfactory. Most notably, the absence of national legislation, bilateral and multilateral agreements, as well as regional agreements which are aimed at facilitating and promoting MSR, are major shortcomings in a regime that is intended to be a model of international collaborative and cooperative endeavor. See E. Tirpak, Results of IOC Questionnaire N°3 on the Practice of States in the Fields of Marine Scientific Research and Transfer of Marine Technology: An update of the 2003 analysis by Lt. Cdr. Roland J. Rogers. Presented at Fifth Meeting of the Advisory Body of Experts on the Law Of The Sea (IOC/ABE-LOS V), Buenos Aires, Argentina, 11–15 April 2005; and by the same author, Practices of States in the Fields of Marine Scientific Research and Transfer of Marine Technology *An Update of the 2005 Analysis of Member State Responses to Questionnaire No. 3* IOC/ABE-LOS VIII, Paris, 21–25 April 2008.The results of the survey are available at: Available at: http://ioc3.unesco.org/abelos/index.php?option=com_content&task=view&id=45&Itemid=56

146 The 16 of the 22 coastal Member States replied to the survey (Belgium, Bulgaria, Denmark, Finland, France, Germany, Ireland (2008), Lithuania, The Netherlands, Poland, Portugal, Romania, Slovenia, Spain, Sweden, and the United Kingdom). The non-respondents were Cyprus, Estonia, Greece, Italy, Latvia, and Malta.

Professor Soons published his original study in the early 1990s.[147] In general, it is evident that state practice in the EU varies considerably and there is no uniform approach by Member States to the regulation and management of foreign vessel MSR in sea areas under their sovereignty and jurisdiction. A summary of the information provided by Member States is shown in Table 1 below.[148]

Significantly, 13 of the Member States who respond to the IOC Survey indicated that they have adopted some form of legislation governing foreign MSR. Again this legislation differs to a significant extent with some Member States such as Poland and Latvia setting a high standard by adopting specific laws which replicate many of the MSR provisions in the 1982 Convention.[149] Other Member States such as the Netherlands, the United Kingdom have remained true to their original negotiation position at UNCLOS III by not enacting national legislation regulating the activities of foreign vessels engaged in MSR. The administrative practice of both these States, nonetheless, appears to follow the scheme set down by the 1982 Convention very closely.[150] One noteworthy point is that the United Kingdom does not consider "as a matter of law" that hydrographic survey constitutes MSR under the 1982 Convention.[151] This is similar to the position taken by the United States on this issue.[152] As mentioned above, the Netherlands has been a longstanding advocate of the adoption of simplified reciprocal arrangements between EU Member States governing vessel based MSR.[153]

A number of Member States such as Ireland have not adopted national legislation on MSR but utilise their laws on the continental shelf and fisheries to address the matter indirectly. The position in relation to Spain appears to be slightly oblique in so far the IOC Survey indicates that there are no specific measures implementing UNLOS MSR provisions but at the same time it lists *Royal Decree 799/1981* which is clearly relevant to the subject of foreign vessel

[147] A. Soons, "Regulation of Marine Scientific Research by the European Community and its Member States" (1992) 23 *Ocean Development and International Law* 259.

[148] Additional information has been obtained from the DOALOS website and the academic works cited in footnotes 14 and 17 *infra.*

[149] IOC Survey, Responses from Poland and Latvia. Available at: http://ioc3.unesco.org/abelos/index.php?option=com_content&task=view&id=45&Itemid=33

[150] First noted by M. Geoffrey, United Kingdom Material International Law 1985, *British Yearbook of International Law*, 1985, pp. 500–503.

[151] See V. Lowe, "The United Kingdom and the Law of the Sea" in T. Treves (ed.), *The Law of the Sea, The European Union and its Member States* at p. 552.

[152] J.A. Roach, "Marine Scientific Research and the New Law of the Sea" (1996) 27 *Ocean Development and International Law* 59 at 60.

[153] A. Soons, "Regulation of Marine Scientific Research by the European Community and its Member States" (1992) 23 *Ocean Development and International Law* 259.

based MSR.[154] At the time of writing, the law in Spain governing foreign vessel MSR and underwater cultural heritage is the subject of prompt release proceedings at ITLOS in *The M/V "Louisa" Case (Saint Vincent and the Grenadines* v. *Kingdom of Spain)*.[155] Elsewhere in Iberia, Portugal changed its position between UNCLOS I and III from a view supporting freedom of scientific research to one which now reflects the qualified coastal State consent approach to MSR in sea areas under national jurisdiction.[156] Today Portugal addresses foreign MSR by means of its continental shelf legislation and a licence must be obtained from the appropriate Ministerial authority in order to conduct oceanographic or other research on the continental shelf.[157]

In Scandinavia, state practice is more or less typical of Member State practice elsewhere in the EU. Thus, for example, Sweden which was a leading advocate of freedom of scientific research at UNCLOS III, addresses MSR by means of national legislation concerning the EEZ, the continental shelf, and the high seas but again has not adopted specific national legislation on the subject of MSR.[158] Similarly, Finland has no specific legislation but relies upon a range of measures such as the Continental Shelf Act of 1965, the Surveillance Decree of 1989, as well as fisheries legislation to address MSR in sea areas under national jurisdiction. At the other side of the Baltic Sea, Denmark has a diffuse range of legal instruments that are relevant to MSR but relies upon administrative procedures and institutional arrangements for regulating the conduct of MSR by non-nationals in maritime zones under her national jurisdiction.[159]

Germany has a strong tradition in the marine sciences and has adopted the Federal Mining Law which concerns the approval of research activities on the continental shelf which do not relate to the exploitation of resources as well as *Meeresforschungsgesetz*, the Marine Research Law, authorizing the Ministry of Transport to regulate MSR in the German territorial sea and in the EEZ in accordance with Art. 245 to 255 of the 1982 Convention. At the time of the IOC Survey, no regulations had been issued under this law and this appears to be the current position at the time of writing. In practice, Germany relies upon an administrative procedure for foreign vessel MSR that is managed by the *Bundesamt für Seeschifffahrt und Hydrographie* in conjunction with the

---

[154] *Spanish legislation: R.D. 799/1981, 27 febrero (B.O.E. 8 mayo 1981)*. This measures is discussed by V. Bout, R. Bermejo, "L'Espagne et le droit de la mer" in T. Treves (ed.), *The Law of the Sea, The European Union and its Member States* at pp. 490–491.

[155] Available at http://www.itlos.org/start2_en.html

[156] M.E. Goncalves, "Le Portugal et le droit de la mer" in T. Treves (ed.), *The Law of the Sea, The European Union and its Member States* at pp. 443–444.

[157] Arts 5 and 6 Decree No 49–369 of 11 November 1969.

[158] IOC Survey, Response Sweden. Also, see, M. Jacobsson, "Sweden and the Law of the Sea" in T. Treves (ed.), *The Law of the Sea, The European Union and its Member States* at p. 553.

[159] IOC Survey, Response Denmark.

Federal Foreign Office and the Federal Ministry of Transport, Building, and Housing.[160]

In the Mediterranean Sea, neither Italy nor Greece responded to the IOC survey. This is surprising in light of their vested interests and the well-established MSR communities in both countries. At the various Law of the Sea Conferences, Italy supported the concept of freedom of scientific research in sea areas under coastal State jurisdiction and was the first country to advance the principle of tactic consent at the Seabed Committee in 1973. In order to address practical matters, the Italian Ministry of Foreign Affairs issued a Note concerning the regulation of scientific research by foreign vessels in areas under Italian jurisdiction in 1984.[161] As pointed by Judge Treves, this follows the general scheme of the 1982 Convention in many respects but exceeds what is set down in the 1982 Convention on a number of points.[162] In line with other international agreements, the 1982 Convention is implemented into Italian law by statute and the provisions therein thus supersede the Note as a matter of law.[163]

Similar to Italy, Greece is another EU Member State with a strong tradition in MSR and marine related research. Again an administrative approach has been adopted and is set out in a *Note Verbale* issued by the Ministry of Foreign Affairs in Athens in 1978.[164] There have been a number of incidents regarding research by third countries in areas of the territorial sea that are claimed by both Greece and Turkey and this subject continues to be the source of controversy in the eastern Mediterranean Sea.[165]

Disappointingly, some of the EU Member States that participated in the survey did not provide copies of their national legislation as it applies to MSR as requested by the IOC. This makes it difficult to obtain a comprehensive overview of state practice in the EU. From the limited information available, however, it appears that only 2 Member States (Germany and Poland) appear

160 Available at http://www.bsh.de/en/Marine_uses/Science/Research_activities/index.jsp

161 T. Treves, "Italy and the Law of the Sea" in T. Treves (ed.), *The Law of the Sea, The European Union and its Member States* at p. 358.

162 *Ibid.*

163 *Ibid.*

164 UN OALOS, National Legislation, Regulations and Supplementary Documents on Marine Scientific Research in Areas under National Jurisdiction, 1989, p. 123. See *inter alia*: T. Kairitis (ed.), *Greece and the Law of the Sea* (Dordrecht, Kluwer International Law, 1997); E. Roucounas, Greece and the Law of the Sea in T. Treves (ed.), *The Law of the Sea, The European Union and its Member States* at pp. 248–249.

165 M. Gorina-Ysern, An International Regime for Marine Scientific Research, p. 275. This issue was raised before the International Court of Justice in the Aegean Sea Continental Shelf case, Request for Indication of Interim Measures of Protection. The Court did not issue any interim measures. See http://www.icj-cij.org/docket/files/62/6221.pdf

to have specific regulatory measures implementing Part XIII. This is not fully representative of the overall position as can be seen from the information presented in Table 1 below as at least 12 Member States have some form of legislation that address MSR but this in the main has a much broader material scope (*ratione materae*) in so far as it addresses matters such as the continental shelf, fisheries and the EEZ. Of the 16 Member States that replied to the survey, all require consent to be sought by means of official channels for foreign vessel based MSR in sea areas under their sovereignty and jurisdiction. Five Member States utilise the ICES Standard Form and the remainder utilise a specialised form which shares similarities with the UN Standard Form A. The Helsinki Commission has adopted the ICES Form. On the whole, the level of requests for foreign vessel based request is impressive with some Member States such as Sweden and Denmark receiving up to 300 and 200 requests respectively for authorisation over the five-year period 1998–2002. The level of approvals is equally impressive with almost all request approved by Member States and with only one member States, Denmark, recording a less than 98% approval rating at 95%. This trend is consistent with the general trend of IOC Member States which showed very high approval rates for MSR applications.[166] All of the EU Member States surveyed, apart form Finland, Lithuania and Slovenia, have benefited from the procedure of implied consent as set out in Article 252 of the 1982 Convention to conduct research in the waters of another coastal State. Ten Member States have had observers embarked on foreign research vessels serving multiple purposes. Nine Member States require researchers to provide the relevant authorities with copies of data and samples in accordance Article 249 (1c) of the 1982 Convention. Practice on this matter appears to vary considerably with some Member States such as Finland limiting their request to data on sea bottom mapping / profiling. Overall, however, the sharing of data between researching States and coastal Member States does not appear to pose any specific problem or impediments in the EU. From the information presented by EU Member States, there appear to be a number of instances where there has been the suspension or cessation of research for non-compliance with Articles 248 and 249 of the 1982 Convention. Namely, Belgium and France, with Finland rerouting research cruises for grounds relating to military purposes or concerns.

Interestingly from a law of the sea perspective, there is no generally accepted definition of what constitutes "fundamental MSR" in Member State or EU law. This omission does not seem to create any practical problems regarding

[166] E. Tirpak, Results of IOC Questionnaire N°3 on the Practice of States in the Fields of Marine Scientific Research and Transfer of Marine Technology: An update of the 2003 analysis by Lt. Cdr. Roland J. Rogers. Presented at Fifth Meeting of the Advisory Body of Experts on the Law Of The Sea (IOC/ABE-LOS V), Buenos Aires, Argentina, 11–15 April 2005.

the regime that is applied by the Member States. In general, it appears that the practice of EU Member States is more or less consistent with the general scheme set down in Part XIII of the 1982 Convention. Furthermore, a brief perusal of national legislation and administrative practices appears to suggest that the majority of Member States appear to assert their jurisdiction over MSR in very general terms. The principal weakness in the current regime appears to be the absence of harmonisation regarding the administrative and procedural requirements governing foreign vessel based MSR projects. Importantly, undertaking MSR in the regional seas which surround the EU does not pose the same range of problems that are now being encountered elsewhere in the world such as the South China Sea or the Indian Ocean. Indeed, several EU Member States have adopted an approach similar to the United States aimed at fostering MSR in sea areas both within and beyond national jurisdiction. In other words, they have ensured that all EU Member States, have the right to conduct MSR subject to the rights and duties of other States as provided for in the 1982 Convention.

8. *Member State capacity to undertake ship-based MSR*

The capacity of the EU to undertake ship-based MSR compares very favourably to the capacity of other global maritime powers such as the United States and the Russian Federation. Such a comparison may not be apposite in view of the fact that research vessels fly the flag of the Member State in which they are registered and therefore it is somewhat misleading to talk about the "capacity of the EU". As such, there is no EU research fleet *per se* as there is no EU registry for research vessels apart from the national shipping registries in the Member States. Accordingly, it may be more appropriate to talk about the research vessel capacity of the Member States as opposed to the EU. That being said, there are however a number of pan-European administrative and organisational structures which are concerned with the management and operation of research vessels. One such entity is the *Marine Board of the European Science Foundation*, which represents 31 organisations from 19 different countries in Europe involved in MSR. In light of the diversity of interests that it represents, the Marine Board has a wide brief, which extends to defining common priorities and activities that impact upon the research agendas adopted by the Member States and the EU. Importantly, the Marine Board has undertaken important work aimed at promoting a more integrated approach to the utilization of European research infrastructure including research vessels. Much of progress to date can be attributed to a Working Group established by the Marine Board in 2007 tasked with examining the use of European research vessels and their associated equipment, and mandated with making recommendations regarding their enhanced use and improved management at a European level. The Working Group produced a position paper entitled: *European Ocean Research Fleets – Towards a Common Strategy and Enhanced Use,* which made wide ranging recommendations on the subject.[167]

In 2007, the research fleet was made-up of 46 vessels including 11 of Global class, 15 of Ocean class and 20 of Regional class (see Figures 2 and 4 below). This particular classification is similar to the one used in the United States and using this as a comparator it is evident that the size of the European fleet is relatively impressive and compares very favourably to size and number of research vessels available in the United States. The principal problem associated with the European research fleet relates to the age of vessels. This may be contrasted with the assessment of the large exchangeable equipment deployed on research vessels such as underwater submersibles which is described in the report as "state-of-the-art, performing excellently, and is more extensive than elsewhere in the world".[168]

From the viewpoint of our discussion regarding the need to undertake transboundary MSR to support the implementation of ecosystem-based management under the MSFD, it is significant to note that the Expert Group found that national authorities in the Member States are the principal funding bodies for ship-time.[169] Furthermore, they expressed the view that this situation was unlikely to change in the near future and the onus rested with the same national authorities to generate further "European integration" regarding the utilisation of ship resources and other infrastructure.[170] The Expert Group made several substantive recommendations that are worthy of enumeration here in light of the practical difficulties encountered in undertaking ecosystem-based management on a transboundary basis with the limited resources that are available in the Member States to undertake deep-ocean science. Firstly, they urge national authorities in the Member States to promote and support the co-ownership national equipment pools and to open possibilities to barter/charter national fleets.[171] Secondly, they call on the Marine Board to "promote the integration of the use of European fleets; its Member Organisations to find ways and means

---

[167] Marine Board, *European Ocean Research Fleets – Towards a Common Strategy and Enhanced Use* (Ostend, March 2007). Available at: http://www.esf.org/index.php?eID=tx_nawsecuredl&u=0&file=fileadmin/be_user/research_areas/marine/pdf/Publications/MBPP10_OFWG.pdf&t=1291123536&hash=92aa612744e7e9611da47b2934a7bf61

[168] *Ibid.* at p. 10.

[169] *Id.*

[170] *Id.*

[171] *Id.* at p. 11.

to enhance coordination of fleets and equipment scheduling, to launch transnational technical teams for deployment of heavy equipment, and to elaborate together proposals, on inter-operability for instance, and to present them to the European Commission."[172] Thirdly, they call upon the European institutions to support new infrastructure projects dedicated to inter-operability.[173] Fourthly, they recommended the re-organisation of the various European groups concerned with the exchange of equipment and the operation of research vessels into two specific groups, the Ocean Facilities Exchange Group and the European Research Vessel Operators Group.[174] Overall, the central thrust of these recommendations is to improve efficiency and to contribute to the enhanced integration of critical infrastructure at a pan-European level. This is entirely consistent with the requirements of delivering ecosystems-based management under the MSFD which requires policy-makers to obtain comprehensive scientific knowledge on the status of the marine environment.

Since the publication of the Marine Board position paper there have been a number of other initiatives at a pan-European level aimed at improving the efficiency and inter-operability of European research infrastructure. In 2009, for example, the European Commission financed a project under the 7th Framework Research Programme entitled "Towards an Alliance of European Research Fleets" (the "Eurofleets Project") which brings together 24 partners from 16 Member States and associated countries who own or operate research vessels with a view to enhancing their coordination and promoting the cost-effective use of their facilities.[175] The project has a budget of €7 million and is in the process of developing a common strategic vision for European research fleets and their associated heavy equipment. One of the project tasks is to promote a common language among European research fleets by reinforcing common standards and experimental protocols. A key project objective is to improve access to research vessels and their associated equipment by facilitating transnational access to infrastructure and facilities in the Member States.

[172] *Id.*

[173] *Id.*

[174] *Id.*

[175] Available at http://www.eurofleets.eu/np4/15

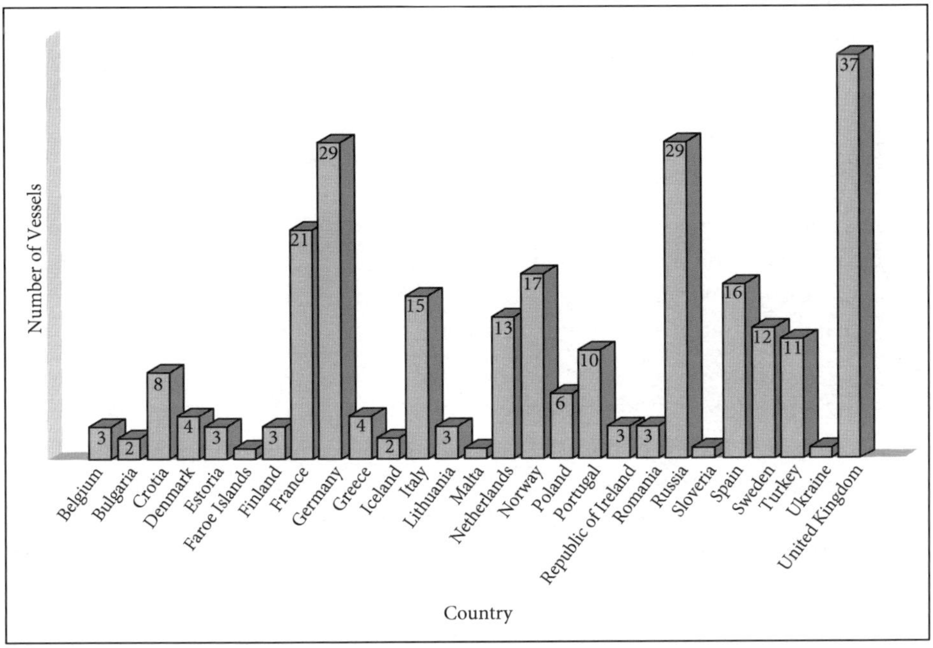

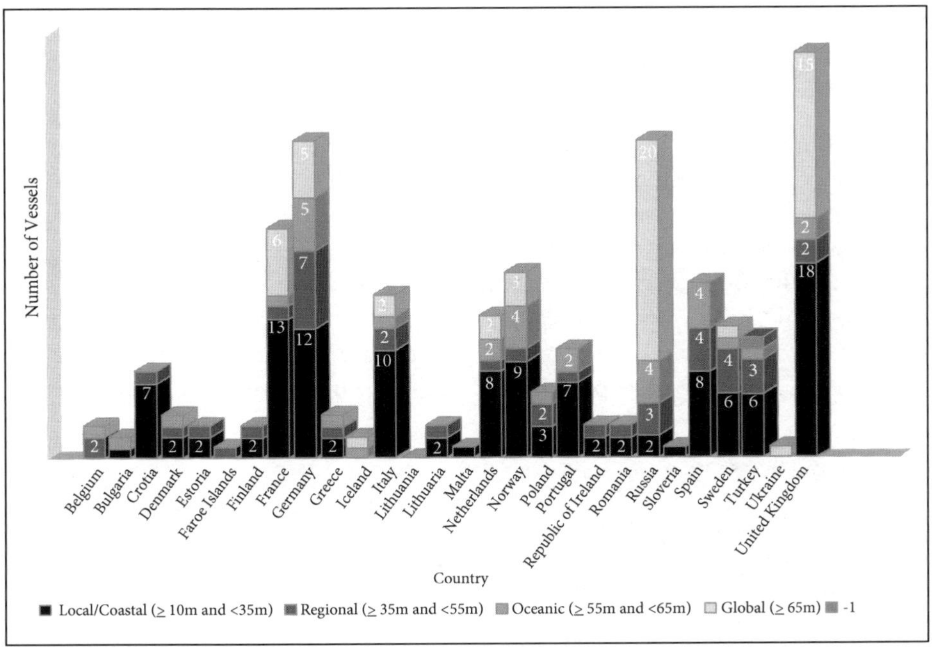

Sources Figures 2 & 4: EurOcean Database on European Research Vessels[176]

[176] Available at http://www.rvinfobase.eurocean.org/

Part III
Harmonising Member State Practice: Why, What and How?

9. *Why do Member States need to harmonise national procedures?*

Apart from implementing the European Research Area, there appears to be several valid reasons why the Member States in the EU need to streamline current procedures governing ship-based MSR. Some of the principal reasons that support harmonisation are mentioned here.

9.1 *Implementing international law*

As a start point, the simplification of current procedures and practices of the Member States in relation to MSR will accord with international legal obligations that arise for the EU and the Member States under the scheme set down in Part XIII of the 1982 Convention.[177] This approach will also build upon the sterling work undertaken by the Member States and the EU in promoting and facilitating the work of international bodies such as the IOC and ICES which are mandated to undertake scientific research at global, regional and sub-regional levels.

9.2 *Implementing the EU Treaty right to provide and receive a service*

From a European law perspective, harmonisation will sit very comfortably with treaty provisions which prohibit discrimination on the grounds of nationality and aim to eliminate restrictions to trade within the EU.[178] Clearly, the market for research ship-time is a European market and it may therefore be appropriate to say a little more about the applicable Treaty regime. The free movement provisions in the European Treaties guarantees the right of workers such as scientists to move freely from one Member State to another for the purpose of work.[179] This is a core principle of EU law and derogations can only be

[177] Arts 243 and 255, 1982 Convention.

[178] Art 18 of the TFEU. The Court has held that this provision is directly effective in *Baumbast and R v Secretary of State for the Home Department* [2002] ECR 1-7091.

[179] The concept of who constitutes a "worker" has a broad and unique meaning under European law and definitely encompasses members of the scientific community whose work normally entails performing services of economic value under the direction of another person in return for remuneration. On the meaning of the term "worker" see, *inter alia*: Case 53/81 *Levin* v. *Staatssecretaris van Justitie* [1982] ECR 1035; Case 139/85 *Kempf* [1986] ECR 1741; Case 3/87 *Agegate* [1989] ECR 4459; Case 196/87 *Steymann* [1988] ECR 6159; Case 344/87 *Bettray* [1989] ECR 1621; Case C-413/01 *Ninni-Orasche* [2003] ECR I-13187; Case C-456/02 *Trojani v. CPAS* [2004] ECR I-7573.

justified on the grounds set out in the Treaties and secondary EU legislation.[180] In practice, research vessels only move to another Member States temporarily and often do so to undertake research work commissioned by public and private bodies in another Member State or which is paid for by the EU under the framework research programmes.[181] Therefore the provisions in the TFEU which protects the right to provide and receive a service on a cross-border basis without restrictions are applicable to research services.[182] Briefly stated, EU Treaty provisions on this subject apply to both providers and recipients of services and are aimed at ensuring that the rules that are normally applied in a host Member State to service providers that resident in that Member State are also applied to the activities of a temporary nature pursued by persons who are normally resident in another Member State. Services may be provided by sole traders, companies or partnerships and include activities of an industrial, commercial or professional character normally undertaken on a remunerated basis.[183] These are important considerations in the case of ship time on board research vessels which tends to be expensive, publically funded, and may entail additional costs if it includes the use of large equipment such as ROVs and submersibles. Significantly, the Court has held that publically funded services such as education and research come within the scope of the Treaty provisions and a service may be provided or received on a temporary or infrequent basis.[184] *A priori*, all discrimination based on nationality in relation to such services whether direct or indirect is prohibited under the TFEU.[185]

A preliminary assessment suggests that the different authorisation requirements described above that apply to research ships flying the flag of a Member State offering a scientific service in another Member State do not sit comfortably with the Treaty provisions which guarantee the freedom to provide and

[180] The right is not absolute and is subject to some important qualifications under Article 45(4) of the TFEU and under secondary legislation including Regulation (EEC) No 1612/68 of the Council of 15 October 1968 on freedom of movement for workers within the Community OJ 257, 19.10.1968, pp. 2–12; Directive 2004/58/EC of the European Parliament and of the Council of 29 April 2004 on the right of citizens of the Union and their family members to move and reside freely within the territory of the Member States amending Regulation (EEC) No 1612/68 and repealing Directives 64/221/EEC *OJ L 158, 30.4.2004. Article 46 of t*he TFEU provides a legal basis for the European Parliament and Council to issue directives or make regulations setting out the measures required to bring about the free movement policy.

[181] As seen above, the ship time is normally paid from public funding in the Member States. See note 168 *infra* at p. 10.

[182] Art 56 of the TFEU.

[183] Art 57 of the TFEU.

[184] In Case 286/83 *Luisi and Carbone v Ministero del Tesoro* [1984] *ECR* 377, the ECJ held that education can be a service if it is provided by a private body on a commercial basis.

[185] Case 205/84 *Commission v Germany* [1986] ECR 3755.

receive a service in another Member Treaty. In practice, they make it more difficult for ship operators to reach potential customers in a host Member State and apply different rules than those that apply to a ship operator established in that Member State. There is important secondary legislation in this particular field in the form of the Services Directive which requires Member States to remove unjustified and disproportionate burdens including administrative burdens when a service provider wants to supply services across borders in another Member State, without setting up an establishment there.[186]

The Treaty sets down a number of derogations which allow Member States to impose restrictions on the free movement provisions regarding posts that are connected with the exercise of official authority, or on the grounds of public policy, security or public health.[187] In the context of free movement of workers, however, both the European Court of Justice and the European Commission have interpreted these restrictions very narrowly.[188] Suffice to note here that research for non-military purposes or research undertaken on behalf of a national research agency do not come within the scope of the exceptions.[189] From a legal viewpoint, streamlining the consent procedures as suggested in this paper will be fully consistent with the achievement of a fundamental aspect of the EU Treaties as it will facilitate the freedom to provide and receive a scientific service across the EU.

9.3 *Implementing the ecosystems approach*

As is evident from our discussion so far, harmonisation will also facilitate the implementation of the ecosystems based approach to management of human

---

[186] Directive 2006/123/EC of the European Parliament and of the Council of 12 December 2006 on services in the internal market, OJ L 376, 27.12.2006, pp. 36–68. Under the Directive, service providers are able to obtain information and complete administrative formalities through points of single contact in each Member State. The EU has also adopted a Directive (referred to as the "Posted Workers Directive") which sets down the rules which applies to workers which are posted from State of origin to provide a service in another Member State. Directive 96/71/EC of the European Parliament and of the Council of 16 December 1996 concerning the posting of workers in the framework of the provision of services. OJ L 018, 21.01.1997 p. 1.

[187] Art 62 of the TFEU applies 51–54 of the treaty to the provisions on services.

[188] See COM (2002) 694 and the cases cited therein including Case 152/73, Sotgiu ECR [1974] 153; Case 149/79, Commission v Belgium I ECR [1980] 3881; Case 149/79, Commission v Belgium II ECR [1982] 1845; Case 307/84, Commission v France ECR [1986] 1725; Case 66/85, Lawrie-Blum ECR [1986] 2121; Case, 225/85 Commission v Italy ECR [1987] 2625; Case C-33/88, Allué ECR [1989] 1591; Case C-4/91, Bleis ECR [1991] I-5627; Case C-473/93, Commission v Luxembourg ECR [1996] I-3207; Case C-173/94, Commission v Belgium ECR [1996] I-3265; Case C-290/94, Commission v Greece ECR [1996] I-3285.

[189] Case 225/85 *Commission* v. *Italy* [1987] ECR 2625.

activities in the marine environment. This will be achieved through the provision of timely data, better knowledge of the marine environment, and scientific information regarding the impact of EU policies in the marine environment.[190] In this context it is worth noting that the *2009 European Commission's Progress Report on the EU's Integrated Maritime Policy* emphasises that there can be no maritime policy without proper data and knowledge on Europe's seas and coast.[191]

At this juncture, it may be appropriate to say a little more about the ecosystem approach as it has the potential to shape the future development of EU policy on ship-based MSR. In very general terms, the ecosystems approach is intended to provide for the conservation, management and exploitation of marine aquatic resources while maintaining the quality, structure and functioning of marine ecosystems.[192] The successful implementation of the approach is utterly contingent upon having good quality scientific data regarding the functioning of marine ecosystems. As noted in the OSPAR Quality Status Report 2010, "the implementation of the ecosystem approach requires a good understanding of the ecosystem and its dynamics and the development of appropriate indicators and scientific methodologies to enable evaluation of the quality status of the ecosystem in response to pressures from human activities".[193]

As noted above, the EU has taken a broad brush perspective to implementing this new normative concept for environmental management and there are several secondary legal instruments that assist the EU and the Member States in implementing the ecosystem approach including the Habitats and Birds Directives, the Water Framework Directive and the MSFD. These instruments are very much science driven and require Member States to achieve good environmental status of all marine waters by 2020 at the latest in the North East Atlantic, the Mediterranean Sea, the Baltic Sea and the Black Sea.[194] One of

---

[190] Art 192 of the TFEU.

[191] Report from the Commission to the Council, the European Parliament, the European Economic and Social Committee and the Committee of the Regions, Progress Report on the EU's Integrated Maritime Policy, COM (2009) 540, Brussels, 15 October 2009, at p. 7.

[192] R. Long, "The EU Marine Strategy Framework Directive: A New European Approach to the Regulation of the Marine Environment, Marine Natural Resources and Marine Ecological Services", International Bar Association, (2011) *Journal of Energy and Natural Resources Law* 29 (1) pp. 1–45.

[193] Available at: www.ospar.org. This report reviews all aspects of human influence on the quality of the marine environment of the OSPAR maritime area which is divided into five regions (the Arctic Waters, Greater North Sea, Celtic Seas, Bay of Biscay and Iberian Coast, Wider Atlantic).

[194] Directive 2008/56/EC of the European Parliament and of the Council of 17 June 2008 establishing a framework for community action in the field of marine environmental policy (Marine Strategy Framework Directive) OJ L 164/19, 25 June 2008. For commentary on

the first steps under the Directive is that Member States must "establish and implement coordinated monitoring programmes for the ongoing assessment of the environmental status of their marine waters by 2014."[195] Significantly, such monitoring programmes must be compatible within marine regions or sub regions and must build upon, and be compatible with, relevant provisions for assessment and monitoring laid down by EU legislation, including the Habitats and Birds Directives, or under international agreements.[196] With a view to facilitating coherence and coordination at a regional level, Member States must ensure that: (a) monitoring methods are consistent across the marine region or sub region so as to facilitate comparability of monitoring results; (b) relevant transboundary impacts and transboundary features are taken into account. Elaborate and indicative lists of the elements that need to be provided in the monitoring programme are set out in Annex III and Annex V of the Directive. These by definition will require a high level of scientific cooperation across a broad range of scientific disciplines and across borders. Therefore it comes as no surprise to find that Member State cooperation and coordination with third countries by means of the regional seas agreements are at the heart of the scheme introduced by the Directive.[197] The ultimate aim is the integration of the conservation objectives, management measures and monitoring and assessment activities at the level of the various regional seas conventions with a view to achieving good environmental status by 2020.

The importance of MSR is noted in the preamble of the MSFD which points out that "strategies will be effective only if they are devised on the basis of a

---

this Directive from a political science perspective, see R. Long, The EU Marine Strategy Framework Directive: A New European Approach to the Regulation of the Marine Environment, Marine Natural Resources and Marine Ecological Services", (2011) *Journal of Energy and Natural Resources Law* 29 (1) pp. 1–45; L. Juda, 'The European Union and the Marine Strategy Framework Directive: Continuing the Development of Ocean Use Management', (2010) 41 *ODIL* 34–54; N. Westaway, 'The New European Marine Strategy Framework Directive', (2008) 10 *Env L Rev* 218–224; S Fletcher, 'Converting science to policy through stakeholder involvement: an analysis of the European Marine Strategy Directive', (2007) 54 *Marine Pollution Bulletin* 1881–1886; L.D. Mee *et al.*, 'How good is good? Human values and Europe's proposed Marine Strategy Directive', (2008) 56 *Marine Pollution Bulletin* 187–204; A. Borja, 'The new European Marine Strategy Directive: difficulties, opportunities, and challenges', (2006) 52 Marine *Pollution Bulletin* 239–42.

[195] Art 5.2(a)(iv) of Directive 2008/56/EC.

[196] Art 11(1) of Directive 2008/56/EC.

[197] In particular, the Convention on the Protection of the Marine Environment of the Baltic Sea Area; the Convention for the Protection of the Marine Environment of the North-East Atlantic; the Convention for the Protection of the Marine Environment and the Coastal Region of the Mediterranean; and the Protocol for the Protection of the Mediterranean Sea Against Pollution from Land-Based Sources; 1992 Convention on the Protection of the Black Sea against Pollution.

sound knowledge of the state of the marine environment in a particular area and are tailored as closely as possible to the needs of the waters concerned in the case of each Member State".[198] In 2010, the Commission laid down criteria and methodological standards to be used by the Member States for monitoring and assessment of the marine environment.[199] There is an express legal obligation under this instrument and the MSFD regarding the sharing of data and information in so far as Member States must provide the Commission with access and use rights in respect of data and information resulting from the initial assessments and from the ongoing monitoring programmes of the status of the marine environment.[200] In addition, such information and data must also be made available to the European Environment Agency for the performance of its tasks.[201]

9.4 *Implementing maritime spatial planning and ICZM*

Harmonisation will also complement initiatives such as maritime spatial planning (MSP) and integrated coastal zone management (ICZM) which are heavily dependent on good quality scientific evidence and data.[202] In 2008, the Commission adopted the "Roadmap on Maritime Spatial Planning: Achieving Common Principles in the EU" (the "Roadmap") which sets down 10 key principles and seeks to promote the development of a common approach among Member States in the implementation of MSP at national and EU level.[203] Principle 5 is the streamlining of the application process for licences and consents for offshore activities at a national level in the Member States.[204] The Roadmap points out that "cooperation across borders is necessary to ensure coherence of plans across ecosystems. It will lead to the development of common standards and processes and raise the overall quality of MSP".[205] Furthermore, that "MSP has to be based on sound information and scientific knowledge."[206] Since the publication of the Roadmap, the Commission have launched two preparatory actions in the Baltic Sea and in the North Sea/North East Atlantic. These aim to develop the cross-border cooperation aspects and economic benefits of MSP.

---

198 Recital 23 of the Preamble.

199 Commission Decision of 1 September 2010 on criteria and methodological standards on GES of marine waters, OJ L 232/14, 2.9.2010.

200 Art 19(3) of Directive 2008/56/EC.

201 Art 19(3) of Directive 2008/56/EC.

202 ICZM Recommendation.

203 Communication from the Commission. Roadmap for Maritime Spatial Planning: Achieving Common Principles in the EU. COM(2008) 791 final. Brussels, 25.11.2008.

204 Para 5.5, COM(2008) 791 final.

205 Para 5.7, COM(2008) 791 final.

206 Para 5.10, COM(2008) 791 final.

In addition, they have commissioned a study on the potential of MSP in the Mediterranean Sea of MSP. In a progress report on the implementation of the EU's IMP, the Commission expressed the view that spatial planning can drastically improve the way we manage our maritime spaces and preserve their ecosystems.[207] Viewed in this light, the streamlining of the procedures for the conduct of ship-based MSR will facilitate and reduce the costs in implementing MSP as it will entail the introduction of a simplified permit system and administrative procedures in the Member States. This will bring about significant cost reductions in the planning of scientific cruises. Furthermore, it will facilitate the implementation of the ecosystem approach. As noted in the Communication from the Commission:

> *The sea is a complex ecosystem that cuts across administrative borders. For balanced long-term management, the whole ecosystem and its determining factors must be taken into account. Planning must seek to protect and enhance the marine environment. Work on MSP at EU level provides an appropriate forum for Member States to discuss and develop a holistic approach to the management of maritime activities in line with ecosystem requirements.*[208]

The Communication goes on to point out that MSP needs to be based on sound information and scientific knowledge and it highlights several scientific and data gathering tools that have been developed in the EU with a view to undertaking adaptive management of the marine environment.[209] These include some of the initiatives described above including: the European Marine Observation and Data Network (EMODNET). In conclusion, the harmonisation of the procedures that apply to foreign vessel MSR will assist the implementation of MSP through the provision of a stable and more coherent regulatory framework for undertaking ship-based MSR on a cross-boundary basis.

10. *What measures ought to be harmonised at an EU level?*

From the review undertaken above, it appears that there is a compelling case supporting the harmonisation and the simplification of the complex and expensive procedures associated with the planning and implementation of MSR projects by vessels flying the flag of a Member State when such projects are going to be undertaken in sea areas under the sovereignty and jurisdiction of another Member State of the EU. But what exactly needs to be harmonised?

---

[207] Progress Report on the EU's Integrated Maritime Policy, COM(2009) 540, Brussels, 15 October 2009 at 11.

[208] COM(2008) 791 final, p. 4.

[209] COM(2008) 791 final, p. 11.

At a rather mundane administrative level, an EU harmonisation needs to address matters such as to how and when scientists are required to submit a research cruise application, the information to be provided by the applicant to the coastal State, as well as the information to be provided to neighbouring land-locked States. There also appears to be a strong case for standardising the designated channels for the submission of such applications. On this particular issue, it is questionable whether is really necessary to work through the designated diplomatic channels as is currently the procedure in the majority of Member States as this normally entails communication by means of the diplomatic mission of the researching State to the Ministry of Foreign Affairs in the coastal State. Surely consideration ought to be given to allowing the researching institutions to communicate directly with a designated authority in the coastal Member State such as an "MSR Clearance Office" which is officially established and resourced for this purpose. This in itself would expedite the application process from the excessive limit of 6 months which is set down by the 1982 Convention to perhaps a more realistic period of 1 month for the processing an application if it is received electronically.[210] Obviously this process could be speeded up further if there is agreement to use a standard EU form modelled on the ICES Standard Form or the UN Draft Standard Form A.[211] As a minimum, the onus should be on the applicant to provide information which fulfils the requirements set down in Article 248 of the 1982 Convention and address matters such as: the objectives of the project; the name and details of the vessel and the scientific equipment embarked; the geographical coordinates of the project and the estimated times of arrival and departure of the vessel from sea areas under coastal State jurisdiction; the name of institution and the lead scientist for the research programme; the European and third-country partners participating in the project; the scope for participation of scientists and observer from the coastal State in the research project. The request for consent should be submitted in the working language of the coastal Member State where the project is going to take place. As a matter of EU law, the "standard EU application form" will have to be made available in all 23 official languages of the Member States.[212]

---

[210] Art 248 of the Convention.

[211] See, United Nations, *Guide for the Implementation of the Relevant Provisions of the UN Convention on the Law of the Sea* (United Nations, Office for Ocean Affairs and the Law of the Sea, New York, 1991).

[212] This in itself should not pose an insurmountable challenge as European legislation is normally published in 23 languages in the Official Journal of the EU prior to coming into force. These are: Bulgarian, Czech, Danish, Dutch, English, Estonian, Finnish, French, German, Greek, Hungarian, Irish, Italian, Latvian, Lithuanian, Maltese, Polish, Portuguese, Romanian, Slovak, Slovene, Spanish and Swedish.

The procedures and timeline for the response of the coastal Member State could also be standardised to address matters such as: the designation of a central MSR Office as a "one-stop shop" in the coastal Member State for the processing of applications and to ensure coordination at a national level. This office could be responsible for circulating the proposed application to national bodies such as the coastguard, government agencies and the appropriate ministries. Clearly, a Member State is required to grant consent for research projects in its exclusive economic zone or continental shelf unless the project comes within the four specified cases set out in the 1982 Convention. Namely, projects of direct significance for natural resource exploration and exploitation; projects involving drilling, use of explosives or the introduction of harmful substances into the marine environment; projects involving artificial islands, installations and structures; or research projects containing information that is inaccurate regarding the nature or objective of the project or where there is outstanding obligations in relation to a previous research project.[213] In view of the fact that the provisions on MSR in the 1982 Convention simply refer to the researching State, it would appear logical if the designated clearance office in the member State monitors compliance by both governmental and non-governmental research institutes with the obligations set down by the 1982 Convention as subsequently implemented into EU law. The EU harmonisation measure should also prescribe an exhaustive list the conditions which may be imposed by the coastal State when granting consent similar to the list enumerated in Article 249 of the 1982 Convention. This could include matters that are to be undertaken during or after a research cruise which are linked to the research undertaken at sea.

In relation to undertaking the research cruise, the EU harmonisation measure could address the following: the terms and conditions for coastal State participation in the research project when practicable; the duty to disclose changes in the research programme to the coastal State; the rights of the coastal State to suspend or to require the cessation of MSR; the removal of installations and equipment; general measures concerning the provision of assistance to research vessels; as well as the rules governing access and assessment of data, samples and research results.

The rights of research institutes in land-locked Member States (Austria, Luxembourg, Slovakia, the Czech Republic and Hungary) to participate in MSR projects could also be addressed in the harmonisation measures. Such measures would follow the general thrust of Art 254 of the 1982 Convention but it needs to be emphasised that research institutes in land-locked states of the EU have precisely the same rights and duties as institutes that are located in coastal

[213] Art 246 5 (a) to (d) of the 1982 Convention.

Member States under the EU Treaties. Indeed, EU secondary legislation such as the MSFD and the Water Framework Directive set down specific requirements for land-locked States regarding their role in the protection and preservation of the marine environment.[214]

Although not specifically provided for in the 1982 Convention, EU research vessels could be required to install and operate a vessel monitoring system with a view to facilitate monitoring compliance with the scheme of regulation set down by the EU harmonisation measure. This is of course is an issue which might provoke some discord among the scientific community and it is clearly beyond the scope of this paper to explore the legal implications of setting down such a requirement. *Prima facie*, however, the imposition of such a requirement would certainly make the task of monitoring the activities of research vessels less onerous for coastal and flag States.

10.1 *What type of measure could be used to harmonise Member State practice?*

There are several potential answers to this question as there are many options open to the EU should it wish to harmonise Member State practices on this matter. In the first instance, the reply will very much depend on whether a non-legislative or legislative approach is the preferred option. In relation to the former which is a softer intervention by the EU, it would be possible to tighten up the existing administrative procedures in the Member States to ensure that they are fully consistent with Part XIII of the 1982 Convention. This would not entail any regulatory action on the part of the EU and would only involve a degree of administrative coordination by the European institutions regarding the current practices in the Member States. This could be achieved by means of a Communication from the Commission setting down best practice on the subject matter or it could be in the form of an Action Plan, Roadmap, or Guidelines which encourage Member States, and other interested parties including the marine scientific community, to take appropriate steps in streamlining current practices regarding foreign vessel MSR. Along the same vein, the Council or the Commission could adopt a non-binding instrument as it has done in other areas of the maritime policy. An example of such an approach is evident the ICZM Recommendation mentioned above.[215] This would be slightly more formal but would not have the force of law in the Member States as it would simply encourage the adoption of a specific line of Member State conduct in

[214] See, for example, Article 6(2) and 6(3) of Directive 2008/56/EC which requires landlocked countries to bring into force only those measures that are necessary to ensure compliance with requirements under Article 6 (Regional Cooperation) and Article 7 (Competent Authorities) of Directive 2008/56/EC.

[215] See discussion on ICZM *infra*.

relation to the administration and control of foreign vessel MSR.[216] Broadly speaking, recommendations are adopted in areas where the EU lacks legal competence or where a transitional period is required before the EU institutions are empowered to adopt appropriate measures. Therefore, in the domain of MSR, where the EU shares competence with the Member States under the Treaties, the adoption of a non-binding legal instrument would not appear to be the most appropriate course of action.

Moving on to the second category, there appear to be two hard law options which both entail the adoption of a secondary European legal instrument following the procedures set down in the EU Treaties. The first is the adoption of a prescriptive instrument in the form of a European Parliament and Council Regulation.[217] The principal advantage of this approach is that regulations are binding in their entirety and directly applicable in all Member States.[218] This approach has a number of clear advantages in so far as regulations are incorporated automatically into the legal systems of each of the Member States and do not require national transposition measures. As a matter of practice, the European institutions generally rely upon regulations in instances where it is necessary to be clear and precise regarding the legal obligations that are created. Furthermore, regulations are directly effective which means that can be applied by the courts of the Member States as soon as they become operative. They are the preferred regulatory option in a number of policy areas such as fisheries and agriculture where there is a requirement to adopt legislation which requires speedy implementation by the Member States.

The second option is to adopt a relatively inflexible directive that leaves the national authorities a degree of autonomy regarding the choice of form and method of achieving desired results in relation to the conduct of MSR.[219] In contrast to regulations, a directive is not directly applicable and therefore requires national transposition measures by each Member State before they become effective in national legal systems. Directives by their very nature are more malleable than regulations as they usually provide Member States with a range of options from which they can choose when adopting their national implementation measure. Directives are the principal means of regulatory intervention under the EU's environmental policy and in many instances they leave Member States considerable discretion regarding national transposition measures. This leads to one obvious weakness which is that a number of EU Member States have tardy records when it comes to meeting their require-

[216] Note however that the European Court of Justice held in Case 322/88 *Grimaldi* [1989] ECR 4407 that recommendations are not devoid of all legal effect.

[217] Art 288(1) of the TFEU.

[218] Art 288(2) of the TFEU.

[219] Art 288(3) of the TFEU.

ments under EU directives and consequently this type of instrument would not appear to be the most appropriate for the task at hand. In any case, within the European legal order, the relevant institution are empowered by the Treaty to choose the relevant instrument for harmonisation once a particular legal basis is identified in the Treaties for such a measure.

10.2 *Finding an appropriate legal basis in the Treaties*

This takes us to the next question which is to identify an appropriate legal basis in the European Treaties in which to root an EU legislative measure aimed at harmonising Member State practice. The legal base in the Treaties will dictate the legislative procedures that must be followed in the European institutions as well as the voting procedures in the Council. In principle, without an appropriate legal base in the Treaties, the European institutions are prevented from adopting a measure that is legally binding on the Member States. Thus, for example, there is no specific legal basis in the Treaties for the Integrated Maritime Policy and most of the initiatives in this regard have consisted of soft law initiatives or else in the form of regulatory measures in the field of EU environmental protection that has its own separate legal basis in the TFEU.[220]

The task of selecting a legal base for draft legislation normally falls on the Commission who must also record the reasons for the legislative proposal, the decision-making process followed, and the institutions and bodies which participated in the legislative process.[221] A brief perusal of the Treaties reveals that there appear to be a number of treaty provisions that could be cited to support the adoption of common rules at an EU level regarding ship-based MSR. At first sight, the determination of a specific legal basis is not a straight-forward exercise as any such measure touches on several treaty provisions as seen previously including the provisions on the European Research Area, the freedom to provide and receive a service, and the EU's environmental policy.

Instructively, the European Court of Justice has set down a number of general principles that allow the European institutions to identify the appropriate legal base for a legislative act when there are a number of possibilities under the Treaties.[222] The choice is not simply dependent on the EU institution's conviction as to the objective pursued but must be based on objective criteria

---

[220] Art 3 of the TEU and Arts 4, 11, and 191 to 193 of the TFEU.

[221] Art 296 of the TFEU. These questions used to be the source of controversy and litigation between the European institutions but since the ratification of the Lisbon Treaty and the application of the ordinary legislative procedure to the majority of EU policy areas, there now appears to be less scope for conflict as this procedure puts the Parliament and the Council on an equal footing in the law-making process.

[222] The principles for the identification of the appropriate legal basis are described in most textbooks on EU law, see, *inter alia*: J. Fairhurst, *Law of the EU*, 8th Ed., (Harlow, Pearson,

which are amenable to judicial review by the Court taking into account the aim and content of the measure.[223] If the EU harmonisation measure seeks to achieve two objectives which are covered by different treaty provisions, then the objective that is considered to be the principal or predominant purpose must be selected as opposed to a purpose that is merely ancillary.[224] The Court has set down a test to resolve the difficulties concerning the identification of an appropriate legal basis which is refereed to as the "centre of gravity doctrine".[225] In effect, this means that the legal basis that is closest to the primary purpose of the instrument must be selected. In very exceptional circumstances where the proposed measure seeks to achieve a number of objectives which are of equal importance and which are inseparably linked, the measure may be rooted in a number of treaty provisions.[226]

If one is to follow the methodology set down by the Court it appears that any EU harmonisation measure aimed at standardising the procedures that apply to ship-based MSR in the Member States could have as its principal aim the implementation of the Treaty provisions on research and technological development.[227] This would allow the European Parliament and the Council, acting in accordance with the ordinary legislative procedure and after consulting the Economic and Social Committee, to adopt a harmonisation measure as a "complement to the activities planned in the multiannual framework programme."[228] Although much of the research conducted in sea areas under Member State jurisdiction and sovereignty is not connected with the framework programmes this would not appear to be an impediment to the adoption of an EU harmonisation measure as it could be argued that such a measure is necessitated to advance the implementation of the European Research Area.[229] In other words, the definition of "common standards" regarding ship-based research will facilitate researchers circulating and co-operating across borders in line with the

---

2010) pp. 125–150; A. Kaczorowska, *European Union Law*, 2nd Ed., (London / New York, Routledge-Cavendish, 2010) pp. 183–197, especially 219–220.

[223] Case C C-176/03 Commission v Council [2005] ECR I-7879; Case C-269/97 *Commission v Council* [2000] ECR I-2257; Case C-300/89 *Commission v Council* (Titanium Dioxide) [1991] ECR I-2867; Case 45/86 *Commission v Council* [1987] ECR 1493.

[224] Case T-99/05 *Spain v Commission* 10 May 2007; Case C-42/97 *Parliament v Council* [1999] ECR I-869.

[225] See *inter alia*: Case C-155/91 *Commission v Council* [1993] ECR I-939; Joined Cases C–164 and 165/97 *European Parliament v Council* [1999] ECR I-1139. For discussion of the application of this doctrine in relation to environmental legislation, see, R. Brady, in M. Nordquist, R. Long, T. Heidar and J. N. Moore (ed.) *Law, Science and Ocean Management* (Boston/ Leiden, Nijhoff, 2007) pp. 110–115.

[226] Case C-178/03 *Commission v European Parliament and Council* [2006] ECR I-107; Case C-281/01 *Commission v Council* [2002] ECR I-2049.

[227] These provisions are set out in Title XIX of the TFEU.

[228] Art 182(5) of the TFEU.

[229] Art 179(1) of the TFEU.

general scheme set down by the Treaties.[230] The TFEU expressly provides that all EU activities under the Treaties in the area of research and technological development, including demonstration projects, must be decided on and implemented in accordance with the provisions of Title XIX of the Treaty.[231] The EU is compelled to stimulate the training and mobility of researchers in the EU.[232] Furthermore, both the EU and Member States are obliged to coordinate their research and technological development activities so as to ensure that they are mutually consistent.[233] The European Commission thus have an explicit legal basis in which to root the proposed harmonisation measure and it is open to the European institutions to select the appropriate measure on how to achieve this objective.

10.3 *Legal constraints: the dual principles of subsidiarity and proportionality*

EU legislative measures harmonising the regulatory or administrative procedures of the Member States in relation to ship-based MSR have to be reconciled with the principles of subsidiarity and proportionality which are cardinal tenets of EU law that influence the decision of the European institutions to adopt draft legislation in any particular field.

The principle of subsidiarity was introduced into the EU Treaties in the mid 1980s with a view to maintaining a degree of equilibrium in the balance of powers between the EU Member States and the EU institutions. Essentially, the principle ensures that EU action is only permissible when particular objectives cannot be better attained at the level of the individual Member States. This ensures that the European institutions acts within the limits of the powers conferred on them by the Member States under the Treaties. The precise wording in the TEU on the principle is as follows: "in areas which do not fall within its exclusive competence, the EU shall act only if and in so far as the objectives of the proposed action cannot be sufficiently achieved by the Member States, either at central level or at regional and local level, but can rather, by reason of the scale or effects of the proposed action, be better achieved at EU level."[234]

[230] Art 179(2) of the TFEU.

[231] Art 179(3) of the TFEU.

[232] Art 180(d) of the TFEU.

[233] Art 181 of the TFEU.

[234] Art 5(3) of the Treaty on European Union. As an aside, it should also be mentioned that there is a Protocol on the application of both principles appended to the Treaties which sets down a number of procedural requirements which must be followed by the European institutions in bringing forward draft legislation. Protocol No 2 to the Treaty on European Union and the Treaty on the Functioning of the EU. Importantly, this provides a mechanism by which the Commission will have to reconsider a proposal if one-third of national parliaments consider that the proposal infringes the principle of subsidiarity.

The application of the principle will depend on which legal basis is selected for the proposed harmonisation measure. So for example, if the proposed measure is aimed at facilitating the provision of scientific services on a cross-border basis, then this is an exclusive EU competence and the principle is thus inapplicable. If on the other hand, the proposed measure is intended to implement the Treaty provisions on research and development as suggested above, then the principle is applicable as the regulation of ship-borne MSR is not within the exclusive competence of the EU but is shared with the Member States.[235] However, it may be contended that this does not pose an insurmountable legal obstacle for a number of reasons. To start with, the rationale underpinning EU legislative intervention in this particular field stems from the trans-national and regional nature of MSR activities which cannot be properly regulated by action at a national level in the Member States. Secondly, an EU legislative measure will facilitate Member States in implementing EU Directives and undertaking a whole range of tasks associated with ecosystem-based management, as well as soft law initiatives such as maritime spatial planning and integrated coastal zone management. Thirdly, it can also be argued that action at an EU level is likely to produce clear benefits by reason of its scale and effects, compared with regulatory action pursued at the level of an individual Member State or at the regions. In this regard, the decision to grant or refuse a particular research cruise will remain a question for the relevant authorities in the Member States following the long-established national administrative arrangements for processing foreign MSR cruise applications.

The principle of proportionality provides that any EU action should not go beyond what is necessary to achieve a legitimate objective. In contrast to principle of subsidiarity described above, it is less elusive as a legal concept in so far as it has a well-established history in both civil and common law jurisdictions. The principle was imported into EU law from the German legal system and it is aimed at ensuring that the content and form of EU action must not exceed what is necessary to achieve the objectives of the Treaties.[236] The suggested harmonisation measure appears to be proportionate since it will enable the Member States to achieve the objectives of a number of EU policies more effectively. In particular, there are tangible symbiotic links between MSR and EU policies such as fisheries, environment, research, climate change, and the EU's integrated maritime policy. Moreover, it should not be forgotten that the principal focus of any putative EU measure ought to be aimed at harmonising national measures and making existing administrative systems interoperable. In this context, some similarities may be drawn between the European integrated maritime surveillance system and the proposed measure.

[235] See discussion on EU competence to regulate MSR in paragraph 3 *infra*.

[236] Art 5(4) of the Treaty on European Union.

Assuming that the proposed measure is clearly predicated on the need for EU-wide action and is not overtly restrictive or onerous, it may be contended that it is unlikely to infringe upon either the principle of subsidiarity or proportionality.

11. *Conclusions*

Over the past three decades, research has become increasingly global and it is now generally accepted that MSR is the foundation of good ocean governance.[237] We have seen on a number of occasions over the past three decades how science can play an important role in resolving high profile disputes at an international level regarding the status of the marine environment and the resources it supports.[238] Surprisingly, however, advances in scientific enquiry into the oceanic environment have not been mirrored by the progressive development of the law as it applies to modern research methods.[239] In this context, the implementation of Part XIII by States Parties to the 1982 Convention appears to be pedantic at best and frequently at odds with the needs of the scientific community. This is borne out by the experience in the EU over the past three decades which demonstrates that getting authorisation for ship-based MSR tends to be a time-consuming business involving cumbersome procedures in the Member States.[240] Although permission is rarely refused, national structures and procedures do not facilitate Member States and the EU in discharging their obligation under Part XIII of the 1982 Convention to create favourable conditions and rules for the conduct of MSR.

The MSR provisions in the 1982 Convention require further implementation by means of state practice and the EU has an enormous capacity to influence the future development of the law in this regard. This paper suggests that the rising cost of undertaking research at sea and the potential efficiencies to be gained from regulatory harmonisation are compelling reasons for setting down common EU standards for foreign vessel MSR. Streamlining administrative procedures and reducing red tape in the EU would lead to shorter times to

[237] Y. Tanaka, *A Dual Approach to Ocean Governance*, (Farnham, Ashgate, 2008) at 209.

[238] See, for example, the *Southern Bluefin Tuna* case (Australia, New Zealand v Japan, 1999) 38 ILM 1624.

[239] In particular, *in situ* and *ex situ* research methods, see D. R. Rothwell, T. Stephens, *The International Law of the Sea* (Oxford, Hart Publishing, 2010) at 321.

[240] As seen above, the European Commission has taken a number of regulatory initiatives to coordinate the policies of Member States in relation to fisheries research and considerable developments have been undertaken within the framework of the Fisheries Data Collection Regulation to ensure the sharing of information and the rationalisation of the resources used for this purpose.

contract and plan vessel time for MSR.[241] This is attractive for companies that face tight deadlines and a harsh fiscal environment in which to market their services.

The case should not be viewed solely in terms of its commercial utility as harmonisation will undoubtedly make a significant contribution to the implementation of EU Treaty provisions on research and innovation as it applies to the marine environment. Most importantly of all it will help the Member States to implement the ecosystem approach on a regional basis in accordance with the scheme established under the MSFD. From the scientific literature, it is evident that the successful implementation of this approach is very much contingent upon obtaining a comprehensive scientific picture of the functioning of marine ecosystems. This is the principal reason why the MSFD and the supplementary Commission Decision require the on-going collection and analysis of a considerable amount of scientific data regarding the environmental status of marine waters. Indeed, the *raison d'être* for the MSFD instrument may partly be attributed to the divergence of approaches across Europe regarding the monitoring and assessment of the status of the marine environment. The regional approach to ecosystems based management under this Directive could be greatly facilitated if there is one consent procedure that is applied to ship-based MSR across the EU.

Similarly, the European Integrated Maritime Policy and the MSFD are predicated on obtaining a sound scientific understanding of the functioning of the ocean environment.[242] The European institutions and international scientific bodies will also benefit from such an approach as they do not have any capacity to collect MSR data on their own and rely upon the resources that are available in the Member States. The streamlining of the administrative procedures that apply to foreign vessel MSR will reduce the cost of obtaining scientific data for policies such as the transport, fisheries, environmental, and climate change policies. This will create a win-win situation for all interested parties including the research community and those responsible for policy implementation in the Member States.

There are a number of potential ways to take this proposal forward within the European institutions. The first point of contact could be the Working Party

[241] This accords with the finding of the Marine Board, *European Ocean Research Fleets – Towards a Common Strategy and Enhanced Use* (Ostend, March 2007) at 37–38.

[242] Recital 11 of the MSFD states that: "it is necessary that Member States cooperate among themselves, as well as with third countries, and coordinate their national programmes with respect to the collection of data regarding the same marine region and regions covering relevant inland waters. Recital 12 goes on to provide that: priorities should be established at Community level, as should the procedures for data collection and processing within the Community, in order to ensure that the entire system is consistent and to optimise its cost-effectiveness by creating a stable multi-annual regional framework.

on the Law of the Sea (usually referred to by its French acronym COMAR) which is made-up of experts from the Member States who undertake much of the advisory within the European institutions on the implementation of the 1982 Convention and its associated agreements.[243] Apart from preparing the ground work for meetings of the Council of Ministers and the Committee of Permanent Representatives, COMAR has a wide mandate and undertakes many of the difficult tasks associated with the providing advice on law of the sea issues at an EU level.

In considering the merit of proposed measure, COMAR will be aware of the importance of introducing a scheme that is expeditious, transparent and does not discriminate between natural and legal persons in the Member States on the basis of nationality. This will speed up the authorisation process for foreign vessel MSR significantly. As a result, ship operators will find it much easier to provide their services across borders in line with their free movement provisions of the EU Treaties. At a practical level, the establishment of an automated electronic system and a "one-stop approach" will allow for the direct and efficient exchange of information between Member States, the various service providers, and the marine scientific community. This in turn will lead to greater efficiency regarding the use of the European research fleet. Additional impetus could also be achieved if the Member States in conjunction with the professional bodies or associations that represent the scientific community agreed a European code of conduct that is applicable to ship-based MSR.[244] Such a code has already been agreed by OSPAR Contracting parties in relation to MSR undertaken in the deep seas and high seas of the OSPAR Maritime Area.[245]

One final question relates to how many Member States ought to be concerned about this issue. The short answer is that this is a matter of concern for all 27 EU Member States, including land-locked States such as Austria which has an active scientific community engaged in researching the functioning of marine ecosystems and has a long-standing diplomatic interest in the legal regime that applies to the conduct of MSR.[246] Indeed, with the advent of phenomena such as climate change and the inherent dangers posed by transboundary hazards such as tsunamis and extreme weather events such as typhoons and hurricanes which originate over the oceans, the legal regime that applies to MSR in the

---

[243] Positions on questions within the EU's competence are adopted by the normal procedure at COMAR. Questions falling under the European Union's foreign policy are governed by Title V of the TEU.

[244] Some Member States have already adopted codes of practice regarding research undertaken in sea areas that are designated for the protection under the Habitats Directive, see, R. Long, *Marine Resource Law*, (Dublin, Thomson Round Hall, 2007) at 680–681.

[245] OSPAR 08/24/1, Annex 6. Available at: www.ospar.org.

[246] See G. Hafner, "Austria and the Law of the Sea" in T. Treves (ed.), *The Law of the Sea, The European Union and its Member States* at 35.

European maritime area ought to be of interest to all States both within and beyond the EU, irrespective of their geographical location. In other words, when it comes to harmonising the procedures that apply to foreign vessel MSR in sea areas under their sovereignty and jurisdiction, it will certainly take more than two Member States to tango.

Table 1 Member State practice in relation to MSR as evaluated by the IOC in 2005.[247]

Member State	Legislation	Consent via Official Channels	Consent Form Spec Form	No. of requests annually 1998–2002	Approx No. of authorisations / approvals 1998–2002	Researching State	Observers	Require Copies of Data / Assessments of Data	Suspension of MSR for Non Compliance with Arts 248- 249
BE*	✓	✓	ICES Form ×	12	57 (almost all)	✓		×	✓
BG*	✓					✓	✓	No Response	×
CY	No Response								
DK*	✓	✓	ICES Form	200	95%	✓	✓	✓	×
EE	No Response								
FR*	✓	✓	No Form	40	Almost all	✓	✓	?	✓
FI*	✓	✓	ICES	20	100%	×	×	*Only if data on sea bottom mapping/ profiling*	Rerouting for military purposes

[247] Compiled from IOC Questionnaire N°3 IOC which was implemented in accordance with Resolution EC-XXXV.7 adopted by the 35th session of the IOC Executive Council (Paris, 4–14 June 2002) and of Resolution A/RES/56/12 of the UN General Assembly. The purpose of the survey and compilation is (i) to assess the problems encountered in the implementation of the marine scientific research (MSR) regime as established by Part XIII of UNCLOS (Section One), (ii) to assist States in establishing generally accepted guidelines, criteria and standards for the transfer of marine technology (TMT) in accordance with Article 271 of UNCLOS (Section Two) and to inform the international community as to the status of MSR and TMT and practical issues raised in their implementation. Available at: http://ioc3.unesco.org/abelos/index.php?option=com_content&task=view&id=45&Itemid=56

Table 1 (*cont.*)

Member State	Legislation	Consent via Official Channels	Consent Form Spec Form	No. of requests annually 1998–2002	Approx No. of authorisations / approvals 1998–2002	Researching State	Observers	Require Copies of Data / Assessments of Data	Suspension of MSR for Non Compliance with Arts 248–249
DK*	✓	✓	No Form	39	All	✓	×	✓	×
EL	No Response								
IRL[248]	No Response								
IT	No Response								
LV	No Response								
LT	✓	✓	Helsinki Commission (Baltic Sea Environment Protection Commission) ×	7–17	100%	×	×	✓	×
MT	No Response								
NL*	×	✓	ICES ×	50	100%	✓	×	×	×
PL*	✓	✓	NO FORM ×	–	–	–	✓	–	–
PT*	✓	✓	× ×	49	100%	✓	✓	✓	×
RO*	✓	✓	× ×	2	100%	✓	✓	✓	×
SI	✓	✓	× ×	1	100%	×	✓	✓	–
ES*	×	✓	× ×	< 10	–	✓	✓	✓	–
SE*	✓	✓	ICES ×	300	98%	✓	×	✓	×
UK*	×	✓	× ×	80–90	2%	✓	×	✓	X

248 Ireland has since submitted a response to the survey.

THE LAW AND PRACTICE RELATING TO MARINE SCIENTIFIC RESEARCH IN NORTHEAST ASIA

Ki-Jun YOU[1]

Abstract

In Northeast Asia, Japan, the People's Republic of China, the Republic of Korea and the Russian Federation are parties to the United Nations Convention on the Law of the Sea (the "Convention"). Therefore, the relevant provisions of the Convention that govern marine scientific research apply to the relations between the four States. However, the situation is not as simple as it appears.

First of all, several legal problems may arise out of the specific situation in Northeast Asia. According to the Convention, all marine scientific research in the Exclusive Economic Zone (EEZ) and on the continental shelf requires the consent of the coastal State. However, in Northeast Asia there are many instances where there is no maritime boundary, with the exceptions of the continental shelf boundary between Japan and the Republic of Korea and the EEZ boundary between the Democratic People's Republic of Korea (DPRK), which is not a party to the Convention, and the Russian Federation. It follows that it may not be very clear who is a coastal State in the absence of maritime delimitation. The same is true for research installations. The most notable case would be that of Socotra Rock, which both China and South Korea have been claiming as part of their EEZ. Under such circumstances, Northeast Asian countries are obliged to cooperate in accordance with Article 123 of the Convention.

Second, the question of marine scientific research is a complex one, which goes beyond this region. The Convention itself has problems within its own system. Since there is no clear definition of marine scientific research within the Convention, sometimes it may not be easily distinguished from "survey activities" or "other internationally lawful uses of the sea." The recent incident where the US Navy surveillance vessel, the Impeccable, was shadowed by Chinese vessels in international waters in the South China Sea, is a salient example. The possible solutions are not easy, though not impossible. One way to solve this problem is to take into account subsequent practice when considering the application of the relevant provisions of the Convention that govern marine scientific research. Another possible way to improve the current state of affairs would be to seek an advisory opinion from the International Tribunal for the Law of the Sea if there is the willingness to do so on the part of the Meeting of the States Parties to the Convention.

[1] Editorial Note: The views expressed herein do not necessarily represent those of the Government of the Republic of Korea. Mr. YOU wrote this paper in an academic capacity and not as a government spokesman. Ki-Jun YOU is Counselor, Permanent Mission of the Republic of Korea to the United Nations. The author's PowerPoint presentation can be viewed at http://www.virginia.edu/colp/pdf/kmi-you.pdf

Introduction

On 23 January 1968, well before negotiations even began on the United Nations Convention on the Law of the Sea (the "LOSC"),[2] the USS *Pueblo*, while carrying out intelligence and oceanographic data collection duties beyond the territorial seas of the Democratic People's Republic of Korea (North Korea) in the East Sea/Sea of Japan, was attacked by North Korean forces. During the attack, the North Korean forces wounded four of the *Pueblo*'s crew and held eighty crew members and two civilian oceanographers captive for eleven months, finally repatriating them on December 23, 1968.[3]

This paper addresses and analyzes legal issues relating to marine scientific research such as the *Pueblo* incident, focusing largely on Northeast Asia. It begins by identifying the rules of international law that govern marine scientific research in Northeast Asia today. It then goes on to deal with the legal issues arising out of the inherent lack of clarity within the LOSC concerning marine scientific research and the possible approaches to deal with such issues. Finally, it considers the legal problems relating to marine scientific research in the context of territorial/maritime boundary disputes in Northeast Asia and the possible solutions thereto.

It must be noted that this paper is not intended to analyze the entire system of marine scientific research under the LOSC. For example, since there are no archipelagic waters[4] or high seas[5] *per se* in Northeast Asia, this paper will not deal with marine scientific research in archipelagic waters[6] or the high seas;[7] rather it will focus on marine scientific research in the territorial sea, as well as in the Exclusive Economic Zone (EEZ) or on the continental shelf. Neither will it review each territorial/maritime boundary dispute in Northeast Asia, since its focus is on the consequences of such disputes rather than on such disputes themselves.

---

[2] United Nations Convention on the Law of the Sea, 1833 *U.N.T.S.* 3 (hereinafter "LOSC").

[3] *See* Department of the Navy – Naval Historical Center, "*Pueblo*," at <http://www.history.navy.mil/danfs/p13/ pueblo-iii.htm>.

[4] LOSC, *supra* note 1, Part IV.

[5] *Ibid.*, Part VII.

[6] *See generally*, R. R. Churchill and A. V. Lowe, *The Law of the Sea (3rd Edition)* Manchester: Manchester University Press, 1999, pp. 404–5.

[7] *Ibid.*, p. 404.

1. *Rules of international law governing marine scientific research in Northeast Asia*

As of 1 October 2010, 161 countries were parties to the LOSC.[8] Given the large number of parties to the LOSC, the question of what is the customary international law relating to marine scientific research appears less important than in the past. In Northeast Asia, in particular, all countries except North Korea have ratified the LOSC.[9] Therefore, all the relevant provisions of the LOSC that govern marine scientific research apply to the relations between the four States (Japan, the People's Republic of China, the Republic of Korea and the Russian Federation). However, the situation in Northeast Asia is not as simple as it appears. If North Korea or such non-regional states as the United States of America, that are not parties to the LOSC, are involved, customary international law still deserves attention. Accordingly, whereas this paper will focus largely on the LOSC, it will also touch briefly upon customary international law where necessary.

2. *Legal issues in Northeast Asia arising out of the inherent lack of clarity within the LOSC concerning marine scientific research and the possible approaches thereto*

2.1 *Legal issues*

On its surface, the question of marine scientific research may appear very straightforward. However, that is not necessarily the case. Since there is no clear definition of "marine scientific research" within the LOSC, sometimes it may not be easily distinguished from "survey activities". The recent incident where the US Navy surveillance vessel, the *Impeccable*, was shadowed by Chinese vessels in the South China Sea, is a salient example.[10]

---

[8] Unlike the other regions, there are few region-specific legal instruments that govern marine scientific research in Northeast Asia, so that this paper will focus, to a large extent, on the United Nations Convention on the Law of the Sea; *See* United Nations Division for Ocean Affairs and the Law of the Sea, *Status of the United Nations Convention on the Law of the Sea, of the Agreement relating to the implementation of Part XI of the Convention and of the Agreement for the implementation of the provisions of the Convention relating to the conservation and management of straddling fish stocks and highly migratory fish stocks, available at* http://www.un.org/Depts/los/reference_files/status2010.pdf.

[9] *Ibid.*

[10] L. Zhu, 'Chinese Practice in Public International Law: 2009', 9 *Chinese Journal of International Law*, (2010) 607, 624.

One school of thought suggests that, since "survey activities" are primarily provided for in Articles 19(2)(j),[11] 40,[12] and 54,[13] such activities do not fall under the marine scientific research regime in Part XIII of the LOSC.[14] Therefore, whereas coastal State consent is required for both marine scientific research and survey activities in the territorial sea and international straits, coastal State consent is required for marine scientific research but not for survey activities in the EEZ. These activities remain within the freedom of the high seas that may be exercised in the EEZ, without coastal State interference, in accordance with Article 58 of the LOSC.[15]

Conversely, the other school argues that since it is not easy to distinguish between "research activities" and "survey activities", in light of the types and potential uses of collectable marine data, the "marine data collecting activities" that the *Impeccable* was carrying out could be categorized as "marine scientific research" which falls under the jurisdiction of the coastal States under the LOSC. Accordingly, China was within its rights to exercise its jurisdiction over such US activities.[16]

Now the question arises as to how to deal with this situation.

2.2 *Possible approaches*

Law-of-treaties approach

If the *Impeccable* incident had been a situation involving States which were both parties to the LOSC, there could have been a law-of-treaties approach to this issue. In this connection, it seems worth reviewing Article 31 of the Vienna

---

[11] LOSC, *supra* note 1, Art. 19. Article 19(2) reads as follows:

> 2. Passage of a foreign ship shall be considered to be prejudicial to the peace, good order or security of the coastal State if in the territorial sea it engages in any of the following activities: ... (j) the carrying out of *research* or *survey activities*... (Emphasis added.)

[12] *Ibid.*, Art. 40. Article 40 reads as follows:

> During transit passage, foreign ships, including marine scientific research and hydrographic survey ships, may not carry out any *research* or *survey activities* without the prior authorization of the States bordering straits. (Emphasis added.)

[13] *Ibid.*, Art. 54. Article 54 reads as follows:

> Articles 39, 40, 42 and 44 apply *mutatis mutandis* to archipelagic sea lanes passage.

[14] *See* United Nations Office for Ocean Affairs and the Law of the Sea, *The Law of the Sea: Marine Scientific Research: A Guide to the Implementation of the Relevant Provisions of the United Nations Convention on the Law of the Sea*, New York: United Nations, 1991, p. 1.

[15] R. Pedrozo, 'Preserving Navigational Rights and Freedoms: The Right to Conduct Military Activities in China's Exclusive Economic Zone,' 9 *Chinese Journal of International Law*, 2010, 22–23.

[16] Z. Haiwen, 'Is It Safeguarding the Freedom of Navigation or Maritime Hegemony of the United States? – Comments on Raul (Pete) Pedrozo's Article on Military Activities in the EEZ,' 9 *Chinese Journal of International Law*, 2010, 31, 36.

Convention on the Law of Treaties of 1969, which shows, as Aust pointed out, that one "naturally begins with the text, followed by the context, and then other matters, in particular subsequent material."[17] A treaty plays the role of "freezing" certain practices in a document which probably will remain unchanged, even if it contains provisions for amendment.

However, State practice may not be static and may evolve subsequently. "[S]ubsequent practice", as provided for in Article 31(3)(b) of the Vienna Convention, is a major element in the interpretation of any treaty. Usually, how a treaty is actually applied by the parties is "a good indication of what they understand it to mean, provided the practice is consistent and is common to, or accepted, expressly or tacitly," by all parties.[18]

Perhaps the most well-known example of the interpretation of a treaty provision by subsequent practice is how UN members have interpreted and applied Article 27(3) of the Charter of the United Nations. Article 27(3) provides that "[d]ecisions of the Security Council on all other matters shall be made by an affirmative vote of nine members including the concurring votes of the permanent members." At first glance this would seem to mean that all five permanent members must vote in favor. However, from as early as 1946, the practice of the Security Council has been "to interpret 'concurring' as meaning 'not objecting'."[19]

In the same vein, it can be suggested that State practices relating to the interpretation and application of the relevant provisions of the LOSC relating to marine scientific research should be reviewed in light of Article 31 of the Vienna Convention. The question then is whether such a case as mentioned earlier can be regarded as an example of "subsequent practice" under subparagraph 3(b) of Article 31. Such a question merits a comprehensive survey and in-depth consideration of State practices and hence is, unfortunately, beyond the scope of this paper.[20]

Customary international law approach

There may be a customary international law approach to this issue, which can be divided into: 1) what the existing customary international law is; and

---

[17] Aust, A., *Modern Treaty Law and Practice* 2nd Ed. Cambridge: Cambridge University Press, 2007, p. 234.

[18] *Ibid.*, p. 241.

[19] *Ibid.*, p. 242.

[20] But *see generally*, United Nations, *The Law of the Sea: National Legislation, Regulations and Supplementary Documents on Marine Scientific Research in Areas under National Jurisdiction*, New York: United Nations, 1989. The UN once compiled a collection of such laws and regulations that govern marine scientific research.

2) whether it is possible for customary international law to continue to exist alongside treaty law.

First, since in the *Impeccable* incident, both a party to the LOSC and a non-party were involved, it seems worth referring to customary international law. It should be noted that, in order for a conventional rule to pass into the corpus of customary law, provisions in a treaty must be fundamentally norm-creating.[21] Churchill and Lowe argued, in this regard, that:

> *. . . the principle of coastal State consent for research in the EEZ and on the continental shelf is now part of customary international law. However, many of the details of the [LOSC] regime, such as the period of notice and implied consent, are not now, and are probably incapable of becoming, part of customary international law because of the paucity of State practice and because they do not seem to have the fundamentally norm-creating character necessary for an emergent rule of customary law. In addition, the question of opposability . . . will be crucial in determining the validity of individual claims.*[22]

That being said, it should still be added that the ambiguity in the principle of coastal State consent for marine scientific research in the EEZ and on the continental shelf that is found in the LOSC remains, even in customary law.

Second, it is interesting to note that the International Court of Justice (ICJ) in the *Nicaragua* case concluded that "customary international law continues to exist alongside treaty law. The areas governed by the two sources of law thus do not overlap exactly, and the rules do not have the same content."[23] Therefore, there can be customary international law concerning marine scientific research existing alongside the LOSC.

One interesting question might arise as to whether excessive claims may create customary international law which is different from the LOSC.

The LOSC is said to be a close-to-universal treaty, sometimes called the "constitution for the oceans". According to Professor O'Connell, "[a] rule of customary law is overridden by a rule of treaty law, and since treaties can only fall into desuetude if the parties so intend, [the LOSC] is not easily subverted by the progress of customary law."[24] Thus, it can be suggested that we should not conclude too easily or hastily that a new customary international law has emerged.

On the other hand, it should be also acknowledged that state practices relating to marine scientific research may evolve and rules may have to be changed. As Churchill and Lowe pointed out within the context of straight baselines,

[21] I.C.J. Reports 1969, p. 3, para. 71.

[22] *See* Churchill and Lowe, *supra* note 5, p. 409.

[23] I.C.J. Reports 1984, p. 14, para. 176.

[24] D.P. O'Connell, *The International Law of the Sea*, Vol. I. Oxford: Clarendon Press, 1982, pp. 46–7.

widespread toleration of misuse of the rules could lead in time to a modification of the rules themselves.[25]

Conclusion

There still appear to be several questions that warrant further examination. Due to constraints of space, however, this paper was not meant to provide a comprehensive analysis of such questions. It is simply to be noted that under Article 297(2) of the LOSC such disputes as the refusal by a coastal State to give permission to conduct marine scientific research in its EEZ or continental shelf are not to be brought before the compulsory procedures entailing binding decisions under Part XV, Section 2.[26] Therefore, one possible way to improve the current state of affairs would be to seek an advisory opinion from the ICJ in accordance with Article 96 of the Charter of the United Nations, or the International Tribunal for the Law of the Sea (ITLOS) if there is willingness to do so on the part of the Meeting of the States Parties to the LOSC.[27]

3. *Legal problems relating to marine scientific research in the context of territorial/maritime boundary disputes in Northeast Asia and the possible solutions thereto*

3.1 *Legal problems*

The question of marine scientific research is a complex one. In other words, even if there is a very sophisticated regime to regulate marine scientific research in the oceans in the first place, some problems may still arise. In Northeast Asia, there are several instances where there is a territorial dispute over islands, including those over the Senkaku/Diaoyu Islands (between China and Japan)[28] and the Kuril Islands (between Russia and Japan).[29] There are also a number of disputes over maritime boundaries which remain unresolved, with the excep-

---

[25] *See* Churchill and Lowe, *supra* note 5, p. 57.

[26] LOSC, *supra* note 1, Art. 297(2).

[27] *See generally* You, 'Advisory Opinions of the International Tribunal for the Law of the Sea: Article 138 of the Rules of the Tribunal, Revisited,' 39 *Ocean Development & International Law*, 2008, 360–371; T.M. Ndiaye, 'The Advisory Function of the International Tribunal for the Law of the Sea,' 9 *Chinese Journal of International Law*, (2010), 584–585.

[28] *See generally* C. Ramos-Mrosovsky, 'International law's unhelpful role in the Senkaku Islands', 29 *University of Pennsylvania Journal of International Law*, (Summer), 2008, 903.

[29] *See generally* G.W. Price, 'Legal Analysis of the Kurile Island Dispute', 7 *Temple International and Comparative Law Journal*, (Fall), 1993, 395.

tions of the continental shelf boundary between Japan and the Republic of Korea and the territorial sea/EEZ boundaries between North Korea and the Russian Federation.[30] It follows that the caveat still remains that it must be determined who is a "coastal State" in the case of a territorial dispute or in the absence of maritime delimitation. The same is true for research installations which are located in undelimited waters.

The most notable case would be that of Socotra Rock, which both China and the Republic of Korea have been claiming as part of their EEZ. Socotra Rock is a submerged rock 4.6 meters (15 ft.) below sea level in the East China Sea where both the claimed EEZs of the Republic of Korea and China overlap.[31] The Korean Ieodo Ocean Research Station, equipped with ocean, weather and environment observation systems, is currently stationed at this location.[32] It is evident that Socotra Rock cannot be claimed as rock or island by any country because it is clear that, according to the LOSC, it is neither a rock "which cannot sustain human habitation or economic life of their own", nor an island which "is a naturally formed area of land, surrounded by water, which is above water at high tide" under the LOSC.[33] Therefore, the issue of the Korean Ieodo Ocean Research Station has more to do with the question as to which country has jurisdiction over Socotra Rock as a coastal State. Once there is a clear maritime boundary between China and Korea, this issue could be resolved very easily. It is to be noted, in this regard, that the two countries have said that they have never had a "territorial dispute."[34]

Therefore, at least some parts – if not all – of the relevant provisions of the LOSC may be of little use in this kind of situation. To resolve this state of affairs, the first and foremost solution would be to resolve territorial/maritime boundary disputes once and for all. One possible option is that, just as Southeast Asian countries brought two cases before the ICJ,[35] Northeast Asian

---

[30] T.L. McDorman, 'Central Pacific and East Asian Maritime Boundaries,' in Colson, D.A. and Smith, R.W. (eds.), *International Maritime Boundaries, Vol. V*, Leiden: Martinus Nijhoff, 2005, 3439, p. 3440.

[31] R. Guo, 'Territorial disputes and resource management: a global handbook,' *Nova Science Publishers, Inc.*, 2007, p. 226.

[32] http://ieodo.nori.go.kr/eng/open_content/main/

[33] LOSC, *supra* note 1, Art. 121.

[34] M. Ha, 'China's Claim to Ieodo Overshadows Hu's Planned Visit,' *Korea Times*, Aug. 15, 2008, available at WLNR.; 'South Korea says China's website's designation could cause controversy,' *BBC International Reports (Asia)* Aug. 9, 2008, available at WLNR.; S. Lee, "Temperature Different Between Korea, China Over Ieodo," *Korea Times*, Aug. 16, 2008, available at WLNR.

[35] See *Sovereignty over Pedra Branca/Pulau Batu Puteh, Middle Rocks and South Ledge (Malaysia/Singapore)* at <http://www.icj-cij.org/docket/index.php?p1=3&p2=3&code=masi&case=130&k=2b>; See also *Sovereignty over Pulau Ligitan and Pulau Sipadan (Indonesia/Malaysia)* at <http://www.icj-cij.org/docket/index.php? p1=3&p2=3&code=inma&case=102&k=df>.

countries may consider bringing cases before an arbitral tribunal, the ICJ or the ITLOS. Alternatively, they may conclude bilateral agreements concerning maritime boundary delimitation like the agreement between China and Vietnam regarding the Gulf of Tonkin.[36] However, such territorial/maritime boundary disputes frequently take a long time to resolve.

3.2 *Possible solutions*

In extreme cases, the States in the region may choose not to regulate, authorize or conduct marine scientific research in any disputed area in order to avoid any problems. However, this approach is highly unlikely, since all States would wish to protect their legal interests.[37] Instead, there are several practical options that may be exercised by the States in the region to deal with this delicate situation.

First, in view of Article 241, which provides that "[m]arine scientific research activities shall not constitute the legal basis for any claim to any part of the marine environment or its resources," they may seek a solution on an *ad hoc* basis. For example, let us suppose that State A intends to undertake marine scientific research in waters, part of which both State A and State B consider as their respective EEZs or continental shelves. Then, State A, when seeking the consent of State B, may add to its diplomatic note the following phrase: "Nothing in the present note shall be construed as affecting the position of the Government of [State A] with respect to its maritime delimitation."

Second, Articles 74(3) and 83(3) of the LOSC provide that "[p]ending agreement…, the States concerned, in a spirit of understanding and cooperation, shall make every effort to enter into provisional arrangements of a practical nature and, during this transitional period, not to jeopardize or hamper the reaching of the final agreement. Such arrangements shall be without prejudice to the final delimitation." This clause requires interested states to seek a solution on a "more permanent" basis. For example, in 2001, China and Japan agreed on a mutual prior notification system for maritime scientific research in waters between the two countries, which provides that China is to give Japan at least two months' notice when its research ships plan to enter waters "near Japan

---

[36] K. Zou, 'The Sino-Vietnamese Agreement on Maritime Boundary Delimitation in the Gulf of Tonkin,' 36 *Ocean Development and International Law*, 13–24 (2005).

[37] *See e.g.* 'Japan, S. Korea end EEZ talks without agreement', *Asian Political News,* Sept. 11, 2006, *available at* WLNR. In April 2006 Japan and the Republic of Korea became involved in a dispute when Japan's coast guard said it planned to conduct a marine survey in undelimited waters in the East Sea/Sea of Japan, which attracted a storm of protest from the Republic of Korea. The two countries subsequently avoided a confrontation by holding a high-level meeting in Seoul where Japan agreed to withdraw its plan to conduct the survey.

and in which Japan takes interest" and that similarly, Japan is to inform China before its vessels enter waters "near" China.[38]

Lastly, the entire maritime area in Northeast Asia, including the East Sea/Sea of Japan, the Yellow Sea and the East China Sea, falls under the definition of "enclosed or semi-enclosed seas" in Article 122 of the LOSC. Therefore, in Northeast Asia, Article 123 of the LOSC could apply. This Article imposes upon the States bordering an enclosed or semi-enclosed sea a duty to cooperate with each other in the exercise of their rights and in the performance of their duties. In other words, let us suppose that some part of "enclosed or semi-enclosed seas" is an area which State C and State D bordering the seas consider as their respective EEZs or continental shelves. When State C and State D intend to undertake marine scientific research in the waters in question, they may conduct joint marine scientific research in any disputed area in accordance with Article 123, without it being interpreted as compromising their positions with respect to maritime delimitation.[39]

Conclusion

In conclusion, this paper has reviewed some of the intriguing legal issues relating to marine scientific research in Northeast Asia. First, it suggested that whereas the LOSC is, to a large extent, applicable to marine scientific research, customary international law could also be relevant. Second, as the recent *Impeccable* incident showed, there are conflicting legal interpretations of the LOSC in relation to marine scientific research. Thus there is a pressing need to somehow resolve this problem, for example, by seeking an advisory opinion from the ICJ or the ITLOS. Finally, at least some part of the relevant provisions in the LOSC may be of little use in the case of territorial/maritime boundary disputes. Accordingly, for the time being, it could be suggested that in view of Article 241, States may seek provisional solutions such as those found in Articles 74(3) and 83(3), or Article 123, of the LOSC.

[38] *See* 'Japan, China agree on 2-month maritime notice system,' *Japan Policy & Politics*, Feb. 19, 2001, *available at* WLNR.; *See also* Valencia, M.J. & Amae, Y., 'Regime Building in the East China Sea,' *Ocean Development & International Law* 34, (2003), 189–208, p. 198.

[39] *See e.g.* S. Park, 'Seoul, Tokyo Plan Joint Survey Near Dokdo,' *Korea Times*, Sept. 11, 2006, *available at* WLNR. Japan and the Republic of Korea agreed to carry out the joint surveys in their respective EEZs.

References

Aust, A., *Modern Treaty Law and Practice (2nd Ed.)*. Cambridge: Cambridge University Press, 2007.

Churchill, R.R. and Lowe, A.V., *The Law of the Sea (3rd Edition),* Manchester: Manchester University Press, 1999.

Guo, R., 'Territorial disputes and resource management: a global handbook,' *Nova Science Publishers, Inc.*, 2007.

Haiwen, Z., 'Is It Safeguarding the Freedom of Navigation or Maritime Hegemony of the United States?-Comments on Raul (Pete) Pedrozo's Article on Military Activities in the EEZ,' *Chinese Journal of International Law* 9, (2010), 31.

McDorman, T.L., 'Central Pacific and East Asian Maritime Boundaries,' in Colson, D. A. and Smith, R.W. (eds.), *International Maritime Boundaries, Vol V.* Leiden: Martinus Nijhoff, 2005, 3439.

Ndiaye, T. M., 'The Advisory Function of the International Tribunal for the Law of the Sea,' *Chinese Journal of International Law* 9, (2010) 565.

O'Connell, D.P., *The International Law of the Sea,* Vols. I & II. Oxford: Clarendon Press, 1982.

Pedrozo, R., 'Preserving Navigational Rights and Freedoms: The Right to Conduct Military Activities in China's Exclusive Economic Zone,' *Chinese Journal of International Law* 9, (2010), 9.

Price, G.W., 'Legal Analysis of the Kurile Island Dispute', *Temple International and Comparative Law Journal* 7, (Fall, 1993), 395.

Ramos-Mrosovsky, C., 'International law's unhelpful role in the Senkaku Islands', *University of Pennsylvania Journal of International Law* 29, (Summer 2008), 903.

United Nations Division for Ocean Affairs and the Law of the Sea, *Status of the United Nations Convention on the Law of the Sea, of the Agreement relating to the implementation of Part XI of the Convention and of the Agreement for the implementation of the provisions of the Convention relating to the conservation and management of straddling fish stocks and highly migratory fish stocks, available at* <http://www.un.org/Depts/los/reference_files/status2010.pdf>.

United Nations Office for Ocean Affairs and the Law of the Sea, *The Law of the Sea: Marine Scientific Research: A Guide to the Implementation of the Relevant Provisions of the United Nations Convention on the Law of the Sea,* New York: United Nations, 1991.

United Nations, *The Law of the Sea: National Legislation, Regulations and Supplementary Documents on Marine Scientific Research in Areas under National Jurisdiction*, New York: United Nations, 1989.

Valencia, M. J. & Amae, Y., 'Regime Building in the East China Sea,' *Ocean Development & International Law* 34, (2003), 189–208.

You, K.-J., 'Advisory Opinions of the International Tribunal for the Law of the Sea: Article 138 of the Rules of the Tribunal, Revisited,' *Ocean Development & International Law* 39, (2008), 360–371.

Zhu, L., 'Chinese Practice in Public International Law: 2009', *Chinese Journal of International Law* 9, (2010) 607.

Zou, K., 'The Sino-Vietnamese Agreement on Maritime Boundary Delimitation in the Gulf of Tonkin,' *Ocean Development and International Law* 36, (2005), 13–24.

Panel VI: Emerging Global Ocean Policy Issues

EMERGING OCEANS POLICY ISSUES

Vice Admiral James W. Houck, JAGC, USN[1]

Abstract

As a maritime nation, the United States is dependent upon the sea for both national security and economic prosperity. Our Navy must be prepared to meet future security challenges. At any one time, more than 40 percent of US Navy ships are underway daily, globally present and persistently engaged. Global maritime security can only be achieved through the integration of national and regional maritime cooperation. Forward presence provides the opportunity to conduct cooperative activities with allies and an expanding set of international partners. The United States needs to be in the best position possible to shape emerging ocean policy issues. These include counter proliferation and irregular challenges at sea such as piracy. They also include pressures for more coastal State assertions of control that threaten to undo the traditional balance with high seas freedoms. Additionally, the United States has national security interests in the Arctic and must be prepared to operate in this unique and harsh environment, either independently or in conjunction with other nations.

Introduction

First, I offer my warm thanks to Dr. Kim, Professor Moore, Professor Soons, and their institutions for co-sponsoring this valuable conference. I also thank Professor Nordquist and his staff for all of their support in making this conference a success.

Today's Navy faces many ocean policy challenges. Some of those challenges such as combating piracy, and maintaining freedom of navigation would have been familiar to the first crew of the U.S.S. *Constitution*; others such as environmental stewardship, Arctic regulation and counter proliferation are more recent developments. The fundamental truth that nations with common interests in international commerce, safety, and security must work together to address common challenges is at the heart of our Cooperative Strategy for 21st Century Seapower.[2] Global security depends upon a partnership of maritime nations sharing common goals and values.

Global maritime security is undergoing significant transformation today, and as the world's foremost maritime power, the United States is both expected and

---

[1] Vice Admiral James W. Houck is the Judge Advocate General of the US Navy and the Department of Defense Representative for Ocean Policy Affairs.

[2] Available online at http://www.navy.mil/maritime/MaritimeStrategy.pdf.

required to lead that transformation. We must lead and manage a maritime security domain in which friendly navies, coast guards, and industry develop common interoperability protocols and information sharing frameworks that in turn enable distributed maritime operations appropriately scaled to meet the challenges of 21st Century, including proliferation of weapons of mass destruction (WMD), terrorism, piracy, and transnational criminal activities such as narcotics and human trafficking.

Earlier this year the Sea Services of the United States promulgated the Naval Operating Concept 2010 (NOC 10) to implement the Maritime Strategy. We have made both of those publications available to conference participants. Continuous innovation, by the United States, its allies and partners, and its adversaries, compels us to have a guide not only for current operations, but also, to have one that is forward looking to anticipate and describe the ways new capabilities can be integrated into joint force efforts to address emerging threats.

Threats to the Maritime Legal Regime

The maritime legal regime that has served us so well for many years is threatened. I would like to address those threats as well as some approaches to deal with them.

The order we have worked well within is being challenged by two camps. The first group consists of lawbreakers. Real-time physical threats are being posed by pirates and by those who would spread WMD. The second group consists of law makers, or rather law remakers. They are those who would convert Exclusive Economic Zones (EEZs) into territorial seas, and who would regulate sovereign immune vessels.

The best response to these challenges is through cooperative engagement and partnership. NOC 10 reaffirms that, in an increasingly complex world, naval forces provide the Nation with the global presence and the freedom of maneuver needed to influence world events. Persistently postured forward, naval forces are continuously engaged with global partners in cooperative security activities aimed at reducing instability and providing another arm of national diplomacy. As the Chief of Naval Operations has stated, the key factor supporting this ability is freedom of navigation upon, over and under the world's seas. And the key to those freedoms is the 1982 UN Convention on the Law of the Sea (UNCLOS).

Counter-Piracy

Twenty years ago few people would have believed that in 2010 piracy would constitute a major threat to international commerce, endangering the lives of civilian mariners and weakening the legitimacy of fragile states. And yet, even as I speak, the United States Navy as a member of a multi-national naval task force (CTF-151) presently under the command of a Pakistani Commodore is patrolling the waters off the coast of Somalia to counter a very real pirate threat. The European Union, NATO and navies from many of the world's maritime nations continue to deploy ships specifically to address the growing piracy problem. The following statistics illustrate both the magnitude of the threat and the scope of the international counter-piracy effort. Between August and June of this year [2010], CTF-151 and other international forces encountered over 1100 pirates, disrupting the attacks of over 600. Thirteen were killed and almost 500 were apprehended and more than 100 pirate vessels were either destroyed or confiscated.

Navy lawyers are involved in every aspect of the United States' counter-piracy efforts. Navy judge advocates and their international counterparts in the coalition environment are on the front lines advising senior leadership on UNCLOS provisions on the suppression of piracy and UN Security Council counter-piracy resolutions regarding piracy off the coast of Somalia. They advise military commanders on the applicable United States rules of engagement as well as the ROE of our coalition partners. Forward deployed Navy lawyers also assist their State Department colleagues in facilitating the transfer of suspected pirates to regional authorities and assist US Department of Justice attorneys in the prosecution of piracy cases in US courts.

While naval forces can have a deterrent effect on the problem, the elimination of the threat will require the development of a stable, effective government in Somalia capable of denying would-be pirates a safe haven and denying those pirates a base of operation. Until such a government is in place, piracy is likely to be a persistent problem in the region. As long as piracy continues to be a threat, there will be a need for the robust international naval response that has developed over the last several years and for the continued global development of national ocean policies that facilitate the prosecution of suspected pirates wherever they are apprehended.

Counter proliferation

Few issues have attained the level of international consensus inspired by the need to counter the proliferation of WMD. Domestically, administrations of both parties have agreed that the greatest single national security threat is the possibility that terrorist organizations could obtain and use a nuclear weapon to carry out a terrorist attack. Additionally, it does not take much imagination to envision terrorist attacks with WMD short of a nuclear weapon that could be almost as devastating as a nuclear attack, both in terms of lives lost and in the damage to the world-wide economy. While counter-proliferation may not garner the attention given to counter piracy, the threat posed by the proliferation of WMD is a far graver danger. Since it was announced in 2003, over 80 nations have committed to the Proliferation Security Initiative, pledging to cooperate in the interdiction of shipments of weapons of mass destruction and related goods to terrorists and countries of proliferation concern. Subsequently, the United Nations Security Council adopted UNSCR 1540 in 2004, calling on all states to prohibit support to non-State actors seeking WMD; adopt effective laws prohibiting the proliferation of WMD to non-State actors and prohibit assisting or financing the spread of WMD. Similarly UNSCR 1929 is the most recent Security Council resolution to address Iran's failure to comply with its international obligations with regard to its nuclear program. The US Navy, among others, has been very active in challenging and inspecting suspect vessels in accordance with applicable UNSC resolutions and continues to provide a significant deterrent to proliferation of WMD.

From advising senior Navy and Department of Defense officials on the details of Security Council Resolutions to ensuring enforcement operations on the high seas are compliant with domestic and international law, Navy judge advocates have been an indispensible part of the United State's effort to counter the proliferation of WMD.

Freedom of Navigation

Piracy is a threat to the freedom of navigation necessary for international commerce and the shipment of vital energy supplies. However, piracy is not the only such threat. Another threat, one which could actually limit the ability of maritime nations to respond to the next global crisis or humanitarian disaster, is the threat of excessive maritime claims. Indeed, one of the most important, and perhaps most contentious issues in ocean law and policy today is the attempt by some coastal States to treat the EEZ like a territorial sea by attempting to exercise complete sovereignty and hamper or exclude normal military activities and exercises within these areas. The trend toward imposing excessive restrictions and limitations on navigational rights and freedoms, in the name of coastal State security or environmental protection, while clearly a minority position, is nevertheless troubling.

The ability of all nations' military forces to operate freely on, under and above the vast military maneuver space of the oceans, including foreign EEZs in which freedom of navigation and overflight apply, is critical to the security interests of all nations as well as the ability to respond to humanitarian disasters around the globe. National security depends on the strategic mobility of military forces and requires the ability to move throughout these global commons at any time without a permission slip.

Customary international law, as reflected in Articles 58 and 87–115 of UNCLOS, provides that high seas freedoms apply in the EEZ, including freedom of navigation and overflight, the laying of submarine cables and pipelines, and other internationally lawful uses of the sea related to those freedoms. Military operations, exercises, and activities have always been regarded as internationally lawful uses of the sea and the right to conduct military operations, exercises, and activities in the EEZ is enjoyed by all nations. The law of the sea also recognizes that warships, naval auxiliaries, other public vessels of a State, as well as State aircraft enjoy sovereign immunity and as such are not subject to foreign regulatory control, arrest, search, inspection, taxation, or customs duties. Nevertheless, some coastal States do not adhere to these bedrock principles of international law and persist in attempting to hinder these activities in the global commons.

In accordance with customary international law, as reflected in the Convention, the United States will exercise the rights of navigation and overflight in the world's EEZs with due regard for the rights and obligations of the coastal State. However, the United States will not agree with coastal State demands for prior permission or notification prior to the conduct of military activities within a foreign EEZ or prior to exercising the right of transit passage through international straits. We will continue to challenge excessive claims through a combination of diplomatic protests, bilateral and multilateral engagement, and operational challenges to demonstrate non-acquiescence. The operational assertions are not intended to be provocative or threatening but are a demonstration of freedoms enjoyed by all nations.

Obviously, the Navy is uniquely situated to challenge these excessive claims as being inconsistent with international law. Navy judge advocates work closely with operational commanders to ensure that all legitimate claims under the provisions of UNCLOS are respected while exercising the full range of navigational freedoms in accordance with international law.

UNCLOS has made great strides in creating a stable common international framework. However, the assertion of and debate over excessive maritime claims will likely continue until coastal and maritime nations reach the conclusion that they have more to gain by adhering to the UNCLOS provisions regarding freedom of navigation, than they do by asserting extraordinary coastal claims that are ultimately counterproductive.

The bad news is that the lack of the United States joining UNCLOS is a national security threat that places us at a disadvantage. It has caused the United States to rely on customary international law that is subject to change over time on the basis of state practice, and it diminishes our ability to provide collaborative leadership. The good news is that the current Administration supports acceding to the Convention. It is clear that the US Navy will continue to operate within the tenets of the Convention.

The Arctic

We have all seen evidence of the dramatic effect of climate change in the Arctic. Arctic sea and air temperatures are rising faster than the global averages. 2007, 2008 and 2009 have been the three lowest years for summer sea ice extent in the Arctic. Melting sea ice has enormous environmental, economic and security consequences. For instance, maritime transportation becomes more viable with less ice. Increased shipping activity leads to heightened chances of accidents and the consequent need for search and rescue and emergency response capabilities.

Of all the world's oceans, perhaps the Arctic best illustrates the importance of having a stable framework for freedom of navigation in accordance with UNCLOS and free from excessive Arctic claims. In 2008, the five Arctic nations declared in Ilulissat, Greenland, that the law of the sea provides the legal framework that governs the Arctic Ocean, and there is no need for a new treaty.

The five also acknowledged that the Arctic Ocean stands at the threshold of significant changes, and climate change and the melting of ice have the potential impact on vulnerable ecosystems, livelihoods of local inhabitants and indigenous communities, and exploitation of natural resources. By virtue of the sovereign claims and jurisdiction in large areas of the Arctic Ocean, the five coastal States are "in a unique position to address these possibilities and challenges." The five committed to an orderly settlement of overlapping maritime boundary claims, and since then Norway and Russia have settled a long-standing dispute regarding their border.

The Arctic is a changing environment and US ability to exert influence and defend national interests in the Arctic depends heavily on a sovereign national presence and continuing engagement, manifested in both special and routine operations. At-sea presence of US assets is a critical means of protecting and furthering the US interests in the Arctic, including: ensuring freedom of navigation; enforcing US laws and treaties; providing for the safety and security of maritime commerce; protecting our maritime borders and areas of maritime jurisdiction; asserting our national maritime jurisdictional claims and countering excessive jurisdictional claims of others; safeguarding our oceans and resources; protecting critical maritime infrastructure (including offshore oil and gas infrastructure); and enhancing our maritime domain awareness. The need for a surface presence will increase substantially along with the corresponding increase in human activity in the Arctic.

Conclusion

The future will undoubtedly present new ocean policy challenges. Those issues I touched on today will remain important ocean policy issues for years to come.

As diverse as these issues are, they do have at least one thing in common. None of these challenges can be addressed by one nation alone. Indeed, it is a broad based international effort that is meeting each of the challenges. It is the willingness of all the world's maritime nations to come together and address these challenges that makes me optimistic that not only will these challenges ultimately be overcome, but also that the United States and our partners are well situated to meet future challenges with the same spirit of cooperation and unity of purpose. The efforts of naval partnerships around the world to meet emerging challenges are leading us into the future by showing that we can join together against common threats to our welfare while still defending our individual sovereign rights.

DEEPWATER HORIZON AND THE ARCTIC: IS THERE A NEED FOR INTERNATIONAL REGULATION?

Larry A. Mayer[1]
Capt. J. Ashley Roach, JAGC, USN (ret.)
Betsy Baker

Abstract

The Deepwater Horizon oil spill in the Gulf of Mexico has focused much attention on the environmental impacts of offshore oil and gas activities and on the effectiveness of the regulatory system controlling oil and gas production in the United States. While unquestionably a tragedy in terms of loss of life and the amount of oil spilled, a series of fortuitous environmental factors actually prevented this disaster from being even worse. Despite several threats, a major hurricane that could have driven large amounts of oil-laden water onto beaches and into fragile marsh environments did not materialize; the warm waters of the Gulf and the presence of numerous natural gas seeps created an environment conducive to the presence of microbes that naturally degrade hydrocarbons, and; the location of the well with respect to the loop current, and the behavior of the loop current during the spill kept the surface expression of the oil constrained within the Gulf rather than carrying it out towards the Atlantic where it could have impacted other US coastlines, the northeast tip of Mexico, Cuba, and the Bahamas.

The potential of the Deepwater Horizon spill to impact other nations raises important questions about the regulatory regime (or lack thereof) for events that cross territorial and maritime boundaries. Of even greater concern is the potential for an event like this to happen in the Arctic where virtually no infrastructure exists and where the geographic, oceanographic and fragile environmental conditions are such that a major spill almost anywhere in the basin would have a catastrophic impact on neighboring states.

Part XII of the Law of the Sea Convention (Articles 192, 194[3] and particularly Articles 208[1,5] and 214) offers a start at addressing these issues with its general principles obligating states to adopt laws, regulations and other measures to prevent pollution arising from offshore installations under their jurisdiction and specifying that these laws, regulations and measures be no less effective than international standards. Additionally, the Convention encourages states to establish global and regional rules and standards through competent international organizations or diplomatic conferences. Strong international standards to prevent pollution from shipping have been adopted and are very effective (e.g., the double hull standards instituted by the IMO through amendment of the MARPOL Convention), but an equivalent international convention does not exist for the activities of oil platforms like the Deepwater Horizon.

---

[1] Larry Mayer is a Professor and Director of the Center for Coastal and Ocean Mapping at the University of New Hampshire. Capt. J. Ashley Roach, JAGC, US Navy (ret.) and Betsy Baker, Vermont Law School, co-authored this paper with Professor Mayer. The authors' PowerPoint presentation can be viewed at http://www.virginia.edu/colp/pdf/kmi-mayer.pdf. See also in this volume "The Sky is Falling or is It? Dissection of the Gulf of Mexico 'Macondo' Oil Spill" by Q. Dokken.

In the absence of an international (or even regional for the Gulf of Mexico and the Arctic – at least with respect to pollution from platforms) convention, we must fall back upon the regulations, standards and practices of the state to ensure compliance with the principle of Part XII of the LOS Convention. Unfortunately, as demonstrated by the Deepwater Horizon incident, the current US regulatory regime appears to be inadequate.

While numerous reviews and modifications of the US oil and gas regulatory procedures are currently underway, several things are already clear. The conflict of interest associated with having the same agency responsible for regulations also responsible for revenue collection has already been recognized and is now being addressed. More fundamentally though, the US approach to establishing regulations appears to be flawed. The technology associated with deepwater drilling and oil extraction is so advanced that the expertise needed to understand this technology often resides only within the industry and not within the government – largely due to the large pay differential between government and industry employees. Despite this lack of expertise, the US approach to regulation is prescriptive, i.e., it specifies the means and minimum steps necessary for compliance. Prescriptive regulations often set the lowest acceptable safety level and if there is not a full understanding of the technology by the regulators, these levels may not assure safety (as made apparent by the DWH incident). Other nations, particularly Norway, have created independent oversight bodies (with employees paid on par with industry workers) and have adopted mostly performance- and risk-based standards which allow the operator the freedom to optimize the approaches to safety but also require a systematic risk management plan. This approach encourages continuous development and adaptation of new technology and best practices and has resulted in an enviable safety record for Norwegian operations.

As the United States seeks to revamp its regulatory system and move towards more effective safety practices, there may be an opportunity to establish an international framework for the safety of offshore drilling platforms that lives up to the principles of article 208 of the Law of the Sea Convention. To carry out the mandate of Article 208 of the LOS Convention, and consistent with the competence of the IMO granted by its Constitution, in light of the Deepwater Horizon incident, the IMO Assembly, which next meets in late November 2011, could task the Maritime Safety Committee to revise and update the MODU Code to incorporate guidance relating to drilling operations, both generally and in the Arctic.

Introduction

For three months, between 20 April and 15 July 2010, after a catastrophic blowout leading to the sinking of the Deepwater Horizon drilling rig, the Macondo 252 oil well spewed almost 5 million barrels of crude oil into the Gulf of Mexico. The initial explosion led to the death of 11 men working on the platform. The subsequent oil spill had immediate impact on the environment, ecosystem, and economy of the Gulf. The long-term environmental and economic ramifications of the spill are yet to be determined.

While unquestionably a tragedy of great proportion, a series of fortuitous environmental factors prevented this disaster from being even worse. A major hurricane that could have driven large amounts of oil-laden water onto beaches and into fragile marsh environments did not materialize. The warm waters of the Gulf and the presence of numerous natural gas seeps created an environment conducive to the presence of microbes that naturally degrade hydrocarbons. And, the location of the well with respect to the loop current, and the behavior of the loop current during the spill, kept the surface expression of the oil constrained within the Gulf rather than carrying it out towards the Atlantic where it could have impacted other US coastlines, Cuba, and the Bahamas.

Hurricane Season

Hurricane season in the Gulf of Mexico is typically between June and November. The Macondo spill began in late April and was not capped until mid-July, 45 days into hurricane season. As noted in Figure 1 depicting the path of major (Category H3 or above) hurricanes since 1990, the site of the Macondo spill was directly under the path of many of these major hurricanes. During the time frame of the Macondo spill, however, only one hurricane (Alex) developed (25–29 June 2010) and its path crossed the Yucatan Peninsula and then travelled far south of the spill site into Mexico. Two tropical storms developed soon after the capping of the well (Bonnie – 22–24 July and Colin – 2–8 August). Bonnie's track brought it close to the spill site but by the time it approached the spill its winds had greatly diminished; Hurricane Colin never entered the Gulf of Mexico, tracking up the Atlantic instead.[2] Had a hurricane tracked over, or west of, the spill site it would have wrought havoc with the cleanup efforts and, most critically, would have brought much more oil onto coastal beaches and into the fragile marshes greatly exacerbating the environmental and economic damage of the spill.

An Environment that Favors Biodegradation

The Gulf of Mexico is an oil rich environment and hundreds of thousands of barrels of oil and gas leak into the Gulf through natural seepage each year.[3] The presence of this oil along with relatively warm water temperatures in the Gulf of Mexico creates an environment that is very favorable for bacteria that have developed the ability to metabolize and thus degrade hydrocarbons including the most toxic types (polycyclic aromatic hydrocarbons – PAHs). At Gulf

[2] Information about the historic record of hurricanes and the nature of storms during the period from 20 April to August 2010 is available from the National Hurricane Center (http://csc.noaa.gov/hurricanes/#app=1834&3e3d-selectedIndex=0).

[3] Mitchell, R., MacDonald, I.R., Kvenvolden, K., 2000, Estimates of Total Hydrocarbon Seepage into the Gulf of Mexico Based on Satellite Remote Sensing Images, OS41I-02, Proceedings of the Ocean Sciences Meeting, American Geophysical Union.

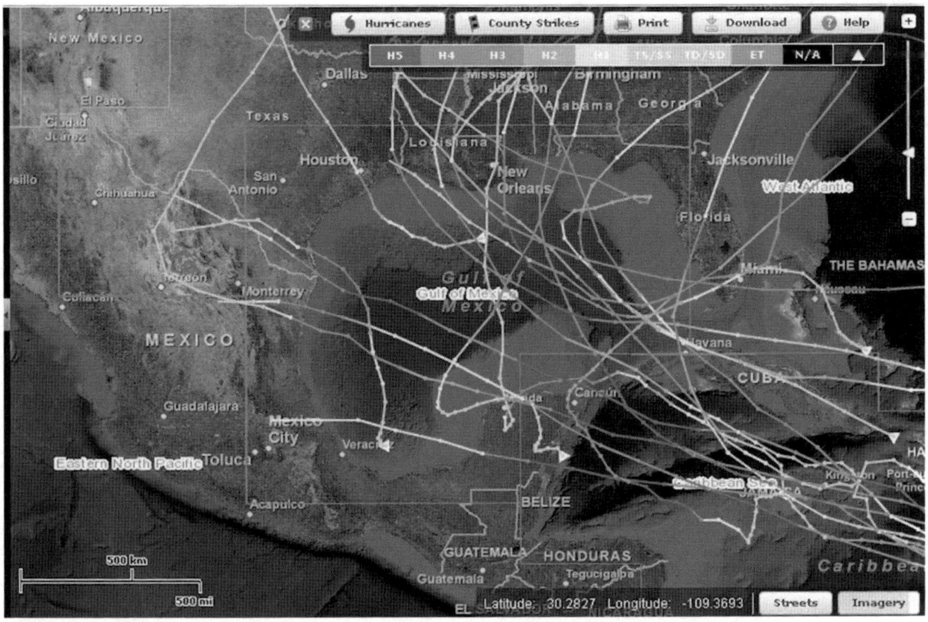

Source: http://csc.noaa.gov/hurricanes/#app=1834&3e3d-selectedIndex=0

Figure 1. Tracks of major hurricanes 1900–2008 in the Gulf of Mexico. Yellow dot represents Site of Macondo 252 well.

water temperatures, it is thought that the "half-life" of hydrocarbons (the time it takes for half of the oil to degrade) is on the order of several days.[4] A report issued by the U.S. federal government on 4 August 2010 concluded that of the approximately 5 million barrels of oil released during the Macondo 252 spill, approximately 25% was the evaporated or dissolved in the water, 24% was dispersed through natural or chemical means and another 25% removed from direct recovery from the well head. The report goes on to say:

> *Dispersed oil in the water column and oil on the surface of the water biodegrade naturally. While there is more analysis to be done to quantify the rate of biodegradation in the Gulf, early observations and preliminary research results from a number of scientists show that the oil from the BP Deepwater Horizon spill is biodegrading quickly. Scientists from NOAA, EPA, DOE and academia are working to calculate more precise estimates of this rate. It is well known that bacteria that break down the dispersed and weathered surface oil are abundant in the Gulf of Mexico in large part because of the warm water, the favorable nutrient and oxygen levels, and the fact that oil regularly enters the Gulf of Mexico through natural seeps.*[5]

[4] http://new.earthgauge.net/wp-content/EG_Gulf_oil_spill_Microbes.pdf

[5] http://www.noaanews.noaa.gov/stories2010/PDFs/OilBudget_description_%2083final.pdf

While much debate continues over the veracity of these estimates and the details of the fate of oil released during the Macondo 252 spill, there can be little doubt that biodegradation is an active process in the Gulf of Mexico that has contributed to the removal of a component of the spilled oil.

Available Infrastructure

The Gulf of Mexico is the locus of a tremendous amount of oil and gas production and exploration activity with nearly 4000 oil and gas platforms currently operating[6] and over 12,000 miles of offshore pipeline on the sea floor.[7] In support of these activities are airports, ports, workers, fabrications facilities, repair and maintenance yards, support vessels, shipyards, and supply bases all attuned to the needs of the offshore oil industry. Within 24 hours of the Deepwater Horizon explosion, the government and industry were able to mobilize more than 30 response vessels, six fire-fighting vessels, skimming capability of more than 171,000 barrels/day, spill-trajectory forecasts, and more than 400,000 feet of oil containment boom.[8] Thousands of workers were also mobilized to serve in clean-up crews around the Gulf. By March 2011, 48,200 responders, 9700 vessels, 127 aircraft, 3.9 million feet of hard boom and 5.9 million feet of soft boom had been involved in Deepwater Horizon-related clean-up activities.[9]

The Loop Current Did Not Intercept the Oil Spill

The Loop Current is a clockwise current that flows northward between Cuba and the Yucatán peninsula into the Gulf of Mexico and then loops from west to east before turning south and leaving the Gulf through the Florida Straits where it can merge with the Gulf Stream. It can be a remarkably fast and powerful current with typical near-surface velocities around 80 cm/sec (1.6 knots) carrying estimated volumes of between 24 and 30 Sv (one Sv [Sverdrup] is equal to one million cubic meters of water per second).[10] The position of the

---

[6] http://oceanexplorer.noaa.gov/explorations/06mexico/background/oil/oil.html

[7] http://www.gomr.boemre.gov/PI/PDFImages/ESPIS/2/2985.pdf

[8] http://www.pewtrusts.org/uploadedFiles/wwwpewtrustsorg/Fact_Sheets/Protecting_ocean_life/Gulf%20and%20Chukchi%20Oil%20Spill%20Response%20April%2030%20FINAL.pdf?n=8646

[9] Capt. James Hanzalik, Federal on Scene Coordinator, Presentation to the NRC Committee on the Impact of the Deepwater Horizon Oil Spill on Ecosystem Services in the Gulf of Mexico, 23 March, 2011, New Orleans, Louisiana.

[10] http://oceancurrents.rsmas.miami.edu/atlantic/loop-current.html

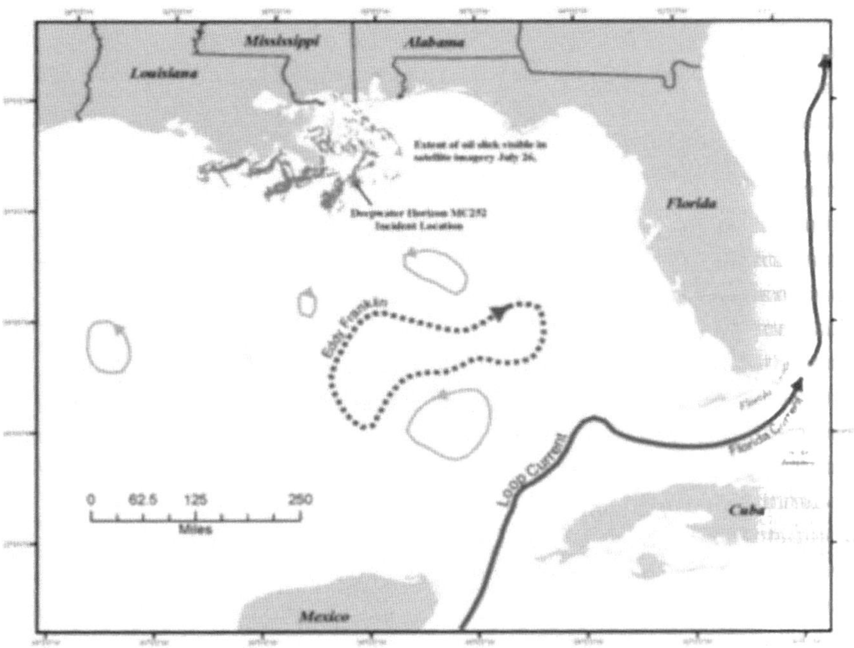

Source: http://oceancurrents.rsmas.miami.edu/atlantic/loop-current.html

Figure 2. Location of Loop Current and Eddy Franklin on 20 July 2010.

Loop Current is very variable and one of the great fears during the Deepwater Horizon/Macondo 252 spill was that the current would intercept the oil spill and carry oil out of the Gulf impacting Cuba, the Bahamas and the Florida Keys (and potentially up the east coast of the United States). Fortunately, during the time of the spill the loop current spun off an eddy that isolated the spill from the main body of the loop current and oil was not carried out of the Gulf (Figure 2).[11]

Had the spill impacted Cuba, the Bahamas, and other coastal States, it would have grown beyond a US environmental tragedy to become an international incident that would have severely tested the framework of international environmental law. As outlined above, nature was cooperative during the Deepwater Horizon/Macondo incident and there was no immediate impact on other coastal States (time will tell if there will be long-term impacts) but there is currently greatly increased interest and activity in another oil-rich region – the Arctic – where the environmental and oceanographic conditions are such that

[11] http://www.noaanews.noaa.gov/stories2010/20100730_threat.html

a potential spill could be much more catastrophic and would inevitably impact other coastal States.

Conditions in the Arctic

Recent studies by the US Geological Survey have estimated that the Arctic contains about 22 of percent of the world's undiscovered, but recoverable hydrocarbon resources. This is broken down as 13 percent of the world's undiscovered oil, 30 percent of the undiscovered natural gas, and 20 percent of the undiscovered natural gas liquids. About 84 percent of the estimated resources are expected to occur offshore.[12] These studies and independent exploration by the oil industry have focused much attention on the Arctic as a viable locale for oil and gas extraction – particularly in the shelf regions off Russia where 43 of the 61 significant Arctic oil and gas fields are located and in the region of the Chukchi and Beaufort Seas off North America where Shell Oil Company recently spent 2.1 billion dollars for lease blocks in the Chukchi Sea alone.[13]

While the greatest potential for oil and gas recovery in the Arctic is in waters much shallower than the 1500 m depth of the Macondo 252 well, the environmental and logistical concerns associated with the extraction of hydrocarbons in the Arctic are extensive. The potential of an oil spill in the Arctic is particularly concerning as many of the conditions discussed above that prevented the Deepwater Horizon spill from being even more catastrophic than it was, are not found in the Arctic.

First and foremost, unlike the relatively benign (with the exception of an occasional hurricane or tropical storm) weather of the Gulf of Mexico, the Arctic is a region of extreme weather conditions, very low temperatures, ice, and many months of complete darkness. Each of these factors could turn even a minor spill into a major environmental incident. The presence of ice can present very serious challenges to attempts to respond to an oil spill, none the least of which is the simple question of determining the location of the oil as it is typically hidden beneath the ice.[14] When ice is not present, fog, strong winds, waves, and low temperatures can impede attempts at recovery by rendering mechanical recovery equipment like booms and skimmers ineffective or preventing responders from accessing the spill area. Limited daylight can also render response impossible. It is estimated that in the Arctic, temperature alone

[12] Gautier, D. *et al.*, 2009, Assessment of Undiscovered Oil and Gas in the Arctic, Science 29 May 2009: Vol. 324 no. 5931 pp. 1175–1179 DOI: 10.1126/science.1169467.

[13] Nelson, K. 2008, Chukchi High Five, Petroleum News, Feb. 2008.

[14] National Commission on BP Deepwater Horizon Oil Spill and Offshore Drilling: The Challenges of Oil Spill Response in the Arctic, Staff Working Paper No. 5, 2011.

(work stops at temperatures below –45 degrees) would prevent operations 50% of the time in January and 64% of the time in March.[15] Even when responders can gain access to a spill area and locate the oil, many questions remain about the efficacy of non-mechanical (burning and dispersants) oil removal techniques in cold, ice-covered waters.

One of the most effective processes in mitigating some of the impacts of the Deepwater Horizon oil spill was the abundance of bacteria capable of biodegradation of oil. The cold temperatures of the Arctic, however, create an environment where spilled oil will be more viscous and where natural biodegradation processes are most likely much slower than in the relatively warmer waters of the Gulf of Mexico.

In addition to the environmental factors that would inhibit the response to an oil spill in the Arctic, the infrastructure available to respond to a spill in the Arctic is virtually non-existent compared to the infrastructure that was available in the Gulf of Mexico when the Deepwater Horizon platform exploded. The largest community in proximity to the Chukchi Sea is Barrow, with a population of less than 5,000 people and no oil response infrastructure. The nearest Coast Guard base is about 1,000 miles from the Chukchi area and at present the U.S. Coast Guard has only one icebreaker, operating seasonally, in the Arctic (the USCG Cutter *Healy*).[16]

Thus, as catastrophic as the Deepwater Horizon spill was, a major spill in the Arctic has the potential to be much worse, impacting one of the most fragile environments on the planet. In addition, depending on where the spill occurred, the counterclockwise flow of the Arctic Ocean Boundary Current would likely spread the spill and impact neighboring coastal States.[17] Given this potential for environmental disaster on an international scale, we must ask if there is a regulatory framework that can address these concerns (as well as those associated with the Deepwater Horizon and other events like it).

The Regulatory Context that Led to Deepwater Horizon

Part XII of the Law of the Sea Convention (Articles 192, 194(3) and especially Articles 208(1,5) and 214) offers general principles obligating states to adopt

[15] Shell, Chukchi Sea Regional Exploration for Oil Discharge Prevention and Contingency Plan (May, 2009), as reported in National Commission on BP Deepwater Horizon Oil Spill and Offshore Drilling: The Challenges of Oil Spill Response in the Arctic, Staff Working Paper No. 5, 2011.

[16] National Commission on BP Deepwater Horizon Oil Spill and Offshore Drilling: The Challenges of Oil Spill Response in the Arctic, Staff Working Paper No. 5, 2011.

[17] Gobeil, C., *et al.*, 2001, Atlantic Water Flow Pathways Revealed by Lead Contamination in Arctic Basin Sediments, Science 17 August 2001: 1301–130.

laws, regulations and other measures to prevent pollution arising from offshore installations under their jurisdiction and specifies that these laws, regulations and measures be no less effective than international standards. Article 208 also encourages states to establish global and regional rules and standards through competent international organizations or diplomatic conferences. Unfortunately an international convention does not exist for oil platforms like Deepwater Horizon.

In absence of international convention we must look to the coastal State for establishing standards and regulations. But as the Deepwater Horizon spill demonstrated, US regulations and regulatory processes were clearly inadequate. Since the spill, there has been a tremendous amount of scrutiny of the US regulatory process and in particular, the agency responsible for regulating US offshore drilling activities at the time of the spill – the Minerals Management Service (MMS). Serious problems were identified with the approach and behavior of MMS regulators, many of these related to a fundamental conflict of interest in the structure of MMS that allowed the single agency to be the regulator of the offshore oil industry while at the same time being charged with collecting revenue from that industry (MMS was the second largest source of income to the US Treasury after the Internal Revenue Service).[18] Soon after the Deepwater Horizon spill the US government recognized the flaw in this aspect of the regulatory process. Secretary of Interior Salazar reorganized the MMS, creating three separate entities, one responsible for sustainable development and evaluation of outer shelf resources, one with regulatory responsibility, and one with revenue collection responsibility.[19]

The conflict of interest at MMS was not the only problem with the US regulatory process. The technologies associated with offshore drilling, particularly those used in very deep waters like the Macondo 252 well site in the Gulf of Mexico, are phenomenally complex. In the United States, the high-level technical expertise needed to design, build, implement, and evaluate deep-water drilling technology lies in the industry, not in the government, as those with these very specialized skill sets are paid much higher salaries in the private sector. This lack of technical expertise amongst the regulators is amplified by the fact that the US approach to the regulatory process is a prescriptive one whereby the regulators specify the means and minimum steps necessary for compliance at the lowest acceptable safety level. Risk is typically only explored with respect to worst-case scenarios and these worst-case scenarios are often so extreme that they are dismissed as being unlikely. Prescriptive regulations are explicit with respect to the specific technical requirements for structures, technical equip-

[18] Eilperin, J. and Highman, S., "Seeking answers in MMS's flawed culture," Washington Post, 25 August 2010.

[19] http://www.doi.gov/news/pressreleases/Salazar-Divides-MMSs-Three-Conflicting-Missions.cfm

ment and operations needed to prevent accidents and mitigate hazards. The regulatory authorities define the requirements and monitor compliance with no specific requirements to establish a safety management system or detailed risk analyses.[20] Thus, the regulations tend to be complex and, if the regulators are not fully knowledgeable of the technologies involved, they can be inadequate. In MMS's case they would often defer to industry for recommendations to establish minimum standards,[21] a path that eventually led to the Deepwater Horizon spill.

In contrast to the current prescriptive approach used in the United States, Norway, a major player in the offshore oil industry and a leading developer of offshore technology, uses a performance and risk-based regulatory system. In a performance based system, the regulators define the safety standards (i.e., the end result, not the specific approach to achieving it) and acceptance criteria which companies must achieve. It becomes the responsibility of the operators to demonstrate how the equipment and approach they are using will comply with the regulated safety standards. This allows the operators freedom to optimize approaches to safety but demands a stringent and systematic risk management plan across all levels of operation (not just the worst-case scenario). This approach encourages continuous development and adaptation of new technology and best practices. The result is a much simpler regulatory system and an excellent safety record for Norwegian operations.[22]

This brief comparison of the standards and approaches to regulation used by the United States and Norway (and the safety records resulting from the different approaches) indicates that the US regulatory approach is not as effective as the Norwegian.[23] While the Norwegian regulations and measures have not been adopted as "international standards," they are amongst the most effective in the world, and as such, the United States has clearly not fulfilled the spirit of article 208 of the Law of the Sea Convention:

---

20 OLF/NOFO, 2010 – "Summary of differences between offshore drilling regulations in Norway and U.S. Gulf of Mexico," Report no/DNV Reg No.: 2010-1220/ 12P3WF5-9, Rev 02, 2010-08-26, Det Norske Veritas.

21 Eilperin, J. and Highman, S., "Seeking answers in MMS's flawed culture," Washington Post, 25 August 2010 and OLF/NOFO, 2010 – "Summary of differences between offshore drilling regulations in Norway and U.S. Gulf of Mexico," Report no/DNV Reg No.: 2010-1220/ 12P3WF5-9, Rev 02, 2010-08-26, Det Norske Veritas.

22 OLF/NOFO, 2010 – "Summary of differences between offshore drilling regulations in Norway and U.S. Gulf of Mexico," Report no/DNV Reg No.: 2010-1220/ 12P3WF5-9, Rev 02, 2010-08-26, Det Norske Veritas.

23 For an analysis of the effectiveness of the Norwegian approach, and a discussion of potential limits to its applicability in the United States context, see Baram, M., "Preventing Accidents in Offshore Oil and Gas Operations: The U.S. Approach and Some Contrasting Features of the Norwegian Approach," Boston University School of Law Working Paper No. 09-43 (December 1, 2010), SSRN Id. 1705812.

1. Coastal States shall adopt laws and regulations to prevent, reduce and control pollution of the marine environment arising from or in connection with seabed activities subject to their jurisdiction and from artificial islands, installations and structures under their jurisdiction, pursuant to articles 60 and 80.
2. States shall take other measures as may be necessary to prevent, reduce and control such pollution.
3. Such laws, regulations and measures shall be no less effective than international rules, standards and recommended practices and procedures.

The horrific events of the Deepwater Horizon spill have focused much attention on the U.S. regulatory framework for the offshore oil and gas industry. Many committees and panels are evaluating this structure and there is already discussion of an evolution towards a more performance based approach to regulation beyond the Safety and Environmental Management Systems regulations promulgated by BOEMRE under the Outer Continental Shelf Lands Act in October 2010.[24] This may help the situation in the United States, but there are many players in the growing world of offshore oil and gas exploitation, opening the question of whether it is possible to establish an international framework for regulating offshore oil and gas platforms.

An International Regulatory Framework for Offshore Oil Spills Like Deepwater Horizon?

As outlined above, Article 208 of the Law of the Sea Convention addresses pollution from seabed activities subject to national jurisdiction. Paragraph 1 requires coastal States to adopt laws and regulations to prevent, reduce and control pollution of the marine environment arising from or in connection with seabed activities subject to their jurisdiction and from artificial islands, installation and structures under their jurisdiction. Article 208.3 further requires that such laws, regulations and measures are to be no less effective than international rules, standards and recommended practices and procedures. Article 208.5 requires States, "acting especially through competent international organizations or diplomatic conference," to establish global and regional rules, standards

[24] Department of the Interior, Bureau of Ocean Energy Management, Regulation and Enforcement, 30 CFR Part 250, Oil and Gas and Sulphur Operations in the Outer Continental Shelf – Safety and Environmental Management Systems; Final Rule, 75 Fed. Reg. 63610, October 15, 2010. The Notice of Proposed Rule making was published (74 FR 28639) and its public comment period closed (September 2009) well before the Deepwater Horizon incident.

and recommended practices and procedures to prevent, reduce and control pollution of the marine environment referred to in paragraph 1 of Article 208. Paragraph 5 also requires that such rules, standards and recommended practices and procedures be re-examined from time to time as necessary.[25] The International Maritime Organization is understood to be the "competent international organization" referred to in Article 208.5.

The IMO and the Arctic Council have to date addressed some, but not all, of these requirements.

The purposes of the IMO, as set out in Article 1 of its constitutive instrument, the Convention on the International Maritime Organization, as amended, include the encouragement and facilitation of "the general adoption of the highest practicable standards in matters concerning the maritime safety…and prevention and control of marine pollution from ships…". Article 15 sets out the functions of the Assembly, which include in paragraph (j) "to recommend to Members for adoption regulations and guidelines concerning maritime safety, the prevention and control of marine pollution from ships and other matters concerning the effect on shipping on the marine environment assigned to the Organization by or under international instruments…".

In December 2009, at its twenty-sixth meeting, the IMO Assembly adopted a revised "Code for the Construction and Equipment of Mobile Offshore Drilling Units, 2009 (2009 MODU Code)".[26] This 146-page non-binding document provides international guidelines for mobile offshore drilling units of new construction which will facilitate the international movement and operation of these units. It is also designed to ensure a level of safety for such units and for personnel on board, equivalent to that required by the International Convention for the Safety of Life at Sea, 1974, as amended, and the Protocol of 1988 relating to the International Convention on Load Lines, 1966, for conventional ships engaged on international voyages. However, this Code does not include any guidelines for the drilling of subsea wells or the procedures for their control, as such drilling operations are subject to control by the coastal State.[27]

---

[25] Article 214 of the LOS Convention requires States to enforce their laws and regulations adopted in accordance with article 208. It also requires them to adopt laws and regulations and to take other measures necessary to implement applicable international rules and standards established through competent international organizations or diplomatic conference to prevent, reduce and control pollution of the marine environment arising from or in connection with seabed activities subject to their jurisdiction and from artificial islands, installations and structures under their jurisdiction.

[26] IMO Assembly resolution A.1023(26), Dec. 2, 2009, IMO document A26/Res.1023, Jan. 18, 2010 (hereafter MODU Code).

[27] MODU Code, Preamble.

The Code does address the following subjects:

- construction, strength and materials;
- subdivision, stability and freeboard;
- machinery installation for all types of units;
- electrical installations for all types of units;
- machinery and electrical installation in hazardous areas for all types of units;
- machinery and electrical installations for self-propelled units;
- periodically unattended machinery spaces for all types of units;
- fire safety;
- life-saving appliances and equipment;
- radio-communication and navigation;
- lifting devices, personnel and pilot transfer;
- helicopter facilities; and
- operations.

In April 2009, the Arctic Council endorsed a revised set of "Arctic Offshore Oil and Gas Guidelines" prepared by the Protection of the Arctic Marine Environment (PAME) Working Group.[28] These non-binding guidelines are "intended to be of use to the Arctic nations for offshore oil and gas activities during planning, exploration, development, production and decommissioning."[29] Chapter 6 of the Guidelines addresses operating practices and chapter 7 deals with emergencies, while chapter 10 provides a comprehensive bibliography. Chapter 5 focuses on the transition from prescriptive to performance and risk-based regulatory systems. In February 2011 the PAME working group approved a project for comparing "existing Arctic health, safety and environmental management systems, and best practices requirements for offshore drilling operations and possibly developing a corresponding set of expanded guidance for Arctic States beyond what is already in the Arctic Offshore Oil and Gas Guidelines, 2009."[30]

To carry out further the mandate of article 208 of the LOS Convention, and consistent with the competence of the IMO granted by its Constitution, in light of the Deepwater Horizon incident, the IMO Assembly, which next meets in late November 2011, could task the Maritime Safety Committee to

[28] Arctic Council Protection of the Arctic Marine Environment Working Group, Arctic Offshore Oil and Gas Guidelines, April 29, 2009, available at http://www.pame.is/images/stories/FrontPage/Arctic-Guidelines-2009-13th-Mar2009.pdf (hereafter Arctic Guidelines).

[29] Arctic Guidelines, p. 4, para. 12.

[30] Arctic Council Protection of the Arctic Marine Environment Working Group Work Plan 2011–2013, Annex 3, p. 12, Final agreed version as per PAME I-2011, February 2011.

revise and update the MODU Code to incorporate guidance relating to drilling operations, both generally and in the Arctic.

If, after time and experience with such expanded guidelines, there was a desire to make them mandatory, the guidance provided in IMO resolution A.911(22), uniform wording for referencing IMO instruments, should be followed.[31]

[31] Uniform wording for referencing IMO instruments, IMO resolution A.911(22), Nov. 29, 2001, IMO document A22/Res.911, Jan. 22, 2002.

Panel VII: Commentary and Review of the Conference

THE PARTICULARLY SENSITIVE SEA AREA (PSSA): HISTORY AND DEVELOPMENT[1]

Haryo Budi Nugroho[2]

I. *Introduction*

The oceans comprise approximately 71 percent of the Earth's surface[3] and have had a great significance for human life since time immemorial. The oceans play a very vital role as a source of food, minerals and oil. Another source of importance of the oceans that is sometimes considered less significant is their role as a route for navigation. This freedom of navigation through the oceans is also a common heritage of mankind that is often forgotten.[4] The oceans connecting all parts of the world enable mankind to explore new places and trade between continents and islands.

The importance of the oceans as a natural resource is threatened by pollution. Problems of pollution have been acknowledged as common for all states. International law has developed various kinds of instruments to deal with this problem of marine pollution. The United Nations Convention on the Law of the Sea (UNCLOS) 1982, for example, contains a special part called the Protection and Preservation of the Marine Environment (Part XII). UNCLOS 1982 has been recognized as the umbrella convention for the protection of the marine environment.[5] Specific international instruments are also designed to

[1] This is an abridged version of an independent research paper by the author with the same title prepared at the University of Virginia School of Law in 2010 before the Strait of Bonifacio was designated as a PSSA.

[2] Haryo Nugroho is an SJD Candidate at the University of Virginia School of Law and a Rhodes Academy of Oceans Law and Policy Graduate, class of 2010. The author would like to thank Prof. John Norton Moore for his guidance and advice during the research. The views in this study are exclusively that of the author and are not in any way a reflection of the view of the Government of the Republic of Indonesia.

[3] Markus J. Kachel, *Particularly Sensitive Sea Areas: the IMO's Role in Protecting Vulnerable Marine Areas* 6 (Springer-Verlag Berlin Heidelberg 2008).

[4] "Common Heritage of Mankind" usually refers to the legal status of resources in common space areas such as the ocean floor, outer space, the moon and Antarctica, *see* McDorman *et al.*, *International Ocean Law Materials and Commentaries* 22 (Carolina Academic Press 2005).

[5] Agustin Blanco-Bazán [1], "The Environmental UNCLOS and the Work of IMO in the Field of Prevention of Pollution from Vessels," *International Marine Environmental Law, Institutions, Implementation and Innovation* 34, Andree Kirchner, ed., (Kluwer Law International 2003).

address the marine environmental problems caused by different kind of sources. Examples include the Convention for the Prevention of Marine Pollution from Land Based Sources,[6] the Convention on the Prevention of Marine Pollution by Dumping of Waste and other Matter,[7] and the International Convention for the Prevention of Pollution from Ships 1973[8] as modified by the Protocol of 1978 (MARPOL 73/78).[9]

In this sphere, "special area" regimes were developed to protect specific areas that are more vulnerable to environmental degradation. Both the MARPOL 73/78 and the UNCLOS 1982 have similar features of a "special area." In MARPOL 73/78, a "special area" is defined as "a sea area where for recognized technical reasons in relation to its oceanographical and ecological condition and to the particular character of its traffic the adoption of a special mandatory method for the prevention of sea pollution by oil, noxious liquid substances, or garbage as applicable is required."[10] On the other hand, UNCLOS 1982, Article 211 (6)(a), stipulates that a State can adopt "special mandatory measures for the prevention of pollution...for recognized technical reasons in relation to its oceanographical and ecological condition, as well as its utilization or the protection of its resources."[11]

Aside from multilateral treaties and conventions, the International Maritime Organization (IMO) has continuously developed measures that can be taken to improve marine environmental protection efforts. In 1991, the IMO Assembly introduced the concept of Particularly Sensitive Sea Area or PSSA. PSSA is defined as an "area that needs special protection through action by IMO because of its significance for recognized ecological, socio-economic, or scientific attributes where such attributes may be vulnerable to damage by international

[6] The Convention for the Prevention of Marine Pollution from Land Based Sources, Jun. 4, 1974, 1546 U.N.T.S. 120.

[7] The Convention on the Prevention of Marine Pollution by Dumping of Waste and other Matter, Dec. 29, 1972, 1046 U.N.T.S. 120.

[8] The International Convention for the Prevention of Pollution from Ships, Nov. 2, 1973, 1340 U.N.T.S. 184.

[9] Protocol of 1978 relating to the International Convention for the Prevention of Pollution from Ships 1973, Feb. 17, 1978, 1340 U.N.T.S. 61, 62.

[10] Int'l Maritime Org. [IMO], *Guidelines for the Designation of Special Areas and the Identification of Particularly Sensitive Sea Area*, Annex, IMO Assemb. Res. A. 720 (17), 16 (Jan. 9, 1992). In MARPOL 73/78, the type of Special Area is differentiated by the type of pollution that particular area is vulnerable from. Different types of pollution will be dealt with different requirement of special measures as specify in its annexes. For this purpose, the term "MARPOL 73/78 Special Area" will also include the SOx (*sulphur oxide*) Emission Control Areas (SECA) under Annex VI in which a stricter SOx emission standard is applied.

[11] United Nations Convention on the Law of the Sea [UNCLOS] art. 211 (6) (a), Dec. 10, 1982, 1833 U.N.T.S. 3. For the purpose of this paper it will be referred to as UNCLOS 1982 Special Area.

shipping activities."[12] Although PSSA may sound similar to "special area," this terminology is different, and should not be confused with the Special Area under the MARPOL 73/78 and the Special Area under Article 211 of the UNCLOS 1982.

Along with the introduction of the concept of PSSA in 1991, the Great Barrier Reef of Australia was identified as the first PSSA. Today, there are twelve PSSAs. The development of PSSA has been an important issue, since PSSA is not the only regime addressing marine pollution caused by shipping activities, thus it raises the question of whether it will overlap with the previous regime. The next issue raised by PSSA is to what extent it serves as an effective remedy in protecting the environmental attributes of a marine area. The balance between environmental and navigational interests is what's at stake in this designation. It is important to maintain the balance of interests, as well as the rule of law in this context.

This study will examine the correlation between PSSA, MARPOL 73/78 Special Area and UNCLOS 1982 Special Area. Other facts to consider in the development of PSSAs are that during the period of 1991 to 2001, there were only two designations of PSSAs, but from the period of 2002 to 2007 there were ten designated PSSAs.[13] These are facts that must be analyzed in order to see the effectiveness of future PSSA applications.[14]

This paper is aimed at a theoretical as well as a practical analysis of reviewing PSSA instruments. Part II of this paper gives the history of PSSA development. Part III of this paper elaborates on the IMO Guidelines for the Identification and Designation of PSSAs in IMO Assembly Resolution A. 982 (24), as well as a comparative analysis between PSSA, MARPOL 73/78 Special Areas and UNCLOS 1982 Special Areas. Part IV of this paper offers analysis and recommendations for the implementation of PSSA.

II. *The History of PSSA*

A. *Development of International Environmental Awareness*

Among many international law instruments, the Declaration of the United Nations Conference on the Human Environment (Stockholm Declaration

[12] IMO, *Revised Guidelines the Identification and Designation of Particularly Sensitive Sea Area*, Annex, ¶ 1.2, IMO Assemb. Res. A. 982 (24), (Dec. 1, 2005).

[13] For the updated chronological list of PSSAs designations *see* www.imo.org.

[14] The doubt over the utility of PSSA was raised by Churchill and Lowe in 1999; see R.R. Churchill & A.V. Lowe, *The Law of the Sea* p. 395 (Manchester University Press 3rd ed. 1999) (1983).

1972) was one of the first instruments that obligated States to undertake preventive measures with regard to marine pollution.[15] Throughout this decade, several vessel incidents occurred that resulted in catastrophic results to the marine environment. To name a few, there were the *Amoco Cadiz*[16] and the *Oceanic Grandeur*.[17] These incidents triggered several other conferences that tried to address marine pollution prevention and vessel traffic regulation. Also in this decade, the Third United Nations Conference on the Law of the Sea was in session with the Third Committee dealing with the marine environment and scientific matters in particular. This Conference resulted in UNCLOS 1982 in which Part XII comprehensively dealt with marine environment problems and not only regulated the general obligations of States, but also other matters including international cooperation (Section 2) as well as international rules and national regulation to prevent, reduce and control pollution of the marine environment (Section 5).

B. *Embodiment of the PSSA Concept*

It was the International Conference on Tanker Safety and Pollution Prevention (TSPP), London, 1978, where the issue of PSSAs was first raised. At this Conference, Sweden proposed to bestow special attention to areas that have particular value due to their "renewable natural resources or their importance for scientific purposes."[18] The Conference therefore adopted Resolution No. 9 of TSSP, which invited the IMO (IMCO at that time)[19] to

---

[15] This notion was embodied in Principle 7 and 21, Stockholm Declaration of the United Nations Conference on the Human Environment, June 16, 1972, U.N. Doc. A/CONF.48/14 (1972), 11 I.L.M. 1416 (1972). Prior to this Declaration, one of the biggest marine incidents happened in 1967, the grounding of the *Torrey Canyon*. That raised the awareness of the international community on the importance of marine environment protection.

[16] During the 38th Session of the Third Committee of the Third United Nations Conference on the Law of the Sea, *the Amoco Cadiz* incidents received great attention from the delegations and raised concern to enhance measures to address marine environment protection while still maintaining the balance between this interest and the interest of international navigation, *see* the Chairman of the Third Committee's Report to the Plenary *Reports of the Committees and Negotiating Groups on Negotiations at the Seventh Session Contained in Single Document both for the Purpose of Record and for the Convenience of Delegation 1*, Doc. A/CONF.62/RCNG/1 (May 19, 1978).

[17] This incident caused a major oil spill in the Torres Strait that latter become one of the designated PSSA. *See* Peter Ottesen *et al.*, "Shipping Threats and Protection of the Great Barrier Reef Marine Park—the Role of the Particularly Sensitive Sea Area Concept," 9 Int'l J. Marine & Coastal L. 511, 507–522 (1994).

[18] Gerard Peet, "Particularly Sensitive Sea Areas – A Documentation History," 9 Int'l J. Marine & Coastal L. 475, 469–506 (1994).

[19] IMO was established under the name "Inter-Governmental Maritime Consultative Organization" but the name was changed to IMO in 1982, *see* Introduction to IMO at http://www .imo.org/ (last visited Apr. 22, 2010).

> *... [make] an inventory of sea areas around the world which are in special need of protection against marine pollution from ships and dumping, on account of the areas' particular sensitivity in respect of their renewable natural resources or in respect of their importance for scientific purposes.*[20]

The TSSP was the conference that adopted the 1978 Protocol to the 1973 MARPOL Convention (MARPOL 73/78). Resolution No. 9 did not explain the relation between these two features, although Sweden suggested in its proposal that these would be complementary to the MARPOL 73/78 Special Area.[21]

IMO continues to prepare studies for the realization of the PSSA concept. The task to formulate the concept of the PSSAs was entrusted to the Marine Environmental Protection Committee (MEPC).[22] During the period of 1978–1985, MEPC did not make any significant progress in addressing this matter, but focused more on further research and consideration of what would be the next appropriate step.[23] The Group of Experts on the Scientific Aspects of Marine Pollution (GESAMP) suggested that making an inventory would not be suitable at this stage; rather IMO should develop guidelines for the identification of a Particularly Sensitive Sea Area.[24]

It should also be noted that during this period of time, UNCLOS 1982 was in a negotiating stage. UNCLOS 1982 also developed a provision concerning Special Areas (UNCLOS 1982 Special Area) namely in Article 211 (6) (a).[25] During the negotiation process the proposition of "special area" was understood as a MARPOL 73/78 Special Area.[26] However the language was kept open to

[20] Int'l Conference on Tanker Safety & Pollution Prevention, London 1978, Resolution 9: Protection of Particularly Sensitive Sea Areas, ¶ (b)(i).

[21] Gerard Peet, *supra* note 18 at 475.

[22] Nihan Ünlü, *Particularly Sensitive Sea Areas: Past, Present and Future*, http://www.imo.org/includes/blastDataOnly.asp/data_id%3D17988/Particularly.pdf (last visited Feb. 19, 2010).

[23] Gerard Peet, *supra* note 18 at 475.

[24] *Id.*

[25] Until today, in relation to Article 211 (6) (a), the IMO has not made any proposition of its implementation, nor is there any state that has invoked this provision. However MARPOL 73/78 Special Area is similar to this provision and the PSSA Guidelines mentioned in this article were one consideration in adopting Associated Protective Measures (APMs), *see* E.J. Molenaar, *Coastal State Jurisdiction over Vessel-Source Pollution* 407–408 (Kluwer Law International 1998).

[26] GR. J. Timagenis, *International Control of Marine Pollution* Vol. 2 612–613 footnote 73 (Oceana Publication 1980). However this note did not explain why Article 211 (6) (a) gives specific provision regarding the procedure and time scope for special area proposals that are different from MARPOL 73/38 Special Area Guidelines. Note also that the IMCO in its general statement during the Plenary Meeting on the Second Session of the Third United Nations Conference on the Law of the Sea, June 28, 1974, mentioned the "special area" feature of the MARPOL 73 as one of the important achievement made by the IMCO, *see* the Official Record in the *Third United Nations Conference on the Law of the Sea Official Records Volume I* at 66,

include other types of special areas that either already existed or would be created in the future,[27] presumably including PSSAs as well.

The discussion under the MEPC took place from 1986 to 1991.[28] During its Twenty-Third Session, the MEPC received proposals from Friends of the Earth International (FoEI), an observer NGO, which suggested PSSAs could serve as a tool of aligning international instruments that deal with marine environmental protection.[29] The same spirit was in a proposal by Germany, which suggested that the concept of 'particularly sensitive sea areas' should be incorporated into MARPOL 73/38.[30] The Twenty-Third Session then wound up with a conclusion requesting States to provide information regarding their national marine protected areas including the criteria, the protective measures, and the geographical description of the areas that would become the basis for the IMO's work on formulating the PSSA concept and its protection measures.[31]

During this period of time, several international organizations and NGOs were also involved in working on the PSSA concept.[32] One of the highlights of this effort was a seminar held in Malmö, Sweden, from September 25–28, 1990.

U.N. Sales No. E.75.V.3 (1975). However, from the information in the Official Records, the issue of "particularly sensitive areas" referred to by Resolution No. 9 was not raised.

27 *Id.*

28 IMO Assemb. Res. A. 982 (24), *supra* note 12 annex ¶ 1.1. Nihan Ünlü, *supra* note 22. *See also* Markus J. Kachel, *supra* note 3 at 157. It is during this period that Australia began its proposal to identify the Great Barrier Reef as a PSSA, *see* IMO, MEPC, *Identification of the Great Barrier Reef as a Particularly Sensitive Sea Area*, MEPC 30/19/4 (Sep. 19, 1990).

29 Gerard Peet, *supra* note 18 at 476–477; Kristina M. Gjerde and David Ong, "Protection of Particularly Sensitive Sea Areas under International Marine Environmental Law, Report of the International Meeting of Legal Experts on Particularly Sensitive Sea Areas University of Hull, 20–21 July 1992," 26 *Marine Pollution Bulletin* 10, 9–13 (1993). Peet also mentioned that the effort to bring the discussion of the PSSA in the MEPC began in the 22nd session of the MEPC, and has been supported by other NGOs including the International Union for the Conservation of Nature and Natural Resources (IUCN).

30 *See* Gerard Peet, *supra* note 18 at 477. At a latter stage, this proposal also came from Friends of the Earth International and Norway; however MEPC did not approve this suggestion (*see* MEPC 35/21) and maintained PSSAs separate from MARPOL 73/78, *see id.* at 493 and 501.

31 IMO, MEPC, *Report of the Marine Environment Protection Committee on its Twenty-Third Session*, Annex 13, MEPC 23/22 (Jul. 11, 1986).

32 Markus J. Kachel, *supra* note 3 at 157, mentions that the Intergovernmental Oceanographic Commission of UNESCO (IOC), FoEI, and the World Conservation Union (IUCN) are involved in the process. *See also* Angelo Merialdi, "Legal Restraints on Navigation in Marine Specially Protected Areas," *Marine Specially Protected areas the General Aspects and the Mediterranean Regional System* 36, Tullio Scovazzi ed. (Kluwer Law International 1999).

The result, known as the Malmö Declaration, went further by recommending actions that can be taken to protect PSSAs such as:[33]

- Regulation of navigation that includes closure of shipping routes, speed restriction or pilotage;
- Development of contingency plan;
- Imposing environmental fees;
- Strict regulation of maritime activities; and
- Strict regulation with regard to exploitation of resources.

These actions to protect the PSSAs were later recognized as Associated Protective Measures (APM).

These series of discussions finally led to IMO Assembly Resolution A 720 (17) concerning *Guidelines for the Designation of Special Areas and the Identification of Particularly Sensitive Sea Areas* in 1991.[34] The term "identification" was used because the PSSA did not possess a legally binding foundation, it only relied on the Resolution No. 9 of TSSP and IMO Resolution,[35] noting that UNCLOS 1982 had not yet entered into force.[36]

Besides the Great Barrier Reefs (Australia) being identified as a PSSA along with the adoption of this Resolution, the Archipelago of Sabana-Camaguay (Cuba) was identified as a PSSA in 1997 using the procedure in IMO Assembly Resolution A. 720 (17).

C. *Evolution of the PSSA Guidelines*

After the adoption of the Assembly Resolution A. 720 (17), there are two important developments in international environmental law. They are the adoption of the Agenda 21 during the United Nations Conference on Environment and Development (UNCED) in Rio de Janeiro, June 1992, and the entry into force of the UNCLOS 1982 in November 1994.

---

[33] Extract of the Malmö Declaration in the IMO, MEPC, Report of the International Meeting of Legal Expert on Particularly Sensitive Sea Area, University of Hull, 20–21 July 1992, Annex 3, MEPC 33/INF.27 (Sep. 1, 1992), *see also* Ryan P. Lessmann, "Current Protections on the Galapagos Islands are Inadequate: the International Maritime Organization Should Declare the Islands a Particularly Sensitive Sea Area," 15 Colo. J. Int'l Envtl. L. & Pol'y 146, 117–152 (2004).

[34] IMO Assemb. Res. A. 720 (17), *supra* note 10.

[35] Gerard Peet, *supra* note 18 at 482. E.J. Molenaar, *supra* note 25 at 438; Agustin Blanco-Bazán [2], *the IMO Guidelines on Particularly Sensitive Sea Areas (PSSAs) their Possible Application to the Protection of Underwater Cultural Heritage*, 20 Marine Policy 346, 343–349 (1996).

[36] The UNCLOS 1982 was entered into force on November 16, 1994.

Agenda 21 is significant because it gives a further specific mandate in relation to the PSSA concept. It stipulates that States, individually, together with other States, or within IMO are to deal with pollution matters "...caused by ships in particularly sensitive areas identified by IMO and taking action, where necessary, to implement applicable measures...to ensure compliance with generally accepted international regulations.[37]

The entry into force of the UNCLOS 1982 also affected the PSSA concept. Previously the obligation to protect the environment was based on declarations. By the entry into force of UNCLOS 1982, States now have a treaty obligation to protect and preserve the marine environment.[38] Therefore all measures taken in relation to the ocean were to be in conformity with the provisions of the UNCLOS 1982.

Taking into consideration this development and other factors, the IMO continued its work to develop the PSSA concept. In 1999 IMO revised the PSSA guidelines by Assembly Resolution No. A. 885 (21) concerning *Procedures for the Identification of Particularly Sensitive Sea Areas and the Adoption of Associated Protective Measures and Amendments to the Guidelines Contained in Resolution A. 720 (17)*. However, no PSSA was identified using Resolution No. A. 885 (21) in particular.

In 2001, the IMO adopted Assembly Resolution No. A. 927 (22) concerning *Guidelines for the Designation of Special Areas under MARPOL 73/78 and Guidelines for the Identification and Designation of Particularly Sensitive Sea Area*[39] and revoked both Resolution No. A. 720 (17) and No. A. 885 (21). One of the significant changes that the Guidelines made was using the term "designate" as opposed to the previously used term "identify." In this regard, it seems that PSSAs had been elevated from a simple mechanism to coordinate IMO related measures to a more tangible environmental measure.[40]

Under these new guidelines, there were nine PSSAs identified, namely the area around the Malpelo Islands (Columbia), the area around the Florida Keys (United States), the Wadden Sea (the Netherlands, Denmark, and Germany),

---

[37] Agenda 21, Section III Chapter 17.30. (A)(iv), UNCED, U.N. Doc. A/CONF.151/26 (1992), reprinted in 31 I.L.M. 874 (1992), available at http://www.un.org/esa/sustdev/agenda21.htm.

[38] UNCLOS 1982, *supra*, note 11 Arts. 192 and 194.

[39] IMO, *Guidelines for the Designation of Special Areas under MARPOL 73/78 and Guidelines for the Identification and Designation of Particularly Sensitive Sea Area*, IMO Assemb. Res. A 927 (22) (Nov. 29, 2001).

[40] *See further* Julian Roberts, *Marine Environment Protection and Biodiversity Conservation: the Application and Future Development of the IMO's Particularly Sensitive Sea Area Concept 4–5* (Springer-Verlag Berlin Heidelberg, 2007). The book further suggests that this is the result of public pressure from NGOs and environmentally focused coastal States. This seems to be true due to the fact of the role played by international organizations and NGOs as well as Sweden in particular in initiating the discussion of PSSAs within the IMO.

the Paracas National Reserve (Peru), the Western European Waters (Belgium, France, Ireland, Portugal, Spain, United Kingdom), the Canary Islands (Spain), the Baltic Sea Area (Denmark, Estonia, Finland, Germany, Latvia, Lithuania, Poland, and Sweden), the extension of the Great Barrier Reefs PSSA to include the Torres Strait (Australia and Papua New Guinea), and the Galapagos Archipelago (Ecuador).

In the next and current Guidelines, Assembly Resolution No. A. 982 (24) *Revised Guidelines for the Identification and Designation or Particularly Sensitive Sea Areas*, which was adopted in 2005, the IMO decided to separate the guidelines for the identification and designation of PSSAs from the MARPOL 73/78 Special Area.[41] The latest PSSA, the Papahānaumokuākea Marine National Monument, was designated using Resolution No. A. 982 (24).[42] When this paper was written, Resolution No. A. 982 (24) continued to remain in force and serves as the basic guidelines in PSSA identification and designation.

III. *Designation and Comparison with Other Special Areas*

A. *Designation of PSSA*

The latest PSSA Guideline, IMO Assembly Resolution No. A. 982 (24),[43] in principle has two main aspects: the elements of PSSA and the procedure for PSSA designation. Therefore, this part will be divided into two sections accordingly.

1. *Elements of a PSSA*

The Guidelines define a PSSA as "...an area that needs special protection through actions by IMO because of its significance for recognized ecological, socio-economic, or scientific attributes where such attributes may be vulnerable to damage by international shipping activities."[44] From that definition, it can be implied that there are three elements in PSSAs: Attributes; Vulnerability; and an IMO action that is referred to as an Associated Protective Measure.

a. Attributes

In principle, Attributes are the elements that make the area particularly special. The Guidelines use this term interchangeably with "criteria" referring to the

---

[41] For the latest update of the current PSSA guidelines, *see* www.imo.org.

[42] IMO MEPC Res. 171 (57), Apr. 4, 2008.

[43] The IMO always puts the Guidelines under review according to the IMO Assemb. Res. A. 982 (24).

[44] IMO Assemb. Res. A. 982 (24), *supra* note 12, Annex ¶ 1.2.

same understanding about what is so special or significant about the proposed area. To be considered as a PSSA, the proposed area must at least meet one of these criteria: Ecological Criteria; Social, Cultural and Economic Criteria; and Scientific and Educational Criteria.

The consideration for social, cultural and economic as well as scientific and educational criteria are new aspects with regard to special area designation. The Guidelines further elaborate that social or economic dependency can be met if environmental quality and marine resources serve as a significant basis for the source of income of people in the area, which includes fishing, tourism,[45] or the traditional way of living.[46] The cultural heritage criterion was added to address the concern to protect the underwater cultural heritage that is not properly addressed by the UNESCO Agreement for the Protection of Underwater Cultural Heritage.[47]

The IMO also mentions in the Guidelines that it will take into consideration whether the proposed area has received international acknowledgment, which can be in a form of the World Heritage List or Biosphere Reserve within the framework of UNESCO.[48] In practice, other international or regional frameworks that are considered by the IMO include the List of Wetlands of International Importance of the Convention on Wetlands of International Importance (RAMSAR Convention).[49]

b. Vulnerability

Firstly it should be noted that vulnerability was caused by international shipping activities; otherwise national legislation was deemed sufficient national regulation.[50] The PSSA regime is designed to prevent environmental degradation

---

[45] *Id.* ¶ 4.4.12. This is one of the criteria that often invoked by States in PSSA applications, for example in the Canary Islands, *see further* IMO, MEPC, *Designation of the Canary Islands as a Particularly Sensitive Sea Area*, Annex 1 ¶ 2.2.2, MEPC Res. 134 (53) (Jul. 22, 2005).

[46] IMO Assemb. Res. A. 982 (24), *supra* note 12, Annex at ¶ 4.4.13. This proposition was applied in the Torres Strait that includes the consideration of the indigenous people living in the area, *see further* IMO, MEPC, *Designation of the Torres Strait as an Extension of the Great Barrier Reef Particularly Sensitive Sea Area*, Annex 1 ¶ 2.2 & 2.3, MEPC Res. 133 (53) (Jul. 22, 2005).

[47] IMO, MEPC, *Report of the Correspondence Group of the Identification and Protection of Special Areas and Particularly Sensitive Areas,* Annex ¶ 4.4.14 (*bis*), MEPC 53/8/2 (Apr. 15, 2005) (*submitted by* the United States).

[48] IMO Assemb. Res. A. 982 (24), *supra* note 12, Annex ¶ 6.2.

[49] Among others, the Paracas National Reserve PSSA, Resolution MEPC. 106 (49) (Jul. 18, 2003), ¶ 2.4.1.

[50] *See* IMO, MEPC, *Draft Guidance Document for Submission of PSSA Proposals*, Annex ¶ 2.1, MEPC 47/8/1 (Dec. 10, 2001) (*submitted by* the United States). This Document latter was used as Annex to *Guidance Document for Submission of PSSA Proposal to IMO*, MEPC/Circ.398 (Mar. 27, 2003) that is complimentary to the IMO Assembly Resolution A. 927 (22).

from shipping activities that include operational discharge, accidental or intentional pollution and physical damage to marine environments or organisms.[51] However, the designation as PSSA will not address whether the area should be protected from dumping.[52]

Similar to the Attributes element, the Guidelines also categorized the vulnerability element into two factors, namely:

1. Vessel traffic characteristics:
   - Operational factors (type of maritime activities that reduce the safety of navigation);
   - Vessel types;
   - Traffic characteristic; and
   - Harmful substances carried.
2. Natural factors:
   - Hydrographical;
   - Meteorological; and
   - Oceanographic.[53]

In addition to these factors, the State may also include other factors that affect the vulnerability of the proposed areas including evidentiary assessments of potential damage, past incidents, expected effect of PSSA designation on its adjacent areas, natural sources of pollution and other measures already enforced in the proposed area.[54]

c. Associated Protective Measures (APM)

In a PSSA designation, the proposing State can suggest that the IMO implement an Associated Protective Measures (APM) in the proposed area. The IMO then will determine whether this measure is appropriate to be implemented in the area. The primary responsibility within the IMO to examine the proposal lies within the MEPC, but when the APM proposal involves the competence of other committees, mainly the Maritime Safety Committee (MSC) and the

[51] IMO Assemb. Res. A. 982 (24), *supra* note 12, Annex ¶ 2.1. The Guideline further explain that shipping activities can introduce harmful substances even from normal activities including anti-fouling systems, harmful aquatic organisms, pathogens and even noise, *see id.* ¶ 2.2.

[52] *Id.* Annex ¶ 4.2, the Guideline mentioned that this matter is already addressed by the London Convention 1972, *supra* note 7 and the 1996 Protocol.

[53] IMO Assemb. Res. A. 982 (24), *supra* note 12, Annex ¶ 5.1.

[54] *Id.* ¶ 5.2. For example on the application of the designated PSSA *see further* IMO, MEPC, *Designation of a Western European Particularly Sensitive Sea Area*, MEPC49/8/1 (Apr. 11, 2003) (*submitted by* Belgium, France, Ireland, Portugal, Spain, and the United Kingdom) Annex 1 ¶ 4.9 for additional information and Annex 2 for existing measures and a list of past incidents.

Legal Committee, the proposal will be referred to them for consideration and approval.

Basically APMs shall be limited to measures that have previously been adopted by IMO. These measures include:

- designation of the area as MARPOL 73/78 Special Area or SOx Emission Control Area;[55]
- adoption of ship routeing under the International Convention for the Safety of Life at Sea (SOLAS), General Provisions on Ships' Routeing and the Guidelines and Criteria for Ship Reporting Systems; and
- new measures to be adopted, as far as the legal basis for such measures is available.[56]

In practice, the pilotage system has also been adopted as an APM.[57]

In the event that measures are already enforced to address the vulnerability of the area by international shipping activities, then the proposing State may propose amendment of the existing measure.[58]

2. *Procedure for PSSA Designation*

Resolution No. A. 982 (24) also regulates the procedure of PSSA designation. In principle, the State (or States if the proposed area covers more than one State's territory or jurisdiction)[59] shall submit a proposal to the IMO comprised of two parts. The first one is the description of the area and how it meets the attributes and vulnerability elements, and the second one is what proposed

[55] SOx Emission Control Area (SECA), regulated by Annex VI of MARPOL 73/78, is the area where the standard of emission of sulphur oxide is stricter than other area. Example of a PSSA that is also a MARPOL Special Area is the Baltic Sea, *see further* IMO, MEPC, *Designation of the Baltic Sea area as a Particularly Sensitive Sea Area,* MEPC Res. 136 (53) (Jul. 22, 2005).

[56] IMO Assemb. Res. A. 982 (24), *supra,* Annex ¶ 6.1.

[57] *See* IMO Assemb. Res. A. 720 (17), *supra* note 10, Appendix C that adopted recommended pilotage as one of the Great Barrier Reefs' APM.

[58] IMO Assemb. Res. A. 982 (24), *supra* note 12, Annex ¶ 7.2.

[59] The previously adopted PSSAs that comprise more than one State territory or jurisdiction are the Wadden Sea (the Netherlands, Denmark, and Germany, *see* IMO, MEPC, *Identification of the Wadden Sea as a Particularly Sensitive Sea Area,* MEPC Res. 101(48) (Oct. 11, 2002), the Western European Waters (Belgium, France, Ireland, Portugal, Spain, and the United Kingdom, *see* IMO, MEPC, *Designation of the Western European Waters as a Particularly Sensitive Sea Area,* MEPC Res. 121 (52) (Oct. 15, 2004), the Baltic Sea Area (Denmark, Estonia, Finland, Germany, Latvia, Lithuania, Poland, and Sweden, *see* IMO MEPC Res. 136 (53) *supra* note 55), and the Torres Strait (Australia and Papua New Guinea, *see* IMO MEPC Res. 133 (53) *supra* note 46).

APMs are to be implemented in the area and whether the IMO is competent to adopt such measures.[60]

The application should also include previously adopted measures, whether national or international instruments, that aim to protect the proposed area.[61] Most of the designated PSSAs have been previously designated as national parks and several IMO measures may have been previously adopted in that area. For example, the Great Barrier Reefs have been designated as a Marine Park since 1975 and Annex I MARPOL 73/78 has made special recognition in its provision.[62]

Upon the receipt of such a proposal, the IMO, in this case the MEPC, that bears the primary responsibility, shall consider whether the proposed area has met the criteria of a PSSA. With regard to the APM, the MEPC refers the matter to the relevant committee, sub-committee or the IMO Assembly itself, depending on the competence of each in addressing the measures, to determine whether the proposed APM can be implemented in the proposed area. While waiting for approval regarding an APM, the MEPC may designate "in principle" the proposed area if the area is considered to possess the required attributes that are vulnerable to international shipping activities.

When all approvals are received, the MEPC will adopt a resolution for the designation of a PSSA and its APM. Sometimes it will be accompanied by a resolution of the relevant committee (for example, the MSC) for adoption of an APM under its competence.

B. *Comparison with MARPOL 73/78 Special Area, UNCLOS 1982 Special Area*

The development of MARPOL 73/78 Special Areas, UNCLOS 1982 Special Areas and PSSA were actually based on the same principle. Two important aspects of these measures are to acknowledge the special circumstances of the area and to elevate protection where the normal environmental protection regime is not sufficient to protect the area. However, the international community wanted to separate these three similar regimes, but to keep them interrelated in some points.

---

60 IMO Assemb. Res. A. 982 (24), *supra* note 12, Annex ¶ 7.5.

61 *Id.*, Annex ¶ 7.8. *See also* MEPC49/8/1, *supra* note 54, Annex 2.

62 Peter Ottesen *et al., supra* note 17 at 511. Ottesen *et al.* further mentioned that Regulation 1(9) and 9 of Annex I of MARPOL 73/78 accommodate the situation of the Great Barrier Reefs that defines "nearest land" as the outer limit of the Great Barrier Reefs, *see id.* at 515.

1. *MARPOL 73/78 Special Areas*

MARPOL 73/78 defines Special Areas as

> *a sea area where for recognised technical reasons in relation to its oceanographical and ecological conditions and to the particular character of its traffic, the adoption of special mandatory methods for the prevention of sea pollution by oil, noxious liquid substances, or garbage, as applicable, is required.*[63]

It appears that the MARPOL 73/78 Special Area is designed specifically to deal with a specific type of pollutant depending on the scope of its respective Annex. Special Area under Annex I deals with pollution by oil, Annex II deals with pollution by noxious liquid substances, Annex V deals with pollution by garbage, and Annex VI deals with air pollution by sulphur oxide (and particularly refer to SOx Emission Control Areas).

With regard to the scope of the area, the Guideline for Designation of Special Areas stipulates that it can cover a "maritime zone of several States, or even an entire enclosed or semi-enclosed sea."[64] From this stipulation, it can be inferred that the scope of the MARPOL 73/78 Special Area can include territorial seas, contiguous zones, EEZs, or even high seas since there is no limitation on the regime of water in which it can be implemented.

From the definition it also can be inferred that the considerations for the MARPOL 73/78 Special Area were oceanographical, ecological, and vessel traffic conditions. With regard to this criterion, the Guidelines provide that oceanographic criteria includes circulation patterns, temperature and salinity stratification, long residence time caused by low flushing rates, extreme ice states and adverse wind conditions.[65] The ecological criteria include the consideration of whether the area is a habitat of endangered species or an area of high natural productivity, with significance for marine life cycle (spawning, breeding, nursery, or transit for marine species). Lastly, to fulfill the element of traffic characteristic, the Guidelines explain that simply implementing the regular operational standard under MARPOL 73/78 is not sufficient to protect the environment of the Special Area.

The special measures provided in the MARPOL 73/78 Special Areas impose stricter discharge requirements, or even no discharge in the Special Area.[66] The requirement for Special Area designation also includes that in that area, adequate

[63] IMO Asemb. Res. 927 (22), *supra* note 39, Annex I ¶ 2.1. The way that the MARPOL 73/78 was designed was to classify the type of pollution to be dealt with in different Annexes of the MARPOL 73/78. Thus the measures for each Annex Special Area are also differentiated to better address the problem. Some areas can be a Special Area under more than one Annex.

[64] IMO Asemb. Res. 927 (22), *supra* note 39, Annex I ¶ 2.2.

[65] *Id.* at ¶ 2.4.

[66] IMO, MEPC, *Additional Protection for Particularly Sensitive Sea Area*, Annex ¶2.4.2, MEPC 46/6/1 (Jan. 19, 2001) (note by the Secretariat).

reception facilities for discharge shall be available in ports of States bordering the Special Area.[67]

2. *UNCLOS 1982 Special Area*

The UNCLOS 1982 Special Area has provisions similar to the MARPOL 73/78 Special Area. Article 211 (6) a of the UNCLOS 1982 describes a special area as follows:

> *. . . clearly defined area of their respective exclusive economic zone is an area where the adoption of special mandatory measures for the prevention of pollution from vessels is required for recognized technical reasons in relation to its oceanographical and ecological conditions, as well as its utilization or the protection of its resources and the particular character of its traffic . . .*

Briefly, the MARPOL 73/78 Special Area and the UNCLOS 1982 Special Area have similar elements: oceanographical, ecological, and vessel traffic characteristics. The significant difference between the two is the scope of the area. The UNCLOS 1982 Special Area is clearly stipulated to cover the EEZ only; in MARPOL 73/78 it can cover a broader maritime zone. UNCLOS 1982 Special Area also requires that a Special Area be designated if in that area the application or regular operational standard regarding pollution from vessels, that is referred to in Article 211 (1),[68] is insufficient.

Additionally, Article 211 (6) (a) provides a time limit period of twelve months from receiving the request for the designation of the Special Area and fifteen months from receiving the request for implementation of the special measures.[69]

3. *Comparison of PSSAs and Their Associated Protective Measures*

In general, the PSSA is broader in its implementation. With regard to its element for designation, MARPOL 73/78 Special Area and UNCLOS 1982 Special Area only considered oceanographic and ecological conditions, whereas PSSA additionally considers socio cultural, economic, and scientific and educational aspects.[70] The second significant difference is that the criteria for designation under MARPOL 73/78 and UNCLOS 1982[71] Special Area are cumulative. In the PSSA the proposed area only needs to fulfil at least one criterion. The third difference is regarding the type of "pollution." In MARPOL 73/78 Special

---

[67] IMO Assemb. Res. 927 (22), *supra* note 39, Annex I at ¶ 2.7.

[68] UNCLOS 1982, *supra* note 11, Art. 211 (1) stipulates that States through the competent international organization (that is the IMO) are obliged to set international standards to prevent, reduce and control pollution from vessels.

[69] *Id.*, Art. 211 (6) (a).

[70] IMO Assemb. Res. A. 982 (24), *supra* note 12, Annex ¶ 4.4. & 5.17.

[71] *See* E.J. Molenaar, *supra* note 25 at 403.

Areas, the types of pollutants are limited to oil, noxious liquid substances, garbage, and sulphur oxide (SOx). The scope of PSSA protective measures includes a wider variety of hazards to the marine environments that includes physical damage and even noise.[72]

With regard to the area that is covered by PSSAs, the Guidelines mention that PSSAs can cover both the territorial sea and beyond the territorial sea.[73] In contrast, the UNCLOS 1982 Special Area can only cover the EEZ. Compared with MARPOL 73/78 Special Area, most areas designated as Special Areas are enclosed or semi enclosed sea.[74] Previously designated PSSAs show a broader application that not only covers enclosed and semi enclosed seas but also other areas such as straits used for international navigation as in the Torres Strait.

The most limited provision that can be applied with regard to "special areas" can be found in MARPOL 73/78. The measures in MARPOL 73/78 are limited to the measures listed in its respective Annex that in principle have stricter discharge standards and reception facilities in ports in that area. The UNCLOS Special Area and PSSA give broader options for States in proposing to IMO the types of measures to be adopted in the Special Area or in the PSSA. In this regard, the PSSA Guidelines stipulate that such measures (APM) shall be measures that are already adopted or within the competence of the IMO to adopt. Such measures include the designation of a MARPOL 73/78 Special Area, routeing and reporting system or any other measure that has a legal basis.[75]

The last major difference between the MARPOL 73/78 Special Area, UNCLOS 1982 Special Area and PSSA is the legal basis of its application. As a convention, both the MARPOL 73/78 Special Area and UNCLOS 1982 Special Area have an inherent legal basis by themselves. On the other hand, the PSSA which was designated by the IMO relied on other international legal instruments to confer a legal basis for the application of its APMs. From the PSSA Guidelines, it is clear that the legal basis to have a MARPOL 73/78 Special Area with APMs is returning to the MARPOL 73/78. Meanwhile the other APMs, namely the ships' routeing and reporting system, will rely on the

---

[72] IMO Assemb. Res. A. 982 (24), *supra* note 12, Annex ¶ 2.1 & 2.2. In the MEPC 33/INF.27, *supra* note 33 at ¶ 5.2.3, it was suggested that noise and physical disturbance do not fall under the definition of "pollution" under the UNCLOS 1982. Thus the scope of the UNCLOS 1982 Special Area is also different from the PSSA. However, the definition of "pollution" under UNCLOS 1982 includes "energy" as a form of pollution. Thus it can be suggested that noise and physical disturbance fall under that definition.

[73] IMO Assemb. Res. A. 982 (24), *supra* note 12, Annex at ¶ 4.3.

[74] Nihan Ünlü, *supra* note 22, argues that the MARPOL 73/78 Special Area was designed especially for enclosed and semi enclosed seas. *See also* Agustin Blanco-Bazán [2], *supra* note 35 at 346.

[75] IMO Assemb. Res. A. 982 (24), *supra* note 12, Annex ¶ 6.1.2.

mandate given to the IMO under the SOLAS 1974.[76] Lastly, with regard to the other measures that are still open for new proposals, the PSSA Guidelines mentioned that they shall be consistent with the provision of UNCLOS 1982, in particular Article 211 (6), which is the same article that regulates the UNCLOS 1982 Special Area.

C. *Summary of Distinction in Forms of Special Areas*

In principle, all of the three special areas are concepts to try to address the unique condition of a sea area for which the usual environmental standards will not be sufficient. The concept of PSSA appears to try to merge all of the IMO competence into one mechanism with a broader scope in terms of area coverage and criteria, as well as the type of APM. In terms of legal basis, because the PSSA is basically a merged concept of the IMO competence, it relied on other international instruments.

In practice, currently there are 12 designated MARPOL 73/78 Special Areas and SOx Emission Control Areas. As a comparison there are 12 designated PSSAs with various APMs such as recommended compliance with pilotage systems, routeing measures, reporting systems, and designations as MARPOL 73/78 Special Area and SOx Emission Control Area. Although included in the PSSA Guidelines, up until now no area has been designated as an UNCLOS 1982 Special Area exclusively.

IV. *Analysis and Recommendation*

A. *Analysis of the PSSA Regime*

After observing the history and development of the PSSA concept, the main issue at present is to evaluate their compatibility in addressing the goals that were previously elaborated in Part II. We now explore how these interests and goals can be maximize by implementing these regimes, especially the PSSA.

The first aspect is how the PSSA accommodates the interests of navigation (both freedom and safety), environmental protection, protection of cultural heritage and following the rule of law as embodied in UNCLOS 1982. In its

[76] *Id. See further* Chapter V of the SOLAS 1974 (as amended), *supra*, Regulation 10 and 11. The PSSA Guideline also mentioned about the General Provisions on Ships' Routeing and the Guidelines and Criteria for Ship Reporting Systems, in this regard it refers to the decision made by the IMO (IMO Assemb. Res. 572 (14) as amended for General Provisions on Ship's Routeing and MSC Res. 43 (64) as amended for the Guidelines and Criteria for Ship Reporting System) pursuant to the mandate given by the SOLAS 1974 Convention.

Guidelines it is clear that all of these aspects were considered before designating an area as a PSSA, and the adoption of APM.

On the question of the legal basis for the PSSA in particular, it only relied on the IMO Assembly Resolution as mandated by the Resolution No. 9. Nevertheless, international law, including UNCLOS 1982, can become a legal basis for the PSSA as an application of the State's obligation to protect the environment. It should be noted also that the application of the PSSA in the respective maritime zones should also conform to the provision of the UNCLOS 1982.[77]

As for specific applications of the APM, the IMO did make it clear that it should be within the competence of the IMO or other measures that have legal basis. Moreover, the IMO requires that if there are questions of legality, the matters are referred to its Legal Committee to ensure compatibility with international law. Thus, it can be concluded that the PSSA and the APM are in conformity with international law.

Two of the most important advantages of the PSSA are that it can become a comprehensive marine environmental protection regime[78] and that it can cover aspects that are not previously covered by the other Special Areas. The PSSA collaborates all measures within the competence of IMO into one framework and the labeling of "PSSA" itself can increase awareness from ships when navigating in the area.[79]

Throughout the process of the embodiment of the PSSA concept, it appears that besides covering unique areas that were not previously covered by the MARPOL 73/78 Special Area, it sought to accelerate the response toward environmental protection while the UNCLOS 1982 was not yet in force. However, it should be noted that this was positive progress as later it evolved to be in line with the provision of UNCLOS 1982.[80]

The progressive development of the PSSA designation also requires attention. As mentioned earlier, in the period between 2002 and 2007, there were ten designations of PSSAs as opposed to the period between 1991 and 2001, when there were only two designations of PSSAs. On the one hand, the advent of the PSSA was a positive development as the international community increasingly began to apply this concept. On the other hand, if too many PSSAs were designated, it would diminish the "special" characteristic of the PSSA. The PSSA might even lose its awareness-raising effect because it would then function in the same way as an ordinary protected area.

[77] *See also* Patricia Birnie, Alan Boyle and Catherine Redgwell, *International Law & the Environment* 416 (Oxford University Press 3rd ed. 2009).

[78] *See also* MEPC 33/INF.27, *supra* note 33, ¶ 10.1.1.

[79] Julian Roberts, *supra* note 40 at 5.

[80] IMO Assemb. Res. 982 (24), *supra* note 12, Annex ¶ 7.9.

Despite the positive value of the PSSA concept, much still needs to be further developed to better achieve its goals or in maximizing the output of these measures to various interests. The downside of the PSSA and recommendations on how to develop it will be further discussed in the following section.

B. *Recommendations*

1. *Provide Clear Explanation of the PSSA Legal Basis in the PSSA Guidelines*
The most important development that the PSSA Guidelines should further is clarification of the legal basis for the PSSA and the relation between the PSSA and the UNCLOS 1982 and the MARPOL 73/78. Despite this unclear relationship between the MARPOL 73/78 Special Area, UNCLOS and PSSA, the MEPC decided not to include an explanation about the interrelation of these three measures.[81]

Throughout this study, it is clear that the PSSA concept was authorized by international law, especially in the UNCLOS 1982 Articles 192 and 194, with regard to the State's obligation to protect the environment. Although the UNCLOS 1982 may be viewed to serve as an "umbrella" on marine environment protection, it still needs to be further implemented through tangible regulation by the IMO as the competent international organization.[82]

The current Guideline did not include the mandate given by the UNCLOS 1982 as an "umbrella" convention. The least that the Guideline does is only use Article 211 of the UNCLOS 1982 for becoming legal basis of the APM. However, the PSSA area not only deals with EEZ as stipulated in Article 211, but includes other maritime zones such as the territorial sea. Additionally, Article 211 does not provide a basis for the protection of cultural heritage, although it can be the case if the present of the cultural heritage is in a location that can

[81] MEPC, *Report of the Marine Environment Protection Committee on its Forty-Fifth Session*, ¶ 6.4, MEPC 45/20 (Oct. 16, 2000). Noted also that the Division for Ocean Affairs and the Law of the Sea of the Office of Legal Affairs of the United Nations (UN DOALOS) once submitted a document to try to clarify the complexity of this matter, *see* IMO, MEPC, *Relationship between the 1982 United Nations Convention on the Law of the Sea and the IMO Guidelines for the Designation of Special Areas and the Identification of Particularly Sensitive Sea Areas*, MEPC 43/6/2 (Mar. 31, 1999) (*submitted by* UN DOALOS).

[82] Daniel Bodansky, "Protecting the Marine Environment from Vessel-Source Pollution: UNLOS III and Beyond," 18 Ecology L. Quarterly 719, reprinted at Ted McDorman *et al.*, *International Ocean Law Materials and Commentaries* 215 (Carolina Academic Press 2005). Other views perceive the PSSA as non-legally binding, *see further* Helene Leferbvre-Chalain, "Fifteen Years of Particularly Sensitive Sea Areas: a Concept in Development," 13 Ocean & Coastal L.J. 60, 47–69 (2007). For the discussion within the MEPC regarding the legal basis for PSSA *see further* MEPC 53/8/2, *supra* note 47 at ¶10–14.

become a navigational hurdle. Therefore, it is also necessary to relate to other provisions of the UNCLOS 1982.[83]

Other than that, the Guidelines should make clear whether the APM can become the generally accepted international rule and standard of design, construction, manning or equipment. This might become one of the areas that the PSSA concept can be developed further to enhance the protection measure.

2. *Further Application of the MARPOL 73/78 Special Areas, the UNCLOS 1982 Special Areas, and the PSSA*

Beyond designation as MARPOL 73/78 as APM under PSSA, these two regimes are not mutually exclusive. To cover all areas that need special protection, it is suggested to maintain the two regimes separately. The MARPOL 73/78 Special Area is best suited for areas where environmental degradation can occur due to technical characteristics, without necessarily having unique environmental features involved. On the other hand, the PSSA is designed for areas that have a unique environment quality or have a cultural heritage aspect, but do not necessarily possess a technical characteristic as do the MARPOL 73/78 Special Areas. Other than that, the PSSA does not require adequate reception facilities; thus the implementation of the PSSA is relatively less restrictive than MARPOL 73/78 Special area concept.

With regard to the UNCLOS 1982 Special Area, the history of the negotiation supports understanding of the MARPOL 73/78 Special Area and anticipates its future "special area" regime. Thus, it is sufficient to perceive the MARPOL 73/78 Special Area and the PSSA as an implementation of the UNCLOS 1982 Special Area.[84] Taking into account the process and procedure for the PSSA and the MARPOL 73/78 Special Area through the IMO and involving all States, it can be viewed that they are in part an application of the UNCLOS 1982 Special Area.[85]

3. *Stricter Procedure in the PSSA Designation*

It was previously mentioned that in the period of 2002 to 2007, there were ten designations of PSSAs. This might be seen as an overloaded expansion of the PSSA. The first impact of this over-designation is that the PSSA will lose its

---

[83] The duty to protect underwater cultural heritage is mandated in Article 303 of UNCLOS 1982.

[84] The view was also expressed by the IMO Secretariat that the UNCLOS 1982 Special Area anticipates that in the future, the IMO will develop special international rules, standards and navigational practices for use in such areas, *see* MEPC 46/6/1, *supra* note 66, Annex at ¶ 2.4.9.

[85] The word "in part" here is to acknowledge that with regard to the UNCLOS 1982 Special Area, there are some differences in relation to the scope of the Special Area that only deals with the Special Area in the EEZ.

unique status and the awareness that supposedly increased by this status. The international community will no longer consider the PSSA as having special character and will consider the PSSA as just an ordinary measure.

The second impact of over-designation of the PSSA is that there will be overwhelming APMs that will hamper navigation too much. Without sacrificing the need for environmental protection, the PSSA designation should not hamper navigational freedom.

When too many places have the same level of vulnerability, then it is suggested the entire international standard relating to navigation and marine pollution prevention that applies to the whole ocean area be reviewed. Then States, both coastal and maritime, can determine appropriate elevations of that standard through the IMO as agreed and applied to all parts of the oceans. With this approach, the PSSA will maintain smaller numbers of areas with higher levels of characteristic than other areas with stricter criteria. Thus the particularity of the PSSA can be maintained while the increasing environment protection interest is also accommodated.

4. *Maintaining the Balance of Interest and the Rule of Law within the Framework of the UNCLOS 1982 and the IMO*

Maintaining the balance of interest and the Rule of Law with regard to ocean management needs to be the ultimate goal considered in applying the PSSA, along with its other APMs that might become available in the future. The current system, that is States working together within the framework of the IMO in conformity with the provision of the UNCLOS 1982, needs to be preserved. The PSSA mechanism has served as the forum for States to meet and adjust their navigation as well as environmental interests. This mechanism ought to be maintained to prevent States taking unilateral action that can create detriments to other States.

V. *Conclusion*

The PSSA concept appears to be an appropriate compliment to the previously established MARPOL 73/78 Special Area. It implements mandates under international law to protect environments in general and specifically, particularly unique areas. The PSSA also appears to be an implementation of UNCLOS 1982 in relation to the measures that can be taken in the EEZ. The relationship between these instruments should be kept clear to avoid confusion.

In applying the PSSA concept, and also the other Special Area concept, it is always important to consider the goal at stake and maintaining the balance between various interests. The most important objective is to maintain the balance to which States agreed under UNCLOS 1982, and preserve the rule of law with regard to management of the ocean. Thus, it is crucial that this process be performed within the framework of the IMO as provided in UNCLOS 1982.

The last concluding point is that the PSSA should be implemented in a manner that can maintain the "specialness" of the PSSA. The large number of the PSSA designations since 2002 raise concern that if too many PSSA are designated, they will lose their unique status. Therefore, for future development, the considerations of PSSA designations should be made stricter to avoid over-designation.

AN OVERVIEW OF TWO CONTEMPORARY ISSUES IN THE LAW OF THE SEA: ISLANDS WITHIN THE CONTEXT OF DELIMITATION AND COMBATING PIRACY OFF THE COASTS OF SOMALIA

Teoman Uykur[1]

The issues under discussion at this Conference involve a wide range of contemporary problems of the law of the sea. For the sake of brevity and precision, I would like to limit my comments to mainly two topics that have been discussed within the Conference, namely, the role of islands and rocks in delimitation, and piracy and armed robbery at sea.

Although these topics may be discussed within the context of different disciplines, they will be approached herein from a legal perspective. Hence, factors of a non-legal nature, such as socio-economic considerations or issues of national security, are not the focus of this presentation. However, to the extent those factors have been taken into account, as in the discussion of whether such factors should affect the delimitation line in question, they will be elaborated upon as well.

Islands as a Geographical Special Circumstance in Maritime Delimitation

I would like to address the topic of islands and rocks particularly within the context of maritime delimitation. The issue has been a point of controversy since the negotiations of the Third Conference on the Law of the Sea, and the debate is far from being over today. Hence, after a brief recollection of the history of the negotiations on the islands provisions at the Third Conference, I will offer my comments on the value of different types of islands in delimitation in light of relevant case law.

Within the context of the law of maritime delimitation, the main points of controversy regarding islands have been whether an island would be entitled to generate the same maritime jurisdictional zones as a mainland, and whether certain criteria should be applied to distinguish islands among each other.

---

[1] Counselor, Permanent Mission of Turkey to the United Nations Office in Vienna. The views and comments expressed here are of a personal nature only, and do not necessarily represent the position of the Ministry of Foreign Affairs of Turkey or of any other official authority.

During the years the Third Conference was ongoing, some proposals were made to differentiate islands, based on their size,[2] location[3] or population. The negotiations on islands during the Third Conference demonstrated a divergence of positions between two sides, namely, states which argued for the equal treatment of islands with mainland, and states calling for giving islands lesser maritime zones than the mainland.[4] While some states, particularly those looking for extended maritime zones due to their insular territories in distant locations, were advocating the former view, others who wanted to limit maritime areas attached to islands were in favor of attributing value to certain factors, including the size and population of the island in question, as a precondition to attach any maritime zone to an island.[5] These debates should be considered in conjunction with the important novel concept of the Exclusive Economic Zone (EEZ) and equally crucial developments regarding the continental shelf during the Third Conference. It was clear that the Convention to come out of the Conference would mark a crucial turning point in some way in attaching maritime areas to insular features. Hence, states were aware of the importance that islands would carry in creating jurisdiction over vast areas of oceans and seas.

The resulting Article 121 of the United Nations Convention on the Law of the Sea[6] (LOSC) contains both old and new elements. On the one hand, it repeats the definition of an island already contained in Art. 10 of the Convention on the Territorial Sea and Contiguous Zone[7] of 1958. On the other hand, it introduces a new paragraph which confirms that islands would generate the same maritime zones as the mainland territory of a state. The third paragraph, which has always created long discussions, specifies that "rocks which cannot sustain human habitation or economic life of their own" would not generate an EEZ or continental shelf.

---

[2] Robert D. Hodgson & Robert W. Smith, *The Informal Single Negotiation Text (Committee II): A Geographical Perspective*, 3 Ocean Dev. & Int'l L. 225, 230 (1976).

[3] Northcutt Ely, *Seabed Boundaries Between Coastal States: The Effect to be Given Islets as "Special Circumstances"*, 6 Int'l Lawyer 219.

[4] For the history of negotiations on the provision of the LOSC concerning islands *see* 3 United Nations Convention on the Law of the Sea, 1982: A Commentary 321–40 (Myron H. Nordquist, ed., 1995); UN Off. for Ocean Aff. & L. of the Sea, The Law of the Sea, Régime of Islands, Legislative History of Part VIII (Article 121) of the United Nations Convention on the Law of the Sea, UN Sales No. E.87.V.II (1998).

[5] *Id.* at 13, 26.

[6] Opened for signature on Dec. 10, 1982 in Montego Bay, entered into force on Nov. 16, 1994; UN Doc. A/CONF.62/122, *reprinted in* 1833 U.N.T.S. 3; 21 I.L.M. 1261 (1982), *and* The Law of the Sea: Official Text of the United Nations Convention on the Law of the Sea with Annexes and Index, U.N. Sales No. E.83.V.5 (1983).

[7] Done at Geneva on Apr. 29, 1958, entered into force on Sept. 10, 1964; 15 U.S.T. 1606 (1964); T.I.A.S. 5639; 516 U.N.T.S. 205.

It has been stated that the last paragraph of Art. 121 is the crucial part of this provision.[8] Indeed, the discussion on the meaning and scope of a rock has not come to an end even almost three decades after the adoption of the LOSC. The fact that a definition of a rock distinguishing it from other insular formations is not provided in the Convention leaves even more room for debate. The question has thus been addressed in academia and case law as touched on below.

The question of islands in the context of delimitation may be approached from two perspectives: the maritime areas to be attached to "rocks" and the effect of islands in delimitation. Regarding the first question, it calls to attention that the first paragraph of Art. 121 of the LOSC, which provides the definition of an island, repeats Art. 10(1) of the Convention on Territorial Sea and Contiguous Zone of 1958. The second and third paragraphs of Art. 121 of the LOSC are the products of the Third Conference. While the second paragraph affirms the entitlement of islands to areas of jurisdiction, the third one brings forward certain exclusions of entitlement for rocks. Thus, the difference between an "island" and a "rock" becomes crucial in terms of determining whether a particular insular feature would generate any maritime zones beyond the territorial sea.

There has been extensive debate among scholars in the period following the adoption of the LOSC on the definition of a "rock".[9] The definition of the concept and its differentiation from an island has been approached from various viewpoints. While some scholars emphasized the importance of a self-sustaining population, and even suggested a certain number of people live permanently

---

[8] Commentary, *supra* note 4, at 338.

[9] Barbara Kwiatkowska & Alfred H.A. Soons, *Entitlement to Maritime Areas of Rocks Which Cannot Sustain Human Habitation of Their Own*, 21 Neth. Y.B. Int'l L. 139 (1990); Alex G. Oude Elferink, *Clarifying Article 121(3) of the Law of the Sea Convention: The Limits Set by the Nature of International Legal Processes*, 6 Boundary and Security Bull. 58 (1998); Alex G. Oude Elferink, *Is It Either Necessary or Possible to Clarify the Provision on Rocks of Article 121(3) of the Law of the Sea Convention?*, in Borderlands Under Stress 399 (M. Pratt & J. Brown eds., 2000); Jonathan I. Charney, *Rocks That Cannot Sustain Human Habitation*, 93 Am. J. Int'l L. 863 (1999); Robert Kolb, *L'Interprétation de L'Article 121, Paragraphe 3, de la Convention de Montego Bay sur le Droit de la Mer: Les "Rochers qui ne se Prêtent pas à L'Habitation Humaine ou à une Vie Économique Propre…"*, 40 Annuaire Français de Droit International 876 (1994); Syméon Karagiannis, *Les Rochers Qui Ne Se Prêtent Pas À L'Habitation Humaine Ou À Une Vie Économique Propre Et Le Droit De La Mer*, 29 Revue Belge De Droit International 559, 564–79 (1996); Jon Van Dyke & Robert A. Brooks, *Uninhabited Islands: Their Impact on the Ownership of the Oceans' Resources*, 12 Ocean Dev. & Int'l L. 265, 247 (1983); John Briscoe, *Islands in Maritime Boundary Delimitation*, 7 Ocean Y.B. 14 (1988); Derek Bowett, *Islands, Rocks, Reefs, and Low-Tide Elevations in Maritime Boundary Delimitations, in* 1 International Maritime Boundaries 155 (Jonathan Charney & Lewis Alexander eds., 1993).

on the feature to qualify as an island,[10] there were some other arguments for taking the criteria of "residing households, vegetation and potable water" or analyzing the geological structure of the feature, i.e., whether it is indeed made of "rock" or sand.[11] None of these suggestions or arguments has found sufficient support so far.

In face of the fact that the LOSC itself did not provide for more concrete criteria in Art. 121(3), it may well be argued that the question of the islands qualified to generate maritime zones was purposefully left to elaboration within the overall context of each particular dispute. Indeed, numerous cases of small islets in different geographical settings worldwide would render any concrete reference point unworkable, be it number of population, geographic size or sustainable economic activities over the islet. Any numeric expression of aforementioned criteria could also open the way for claims on abuse of rights, as one side accuses the other for implanting population to meet the required minimum number. Hence, the issue should be evaluated within all relevant circumstances without referring to a single stringent criterion.[12]

As a final point with regard to the third paragraph of Art. 121, a lingering question needs to be addressed. It has been debated whether this particular provision has become or may in the future become a rule of customary inter-

---

[10] Jon Van Dyke, *Legal Status of Islands with reference to Article 121(3) of the UN Convention on the Law of the Sea*, Presentation made at Seoul, Korea on Dec. 9, 1999, at http://seasteading.org/seastead.org/localres/misc-articles/DykeLegalStatusOfIslands.html (visited Feb. 7, 2011). The author proposed the figure of 50 people permanently residing on the insular feature to distinguish it as an island from a rock.

[11] In-seop Jeong, *Dokdo, Islands or Rocks?: A Patriotic Misunderstanding*, Northeast Asian History Foundations News, <http://english.historyfoundation.or.kr/data/Newsletterlist/1005_eng/sub01.html> (last visited Feb. 7, 2011). The author criticizes the suggestions of solid criteria of the existence of vegetation (forestry) or potable water on the insular feature. While he acknowledges that these considerations may carry certain weight in determining whether an island is entitled to its own jurisdictional zones, the author states that these are not sufficient legal conditions *per se*.

[12] In analyzing the third paragraph of Art. 121, Kolb suggests a three-stage criteria to differentiate islands and rocks:

(i) the island should allow permanent residence of organized social groups of a certain significance;
(ii) those rocks which have been made artificially habitable through some kind of interference to that end, should not be regarded as "islands" (the author also refers to the "abuse of rights" theory in this context as stated in Art. 300 of the LOSC);
(iii) in cases of doubt, the insular feature should be counted as a rock.

Kolb, *supra* note 9, at 904–5.

This approach seems plausible from a restrictive perspective which cautions against the disproportionate expansion of maritime zones under national jurisdiction. However, the third prong, that is, attaching a nature of a residual rule to paragraph 3 by counting a feature as a "rock" in case of doubt, remains open for criticism.

national law. The general tendency in academic writings has so far put forward a negative answer to this query. While some authors have emphasized that this paragraph was a result of a compromise between conflicting positions within the negotiation history of the LOSC, and consequently, it is incapable of generating a rule of customary law;[13] other scholars came to the same conclusion by taking into account the inconclusive state practice so far.[14] Still, at least one scholar has argued that the rule in paragraph 3 should be regarded as part of customary law, on the premise that the liberty of states to deviate from this rule does not contravene with its customary nature.[15]

When the ICJ had to address this question in its decision between Qatar and Bahrain, it sufficed to state the customary character of only paragraph 2 of Art. 121, but not paragraph 3 of the same provision.[16] This careful emphasis made by the Court could be taken as an indication that there is neither consensus on the *opinio juris* element nor enough state practice to sustain a claim as to the customary nature of this particular paragraph, as of now.

On a more general level, the impact of islands on delimitation may be discussed with reference to geographical considerations, particularly in relation to their location and size. This categorization is more workable not only because an increasing number of delimitation disputes have been settled mainly on the basis of geography, but also because the theoretical analyses of the issue have followed a similar approach as well.[17]

Against the backdrop of rather imperfect guidance on the level of multilateral treaty law in this field, there are basically two courses of developments that provide tools for analyzing delimitation law, that is, state practice and case law. Before suggesting certain observations regarding islands' impact on delimitation, a brief recollection of developments in these two tracks might be helpful.

---

[13] Kwiatkowska & Soons, *supra* note 9, at 180.

[14] Elferink, *Clarifying Article 121(3)...*, *supra* note 9, at 59.

[15] Charney, *Rocks that cannot sustain...*, *supra* note 9, at 872–73.

[16] Maritime Delimitation and Territorial Questions (*Qatar v Bahr.*), 2001 I.C.J. 97, para. 185 (Mar. 16). In its more recent judgment, the Court avoided the question by stating that it was not a relevant point for the settlement of the dispute at hand, *Rom. v. Ukr.*, 2009 I.C.J. Interestingly, both parties made some lengthy arguments to persuade the Court on whether Serpents Island could generate an EEZ and continental shelf of its own.

[17] *See* both Bowett, *supra* note 9, and Victor Prescott & Gillian Triggs, *Islands and Rocks and their Role in Maritime Delimitation, in* 5 International Maritime Boundaries 3245, 3246 (David A. Colson & Robert W. Smith eds., 2005). It has been pointed out that socio-economic factors have a rather limited role in maritime delimitation, except in *Anglo-Norwegian Fisheries Case* of 1951, *id.* In this case, the Court stated in connection with the delimitation process that "certain economic interests peculiar to a region" have to be taken into account, *Fisheries Case* (U.K. v Nor.) 1951 I.C.J. 3, 21 (Dec. 18).

It has been stressed in comprehensive studies of state practice that parties to delimitation agreements have chosen various methods in dealing with islands. In situations where islands did not give a significant advantage to one party over the other, islands were given full effect.[18] In other examples of bilateral agreements, states have given full or partial status to some islands while discounting certain others. This latter method was helpful particularly in situations where islands would either complicate the delimitation line, or distort the equidistance line significantly. An example of this situation was the agreement between France and the United Kingdom with regard to Jersey Island,[19] where the parties first had to agree on the sovereignty over a number of islets and then determine to what extent islets could be given an effect on the delimitation line. In other examples, states discounted all islands involved in the area of delimitation[20] especially to avoid their disproportionate effect on the resulting line.

In recent case law, islands have either played a role to some extent in the delimitation process, or have been a point of discussion as to their possible effect on delimitation. The latest example of Serpents Island in the case between Romania and Ukraine was noteworthy, as the off-shore Ukrainian island had the potential to move the delimitation line in favor of its sovereign state if it were given a full effect. A lengthy debate put forward through memorials and counter-memorials by both sides in the dispute demonstrated the pivotal role this tiny islet could have played in the overall delimitation. In its judgment of February 2009, the ICJ gave considerable weight to the discussion of "relevant coasts" and in relation to the Serpents Island, stated that the islet's coasts need not be taken into account in calculating the relevant coasts of Ukraine.[21] Regarding the more crucial issue of whether the Island should generate an EEZ and continental shelf, the Court declared that the overall circumstances of the area of delimitation made it inequitable to attach any maritime jurisdiction

[18] Such examples include the agreements between Albania-Italy; Mexico-United States, and Oman-Pakistan. Further examples involving a group of islands, or a mainland and an offshore island, Prescott & Triggs, *supra* note 17, at 3247–49.

[19] *Id.* at 3253.

[20] As in Thailand-Vietnam boundary agreement of 1997, where the islands of both sides were not given any effect on the boundary line, except a larger Vietnamese island, Phu Quock, close to its own mainland, *id.* at 3256–57.

[21] Maritime Delimitation in the Black Sea (Rom. v. Ukr.), 2009 I.C.J. 59 (Feb. 3), at <http://www.icj-cij.org>. The Court stressed that the coast of Serpents Island was so short that it would not make any difference on the overall length of Ukrainian coasts, *id.* at 97–98, para. 102. When it came to taking the islet as a base point, the Court decided not to consider it as a base point in determining the provisional equidistance line. "To count Serpents' Island as a relevant part of the coast would amount to grafting an extraneous element onto Ukraine's coastline; *the consequence would be a judicial refashioning of geography*, which neither the law nor practice of maritime delimitation authorizes" *id.* at 110, para. 149 (emphasis added).

zone beyond its 12-mile territorial sea. Hence the final boundary line, which is a single all-purpose line, was determined without taking into account Serpents Island. The only effect given to this island was the curvature it caused on the delimitation line to effectuate the 12-mile territorial sea of the Island.

The presence of Serpents Island as a single feature off the coastal junction point of the land boundaries of Ukraine and Romania, presented a less complicated geographical setting in comparison to other disputes with numerous islands scattered in a wide geographical area. However, the situation of the Serpents' island still triggered lengthy arguments on both sides' memorials. One example of a more complex dispute involving islands was between Eritrea and Yemen. The Arbitral Tribunal settled the dispute in two phases, where the first phase involved the sovereignty dispute over the islands,[22] and where the second phase concerned the delimitation in the Red Sea.[23] In the second phase the presence of groups of islands, some of which were closer to their respective mainland, others straddling on the midpoint of the two mainland, was the major issue calling for a decision by the Tribunal. In its judgment, the Tribunal tackled the problem of islands in a differentiated way. Firstly, concerning the Dahlak Islands of Eritrea in the northern sector, which were close to the Eritrean mainland, the Tribunal regarded them as forming part of the Eritrean baseline system. Thus, these islands were taken as base points in determining the equidistance line. Regarding the Yemeni mid-sea islands of Jabal Zukar/ Hanish, on the other hand, the Tribunal opined that it would create an inequitable result if they were taken as base points while determining the equidistance line. Hence, unlike Dahlak Islands, the Yemeni islands were not deemed determinative upon the equidistance line.

The judgment of the ICJ in Qatar / Bahrain case was also noteworthy with regard to the question of islands in the context of delimitation. The overall geographical setting involved a peninsular state (Qatar) facing an insular state (Bahrain). The two complicating factors of this dispute were the argument propounded by Bahrain that it was an archipelagic state, and the presence of numerous islands and low tide elevations in the area. In its judgment, the Court analyzed the area in two segments. In the southern segment, the two sides were so close to each other that there was an overlap of their territorial sea claims. The Court, having decided to affirm the Bahraini sovereignty over Hawar Island, ruled that the delimitation line should be the equidistance line between the mainland of Qatar and Hawar Island. Except in the sector where it has adopted the equidistance line between the mainland Qatar and Hawar, which were very close to one another, the Court gave limited effect to islets in

[22] 114 I.L.R. 2.

[23] 40 I.L.M. 983–1019 (2001); 119 I.L.R. 417.

this section to limit the inequitable consequences insular features might have created. Regarding the northern sector where the distance between the two sides were larger than their territorial sea claims, hence EEZ and continental shelf claims were overlapping, the Court again followed the equidistance line and checked it against any possible inequitable results. Therefore, the resulting delimitation line was basically an equidistance line, with certain adjustments. This approach taken by the Court was in principle in conformity with what had been requested by both sides, since they both framed their respective arguments on the basis of equidistance. Their main difference was on the base points to be taken as reference for an equidistance line, that is, the question whether to take islands as base points. By affirming the sovereignty of Bahrain over Hawar, and not enclaving this island, the judgment gave certain advantage to Bahrain in the southern sector. Although the reasons for this outcome were not satisfactorily clear, it may be deduced that the very limited area in this sector where the two sides' territorial sea claims were overlapping, an enclave solution would be impractical. With regard to this judgment, while there were some views that regarded it as a confirmation of equidistance/special circumstances rule[24] as in Art. 15 of the LOSC, others have taken a more critical stance against it by underlining the rather unsatisfactory reasoning of the Court and have indicated that the Court ruled due to the geographical and factual particularities of the case.[25]

Without further entering the specifics of case law regarding the impact of islands on delimitation, the following points may be suggested to illustrate the main trends in addressing this issue in international law:

- The geographic location of an island is crucial in determining its possible weight in the overall delimitation process. This postulate is true both for opposite and adjacent coastal situations.
- Islands situated close to their own mainland have often had an impact of varying degrees on the delimitation line. While Kerkennah Island was given a half effect in the Tunisia/Libya case, Dahlak group was given a full effect in the Eritrea/Yemen case.[26]
- In situations where an island straddles in approximately mid-point of two mainland, both in adjacent and opposite coasts, it is usually semi-enclaved,

---

[24] Barbara Kwiatkowska, *The Qatar v. Bahrain Maritime Delimitation and Territorial Questions Case*, 33 Ocean Dev. & Int'l L. 227, 246 (2002); also Robert Kolb, Case Law on Maritime Delimitation 536–37 (2004).

[25] Malcolm D. Evans, *Case concerning maritime delimitation and territorial questions between Qatar and Bahrain (Qatar v Bahrain)*, 51 Int'l & Comp. L.Q. 709, 718 (2002).

[26] But Filfla Island of Malta was given no effect, despite the fact that it formed part of Maltese baseline system, Continental Shelf (Libya v Malta) 1985 I.C.J. 39, para. 64 (Jun. 3).

so as to leave it a certain territorial sea area, but not allowing a further area of jurisdiction. Recent examples include Nicaragua/Honduras case (a group of Honduran cays vis-à-vis Edinburgh Cay of Nicaraguan),[27] and Ukraine/Romania case (Serpents Island).[28]

- It is more likely to confront questions of equitableness of a delimitation line in cases of islands close to the mainland of another state. In such circumstances, solutions arrived through negotiations and adjudicatory means provide various examples. In some cases, the islands on the wrong side were completely enclaved (as in Anglo-French arbitration, Channel Islands), while in some other instances islands were given a seaward projection only (Canada/France case, St. Pierre and Miquelon Islands). Yet in at least one case, that is, between Qatar and Bahrain, Hawar Island was taken as a base point in determining the equidistance line. In the Torres Strait Treaty between Australia and Papua New Guinea, on the other hand, the Australian Islands close to the Papuan mainland were given a limited jurisdictional area, while delimitation lines for seabed and water column differed from one another. The variety of solutions in each of these disputes suggest that the overall geographical setting, particularly the size of area of delimitation and considerations of access to high seas, played a significant role in determining the final line. Thus, an equitable result as referred in Articles 74 and 83 of the LOSC may be achieved by using different methods.
- Finally, the proportion of relevant coastal lengths of the two sides is taken into consideration, both in constructing the (provisional) equidistance line, and in testing the equitableness of it. This comparison of relevant coasts played an increasingly determinative role in delimitation cases. The most significant examples include the Libya/Malta case, as well as the Jan Mayen case between Norway and Denmark.[29]

---

[27] Case Concerning Territorial and Maritime Dispute Between Nicaragua and Honduras in the Caribbean Sea (Nicar. v Hond.) 2007 I.C.J. 1 (Oct. 8), sketch map 8 attached to the judgment, *id.* at 107.

[28] *Supra* note 21. An earlier example of a delimitation through bilateral agreement using a semi-enclave solution was the Agreement Concerning the Sovereignty over the Islands of Al-Arabiyah and Farsi and the Delimitation of the Boundary Line Separating the Submarine Areas Between the Kingdom of Saudi Arabia and Iran, 8 I.L.M. 493 (1969).

[29] However, it should be noted that the ratio of relevant coasts of both sides is not necessarily reflected in a mathematical precision to the relative distance of the delimitation line from two coasts. In the Jan Mayen case, the final delimitation line did not reflect the exact coastal proportion, although the Court confirmed that the ratio between the relevant coasts was 1 to 9.1 (or 9.2 depending on the calculation method), Maritime Delimitation in the Area Between Greenland and Jan Mayen (Den. v Nor.), 1993 I.C.J. 31, para. 61 (Jun. 14). "It should, however, be made clear that taking account of the disparity of coastal lengths does not mean a direct and mathematical application of the relationship between the length of the coastal front of eastern Greenland and that of Jan Mayen", *id.* at 35, para. 69.

Combating Piracy off the Coasts of Somalia, the Gulf of Aden and the Indian Ocean

The problem of piracy or armed robbery at sea has been forgotten for centuries except in certain sea areas around the Asian continent, notably in the region of the Strait of Malacca where armed attacks at sea have been reported even in modern times.[30] However, this problem has reemerged since 2005 off the coast of Somalia,[31] and has increasingly been a source of concern for the international community far beyond its geographical area. Indeed, maritime routes crucial for international shipping have been adversely affected by acts of piracy and armed robbery off the coasts of Somalia, the Gulf of Aden and in the western Indian Ocean to such an extent that no nation involved in maritime activities finds itself immune from this rather unanticipated problem.[32]

The situation in Somalia, and in particular the ongoing incidents of piracy and armed robbery, has been on the agenda of the United Nations and other international and regional organizations. The UN Secretary General, upon the request of the Security Council, has so far issued a number of reports, which reflect the current situation, complete with latest statistical figures and

---

[30] For recent figures regarding piracy incidents in Asia, *see* The Regional Cooperation Agreement on Combating Piracy and Armed Robbery against Ships in Asia, 2010 Annual Report (2011). The areas where the highest number of piracy incidents were reported include coasts off Bangladesh, Vietnam, and East Coast region of Malaysia, *id.* at 10. For a discussion of the problem in the region of Strait of Malacca and some suggested solutions, *see* Carrie R. Woolley, *Piracy and Sovereign Rights: Addressing Piracy in the Straits of Malacca without Degrading the Sovereign Rights of Indonesia and Malaysia*, 8 Santa Clara J. Int'l L. 447 (2010).

[31] There was an acute increase in acts of piracy and armed robbery off the coasts of Somalia in 2006, and the figures remain at alarming levels since then. For a summary of recent history of events that breed piracy and armed robber in Somalia, *see* the report of the Monitoring Group on Somalia *in* UN Doc. S/2008/769 (2008). The report accounts the worsening security situation in this country since 1992, coupled with ecological disasters caused by toxic waste dumping and depletion of fishing resources by foreign vessels over the years. All these developments paved the way for an acute increase in piracy incidents. Due to its lucrative nature, piracy has attracted an ever-growing number of recruits. While the number of pirates were counted by dozen in 2006, this number increased to 1000 to 1500 by 2008, *id.* at 27–33, paras. 122–47.

[32] Hence there has been a growing interest in international community as well as in academia in dealing with this problem within the larger context of interdiction of ships by non-flag states: Douglas Guilfoyle, Shipping Interdiction and the Law of the Sea, 2009; The International Response to Somali Piracy, (Bibi Van Ginkel & Frans-Paul Van der Putten eds., 2010); Tullio Treves, *Piracy, Law of the Sea, and Use of Force: Developments off the Coast of Somalia*, 20 Eur. J. Int'l L. 399 (2009). For an earlier study, *see* Robert C. F. Reuland, *Interface with Non-National Ships on the High Seas: Peacetime Exceptions to the Exclusivity Rule of Flag-State Jurisdiction*, 22 Vand. J. Transnat'l L. 1161 (1989).

suggestions.[33] The figures as laid down in the UN Secretary General's report[34] on the piracy off the coasts of Somalia are startling. More updated figures appear in the report of the Special Adviser to the UN Secretary-General, which promotes 25 suggestions to tackle the issue of piracy off the coasts of Somalia.[35] The latter report gives an estimated number of at least 1,500 pirates at large in the region,[36] and underlines the emergence of a "piracy industry" in Somalia. An even more worrying fact is that almost 90 percent of the pirates captured by naval forces are later released without any criminal proceeding.[37]

The problems on land are equally alarming. The society is desperately impoverished, particularly young people with no reliable livelihood. They are driven into the hands of criminal groups engaged in piracy. The ransoms paid to pirates to free hostages only fuel the problem by making lawlessness more lucrative and appealing.

Beside the risk imposed on human lives, and on the safety and security of navigation, the ongoing threat of piracy has detrimental effects on maritime commerce as a whole. While the insurance coverage and related premiums have

---

[33] Aside from the reports on the situation in Somalia in general, the most recent reports of the UN Secretary General on piracy and armed robbery Somalia are the following:

- Report of the Secretary-General Pursuant to Security Council Resolution 1897 (2009), U.N.S.C. Doc. S/2010/556, Oct. 27, 2010; and
- Report of the Secretary-General on possible options to further the aim of prosecuting and imprisoning persons responsible for acts of piracy and armed robbery at sea off the coast of Somalia, including, in particular, options for creating special domestic chambers possibly with international components, a regional tribunal or an international tribunal and corresponding imprisonment arrangements, taking into account the work of the Contact Group on Piracy off the Coast of Somalia, the existing practice in establishing international and mixed tribunals, and the time and resources necessary to achieve and sustain substantive results, U.N.S.C. Doc. S/2010/394, Jul. 26, 2010.

While the former report provides a general overview of the situation from a legal perspective, the latter report focuses on the question of prosecuting individuals accused of committing acts of piracy.

[34] *Supra*, Report of the Secretary-General, U.N.S.C. Doc. S/2010/556, at 2, paras. 4–7.

[35] Report prepared by Jack Lang, Special Adviser to the Secretary-General on Legal Issues Related to Piracy off the Coast of Somalia, U.N.S.C. Doc. S/2011/30, Jan. 25, 2011, Annex; *hereinafter* "Report of the Special Adviser".

[36] There are three trends listed in this report indicating an escalation of the problem:

- The growing number of pirates: an estimated number of 1,500 at present;
- Intensification of violence (use of AK47's and rocket launchers); and
- Sophistication of methods used by pirates (use of "mother ships" to increase the range of piracy acts, GPS technology, refueling at sea, counterfeit detectors etc.).

Id. at 13, para. 15.

[37] *Id.* at 13, para. 14.

increased drastically[38] as a result of unprecedented risks for ships navigating off Somalia's coasts, the delays of navigation due to security measures in the region, e.g. convoying, also put additional pressure on the sector.

Within this setting, the international community had to respond to this scourge rapidly and efficiently. There have so far been a number of initiatives on various fronts to address this problem. The deployment of naval assets in the region by international organizations and by individual states have been the most drastic measure in counter-piracy efforts.[39] Forming a transit corridor, patrolled by naval forces, for the protected passage of commercial vessels was another important step taken to secure international shipping.[40] The present paper, however, focuses on the legal response to acts of piracy.

As to the current international legal framework, the most relevant international instruments within the context of piracy and armed robbery at sea are the LOSC (mainly Arts. 100 to 110), the Convention for the Suppression of Unlawful Acts Against the Safety of Maritime Navigation[41] of 1988, the International Convention Against the Taking of Hostages[42] of 1979, and the United Nations Convention against Transnational Organized Crime[43] of 2000. It should be underlined that since existing international treaties do not cover all aspects of contemporary incidents of piracy, customary international law has a significant role to play in this field. Furthermore, the UN Security Council has adopted a number of resolutions, which prescribe measures to fight piracy

---

[38] The premiums have reportedly been quadrupled for the passage through this region, a factor which has forced some shipping companies to reroute their ships through the Cape of Good Hope, *id.* at 17, para. 28.

[39] Following the Security Council resolutions, the North Atlantic Treaty Organization (operations Allied Protector and Ocean Shield), the European Union (EU Operation Atlanta), Combined Task Force (CTF–151), and a number of countries acting in their national capacity in coordination with the TFG have deployed naval forces in the area for patrolling. UN Security Council Res. 1950 (2010), UN Doc. S/RES/1950 (2010), Nov. 23, 2010, preambular para. 9.

The number of attacks thwarted by these naval forces in previous years are as follows:

2008: 126 attacks; 2009: 176 attacks; 2010: 127 attacks. Report of the Special Adviser, *supra* note 35, at 19–20, para. 39.

[40] Information on Internationally Recommended Transit Corridor (IRTC) for Ships Transiting the Gulf of Aden, I.M.O. Safety of Navigation Sub-Com. Doc. SN.1/Circ.281, Aug. 3, 2009. The Safety of Navigation Sub-Committee endorsed the use of the said Transit Corridor by mariners transiting the area, and provided the coordinates of the IRTC together with its chart.

[41] 27 I.L.M. 672. It is mostly referred as "the SUA Convention".

[42] G.A. Res. 146 (XXXIV), U.N. GAOR, 34th Sess., Supp. No. 46, at 245, UN Doc. A/34/46 (1979), *entered into force* June 3, 1983; 1316 U.N.T.S. 205.

[43] Done at New York, 15 November 2000, entered into force on Sept. 29, 2003; UN Doc. A/55/383.

off the coasts of Somalia.[44] Aside from treaties and other legal instruments of a multilateral nature, there are many bilateral agreements concluded between the countries in the region and countries which maintain a military presence in this area.[45] Hence, the current legal framework should be found in various sources.

International organizations, states and inter-state initiatives have addressed the legal aspects of this problem at different levels. While the UN Security Council has been involved in the issue from the beginning, the International Maritime Organization has endorsed a set of rules concerning the suppression of piracy and for the investigation of these crimes.[46] The "Djibouti Code of Conduct" was adopted in January 2009 at an IMO Sub-regional meeting to address maritime security, piracy and armed robbery against ships.[47]

---

44 These resolutions are 1814 (2008), 1816 (2008), 1838 (2008), 1844 (2008), 1846 (2008), 1851 (2008) and 1897 (2009). The Security Council Resolutions taken in 2010 are 1910 (2010), 1916 (2010), 1918 (2010), 1950 (2010) and 1964 (2010).

45 The EU and Kenya signed an agreement on Mar. 6, 2009 in Nairobi, regarding the conditions of transfer of suspected pirates to Kenya. <http://www.consilium.europa.eu/uedocs/cms_data/docs/pressdata/en/esdp/106547.pdf>
However, Kenya later declared that it terminated this agreement due to its lack of capacity to carry out its obligations, <http://articles.cnn.com/2010-10-04/world/kenya.eu.pirates_1_somali-pirates-kenyan-authorities-kenya-s-ministry?_s=PM:WORLD>. Likewise, Kenya also signed agreements of similar substance with the United States and the United Kingdom, Douglas Guilfoyle, *Counter-Piracy Law Enforcement and Human Rights*, 59 Int'l & Comp. L.Q. 141, 163, footnote 171 (2010).

46 The following documents are the result of the work of relevant bodies of the I.M.O.:
- (i) Piracy and Armed Robbery against Ships: Recommendations to Governments for preventing and suppressing piracy and armed robbery against ships, The Maritime Safety Committee, I.M.O. Doc. MSC.1/Circ.1333, Jun. 26, 2009. The "Recommendations" cautions the governments against arming the crew of vessels or using armed security personnel since such measures may escalate the tension during a piracy attack. It also outlines an actions plan in case of an attack.

Regarding criminal jurisdiction, the report gives a list of links to determine the "substantially interested state" which can exercise jurisdiction, *id.* Annex, at 6.
- (ii) Code of Practice for the Investigation of Crimes of Piracy and Armed Robbery against Ships, I.M.O. Assembly Doc. A 26/Res.1025, Jan. 18, 2010. The document provides guidance for states concerning the details of investigation and evidence gathering in piracy cases.

47 Code of Conduct concerning the Repression of Piracy and Armed Robbery against Ships in the Western Indian Ocean and the Gulf of Aden, adopted on Jan. 29, 2009 as the outcome of the IMO Sub-regional meeting on maritime security, piracy and armed robbery against ships for Western Indian Ocean, Gulf of Aden and Red Sea States, held in Djibouti in January 2009; *issued in* International Maritime Organization, Council 102nd session, I.M.O. Doc. C102/14, Apr. 14, 2009, Annex, at 5–16.
There are currently 17 states signatory to the Code of conduct, <http://www.imo.org/OurWork/Security/PIU/Pages/Signatory-States.aspx>, visited Feb. 7, 2011.

One of the most notable descriptions of the current situation regarding piracy off the coast of Somalia was provided in the relevant reports of the UN Secretary-General. While the latest reports concern mainly the situation in Somalia in general,[48] a particular one focuses on the possible judicial means for the prosecution and imprisonment of persons responsible for piracy,[49] The Secretary-General's report on the criminal proceeding against piracy draws heavily on the work carried out by the Contact Group on Piracy off the Coast of Somalia, and on the proposals made by countries during its meetings. Thus, the report envisions seven possible ways to deal with piracy in terms of criminal proceedings.[50]

The possible solutions laid down in the report of the Secretary-General dwells on the combination of national and international elements to achieve an efficient and reliable criminal proceeding commensurate with international standards for a fair trial. The suggested ways range from using national courts of one or more countries in the region with the support of the United Nations, to setting up mixed courts that combine international and national judges, to creating a new regional or international court.[51]

---

[48] *Supra* note 33; also Report of the Secretary-General on Somalia, U.N.S.C. Doc. S/2010/447, Sept. 9, 2010.

[49] Report of the Secretary-General, *supra* note 32, UNSC Doc. S/2010/394, Jul. 20, 2010. The report was prepared in response to the request by the Security Council in its resolution 1918 (2010). The remarkably long heading for the report summarizes its content, and reveals the sensitive aspects of the issue, e.g., "time and resources" needed for setting up a judicial mechanism.

[50] The options are as follows:

(i) The enhancement of United Nations assistance to build capacity of regional States to prosecute and imprison persons responsible for acts of piracy and armed robbery at sea off the coast of Somalia;
(ii) The establishment of a Somali court sitting in the territory of a third State in the region, either with or without United Nations participation;
(iii) The establishment of a special chamber within the national jurisdiction of a State or States in the region, without United Nations participation;
(iv) The establishment of a special chamber within the national jurisdiction of a State or States in the region, with United Nations participation;
(v) The establishment of a regional tribunal on the basis of a multilateral agreement among regional states, with United Nations participation;
(vi) The establishment of an international tribunal on the basis of an agreement between a State in the region and the United Nations; and
(vii) The establishment of an international tribunal by the Security Council resolution under Chapter VII of the Charter of the United Nations.

Id. The advantages and disadvantages of each option are discussed in the report, adding previous experience with international courts, mixed tribunals, (e.g. Special Panels for East Timor, UNMIK trial panels in Kosovo, War Crimes Chamber in Bosnia and Herzegovina, the Lockerbie Court) and state practice so far.

[51] *Id.* at 19–37, paras. 35–107.

Given the long process and high costs of creating a new international tribunal, as the world experienced in previous *ad hoc* tribunals set up in 1990s, and in face of the current inability of Somalia to take effective action to bring suspected individuals before justice, those options calling for a regional initiative with the support of the United Nations seem to provide more practical and plausible solutions in addressing this problem. In more concrete terms, countries in the region should take the principal role in trying and incarcerating individuals responsible for piracy. This will enable the problem to be contained within the region to the extent possible, by keeping law enforcement actions, prosecution and enforcement of sentences in that particular geography. It will also help avoid problems of costly and cumbersome transfer of suspects, evidence, witnesses and those sentenced.[52]

Regardless of the option chosen, the support of the international community, in particular, the United Nations, is essential. In all phases of the legal process, starting from the law enforcement stage of detaining the suspects, collecting the evidence, interrogating the witnesses, through the trial stage where the needs of a fair trial, including the provision of legal assistance, interpretation, and observing the right to defense, to the post-trial phase of enforcement of sentence at a correction facility or in other institutions commensurate with the age and mental situation of the convicted, the universally accepted standards of human rights and the rule of law should be observed. The United Nations and other collective initiatives have a crucial role to play in supporting the countries of the region, all of which are having difficulty coping with the vast administrative, financial and infrastructure-related burdens placed on them by ongoing piracy. The recent examples of renovation of Shimo La Tewa Court, the Mombasa Court, and furnishing the courtrooms with modern standard equipment by support from the UN Office of Drugs and Crime illustrate how international institutions can assist in capacity-building of countries.[53] A similar approach may be followed in designing more comprehensive judicial mechanisms as well.

There are several driving forces that shape the international efforts to address piracy from a legal perspective. On the one hand, the security threat against navigation in that particular area has become so untenable that a number of states that have the capability to send naval forces there did so. On the other hand, there is a general demand among the asset contributing states that the

[52] There are even more unusual problems emerging with the transfer of suspects overseas, as in the example of asylum requests by the suspects addressed to the country where they face prosecution.

[53] UNODC, Counter-Piracy Programme: Support to the Trial and Related Treatment of Piracy Suspects, Issue Four, October 2010; available at <http://www.unodc.org/documents/easternafrica//piracy/CPP_Brochure_4.pdf> (visited Feb. 7, 2011).

primary responsibility to incarcerate and prosecute individuals must rest with the countries in the region.[54] Naval forces deployed in the area may not be essentially designed or trained for law-enforcement action. Nor are their physical means or conditions onboard adequate for detention of individuals over a long period of time.[55] Furthermore, once collected, the protection of evidence by the authorities of a country in the region might presumably be more convenient for the purposes of a prompt legal process. The same is true for the examination of witnesses. These facts also play a role in the demand for handing over suspects to countries in the region shortly after their capture without transferring them over longer distances.

Yet another problem is the lack of capacity or extremely limited resources on the part of countries in the region. It is true that certain countries in the region, namely Kenya and Seychelles, have shouldered a considerable burden in the incarceration, trial, and execution of sentences. However, the ongoing problem requires allocation of more resources, professional support from the international community in judicial proceedings, and preparing the infrastructure for carrying out sentences. The burden is obviously beyond what can be achieved by a single nation.

From a standpoint of a country contributing to the international efforts to deal with piracy, there are two different legal layers that call for action, i.e., its domestic law and international law, particularly when sending naval forces to the region. To illustrate that two-track legal work, Turkey's contribution to the

---

[54] This is without prejudice to instances where pirates might have attacked or in some way inflicted damage to the nationals, assets or naval forces of a state. In these cases, it may be argued that the nationality connection of the victim or the interest of the state whose assets had been directly threatened outweigh other competing national jurisdictions.

In an incident where eleven suspected Somali pirates were accused of separate attacks on two US Navy ships off the coast of Africa, they were transferred overseas and indicted in the US federal courts in Norfolk, VA in April 2010, <http://www.cbsnews.com/stories/2010/04/23/world/main6425010.shtml>.

[55] Long period of detention on board a military vessel was the focal question in the case of *Medvedyev and Others v France*, ECtHR, Application # 3394/03, Fifth Section, (Judgment) Jul. 10, 2008, available at <http://www.ehcr.coe.int/eng>. The applicants' claim was that it had taken too long to bring them before "a judge or other officer authorised by law to exercise judicial power" as required by Art. 5 § 3 of the European Convention on Human Rights. The Grand Chamber of the ECHR found no violation on the part of France, taking into account of the fact that the vessel involved in illegal substance trafficking has been detained at a considerable distance from the coasts of France. The Court, however, found violations on other counts. The judgment is indicative of the fact that detention of suspects onboard for a long period of time by military or law-enforcement authorities may be disputed from a human rights perspective.

For further comments on the human rights implications of combating piracy, *see* Guilfoyle, *Counter-Piracy Law Enforcement…*, *supra* note 45, at 152–67.

multi-national forces to combat piracy off the coast of Somalia may be given as an example.

As a non-permanent member of the UN Security Council in 2009 and 2010, Turkey has taken part in the decision making process of the Council in relation to Somalia, and piracy thereof.[56] Following the adoption of the Security Council resolution 1851 (2008) under Chapter VII of the UN Charter, Turkey decided to contribute to the naval forces deployed in the area in question. The Turkish Constitution (article 92) requires that deployment of forces abroad be authorized by an act of the Turkish Grand National Assembly. The Turkish Parliament took that action in February 2009 by adopting a Parliamentary Act[57] which authorized the sending of naval assets to this area, and outlined the conduct of necessary operations and modalities of taking action to prevent or suppress acts of piracy as circumstances warranted. Pursuant to this Act, the Turkish naval frigate *TCG Giresun* was deployed to the Gulf of Aden and neighboring areas, and joined the Command Task Force 151 (CTF 151) within the framework of the Combined Maritime Forces.

Turkish naval frigates have continued to take part both in the CTF 151 and in the NATO operations in this area. At times, the Turkish navy has assumed the command of the international force. Most recently, the Turkish frigate *TCG Gaziantep* carried out the task of commanding the CTF 151 from September 1 to December 1, 2010. During 2010, Turkish frigates have conducted 10 operations against pirate ships, disabling 66 suspects of piracy.[58]

While the above mentioned Parliamentary Act provided the legal basis for these operations, Turkish criminal law, on the other hand, provides for the prosecution of pirates under certain conditions. The relevant jurisdictional provision in the Turkish Penal Code is Art. 13, whereby it is stipulated that Turkish law applies in cases of seizing control or hijacking of air or sea transport vehicles.

---

[56] For an overview of the discussions in Security Council under the Presidency of Turkey, see Letter dated 18 October 2010 from the Permanent Representative of Turkey to the United Nations addressed to the President of the Security Council, U.N.S.C. Doc. S/2010/546 (Oct. 21, 2010), at 5.

[57] Decision of the Turkish Grand National Assembly, Act No. 934 of Feb. 10, 2009, OFFICIAL GAZETTE, Feb. 13, 2009; 27140 (Turk.). The authorization given by the Turkish Parliament had a one-year time limit. Accordingly, the said authorizing act was renewed by the Parliament in February 2010 for another one-year period; Decision of the Turkish Grand National Assembly, Act No. 956 of Feb. 2, 2010, OFFICIAL GAZETTE, Feb. 5, 2010; 27484 (Turk.). The authorization for the deployment of naval forces off Somalia was renewed for another year by the Turkish Parliament on Feb. 7, 2011, Decision of the Turkish Grand National Assembly, Act No. 984 of Feb. 7, 2011, OFFICIAL GAZETTE, Feb. 10, 2011; 27842 (Turk.).

[58] For the figures pertaining to the number of attacks, taking of hostages, action taken against these incidents by Turkish naval assets, and for other related statistical data, *see* <http://www.dzkk.tsk.tr>.

Art. 223§2 of the same Code requires a 2 to 5-year term of imprisonment for the crime of hijacking a vessel.[59]

Conclusion

The two distinct subjects of international law of the sea touched on in this paper, that is, the islands' impact on maritime boundaries, and piracy off the coast of Somalia, are likely to remain on the agenda of the international community for the foreseeable future. Both of these problems require the continuous attention of experts, while the public at large will continue to follow the developments and will likely be affected by their consequences. The delimitation issue is a crucial factor to determine the nature of neighborly relations between states. Piracy, on the other hand, is a criminal act, which has to be addressed through concerted actions between states. The requirement for international cooperation to deal with them might be the main common feature of these two concerns.

The law of maritime delimitation, as it has developed so far, demonstrates that the position of islands vis-à-vis the mainland within the general geographical context carries a determinative role. Although a number of observations may be suggested as above, it is still too early to regard such observations as providing binding rules. However, it may be stated at this stage of the development of delimitation law that islands are often given reduced maritime areas, even no maritime area beyond the territorial sea, particularly where they would create an inequitable result to the detriment of a neighboring country. In relation to the latter situation, there are examples of limiting the territorial sea far less than the stated maximum breadth of 12 miles to avoid an inequitable outcome.

Regarding the issue of piracy, there is a general consensus in the international community on the need for a determined action for its elimination, and for eradicating the conditions that breed this global problem. The debate is more on the modalities of carrying out this task. There is an undeniable need at present for enhancing law enforcement and judicial mechanisms at both national and regional levels. This goal may be achieved with the support of the international community for the countries in the region, first and foremost Somalia, to deal with piracy efficiently on the basis of the rule of law.

[59] Türk Ceza Kanunu [Turkish Penal Code], Law No. 5237 of Sept. 26, 2004, Official Gazette, Oct. 12, 2004; 25611 (Turk.). An English summary of the clauses on piracy is available at <http://www.un.org/Depts/los/LEGISLATIONANDTREATIES/PDFFILES/TUR_penal_criminal_procedure.pdf>. The nationality of the suspect is immaterial in terms of Art. 13 of the Penal Code for the purpose of prosecution. Nevertheless, a constitutional rule prohibits the extradition of a Turkish citizen to another country.

REVIEW OF THE CONFERENCE: GLOBALIZATION AND THE LAW OF THE SEA

Fernanda Millicay[1]

We began this Conference with a presentation on globalization, on the importance of respect for the rule of law in a globalized world, and on UNCLOS, as a norm that represents a very delicate balance between freedoms and obligations which rules two thirds of the Earth's surface. It was highlighted that it is universally accepted even by some very relevant non-Parties that agree to be bound by its rules on the basis of customary international law.

During the Conference, we had the opportunity to address several of the present challenges of the law of the sea. I would like to highlight some of them:

Islands-Rocks

The different presentations on Islands and Rocks depicted various perspectives from which they are an interesting case, not only for the application of UNCLOS. Here, I would distinguish three perspectives posed in the panel:

– Islands over which there is a sovereignty dispute: this is not a case "of islands in the context of the establishment of the outer limit of the continental shelf", but one of sovereignty. The question here does not relate to the nature of the territory (i.e. an island) but to the fact that sovereignty over such territory is disputed. In such cases, in what relates to the continental shelf, Annex I of the Rules of Procedure of the Commission on the Limits of the Continental Shelf applies by virtue of there being a dispute over the territory. As a matter of fact, the Commission on the Limits of the Continental Shelf (CLCS) decided not to consider and qualify the submission made by the United Kingdom in relation to the archipelagoes subject to the sovereignty

[1] Fernanda Millicay is an Argentine lawyer (University of Buenos Aires) and diplomat. She is a Rhodes Academy Oceans Scholar (2004). In 2003, she was granted the 18th Hamilton Shirley Amerasinghe Memorial Fellowship on the Law of the Sea by the United Nations. Presently, she is Legal Adviser of the Permanent Mission of Argentina to the United Nations. The opinions expressed in this presentation are personal, and do not purport to reflect positions of the Argentine government.

dispute between Argentina and the United Kingdom in the South West Atlantic which are mentioned by Judge Anderson in his paper;[2]
- What value to attribute to islands, which entails the question of islands projecting maritime areas *vis á vis* the continental mass for the purposes of maritime delimitation; and
- the question of rocks *vis á vis* islands in the context of article 121 of UNCLOS.

The latter was an issue posed to the International Seabed Authority and the Meeting of States Parties to UNCLOS. Besides the fact that the ISBA has no competence in relation to the delimitation of the continental shelf, there is one additional aspect I would like to highlight in addition to the presentation by my fellow scholar from Turkey on whether to address the issue of Okinotori under the settlement of disputes section of UNCLOS: the issue, from the point of view of the interpretation of the Convention, was taken to the Meeting of States Parties to UNCLOS (SPLOS). Although SPLOS did not take a decision on the matter due to lack of consensus, many Parties coincided with regard to the clear competence of SPLOS – as the body comprising all Parties to the Convention – to interpret the Convention.

Piracy

As regards piracy, it would be worthwhile to remind ourselves that UNCLOS codified a very well accepted norm of customary international law. But while the provisions of UNCLOS constitute the basic norms, when piracy takes place as part of a bigger phenomenon, i.e. a specific situation that is not one of "pure" piracy, other norms may apply. I am referring to the situation off the coast of Somalia, where piracy is only one symptom of a bigger problem. The situation off Somalia gave rise to the involvement of the UN Security Council not due to the acts of piracy and armed robbery against ships, but due to a threat to international peace and security. Therefore, the UN Charter came into play in relation to acts at sea and the Security Council authorized under Chapter VII exceptional remedies that are not in line with UNCLOS. But at the same time, the Security Council stated very clearly that the remedies authorized by it

[2] The Malvinas, South Georgias and South Sandwich Islands are part of the territory of Argentina. Having been illegally occupied by the United Kingdom, the United Nations and other international organizations have recognized that there is a sovereignty dispute between the latter and Argentina over those archipelagoes (i.e. GA Resolution 2065 and concurrent resolutions of the GA, the OAS and other bodies). The decision of the CLCS can be found in Document CLCS/66.

> *"...apply only with respect to the situation in Somalia and shall not affect the rights or obligations or responsibilities of Member States under international law, including any rights or obligations under UNCLOS, with respect to any other situation"*[3] and underscored that its Resolution 1851(2008) *"shall not be considered as establishing customary international law."*[4]

Another important aspect of piracy – which is applicable to Somalia and to other regions where piracy takes place – is that of the capacity-building is necessary to combat and prosecute such acts. One of the aspects in which progress has to be made is the incorporation of piracy as a punishable offence under domestic penal codes.

Marine Scientific Research

We were presented some of the present realities about marine scientific research and some proposals were suggested regarding the application of UNCLOS. One of them is that some of the research activities at sea are "not MSR" as they were not foreseen at the time of the negotiation of UNCLOS. Also, the panelists illustrated regional and global approaches to marine scientific research.

One of the conclusions arising from the panel is that the point of departure for facing these new challenges is UNCLOS. Therefore, we can conclude that the correct interpretation of UNCLOS is that even though some kinds of research activities were not foreseen when the Convention was negotiated, they must be accommodated within the legal regime provided by UNCLOS in its Part XIII.

Advisory Opinion Requested by the ISA at the Seabed Disputes Chamber

The Legal Counsel of the International Seabed Authority (ISA) presented this new development, which is of relevance to the whole regulatory system established by the Convention. He did so in an objective and impartial manner as he is an official of the Authority.

But non-ISA officials are allowed to be less cautious in our evaluation of the proceedings that are underway. I would therefore like to highlight the utmost importance of this first interaction of these two organs established by the Convention in the manner provided by it.

---

[3] S/RES/1851(2008) para.10.

[4] Idem 3 *supra*.

On the one hand, the mere request reflects the trust of the international community – represented at the ISA – in the maturity of the Tribunal. Some years ago, it was unfortunate to hear some voices arguing the Tribunal "was not mature yet" and that it could become a mechanism only for prompt release cases. Reality shows the international community is convinced ITLOS is not only a very specialized but also a mature tribunal: in the last years cases that entail the interpretation of substantive provisions of UNCLOS were brought to it, including one on maritime delimitation.

The request for an advisory opinion also reflects the strong commitment of the international community to the legal regime established by UNCLOS for the international seabed area, which includes this unique mechanism – very much related to the legal status of the Area and its resources as the "common heritage of mankind"[5] – through which neither Party but a judicial body would resolve the question through interpretation of the provisions of UNCLOS, in particular Part XI.

[5] The Area is defined in Article 1 of UNCLOS as "the seabed and ocean floor and subsoil thereof, beyond the limits of national jurisdiction", and Article 136 provides that "the Area and its resources are the common heritage of mankind".

GLOBALIZATION AND THE LAW OF THE SEA: A BRIEF OVERVIEW

Vita Onwuasoanya[1]

Like my co-panellists and fellow Rhodes Academy scholars who have profited from the knowledge and experience of our eminent speakers, I would like to thank the organizers for inviting me to participate in this Conference which has brought together some of the most distinguished academics and authorities on the law of the sea to discuss some thought-provoking issues that have collectively highlighted the continued importance of the oceans and the rule of law of the oceans in a rapidly changing world.

I will make very general observations with regard to the centrality and continued relevance of the United Nations Convention on the Law of the Sea (UNCLOS) within the context of globalization and the rule of law on the world's oceans and seas.

It is well accepted that UNCLOS together with its implementing Agreements[2] sets out a comprehensive legal regime that deals with all matters relating to the law of the sea, conscious "that the problems of ocean space are closely interrelated and need to be considered as a whole".[3] In doing this, it brings together the political, economic, social, scientific and technological aspects of marine affairs.

As recognised by the General Assembly of the United Nations, the Convention contains a comprehensive set of international rules for ocean spaces and for the uses of their resources and remains of strategic importance as the basis for national, regional and global action and cooperation in the marine sector.[4] Thus, its integrity needs to be maintained.

---

[1] Legal Officer, Division for Ocean Affairs and the Law of the Sea, Office of Legal Affairs, United Nations. The views expressed are those of the author and do not reflect the position of the United Nations.

[2] See the 1994 Agreement relating to the Implementation of Part XI of the United Nations Convention on the Law of the Sea of 10 December 1982 and The United Nations Agreement for the Implementation of the Provisions of the United Nations Convention on the Law of the Sea of 10 December 1982 relating to the Conservation and Management of Straddling Fish Stocks and Highly Migratory Fish Stocks, available at http://www.un.org/Depts/los/index.htm last visited 28/01/11.

[3] See United Nations Convention on the Law of the Sea of 10 December 1982, preamble.

[4] See General Assembly resolution A/64/71 of 4 December 2009, preamble.

The presentations from our esteemed panellists have demonstrated that UNCLOS has a number of features and benefits. For example, with regard to combating crimes at sea, it sets limits and provides rules for what States can do in each of the various maritime zones. Since international cooperation is a key to combating crimes at sea, it is very helpful when States have a common understanding of the basic rules for, *inter alia*, legislative jurisdiction and enforcement jurisdiction. It is also important to have clarity with regard to maritime delimitation issues, and in this regard, the Convention not only sets out the relevant rules, but also provides a number of options for the peaceful resolution of maritime disputes (Part XV). The Convention also sets out a detailed regime for addressing intentional and unlawful damage to the marine environment (Part XII), as well as a specific provision for the protection of the Arctic marine environment from vessel source pollution (article 234). The marine scientific research (MSR) regime under Part XIII is also important for the benefit of all States.

The conference has also given us the opportunity to discuss a number of interesting and sometimes provocative issues, some of which represent new and evolving challenges to the use and management of the oceans, such as the resurgence of piracy and the increasing possibilities for maritime terrorism; the developments in the Arctic including the degree of application of Article 234 of UNCLOS; issues relating to responsibility for the regulation of ship-source and greenhouse gas emissions trading; the ambiguities that may arise in distinguishing between islands and rocks under Article 121 of UNCLOS, including during the delimitation of maritime boundaries; and, the lack of a definition of MSR under UNCLOS as well as the challenges associated with the implementation of Part XIII. It goes without saying that addressing all these issues requires multi-faceted cooperation and clearly points to the increasing interdependence of states in a globalised world.

It is worth noting that there are some other issues the conference was unable to cover for want of time which also represent challenges in the regime of the Convention. Here I would like to make reference to the issue of flags of convenience in light of the prevailing principle of exclusive flag State jurisdiction; the question of marine genetic resources as well as the access and benefit sharing regime related to this; and the growing problem of irregular migration by sea, all of which are very important in an increasingly interconnected world.

Another area the conference did not address is Part X of UNCLOS which contains provisions related to access to the sea by land-locked and geographically disadvantaged States. Indeed, a recent report of the United Nations Office of the High representative for the Least Developed countries, Landlocked Developing Countries and Small Island Developing States demonstrated that the effects of globalisation, including the economic crisis, are more deeply felt by such states due to increased trade and importation costs as a result of their compromised access to the sea.[5] Thus, these states have a very vested interest in the effective implementation of UNCLOS and the realization of the rule of law on the oceans.

Considering the fact that UNCLOS is one of the most widely ratified international treaties, and mindful of the fact that one of the most recent ratifications is from a land-locked State,[6] it is important that land-locked and geographically disadvantaged States be engaged with more deliberately not only with regard to Part X, but also with regard to the Area as the common heritage of mankind, and indeed with regard to the entire Convention, including by encouraging them to adopt legislation to implement the relevant provisions of the Convention. This will contribute to ensuring the full, effective and comprehensive implementation of the Convention.

Mindful of the delicate balance of interests UNCLOS represents and upon which the international community is of necessity dependent and interdependent, international cooperation is all the more important in addressing new and emerging threats and challenges and in finding effective solutions for the sustainable use and management of our oceans and seas by all.

As noted by Michael Lodge and Vice Admiral Houck, ocean governance cannot and should not be taken for granted and there is therefore no room for complacency. The faith of the international community in the Convention as a robust and living document capable of accommodating and guiding states in addressing perceived gaps and new challenges is demonstrated in a number of ways including the varied mechanisms that are evolving to address issues such as piracy off the coast of Somalia, measures to address illegal, unreported and unregulated fishing including through the use of port State measures and, as noted by Mr. Lodge, by the recent request for an Advisory Opinion by the International Seabed Authority to the Seabed Disputes Chamber of the International Tribunal for the Law of the Sea. This should reinforce our confidence in the ability of the international community to use, apply and implement the Convention in order to respond to the challenges posed, as well as the opportunities offered, by globalisation.

---

[5] See "The Impact of the Global Financial and Economic Crises on the Development Prospects of the Landlocked Developing Countries", Report prepared by John Serieux for the United Nations Office of the High Representative for the Least Developed countries, Landlocked Developing Countries and Small Island Developing States (UN-OHRLLS), 2009.

[6] Malawi deposited the 161st instrument of ratification on 28 September 2010. See http://www.un.org/Depts/los/reference_files/chronological_lists_of_ratifications.htm# last visited 28/01/11.